Microsoft® Windows® Millennium Edition fast&easy™

Diane Koers

A DIVISION OF PRIMA PUBLISHING

©2000 by Prima Publishing. All rights reserved. No part of this book may be reproduced or transmitted in any form or by any means, electronic or mechanical, including photocopying, recording, or by any information storage or retrieval system without written permission from Prima Publishing, except for the inclusion of brief quotations in a review.

A Division of Prima Publishing

Prima Publishing and colophon are registered trademarks of Prima Communications, Inc. PRIMA TECH and Fast & Easy are trademarks of Prima Communications, Inc., Roseville, California 95661.

Publisher: Stacy L. Hiquet
Marketing Manager: Judi Taylor
Associate Marketing Manager: Heather Buzzingham
Managing Editor: Sandy Doell
Acquisitions Editor: Rebecca Fong
Project Editor: Heather Talbot
Technical Reviewer: Kyle Bryant
Copy Editors: Heather Talbot, Jeff Riley
Interior Layout: Marian Hartsough
Cover Design: Prima Design Team
Indexer: Katherine Stimson
Proofreader: Anne Owen

Microsoft and Windows are registered trademarks of Microsoft Corporation.

Important: Prima Publishing cannot provide software support. Please contact the appropriate software manufacturer's technical support line or Web site for assistance.

Prima Publishing and the author have attempted throughout this book to distinguish proprietary trademarks from descriptive terms by following the capitalization style used by the manufacturer.

Information contained in this book has been obtained by Prima Publishing from sources believed to be reliable. However, because of the possibility of human or mechanical error by our sources, Prima Publishing, or others, the Publisher does not guarantee the accuracy, adequacy, or completeness of any information and is not responsible for any errors or omissions or the results obtained from use of such information. Readers should be particularly aware of the fact that the Internet is an ever-changing entity. Some facts may have changed since this book went to press.

ISBN: 0-7615-2739-7
Library of Congress Catalog Card Number: 99-069405
Printed in the United States of America

00 01 02 03 04 DD 10 9 8 7 6 5 4 3 2 1

*To my friends
at Buck Creek Christian Church*

Acknowledgments

I am deeply thankful to the many people at Prima Publishing who worked on this book. Thank you for all the time you gave and for your assistance.

To Rebecca Fong for the opportunity to write this book and her confidence in me. Rebecca, I hope your dreams come true. Thank you to Heather Talbot for her assistance (and patience) in the book development; to Jeff Riley for his help making this book grammatically correct, and to Kyle Bryant for checking all the technical angles.

Lastly, to my husband. Thank you again, Vern, for all your support and never-ending faith in me. For over thirty years, you've believed in me.

About the Author

DIANE KOERS owns and operates All Business Service, a software training and consulting business formed in 1988 that services the central Indiana area. Her area of expertise has long been in the word processing, spreadsheet, and graphics area of computing as well as providing training and support for Peachtree Accounting Software. Diane's authoring experience includes nine other Prima Publishing *Fast & Easy* books (including *Windows 98 Fast & Easy, WordPerfect 9 Fast & Easy, Office 2000 Fast & Easy*) and she has co-authored Prima's *Essential Windows 98*. She has also developed and written software training manuals for her clients.

Active in her church and civic activities, Diane enjoys spending her free time traveling and playing with her grandsons and her three Yorkshire Terriers.

Contents at a Glance

Introduction xvii

PART I
UNDERSTANDING BASIC WINDOWS
OPERATIONS 1

Chapter 1	Starting Windows Millennium Edition. 3
Chapter 2	Discovering Desktop Components. 9
Chapter 3	Recognizing Parts of a Window 23
Chapter 4	Using Windows Menus and Dialog Boxes 33
Chapter 5	Multitasking and Shutting Down Windows. 49

PART II
WORKING WITH THE ACCESSORIES 61

Chapter 6	Using the Calculator 63
Chapter 7	Using WordPad 71
Chapter 8	Painting with the Paint Program 93
Chapter 9	Playing Around with the Games 107

CONTENTS AT A GLANCE

PART III
DISCOVERING THE WINDOWS TOOLS 117

Chapter 10	Using Windows Help 119
Chapter 11	Using Windows System Tools 131
Chapter 12	Organizing Files and Folders 149
Chapter 13	Finding Files, Folders, and People 173
Chapter 14	Discovering Multimedia. 183

PART IV
CUSTOMIZING WINDOWS. 207

Chapter 15	Customizing the Desktop 209
Chapter 16	Tinkering with the Control Panel 231
Chapter 17	Having Fun with the Control Panel 261
Chapter 18	Working with Printers 279

PART V
USING THE INTERNET 301

Chapter 19	Connecting to the Internet 303
Chapter 20	Surfing with Internet Explorer. 323
Chapter 21	E-mailing with Outlook Express 339
Chapter 22	Using the Windows Address Book 365

| Appendix A | Upgrading to Windows Millennium . . . . 381 |

Glossary. 392
Index 401

Contents

Introduction xvii

PART I
UNDERSTANDING BASIC WINDOWS
OPERATIONS 1

Chapter 1 Starting Windows Millennium Edition 3
Starting Windows Millennium Edition. 4
Using Windows Millennium Edition on a Network 5
Making Selections with the Mouse 5

Chapter 2 Discovering Desktop Components 9
Opening the My Computer Icon. 10
Browsing the Network Places 15
Working with the Taskbar 17
    Using the Start Button 17
    Discovering the Quick Launch Bar 19
    Investigating the System Tray 20
Looking at Other Desktop Items 21

Chapter 3 Recognizing Parts of a Window. 23
Identifying Window Components 24
Using Scroll Bars 26

CONTENTS

Manually Resizing Windows 28
Maximizing a Window 30
Minimizing a Window 31
Moving a Window 32

Chapter 4 **Using Windows Menus and Dialog Boxes 33**
Making Menu Choices with a Mouse 34
Using Shortcut Menus 37
Selecting Menu Choices with the Keyboard 39
Working in a Dialog Box 42
Learning Common Windows Commands 46

Chapter 5 **Multitasking and Shutting Down Windows 49**
Opening a Windows Program 50
Opening with the Start Menu 50
Opening from the Desktop 51
Switching between Programs 52
Closing a Windows Program 53
Handling a Locked Up Application 54
Shutting Down Windows the Right Way 55
Shutting Down Windows When Your Computer Locks Up 58
Part I Review Questions 59

PART II
WORKING WITH THE ACCESSORIES 61

Chapter 6 **Using the Calculator 63**
Starting the Calculator 64
Identifying Calculator Buttons 65
Operating the Calculator 66
Copying Values from the Calculator 67
Changing the Style of the Calculator 69
Viewing the Scientific Calculator 69
Returning to the Standard Calculator 70

CONTENTS

Chapter 7 Using WordPad 71
    Staring WordPad 72
    Entering Text 73
    Editing Text 75
        Adding Text 75
        Deleting Text 76
    Inserting the Current Date and Time 77
    Selecting Text 78
    Cutting and Pasting Text 81
    Formatting Text 83
        Changing the Font 83
    Modifying the Alignment 85
        Adding Bullets 86
    Saving a WordPad Document 87
    Printing a WordPad Document 89
    Opening a WordPad Document 91
    Closing the WordPad Document 92

Chapter 8 Painting with the Paint Program 93
    Starting the Paint Program 94
    Discovering the Paint Tools 95
    Drawing with the Paintbrush 97
    Drawing a Rectangle or Circle 98
    Filling in the Background Color 101
    Selecting and Moving an Object 102
    Saving a Drawing 104
    Saving a Drawing as Wallpaper 105
    Printing a Drawing 106

Chapter 9 Playing Around with the Games 107
    Starting Spider Solitaire 108
    Connecting to an Internet Hearts Game 111
    Part II Review Questions *116*

PART III
DISCOVERING THE WINDOWS TOOLS 117

Chapter 10 Using Windows Help 119
- Starting Windows Help 120
- Exploring the Help and Support Window. 120
    - Using the Help Topics 122
    - Utilizing the Help Index 124
    - Searching for Help 125
- Getting Assisted Support 127

Chapter 11 Using Windows System Tools 131
- Scanning Your Hard Disk for Problems. 132
- Defragmenting Your Hard Drive 134
- Using the Maintenance Wizard 137
- Updating Your System. 139
- Using System Restore 144
    - Creating a Restore Point. 144
    - Restoring Your System 146

Chapter 12 Organizing Files and Folders 149
- Looking in the Explorer Window. 150
    - Identifying Explorer Components 151
    - Expanding Folders 153
- Changing the Look of Explorer. 154
    - Changing Display Options 154
    - Displaying Toolbars. 155
    - Changing the Way Files Are Displayed 156
    - Sorting Files 159
    - Modifying Folder Options 160
- Creating a New Folder 162
- Moving or Copying Files and Folders. 164
- Renaming Files and Folders 166

CONTENTS

Sending Files to the Recycle Bin............................168
Deleting Files...168
    Recovering a File from the Recycle Bin.................170
    Emptying the Recycle Bin..............................172

Chapter 13 Finding Files, Folders, and People...............173
Finding a File..174
Looking for a File by Date..............................178
Searching for People in the Address Book................181

Chapter 14 Discovering Multimedia............................183
Using the Windows Media Player..........................184
    Playing a Music CD.....................................184
        Starting a Music CD................................184
        Discovering Visualizations.........................186
        Choosing from the Playlist.........................187
    Exploring the Windows Media Player....................187
    Equalizing Your Settings..............................189
    Listening to Web Radio................................192
    Using the Media Guide.................................193
    Cataloging Media......................................195
        Creating a Media Library...........................195
        Deleting a Library Media File......................197
    Viewing Modes and Choosing Skins......................198
Using the Windows Volume Control........................201
Adding a Media Clip to a Document.......................203
Part III Review Questions..............................206

PART IV CUSTOMIZING WINDOWS........................207

Chapter 15 Customizing the Desktop..........................209
Creating a New Folder...................................210
Moving and Deleting Icons...............................211

Moving an Icon 211
Deleting an Icon 213
Creating a Shortcut 214
Changing an Icon 217
Renaming an Icon 219
Editing the Start Menu 220
Reorganizing the Start Menu 220
Adding an Item to the Start Menu 222
Removing an Item from the Start Menu 227
Customizing the Taskbar 229
Changing Taskbar Options 230

Chapter 16 Tinkering with the Control Panel 231

Opening the Control Panel 232
Changing the Current Date and Time 232
Changing Mouse Response 234
Changing Basic Mouse Responses 235
Changing Mouse Pointers 236
Changing Mouse Visibility 237
Adding and Removing Programs 239
Installing a New Program 239
Uninstalling a Program 241
Creating a Windows Startup Disk 243
Adding Windows Program Components 244
Changing Your Windows Password 246
Setting Up Multiple Users 249
Changing Accessibility Options 253
Changing Keyboard Options 253
Setting Options for the Hearing Impaired 255
Setting Options for the Visually Impaired 257
Using MouseKeys 258
Setting General Accessibility Options 259

Chapter 17 Having Fun with the Control Panel 261
Changing Sounds 262
Enhancing Your Display 264
Changing Backgrounds 265
Selecting a Screen Saver 266
Changing the Colors of Your Windows 269
Integrating Your Desktop with the Web 270
Using Desktop Themes 276

Chapter 18 Working with Printers 279
Installing a New Printer 280
Discovering Printer Properties 285
Sharing a Printer 286
Connecting to a Network Printer 287
Making a Printer the Default 292
Creating a Desktop Shortcut to the Printer 293
Controlling Print Jobs 294
Pausing a Print Job 296
Deleting a Print Job 296
Rushing a Print Job 297
Part IV Review Questions 299

PART V
USING THE INTERNET 301

Chapter 19 Connecting to the Internet 303
Subscribing to an Online Service 304
Signing Up for MSN Internet Access 304
Starting MSN Internet Access 311
Creating a Dial-Up Connection 313
Starting Your Web Browser 320

Chapter 20 Surfing with Internet Explorer 323
- Browsing the Web with Internet Explorer 324
- Exploring the Internet Explorer Window 327
- Playing Favorites 331
  - Adding Favorites 331
- Setting Parental Controls 333

Chapter 21 E-mailing with Outlook Express 339
- Starting Outlook Express 340
- Working with E-mail 340
  - Creating an E-mail Account 340
  - Creating an E-mail Message 345
  - Formatting an E-mail Message 348
  - Attaching Files to E-mail 352
  - Retrieving Incoming E-mail 354
  - Replying to a Message 355
  - Forwarding a Message 357
  - Receiving E-mail with Attachments 358
  - Creating an E-mail Folder 360
  - Moving an E-mail Message 362
  - Deleting an E-mail Message 363

Chapter 22 Using the Windows Address Book 365
- Managing Address Book Contacts 366
  - Adding Contacts 366
  - Editing Contacts 371
  - Deleting Contacts 372
  - Sorting Address Book Contacts 373
  - Printing a Phone List 374
- Closing the Address Book 376
- Sending Mail to a Contact 376
- *Part V Review Questions* *380*

Appendix A Upgrading to Windows Millennium **381**
   Understanding the Upgrade Process 382
   System Requirements 382
   Installing the Windows Millennium Edition Upgrade 383
   Uninstalling Windows Millennium Edition. 388

Glossary **392**

Index **401**

Introduction

This new *Fast & Easy* guide from Prima Publishing helps you unleash the power of Windows Millennium Edition—the newest release of the world's most popular operating system. Microsoft has long had a reputation of delivering the type of products we've asked for so that each time a new version of the software comes out, it has new features to utilize. Windows Millennium Edition (Me) is no exception. This version has everything most users want in an operating system, including better support for devices such as scanners and digital cameras.

Microsoft Windows Millennium Edition Fast & Easy shows you how to accomplish the most common Windows tasks—from playing games to connecting to your favorite Web site. *Fast & Easy* guides use a step-by-step approach and are written in an easy-to-understand common lingo. Each step is accompanied by a visual representation of your screen so that you can follow along to make sure you are on the right track.

This book cannot teach you everything you can do with Windows Millennium Edition, nor will it give you all the different ways to accomplish a task. I would have loved to cover many other features, but space just doesn't permit me to introduce all features. When you are more comfortable with Windows Millennium Edition, you might want to investigate tools such as the System File Protection, System Monitor, or Resource Meter. Other features you may find interesting are Home Networking, Movie Maker, Microsoft Chat, Microsoft Netmeeting, or Newsgroups.

What I *have* tried to do is give you the fastest and easiest way to get everyday tasks done. Isn't that what we are after: to get a job done and go on to the next one at hand?

Who Should Read This Book?

This book can be used as a learning tool or as a step-by-step task reference. The easy-to-follow, highly visual nature of this book makes it the perfect learning tool for a beginning computer user as well as those seasoned computer users who are new to this version of Windows. By using this *Microsoft Windows Millennium Edition Fast & Easy* guide, any level of user can quickly look up steps for a task without having to plow through pages of descriptions.

Added Advice to Make You a Pro

You'll notice that this book focuses on the steps necessary for a task and keeps explanations to a minimum. Included in the book are elements that provide some additional information to help you master the program, without encumbering your progress through the steps:

- Tips offer shortcuts when performing an action, and they describe a feature that can make your work in Windows quicker and easier.

- Notes give you a bit of background or additional information about a feature; they also give advice about how to use the feature in your day-to-day activities.

This book truly is the *fastest and easiest* way to learn Windows Millennium Edition. Enjoy!

—Diane Koers

PART I
Understanding Basic Windows Operations

Chapter 1
  Starting Windows Millennium Edition 3

Chapter 2
  Discovering Desktop Components 9

Chapter 3
  Recognizing Parts of a Window 23

Chapter 4
  **Using Windows Menus and
  Dialog Boxes 33**

Chapter 5
  **Multitasking and
  Shutting Down Windows. 49**

1

Starting Windows Millennium Edition

Using your computer just became easier than it ever has been. If you're upgrading from Windows 3.1 to Windows Millennium Edition, you'll find Windows Millennium Edition (Me) a faster, more logical environment. Making choices requires less effort on your part due to fewer buttons to click and less mouse movement.

If you're upgrading from Windows 95 or 98, you'll notice a few changes to the desktop and in the response time from your computer. In this chapter, you'll learn how to:

- Start Windows Millennium Edition
- Make a selection with the mouse

Starting Windows Millennium Edition

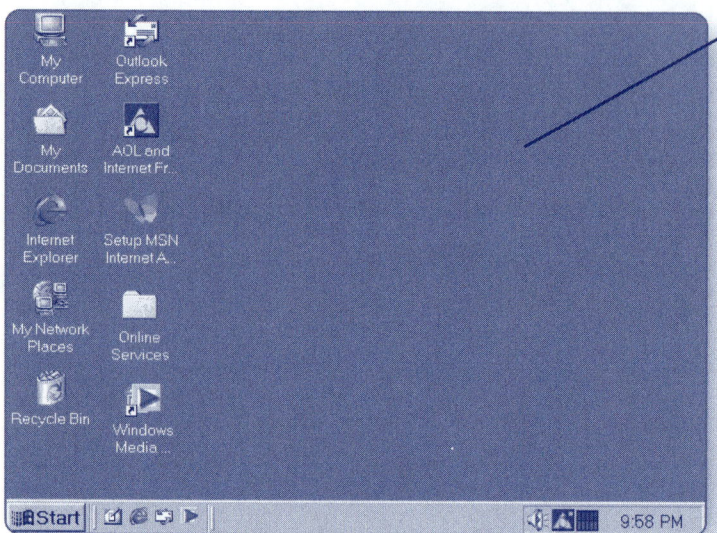

By default, most computers start Windows when you turn on the computer. Also, several diagnostics run at the same time to ensure that certain components of your computer are performing correctly. Depending upon the speed and processor of your computer, this process may take a couple of minutes.

> **NOTE**
>
> If your computer did not shut down properly during the previous session of Windows, when you start your machine the Windows ScanDisk program runs. The Windows program then continues to load. You'll learn more about ScanDisk in Chapter 11, "Using Windows System Tools."

When you start Windows Millennium Edition, the large area you see on your screen is called the desktop. You can customize the desktop by adding shortcuts to your favorite programs, documents, and printers, and by changing its look to fit your mood and personality.

MAKING SELECTIONS WITH THE MOUSE   5

Using Windows Millennium Edition on a Network

If you are on a network, you may be prompted for your user name and network password.

1. Type your **user name** if it's not already displayed. The text you type appears in the User Name text box.

2. Press the **Tab key**. The blinking insertion point appears in the Password box.

3. Type the **password**. A series of asterisks appears.

4. Press the **Enter key**. The Windows Millennium Edition desktop appears.

Making Selections with the Mouse

Although several varieties are available, the most common type of computer mouse is the type that rolls across the desktop, usually on top of a foam pad. Other types of mouse devices include trackballs or touchpads. No matter which type of mouse you have, all have at least two buttons for you to use with the mouse. Some have three buttons, and some have a wheel on the top.

With a standard mouse, your index finger should rest on the left button while the middle finger should rest on the right button.

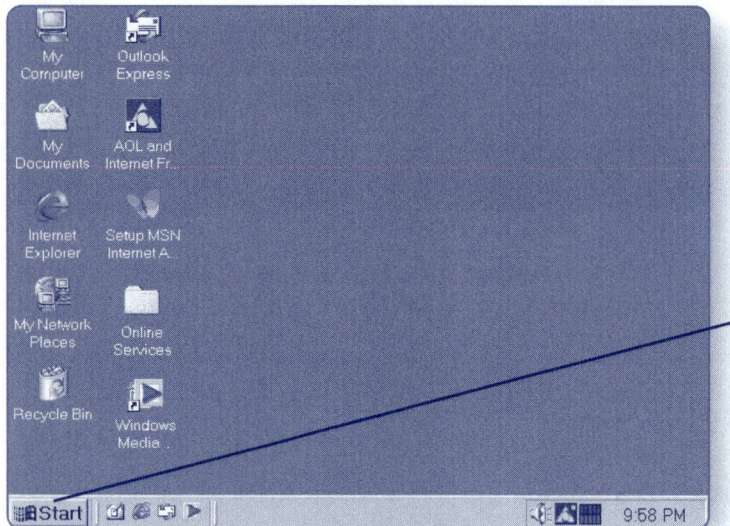

You'll use the left mouse button the most. Use the left button to make selections or choices from the Windows Millennium Edition menus or icons. When you make selections with the mouse, you do one of several things:

- Click the left mouse button once. A single click launches a program or selects an item for modification. For example, you use a single click to activate the Start menu.

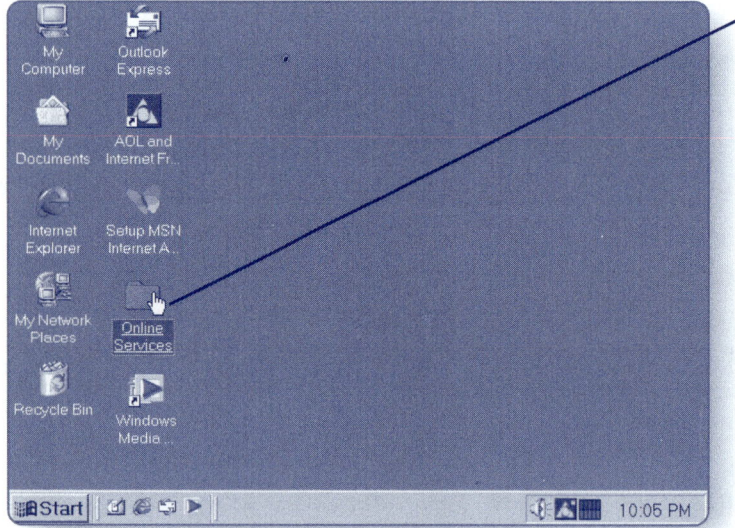

- Click the left mouse button twice (called a double-click). A double-click is the process of pressing the buttons twice (click, click) in rapid succession without moving the mouse while you click. Double-clicking the mouse is often used as a shortcut. Many new features of Windows Millennium Edition eliminate the need to double-click.

MAKING SELECTIONS WITH THE MOUSE 7

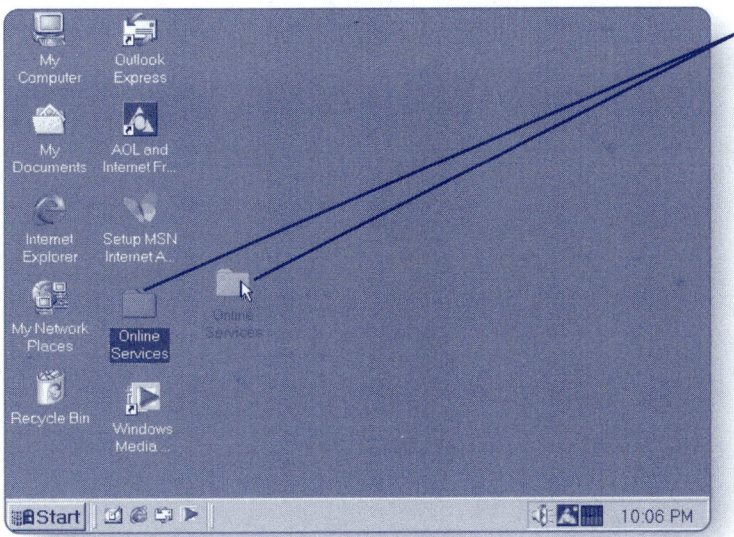

- Click the left mouse button and drag the mouse. You'll accomplish dragging by pointing the mouse pointer at an object, clicking on the left mouse button, and then moving the mouse while keeping the button pressed. Also use this process to select several items at a time or to move an object.

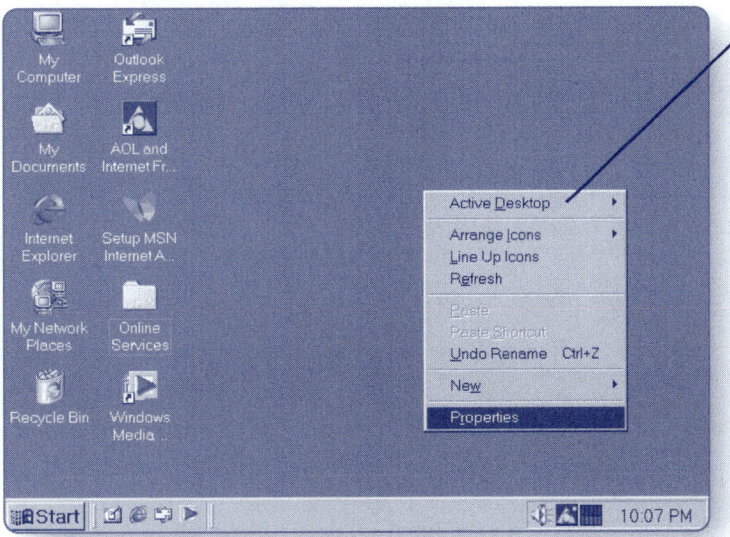

- Click the right mouse button (called a right-click). Right-clicking opens a shortcut menu, which allows you to select common features quickly and easily. Although you make a shortcut menu appear by right-clicking, you make selections from the shortcut menu with the left mouse button.

TIP
All references in this book refer to the left mouse button unless specified otherwise.

2

Discovering Desktop Components

Several pictures or icons are displayed on your computer desktop. You need to recognize these icons in order to operate many of the Windows Millennium Edition features. Depending on the configuration of your computer, you might not have all of these choices or you might have several others. In this chapter, you'll learn how to:

- Open the My Computer icon
- Browse My Network Places
- Work with the Taskbar
- Look at other desktop components

CHAPTER 2: DISCOVERING DESKTOP COMPONENTS

Opening the My Computer Icon

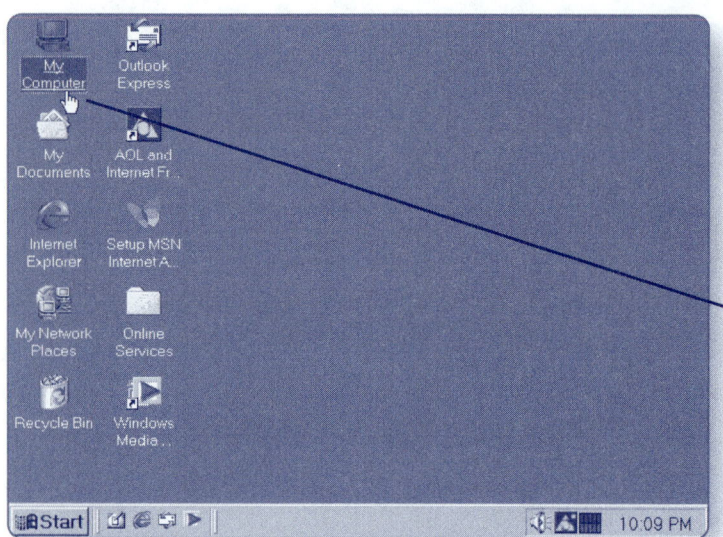

Use the My Computer icon to quickly and easily see everything on your computer. You can also customize your Windows Millennium Edition program through the My Computer icon.

1. Click on the **My Computer icon**. The My Computer window appears.

TIP

If the words "My Computer" are not underlined when you point to them, your Windows Millennium Edition is configured with the Classic style desktop. You need to double-click on icons to open them. In Chapter 17, "Having Fun with the Control Panel," you'll learn how to switch from the Classic style desktop to the Web style desktop. With the Web style desktop, you'll be able to single-click on icons to open them.

OPENING THE MY COMPUTER ICON   11

When a window is open, a button appears at the bottom of the screen in an area called the Taskbar. You'll learn about the Taskbar later in this chapter.

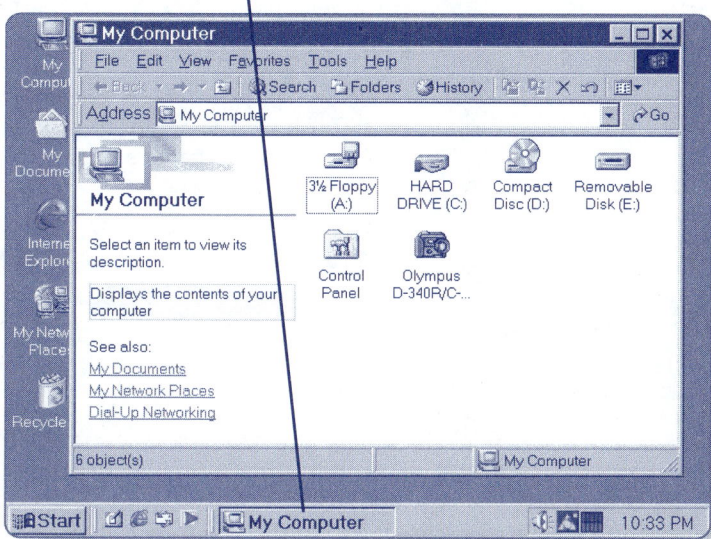

Although you will learn about the different parts of a window in the next chapter, take a look at the contents of the My Computer window. From the My Computer window, you can see each disk drive on your computer, whether your system has a floppy disk drive, a hard disk drive, or a CD-ROM drive. From each of these disk drives you can browse through your files and folders.

NOTE
The following figures show the configuration of my machine. Your computer configuration may be different.

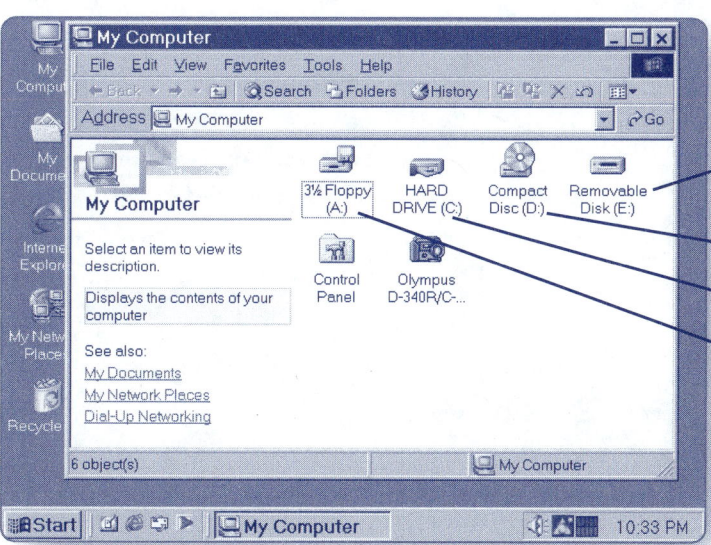

- Drive E (Removable Zip Disk Drive)
- Drive D (CD-ROM)
- Drive C (Hard drive)
- Drive A (3-1/2" Floppy)

12 CHAPTER 2: DISCOVERING DESKTOP COMPONENTS

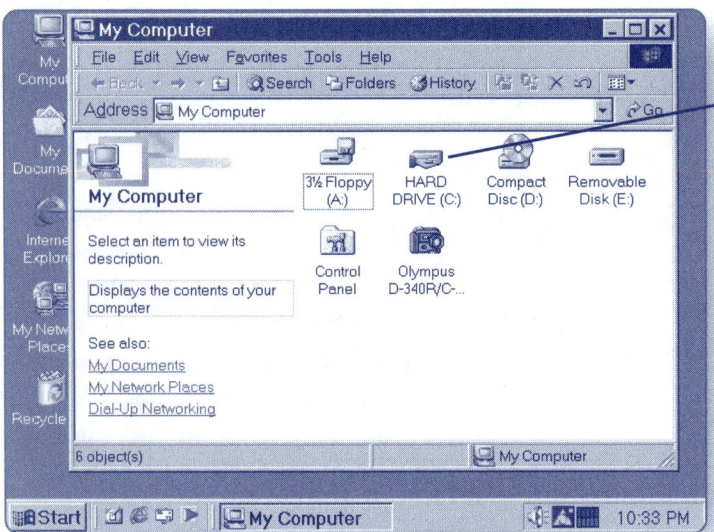

NOTE
If a disk drive icon has a little hand underneath it, it means that disk drive is shared across a network. Other people can access the information on that disk drive. If there is no hand, the drive is not shared.

A few additional items are displayed in the My Computer window. Other items that can be accessed from My Computer include:

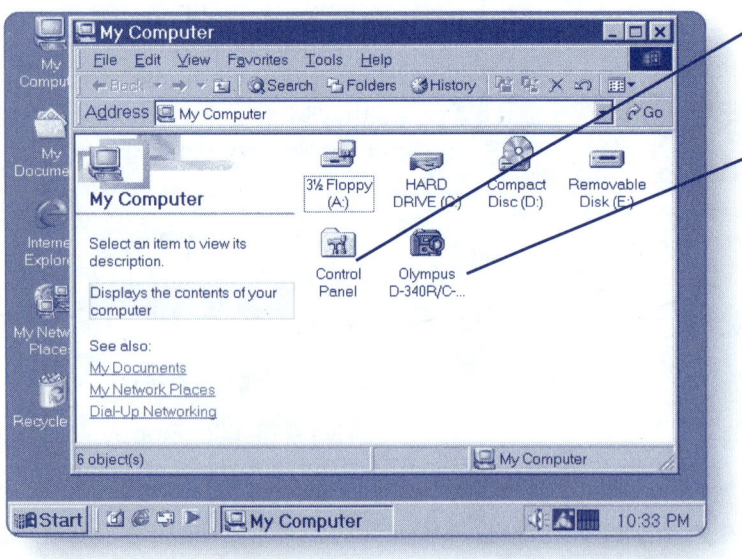

- Control Panel (discussed in Chapter 16, "Tinkering with the Control Panel")
- My Digital Camera—Digital cameras are beyond the scope of this book and will not be covered.

OPENING THE MY COMPUTER ICON   13

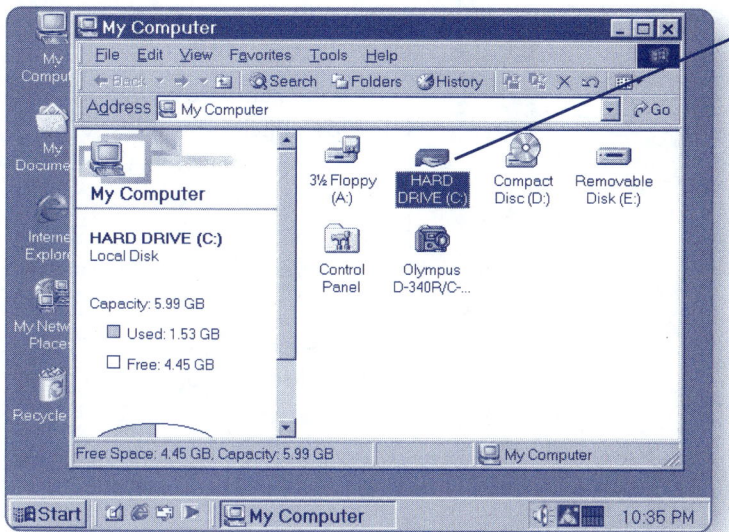

2. Click on a **drive** to view the contents of the drive. The window for that drive appears.

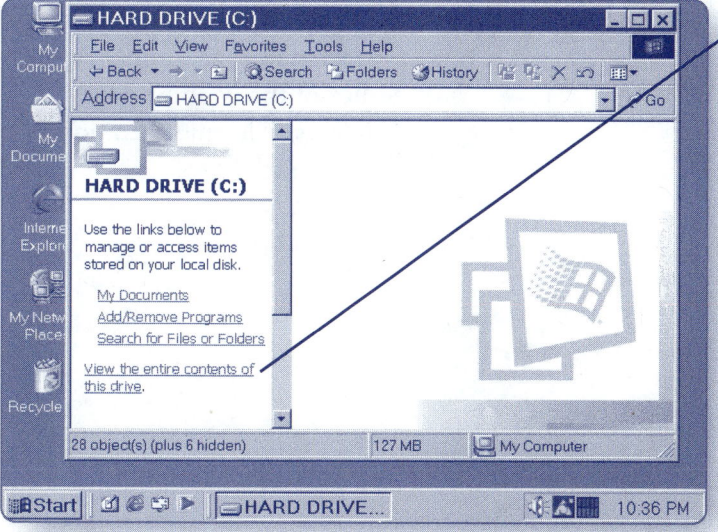

3. Click on **View the entire contents of this drive.** You can view files and other folders in the drive.

14 CHAPTER 2: DISCOVERING DESKTOP COMPONENTS

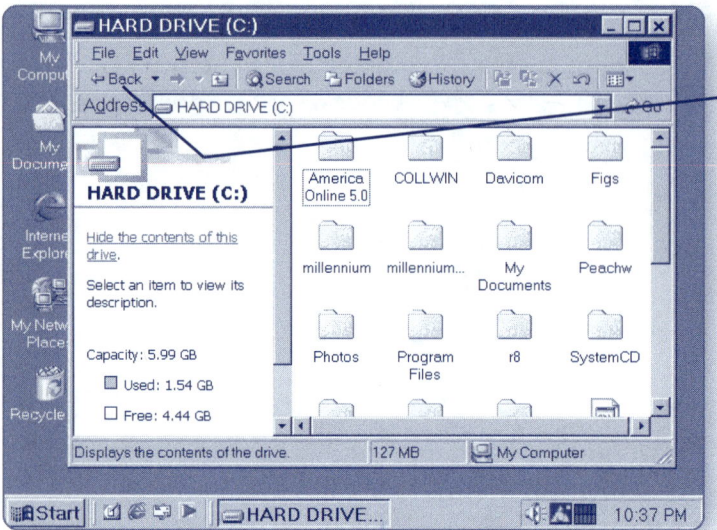

TIP
If you click on the wrong folder, click on the Back button to return to the previous window so that you can try again.

When you are finished looking at the folders, you need to close the windows.

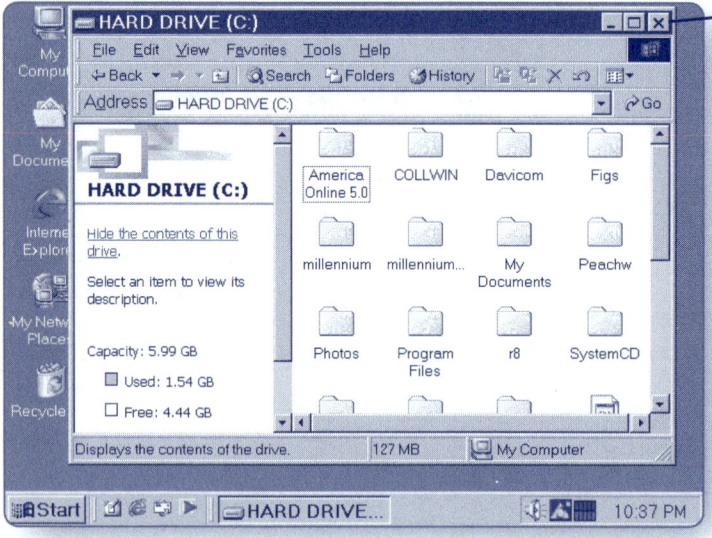

4. Click on the **Close button** ([X]) located in the upper-right corner of the window. The Windows Millennium Edition desktop redisplays.

BROWSING THE NETWORK PLACES   15

Browsing the Network Places

If you are using a network, the My Network Places icon appears on your desktop. You'll use it to browse through the computers on your entire network.

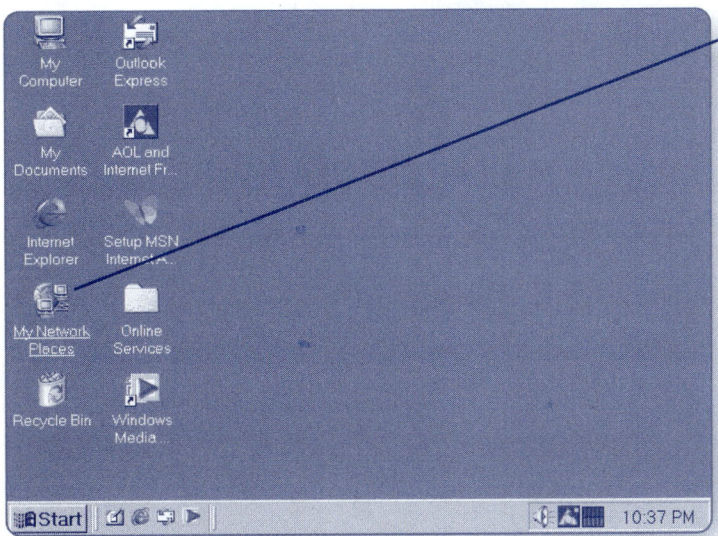

1. Click on the **My Network Places icon**. The My Network Places window appears.

NOTE

If you are not already networked, the first time you launch My Network Places, the Home Networking Wizard may appear. The Home Networking Wizard assists you in connecting your computers. The Home Networking Wizard is beyond the scope of this book and will not be covered.

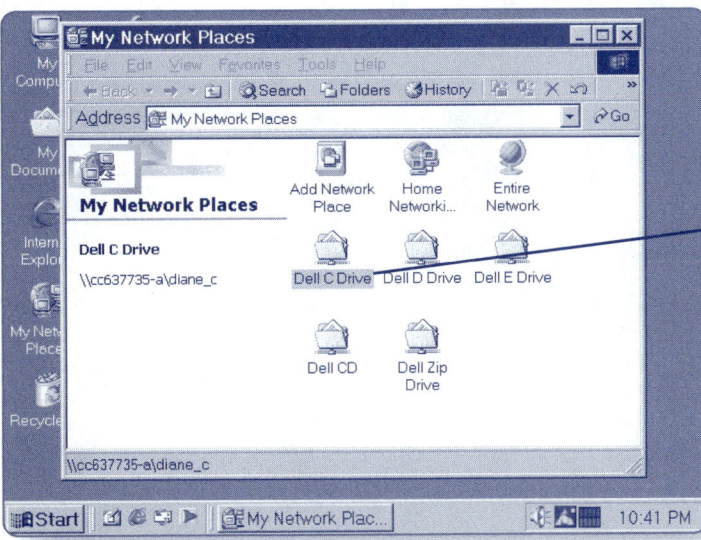

You'll see a listing of each computer drive, folder, or printer to which you are connected.

2. Click on the **drive or folder** you want to access. A listing of files and folders appears.

16 CHAPTER 2: DISCOVERING DESKTOP COMPONENTS

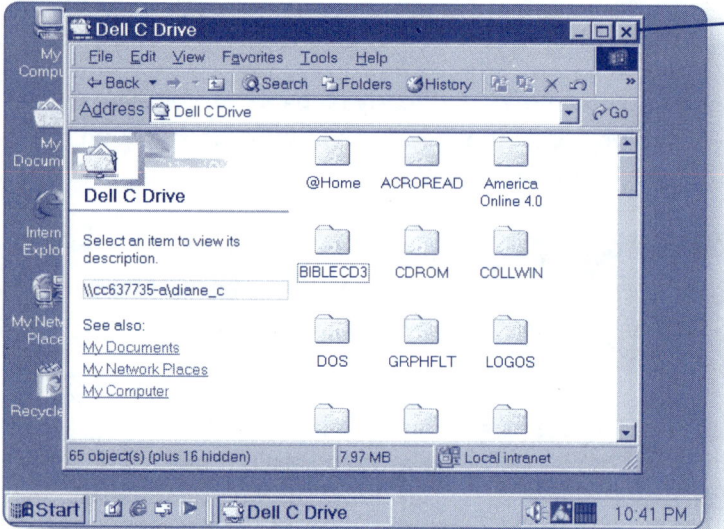

3. Click on the **Close button** (X). The window closes, and the Windows Millennium Edition desktop redisplays.

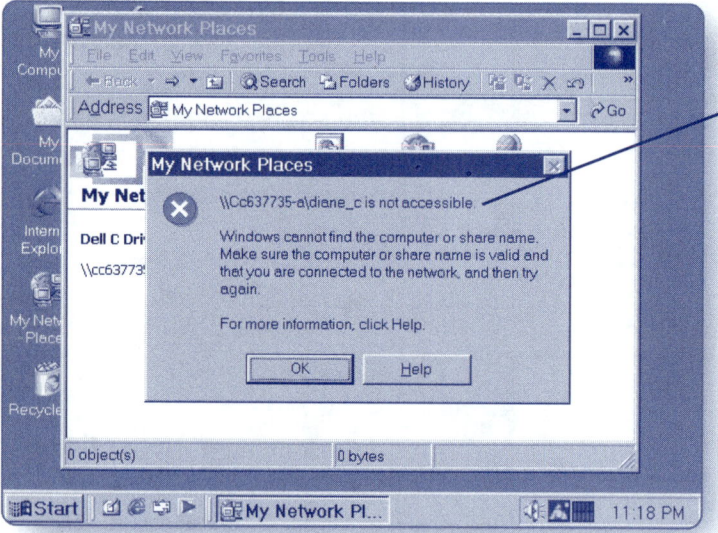

NOTE
If your network is not functioning correctly, you'll receive an error message.

Working with the Taskbar

Windows calls the bar located across the bottom of your screen the Taskbar. It represents several different components. The Taskbar displays the button representing the main Start menu and buttons for each application you have open and running on your computer.

As you move your mouse pointer across any of the buttons on the Taskbar, a small box called a ToolTip appears indicating the name of each button.

Using the Start Button

You generally use the Start button to access your programs and documents. You'll find the Start button located on the lower-left side of your screen.

1. Click on the **Start button**. The Start menu appears.

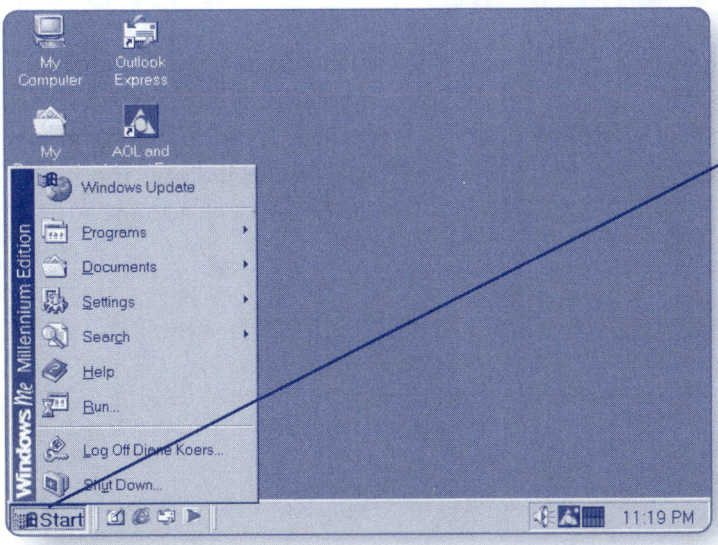

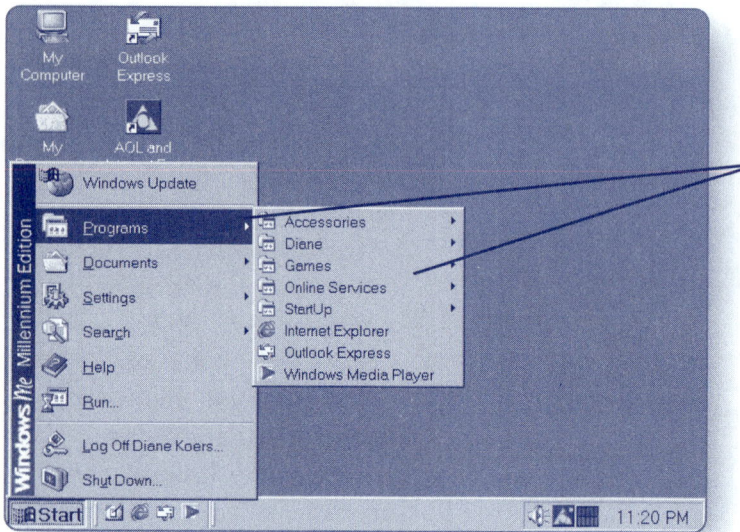

2. Click on the **desired option**. One of three things happens next:

- If you selected Programs, Documents, Settings, or Search, a cascading menu appears allowing you to make another selection. Notice that these items have a small right-facing arrow next to the options. The arrow indicates a cascading menu will appear.

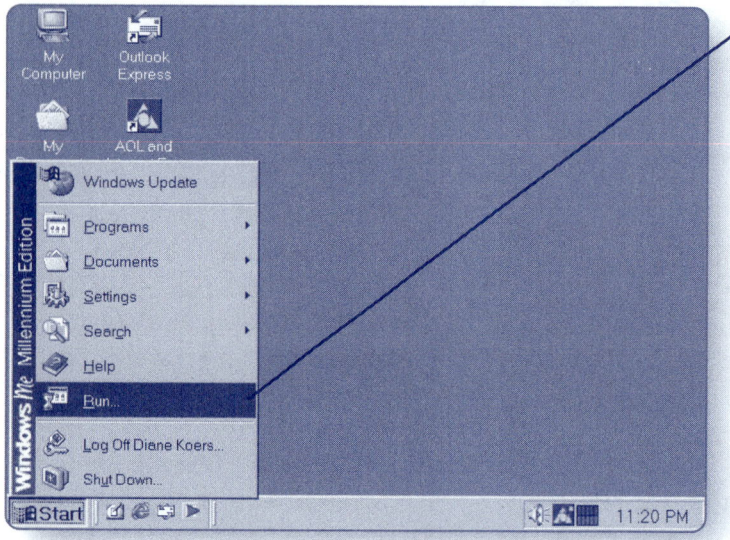

- If you selected Run, Log Off, or Shut Down, a dialog box appears asking you for more information. Dialog boxes are discussed in Chapter 4, "Using Windows Menus and Dialog Boxes." Notice that these items have three dots displayed after the menu choice. The dots are called an ellipsis and indicate that a dialog box will appear.

WORKING WITH THE TASKBAR   19

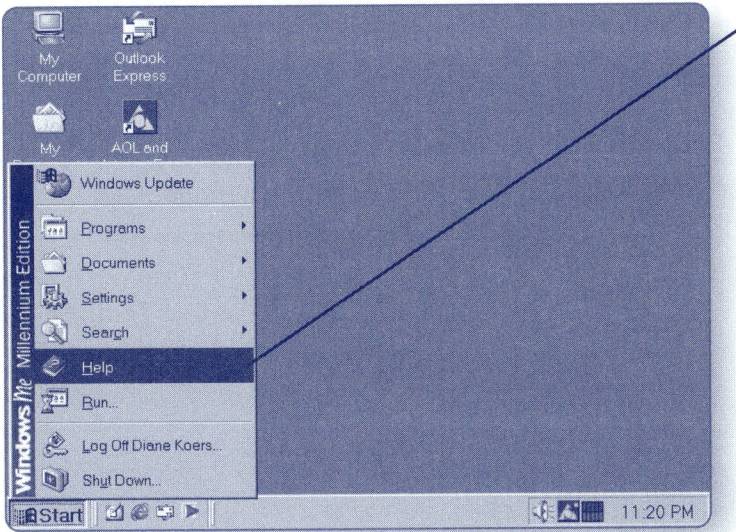

- If you selected Help, the Help and Support system opens. You'll learn about Help in Chapter 10, "Using Windows Help."

NOTE
If you have one of the newer keyboards, you probably have a key between the Ctrl key and the Alt key that has the Windows logo (a flying window) on it. This is the Windows key. You can also open the Start menu by pressing this key.

Discovering the Quick Launch Bar

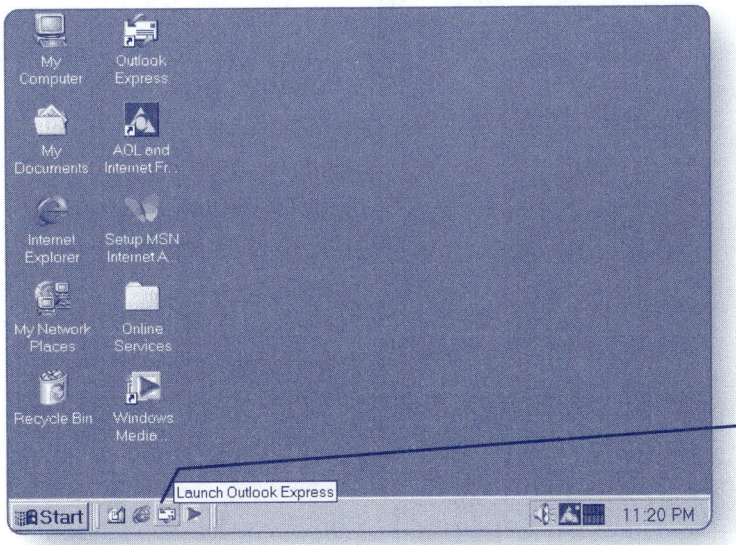

Windows Millennium Edition allows you to add any of four ready-made toolbars to the Taskbar. One of these toolbars, the Quick Launch toolbar, provides shortcuts to several often-used programs, including Internet Explorer and Outlook Express, Windows Media Player, or to display your desktop.

1. Click on any **button** on the Quick Launch bar. The selected program launches.

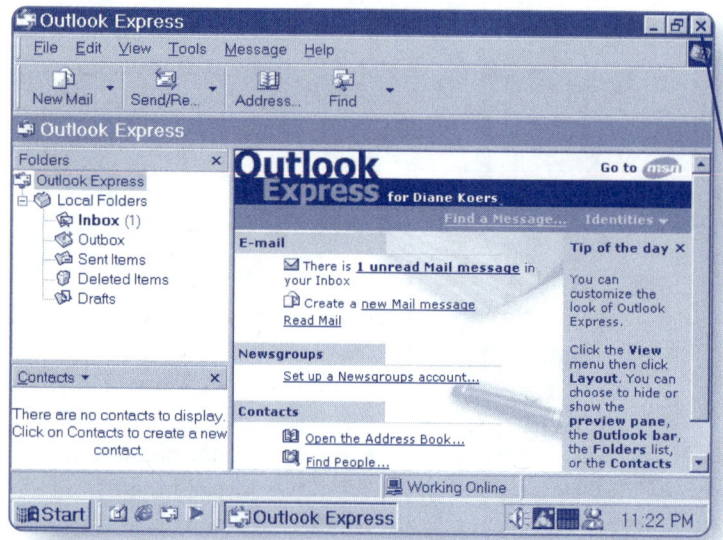

TIP
Position the mouse pointer on top of each Quick Launch button to see a description of that feature.

2. Click on the **Close button** (X). The activated program closes.

Investigating the System Tray

Windows locates the System Tray on the right side of the Taskbar. The System Tray displays a series of icons to help you see what is going on in your system. Items such as the current time, anti-virus programs, and volume control can be modified from the System Tray.

The System Tray can also manage power options, which you'll find particularly helpful if you are using a laptop computer.

Similar to the Quick Launch bar, you can position your mouse pointer on top of a choice in the System Tray to see a description of that feature.

1. Double-click on a **System Tray feature**. A dialog box pertaining to that feature opens.

LOOKING AT OTHER DESKTOP ITEMS   21

2. Make any desired **changes** in the dialog box. In the example shown, we are changing the volume settings.

3. Click on the **Close button** (X). The dialog box closes.

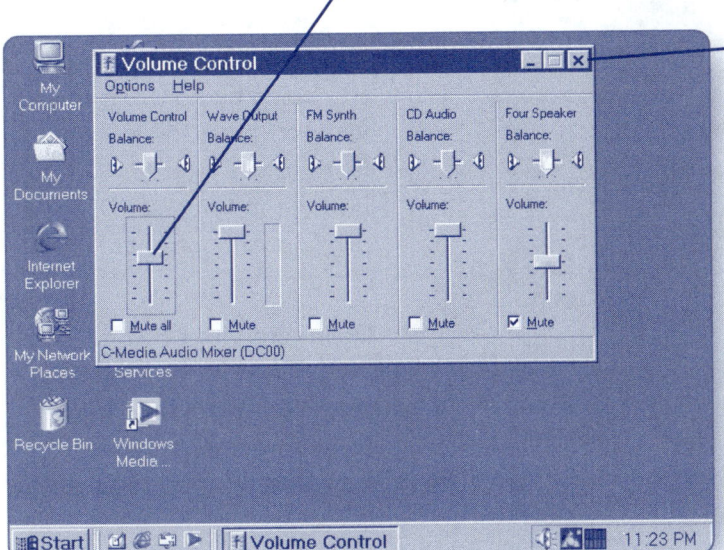

Looking at Other Desktop Items

A couple of other icons on the desktop should be mentioned at this point. You'll learn in detail more about most of these icons in later chapters.

- **Outlook Express.** This icon provides access to a popular e-mail program. If you have Internet access, Outlook Express can help you manage incoming and outgoing e-mail. You'll learn about Outlook Express in Chapter 21, "E-mailing with Outlook Express."

- **My Documents Folder.** Windows created the My Documents folder as a convenient place to store documents or files that you may need to access quickly and easily.

- **Recycle Bin.** This icon represents the place where your files go after they are deleted. Discover the Recycle Bin in Chapter 12, "Organizing Files and Folders."

22 CHAPTER 2: DISCOVERING DESKTOP COMPONENTS

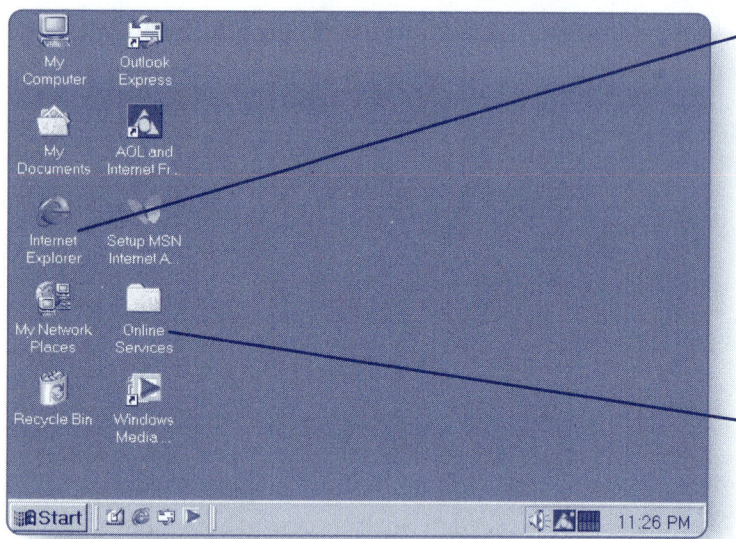

- **Internet Explorer.** The default Web browser supplied with Windows Millennium Edition. A Web browser is necessary if you want to access the Internet. Learn to use Internet Explorer in Chapter 20, "Surfing with Internet Explorer."

- **Online Services Folder.** This folder provides shortcuts to several of the major Internet access providers.

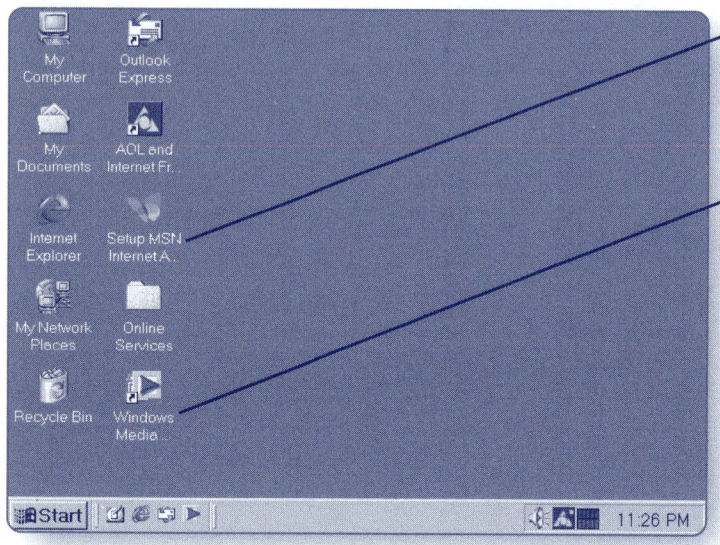

- **Setup MSN Internet Access.** Microsoft Network (MSN) is a popular Internet access provider.

- **Windows Media Player.** Use Windows Media Player to play CDs and video. Learn about Windows Media Player in Chapter 14 "Discovering Multimedia."

3

Recognizing Parts of a Window

Windows Millennium Edition windows have several common components. Each component of a window has a purpose to assist you in one way or another. Some components change the view of the document on the screen; other components speed up a process, such as closing a window. In this chapter, you'll learn how to:

- Identify window components
- Use the scroll bars
- Resize and move a window
- Maximize and minimize a window

Identifying Window Components

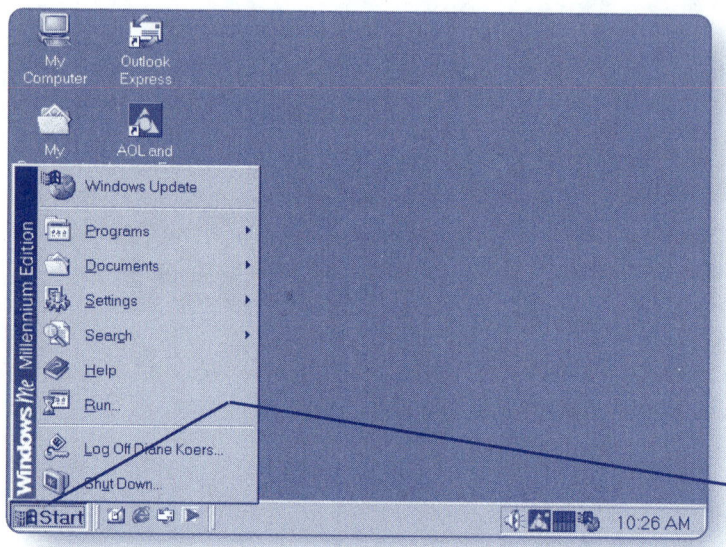

Most of the features listed in this section appear whether the window displays from a program or from a folder. As you position the mouse pointer over many of the buttons, a *ToolTip* displays— a small yellow box reflecting the name of the button.

The WordPad window is an example of a typical window and its components.

1. Click on the **Start button**. The Start menu appears.

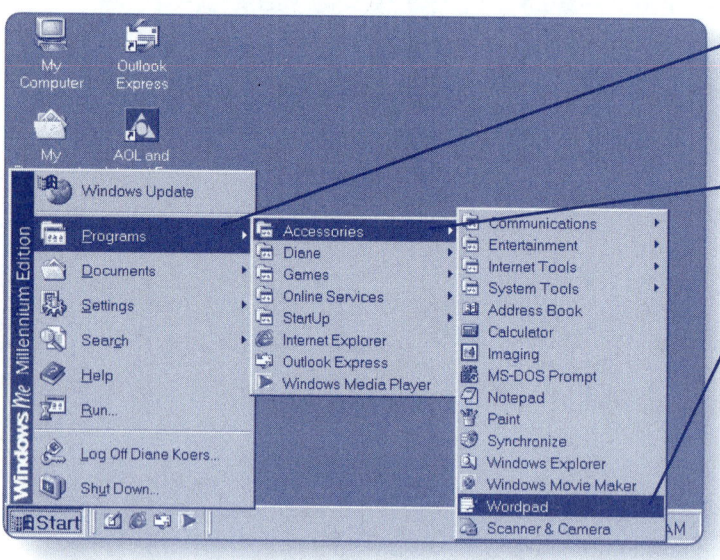

2. Click on **Programs**. The Programs cascading menu appears.

3. Click on **Accessories**. The Accessories menu appears.

4. Click on **WordPad**. The WordPad program begins.

> **NOTE**
>
> You'll learn how to use the WordPad program in Chapter 7, "Using WordPad."

IDENTIFYING WINDOW COMPONENTS 25

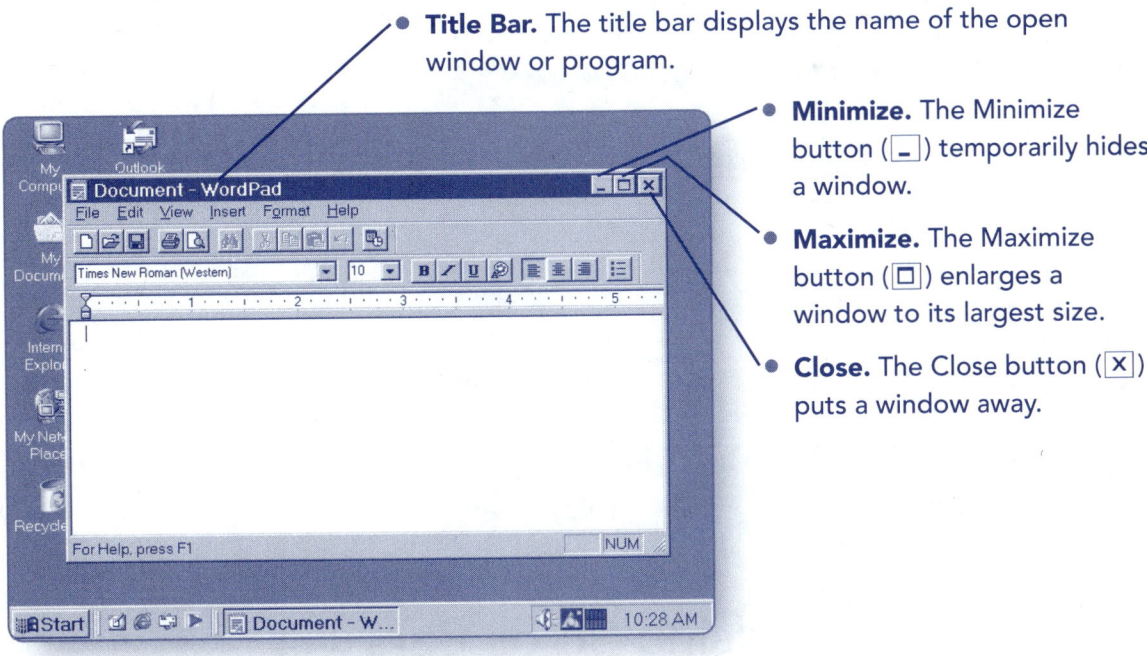

- **Title Bar.** The title bar displays the name of the open window or program.

- **Minimize.** The Minimize button ([_]) temporarily hides a window.

- **Maximize.** The Maximize button ([□]) enlarges a window to its largest size.

- **Close.** The Close button ([X]) puts a window away.

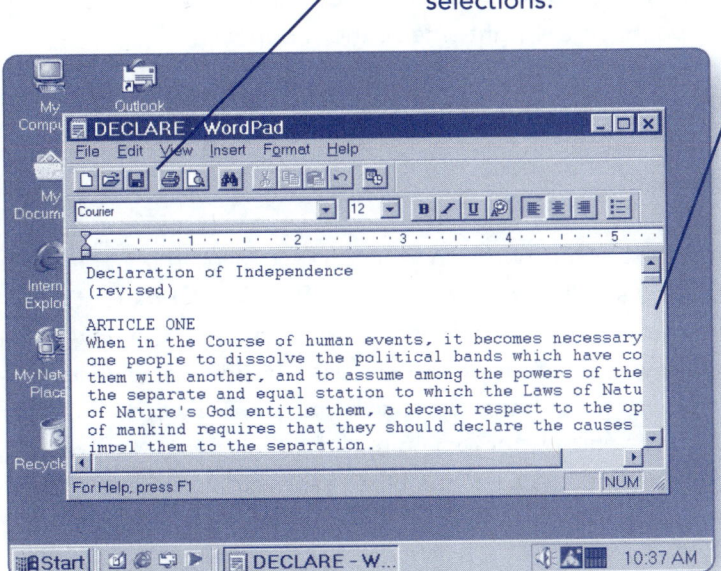

- **Toolbar.** While not all windows have a toolbar, most program windows do. Toolbars are shortcuts to menu selections.

- **Vertical Scroll Bar.** The vertical scroll bar allows you to view a window from top to bottom. In the WordPad program, if you do not have enough text to fill up the screen, you may not see any scroll bars.

CHAPTER 3: RECOGNIZING PARTS OF A WINDOW

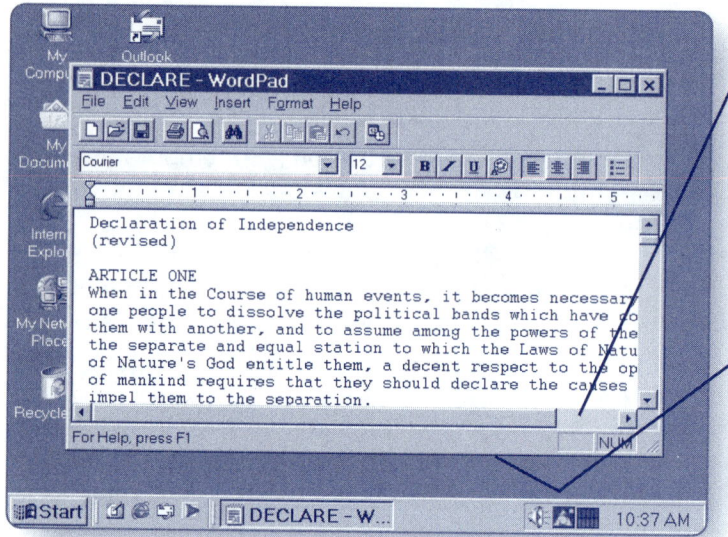

- **Horizontal Scroll Bar.** The horizontal scroll bar allows you to view a window from left to right. In the WordPad program, if you do not have enough text to fill up the screen you may not see any scroll bars.

- **Window Borders.** Window borders frame the perimeter of a window and are used to resize a window.

Using Scroll Bars

Scroll bars appear on a window when there is more to see than displayed in the window. Depending on the window, you may see one or two scroll bars. The horizontal scroll bar appears at the bottom of the window, and the vertical scroll bar appears on the right side of the window.

Although you will look primarily at the vertical scroll bar, all the options listed in this section apply to the horizontal scroll bar as well.

Each scroll bar has two arrows and a box called the *scroll box*. Picture the scroll box as an elevator. If the scroll box is at the top of the bar, this is like being on the top floor. The only direction you can go is down—so use the down arrow to scroll down through the window. If you are in a word processing window, for example, clicking on the down arrow displays one or two lines at a time—sort of like stopping at each floor in the elevator.

USING SCROLL BARS 27

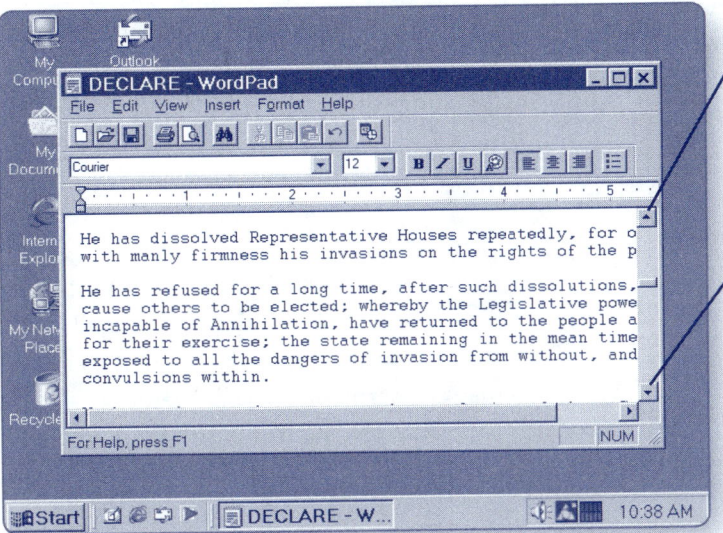

1. **Click** on the **up arrow** (▲) of the vertical scroll bar. The next row of text or objects located farther up in the window appears.

2. **Click** on the **down arrow** (▼) of the vertical scroll bar. The next row of text or objects located farther down in the window appears.

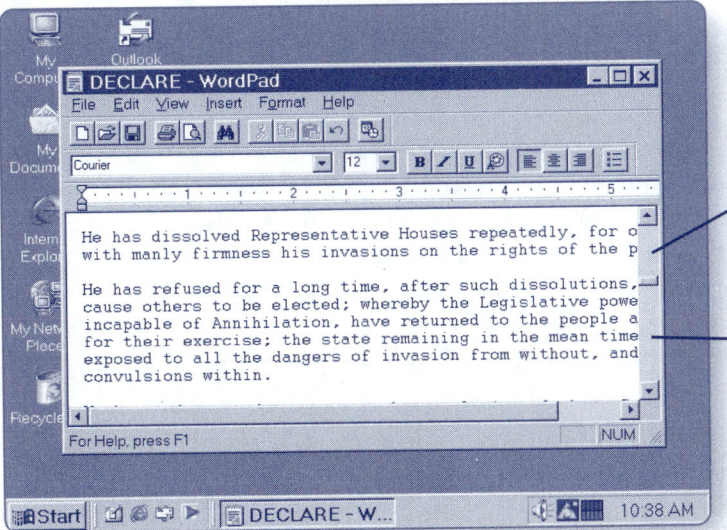

An alternative method is moving the screen up or down one "page" at a time—with a "page" being a window size.

3. **Click** on the **scroll bar** just above the scroll box. The screen moves up one page at a time.

4. **Click** on the **scroll bar** just below the scroll box. The screen moves down one page at a time.

28 CHAPTER 3: RECOGNIZING PARTS OF A WINDOW

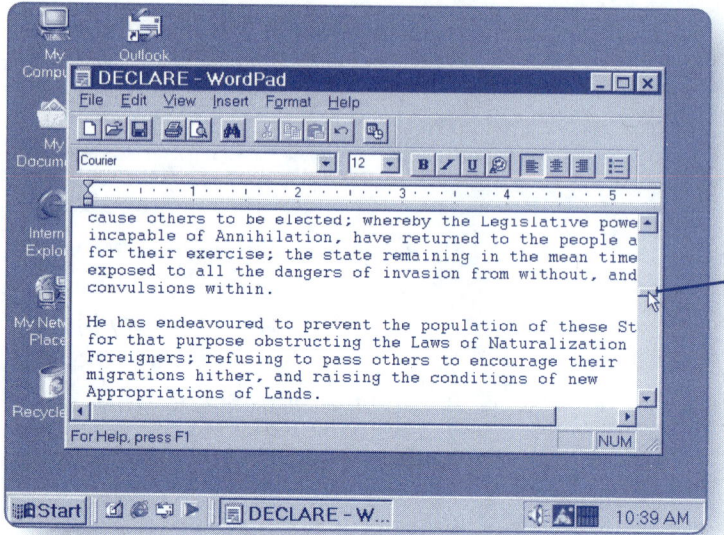

A third method of moving with the scroll bar is to drag the scroll box up or down the bar to quickly move through a window. (Sort of like an "express" elevator.)

5. Press and **hold** the **mouse button** and **drag** the **scroll box** to the top or bottom of the scroll bar. The screen text moves in the direction you are dragging the scroll box.

6. Release the **mouse button**. The text or objects located at the top or bottom of the window appear.

> **TIP**
> You can also drag the scroll box to any point in the scroll bar. The scroll bar is relative to the length of the document or window. For example, if you have a 10-page report and you drag the scroll box about half way down the scroll bar, the screen stops at approximately page five.

Manually Resizing Windows

If a window is too small or too large, you can resize it by using your mouse. However, you cannot resize a window while in the maximized size.

MANUALLY RESIZING WINDOWS   29

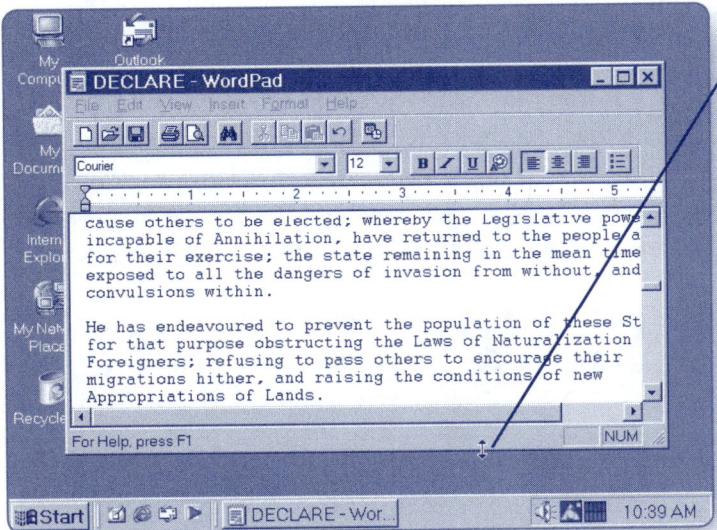

1. Position the **mouse pointer** on an outside edge of a window. The mouse pointer becomes a double-headed arrow.

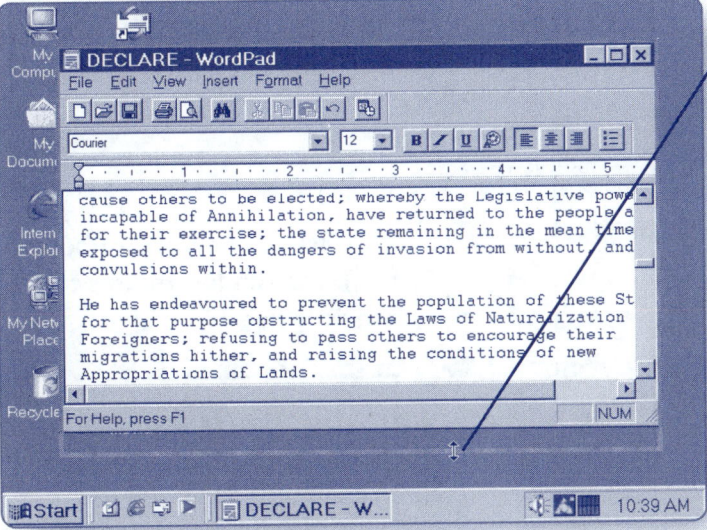

2. Press and **hold** the **mouse button** while moving the mouse. The outline of the window resizes in the direction you move the mouse.

3. Release the **mouse button** when the window is the desired size. The window is resized.

Maximizing a Window

Although you can manually resize a window, *maximizing* the window is a favorite choice for many users. To maximize is to make the window as large as possible—as large as your screen allows. The Maximize button is the middle of the three buttons located in the upper-right corner of the window.

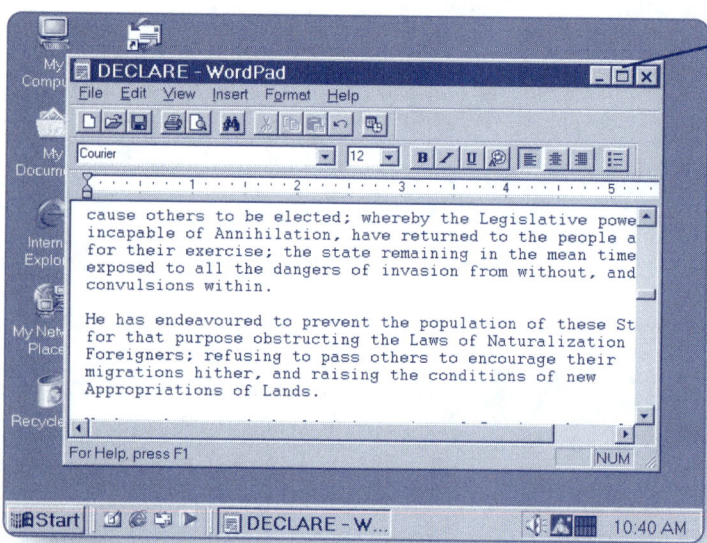

1. Click on the **Maximize button** (☐). The window enlarges.

Notice that the appearance of the Maximize button has changed. When a window is already maximized, the button is called the Restore button.

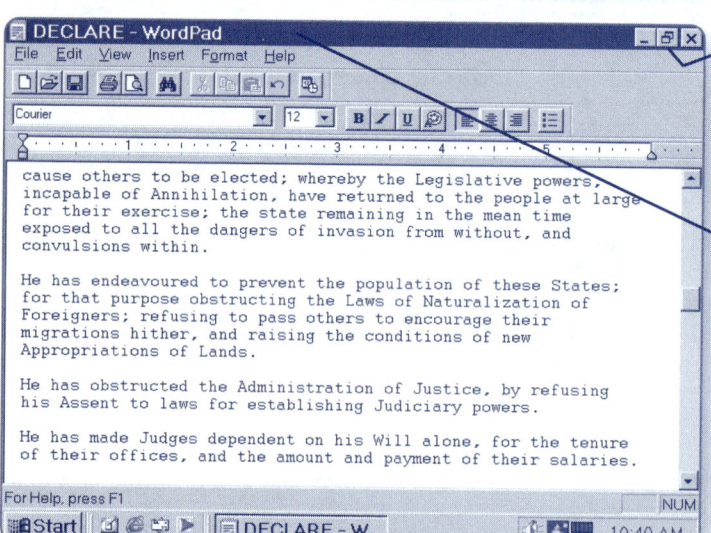

2. Click on the **Restore button** (❐). The window returns to the previous size.

TIP
You can also double-click on the title bar of a window to maximize it. Double-click on the title bar again to restore it.

MINIMIZING A WINDOW   31

Minimizing a Window

Occasionally a window may be on top of something else you need to see on your desktop. You can move a window, as covered in the next section, or you can *minimize* it. Minimizing a window does not close it, but simply sets it aside for later use. Windows calls the first of the three buttons located in the upper-right corner of the window the Minimize button.

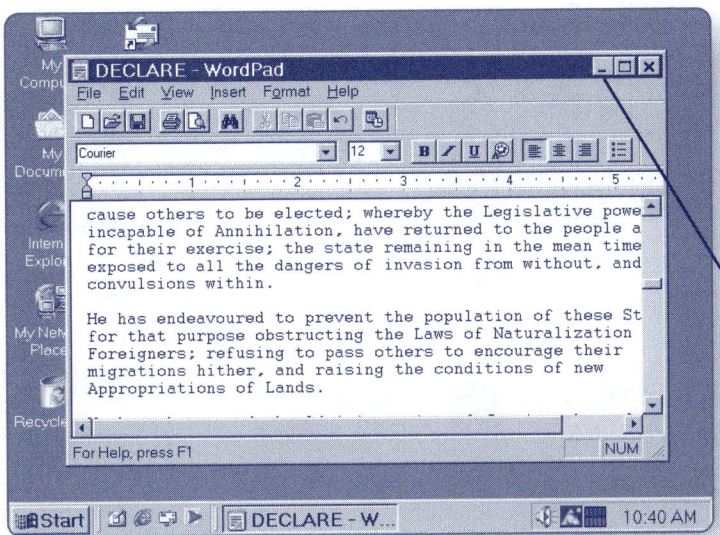

1. Click on the **Minimize button ([_])**. The window temporarily disappears from your screen.

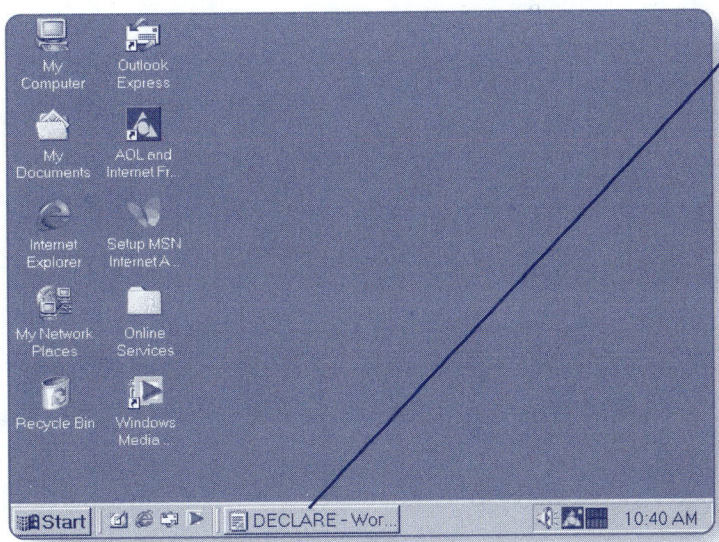

2. Click on the **program application button** on the Taskbar. The window restores to its previous size.

Moving a Window

Besides resizing a window, you can also move a window to a different location on the desktop. A window cannot be moved if it's maximized.

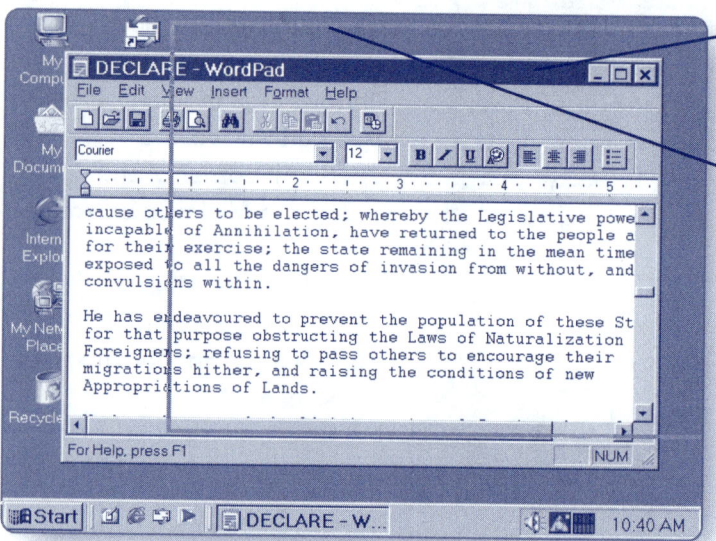

1. Position the **mouse pointer** on the title bar of the window to be moved.

2. Press and **hold** the **mouse button** on the title bar while moving the mouse. An outline of the window appears indicating the new position.

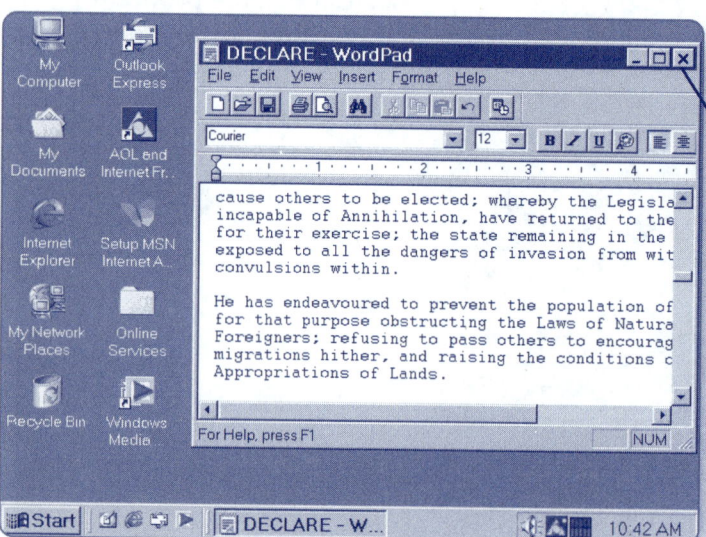

3. Release the **mouse button**. The window moves to a new location.

4. Click on the **Close button** (X). The WordPad program closes.

4

Using Windows Menus and Dialog Boxes

When you go into a restaurant, you make selections from a menu. So it is with a Windows program. Windows programs use the concept of a *menu* to make choices. In this chapter, you'll learn how to:

- Make menu choices with a mouse and a keyboard
- Work in a Windows dialog box
- Learn common Windows Millennium Edition menu commands

Making Menu Choices with a Mouse

When you open an application, the main menus of program options appear at the top of the window in the area called the menu bar. Selecting a choice from the main menu with your left mouse button leads you to another menu selection. Occasionally that second menu leads to a third menu. Windows calls this a *cascading menu*.

Most Windows applications have several menu selections in common. The first one is usually File, the second is Edit, the third is View, and the last one is usually Help. The menu selections in between View and Help vary from application to application.

The Windows Paint program shows us an example of a typical application and its components.

> **NOTE**
> You'll learn how to use the Paint program in Chapter 8, "Painting with the Paint Program."

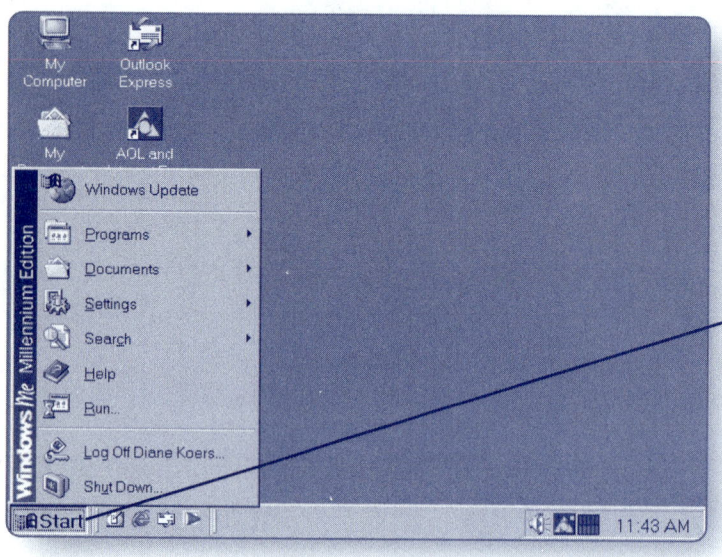

1. Click on the **Start button**. The Start menu appears.

MAKING MENU CHOICES WITH A MOUSE   35

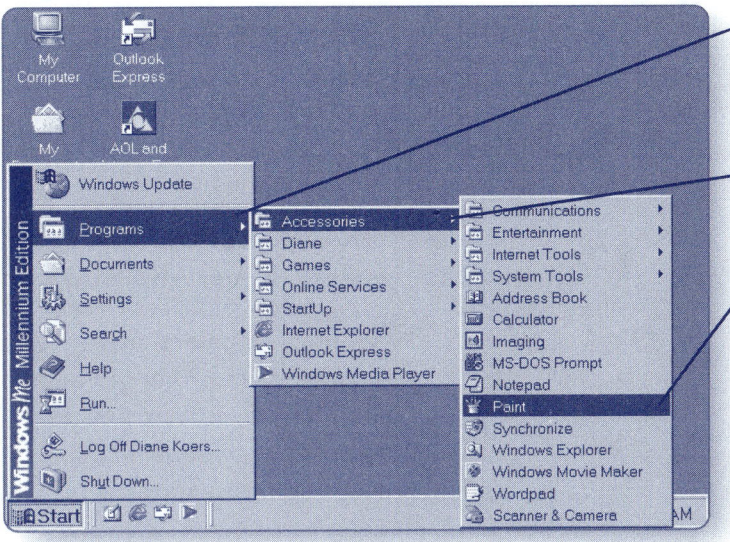

2. Click on **Programs**. The Programs cascading menu appears.

3. Click on **Accessories**. The Accessories menu appears.

4. Click on **Paint**. The Paint program begins.

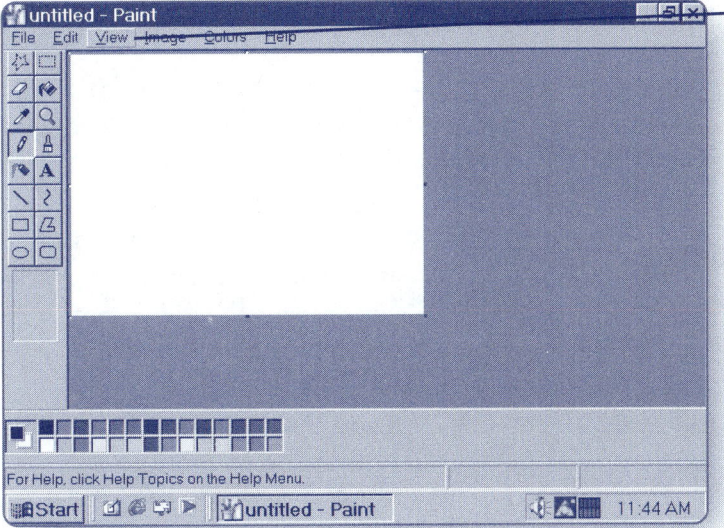

5. Position the **mouse pointer** over the desired menu. The menu becomes three-dimensional in shape.

36 CHAPTER 4: USING WINDOWS MENUS AND DIALOG BOXES

6. Click on the **menu**. The menu selections appear.

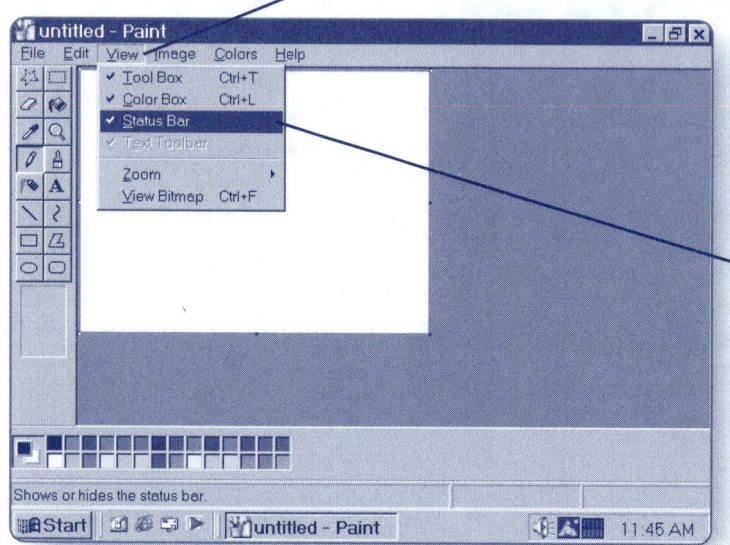

TIP
If you click on a menu in error, click outside of the menu to close it.

7. Choose a **selection** from the displayed menu. One of three things happens: Windows takes the action you requested; a cascading menu appears; or a dialog box opens.

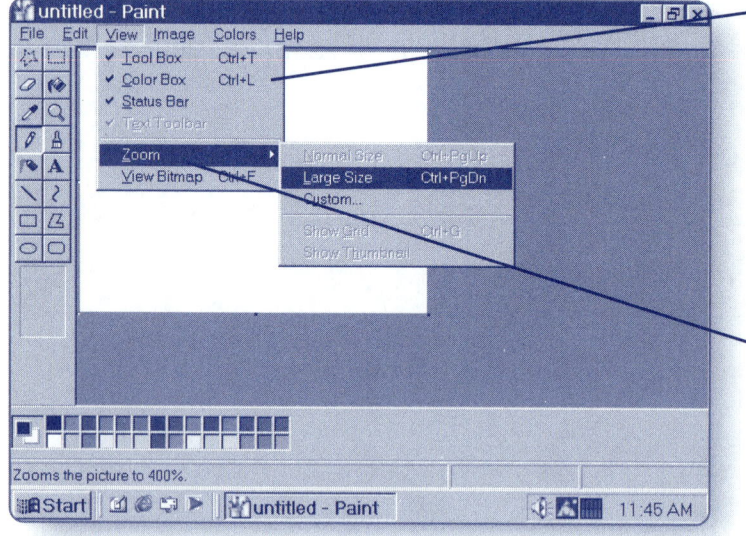

If you choose an item with a check mark beside it, Windows turns off the feature. Check marked items are like toggle switches—a check means the item is active, whereas no check mark means the item is not active.

If you choose a menu item with a cascading menu, you will need to select another choice from that menu.

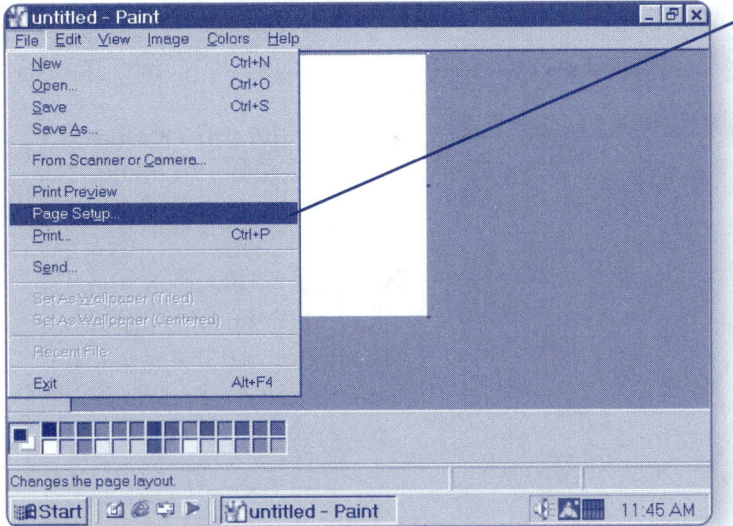

If you choose a menu item with an ellipsis (. . .) following the menu selection, a dialog box opens, prompting you for further information. You'll learn about dialog boxes later in this chapter.

Using Shortcut Menus

Many programs offer a selection when you click the right mouse button. Windows calls this a *shortcut menu*. A shortcut menu is a variable collection of frequently used choices that are relative to your mouse pointer position. For example, if you use Microsoft Word and position your mouse pointer over a word and click the right mouse button, the shortcut menu shows items pertinent to working with text, such as fonts or paragraph choices. However, if you position the mouse pointer on the toolbar and you click the right mouse button, you see choices pertinent to working with different toolbars.

1. Position the **mouse pointer** at the desired location in a document.

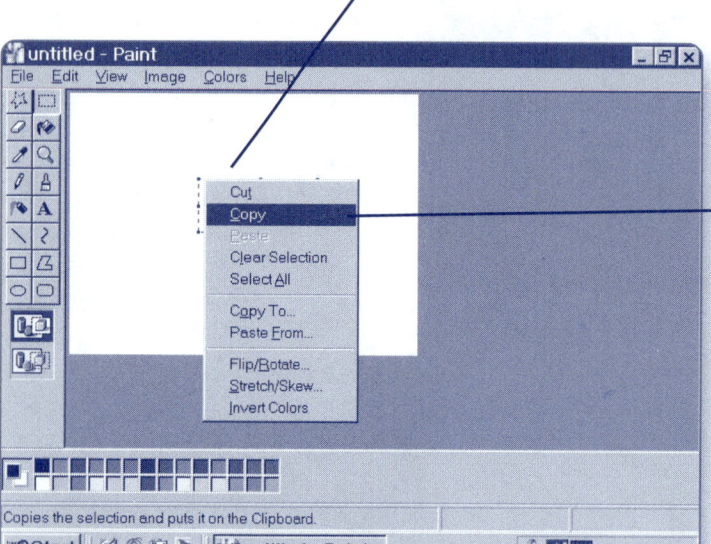

2. Click the **right mouse button**. A shortcut menu appears.

3. Make a **selection** from the shortcut menu with the left mouse button. The requested action happens or a dialog box opens.

TIP
If you open a shortcut menu in error, click anywhere outside of the shortcut menu to close it. No action is taken.

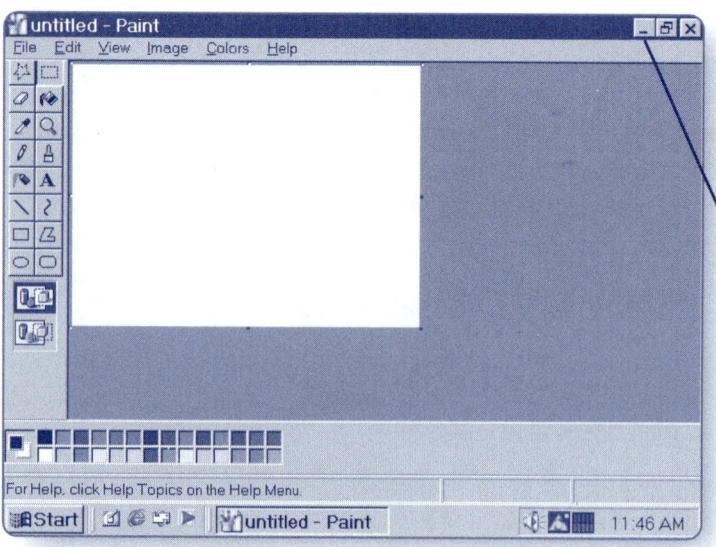

Next we'll show you how to make menu choices with the keyboard. We need to temporarily minimize the Paint program to illustrate this feature.

4. Click on the **Minimize button** (_). The Paint window is minimized.

Selecting Menu Choices with the Keyboard

Many programs offer shortcut keys, such as pressing Ctrl+B to bold a selection or pressing the F1 key for help. The disadvantage of these types of shortcuts is that you must rely on your memory for them. I don't know about you, but the older I get, the shorter my memory gets. However, sometimes it's very cumbersome to take your hands from the keyboard to the mouse, from the mouse to the keyboard, and back and forth.

Fortunately, you do not need to use the mouse to make a selection from the menu. You can use the keyboard to access all menu selections. Notice that each menu selection has an underlined letter. Using the Alt key and the underlined letter gives you control of the menu from your keyboard. Again, remember the magic key: the Alt key.

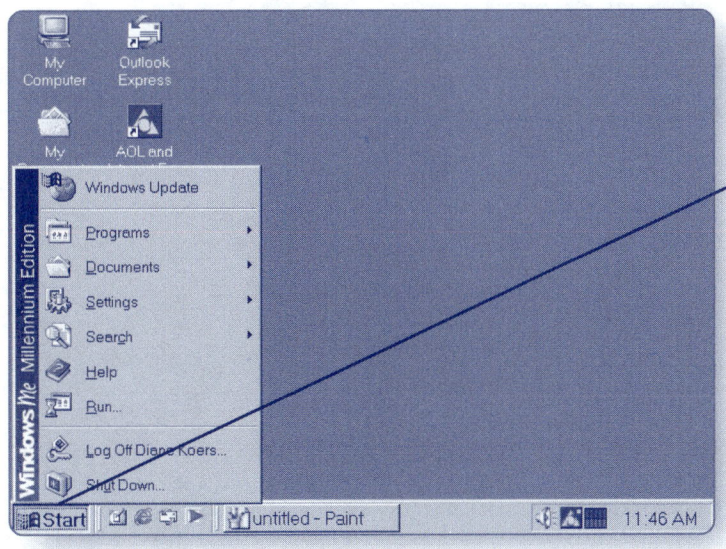

Let's take a look at WordPad for examples of making menu selections with the keyboard.

1. Click on the **Start button**. The Start menu appears.

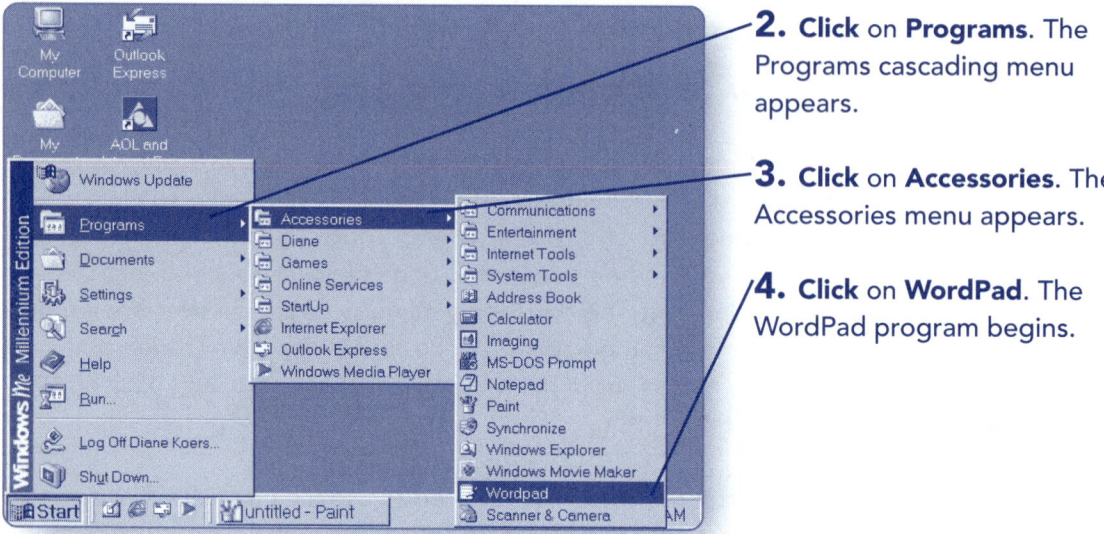

2. Click on **Programs**. The Programs cascading menu appears.

3. Click on **Accessories**. The Accessories menu appears.

4. Click on **WordPad**. The WordPad program begins.

5. Press and **release** the **Alt key**. The first menu (File) is selected with a three-dimensional box around it.

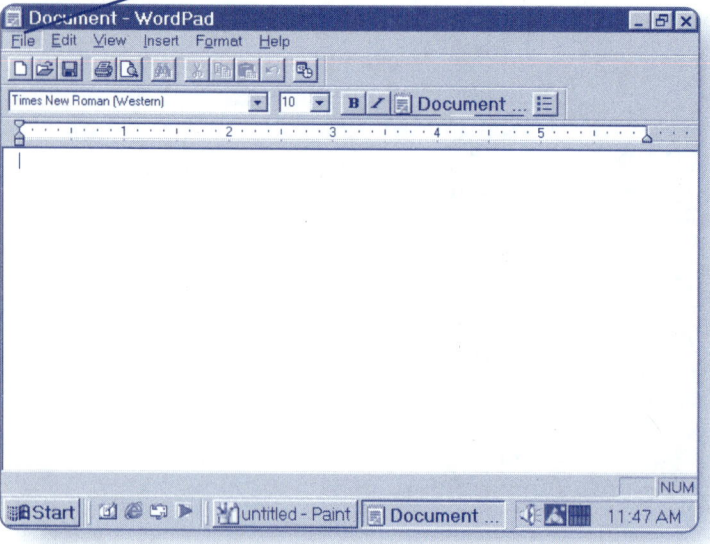

SELECTING MENU CHOICES WITH THE KEYBOARD   41

6. Type the **underlined letter** for the menu you want to select. The menu appears, and the first item in the menu is highlighted. In the figure shown, I pressed the letter "o" for the Format menu.

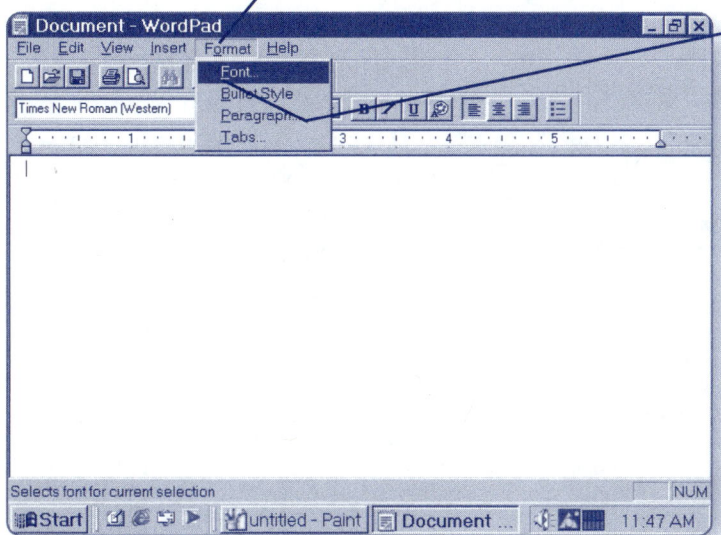

7. Type the **underlined letter** for the item you want to select from the menu. You do not need to press the Alt key again because you are already using the menu. One of three things could happen: The action you requested is taken; a dialog box opens; or a cascading menu appears.

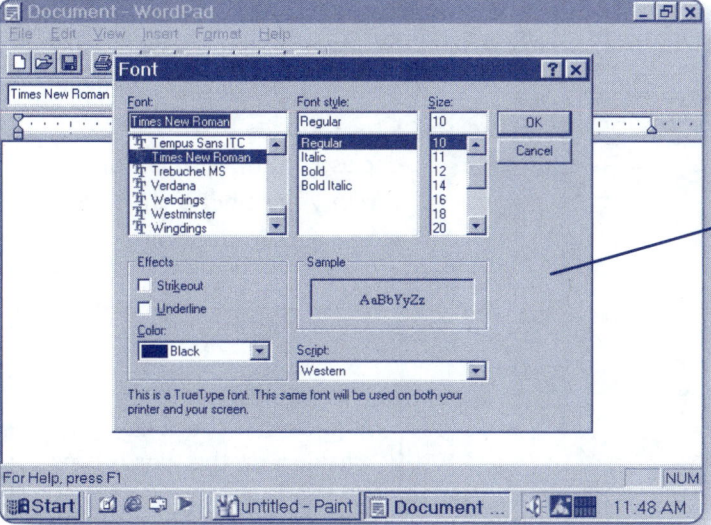

8a. Repeat Step 6 for your next menu selection if a cascading menu appears.

OR

8b. Make any necessary **selections** if a dialog box appears. In our example, we're choosing F**o**rmat and then **F**ont, which results in the dialog box seen in this figure.

Working in a Dialog Box

A menu selection that has three dots after it, called an ellipsis (. . .), indicates that a dialog box opens if you choose that menu item. A *dialog box* prompts you for additional information. Many menu selections open a dialog box. Although each dialog box differs from the next one, common types of selections can be made from a dialog box.

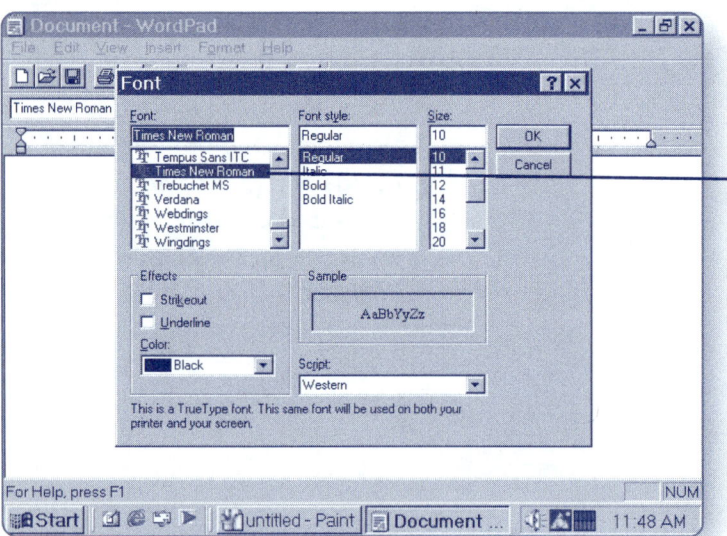

1. Click on the **desired choice** in a scroll box. The item you select displays in the box at the top of the list. *List boxes* enable you to select an item from a displayed list.

If the list is too large to be displayed, a scroll bar becomes available.

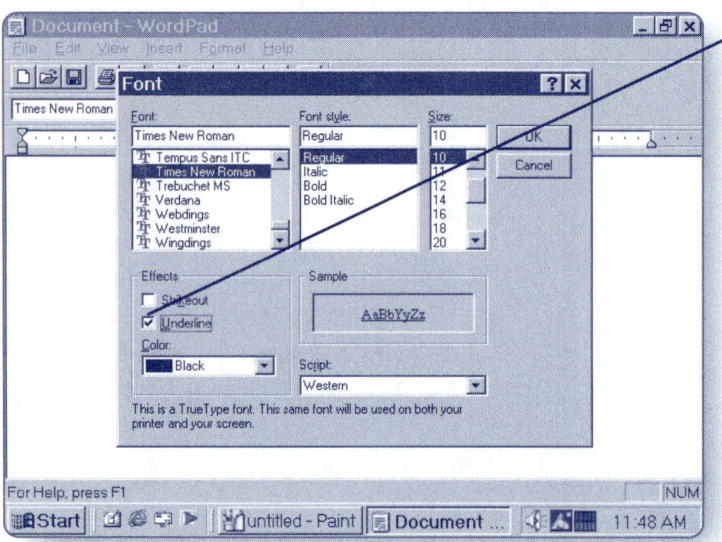

2. Click on the **check boxes** next to your desired choices. *Check boxes* allow you to choose multiple selections. When you select a check box, a ✔ appears in the box.

TIP

You can also make a choice in a check box by clicking on the words next to the box.

WORKING IN A DIALOG BOX   43

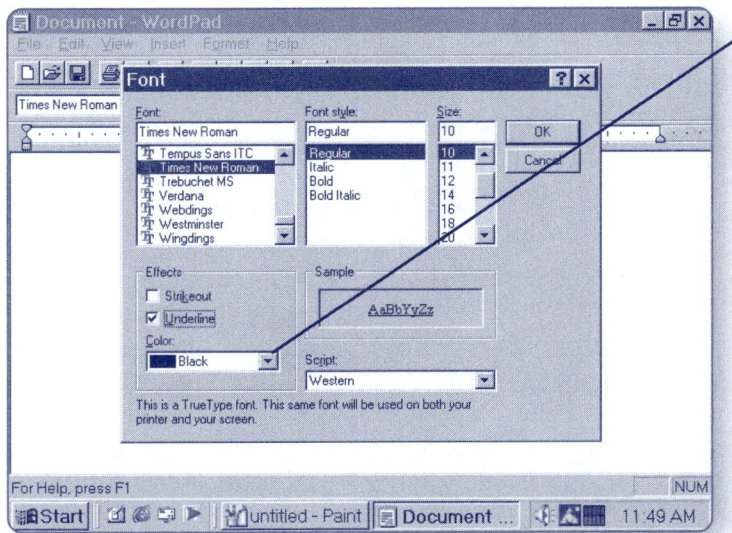

3. **Click** on the **down arrow** (▼) next to a drop-down list box. A list of possible selections appears. *Drop-down list boxes* allow you to select an item from a list that appears. Drop-down list boxes have a small down arrow (▼) to the right of the current selection.

4. **Click** on the **desired choice**. The list of possible selections closes, and the selected choice appears in the drop-down list box.

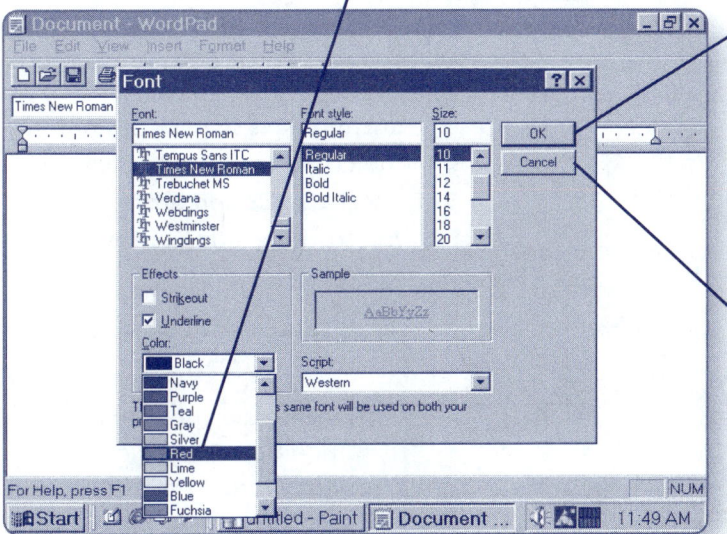

5a. **Click** on the **OK button**. The dialog box closes, and your selections are accepted. The OK button enables you to accept your selections from a dialog box.

OR

5b. **Click** on the **Cancel button**. The dialog box closes, and your selections are ignored. The Cancel button enables you to reject your selections from a dialog box.

CHAPTER 4: USING WINDOWS MENUS AND DIALOG BOXES

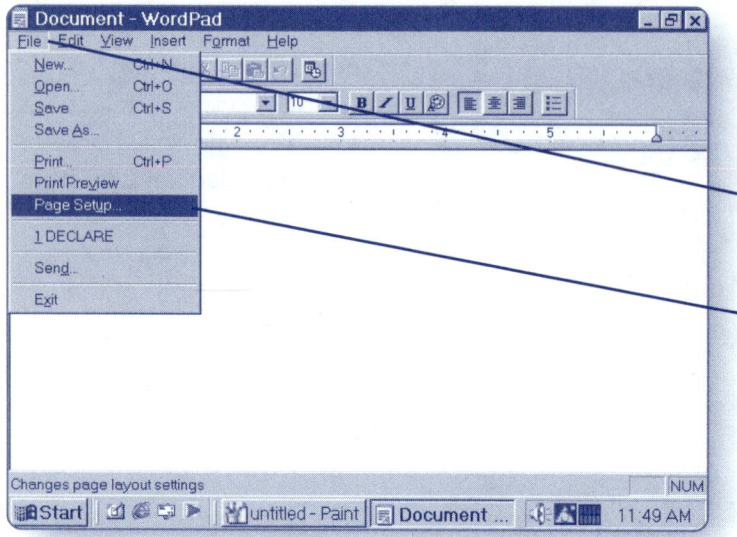

An illustration of another type of dialog box is seen with the WordPad Page Setup dialog box.

6. **Click** on **File**. The File menu appears.

7. **Click** on **Page Setup**. The Page Setup dialog box opens.

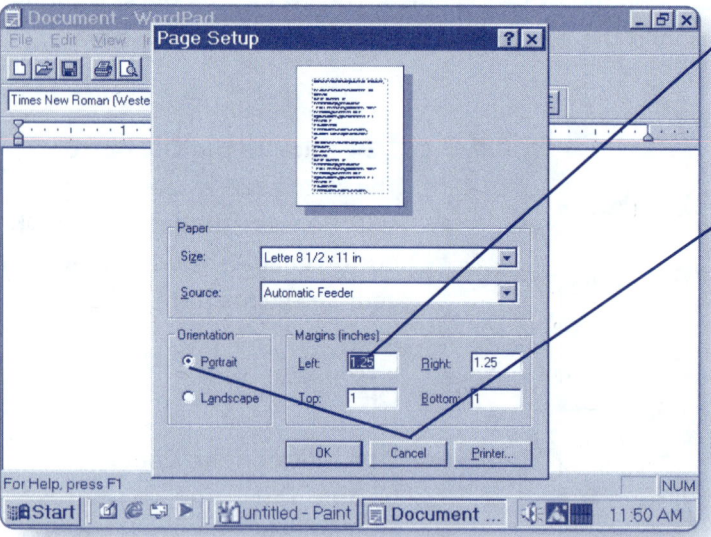

8. **Type** the **desired information** in a text box. *Text boxes* allow you to type specified information in a box.

9. **Click** on the **circle (option button)** next to your desired choice. A small dot appears in the circle. *Option buttons* allow you to choose one of several selections.

TIP
You can also choose an option button by clicking on the words next to the circle.

WORKING IN A DIALOG BOX — 45

NOTE

If you want to use your keyboard to select from a dialog box, use the Tab key to move from section to section of the dialog box. You can then use your down arrow key to select from a list box, drop-down list box, or option buttons; or you can use the spacebar to select/deselect choices with check boxes. Press the Enter key at an OK button to accept the choices or press the Esc key to cancel your selections.

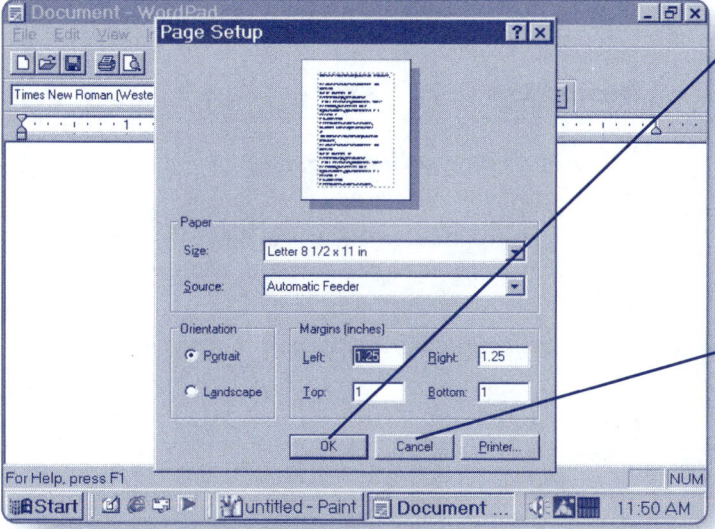

10a. **Click** on the **OK button**. The dialog box closes, and your selections are accepted. The OK button allows you to accept your selections from a dialog box.

OR

10b. **Click** on the **Cancel button**. The dialog box closes, and your selections are ignored. The Cancel button allows you to reject your selections from a dialog box.

Learning Common Windows Commands

Software developers conform to certain conditions in order to designate their products as Windows products. Part of these conditions are common commands that Windows programs can use, whether you're using your word-processing program, spreadsheet, or Internet browser program. The following table illustrates some of the common commands, along with their descriptions and common shortcut keys. Many, but not all, software programs use the same shortcut keys.

Feature	Shortcut	Description
Open	Ctrl+O	Opens an existing document or file. You are prompted for a file name.
Save	Ctrl+S	Saves the current document or file. If it is the first time the document or file has been saved, Windows prompts you for a file name.
Select All	Ctrl+A	Selects the entire text of a document or all files in a folder.
Cut	Ctrl+X	Takes selected text or file and copies it to the Windows Clipboard and removes the original text or file.
Copy	Ctrl+C	Takes selected text or file and copies it to the Windows Clipboard. The original text or file remains in place.
Paste	Ctrl+V	Places the text or file from the Clipboard to the current location in the document or folder.
Undo	Ctrl+Z	Reverses the last action you took in the current program.
Print	Ctrl+P	Prints the current document.
Close	Ctrl+W	Closes the current document, but leaves the program open.
Exit	Alt+F4	Closes the current document and closes the program.
Help	F1	Starts the Help program. The type of help varies according to the specific software you use.

LEARNING COMMON WINDOWS COMMANDS 47

TIP
When a shortcut key begins with Ctrl or Alt, you need to press and hold down the Ctrl or Alt key, and then tap the second required key.

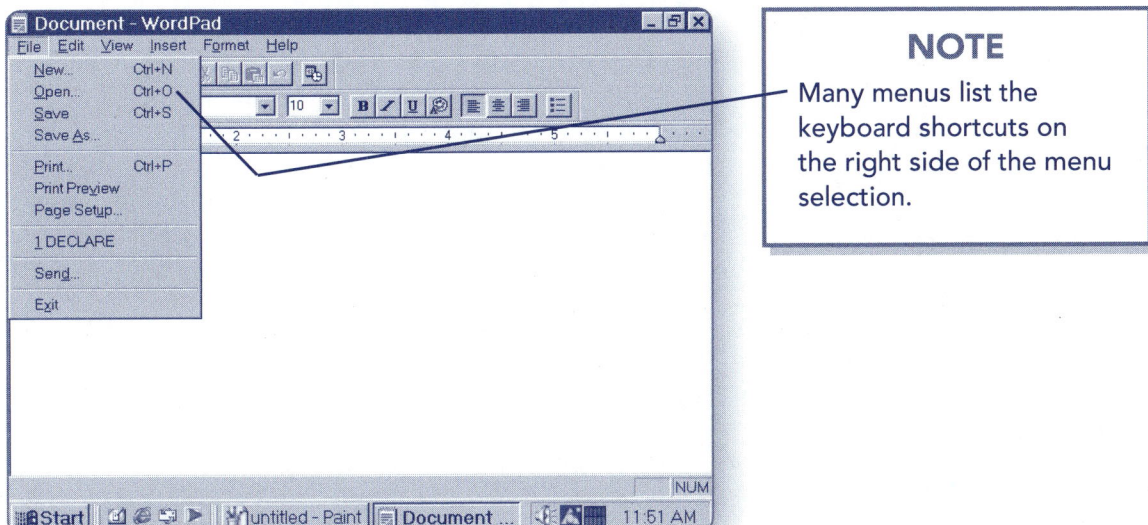

NOTE
Many menus list the keyboard shortcuts on the right side of the menu selection.

5

Multitasking and Shutting Down Windows

Windows has the capability to manage several jobs at one time. This means you can jump to a different program without having to exit the first one, and then return to it later. Sometimes, however, programs or even Windows itself can "lock up" and won't allow you to proceed. In this chapter, you'll learn how to:

- Open and close a Windows program
- Switch between open programs
- Send your PC into hibernation
- Handle a "locked up" program
- Shut down Windows the right way and when your computer locks up

Opening a Windows Program

Windows allows you to have multiple programs operating at the same time in your computer. In this section, while I refer to opening a second program, bear in mind that the same information applies whether it is the first, third, fourth, or thirteenth program you want to open. There are several ways to open additional programs while another one is currently open. It just depends on the location of the shortcut to the second program.

Opening with the Start Menu

Most programs can be accessed from the Start button. Your selections may vary from the following figure.

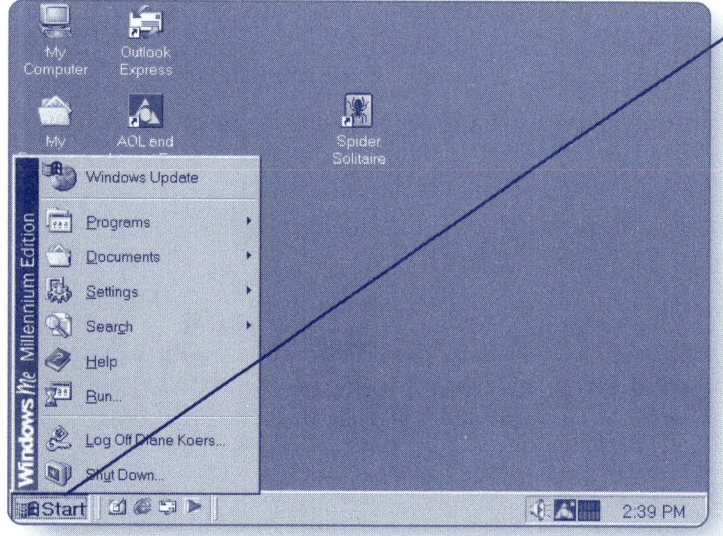

1. **Click** on the **Start button**. The Start menu appears.

OPENING A WINDOWS PROGRAM 51

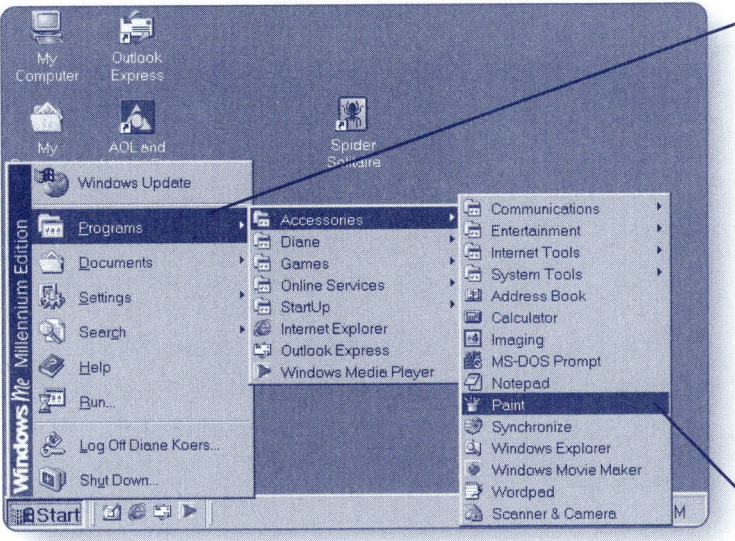

2. Click on **Programs**. The Programs menu appears.

> **NOTE**
> Your program may be buried in one or more additional levels. Continue clicking on the cascading menus until you reach the item for which you are looking.

3. Click on the **program** you want to use. The program opens.

Opening from the Desktop

Suppose you have a shortcut to one of your favorite programs on the Windows desktop. If you had several other programs open and needed to access that shortcut, you would normally need to minimize each of the other programs to get to the desktop. Windows Millennium Edition includes a Show Desktop button on the Quick Launch bar to provide easy access to your desktop. This eliminates the need to do all that minimizing.

1. Click on the **Show Desktop button** on the Quick Launch bar. All current programs are hidden, and your desktop is displayed.

CHAPTER 5: MULTITASKING AND SHUTTING DOWN WINDOWS

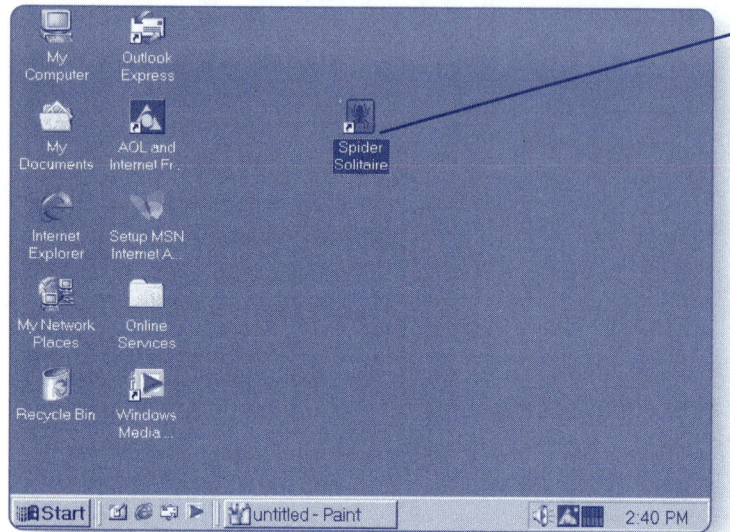

2. Click on the **shortcut** for the program you want to use. The program opens.

> **NOTE**
> Chapter 15, "Customizing the Desktop," shows you how to create desktop shortcuts to your favorite programs.

Switching between Programs

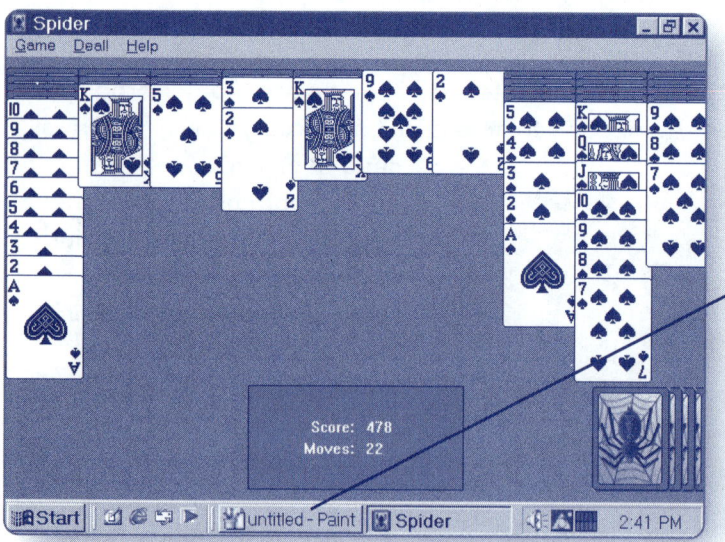

A button appears on the Taskbar for every program you have open. When you have multiple programs open, it is easy to switch back and forth between them.

1. Click on the **button** on the Taskbar for the program you want to make active. The window for that program returns to the front of the screen.

CLOSING A WINDOWS PROGRAM   53

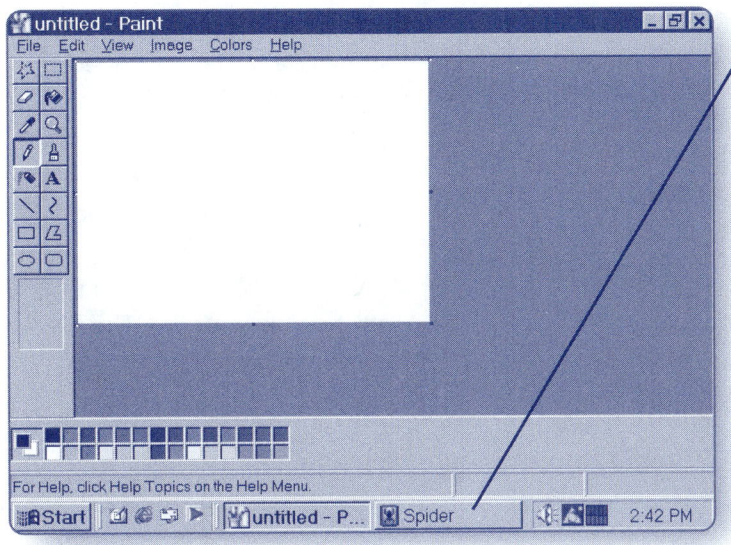

2. Click on a **different button** on the Taskbar. The newly selected program appears in front.

TIP
You can also press Alt+Tab to switch between open programs.

Closing a Windows Program

When you are finished using a Windows program, you should close the program. Keeping it open uses computer resources that you may need for another application.

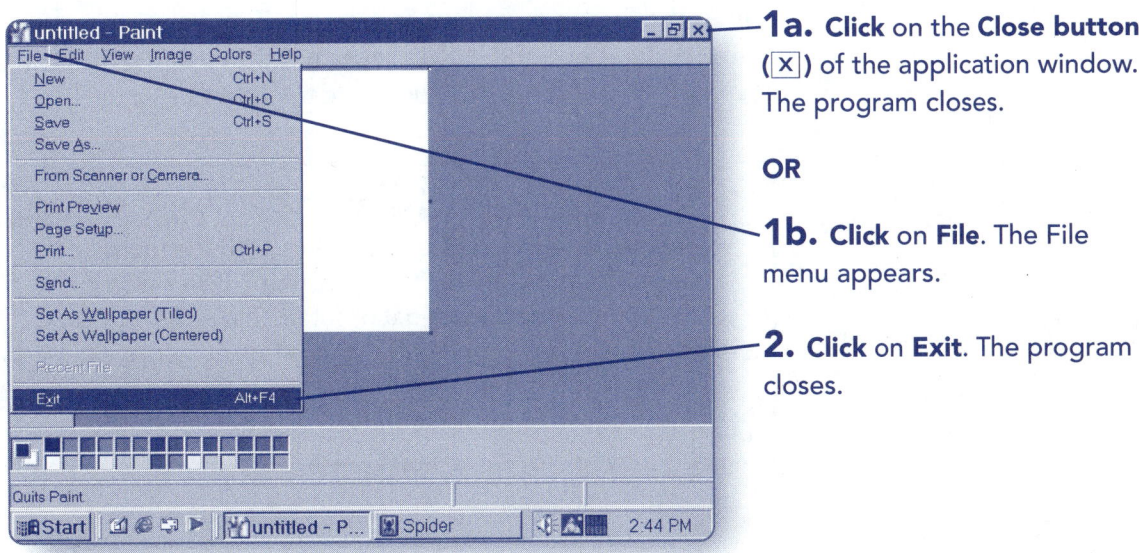

1a. Click on the **Close button** (X) of the application window. The program closes.

OR

1b. Click on **File**. The File menu appears.

2. Click on **Exit**. The program closes.

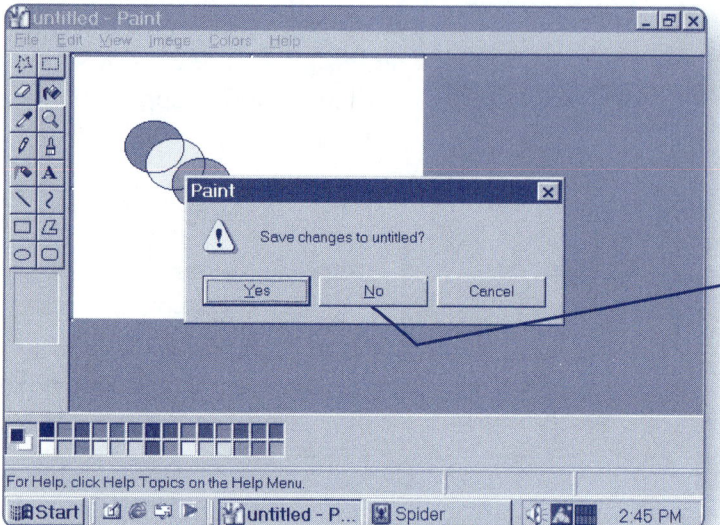

If you are using an application that has data that may need to be saved, Windows prompts you to save that information. You'll learn how to save a file in Chapter 7, "Using WordPad."

3. Click on **No** if you don't want to save your file. The file will not be saved.

Handling a Locked Up Application

As much as you try to avoid it, sometimes application programs simply crash and quit responding. The reasons are varied and far too numerous to mention. The real question is, "How do I get out of it?" If a program locks up and quits responding, you can try to "unfreeze" Windows.

NOTE

Sometimes an error message appears with the words "Illegal Operation" or "Fatal Exception." Don't worry; you didn't do anything illegal or fatal. This is the way Windows lets you know that it doesn't want to play anymore. If you get one of these error messages, follow the instructions on the screen.

1. **Press** and **hold** the **Ctrl key**, while **pressing** the **Alt** and **Delete keys**. (All at the same time.) The Close Program dialog box opens.

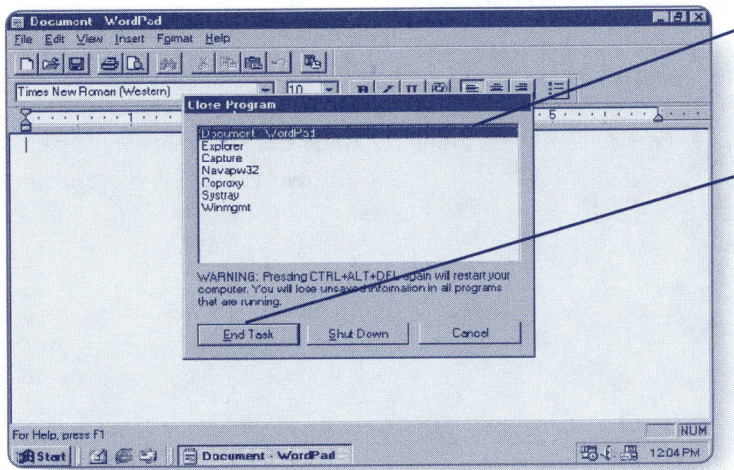

2. **Click** on the **program name** giving you problems. It appears selected.

3. **Click** on the **End Task button**. The selected program shuts down.

You can try restarting the application again. Occasionally, you need to restart your computer to get the application to launch again.

> **TIP**
> A quick way to restart your computer is to press Ctrl+Alt+Del twice.

Shutting Down Windows the Right Way

Windows takes a series of steps when it is time to shut down the computer. One thing you should not do (if at all possible) is just turn off the power. This can cause errors on the hard drive of the computer. It's best to let Windows "do its thing" and shut down using normal procedures.

56 CHAPTER 5: MULTITASKING AND SHUTTING DOWN WINDOWS

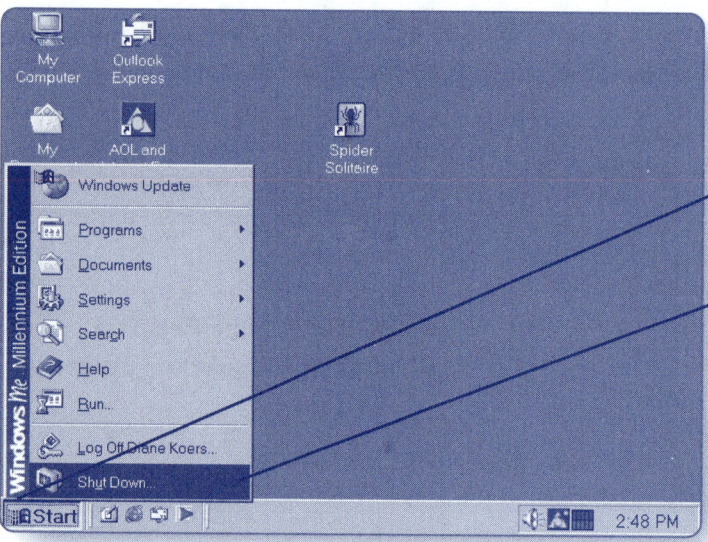

1. **Close** any **open programs**, saving any documents, if necessary.

2. **Click** on the **Start button**. The Start menu appears.

3. **Click** on **Shut Down**. The Shut Down Windows dialog box opens.

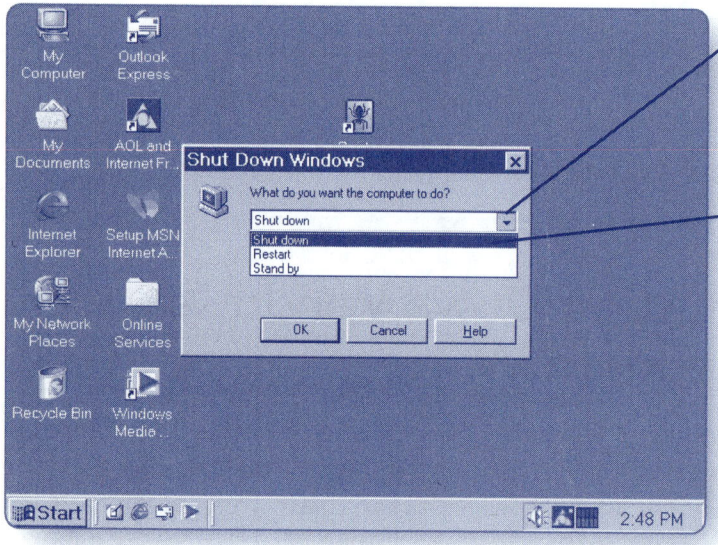

4. If Shut down is not displayed, **click** on the **drop-down arrow**. A list of options appears.

5. **Click** on **Shut down.** The option appears in the list.

SHUTTING DOWN WINDOWS THE RIGHT WAY

> **NOTE**
>
> New to Windows Millennium Edition, hibernation is another feature that may display at shutdown where your computer saves your current Windows settings, writes any information stored in memory to the hard drive, and turns off the computer. Different from the shut down procedure, when the computer is restarted, your desktop appears restored exactly as it was before you chose hibernation. Not all computers can support hibernation. (Mine cannot—that's why the hibernation selection doesn't appear in this figure.)

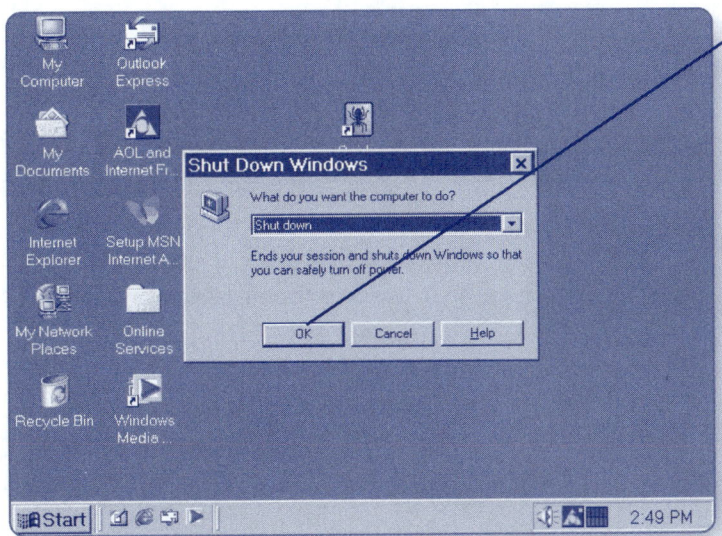

6. Click on **OK**. The computer begins its shut down procedure. You may see a message advising you "It is now safe to shut off your computer."

7. Turn off the **power** to your computer and monitor.

> **TIP**
>
> Some computers have their own power off device. After running its shut down procedure, the power of the machine automatically turns off.

> **NOTE**
>
> To turn your computer back on, press the power button on the machine and the monitor.

CHAPTER 5: MULTITASKING AND SHUTTING DOWN WINDOWS

Shutting Down Windows When Your Computer Locks Up

When the computer gremlin gets into your machine and the Windows program crashes, you can try closing the individual programs. If that doesn't help, there's nothing else you can do but restart your machine.

1a. **Turn off** the **power** to the computer.

OR

1b. **Press** the **restart button** on the front of the computer.

2. Count slowly to **10**. This gives the fans and internal components time to stop.

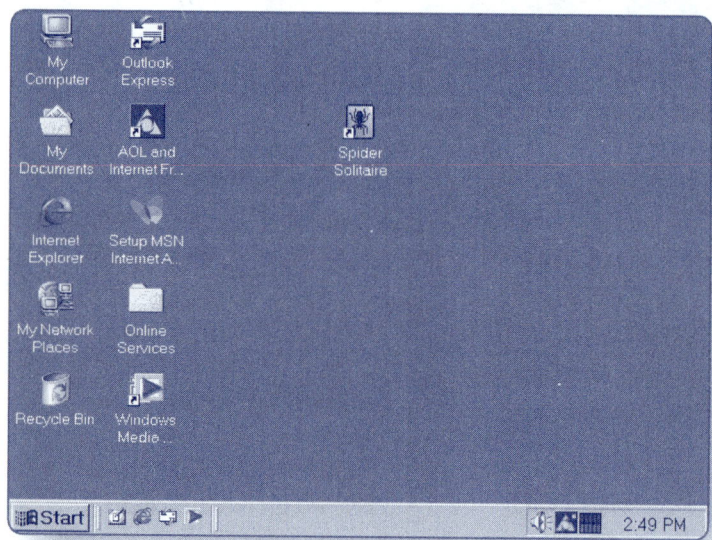

3. Turn on the **computer**. The rebooting process begins again. Your computer automatically runs ScanDisk, a Windows utility used to repair errors on a hard drive.

After the utility has completed its job, Windows continues to load.

Part I Review Questions

1. What character is displayed when you type a password? *See "Starting Windows Millennium Edition" in Chapter 1*

2. What is another word for the little pictures that appear on your desktop? *See "Discovering Desktop Components" in Chapter 2*

3. What does it mean when a disk drive icon has a hand underneath it? *See "Opening the My Computer Icon" in Chapter 2*

4. What is the name of the bar that is displayed at the bottom of your screen? *See "Working with the Taskbar" in Chapter 2*

5. What does the Minimize button do? *See "Identifying Window Components" in Chapter 3*

6. What is usually the first menu choice in a Windows application? *See "Making Menu Choices with a Mouse" in Chapter 4*

7. How do you access a shortcut menu? *See "Using Shortcut Menus" in Chapter 4*

8. How many choices can be selected from a dialog box with option buttons? *See "Working in a Dialog Box" in Chapter 4*

9. What does pressing Ctrl+S usually do in a Windows application? *See "Learning Common Windows Commands" in Chapter 4*

10. What steps should you take before you turn off your computer? *See "Shutting Down Windows the Right Way" in Chapter 5*

PART II
Working with the Accessories

Chapter 6
  Using the Calculator **63**

Chapter 7
  Using WordPad **71**

Chapter 8
  Painting with the Paint Program **93**

Chapter 9
  Playing Around with the Games **107**

6

Using the Calculator

Call me the absentminded professor, but I have trouble keeping track of my pocket calculator. Does that ever happen to you? It does have a way of getting buried beneath papers. Windows offers a calculator available at your fingertips. In this chapter, you'll learn how to:

- Start to use the Calculator
- Identify Calculator buttons
- Copy values from the Calculator to another program
- Change the style of the Calculator program

CHAPTER 6: USING THE CALCULATOR

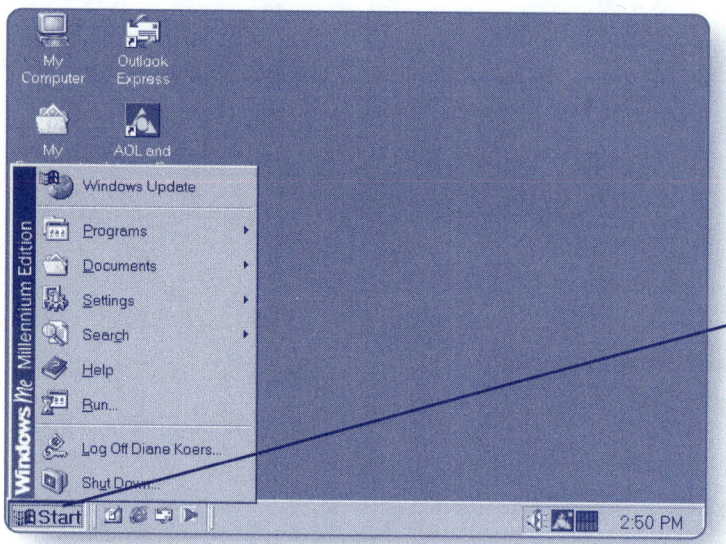

Starting the Calculator

The Calculator program is located in the Accessories folder.

1. Click on the **Start button**. The Start menu appears.

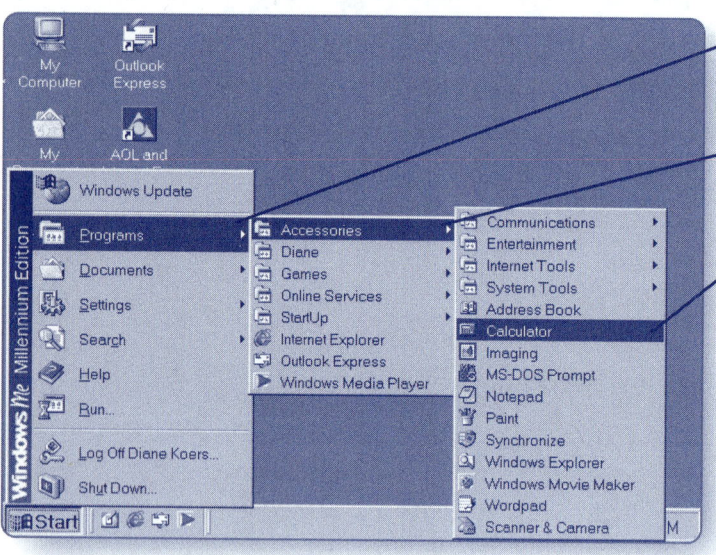

2. Click on **Programs**. The Programs menu appears.

3. Click on **Accessories**. The Accessories menu appears.

4. Click on **Calculator**. The Calculator appears.

Identifying Calculator Buttons

The Calculator program by default is a standard 10-key calculator used to perform basic mathematical functions. Besides the normal 0–9 numeric keys, you should know several other important keys.

Some commonly used Calculator keys (and their keyboard equivalents) are the following:

- + (+): Addition
- - (-): Subtraction
- * (*): Multiplication
- / (/): Division
- = (Enter): Total
- % (%): Displays the result of multiplication as a percentage
- . (.): Adds a decimal point
- Backspace (Backspace): Deletes the last digit of the displayed number
- Clear Entry (Delete): Clears the displayed number
- Clear All (Esc): Clears the current calculation

CHAPTER 6: USING THE CALCULATOR

Operating the Calculator

You can use the keyboard or the mouse to enter values into the calculator. If you are already proficient with a 10-key calculator, you might prefer to use the numeric keypad on the right side of your keyboard. When entering values, be sure to use the decimal point if the value you are entering is not a whole number. For example, to enter the price of a new shirt, type **29.95** not **2995**.

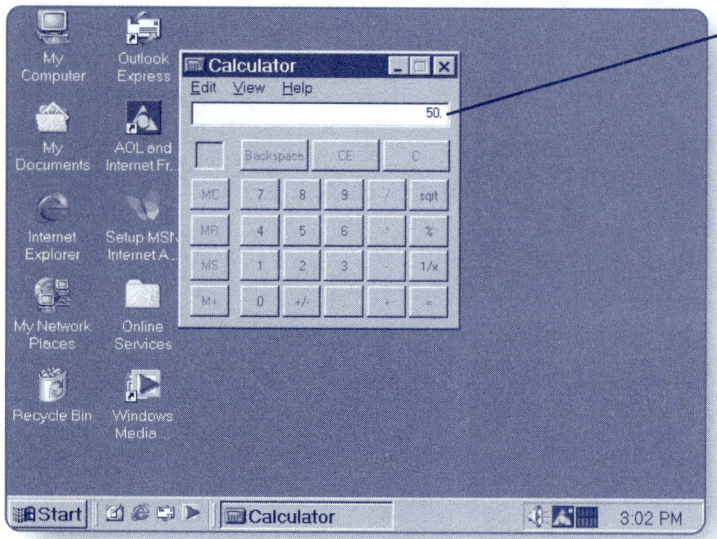

1. **Type** or **click** on the **first value** in the calculation. The number appears in the display box of the Calculator.

2. **Type** or **click** on the **operator** needed. Use + (plus) for addition, - (hyphen) for subtraction, * (asterisk) for multiplication, or / (slash) for division.

3. **Type** or **click** on the **second value** in the calculation. The number appears in the display box of the Calculator.

4. **Type** or **click** on another **operator** and **value**, if needed.

COPYING VALUES FROM THE CALCULATOR

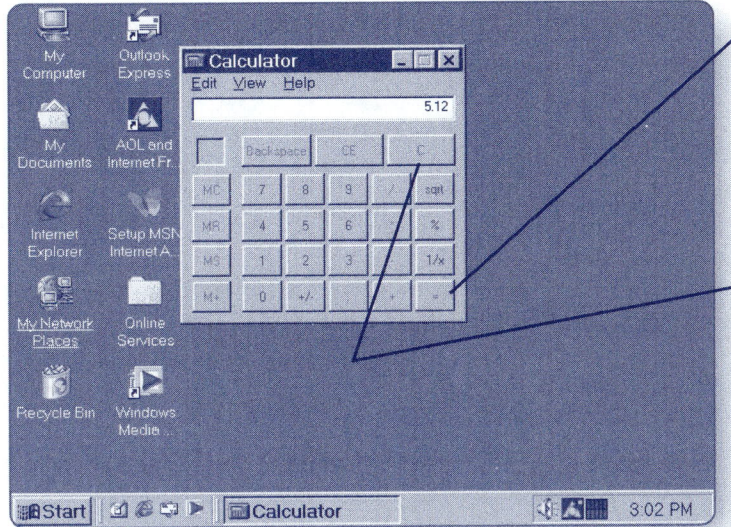

5. Press the **Enter key** or **click** on the **= button**. The result appears in the display box of the Calculator.

TIP

You can clear the totals on the Calculator by pressing the Esc key or by clicking on the Clear All button (C).

Copying Values from the Calculator

Windows includes a feature called the *Clipboard*. The Clipboard is a special holding area to assist you with transferring information from one document to another or from one program to another. This can be accomplished by using two features of Windows called *copy* and *paste*.

The Windows copy and paste functions also work with the Calculator. After you get the results of the calculation, you can then paste it into another document; for example, into a Microsoft Word document.

CHAPTER 6: USING THE CALCULATOR

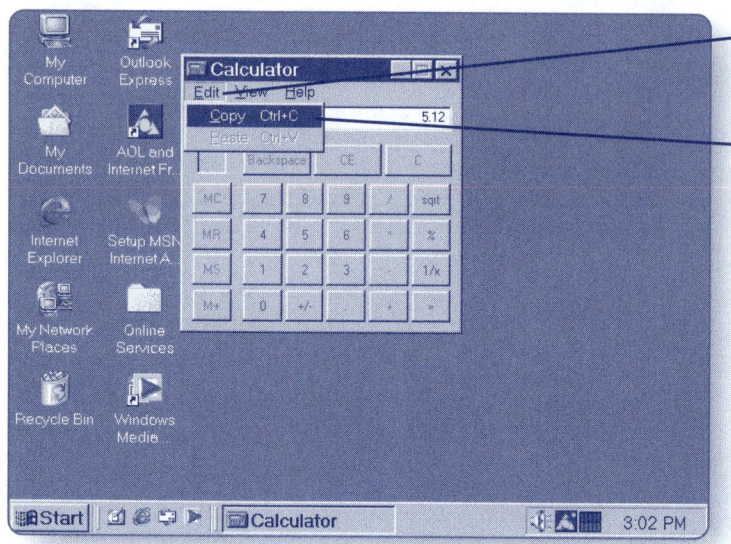

1. Click on **Edit**. The Edit menu appears.

2. Click on **Copy**. The value on the calculator is copied to the Clipboard.

3. Start or **switch** to your word processing or other program. The Calculator may be temporarily hidden from view.

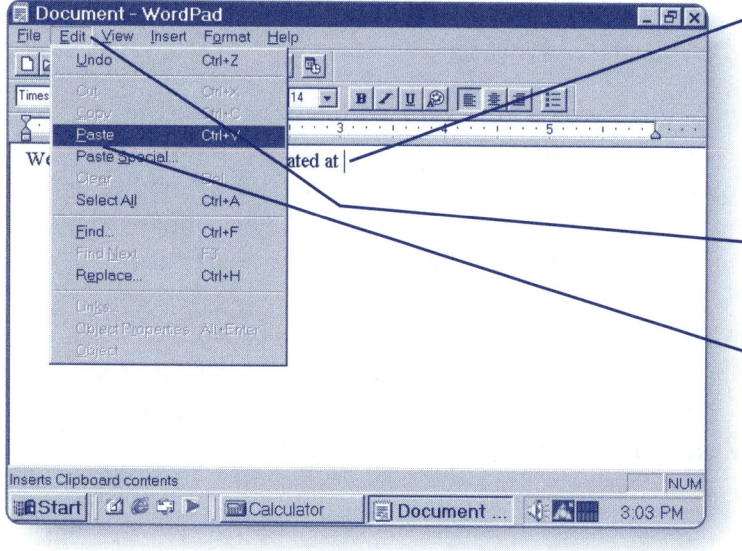

4. Click the **mouse pointer** at the location you want the data to appear. A blinking insertion point appears at the location you clicked.

5. Click on **Edit**. The Edit menu appears.

6. Click on **Paste**. The Edit menu closes.

CHANGING THE STYLE OF THE CALCULATOR   69

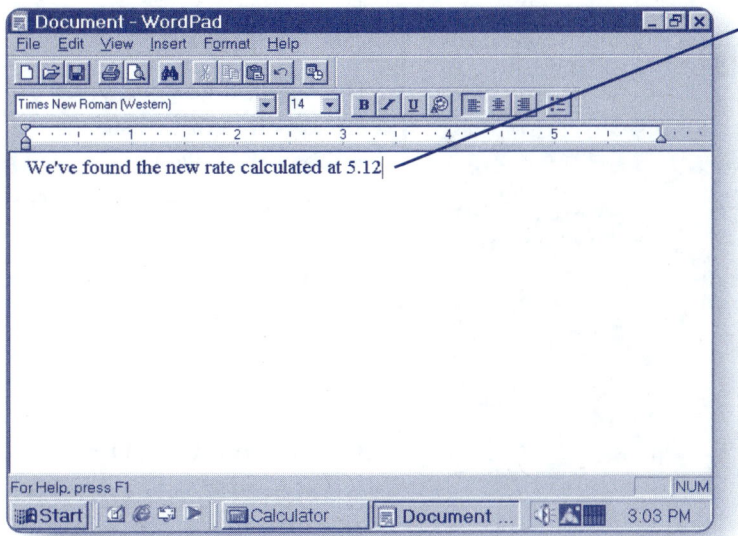

The value from the Clipboard is inserted into your document.

Changing the Style of the Calculator

Besides the standard 10-key calculator, Windows also gives you the option to use a scientific calculator.

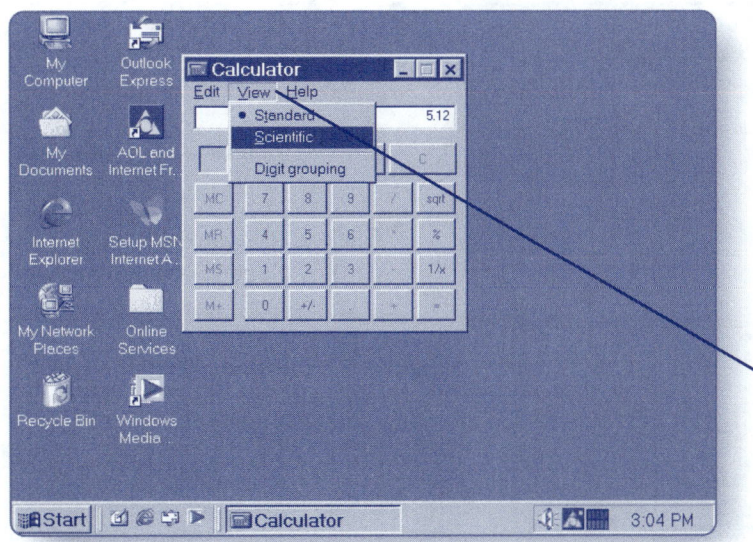

Viewing the Scientific Calculator

This calculator will calculate most trigonometric and statistical functions. The basics of this calculator operate the same as the standard calculator.

1. Click on **View**. The View menu appears.

70 CHAPTER 6: USING THE CALCULATOR

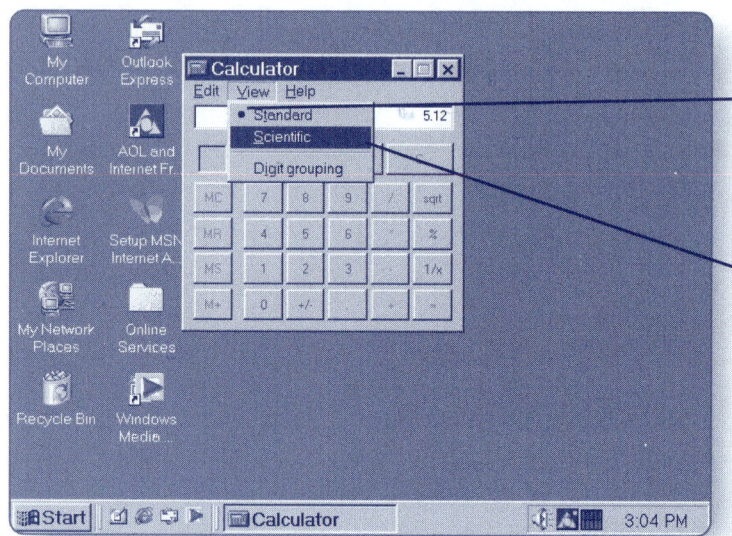

NOTE
The selection on the View menu with a dot beside it is the current view.

2. Click on **Scientific**. The calculator changes to the scientific style.

Returning to the Standard Calculator

If you're not a person who uses the scientific calculator (like me!), even viewing it can be a little overwhelming. You're just two clicks away from having your normal little calculator back.

1. Click on **View**. The View menu appears.

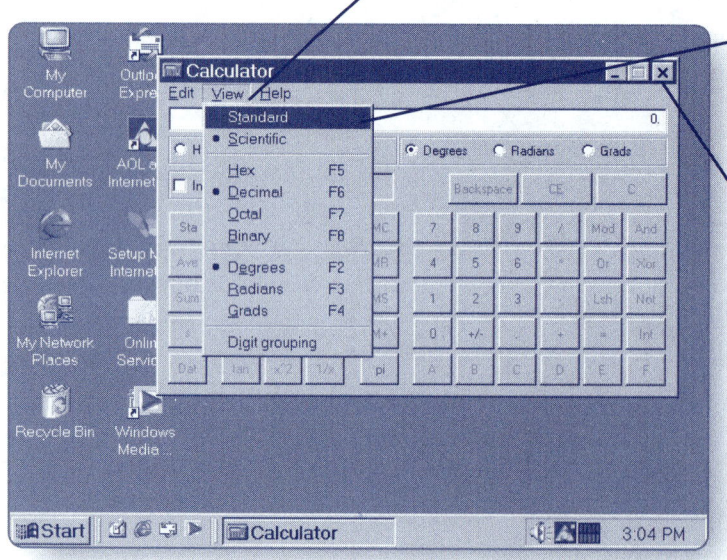

2. Click on **Standard**. The calculator changes to the standard style.

TIP
Click on the Close button ([X]) to close the Calculator.

7

Using WordPad

One of the basic uses of a computer is word processing. Windows includes a small word processing program called *WordPad*. It's a simple program that includes most of the basic features of many popular word processing programs. In this chapter, you'll learn how to:

- Start WordPad
- Enter and edit text
- Insert the current date
- Change the appearance of text
- Add bullet points to a list
- Save and print a document
- Open other WordPad documents

CHAPTER 7: USING WORDPAD

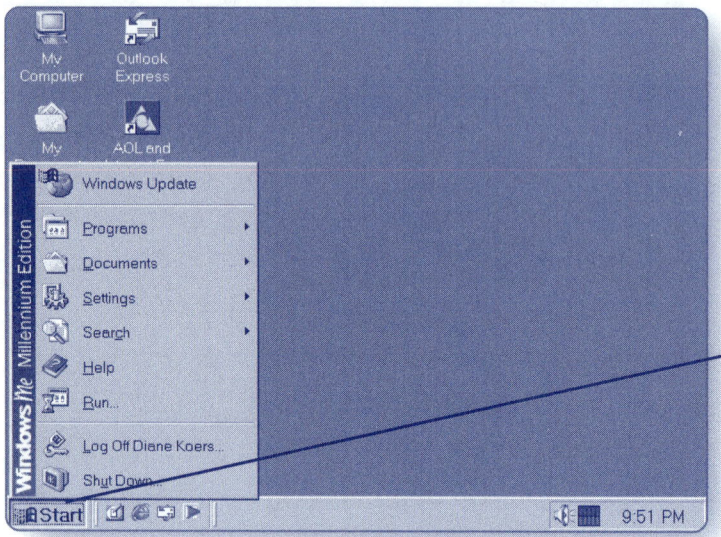

Starting WordPad

WordPad is similar to Microsoft Word. The WordPad program is included with Windows as an accessory.

1. Click on the **Start button**. The Start menu appears.

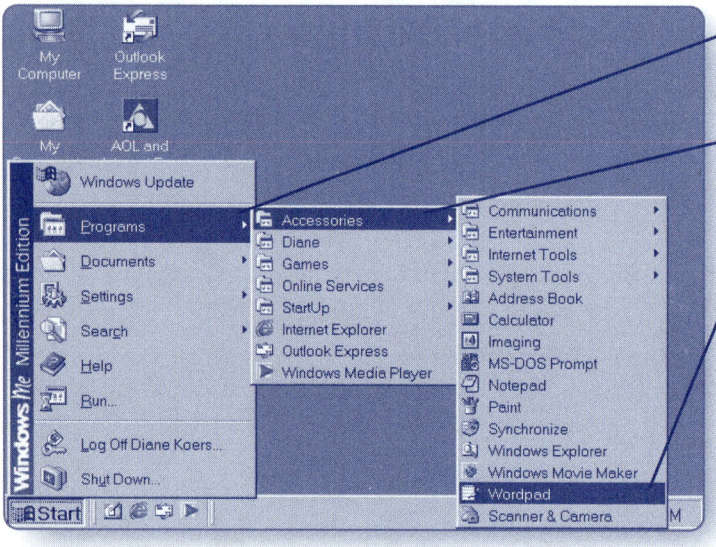

2. Click on **Programs**. The Programs menu appears.

3. Click on **Accessories**. The Accessories menu appears.

4. Click on **WordPad**. The WordPad program begins. A blank document appears, ready to use.

ENTERING TEXT

The WordPad opening screen has several important components.

- Menu bar
- Toolbars
- Ruler
- Document typing area
- Insertion point

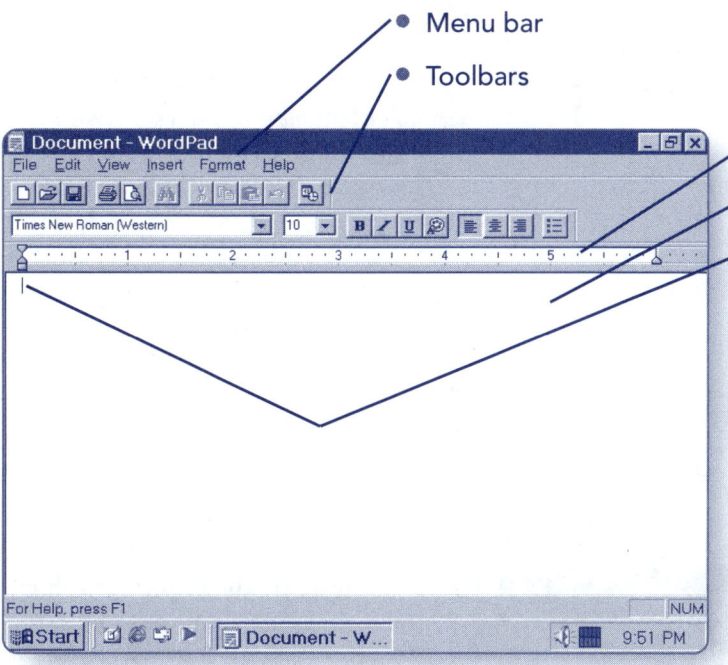

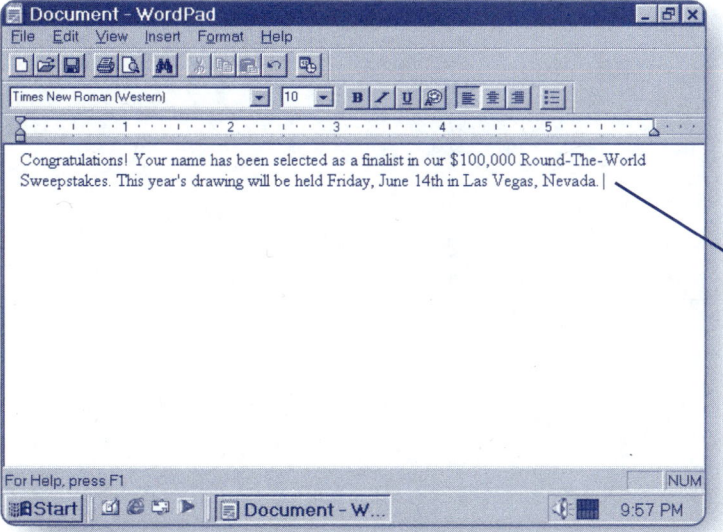

Entering Text

When typing text in a document, WordPad monitors the lines within a paragraph. If the word you are typing does not fit entirely on the current line, WordPad goes to the next line. This feature is called *word wrap*. Press the Enter key only when you get to the end of a paragraph. You can press the Enter key twice if you want an extra blank line between paragraphs. A short line of text—a date or greeting, such as "Dear Mr. Jones"—counts as a paragraph all by itself.

1. Type the desired **text**. The text appears at the location of the insertion point. Do not press the Enter key until you complete the entire paragraph.

74 CHAPTER 7: USING WORDPAD

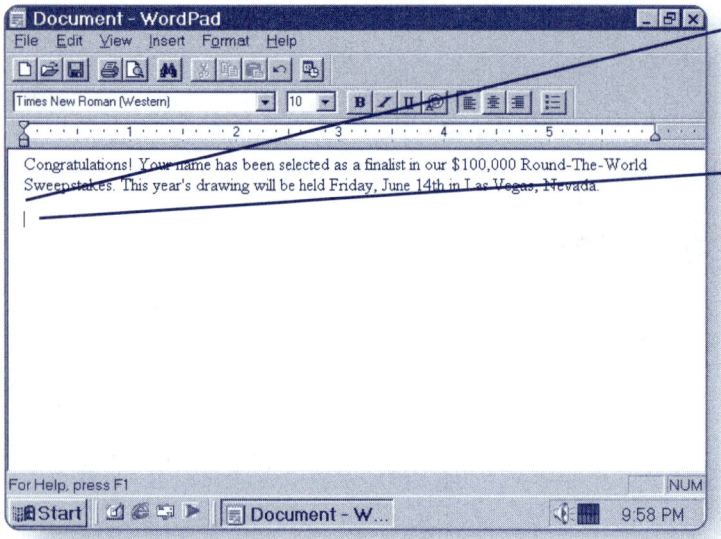

2. Press the **Enter key**. The insertion point moves down one line.

3. Press the **Enter key again.** A blank line appears between the paragraphs, and the insertion point moves down one line.

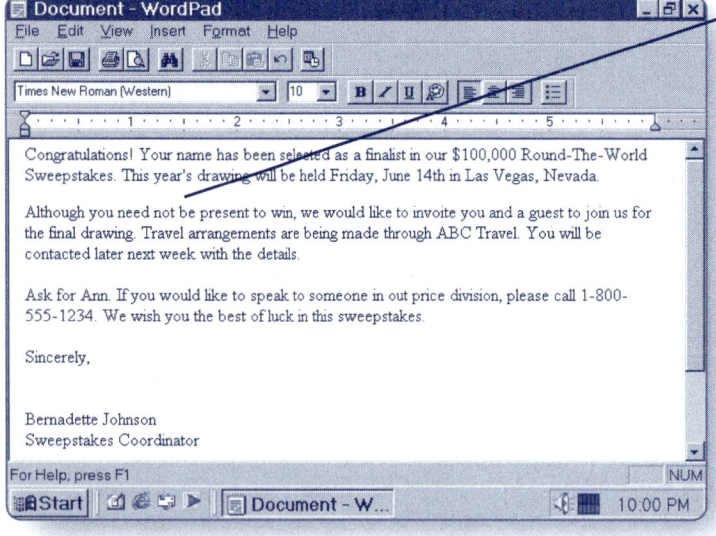

4. Type the **next paragraph** of the document. The text appears on your screen.

5. Repeat steps 2 through **4** for each paragraph of the document.

Editing Text

We all make mistakes. Errors are easy to correct with WordPad, whether you need to add something you forgot or delete something you didn't mean to type.

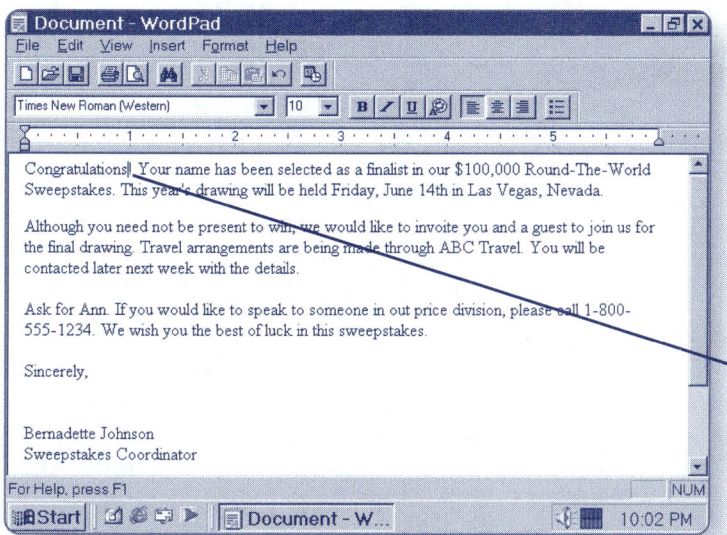

Adding Text

WordPad begins in *insert* mode. This means that when you want to add more text to your document, WordPad makes room for the new text by moving existing text to the right.

1. Click directly in **front of the location** where you want the next text to appear. The insertion point moves to that position.

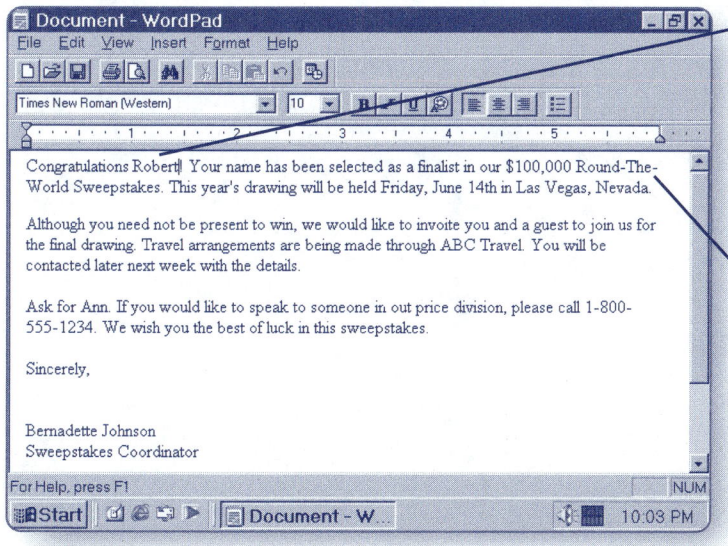

2. Type any new **word** or **phrase**, adding a space before or after as necessary. WordPad inserts the additional words at the position of the insertion point.

Notice how the words previously at the end of the line on which you began typing no longer fit on the first line and have dropped down to the second line.

Deleting Text

Text can be deleted one character, one word, or even one paragraph at a time. You can use one of two keys to delete a single character: the Backspace key or the Delete key. The Backspace key deletes a character to the left of the insertion point, while the Delete key deletes a character to the right of the insertion point.

> **TIP**
> An easy way to remember the difference between the Backspace key and the Delete key is the Backspace key has an arrow on it pointing to the left.

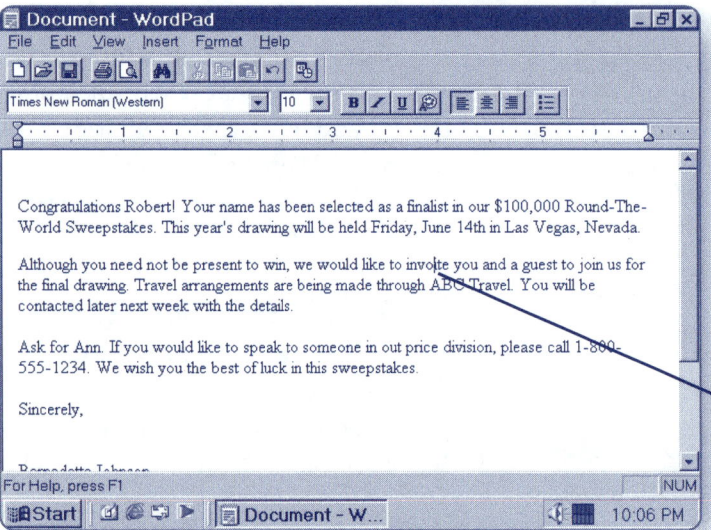

1. Click directly in **front of the character** you want to delete. The insertion point moves to that position.

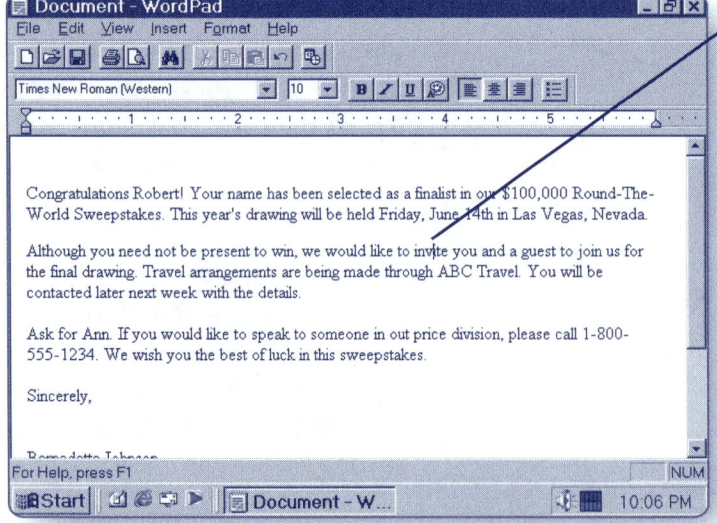

2. Press the **Delete key**. The empty space is filled by the existing text from the right.

Inserting the Current Date and Time

Instead of searching around for a calendar, let WordPad put today's date in your document for you.

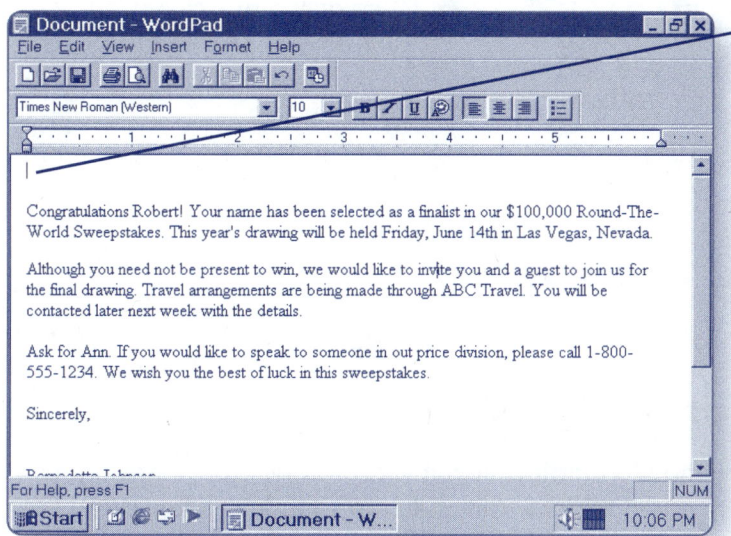

1. Position the **insertion point** at the location where you want the date or time to appear. The blinking insertion point appears.

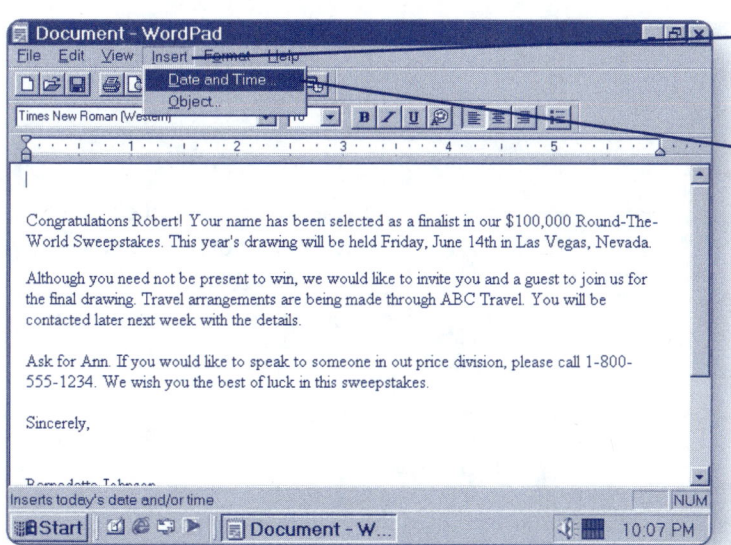

2. Click on **Insert**. The Insert menu appears.

3. Click on **Date and Time**. The Date and Time dialog box opens.

78 CHAPTER 7: USING WORDPAD

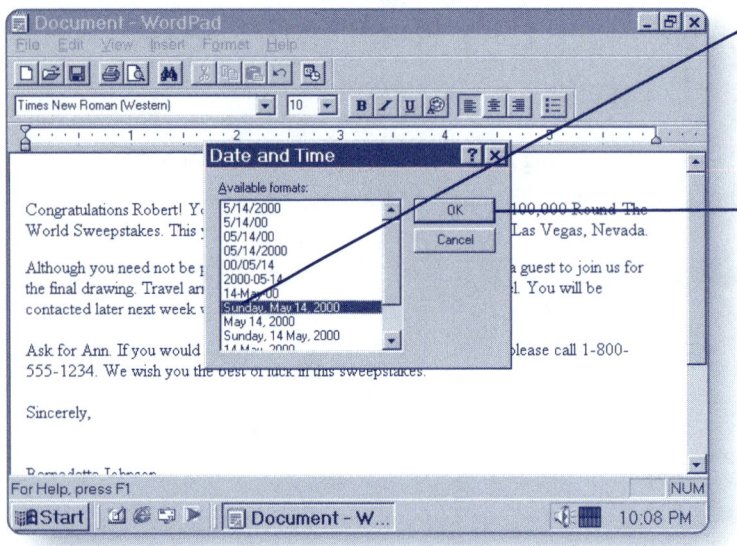

4. Click on the **date and time format** you would like to use in your letter. The format is selected.

5. Click on **OK**. The Date and Time dialog box closes, and WordPad inserts the date into your document.

Selecting Text

To change formatting, alignment, or to delete an area of text, the text needs to be selected prior to modification. WordPad allows you to select a word, a paragraph, the entire document, or any portion of a document.

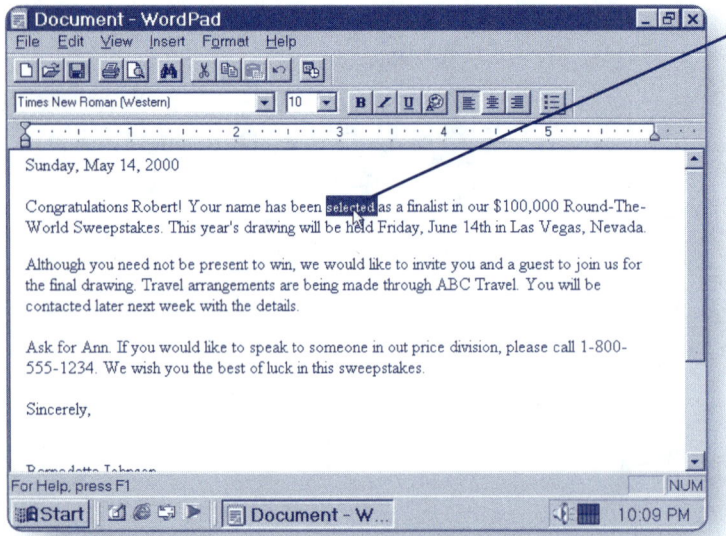

1. Double-click on a **word**. The word is highlighted.

TIP
To deselect text, click anywhere outside of the highlighted area.

SELECTING TEXT 79

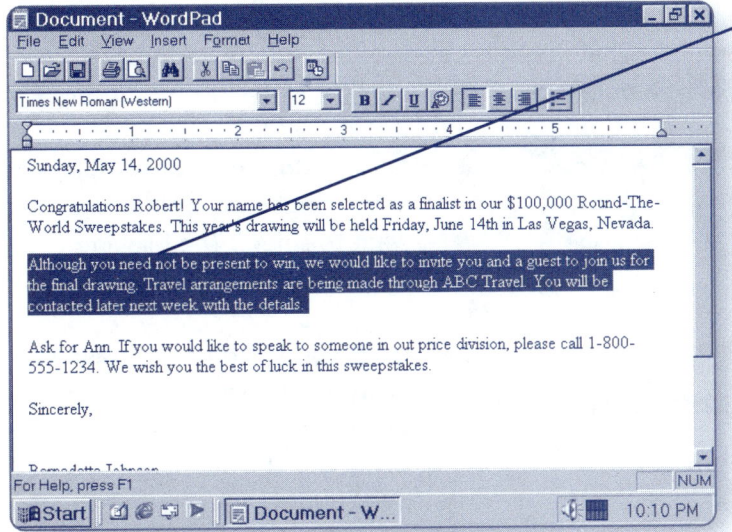

2. **Triple-click** on a **paragraph**. The entire paragraph is selected.

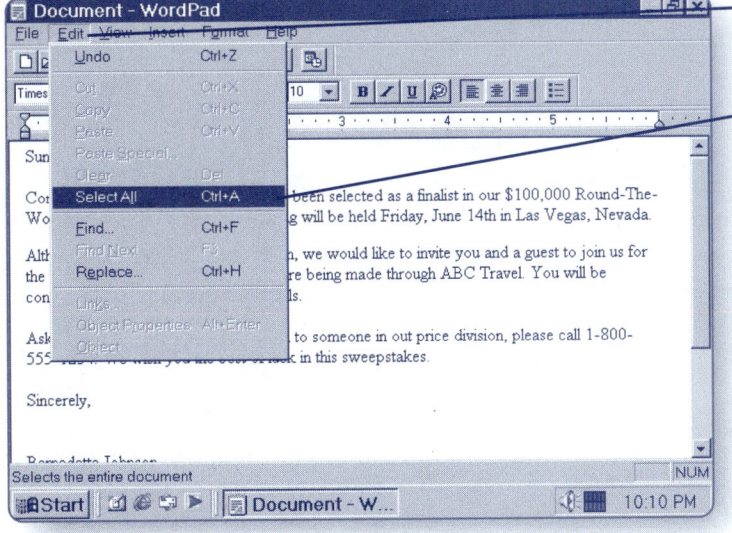

3. **Click** on **Edit**. The Edit menu appears.

4. **Click** on **Select All**. The entire document is selected.

You also have the option of selecting any portion of a document. That might be three words, two paragraphs, or six pages of a document.

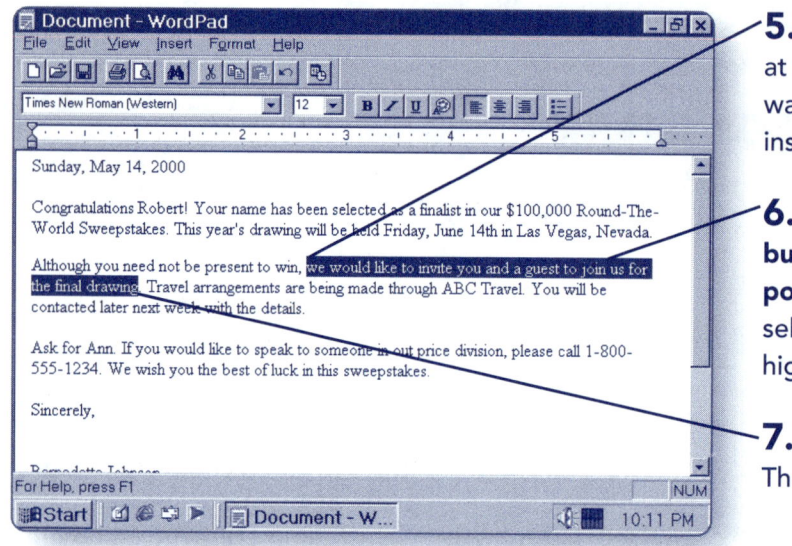

5. **Position** the **mouse pointer** at the beginning of the text you want to select. The blinking insertion point appears.

6. **Press** and **hold** the **mouse button** and **drag** the **mouse pointer** to the end of the selection. The area is highlighted.

7. **Release** the **mouse button**. The text is selected.

NOTE
You can select to the right, to the left, up, or down in the document by moving the mouse pointer in those directions.

CUTTING AND PASTING TEXT   81

Cutting and Pasting Text

If you have mistakenly placed text in the wrong place, don't delete it and retype it, use the Windows Clipboard feature to move it.

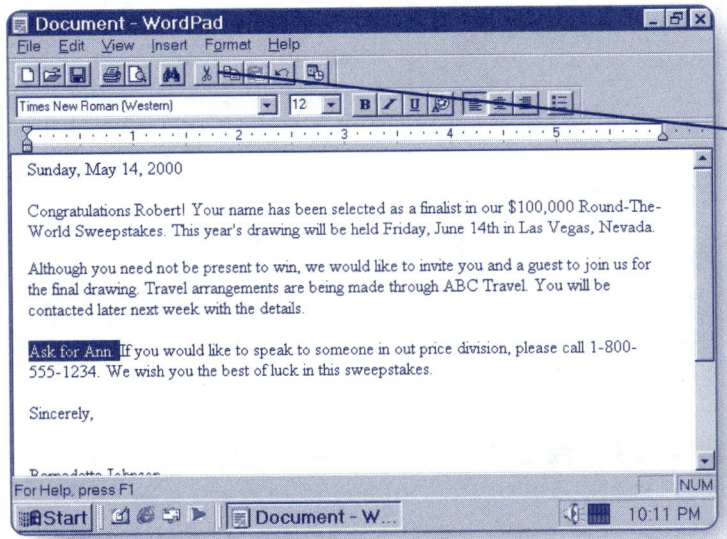

1. **Select** the **text** to be moved. The text is selected.

2. **Click** on the **Cut button**. WordPad removes the selected text from the document.

TIP
Optionally, click on the Edit menu and choose Cut.

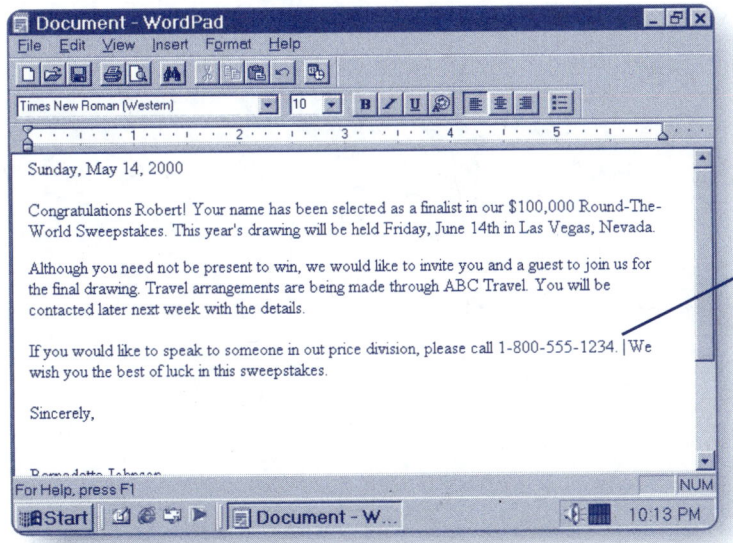

The selected text looks like it disappeared, but it didn't! WordPad placed the text on the Windows Clipboard and is waiting for you to tell it where to be placed.

3. **Position** the **insertion point** where you want the text to be placed. The insertion point moves to that location.

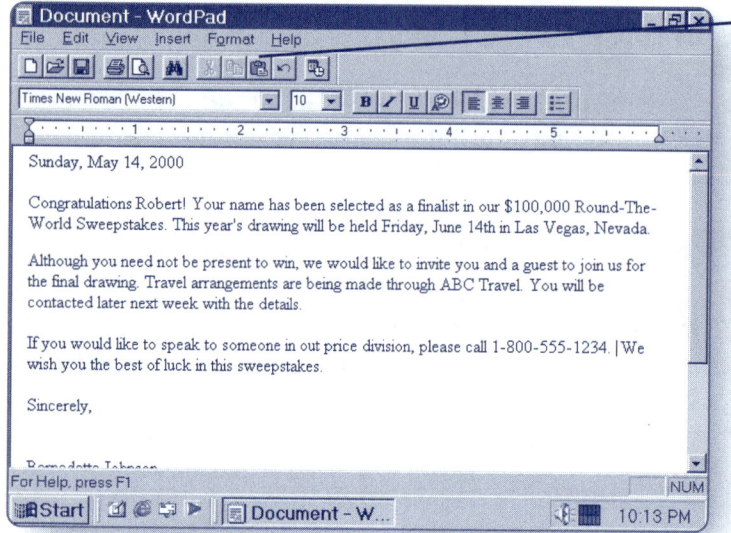

4. Click on the **Paste button**. The text appears in the new location.

> **TIP**
> Optionally, click on the Edit menu and choose Paste.

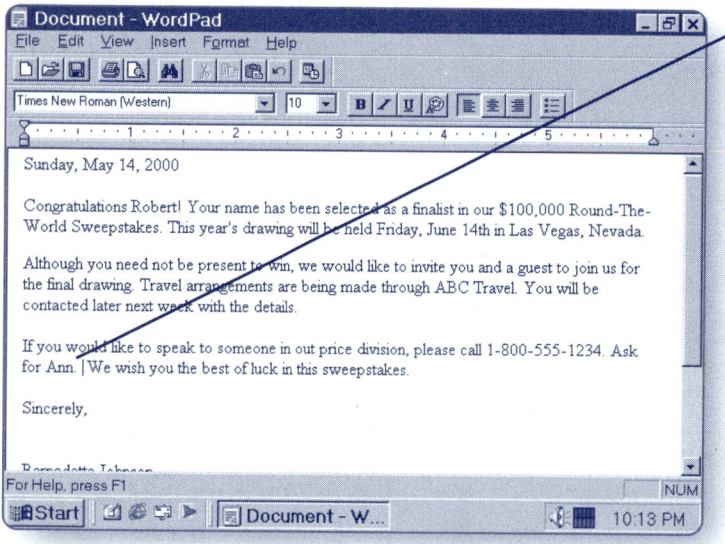

The newly pasted text appears in the location you specified.

Formatting Text

Formatting is changing the appearance of text, such as the font, the color, or such attributes as bolding or underlining. Formatting can also include changing the alignment of text.

Changing the Font

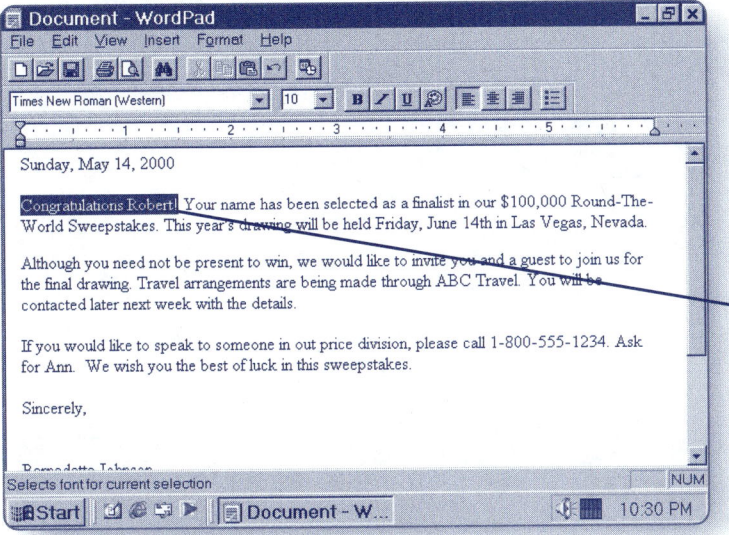

The default font is a 10-point Times New Roman font. Your font choices vary depending on the software installed on your computer.

1. Select the **text** to be formatted. The text is highlighted.

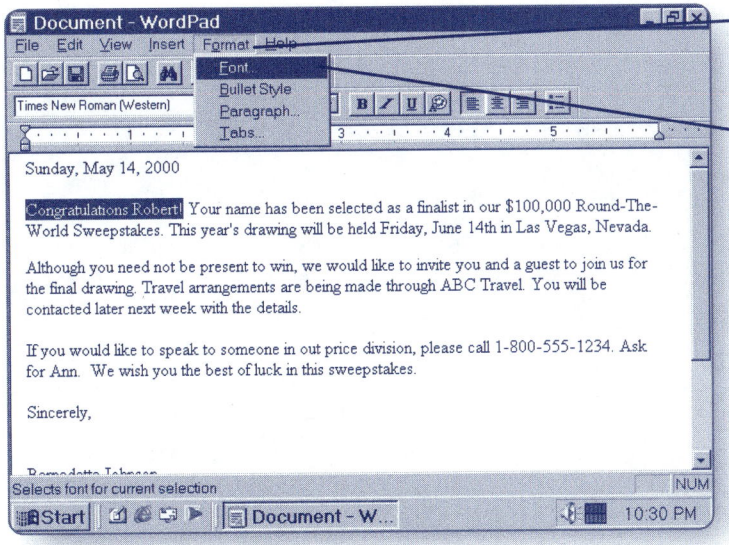

2. Click on **Format**. The Format menu appears.

3. Click on **Font**. The Font dialog box opens.

84 CHAPTER 7: USING WORDPAD

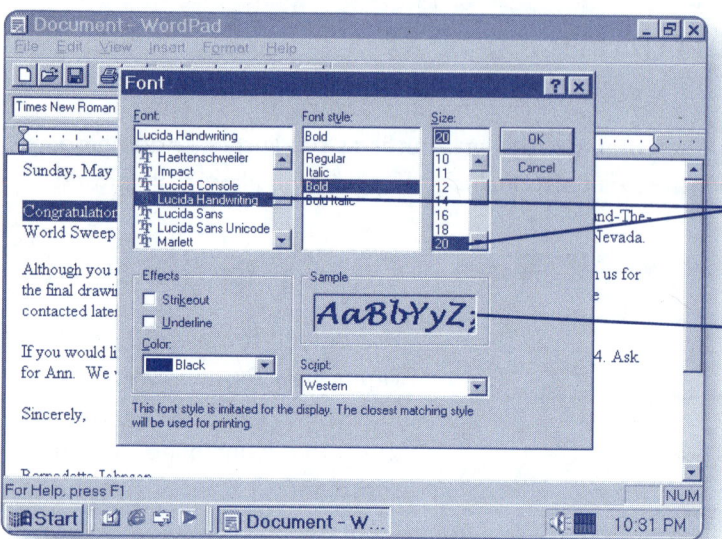

From this dialog box you can select the font, the font style, the size, the color, and special effects.

4. Make any desired **choices**. The options are selected.

The Sample box displays your choices.

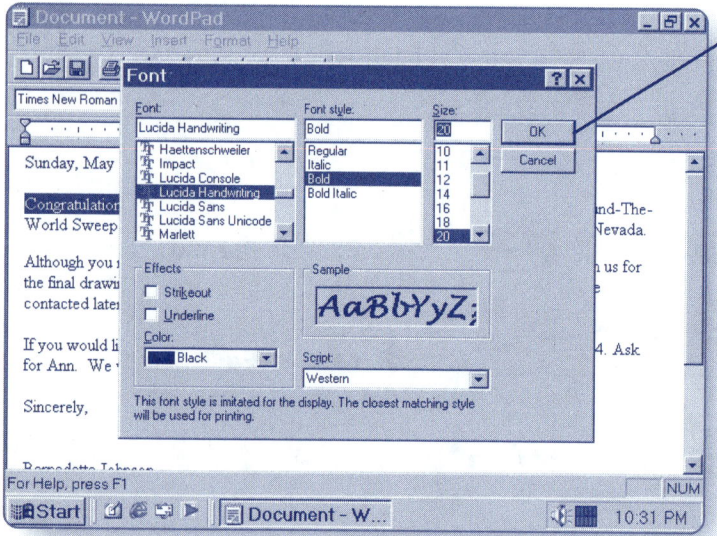

5. Click on **OK**. The dialog box closes, and the font choices you selected are applied to the highlighted text.

Modifying the Alignment

Alignment is the arrangement of text to the margins of a document. It can also be called *justification*. Alignment choices are applied to an entire paragraph and are made from the WordPad toolbar.

Three alignment choices are available:

- Left-aligned text is even with the left margin and uneven on the right margin.

- Center-aligned text is centered between the left and right margins.

- Right-aligned text is even with the right margin and uneven on the left margin.

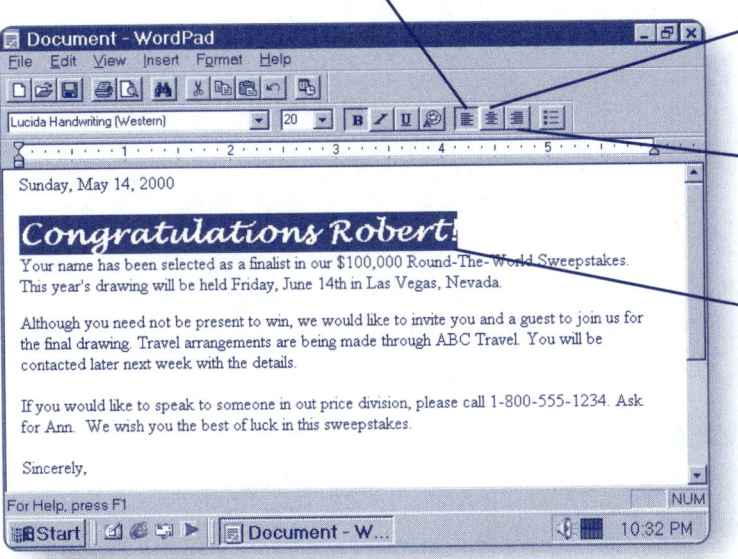

1. Select the **paragraph** you want to modify. The text is highlighted.

TIP
Optionally, you can select multiple paragraphs you want to modify.

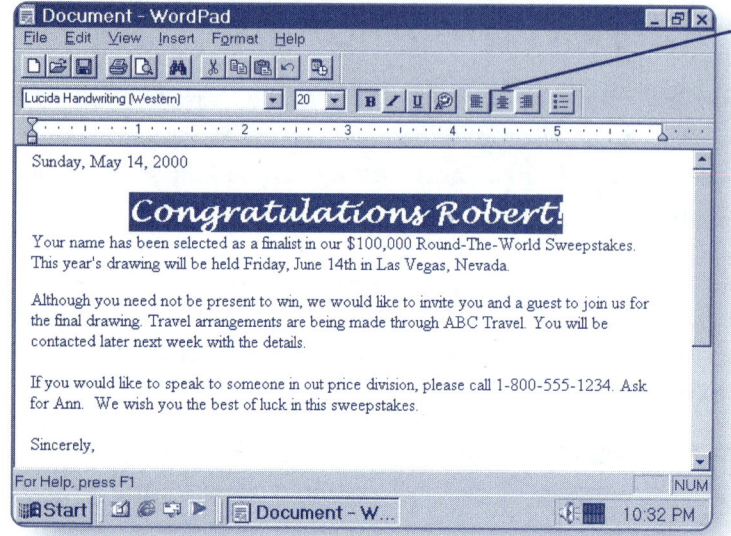

2. Click on the desired **alignment button**. The selected button appears "pushed in" to show the current selection, and the current paragraph is modified.

Adding Bullets

Bullets call attention to specific points in a document. WordPad indicates bulleted items with a small black circle in the front and the text next to it indented.

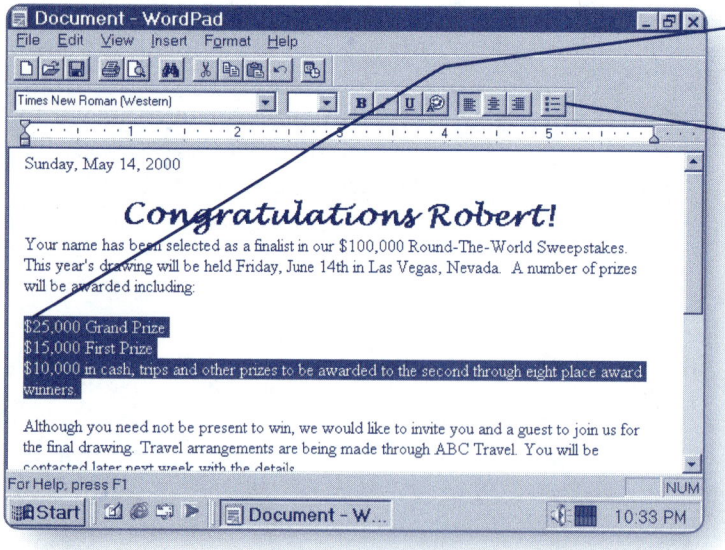

1. Click on or **select** the **paragraphs** you want to bullet.

2. Click on the **Bullets button**. The button appears "pushed in" and bullets are applied to the selected paragraphs.

SAVING A WORDPAD DOCUMENT

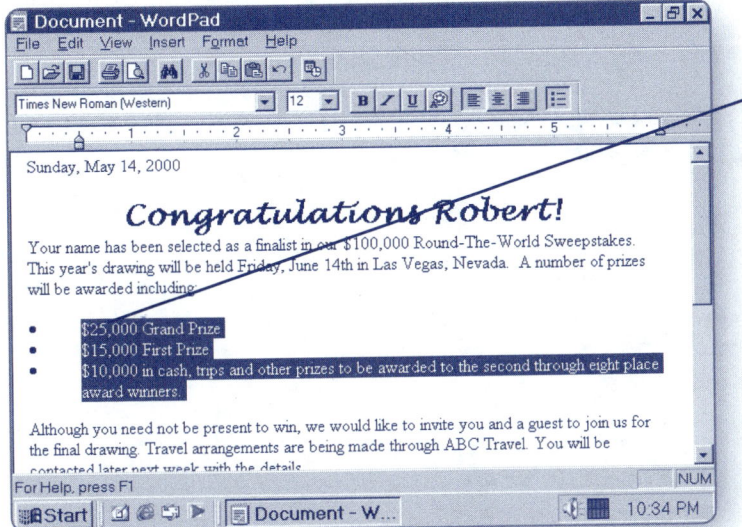

TIP

To remove a bullet, repeat steps one and two.

Saving a WordPad Document

When you work on a document, the changes you make are stored only in the computer memory. That memory is erased when you turn off the computer, if the power fails, or if the computer locks up. To avoid losing a document, you should save it to a file.

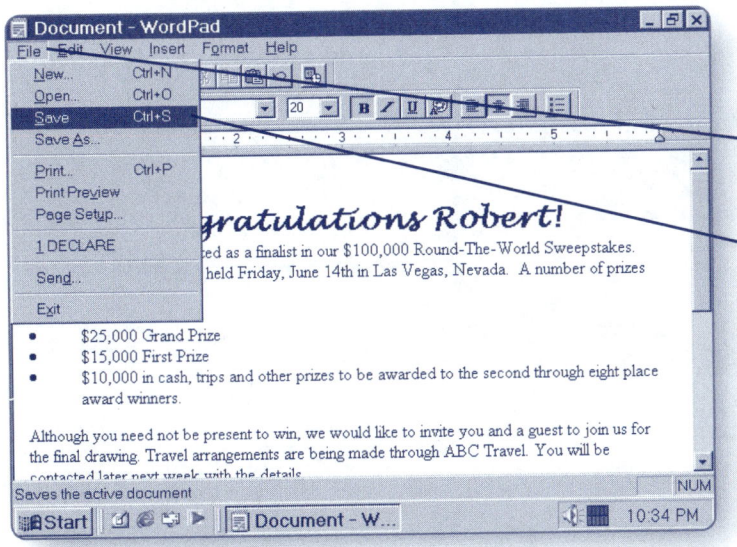

1. Click on **File**. The File menu appears.

2. Click on **Save**. The Save As dialog box opens.

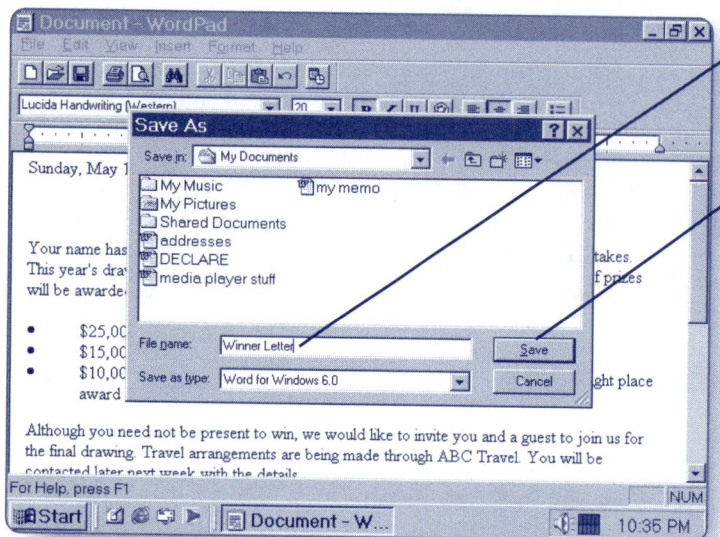

3. **Type** a **descriptive name** for the file in the File name: text box. The text appears.

4. **Click** on **Save**. The file is saved.

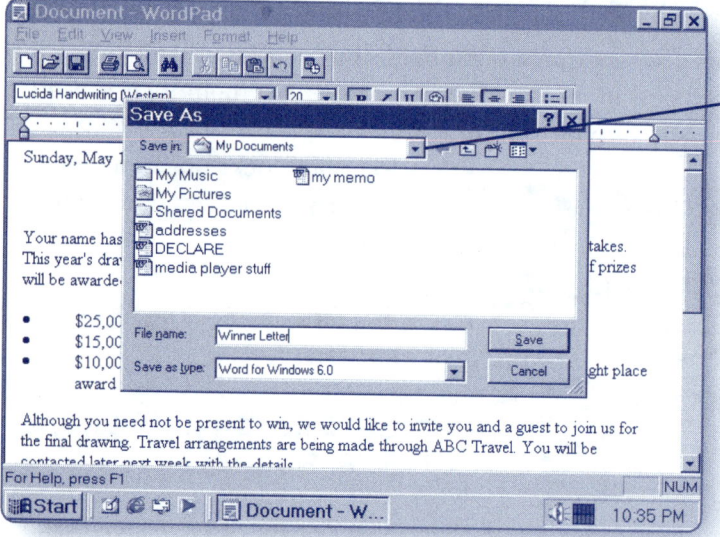

NOTE

The default folder for saving a WordPad file is the My Documents folder stored on the desktop. You can save the file in any other location by clicking on the down arrow next to the Save in: list box and selecting a different folder.

PRINTING A WORDPAD DOCUMENT   89

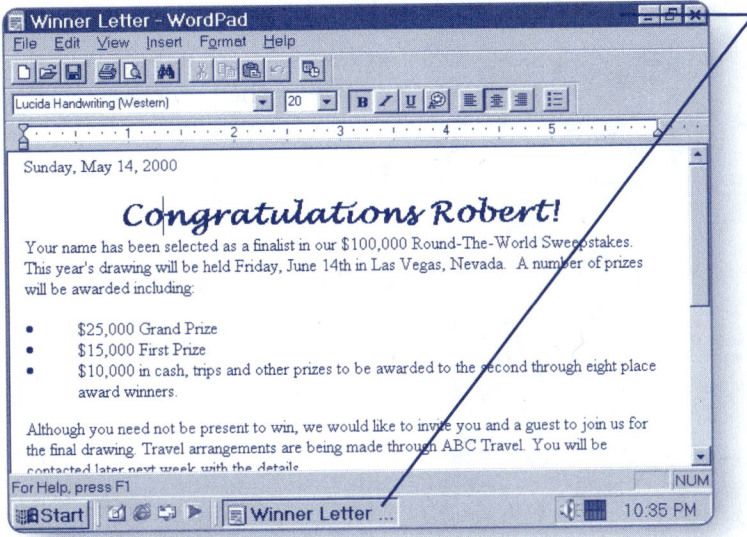

The name of the file now appears in the title bar of the WordPad window and on the Windows Taskbar.

Printing a WordPad Document

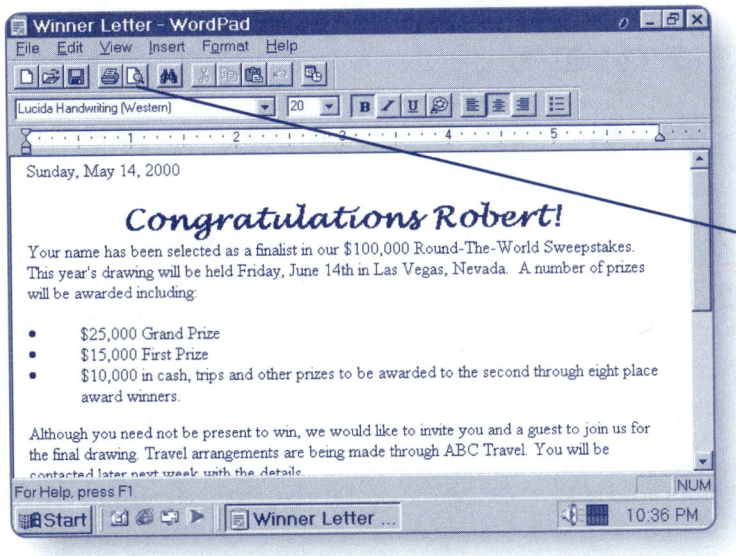

Printing is an expensive process that uses our natural resources. You can use WordPad's print preview feature to review the document prior to printing it.

1. Click on the **Print Preview button**. The screen changes to a non-editable bird's eye view of your document.

TIP
Optionally, click on File and choose Print Preview.

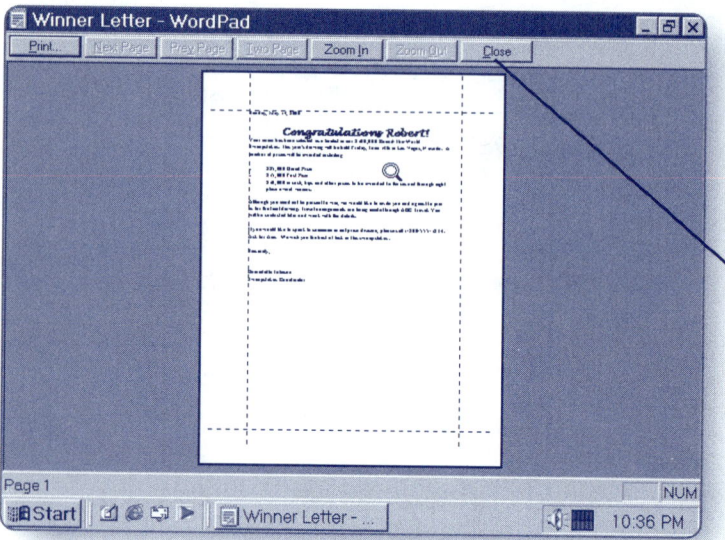

Don't worry if you can't read it very well. You're not supposed to! At this point you are checking out the overall appearance of the document, not the content.

2. Click on the **Close button**. WordPad returns you to the document editing screen.

3. Click on the **Print button** when you are ready to print the document. The document prints with all default settings.

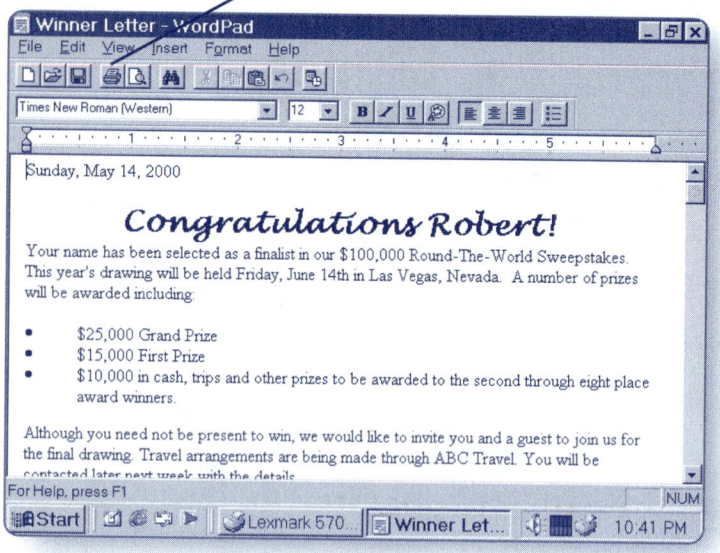

TIP

If you need to change a print setting, click on File, and then Print. The Print dialog box appears prompting you for changes.

Opening a WordPad Document

If you want to work on a previously created and saved WordPad document you must open it. When you open a file, you pull a copy of that file into the computer memory. You can then make any desired changes and save the file again.

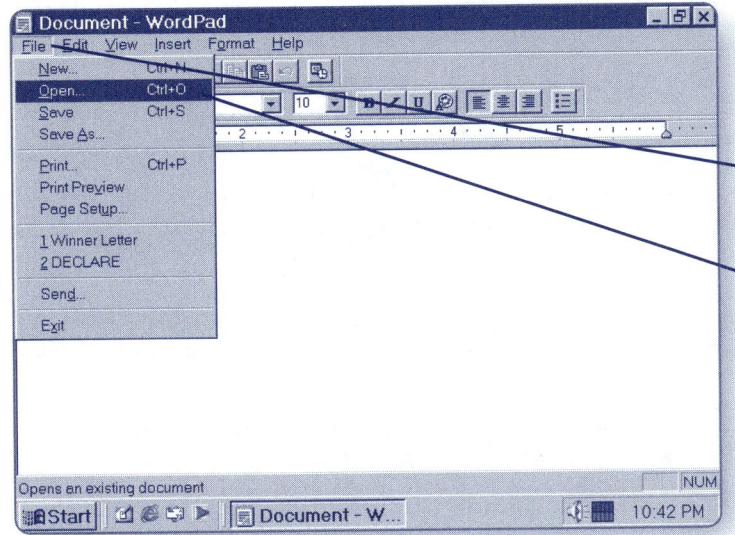

1. Click on **File**. The File menu appears.

2. Click on **Open**. The Open dialog box opens and displays the contents of the My Documents folder.

3. Click on the **name** of the file you want to open. The file name is selected and appears in the File name: text box.

4. Click on the **Open button**. The Open dialog box closes, and the document appears onscreen, ready for you to edit.

Closing the WordPad Program

When you are finished using the WordPad program, you should close it. Keeping a program open unnecessarily uses computer resources that you may need for other areas.

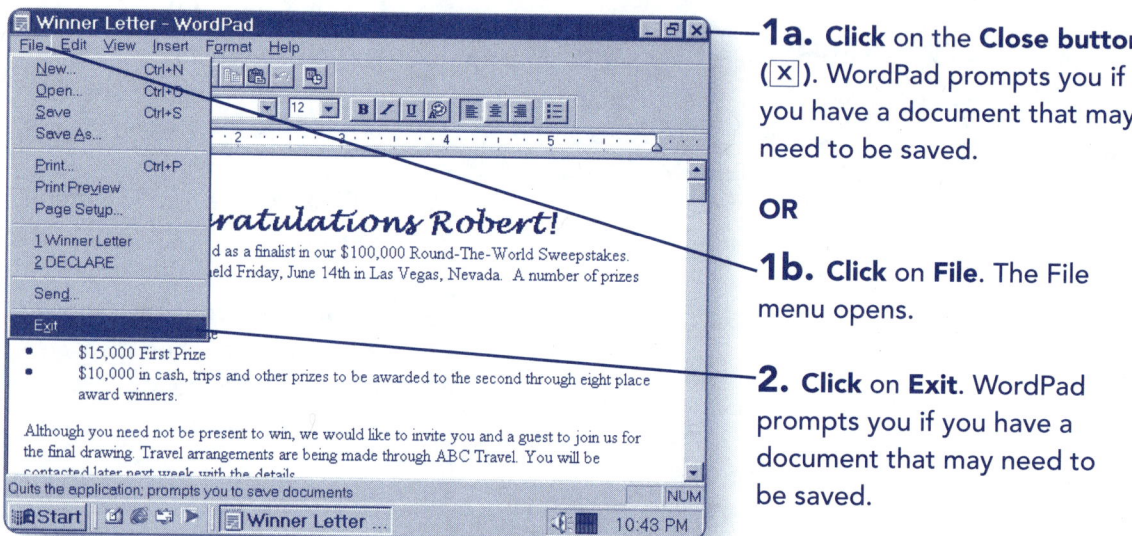

1a. Click on the **Close button** (☒). WordPad prompts you if you have a document that may need to be saved.

OR

1b. Click on **File**. The File menu opens.

2. Click on **Exit**. WordPad prompts you if you have a document that may need to be saved.

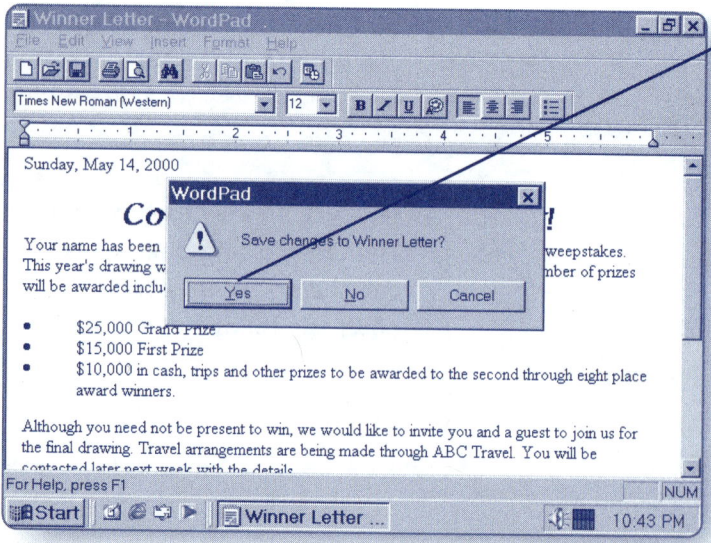

3. Click on **Yes** if you want to save your changes to the document. The program closes and you return to the Windows desktop or to the next open program.

NOTE
If you click on No, the document is not saved and all changes are lost.

8

Painting with the Paint Program

Most of us don't have a lot of artistic skill, so the Microsoft Paint program is included with Windows Millennium Edition. This program is designed to assist you with making drawings. In this chapter, you'll learn how to:

- Identify the paint tools
- Draw with the paintbrush
- Draw a rectangle or circle
- Fill in the background color
- Flip and skew an object
- Select and move an object
- Print and save a drawing

CHAPTER 8: PAINTING WITH THE PAINT PROGRAM

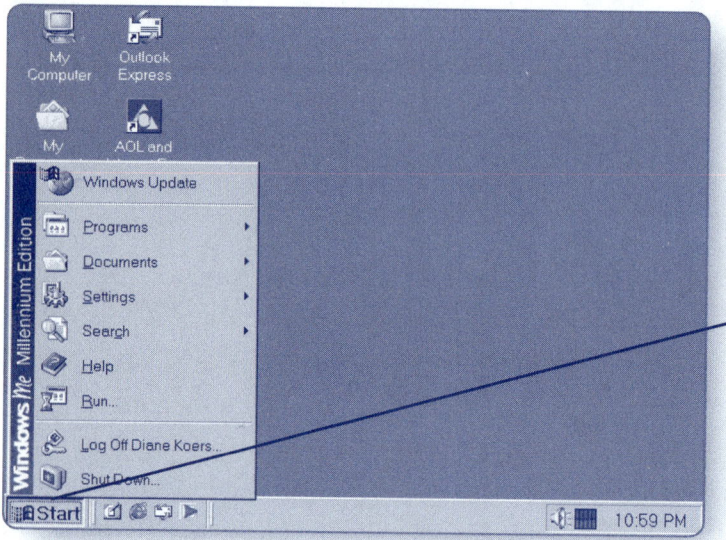

Starting the Paint Program

The Paint program is one of the accessories supplied with Windows.

1. Click on the **Start button**. The Start menu appears.

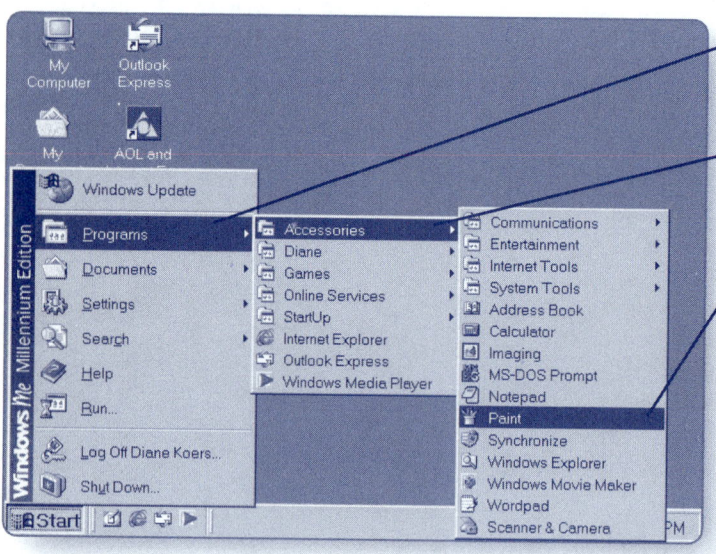

2. Click on **Programs**. The Programs menu appears.

3. Click on **Accessories**. The Accessories menu appears.

4. Click on **Paint**. The Paint program opens with a clean screen.

DISCOVERING THE PAINT TOOLS 95

Discovering the Paint Tools

A feature called the Tool box appears on the left side of your screen. You will use these 16 tools to create or edit the objects you need for your drawing.

> **TIP**
> If the Tool box does not appear, click on View, and then Tool Box.

The first two tools on the top row are selection tools.

Many tools are available to assist you with your drawing. Some of the tools included are the following:

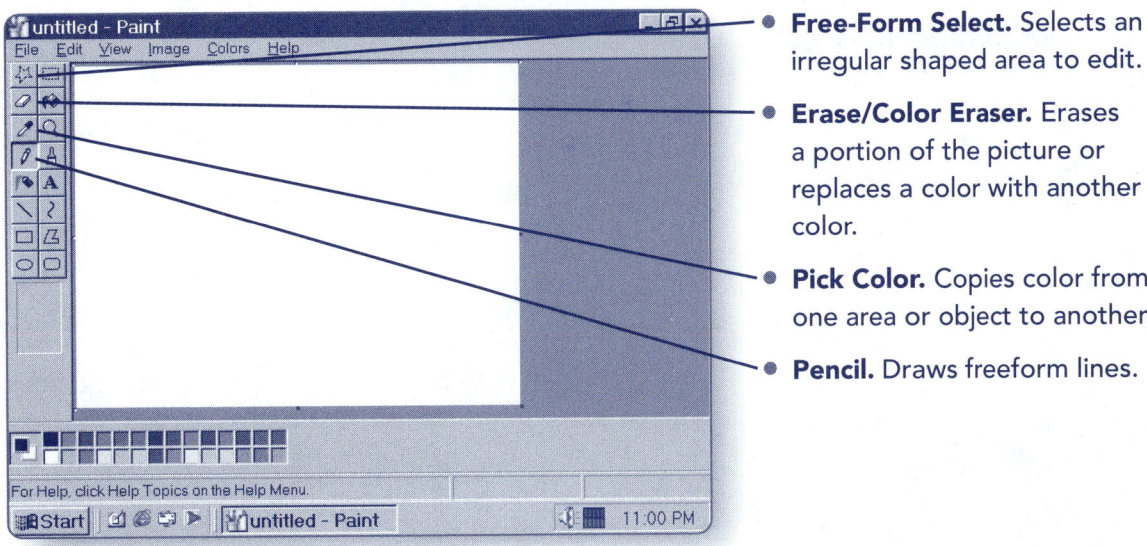

- **Free-Form Select.** Selects an irregular shaped area to edit.
- **Erase/Color Eraser.** Erases a portion of the picture or replaces a color with another color.
- **Pick Color.** Copies color from one area or object to another.
- **Pencil.** Draws freeform lines.

CHAPTER 8: PAINTING WITH THE PAINT PROGRAM

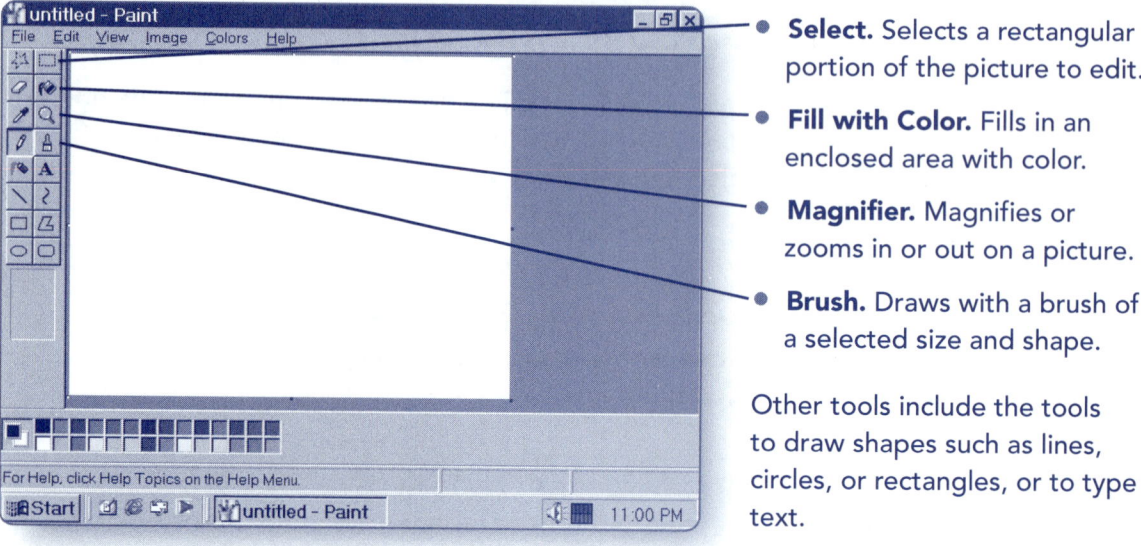

- **Select.** Selects a rectangular portion of the picture to edit.
- **Fill with Color.** Fills in an enclosed area with color.
- **Magnifier.** Magnifies or zooms in or out on a picture.
- **Brush.** Draws with a brush of a selected size and shape.

Other tools include the tools to draw shapes such as lines, circles, or rectangles, or to type text.

> **TIP**
> Position the mouse pointer on top of each tool to see a description of it.

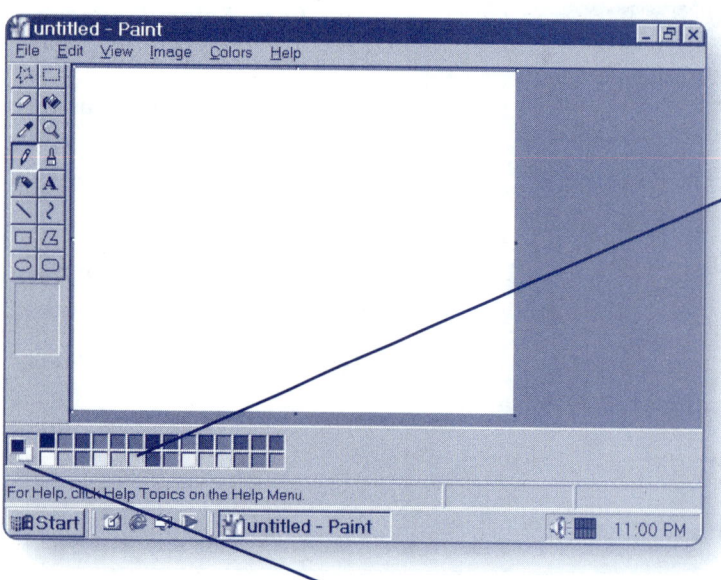

At the very bottom of the screen is the Color box. Clicking on a color with the left mouse button selects a color for the frame or line of an object. Clicking on a color with the right mouse button selects a color for the interior of a filled object.

The currently selected colors are displayed on the left side of the color box.

Drawing with the Paintbrush

The Paintbrush tool is a freeform drawing tool, which means it can have a variable shape or design.

A tool is selected by clicking once on its designated button. When a tool has been selected, many will display any available options at the bottom of the Tool box. For example, if you select the Paintbrush, the various shapes, thickness, and angles will be available for you to choose from. If you select the Rectangle, you can choose from a rectangle with a frame only, filled with a frame, or filled only.

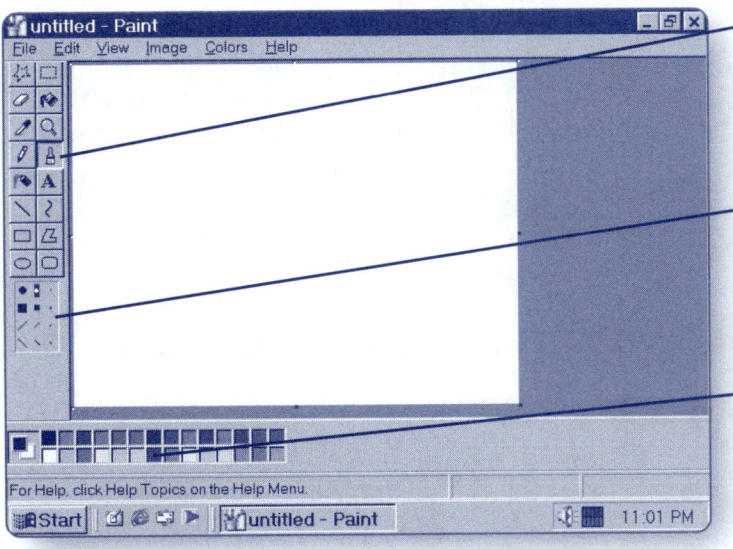

1. Click on the **Paintbrush tool**. The Paintbrush button appears pushed in to indicate the tool is active.

2. Click on a **brush shape** from the bottom of the Tool box. A dark blue box appears around the brush shape.

3. Click on a **color** from the color box. The color appears in the top of the two boxes on the left side of the color box.

4. Press and **hold** the **mouse button** and **drag** the **mouse pointer** on the drawing screen to draw the desired shape or object. The drawing appears onscreen as you move the mouse.

5. Release the **mouse button**. The completed drawn object appears onscreen. *(Author's note: Please don't laugh at my tree. I'm a writer, not an artist!)*

TIP
If you make a mistake, click on Edit, and then Undo to reverse up to the preceding three actions.

Drawing a Rectangle or Circle

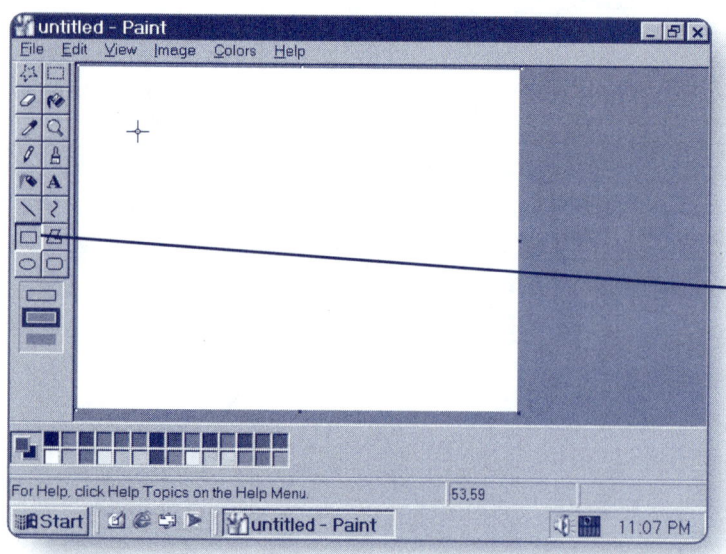

Unless you are a skilled artist, sometimes getting a good-looking drawing with the paintbrush is difficult. That's why the rectangle and other shapes are available to assist you.

1. Click on the **Rectangle tool**, the **Rounded Corner Rectangle tool**, or the **Ellipse tool**. The tool appears selected and the mouse pointer becomes a small cross.

DRAWING A RECTANGLE OR CIRCLE   99

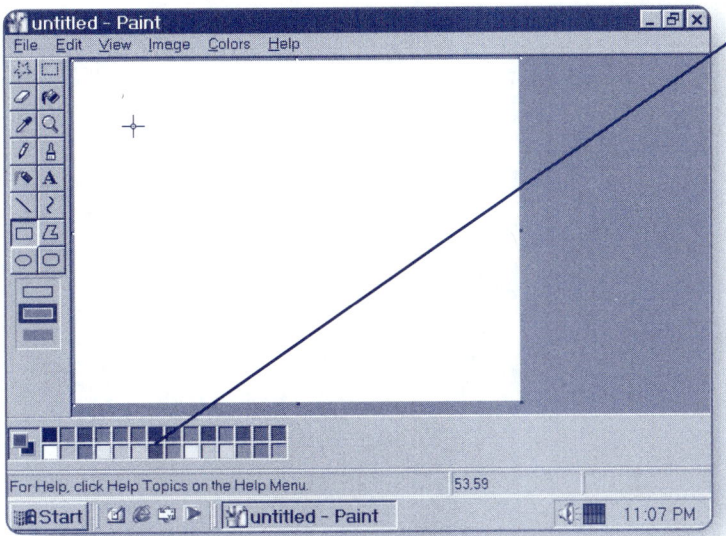

2. Click on a **color** from the color box for the shape's outline. The selected color appears in the top of the two boxes on the left side of the color box.

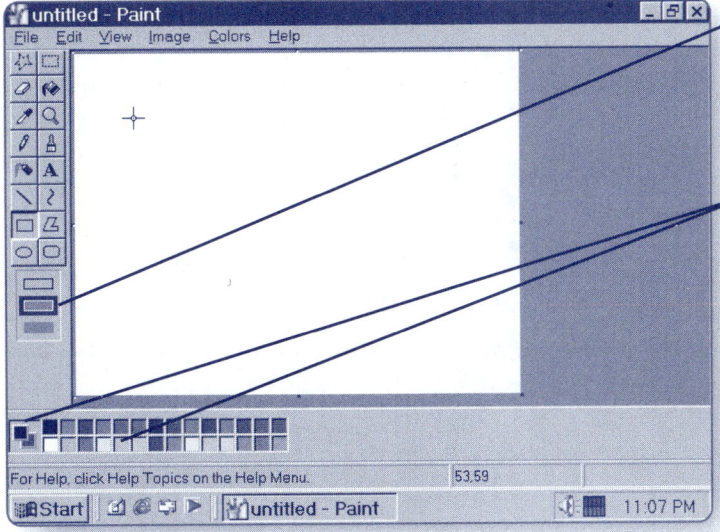

3. Click on a **fill style** from the bottom of the Tool box. A dark blue box appears around the selection.

4. Optionally, **right-click** on a **color** in the color box for the shape fill color. The selected color appears in the bottom of the two boxes on the left side of the color box.

100 CHAPTER 8: PAINTING WITH THE PAINT PROGRAM

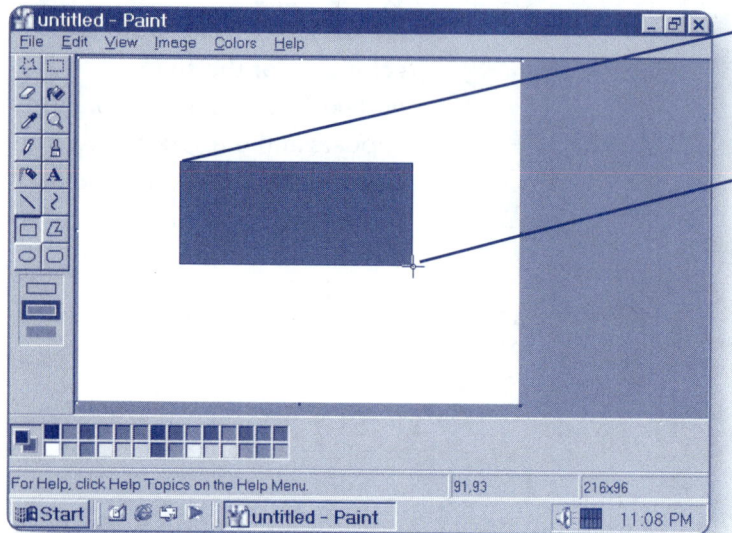

5. **Click** the **mouse** at the location you want the object to begin.

6. **Drag** the **mouse pointer diagonally** in the direction you want. The object appears as you move the mouse.

7. **Release** the **mouse button** when the shape is the correct size. The drawn object appears complete.

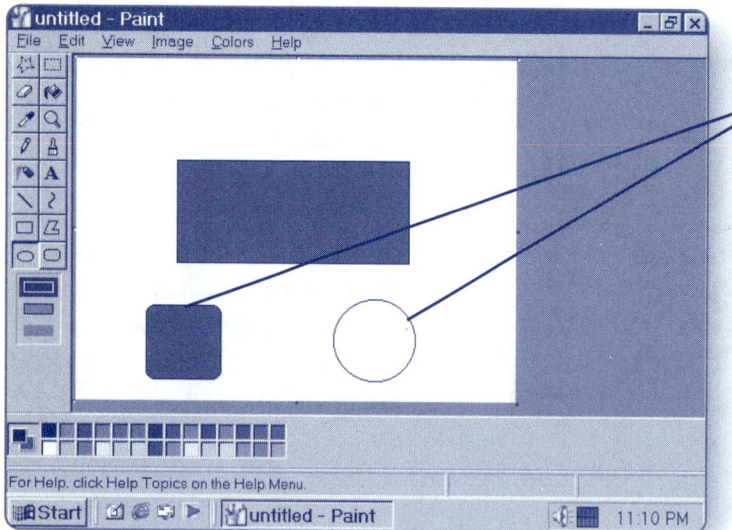

TIP
To draw a perfect square or circle, press and hold the Shift key as you draw the shape. Release the mouse button *before* you release the Shift key.

NOTE
A tool stays selected until a new tool is chosen.

Filling in the Background Color

You can change the interior (fill) color of any closed-in area.

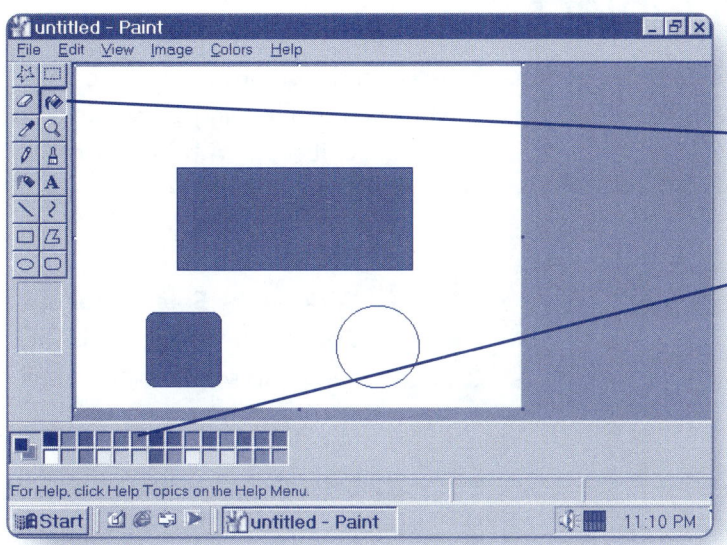

1. Click on the **Fill with Color tool**. The mouse pointer looks like a paint bucket.

2. Click on the desired **fill color** from the color box. The selected color appears in the top of the two boxes on the left side of the color box.

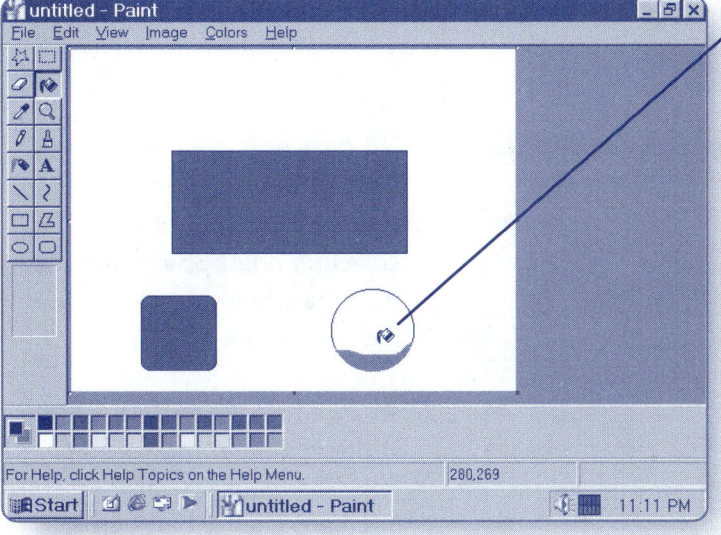

3. Click the **mouse pointer** inside the object to be filled. The interior of the object takes on the new color.

TIP
If you click in the background area of the drawing, the background changes to the new color.

Selecting and Moving an Object

Objects or shapes that have been drawn onscreen can be moved to a new location. The secret to moving an object is to select it first. With Microsoft Paint, you can move all or just part of a drawn object.

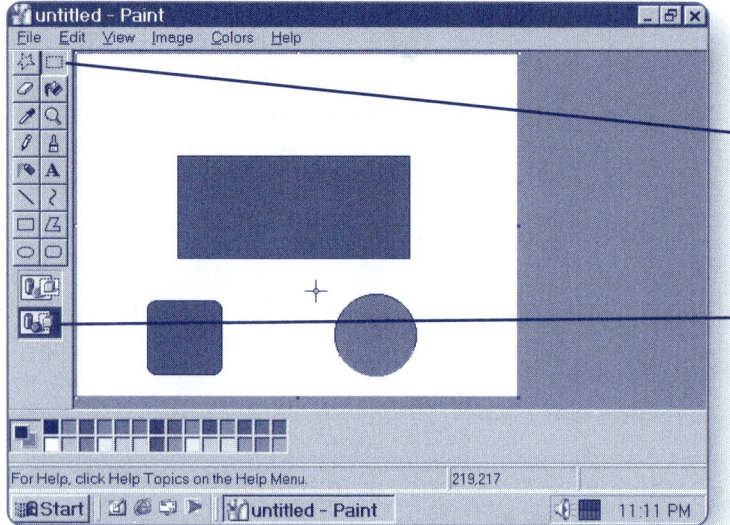

1. Click on the **Select tool** or the **Free-Form Select tool**. The mouse pointer becomes a small white cross.

2. Select whether the **background** of the object you're going to move is to be solid in color or transparent.

3. Click and **drag** around the area of the object to be moved. A dotted line (called the *selection box*) appears around the area when you release the mouse button.

4. Position the **mouse pointer** in the middle of the selection box. The mouse pointer becomes a small black cross with four arrowheads.

SELECTING AND MOVING AN OBJECT 103

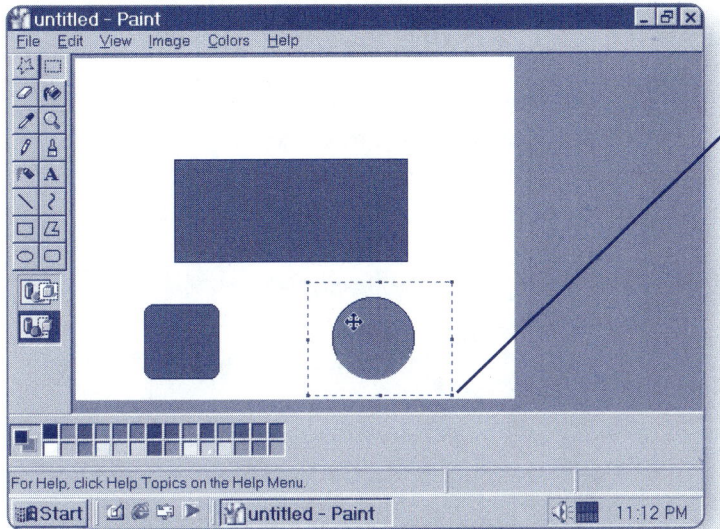

TIP
If you position the mouse pointer over one of the eight small black "handles" on the selection box, it becomes a double-headed arrow. You can resize the object by clicking and dragging the box to the desired size.

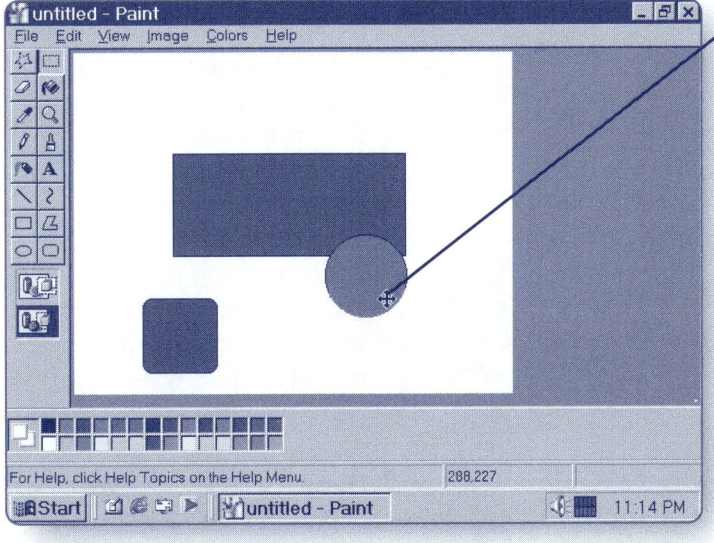

5. Drag the **selection box** to the desired location. The selected object moves.

6. Release the **mouse button**. The object remains selected and is ready for the next editing action.

TIP
To deselect an object, click on any other area of the drawing, or click on another tool.

Saving a Drawing

At this point, the drawing is only temporarily stored in the computer's memory. If you want to work with or refer to it later, you must save the drawing. Although Windows can work with many types of graphic formats, the Microsoft Paint program can save only in a .bmp (bitmap) format.

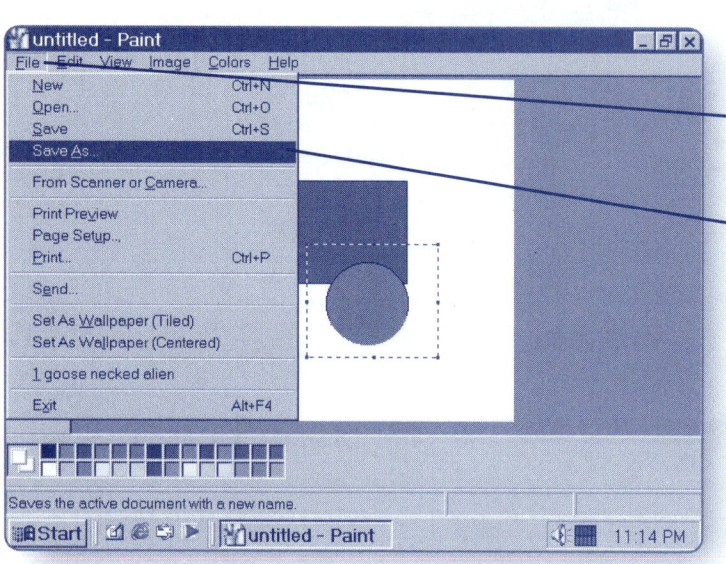

1. Click on **File**. The File menu appears.

2. Click on **Save** or **Save As**. The Save As dialog box opens.

NOTE

The very first time an untitled document is saved, both the Save and Save As commands open the Save As dialog box. After a document has been saved once, the Save command no longer opens a dialog box. The document simply is saved under the same name it was previously given.

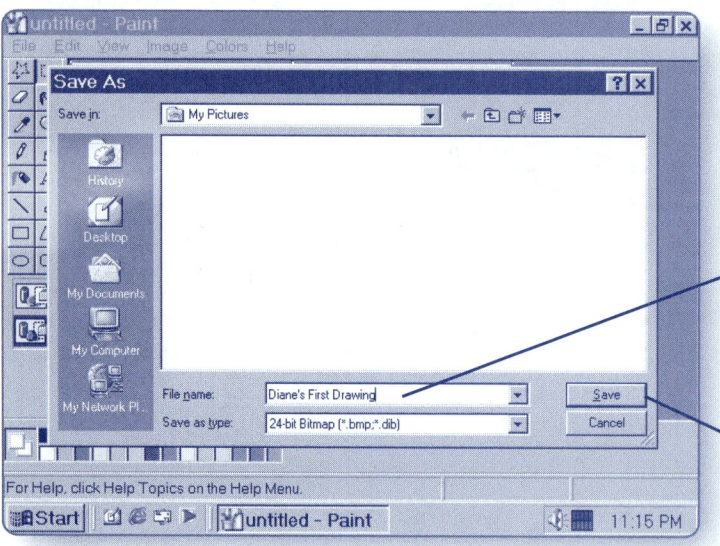

3. Type a **descriptive name** for the drawing in the File name: text box. The name you type appears in the box.

4. Click on the **Save button**. The document is saved and the name appears in the title bar.

Saving a Drawing as Wallpaper

After a drawing has been saved and given a name, you can choose to save the drawing as wallpaper to appear on your Windows desktop. You can select the wallpaper to be tiled or centered.

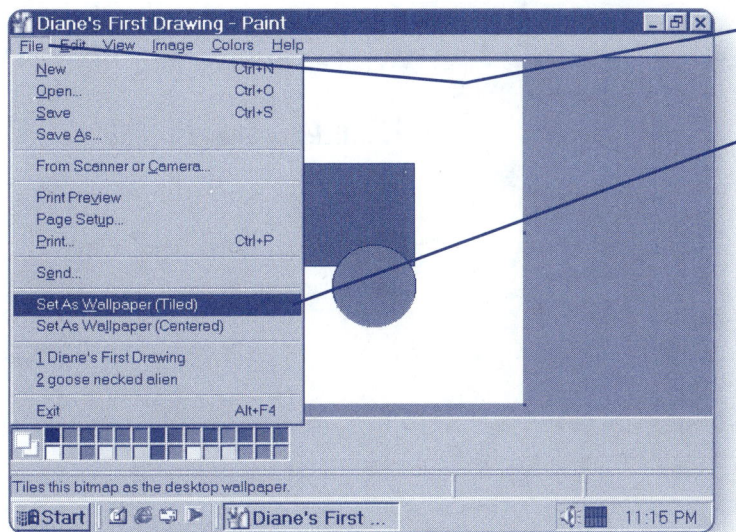

1. Click on **File**. The File menu appears.

2. Click on **Set As Wallpaper (Tiled)** or **Set As Wallpaper (Centered)**. The drawing appears as wallpaper on your desktop.

TIP
To see what the wallpaper looks like, click on the Minimize button ([_]).

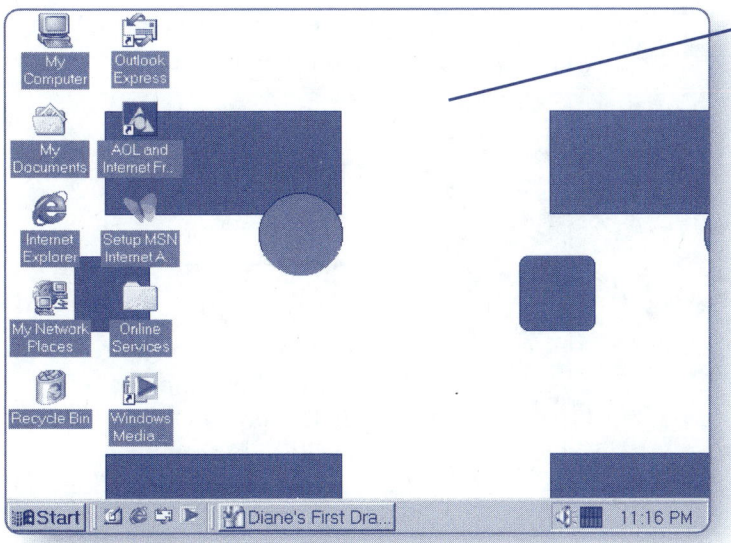

The drawing as it appears on the Windows desktop.

NOTE
Desktop wallpaper is discussed in more detail in Chapter 17, "Having Fun with the Control Panel."

Printing a Drawing

Printing is the final step for many drawing projects. Windows brings more and more consistency between software programs, including the capability and method to print; so printing a drawing is done in the same manner as printing a WordPad document.

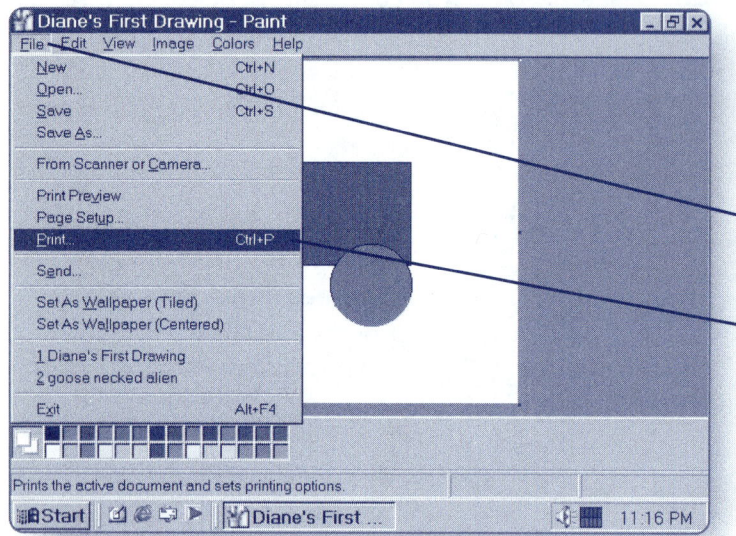

1. Click on **File**. The File menu appears.

2. Click on **Print**. The Print dialog box opens.

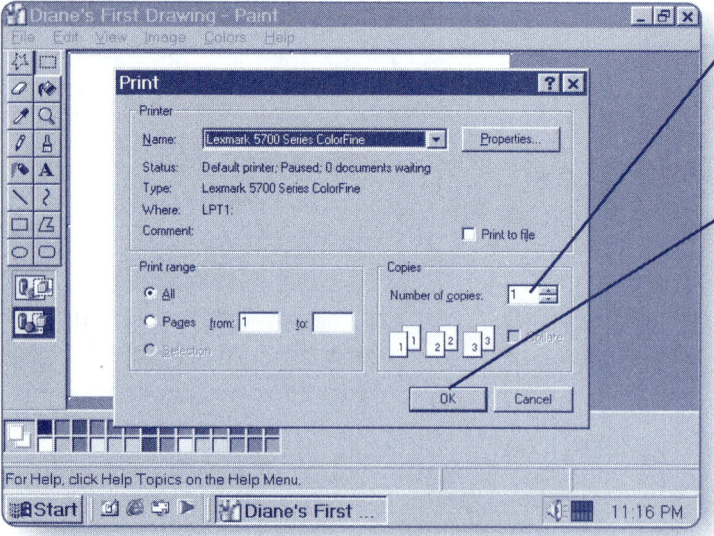

3. Optionally, **type** the **number of copies** to print (if more than one) in the Number of copies: box.

4. Click on **OK**. The document prints.

TIP

Exit the Paint program as any other windows application by clicking on the Close button (X).

9

Playing Around with the Games

I'm sure you've heard the saying, "all work and no play. . . ." Well, Microsoft has included many great games with Windows Millennium. You can play these games alone on your own computer, or with just a click of the mouse, you can play them against an opponent on the Internet.

Stand-alone games include FreeCell, Hearts, Solitaire, Pinball, Minesweeper, and a new game called Spider Solitaire.

Games you can play across the Internet are through a server called the MS Gaming Zone and include Backgammon, Hearts, Spades, and Reversi.

Games serve multiple purposes: one, of course, is to have fun and decrease stress. But more importantly, when you are new to a Windows environment, mastering control of the mouse can be difficult. The Windows Millennium games are great tools for learning to use your mouse. In this chapter, you'll learn how to:

- Start the Spider Solitaire game
- Start Internet Hearts
- Chat with other Internet players

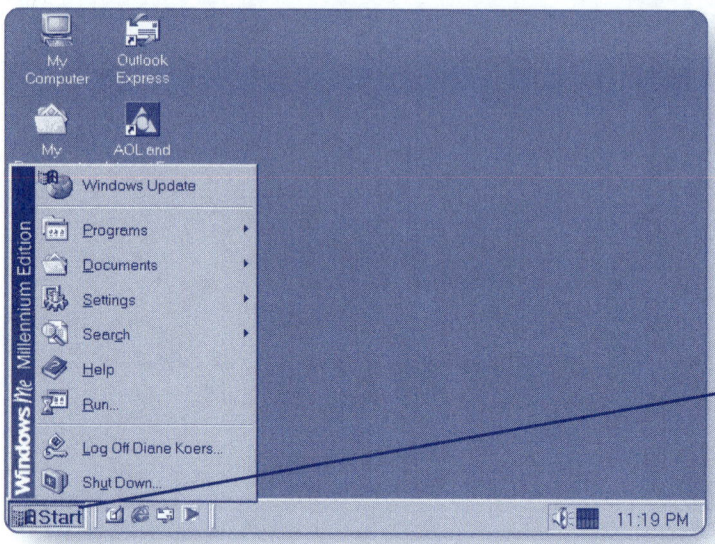

Starting Spider Solitaire

New to Windows Millennium is a cool variation of solitaire called Spider Solitaire. The object of Spider Solitaire is to remove all the cards from the playing area.

1. Click on **Start**. The Start menu appears.

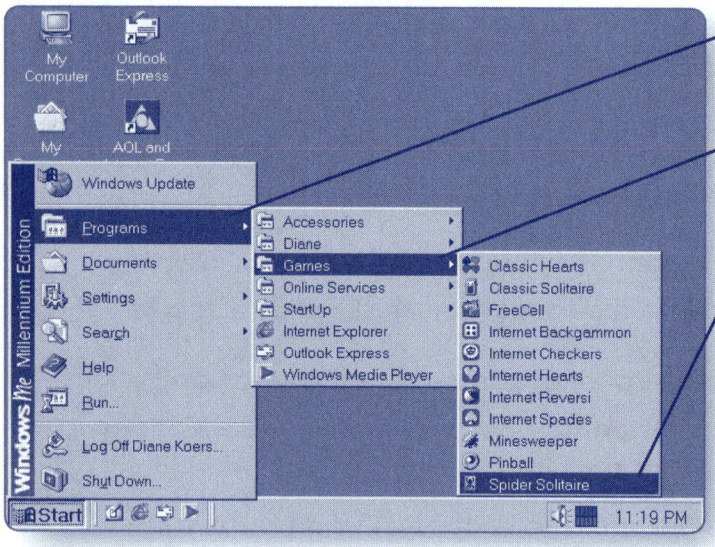

2. Click on **Programs**. The Programs submenu appears.

3. Click on **Games**. The Games submenu appears.

4. Click on **Spider Solitaire**. The Spider Solitaire game launches and a dialog box opens.

TIP

You may have to pause your mouse over the menu down arrow for a moment, to make the Spider Solitaire option appear.

STARTING SPIDER SOLITAIRE 109

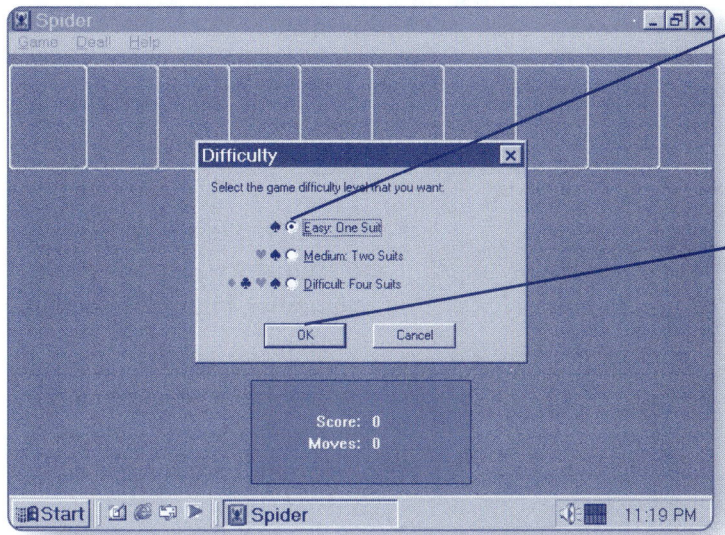

5. Click on the **level of difficulty** you want to play. The option is selected. (Hint: From experience, start with Easy, One Suit.)

6. Click on **OK**. Let the games begin!

The game area is made up of the columns of cards, each with one card turned up.

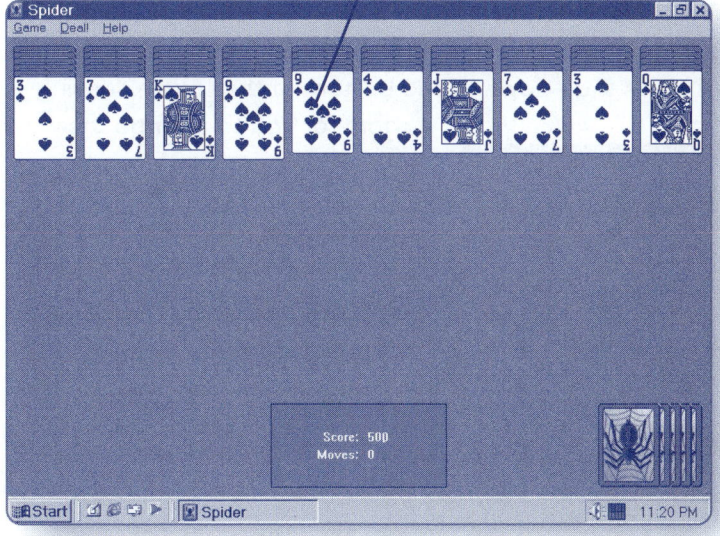

TIP
To move a card, click the card and drag it to the new location.

7. Move cards according to these rules:

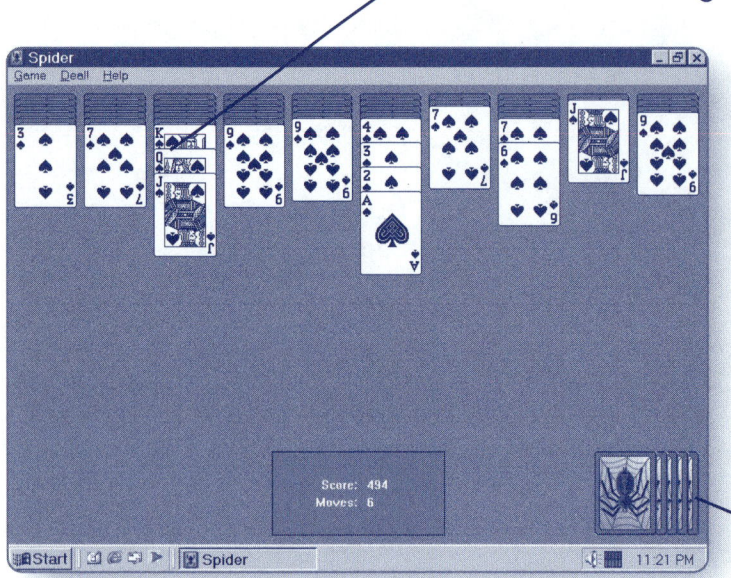

- You can move a card from the bottom of a column to a free space.

- You can move a card from the bottom of a column to a card one higher, regardless of suit or color.

- You can move a set of cards all of the same suit, and in order, as if they were one card.

8. Click on the turned down **deck**, when there are no more moves to make. The next layer of cards is dealt.

To win, move the cards around until you line up each suit of cards in order, King to Ace. When you line up one suit, the line of cards slide down to the bottom of the screen, leaving room for you to arrange the next line of cards.

All finished?

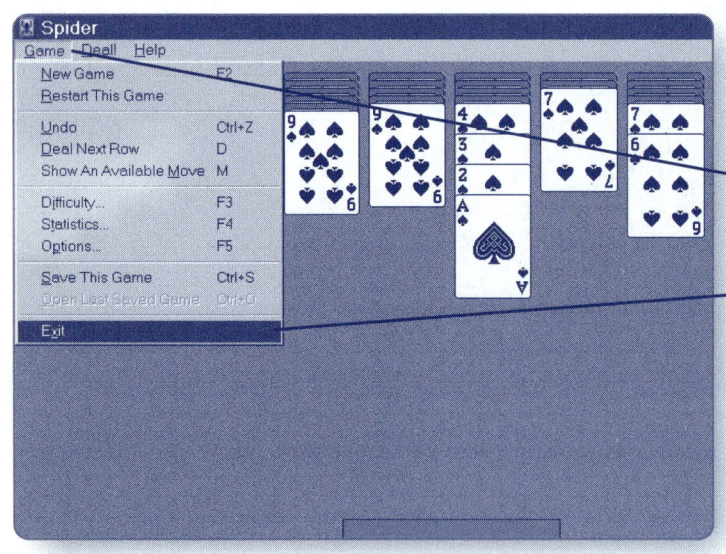

9. Click on **Game**. The Game menu appears.

10. Click on **Exit**. A dialog box appears.

You have the option of saving the current game until next time.

CONNECTING TO AN INTERNET HEARTS GAME   111

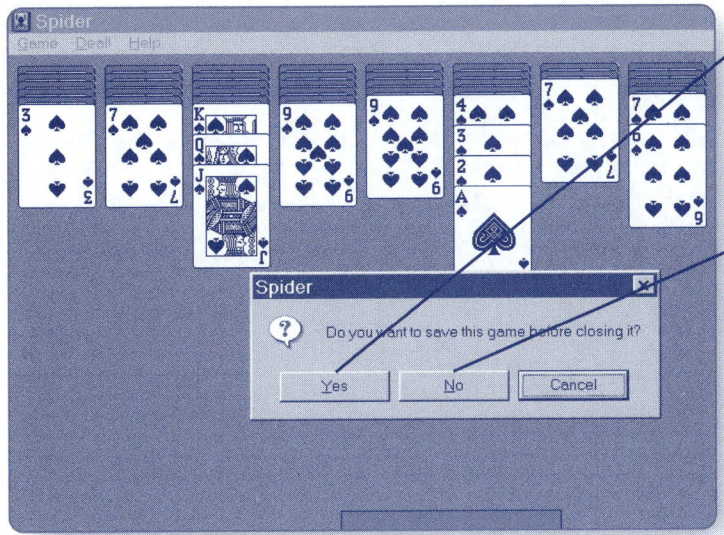

11a. Click on **Yes**. The current game is saved before the program closes.

OR

11b. Click on **No**. The current game is not saved before the program closes.

TIP
To return to the saved game, start Spider Solitaire and then click on Game, Open Last Saved Game.

Connecting to an Internet Hearts Game

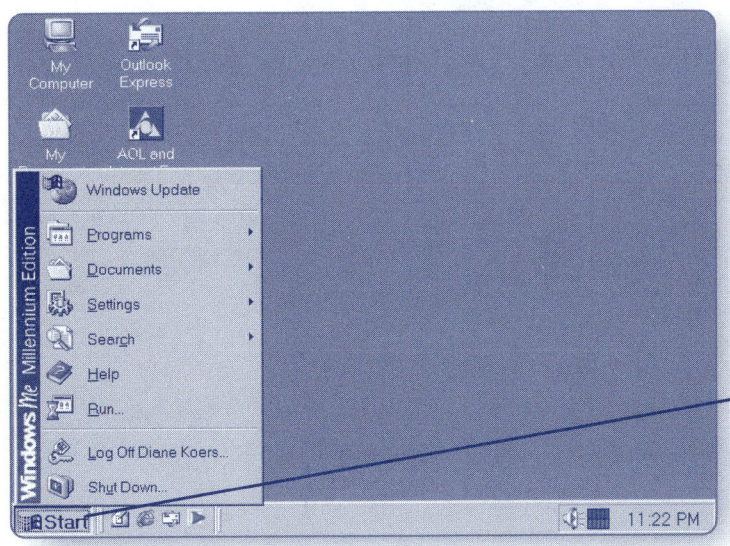

By playing the game of classic hearts, you can play against other players on your network. Not on a network? That's not a problem if you have Internet access. You can join other players across the world. Your identity is anonymous to other players.

1. Click on **Start**. The Start menu appears.

CHAPTER 9: PLAYING AROUND WITH THE GAMES

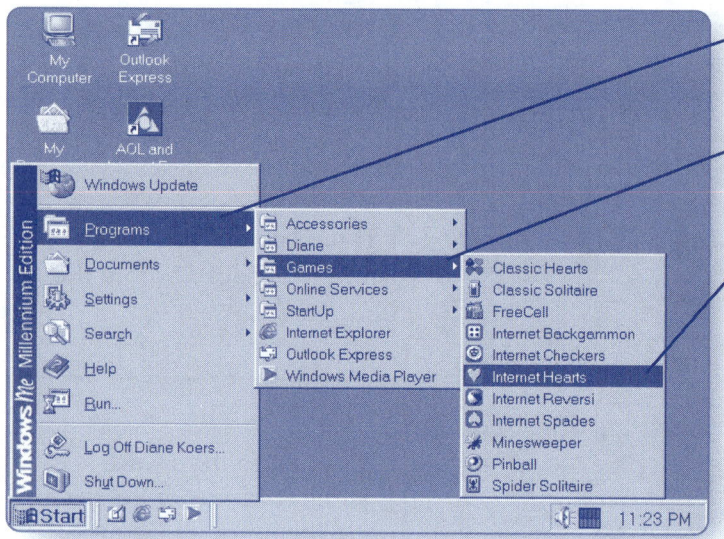

2. Click on **Programs**. The Programs submenu appears.

3. Click on **Games**. The Games submenu appears.

4. Click on **Internet Hearts**. An MSN Gaming Zone dialog box appears.

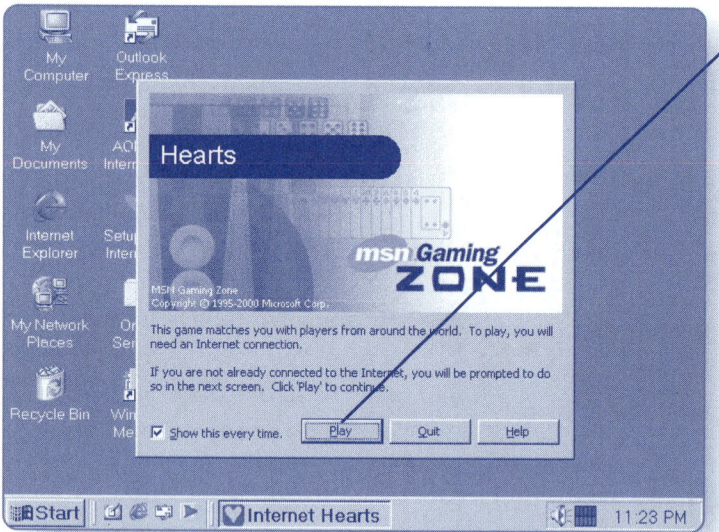

5. Click on **Play**. If you are not already connected to the Internet, a connection is established.

MSN Gaming Zone will then try to contact three other Internet Hearts player who speak your language. Your language is determined during the Windows installation and setup.

CONNECTING TO AN INTERNET HEARTS GAME   113

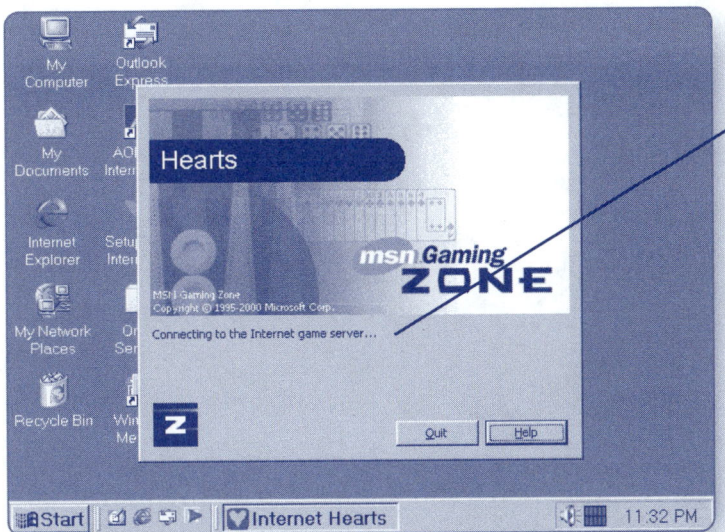

NOTE
Be patient, depending upon the time of day and the number of available players, the process could take several minutes.

When enough players have been contacted, the game board opens. You are assigned a player number. No names are used, just player numbers.

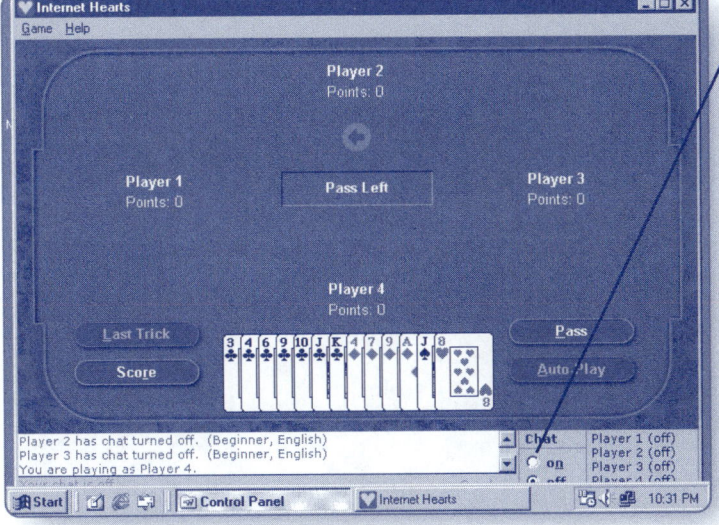

6. Click on **On**. The Chat window becomes activated.

With chat activated, you can type your conversation to the other three players.

114 CHAPTER 9: PLAYING AROUND WITH THE GAMES

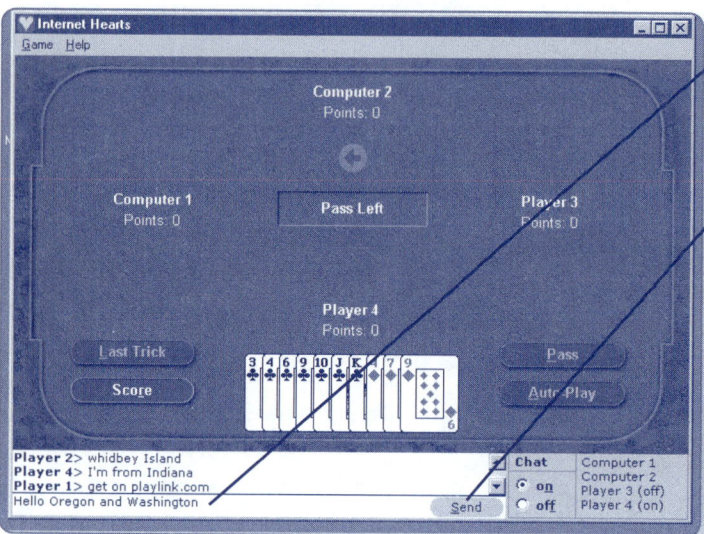

7. **Type** your **message**. The text appears in the bottom part of the chat window.

8. **Click** on **Send or press Enter**. The message is displayed to the other players.

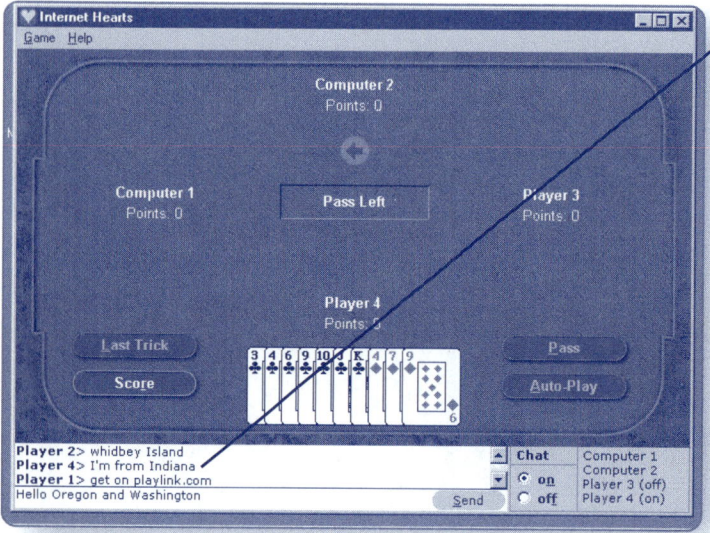

Other players' text is also displayed in the Chat window.

Exit the game in the same manner as other windows applications.

CONNECTING TO AN INTERNET HEARTS GAME 115

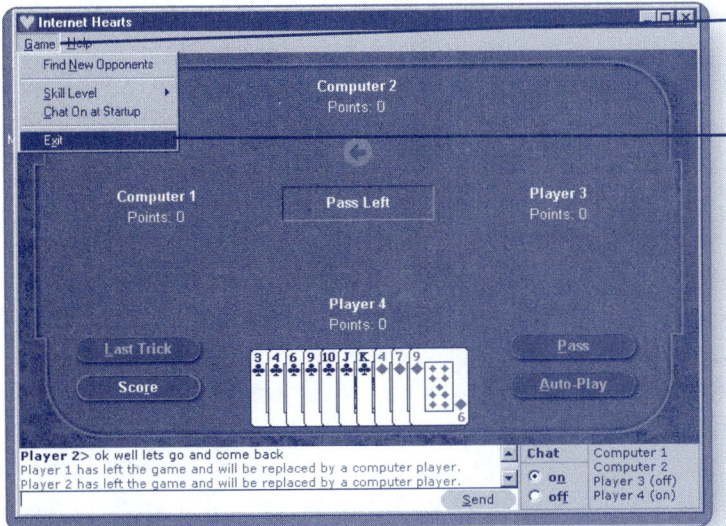

9. **Click** on **Game**. The Game menu appears.

10. **Click** on **Exit**. A confirmation message opens.

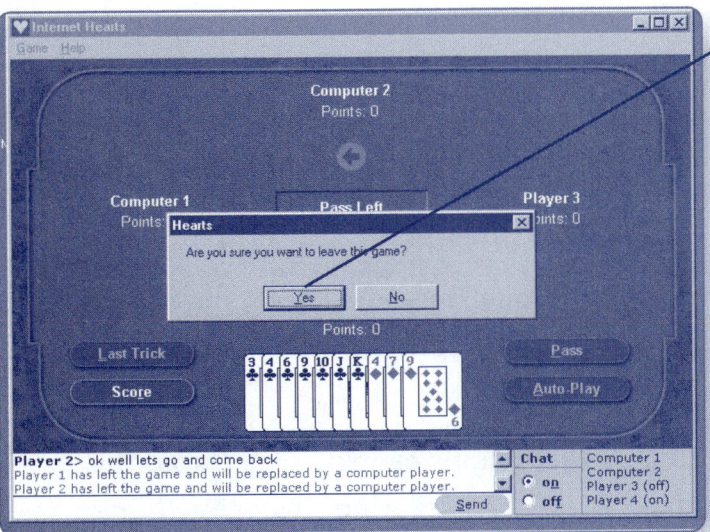

11. **Click** on **Yes**. The Internet Hearts game window closes.

Part II Review Questions

1. What key can be pressed to clear the totals on the Windows calculator? *See "Using the Calculator" in Chapter 6*

2. What are the two types of Windows calculator that can be displayed? *See "Changing the Style of the Calculator" in Chapter 6*

3. How do you access the WordPad program? *See "Starting WordPad" in Chapter 7*

4. In WordPad, pressing the Backspace key will delete text in which direction? *See "Deleting Text" in Chapter 7*

5. What are the three alignment choices available in WordPad? *See "Modifying the Alignment" in Chapter 7*

6. What does the Fill With Color tool in Paint do? *See "Discovering the Paint Tools" in Chapter 8*

7. What key can you press to draw a perfect circle in Paint? *See "Drawing a Rectangle or Circle" in Chapter 8*

8. In a Paint drawing, what can you do when you position the mouse over any of the eight handles on a selection box? *See "Selecting and Moving an Object" in Chapter 8*

9. What Windows Millennium Edition games can you play across the Internet, via the MS Gaming Zone? *See "Playing Around with the Games" in Chapter 9*

10. How do you win a game of Spider Solitaire? *See "Starting Spider Solitaire" in Chapter 9*

PART III
Discovering the Windows Tools

Chapter 10
Using Windows Help **119**

Chapter 11
Using Windows System Tools **131**

Chapter 12
Organizing Files and Folders **149**

Chapter 13
Finding Files, Folders, and People **173**

Chapter 14
Discovering Multimedia **183**

10

Using Windows Help

Although I sincerely hope you find many answers to your Windows Millennium questions from this book, sometimes you need additional information. Windows Millennium includes an informative help center complete with tours, step-by-step instructions, troubleshooters, and helpful links to the Web. In this chapter, you'll learn how to:

- Access the Help and Support window
- Work with the Help index
- Search for specific information
- Get help on the Web

Starting Windows Help

The Windows Help and Support system assists you with general help topics covering such issues as personalizing your computer, connecting to networks, and using the troubleshooting features.

You can access tours, step-by-step instructions, troubleshooters, and Web links through the Help and Support system.

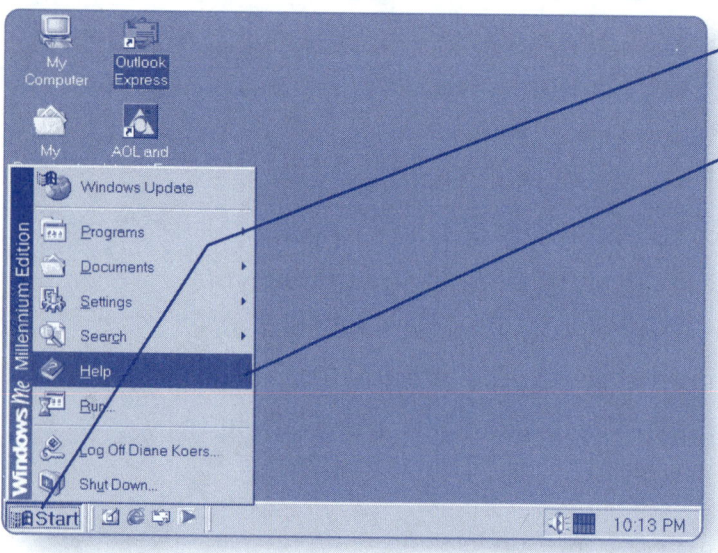

1. **Click** on the **Start button**. The Start menu appears.

2. **Click** on **Help**. The Help and Support window opens.

The first time you run the Help program, it might take a moment or two to generate itself.

TIP
You can also press F1 to access the Windows Help and Support window.

Exploring the Help and Support Window

Let's take a look at some of the components in the Help and Support window. The beginning screen is called the Home screen.

EXPLORING THE HELP AND SUPPORT WINDOW

The top of the screen has navigation buttons and tools:

- **Back.** To view the previous viewed screen.
- **Forward.** To view the next screen.

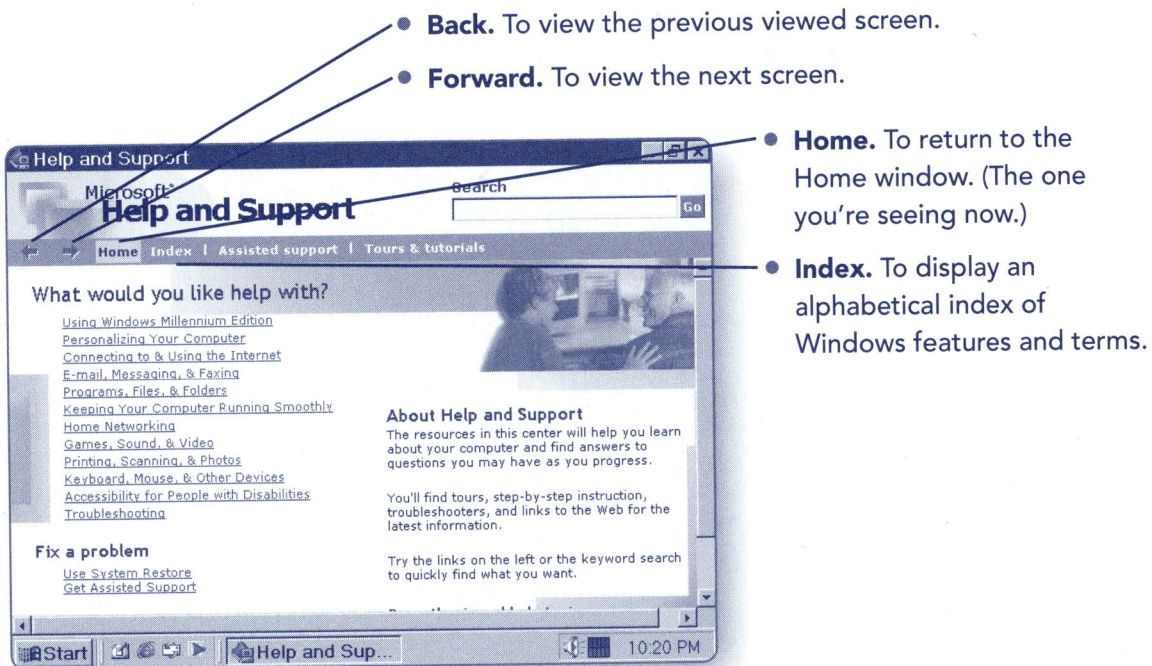

- **Home.** To return to the Home window. (The one you're seeing now.)
- **Index.** To display an alphabetical index of Windows features and terms.

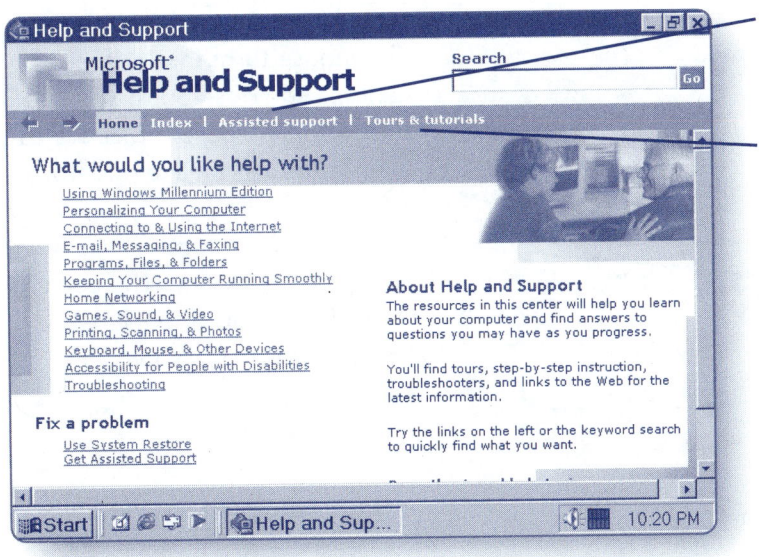

- **Assisted Support.** To take you to the Microsoft Web site for additional assistance.
- **Tours & Tutorials.** To view interactive lessons on a variety of Windows Millennium features.

122   CHAPTER 10: USING WINDOWS HELP

The left side of the screen contains links to various help topics. This area is titled "What would you like help with?"

The right side of the screen contains a search text box in which you can type a keyword to search.

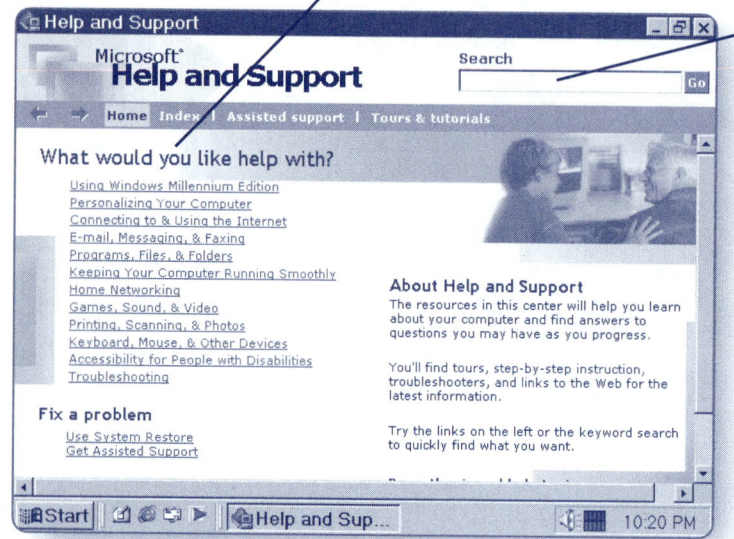

Using the Help Topics

The mouse turns into a small hand as you position the mouse over a topic. These topics are to various links in the Help feature.

1. Click on the **area** in which you need assistance. The Look for Help window appears with information on the topic you selected.

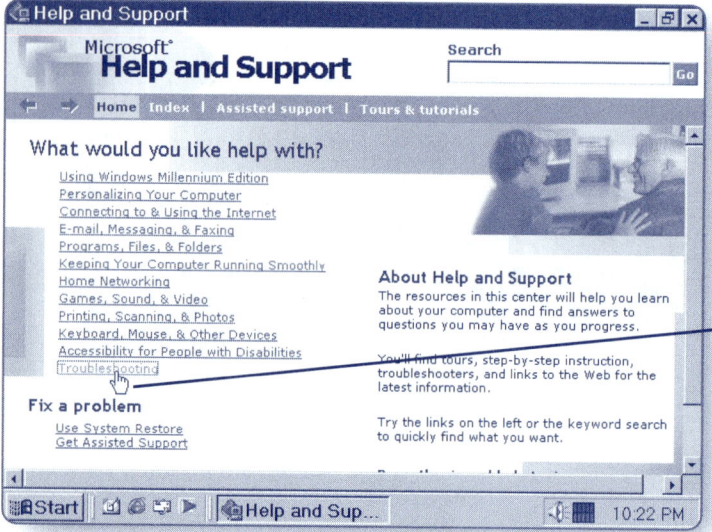

EXPLORING THE HELP AND SUPPORT WINDOW   123

Most areas have multiple choices to select from. Depending on the topic you've selected, you may have several options to click on until you reach the actual Help topics.

A yellow icon with a question mark indicates the Help topics.

2. Click on the **topic** that most closely resembles the information you need. The Help information appears on the right side of the screen.

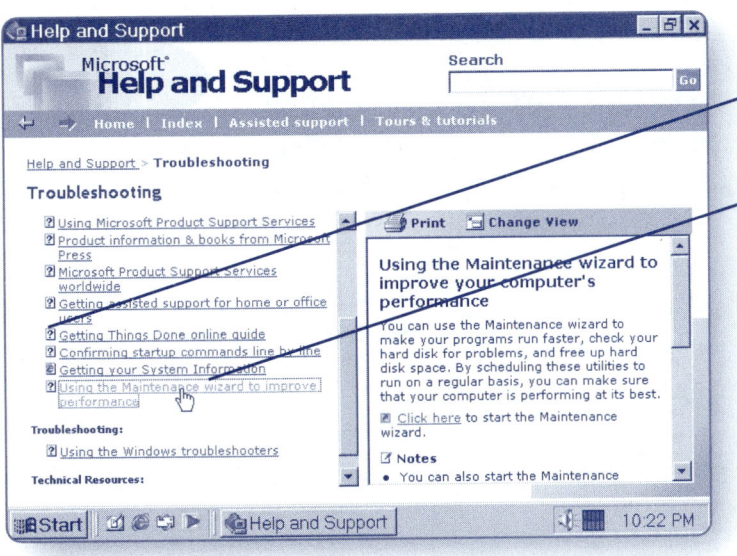

3. Read through the topic **information** following the instructions onscreen.

> **TIP**
> Click on the Print button to print the Help topic information.

4. Click on the **Home button**. The main Help and Support window reappears.

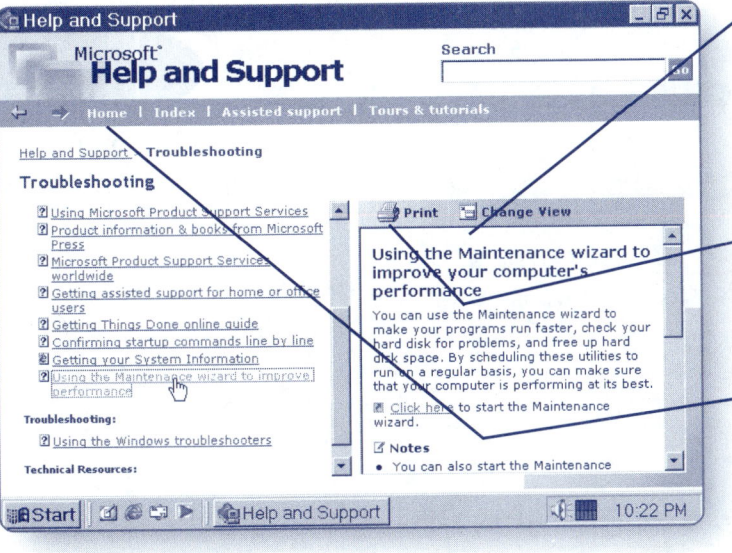

Utilizing the Help Index

The Windows Help Index is a list of every available topic covered in the Windows Help feature.

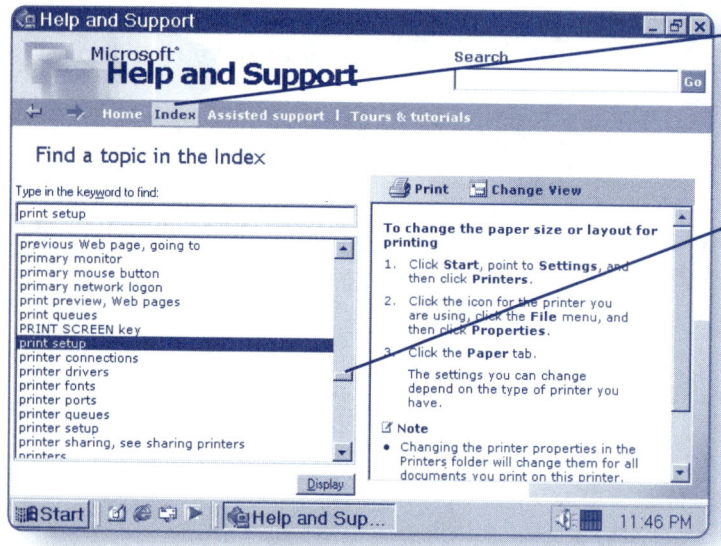

1. Click on the **Index button**. The topics are listed alphabetically with some topics displaying a list of subtopics.

2a. Scroll through the **list of topics** until you find the topic you are looking for.

OR

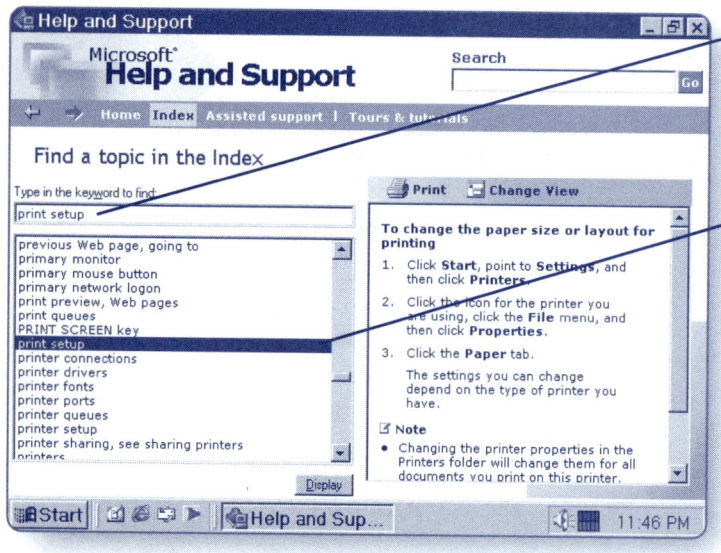

2b. Type the **first word** of the topic you are looking for. The topics jump alphabetically to the word you typed.

3. Double-click on the desired **topic**. The information is displayed on the right side of the screen.

EXPLORING THE HELP AND SUPPORT WINDOW   125

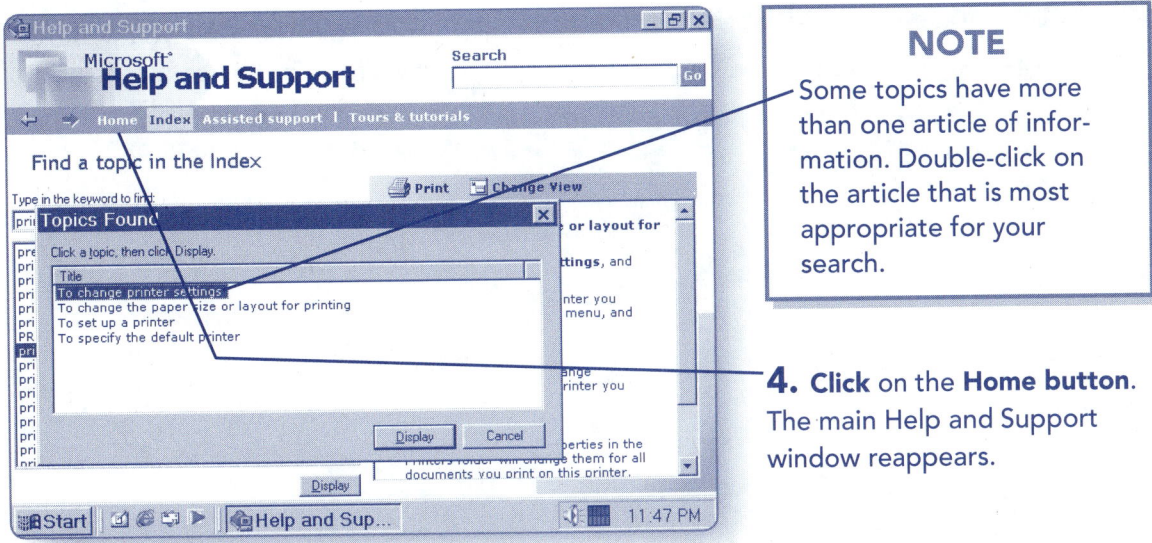

NOTE

Some topics have more than one article of information. Double-click on the article that is most appropriate for your search.

4. **Click** on the **Home button**. The main Help and Support window reappears.

Searching for Help

Another method of help is the Search Help and Support box. If you've used the Internet, you've probably used search engines to help you locate a Web page in which you're interested. The Help and Support search engine works similarly to the Internet search engines.

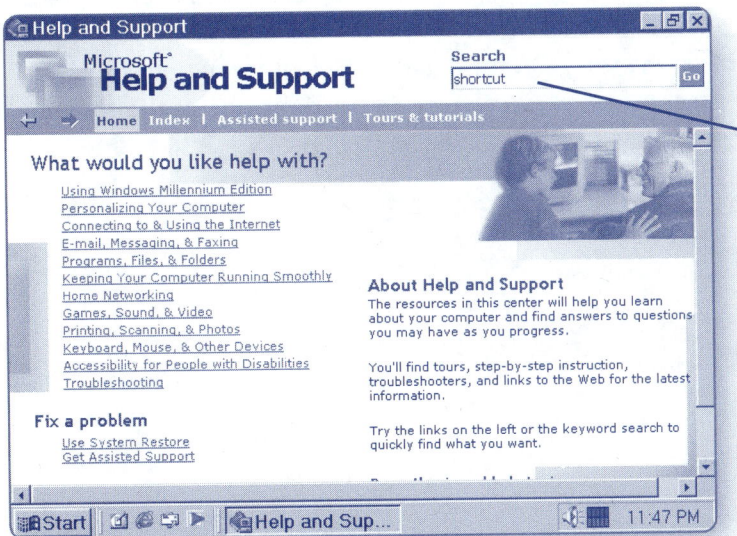

1. **Click** in the **Search Help and Support text box**. A blinking insertion point appears.

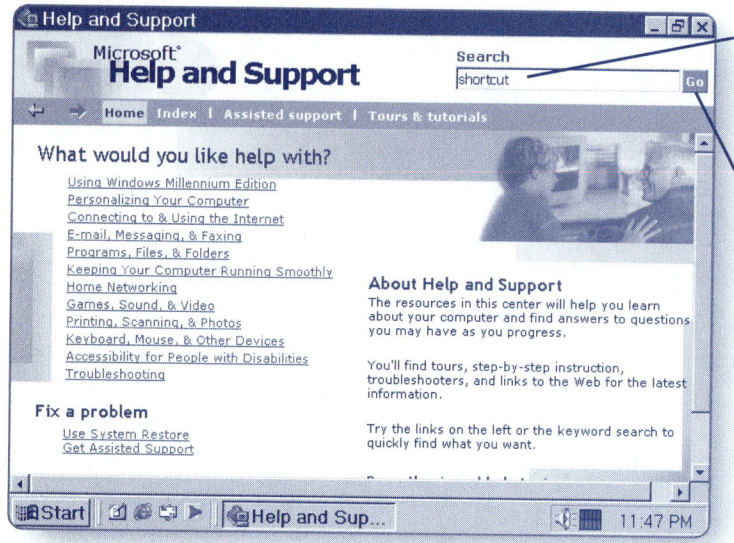

2. Type the **topic** you want to search. The search text can be one word or several. The text appears in the text box.

3. Click on **Go**. A Search Results window appears.

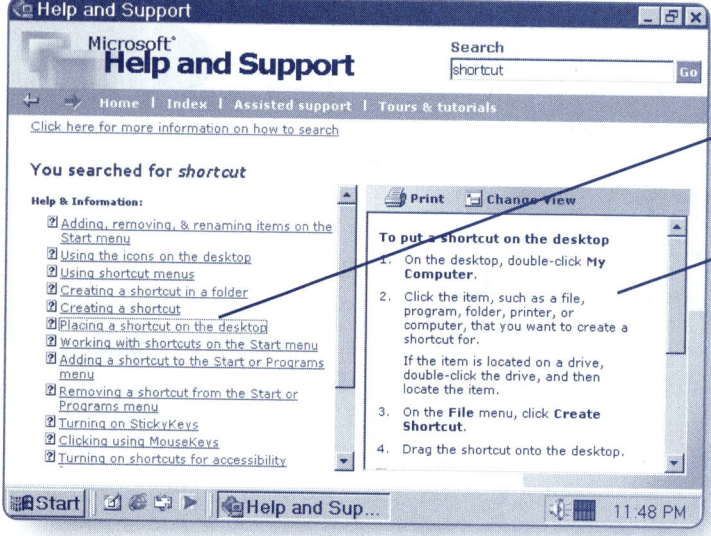

A list of topics that respond to your query are displayed.

4. Click on the **topic** that most closely resembles your request.

The Help information displays on the right side of the screen.

GETTING ASSISTED SUPPORT 127

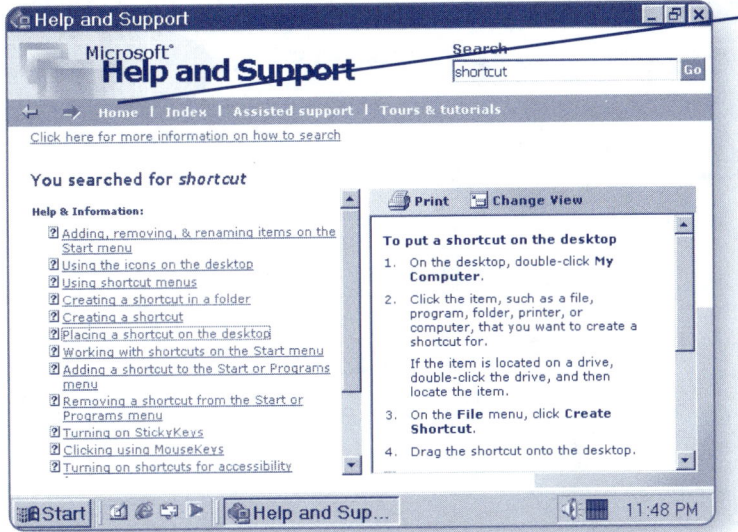

5. Click on the **Home button**. The main Help and Support window reappears.

Getting Assisted Support

Assisted Support is a Web-based help system where you can contact Microsoft support or get in touch with other users of Windows Millennium. You must have an Internet connection to use Assisted Support.

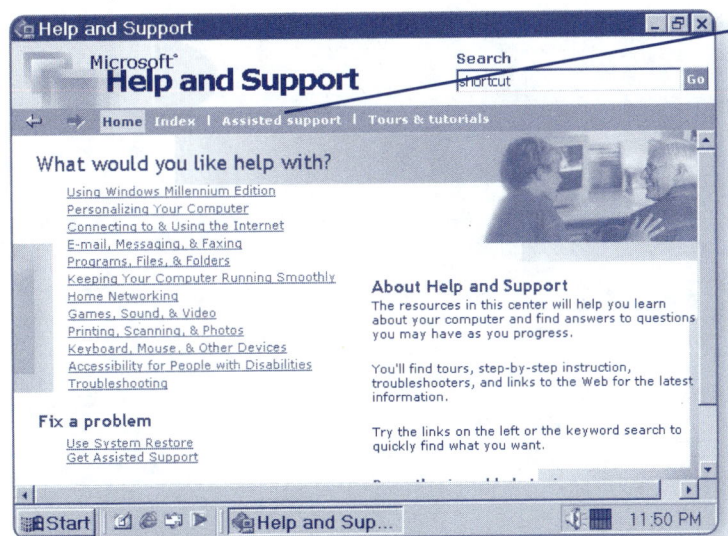

1. Click on **Assisted Support**. The Get Assistance window appears.

The best place to obtain assisted help is through the MSN Computing Central Forums. It's a place where you'll be able to chat or e-mail other people who use computers and want to share their ideas.

128 CHAPTER 10: USING WINDOWS HELP

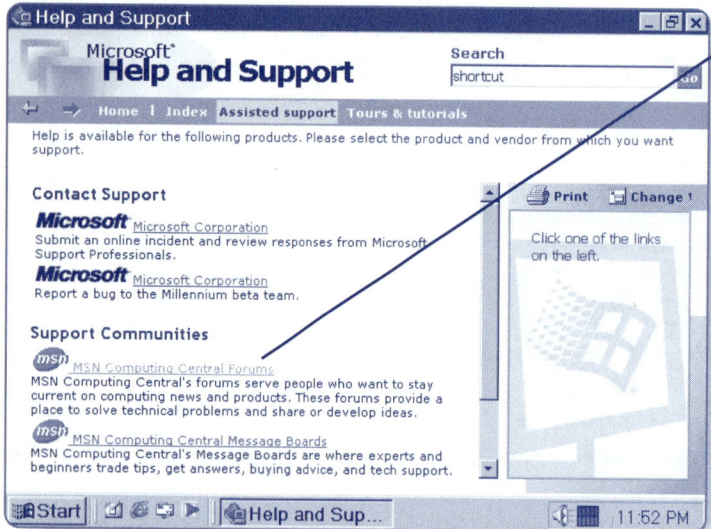

2. Click on **MSN Computing Central Forums**. A list of topics appears on the right.

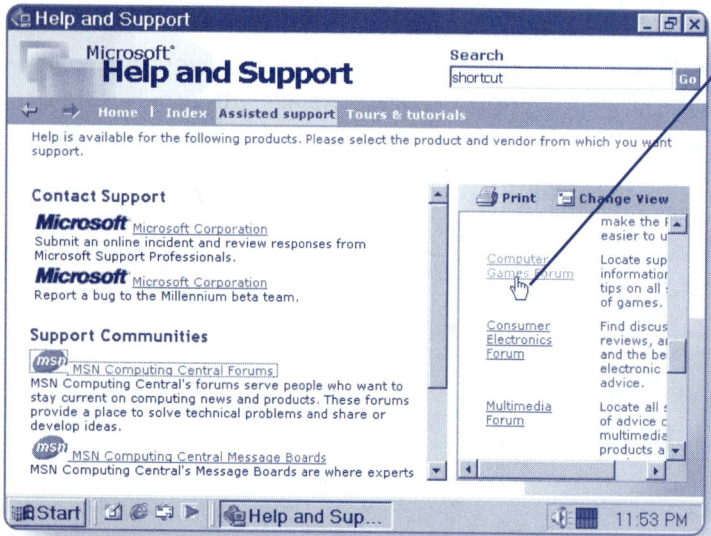

3. Click on the **topic** in which you need help. If you're not already connected to the Internet, a connection is established.

GETTING ASSISTED SUPPORT   129

Your Web browser opens with an MSN Computing Central home page displayed. The page you see will not look exactly as shown. This page is updated frequently.

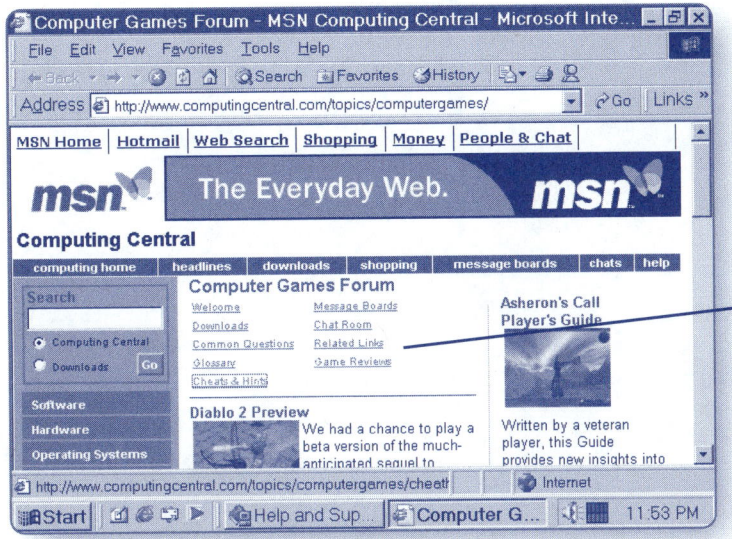

From the home page, you can enter a chat room with other users, read newsletters and reviews, access message boards, review related links, and other options. You can even download free software!

4. Click the **area** you want to explore. The area of help appears.

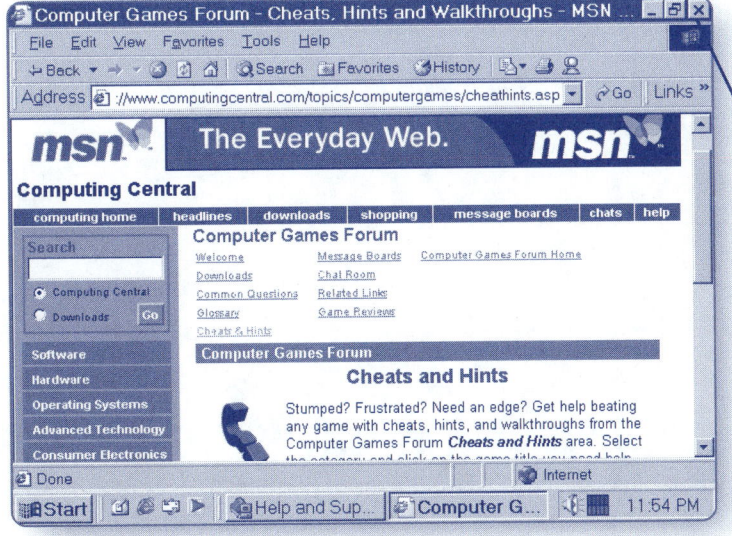

When you're finished exploring MSN Computing Central, close the browser window.

5. Click on the **Close button** (X). The Web browser window closes.

NOTE
You may be prompted to close your Internet connection.

130 CHAPTER 10: USING WINDOWS HELP

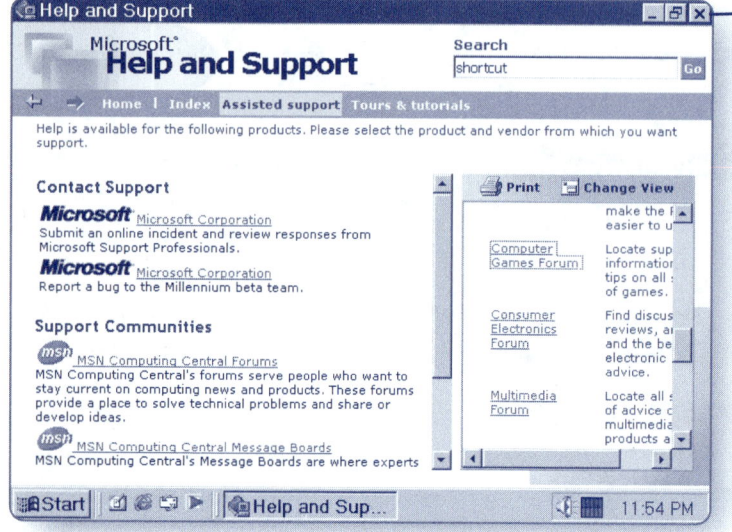

6. Click on the **Close button**. The Help and Support window closes.

11
Using Windows System Tools

Windows has a lot of tools to aid you with the housekeeping and maintenance of your PC. Windows not only makes these tools easily accessible with just a few clicks of the mouse, but many can also be set to run automatically. In this chapter, you'll learn how to:

- Scan your disk for errors
- Defragment your hard disk
- Schedule the Maintenance Wizard
- Use the Windows Update Wizard

Scanning Your Hard Disk for Problems

When you shut down your computer normally, several internal checks and operations occur to make sure everything is closed and filed properly. If Windows is not shut down normally, for example, if the computer locks up or if you turned off the power while in Windows, those internal checks don't get the chance to work. This can cause problems with your computer's hard drive. Windows includes a program to check your hard drive for potential errors.

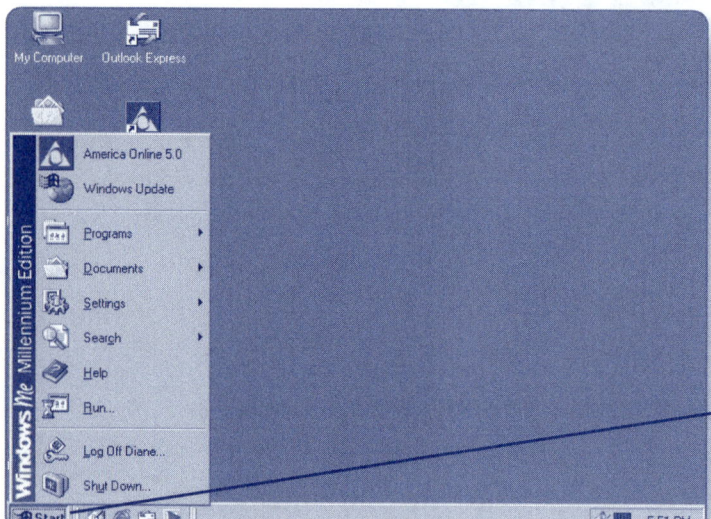

1. Click on the **Start button**. The Start menu appears.

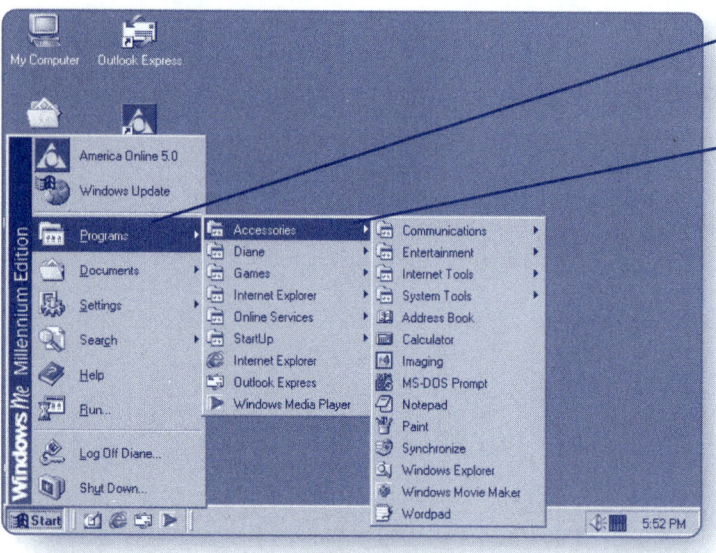

2. Click on **Programs**. The Programs menu appears.

3. Click on **Accessories**. The Accessories menu appears.

SCANNING YOUR HARD DISK FOR PROBLEMS   133

4. Click on **System Tools**. The System Tools submenu appears.

5. Click on **ScanDisk**. The ScanDisk dialog box opens.

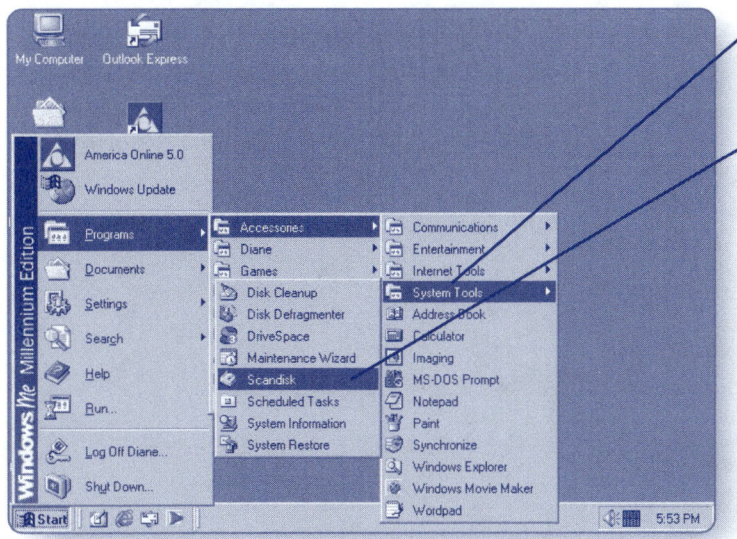

6. Click on the **disk drive** you want to check. The selected drive appears highlighted.

TIP
If you have more than one disk to scan, hold down the Ctrl key and click on each subsequent drive to be checked.

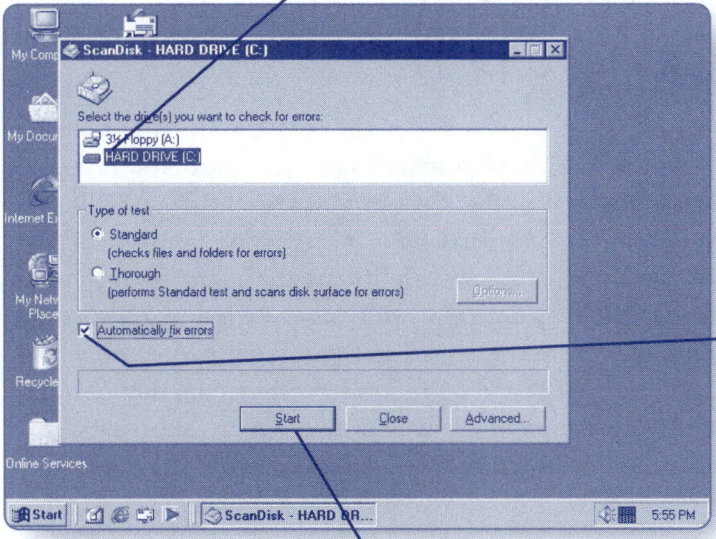

7. Click on the **Automatically fix errors check box,** if it is not already checked. A ✔ appears in the check box.

8. Click on **Start**. The ScanDisk process begins. A progress indicator displays at the bottom of the ScanDisk dialog box. When ScanDisk has finished checking the drive, the ScanDisk Results dialog box appears.

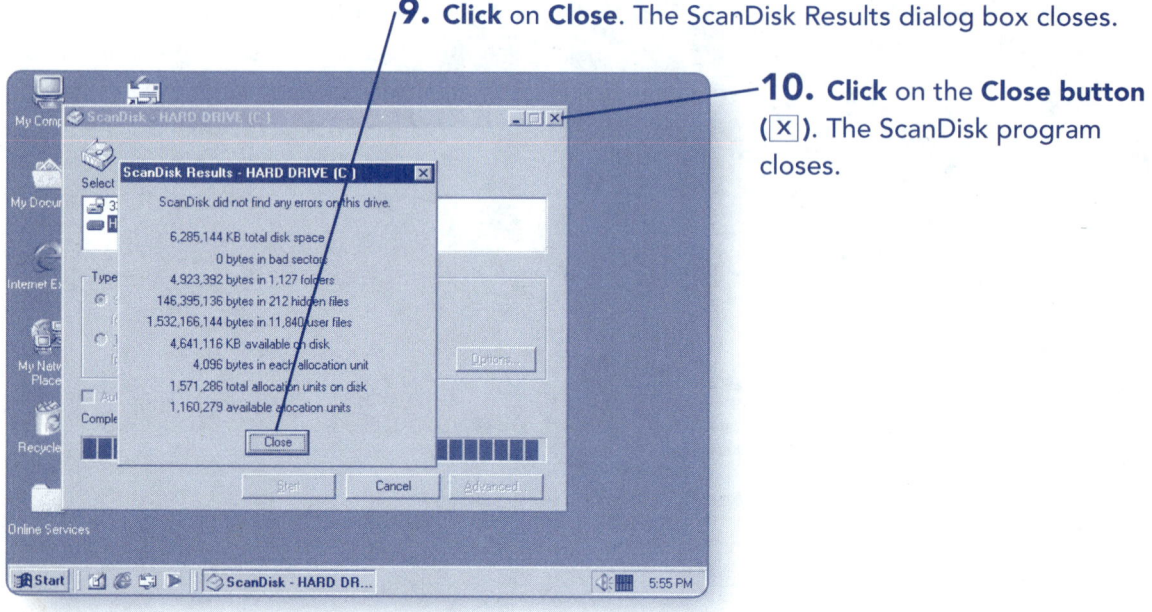

9. Click on **Close**. The ScanDisk Results dialog box closes.

10. Click on the **Close button** ([X]). The ScanDisk program closes.

Defragmenting Your Hard Drive

When a file is stored, the computer puts it in the first available space on the disk drive. If there's not enough room for the entire file, the rest of the file is put into the next available space. A file is fragmented when it is split into more than one location on your hard drive. Defragmenting your hard drive rearranges the way data is stored on your hard disk. Programs and documents are organized so that the entire program or document you want can be read with a minimum number of physical movements of the disk drive. This can substantially improve the performance of your computer.

DEFRAGMENTING YOUR HARD DRIVE   135

> **TIP**
> It's a good idea to run this program every couple of months or after you delete large amounts of data or programs from your hard drive.

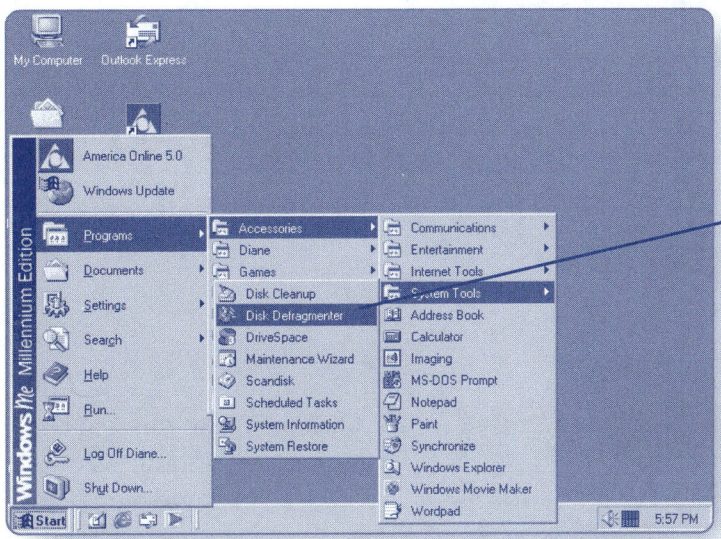

1. Follow steps 1 through **4** in "Scanning Your Hard Disk for Problems." The System Tools submenu appears.

2. Click on **Disk Defragmenter**. The Select Drive dialog box opens.

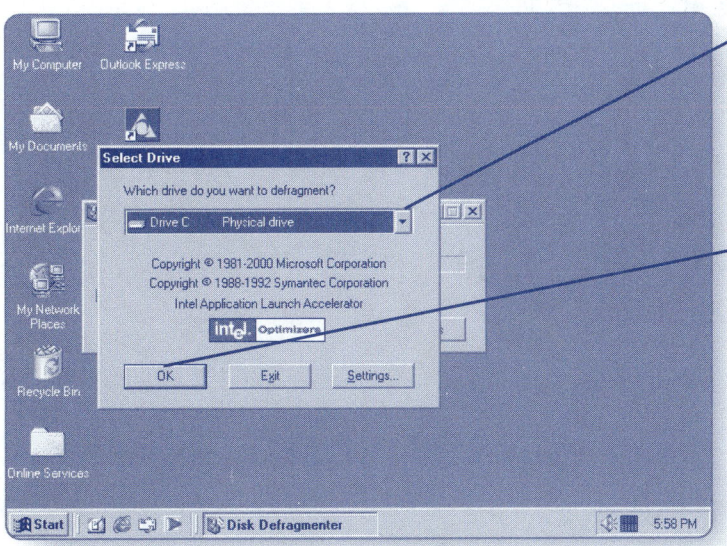

3. If necessary, **click** on the **drop-down arrow (▼)** and **choose** the **drive** you want to defragment. The drive name is displayed.

4. Click on **OK**. The Defragmenting dialog box opens and shows your progress.

CHAPTER 11: USING WINDOWS SYSTEM TOOLS

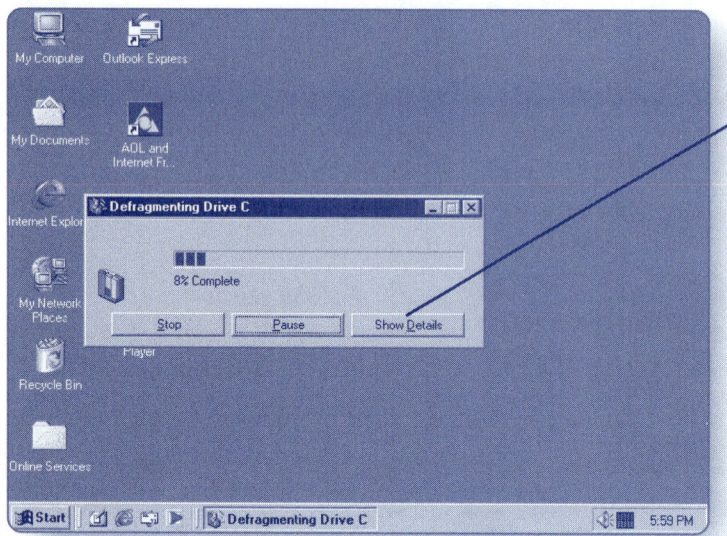

TIP
Optionally, click on Show Details to see a visual representation of the blocks of the hard drive as they are being cleaned up.

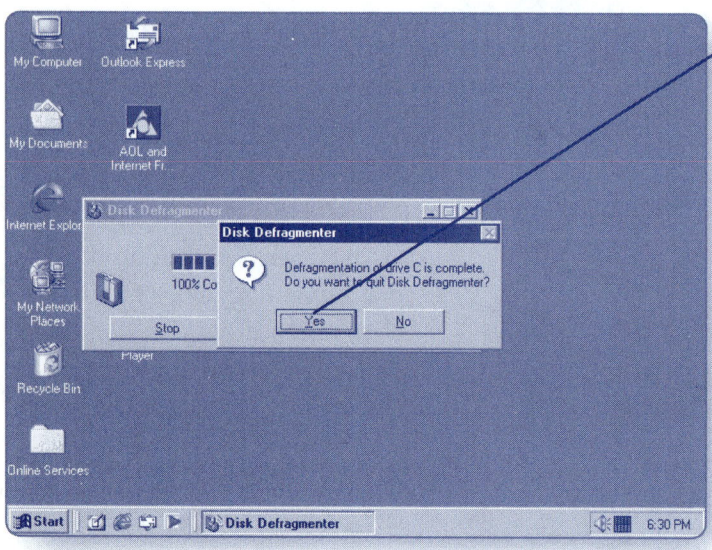

5. Click on **Yes** to quit the Disk Defragmenter program. The Disk Defragmenter dialog boxes close.

Using the Maintenance Wizard

Schedule the Windows Millennium Edition Maintenance Wizard to run Scan Disk, Disk Defragmenter, and delete unnecessary temporary files, automatically, at a time when you won't be using your computer.

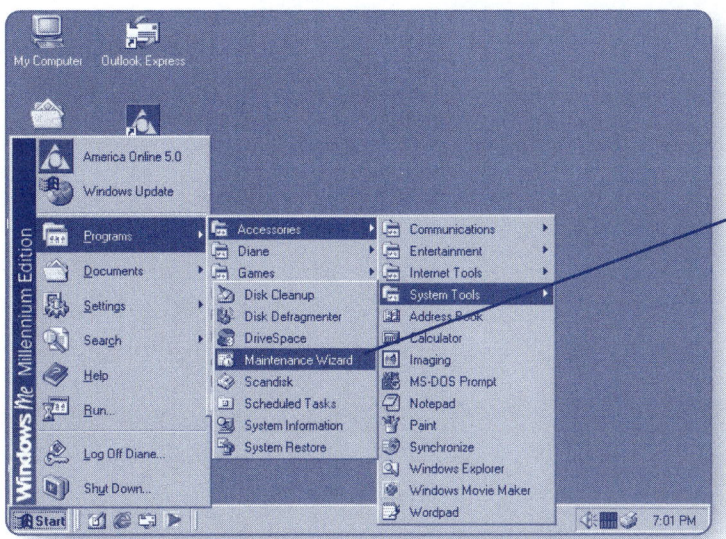

1. Follow steps **1** through **4** in "Scanning Your Hard Disk for Problems." The System Tools submenu appears.

2. Click on **Maintenance Wizard**. The Select Drive dialog box opens.

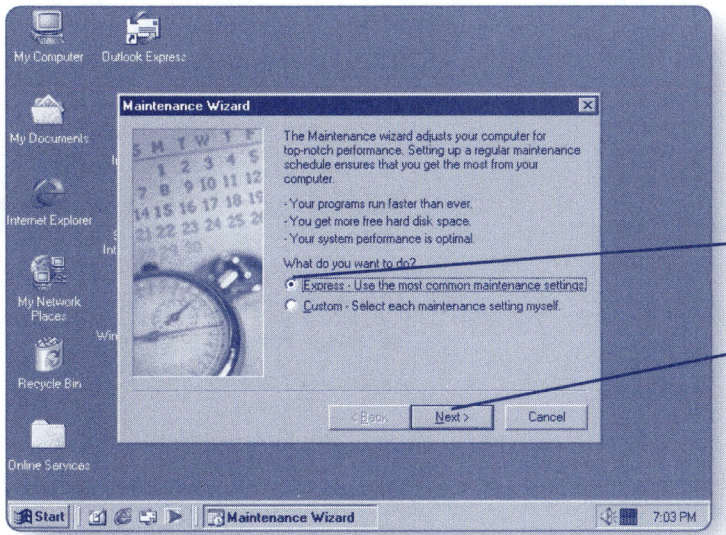

Although you can select and customize the Maintenance Wizard schedule, it's easiest to use the most common maintenance settings.

3. If necessary, **click** on **Express**. The option is selected.

4. Click on **Next**. The Select a Maintenance Schedule screen appears.

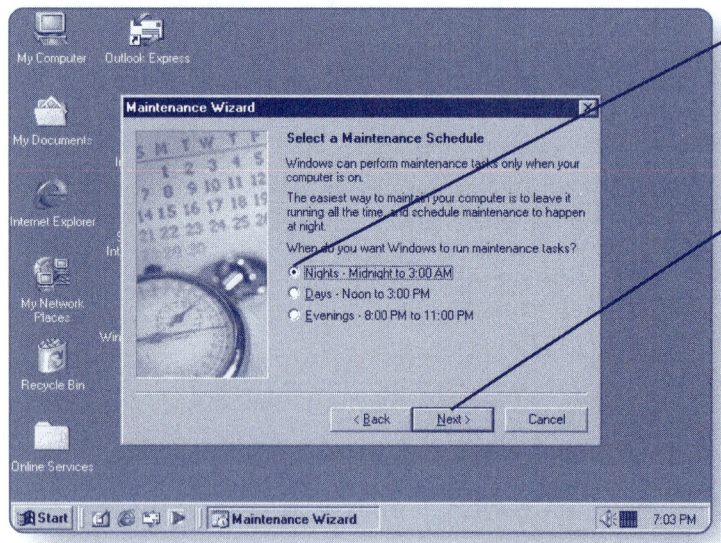

5. Click on a **time** when you're least likely to be using your computer. The option is selected.

6. Click on **Next**. The final screen appears.

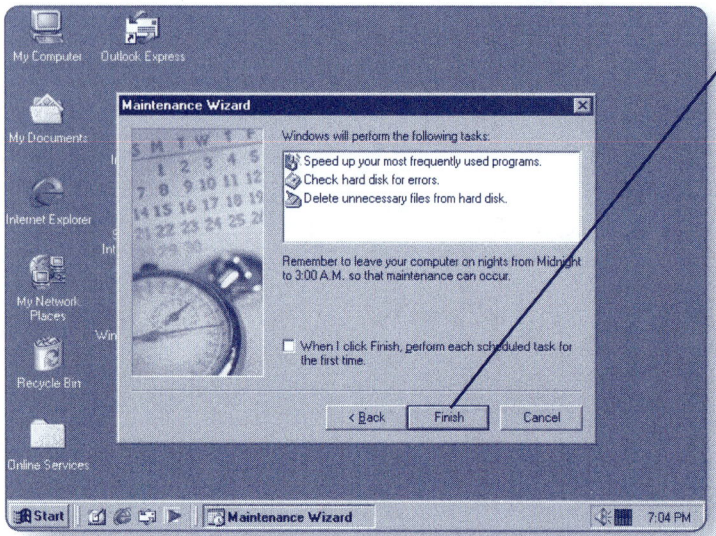

7. Click on **Finish**. The tasks are scheduled to run automatically.

NOTE

Your computer must be powered on for the Maintenance Wizard to run at the designated time.

If you want to modify your Maintenance Wizard time or settings, run the Maintenance Wizard again.

Updating Your System

The Windows Update Wizard is a Web-based service you can use to update your hardware and system software. The Windows Update Wizard compares your hardware and system software files to a Microsoft database to determine whether there are updated files for you to install. Use this to update device drivers, install software upgrades, get service packs, and copy bug fixes and other software patches to your computer. You must have an Internet connection available to use this service.

TIP
Updates change periodically, so you should use the Windows Update Wizard on a regular basis.

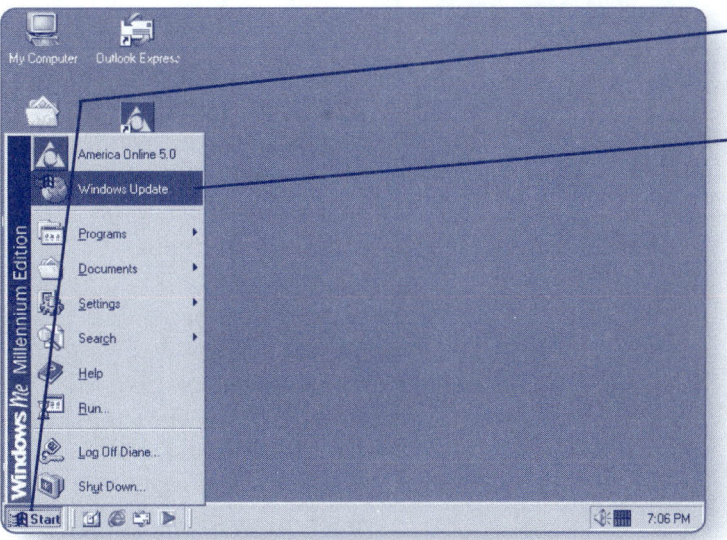

1. Click on the **Start button**. The Start menu appears.

2. Click on **Windows Update**. The Internet Explorer window appears.

NOTE
If you are not already connected to the Internet, your Internet Dial-Up connection is established.

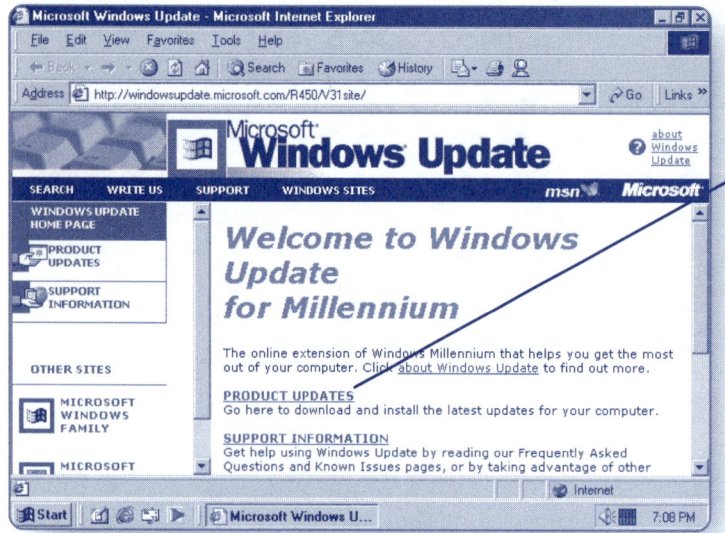

Because Web pages change frequently, your screen may differ from the one shown.

3. Click on **Product Updates**. The Windows Update checks your system for necessary updates.

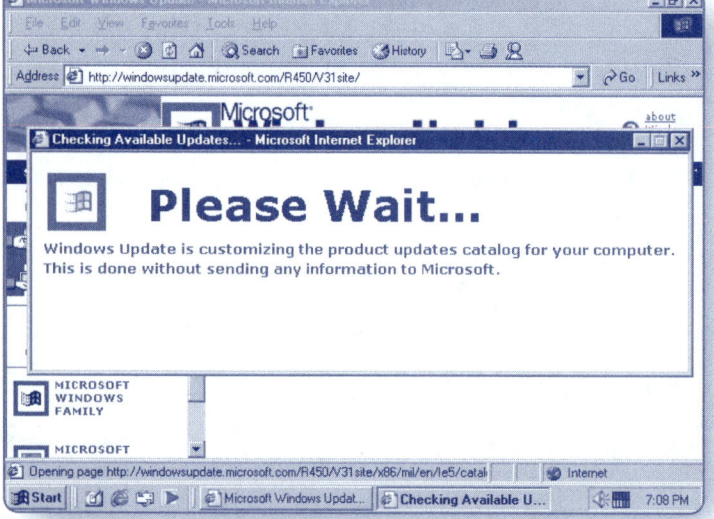

NOTE

How the Windows Update Wizard works: When you visit this site, the Windows Update Wizard downloads an index file onto your computer from the Microsoft server. It compares the available updates from the server with your computer hardware and software. If newer versions are on the server, you are prompted to install the most recent drivers and files available, specific to your computer system.

UPDATING YOUR SYSTEM   141

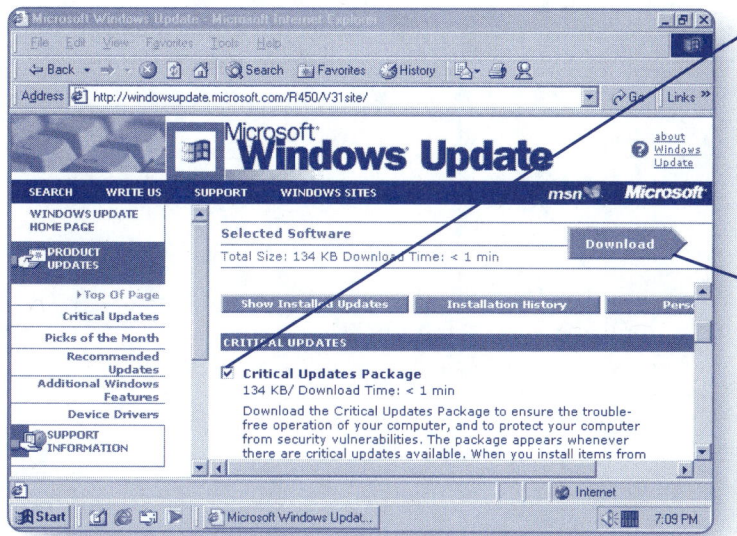

4. Click on any desired **option** to update. A check (✔) appears in the selection boxes.

The total estimated download time appears.

5. Click on **Download**. A download checklist appears.

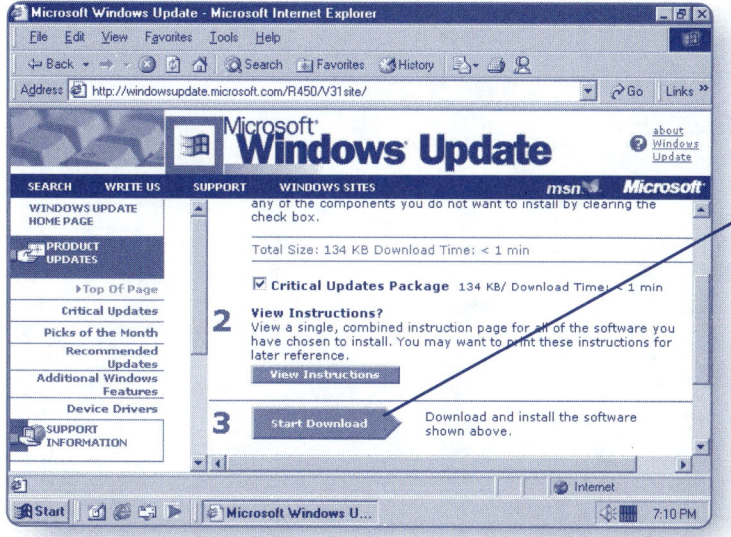

6. Review the checklist **page**. This is to confirm the components you want to update.

7. Click on **Start Download**. A Windows Update dialog box appears.

142 CHAPTER 11: USING WINDOWS SYSTEM TOOLS

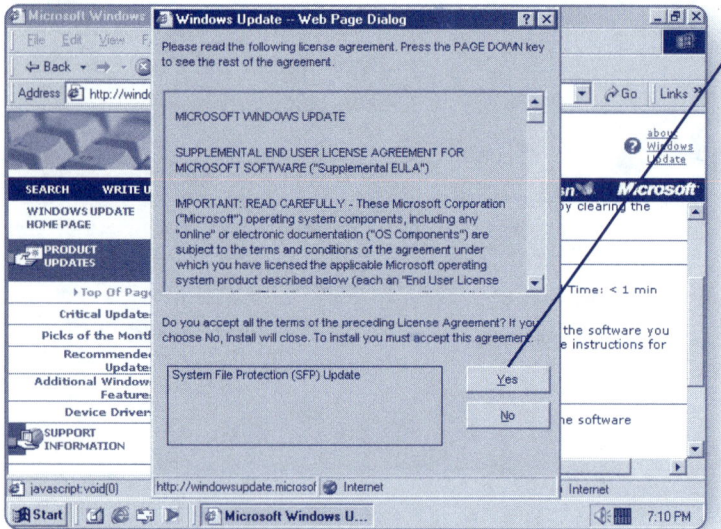

8. **Read** the **agreement** and then **click** on **Yes**. The update process begins.

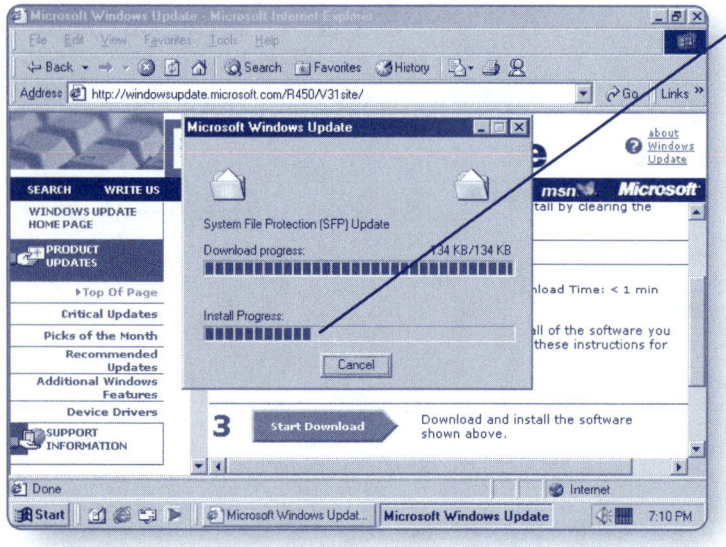

A status bar indicates the progress.

UPDATING YOUR SYSTEM 143

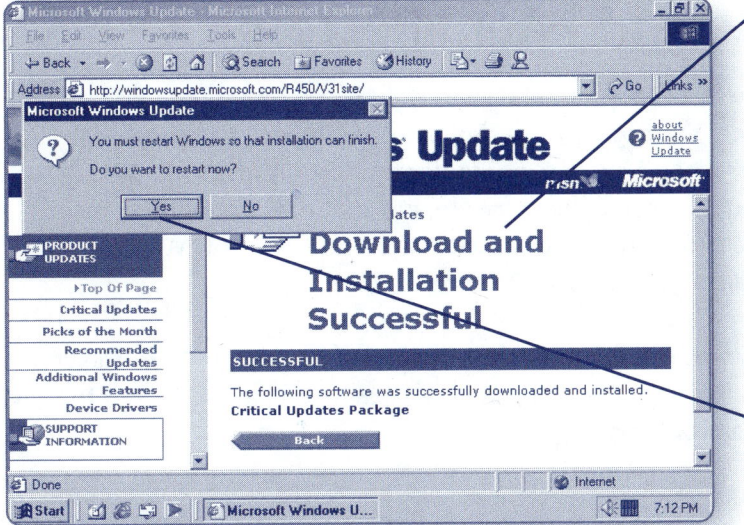

When the process is complete and the update is installed, the Microsoft Windows Update Web page confirms the download and installation.

Depending on the type of update, Windows Update may prompt you to restart your computer.

9a. If you are prompted to restart your computer, **click** on **Yes**. The computer restarts.

OR

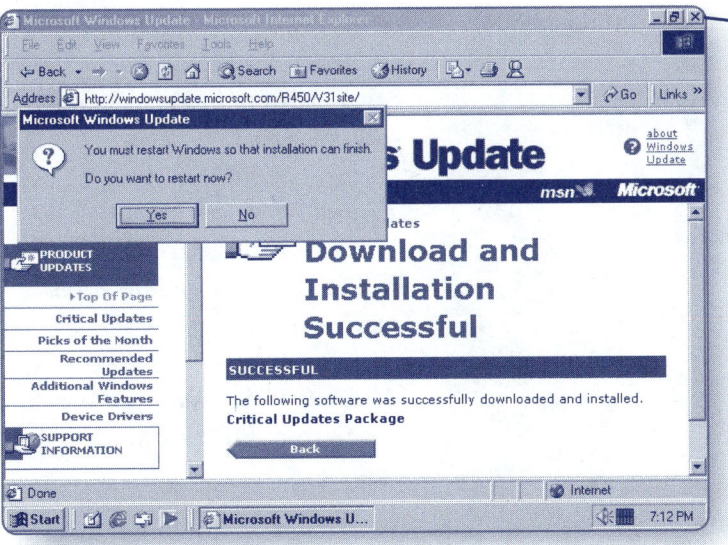

9b. Click on the **Close button** (☒). The Update Wizard window closes.

Using System Restore

We all have moments when we'd like to be able to go back in time. Suppose you loaded a new software package and it disrupted how some of your other programs work. Sure, you could uninstall the software, but that may not entirely resolve the problems. Enter a new feature to Microsoft Windows Millennium: System Restore.

Using the System Restore feature, you can turn back the clock and return your computer settings to an earlier time before the problems began.

Creating a Restore Point

Restore points are basically snapshots of the state of your system. Windows Millennium creates automatic restore points a couple of times a day, but you may want to create your own restore point before you install new hardware or software to your system.

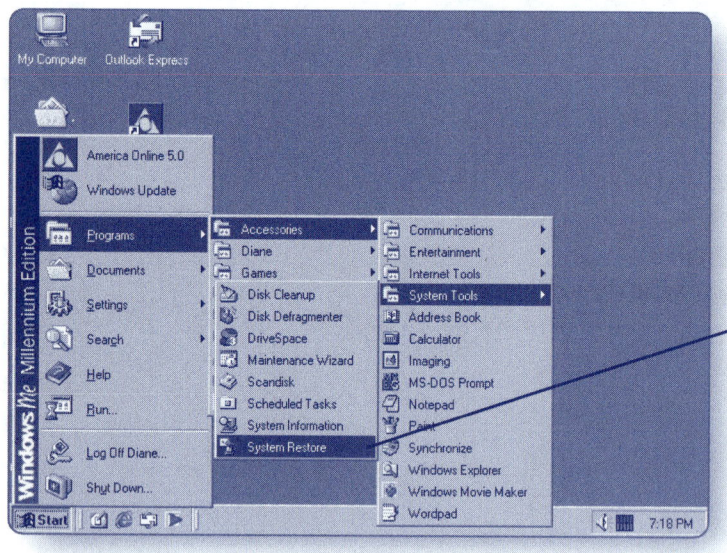

1. Follow steps 1 through **4** in "Scanning Your Hard Disk for Problems." The System Tools submenu appears.

2. Click on **System Restore**. The System Restore window opens.

USING SYSTEM RESTORE 145

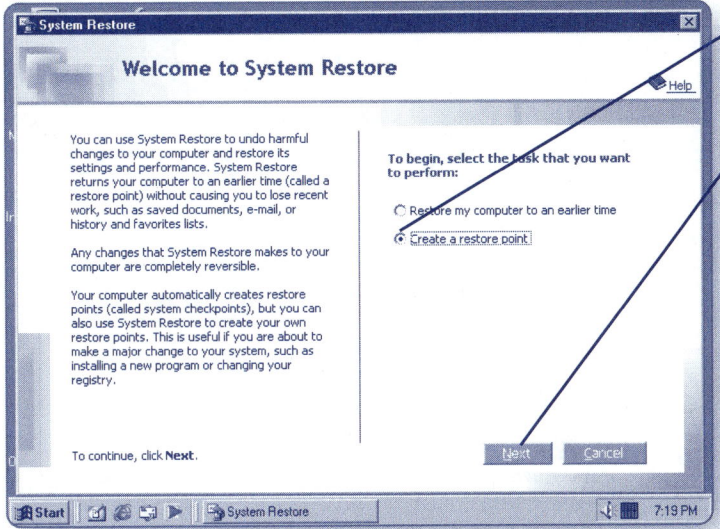

3. Click on **Create a restore point**. The option is selected.

4. Click on **Next**. The Create a Restore Point window appears.

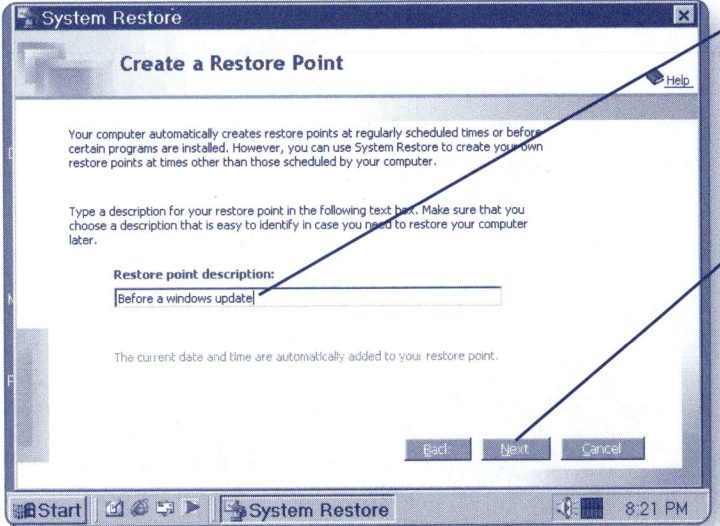

5. Type a **name** for the restore point. Give a description such as "Before the update" or "Before I installed Doom." The date and time are automatically added.

6. Click on **Next**. The Confirm New Restore Point window appears.

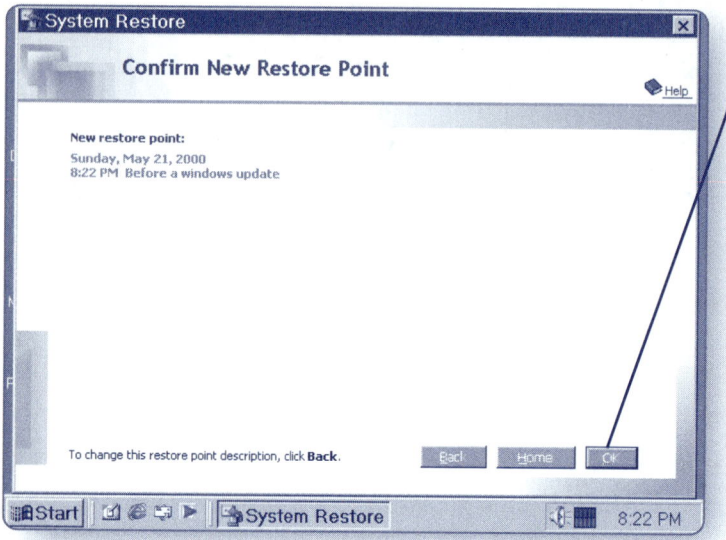

7. Click on **OK**. Windows creates a restore point.

Restoring Your System

Uh-oh—something's not quite right. You installed that new game and now your screen is acting flaky or you cannot access your critical work files. Now's the time you'll be glad you created a System Restore point.

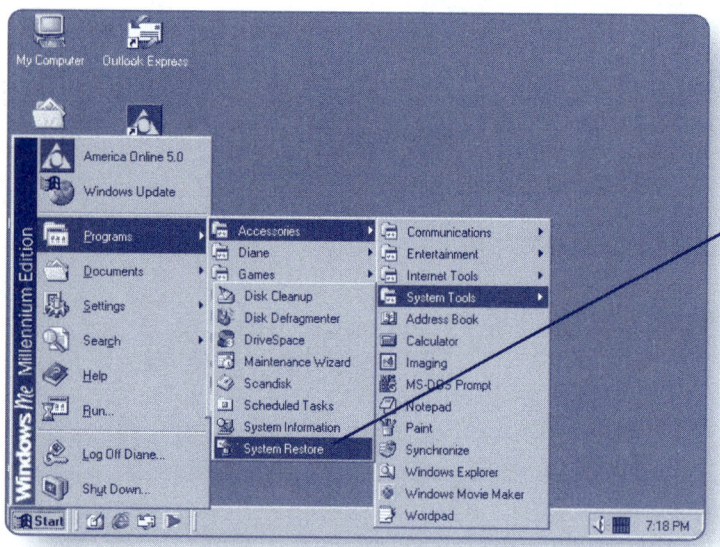

1. Follow steps 1 through **4** in "Scanning Your Hard Disk for Problems." The System Tools submenu appears.

2. Click on **System Restore**. The System Restore window opens.

USING SYSTEM RESTORE 147

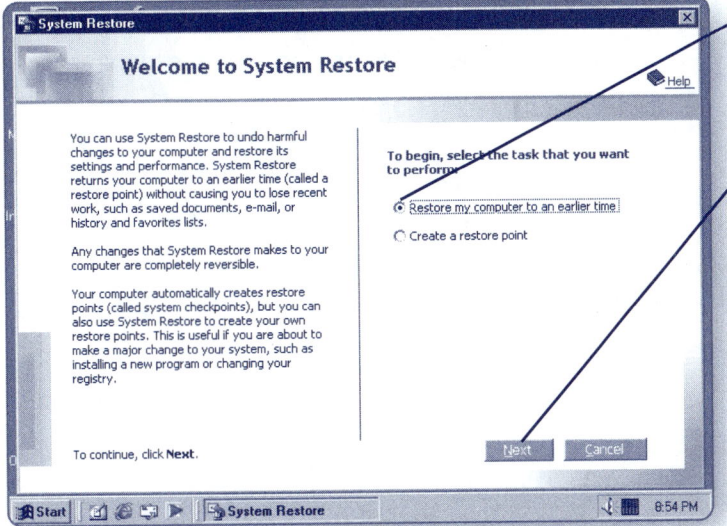

3. Click on **Restore my computer to an earlier time**. The option is selected.

4. Click on **Next**. The Choose a Restore Point window appears.

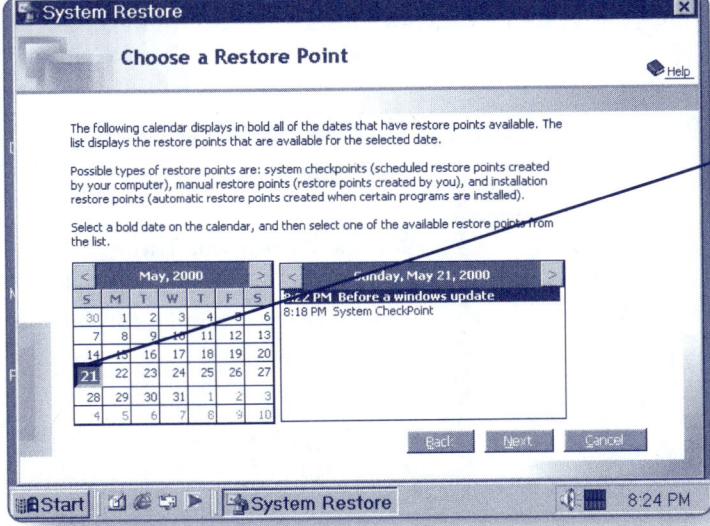

A calendar appears allowing you to choose at what date you want to restore your system.

5. Click on a **date**. A list of all restore points created that day appears.

NOTE

The restore points created automatically by Windows Millennium Edition are called System Checkpoints.

148 CHAPTER 11: USING WINDOWS SYSTEM TOOLS

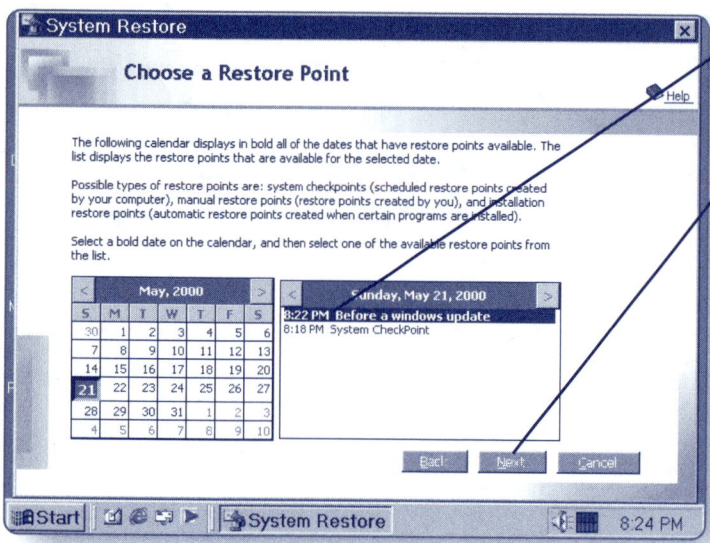

6. **Click** on a **restore point**. The restore point is highlighted.

7. **Click** on **Next**. A message box and the Confirm Restore Point Selection screen appears.

Make sure all applications and documents are closed. Restoring your system does not affect any document data files.

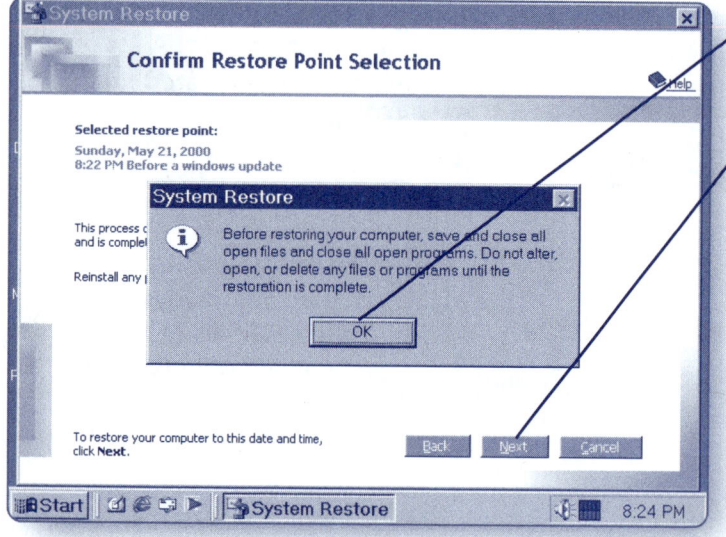

8. **Click** on **OK**. The message box closes.

9. **Click** on **Next**. The restoration process begins. It may take several minutes for the process to complete.

Your computer will restart at the conclusion of the restore process. A message box appears confirming the restore process.

10. **Click** on **OK**. The System Restore window closes.

12

Organizing Files and Folders

The process of organizing files has quite a history. First there was the DOS DIR command with all its switches and syntax. Later came File Manager with Windows 3x, and when Windows 95 came along, so did the Explorer. Each upgrade was simpler than the previous. Windows Millennium has taken this to heart again. Explorer is still here in Windows Millennium, but has become easier to use than ever. In this chapter, you'll learn how to:

- Look at Explorer
- Change the look of Explorer
- Create a new folder
- Move or copy a file or folder
- Delete and rename a file or folder

Looking in the Explorer Window

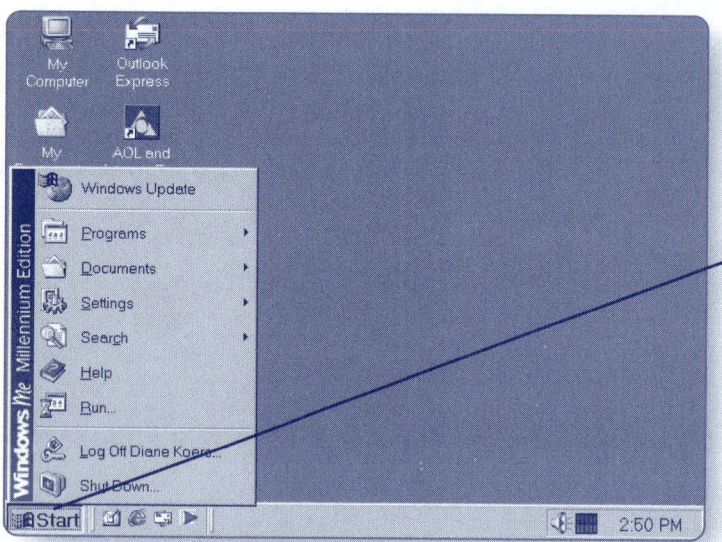

The Windows Explorer is a graphic illustration of the file and folder contents of the storage devices on or connected to your computer.

1. Click on the **Start button**. The Start menu appears.

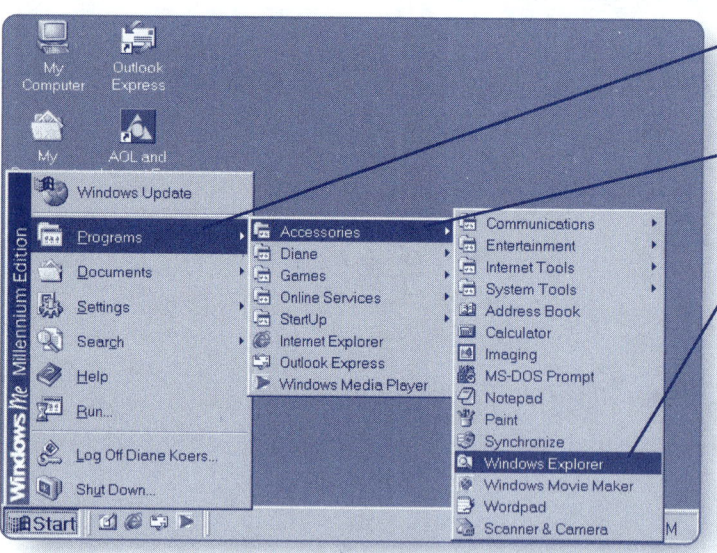

2. Click on **Programs**. The Programs menu appears.

3. Click on **Accessories**. The Accessories menu appears.

4. Click on **Windows Explorer**. The Explorer window opens.

LOOKING IN THE EXPLORER WINDOW

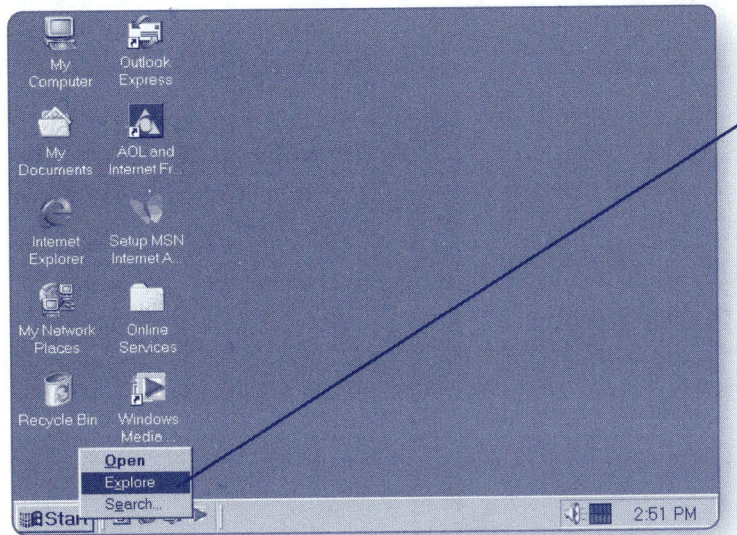

TIP

A quick way to open Explorer is to right-click the Start button, and then click on Explore from the shortcut menu.

Identifying Explorer Components

An assortment of information is displayed in the Explorer window, including the following:

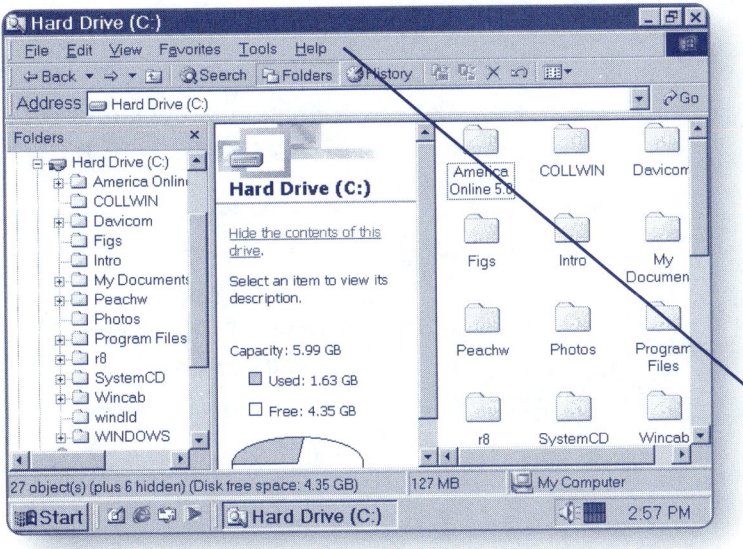

NOTE

Your Explorer window may not display all the elements listed in this section. You'll learn how to change the look of the Explorer window in the next section.

- **Menu bar**. Contains Explorer's drop-down menus.

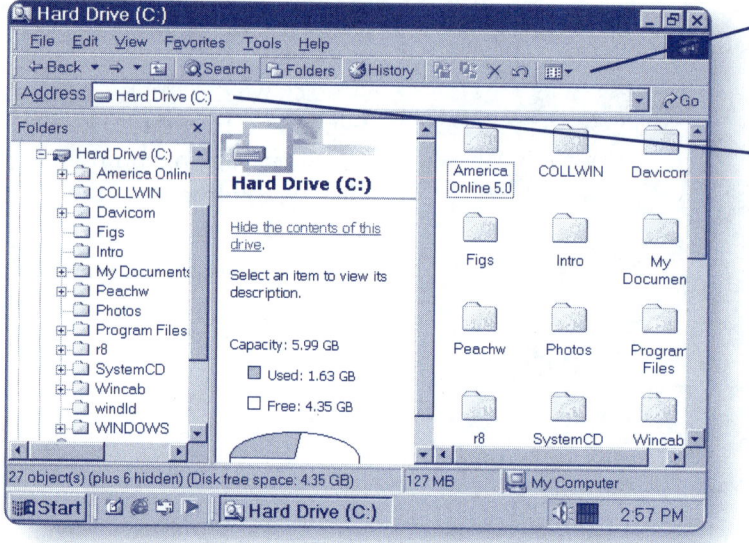

- **Toolbar.** Contains shortcuts to commonly used menu choices.

- **Address bar.** Displays the full path to a Web address or to a file or folder.

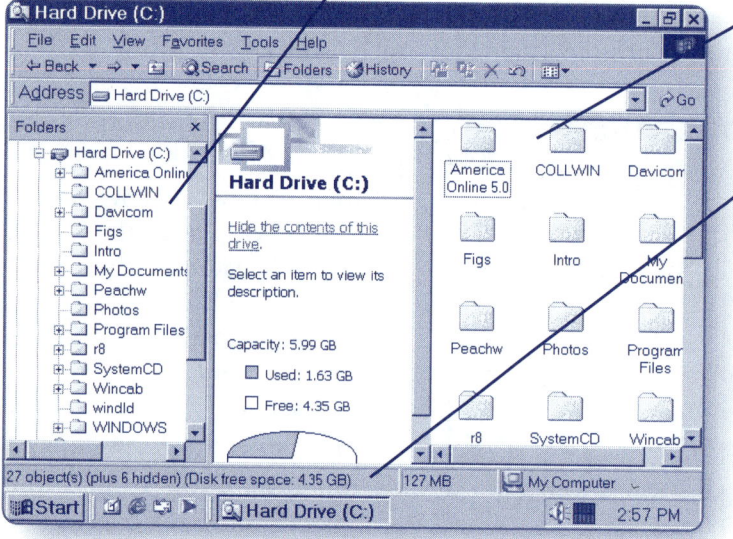

- **Drives and Folders section.** Displays available drives and folders on your computer.

- **Files and Documents section.** Displays the contents of the selected drive or folder.

- **Status bar.** Displays such information as the number and size of selected files.

TIP

Click on any folder in the Drives and Folders section to view its contents.

LOOKING IN THE EXPLORER WINDOW   153

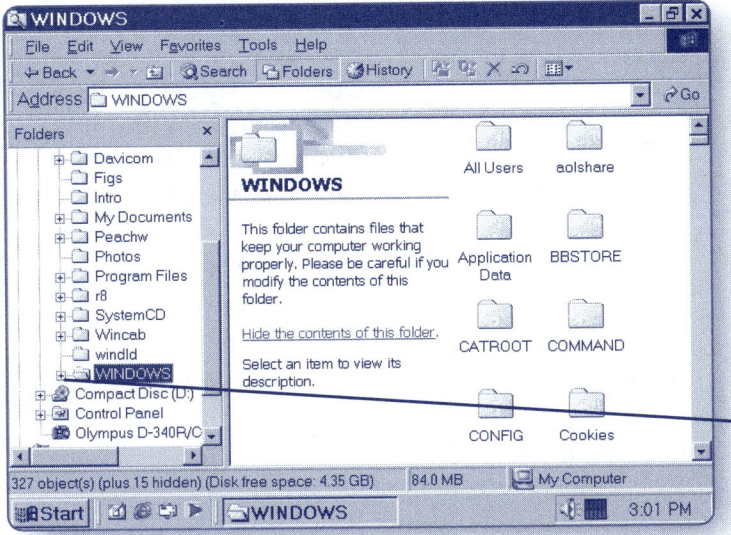

Expanding Folders

You'll notice in the Drives and Folders section that many items have a plus sign next to them. This indicates that there are more folders within them. It's like a tree with its branches, each one expanding off the main branch.

1. Click on a **plus sign (+)**. A listing of subfolders appears.

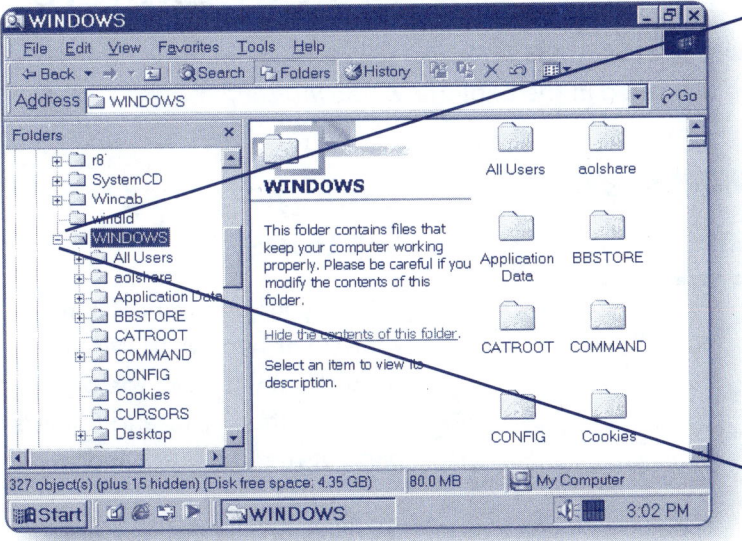

Notice that the plus sign changes to a minus sign. This indicates the folder is already expanded.

NOTE
Some subfolders may have other subfolders. Again, this is indicated with a plus sign.

2. Click on the **minus sign (–)**. The subfolder collapses and a plus sign reappears.

CHAPTER 12: ORGANIZING FILES AND FOLDERS

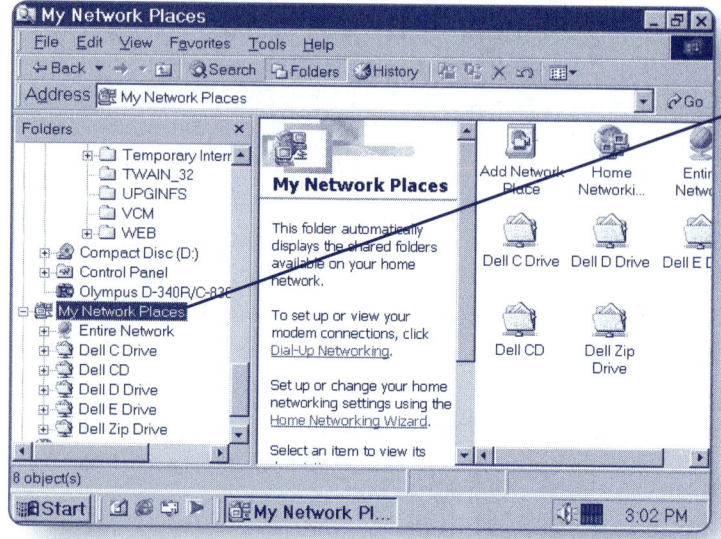

TIP
Open the My Network Places icon from the Drives and Folders section to view the contents of folders on another computer.

Changing the Look of Explorer

Also, you can modify the way the contents of files and folders are displayed in the Explorer window.

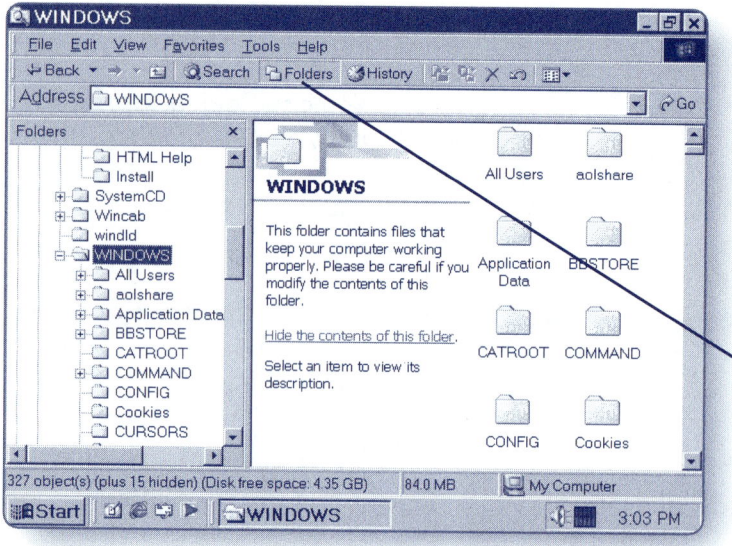

Changing Display Options

What's your preference? One window or two? With Windows Millennium you have the option of hiding the Drives and Folders pane of the Explorer window.

1. Click on the **Folders button**. The Drives and Folders window closes. Only the Files and Documents window remains open.

CHANGING THE LOOK OF EXPLORER   155

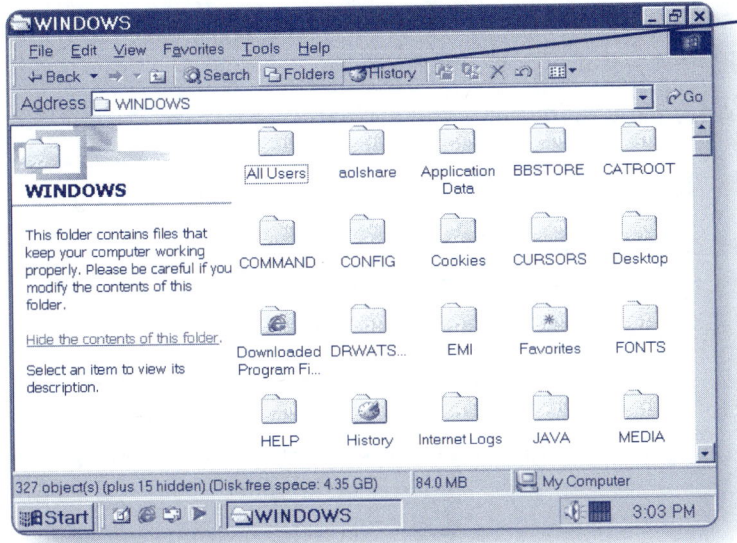

2. Click on the **Folders button** again. The Drives and Folders window reopens. Both the Drives and Folders as well as the Files and Documents windows are now visible.

Displaying Toolbars

The Explorer window has several different toolbars that can be displayed. Toolbars make it easier to get to your programs, files, folders, and favorite Web pages.

By default, two toolbars are displayed in the Explorer window—the Standard toolbar and the Address toolbar. To display or turn off the display of toolbars, look in the View menu.

1. Click on **View**. The View menu appears.

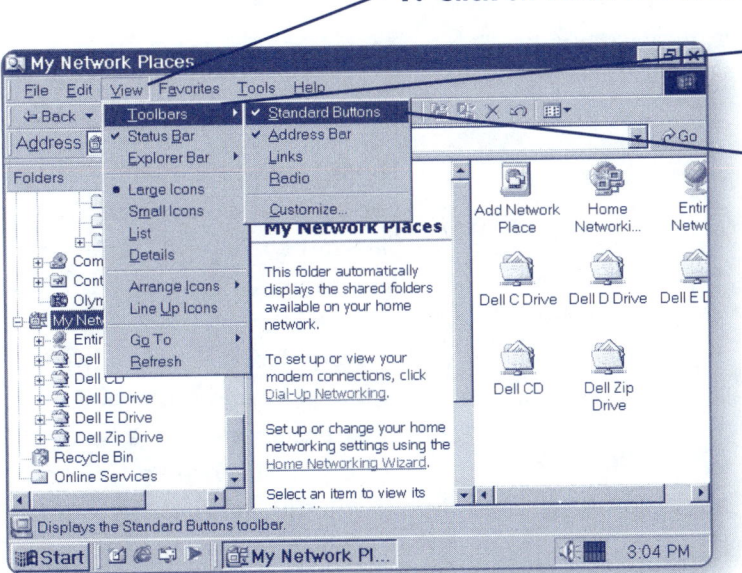

2. Click on **Toolbars**. The Toolbars submenu appears.

3. Click on any desired **toolbar**. The toolbar appears onscreen.

TIP

A ✔ beside an item indicates the choice is active.

You can choose to display one or several of the four types of toolbars.

156 CHAPTER 12: ORGANIZING FILES AND FOLDERS

- **Standard Buttons.** Shows toolbar buttons such as Back, Forward, Cut, Copy, and Paste.
- **Address Bar.** Indicates the current folder being displayed. You can also type a Web page address without opening Internet Explorer first.
- **Links.** Provides shortcuts to important Web sites.
- **Radio.** Allows access to radio stations via the Internet. See Chapter 14, "Discovering Multimedia."

> **NOTE**
> Choosing a toolbar with a ✔ beside it removes the ✔ and turns off that toolbar.

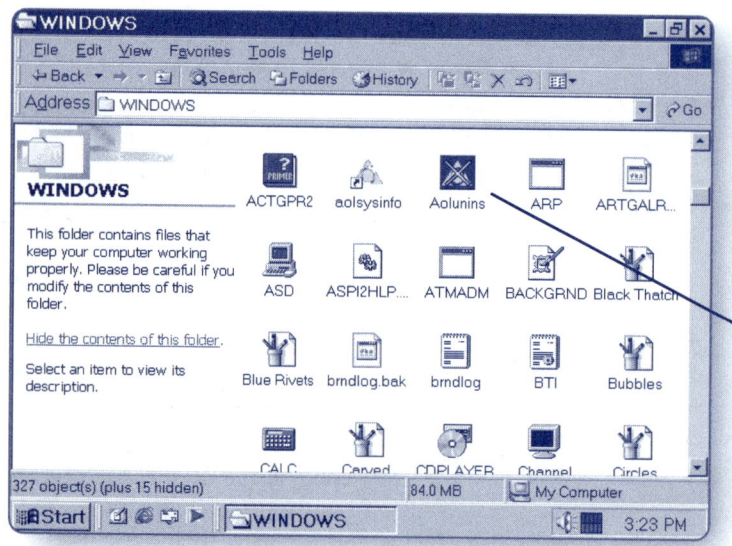

Changing the Way Files Are Displayed

There are five different perspectives of looking at your files in the Files and Documents section:

- **Large Icons View.** Shows the file name and optional extension beneath a large, easy-to-see icon associated with the file. Files are listed in a horizontal multiple-column format.

CHANGING THE LOOK OF EXPLORER 157

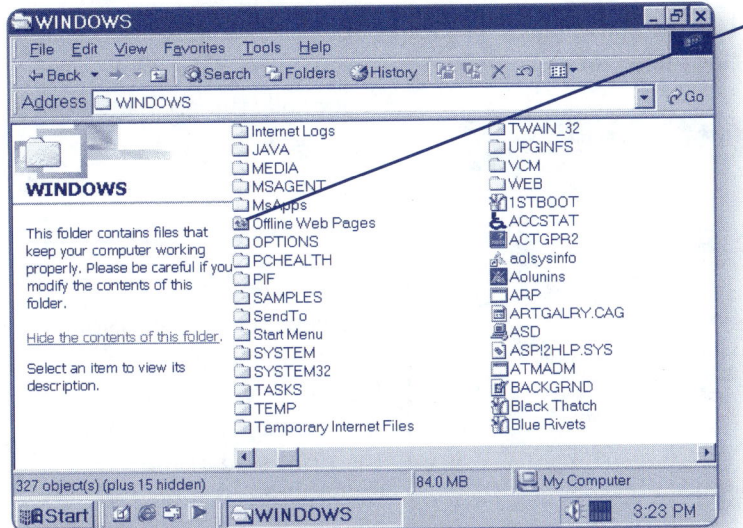

- **Small Icons View.** Shows the file name and optional extension beside a smaller icon associated with the file. Files are listed in a horizontal multiple-column format.

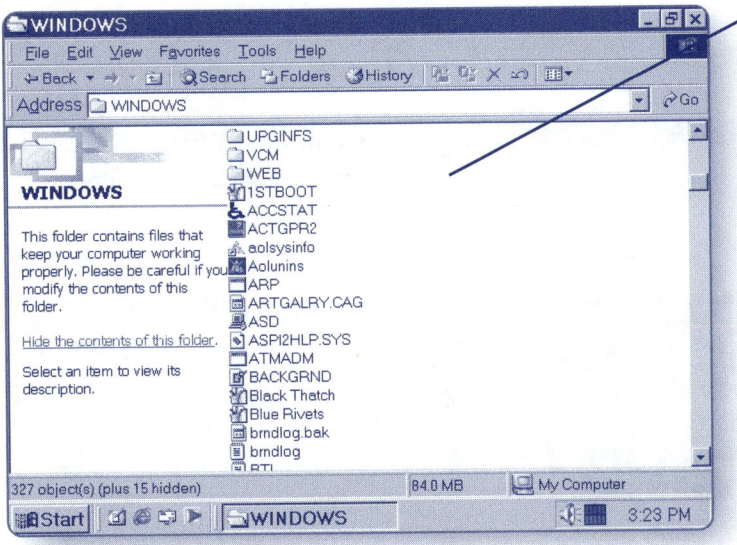

- **List View.** Similar to Small Icon view, but the files are listed in a vertical-column format.

• **Details View.** Displays more information about the files, including the size, type, last modification date, and optionally the attributes of the file. Files are listed in a vertical single-column format.

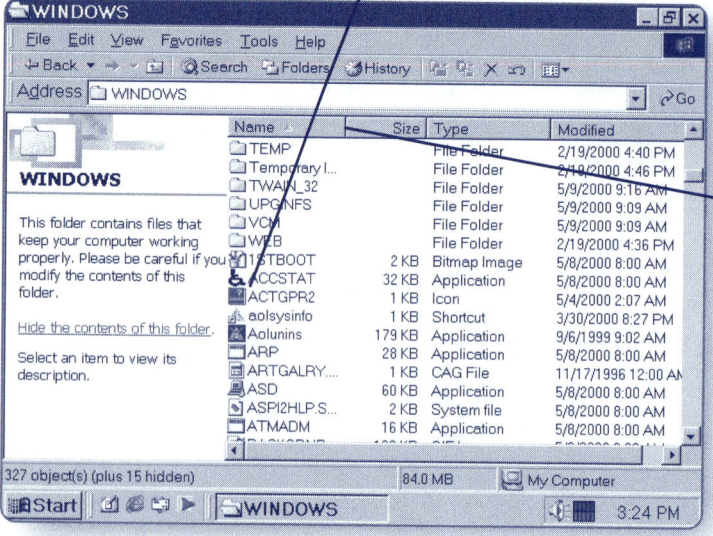

TIP

You can change the display width of any column in Details view by positioning the mouse over the bar on the right side of the column description and clicking and dragging the mouse until the column is the desired width.

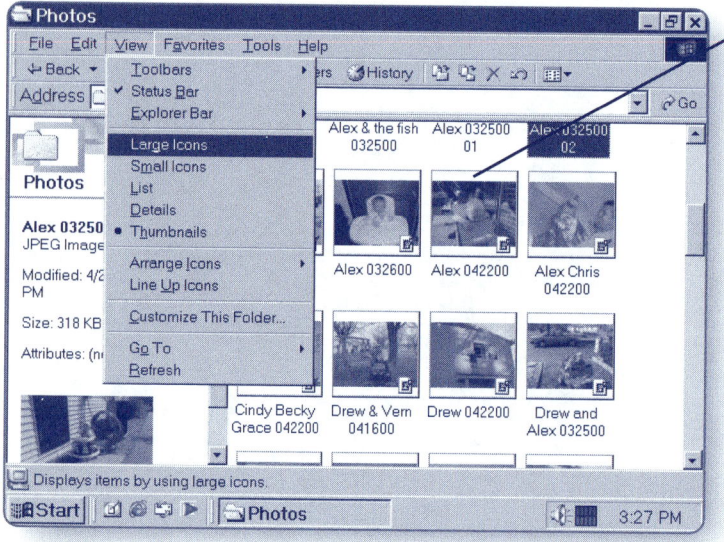

• **Thumbnails View.** Displays graphics files as the files would appear, rather than as an icon.

Choose one of the five perspectives of looking at your files.

CHANGING THE LOOK OF EXPLORER 159

1. Click on **View**. The View menu appears.

2. Click on **Large Icons**, **Small Icons**, **List**, **Details**, or **Thumbnails**. The Files and Documents section changes to the selected view.

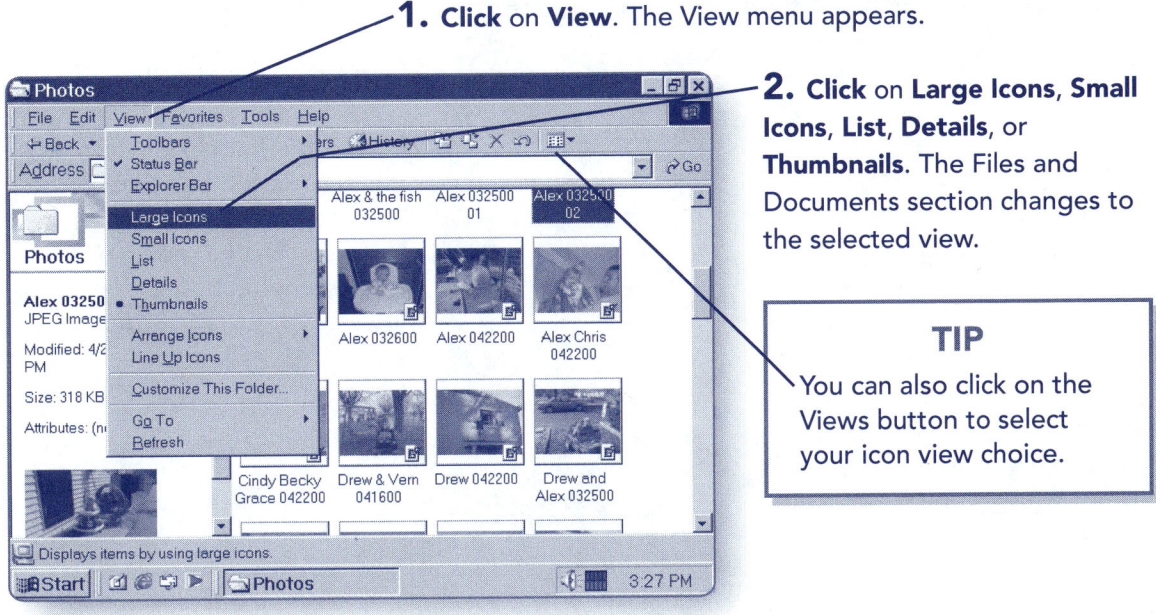

TIP
You can also click on the Views button to select your icon view choice.

Sorting Files

By default, files are sorted in alphabetical order by file name. You can also sort them by type, size, or date. Headings are displayed at the top of each column.

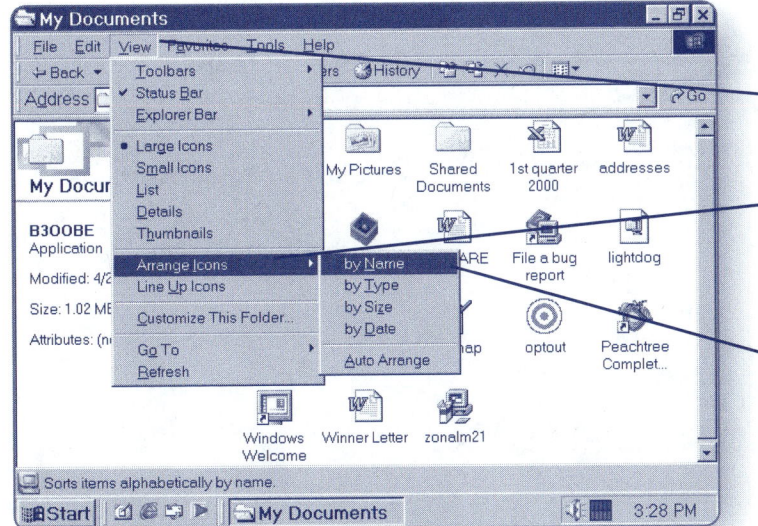

1. Click on **View**. The View menu appears.

2. Click on **Arrange Icons**. The Arrange Icons submenu appears.

3. Click on **by Name**, **by Type**, **by Size**, or **by Date**. The files in the Files and Documents section display in the order you selected.

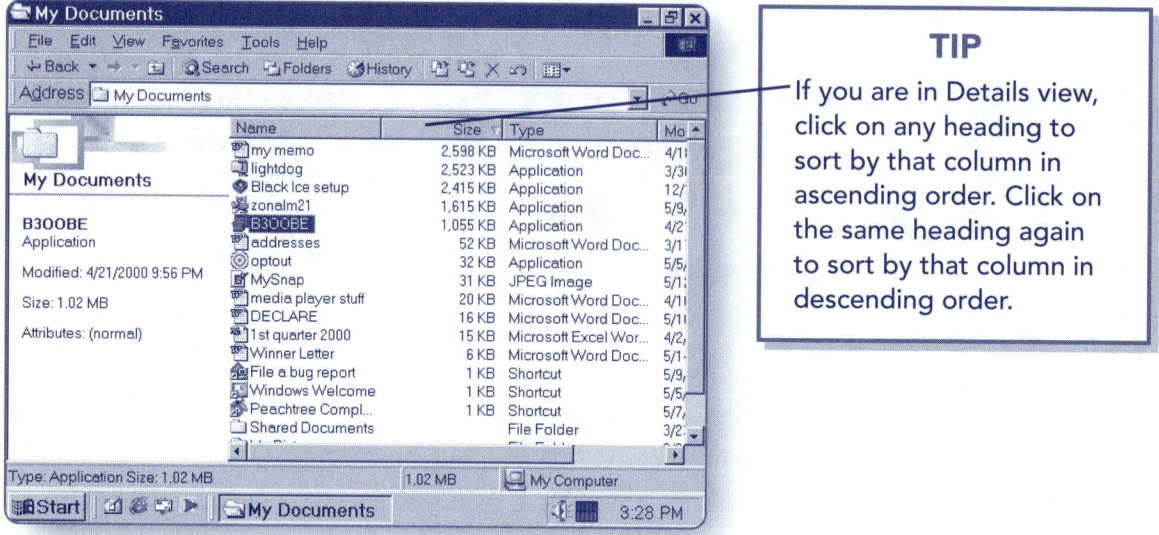

TIP

If you are in Details view, click on any heading to sort by that column in ascending order. Click on the same heading again to sort by that column in descending order.

Modifying Folder Options

By changing the folder options, you can decide whether a file should be accessible with a single-click or double-click, which type of files to display, and whether the file names should display an extension.

1. Click on **Tools**. The Tools menu appears.

2. Click on **Folder Options**. The Folder Options dialog box opens with the General tab displayed.

CHANGING THE LOOK OF EXPLORER   161

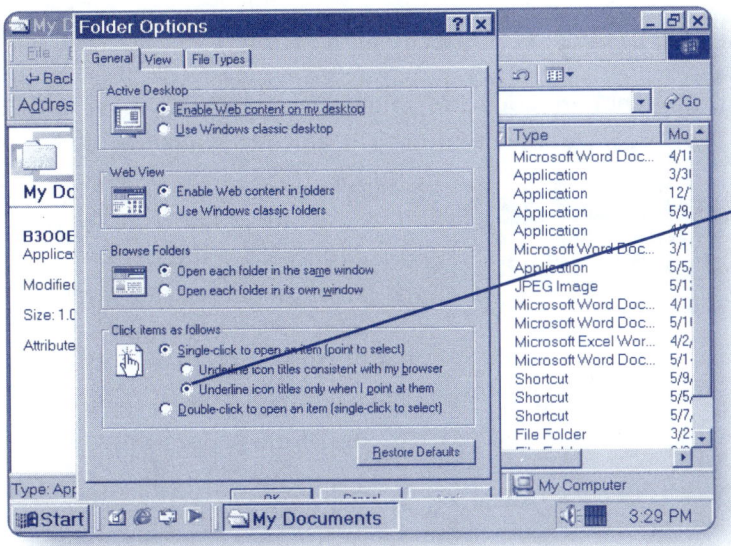

In the "Click items as follows" section, you can determine whether to single-click or double-click to activate an icon.

3. Click on an **option**. The option is selected.

4. Click on the **View tab**. More display options, including showing file extensions in Explorer, appear.

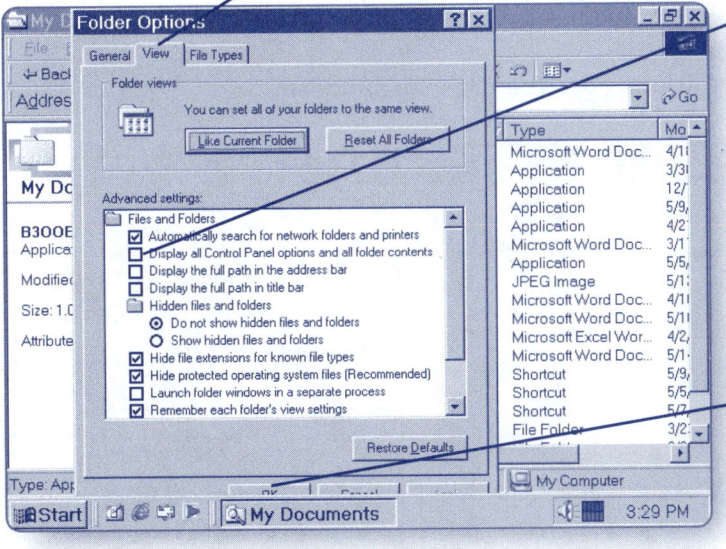

5. Click on any **unchecked options** to select those options. A ✔ appears in the check box.

NOTE
Clicking on an option with a ✔ already displayed turns off the selected feature.

6. Click on **OK**. The Folder Options dialog box closes, and the view changes to your specifications.

162 CHAPTER 12: ORGANIZING FILES AND FOLDERS

Creating a New Folder

Programs that are added to your computer create most folders. For organizational purposes, it's nice to have your own folders to separate your data. For example, most Windows programs store the data files you create in a folder called *My Documents*. It might be handy to have folders in the My Documents folder to separate memos from proposals.

1. Click on the **drive** or **folder** in which you want to create a subfolder. The folder opens and its contents appear. In our example, we'll create a folder in the My Documents folder.

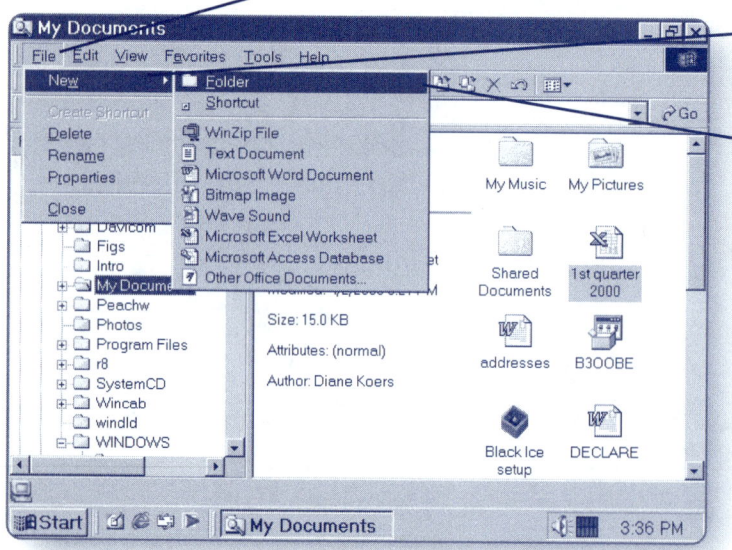

2. Click on **File**. The File menu appears.

3. Click on **New**. The New submenu appears.

4. Click on **Folder**. A new folder appears in the Files and Documents section.

TIP

Another method to create a new folder is to right-click in the Files and Documents section and choose New, and then choose Folder.

CREATING A NEW FOLDER 163

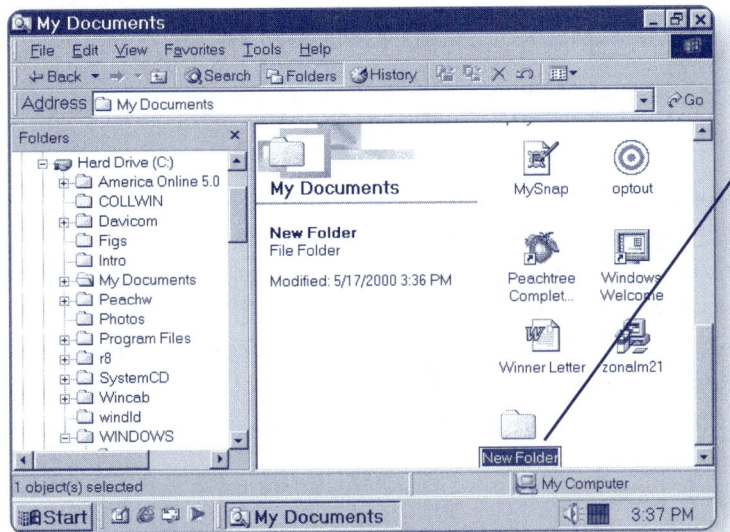

NOTE

The new folder appears and is ready to be given a new name.

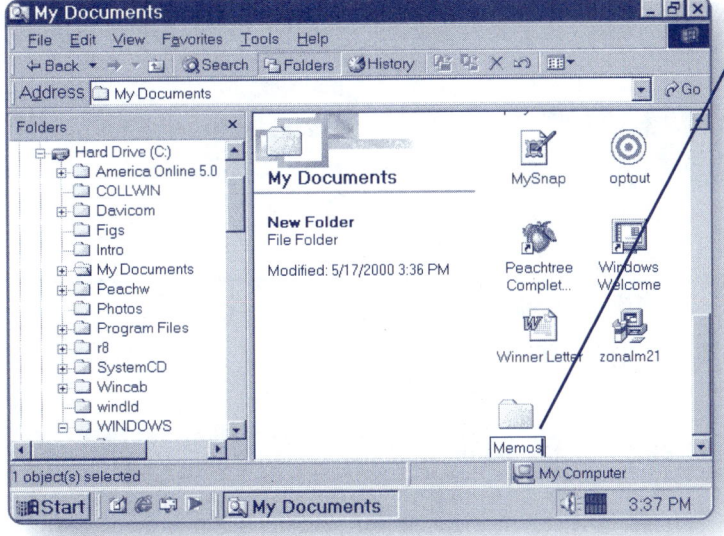

5. Type a **name** for the new folder. The words "New Folder" are replaced with the name you type.

6. Press the **Enter key**. The new folder and its name are accepted and displayed.

Moving or Copying Files and Folders

Files or folders can be moved or copied from one location to another. For example, you can copy a file from your hard drive to a floppy disk. Or you can move a file you've been working on to a network drive. Whether you are working with a file or a folder, the steps are the same. However, if you move or copy a folder, all the contents of that folder are moved or copied as well. In addition, if the folder contains subfolders, the directory structure is also moved or copied to the new location.

1. Display the **Standard toolbar,** if it is not already displayed.

2. Open the **drive** and **folder** that has the file or folder you want to move or copy. The name appears on the right side of the screen.

3. Select the **item** to be moved or copied. The item is highlighted.

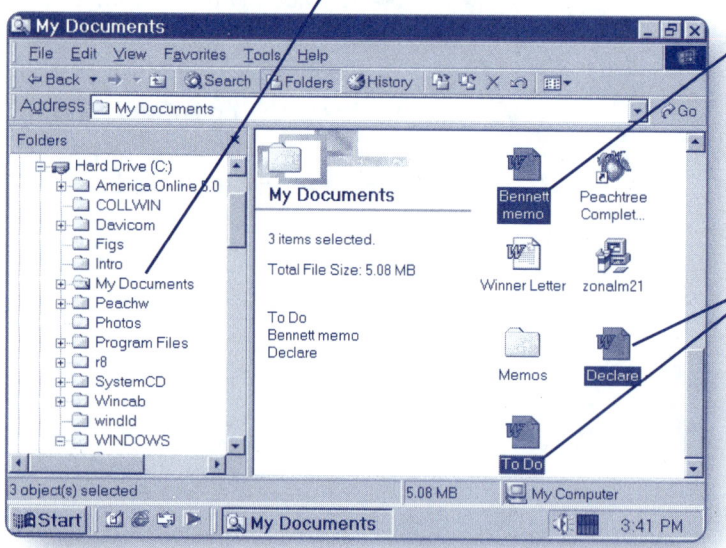

TIP

You can select multiple items to be moved or copied by holding down the Ctrl key while selecting additional items. Release the Ctrl key when you are finished selecting items.

MOVING OR COPYING FILES AND FOLDERS   165

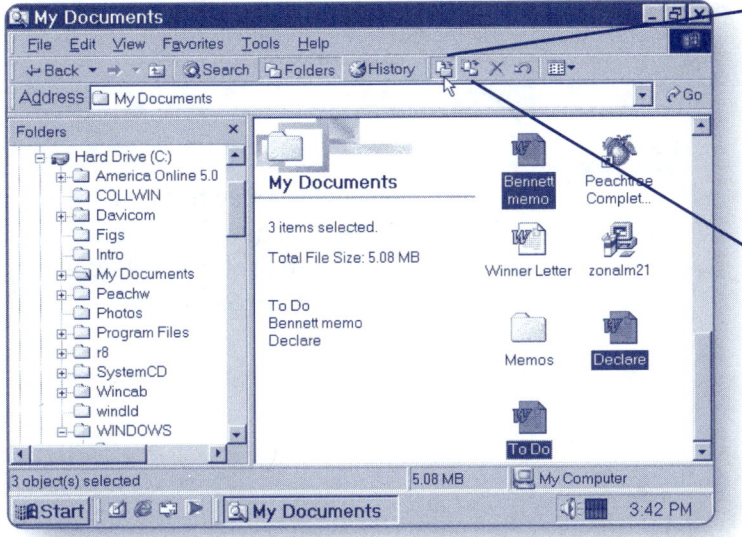

4a. **Click** on the **Move To button**, if you want to move the selected item. The Browse For Folder dialog box opens.

OR

4b. **Click** on the **Copy To button**, if you want to copy the selected item. The Browse For Folder dialog box opens.

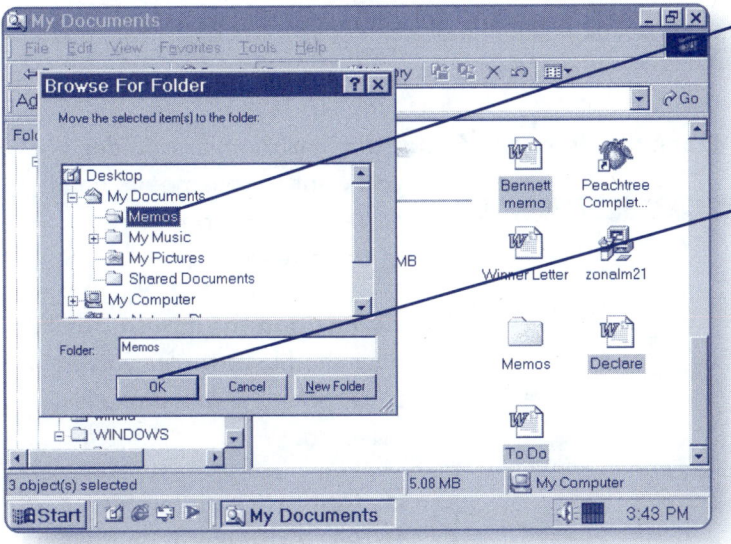

5. **Locate** and **click** on the **drive** or **folder** in which you want to place the file. The drive or folder is selected.

6. **Click** on **OK.** The Browse For Folder dialog box closes.

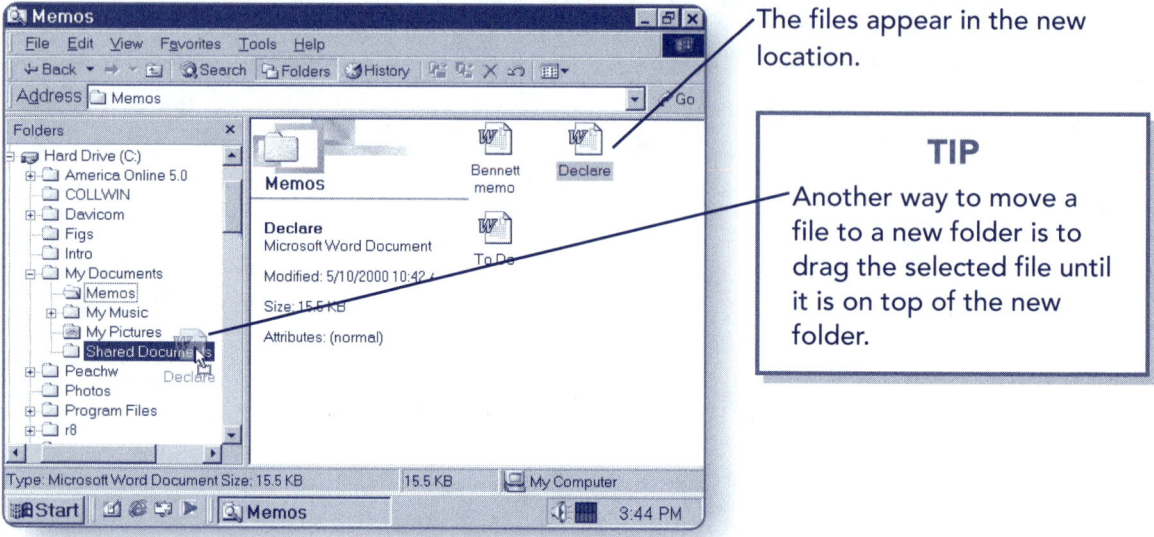

The files appear in the new location.

> **TIP**
>
> Another way to move a file to a new folder is to drag the selected file until it is on top of the new folder.

Renaming Files and Folders

If you have incorrectly named a file, you can easily rename it using the Windows Explorer.

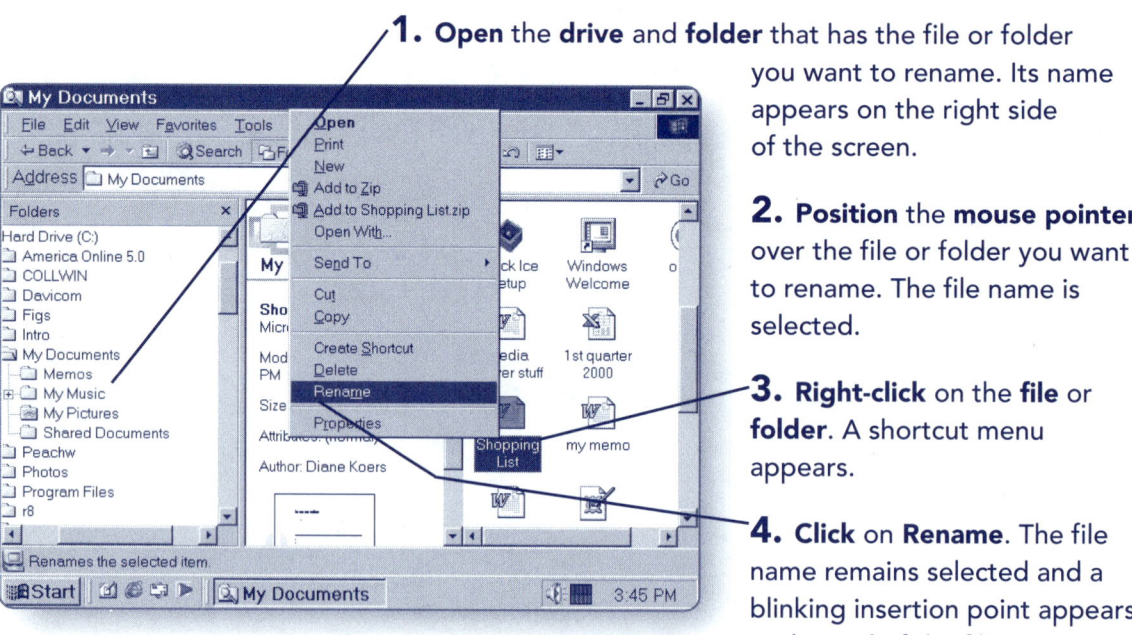

1. Open the **drive** and **folder** that has the file or folder you want to rename. Its name appears on the right side of the screen.

2. Position the **mouse pointer** over the file or folder you want to rename. The file name is selected.

3. Right-click on the **file** or **folder**. A shortcut menu appears.

4. Click on **Rename**. The file name remains selected and a blinking insertion point appears at the end of the file name.

RENAMING FILES AND FOLDERS 167

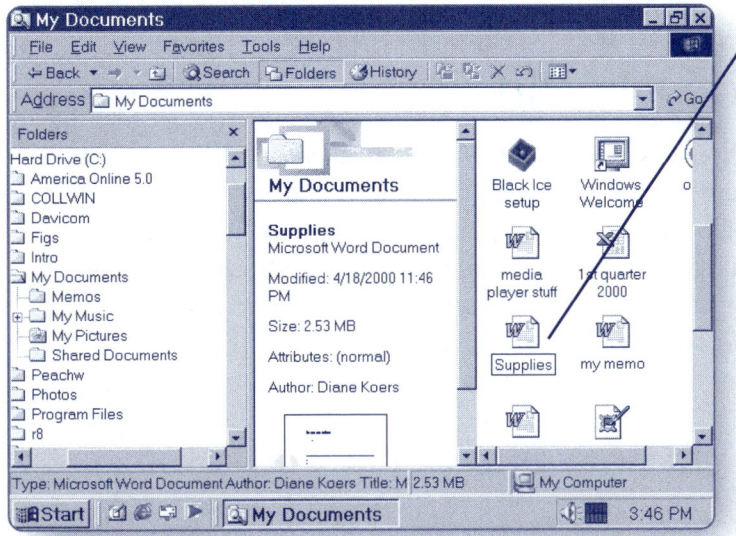

5. Type the **new file name**. The old file name is replaced with the new file name.

If the original file name has an extension, be sure to include that extension with the new file name. If you don't, Windows could lose the association of the file and not know which program to use when opening it. For example, if the file was originally called MYMEMO and you are renaming it MEMO TO BOB SMITH, that's fine; but if it was originally MYMEMO.DOC, you should rename it MEMO TO BOB SMITH.DOC.

6. Press the **Enter key**. Your changes are accepted.

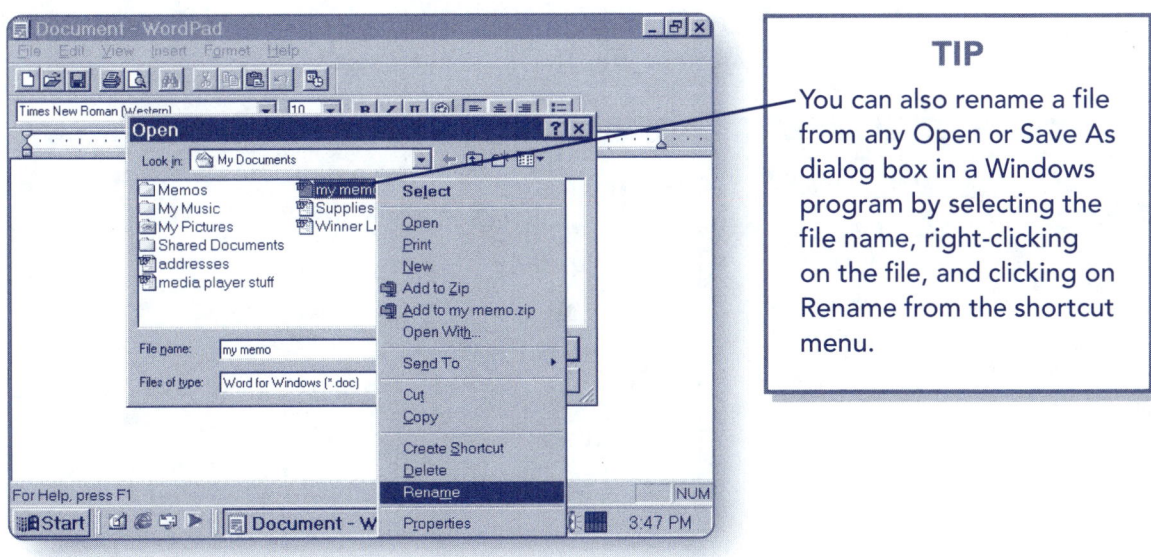

TIP

You can also rename a file from any Open or Save As dialog box in a Windows program by selecting the file name, right-clicking on the file, and clicking on Rename from the shortcut menu.

Sending Files to the Recycle Bin

At home or work you have a wastebasket into which you throw unwanted items. Those items stay in the wastebasket until someone actually takes them out. On your Windows desktop is an icon that looks like a small trash can—the Windows Recycle Bin. It's an area to temporarily hold unwanted items.

Deleting Files

Use the Windows Explorer for an easy way to delete old data files and send them to the Recycle Bin.

1. Open the **drive** and **folder** that has the file or folder you want to delete. The file name appears on the right side of the screen.

2. Position the **mouse pointer** over the file or folder you want to delete. The file name is selected.

3. Click on the **Delete button**. A Confirm File Delete dialog box opens.

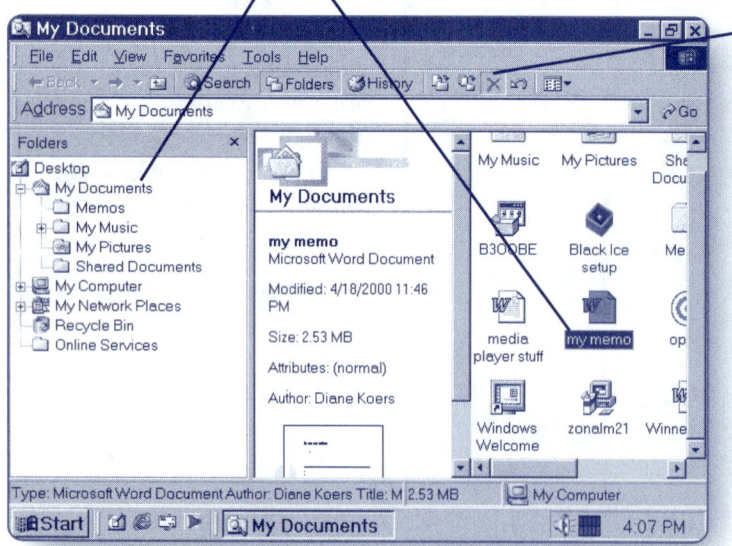

DELETING FILES 169

4. Click on **Yes**. The file is deleted from its folder and placed in the Recycle Bin.

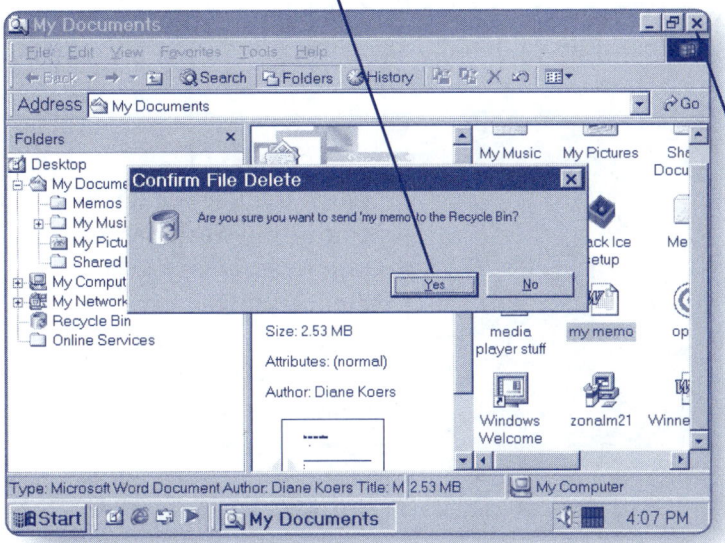

If you are deleting a file from a floppy disk, it is *not* placed in the Recycle Bin. It is permanently deleted.

5. Click on the **Close button** (☒). The Explorer window closes.

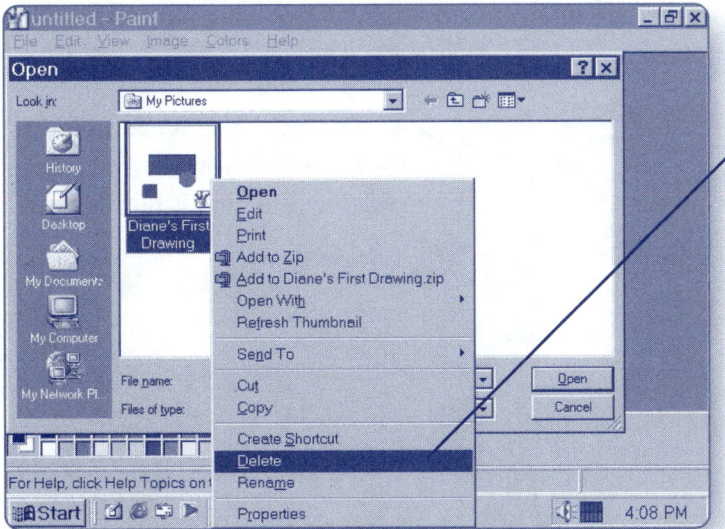

TIP
You can also delete a file from any Open or Save As dialog box in a Windows program by right-clicking on the file name and choosing Delete. A confirmation message will appear.

Recovering a File from the Recycle Bin

At home or work, if you want to recover an item from the wastebasket you can reach in and pull it out. You work with the Windows Recycle Bin the same way.

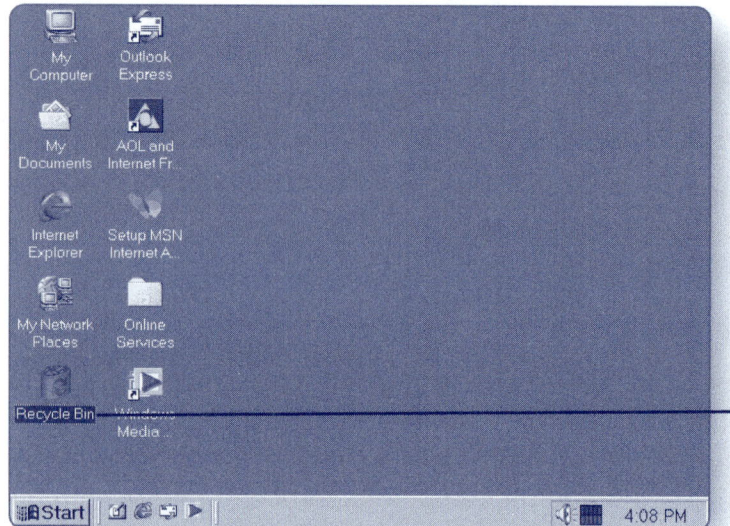

> **NOTE**
> When the Recycle Bin is empty, the wastebasket icon looks empty. When the Recycle Bin has items in it, pieces of paper stick out the top of the wastebasket.

1. Click on the **Recycle Bin icon**. The Recycle Bin window opens, displaying the contents of the Recycle Bin.

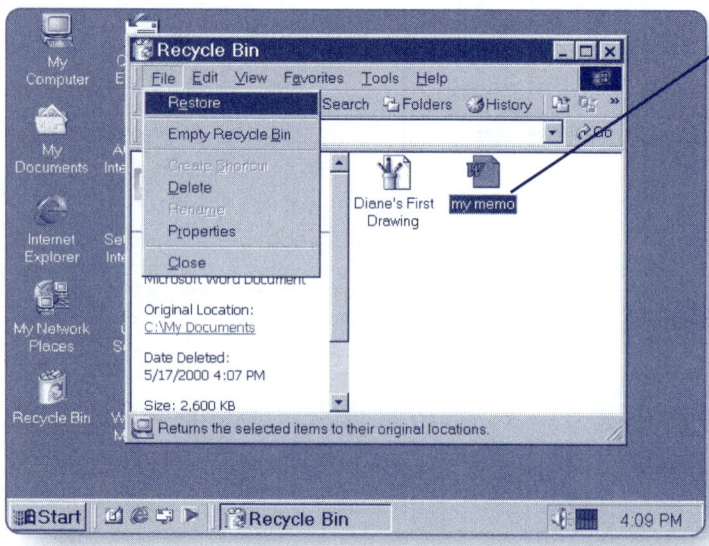

2. Position the **mouse pointer** over the item you want to recover. The item is highlighted.

DELETING FILES

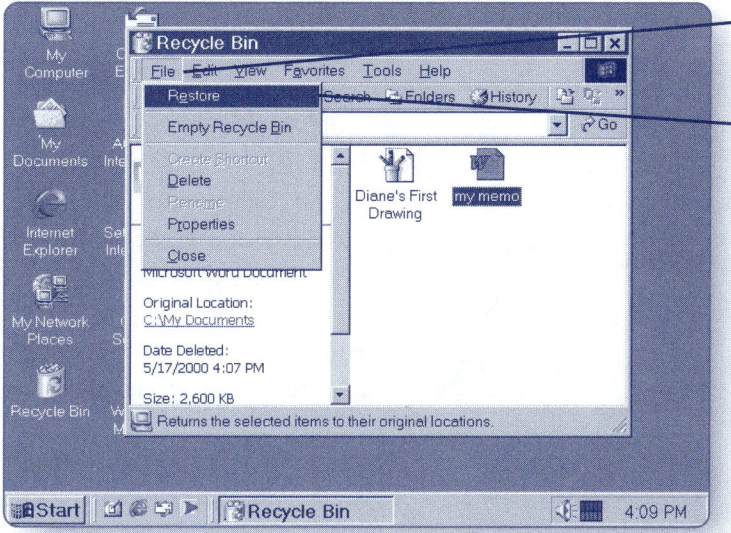

3. **Click** on **File**. The File menu appears.

4. **Click** on **Restore**. The file is removed from the Recycle Bin and placed in the folder from which it was originally deleted.

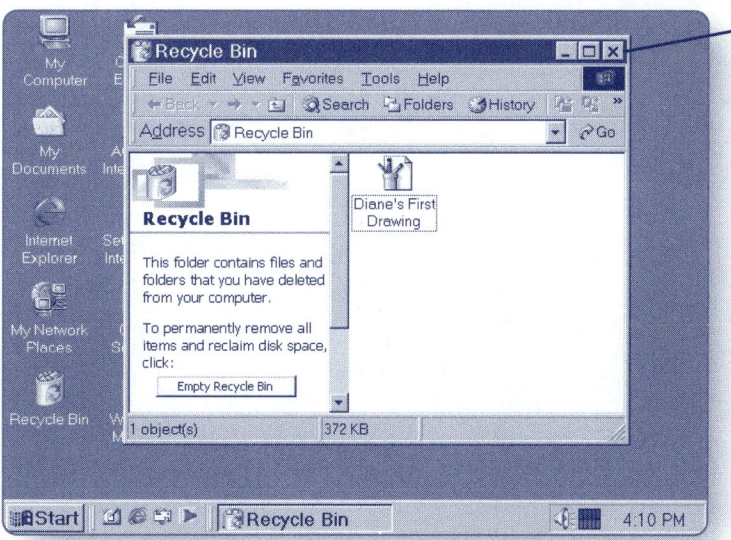

5. **Click** on the **Close button** (X). The Recycle Bin window closes.

Emptying the Recycle Bin

Items stored in the Recycle Bin are using disk space on your computer. It's a good idea to periodically empty the Recycle Bin just like you would periodically empty your wastebasket at home. Be aware, though, that once the Recycle Bin has been emptied, the items that were in it are permanently deleted.

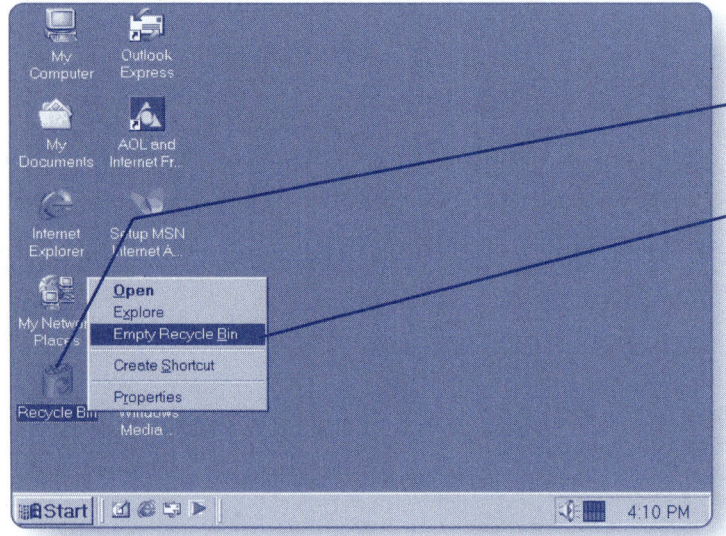

1. Right-click over the **Recycle Bin**. A shortcut menu appears.

2. Click on **Empty Recycle Bin**. A confirmation message appears.

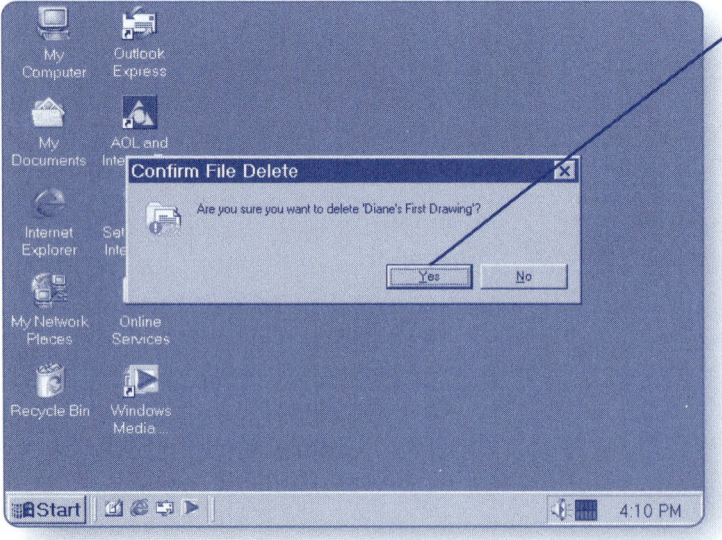

3. Click on **Yes**. The files are permanently deleted from the computer. The Recycle Bin is now empty.

13

Finding Files, Folders, and People

Programs and documents sometimes get buried quite deep in the folder structure of your hard drive. To work efficiently you should know how to find files on your computer. With the Windows Explorer you can let your computer do all the searching for you, whether you're trying to locate a specific file, a group of files, or even a name from the Windows Address Book. In this chapter, you'll learn how to:

- Find a file or folder
- Look for a file by date
- Search for a name in the Address Book

Finding a File

Windows has a powerful tool called the Find feature to help you find those misplaced files and folders.

1. Click on the **Start button**. The Start menu appears.

2. Click on **Search**. The Search submenu appears.

3. Click on **For Files or Folders**. The Search Results window opens.

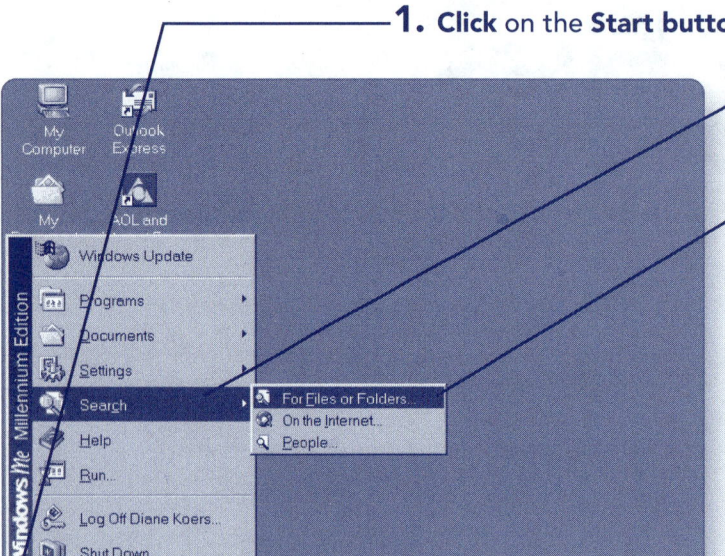

From the Search Results window, you can search for a file (or folder) based on the name of the file or the contents in the file. For example, you can look for a file with the word "bear" in the title or for a document with the word "bear" in its contents. If you search for the word "bear" in the body text, Windows will also list any documents with "bear" in the title.

4. Type any or all of the **file name** or **folder name**. The text is displayed in the Search for files or folders named: text box.

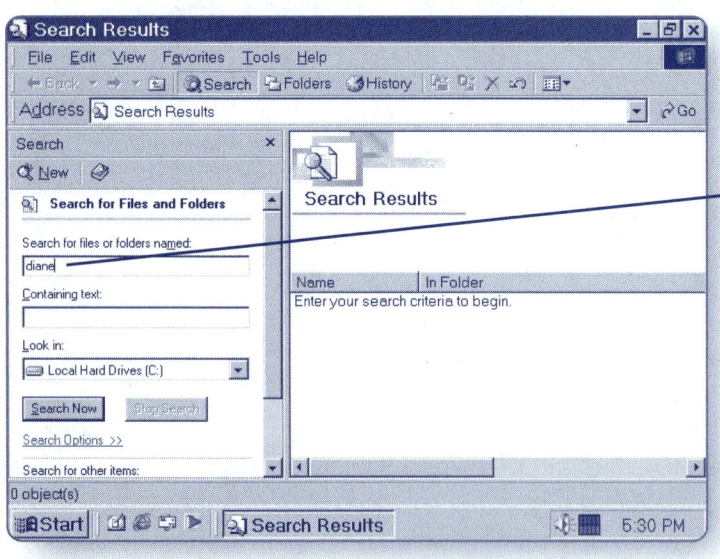

FINDING A FILE 175

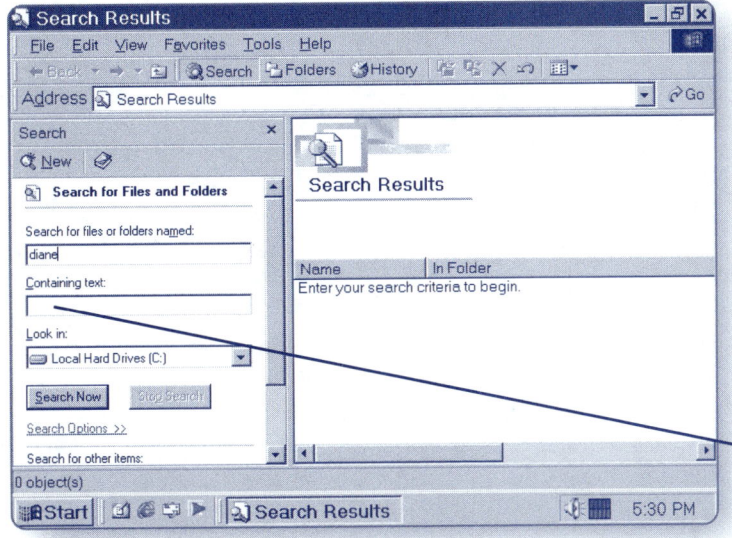

NOTE
If you type multiple words in the Named: list box, Windows will find all files that have any of those words in the file name. If you know the exact file name, enclose it in quotation marks.

5. Optionally, **click** in the **Containing text:** text box. The blinking insertion point appears in the second text box.

6. Type the requested **word or phrase** in the Containing text: text box.

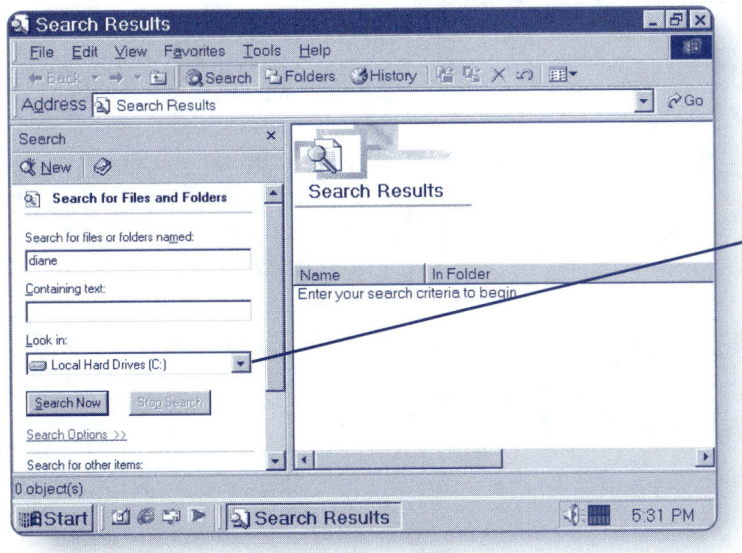

You have the option of specifying where to look for the text. You can search any specific disk drive or the entire computer.

7. Click on the **down arrow** (▼) next to the Look in: list box. A list of locations appears.

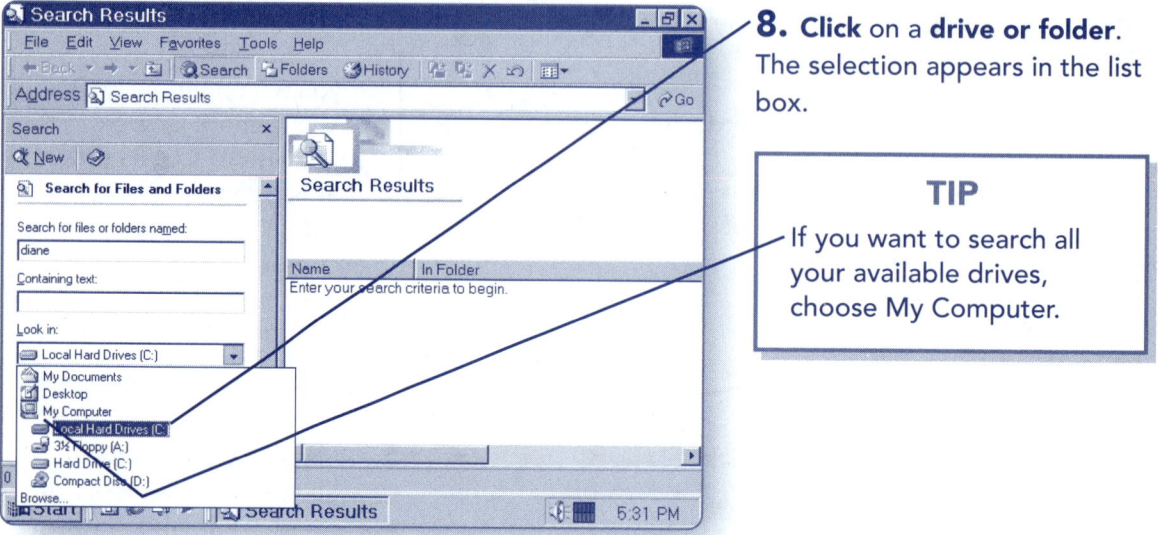

8. Click on a **drive or folder**. The selection appears in the list box.

TIP
If you want to search all your available drives, choose My Computer.

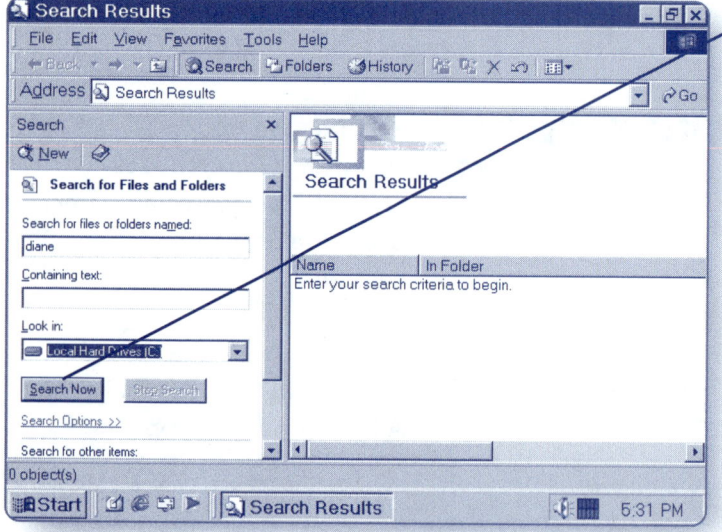

9. Click on **Search Now**. The search begins.

NOTE
If you are searching in the body of the document, the search may be quite lengthy depending on how many files are stored on the searched disk or folder.

FINDING A FILE 177

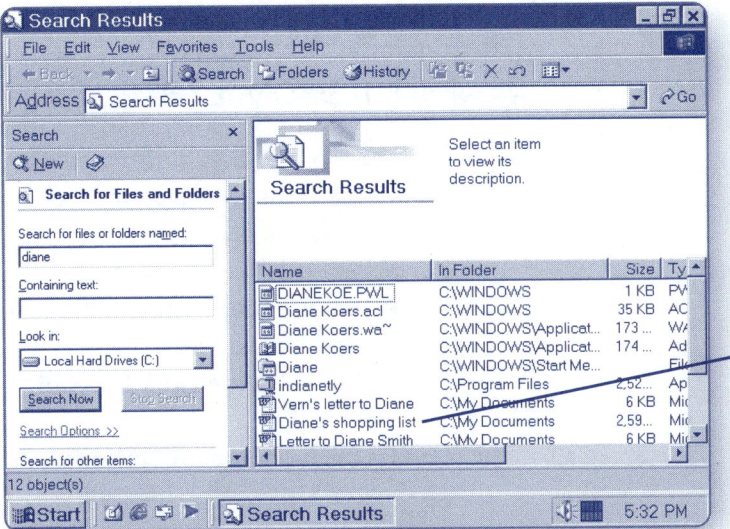

The results of the search are displayed on the lower right side of the window. The name of the file is listed as well as its folder location, size, type, and the date it was last modified.

TIP
Click on a desired file to open it in the application it was created.

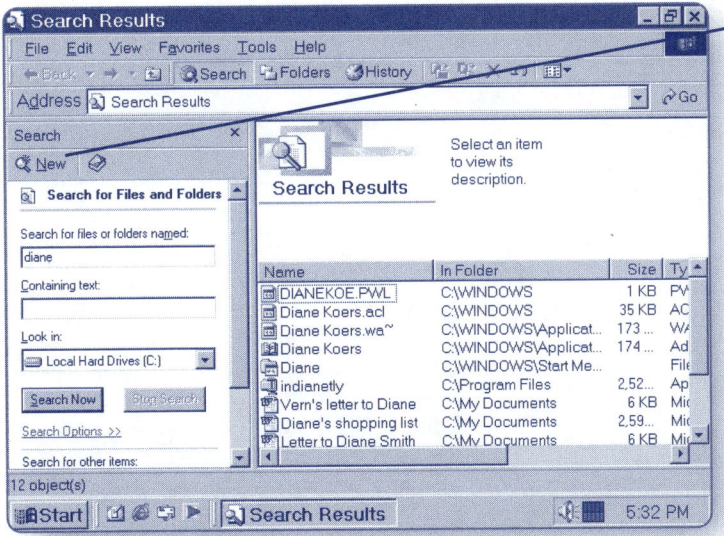

10. Click on **New**. The search conditions are removed and you're ready to create a new search.

CHAPTER 13: FINDING FILES, FOLDERS, AND PEOPLE

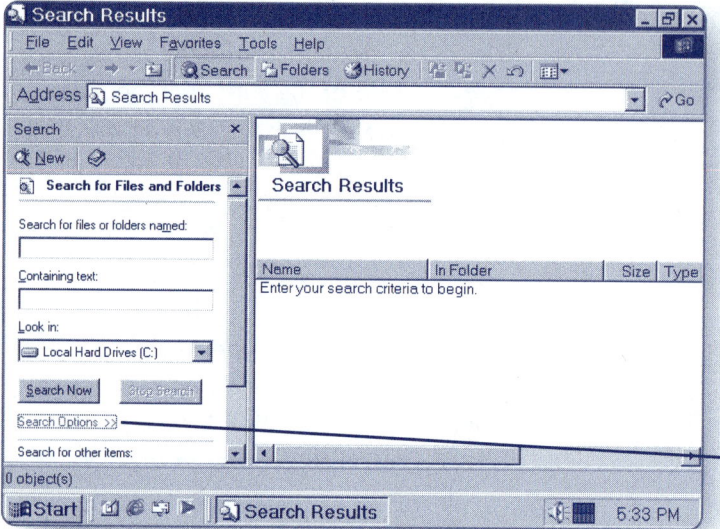

Looking for a File by Date

You can also find files based on the date they were created or even by the last time you modified a file. For example, you might need to find a file you worked on last week. Let Windows do the work for you!

1. Click on **Search Options**. A Search Options box appears.

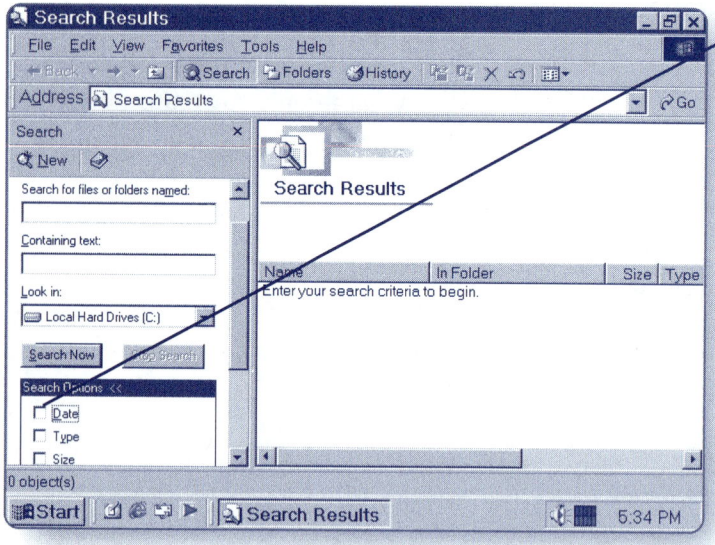

2. Click on **Date**. Options for searching by date appear.

LOOKING FOR A FILE BY DATE   179

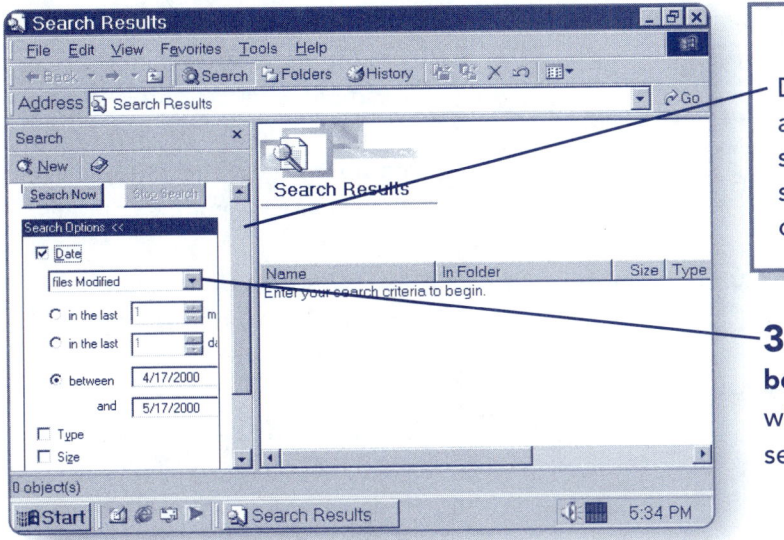

TIP
Depending on your display adapter and screen settings, you may need to scroll down to see the date options in their entirety.

3. Click on the first **drop-down box**. From here you choose what criteria to use when searching.

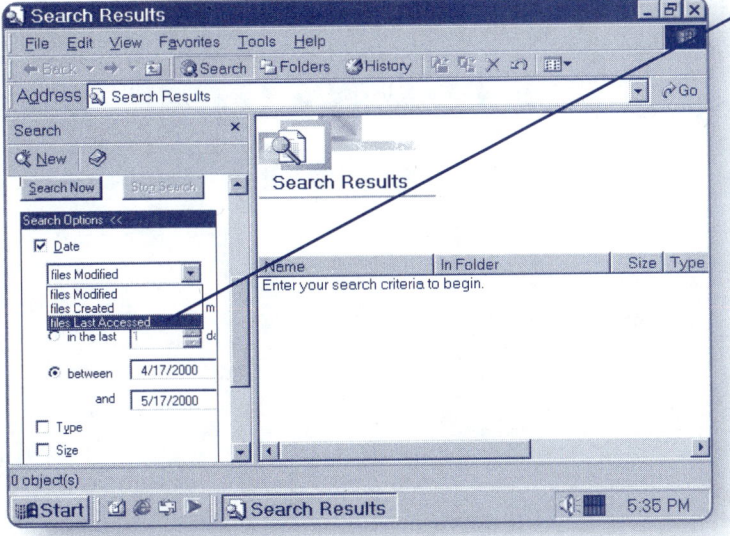

4. Click on **files Modified**, **files Created**, or **files Last Accessed**. Your selection appears in the drop-down box.

CHAPTER 13: FINDING FILES, FOLDERS, AND PEOPLE

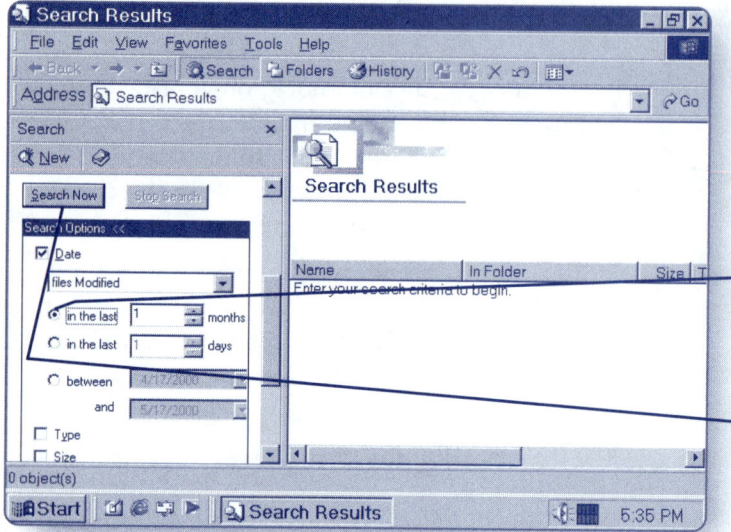

You can specify three types of time frames: Specific dates (for example June 3rd through July 16th), during the previous x number of months, or during the previous x number of days.

5. **Click** on a **time frame** to search. The option will be selected.

6. **Click** on **Search Now**. The search begins and all files meeting your date criteria are displayed in the right pane of the search window.

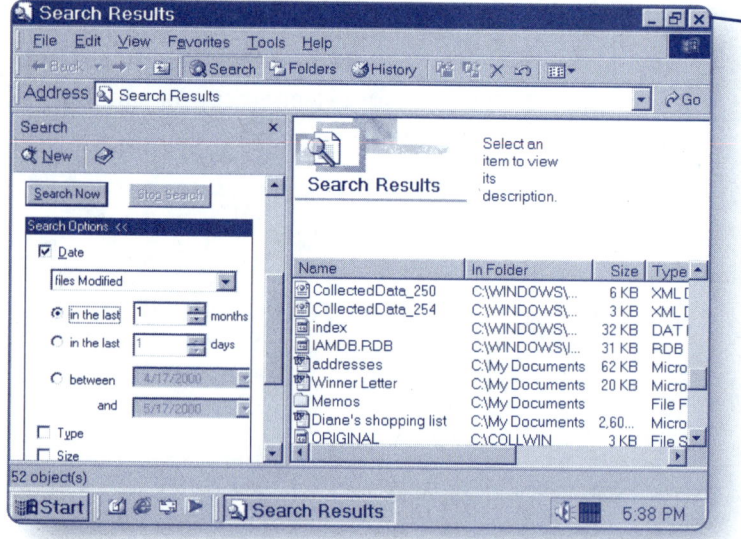

7. **Click** on the **Close button** (X). The Search Results window closes.

Searching for People in the Address Book

You can use the Find feature to search the Windows Address Book for a particular person's name, address, phone numbers, or e-mail addresses. Adding information to the Address Book is covered in Chapter 22, "Using the Windows Address Book."

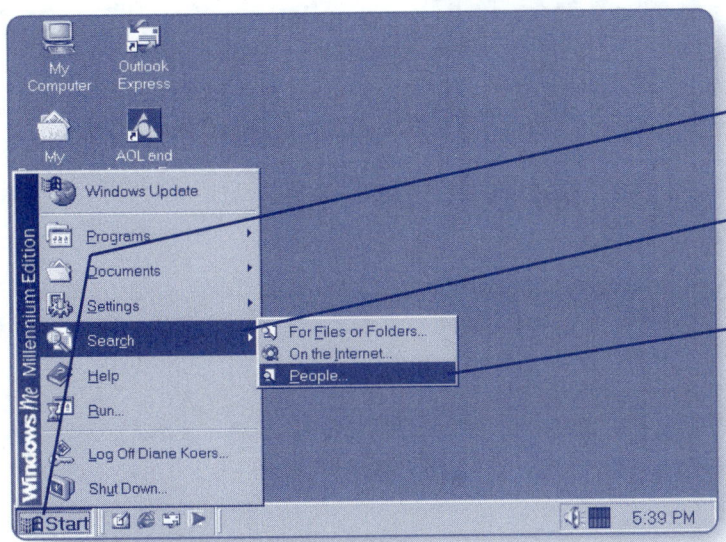

1. Click on the **Start button**. The Start menu appears.

2. Click on **Search**. The Search submenu appears.

3. Click on **People**. The Find People dialog box opens.

Here are a couple of the ways you can search the Address Book:

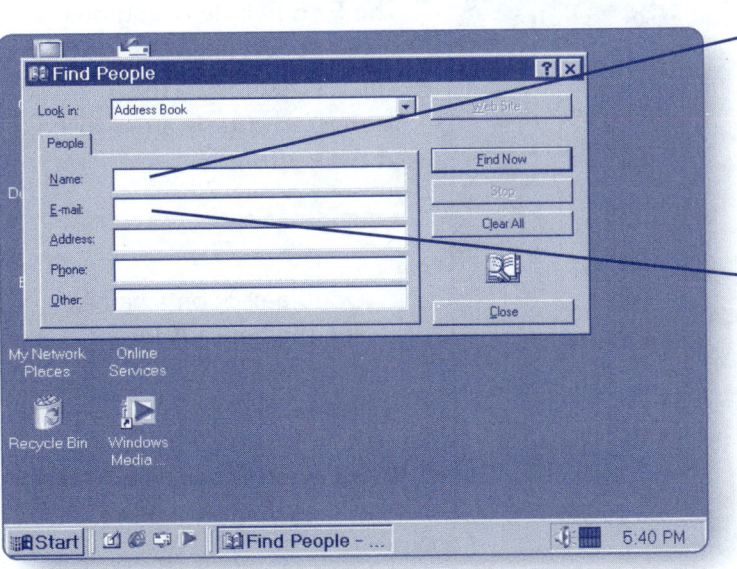

- Type any part of their name. For example, to find anyone with George as part of their first or last name, type George in the Name: text box.

- Type any part of their e-mail address. For example, to find everyone whose e-mail address is at America Online, type AOL in the E-mail: text box.

- Type in both the name and e-mail fields to be more specific. For example, to find your friend George who subscribes to America Online, type George in the Name: text box AND type AOL in the E-mail: text box.

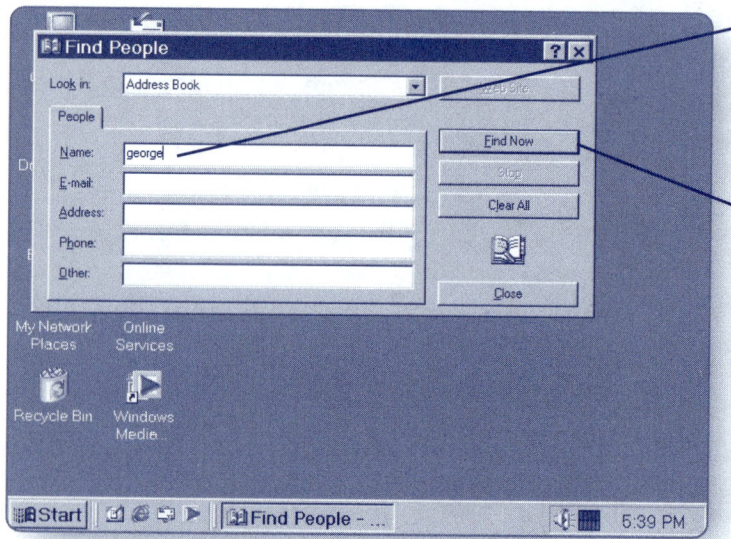

4. Type the **information** you are searching for in the appropriate text boxes. The typed text is displayed.

5. Click on **Find Now**. The search begins.

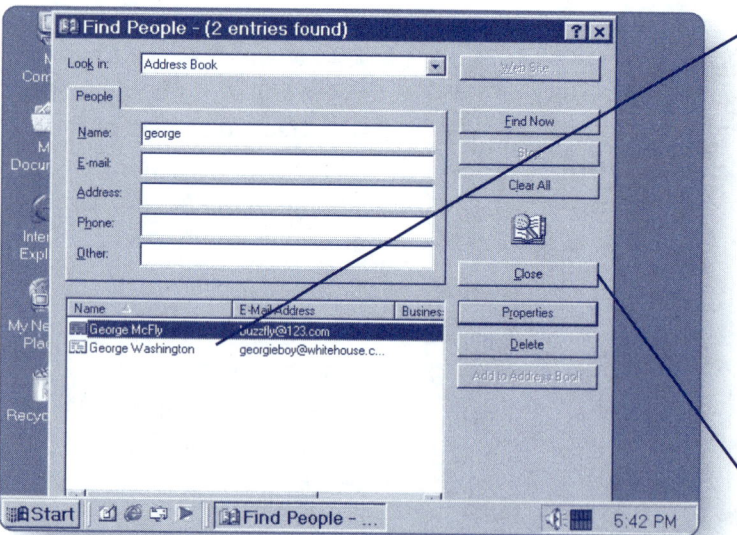

The Find People dialog box expands and any Address Book entries that match the requested criteria are displayed at the bottom.

TIP
Double-click on a name to see the entire Address Book entry.

6. Click on **Close**. The Find People dialog box closes.

14

Discovering Multimedia

One of the most exciting reasons to use a computer today is multimedia. Multimedia is the capability of a computer application to combine with other media, such as video or sound. To enjoy the capabilities of multimedia, your computer needs a CD-ROM or DVD drive, a sound card, and speakers. In this chapter, you'll learn how to:

- Play a music CD
- Use the Media Player
- Listen to Internet radio
- Adjust the sound volume
- Add a media clip to a document

Using the Windows Media Player

Windows Millennium Edition and the Windows Media Player can make beautiful music together. The Windows Media Player is a center for you to listen to CDs, tune in to Internet radio, download music and video from the Internet, or categorize and manage media stored on your computer.

Playing a Music CD

What's your style? No matter whether it's rock and roll, jazz, classical, or the blues, the Windows Media Player gives you several different ways to enjoy your music.

Starting a Music CD

Place your favorite music CD into the computer and listen while you work! With Internet access, the Windows Media Player can locate information about the album and artist you're currently playing.

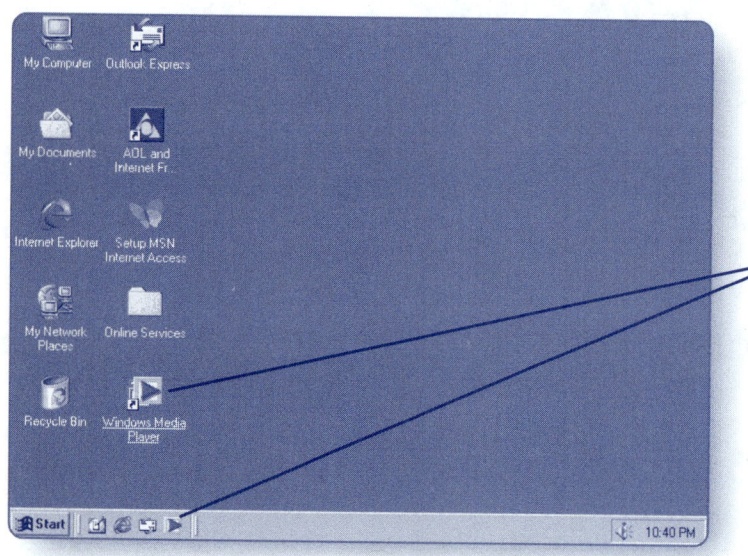

1. Insert the audio **CD** into the CD-ROM drive. The Connect To dialog box appears.

> **TIP**
> To start the Media Player manually, click the Windows Media Player button, either on the desktop or the Quick Launch bar. The Windows Media Player starts.

USING THE WINDOWS MEDIA PLAYER 185

With an Internet connection, Windows Millennium Edition can connect and provide more information about the disc you've inserted.

If you're not already connected to the Internet, you're prompted to connect now.

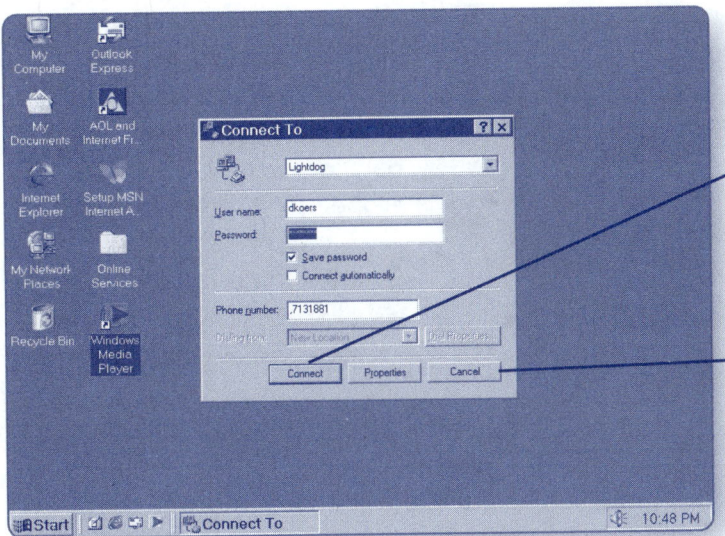

See Chapter 19, "Connecting to the Internet," to establish an Internet connection.

2a. Click on **Connect**. The Windows Media Player appears as your music begins playing.

OR

2b. Click on **Cancel**. If not already open, the Windows Media Player appears and the CD begins playing. Enjoy!

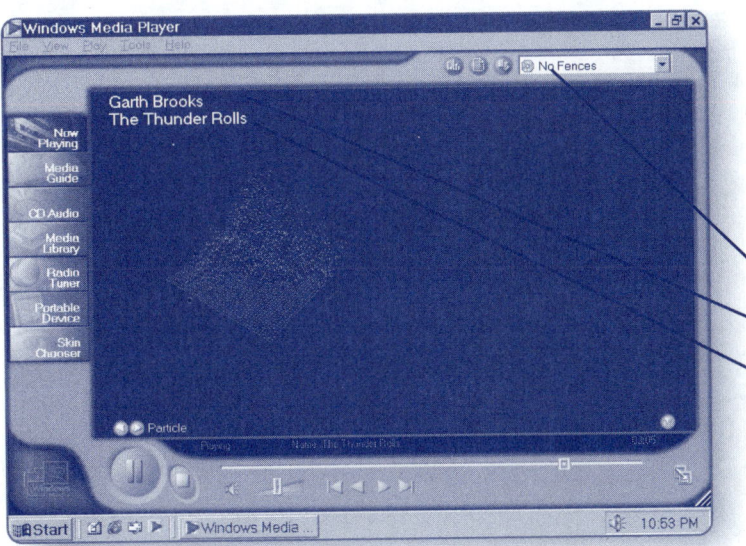

Windows Media Player searches the Internet for information on the current CD. After the Internet connection is established, the Media Player identifies the following:

- The CD title
- The artist
- The current song title

Occasionally, Windows Media Player cannot identify information on the current CD.

186 CHAPTER 14: DISCOVERING MULTIMEDIA

Discovering Visualizations

Visualizations are the splashes of color and geometric shapes you see on the Windows Media Player that change with the beat of the audio currently playing. You can choose from several visualization styles.

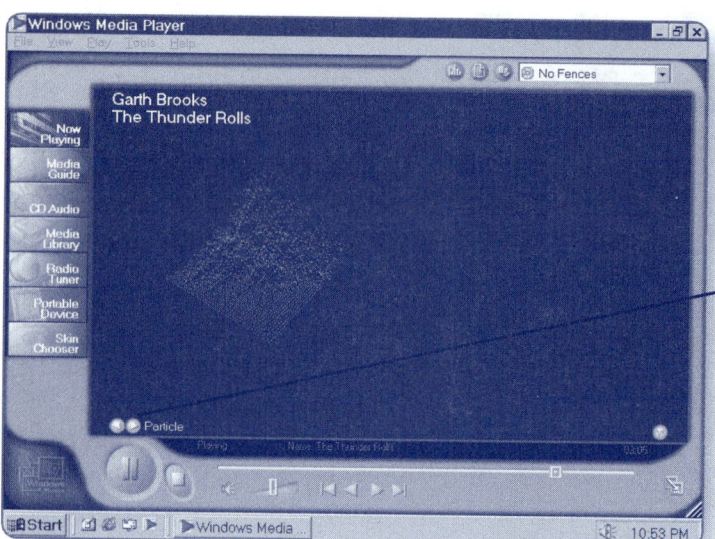

Windows calls the default visualization particle. Other visualization names include: random particle, spike, amoeba, bars, ocean mist, firestorm, and scope.

1. Click the **arrows** below the visualization window. The next available visualization appears.

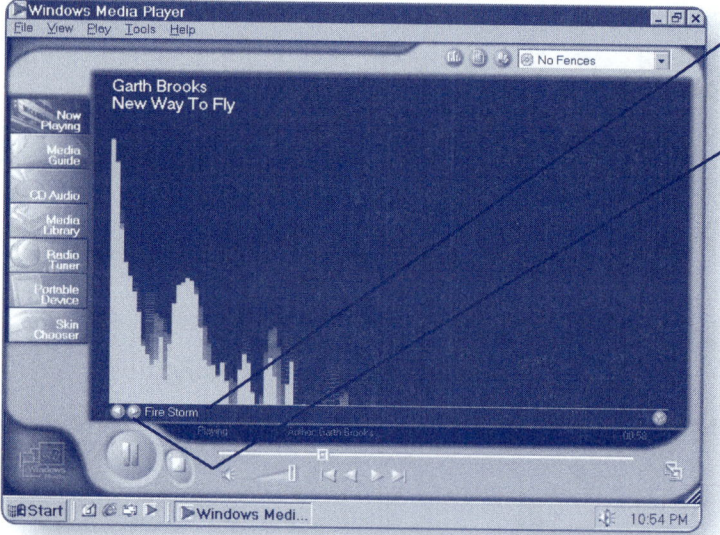

The visualization name appears next to the arrow.

2. Continue clicking a visualization window **arrow** until you arrive at the visualization you want to use. With each click, a different visualization appears.

Choosing from the Playlist

Choose any song you want to hear from your CD.

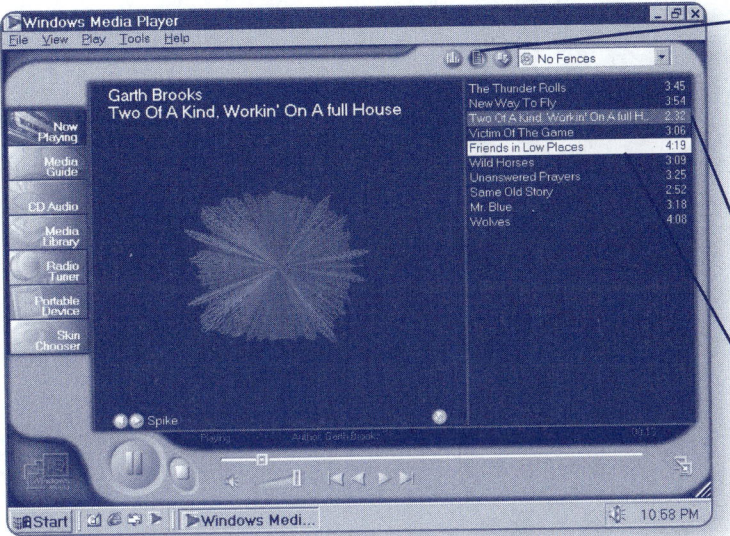

1. Click the **Show Playlist in Now Playing button**. A list of available tracks appears. If you connected to the Internet, Windows Media Player lists these tracks by name.

The current song name is highlighted.

2. Double-click the **track** you want to hear. The track begins playing.

> **TIP**
> Click the Show Playlist in Now Playing button again to close the playlist.

Exploring the Windows Media Player

Windows Media Player is an application that offers a single place to find, organize, and play digital media. It provides easy access to the most common digital media activities, including audio and video playback, CD playback and recording, Internet radio, and transfer of media files to portable devices and removable media.

The Windows Media Player window has many of the same buttons that you see on a standard CD player.

188 CHAPTER 14: DISCOVERING MULTIMEDIA

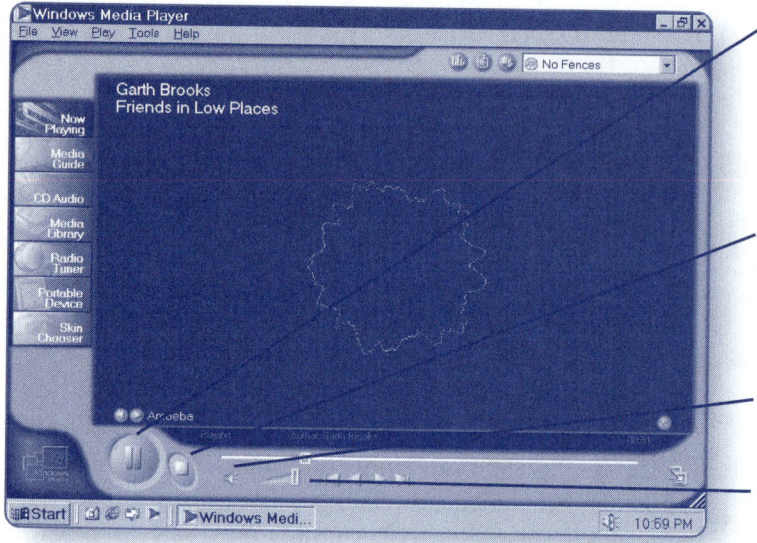

- **Pause/(Play)**. Stops the play, but remembers the current location. (This button turns into Play if the CD is not currently playing a song.)
- **Stop**. Stops the current song. The next time you click the Play button, the CD restarts at the beginning of the disc.
- **Mute**. Turns the volume on or off.
- **Volume Control**. Controls the volume level.

- **Previous Track**. Plays the preceding song.
- **Rewind**. Scans the current song backward.
- **Fast Forward**. Scans the current song forward.
- **Next Track**. Plays the next song.

USING THE WINDOWS MEDIA PLAYER 189

Equalizing Your Settings

Included with Windows Media Player is an integrated 10-band graphic equalizer and other tools to manage your multimedia.

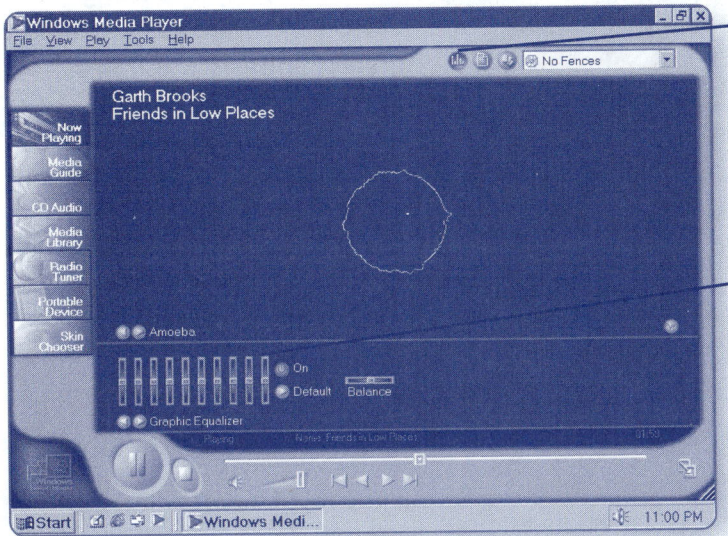

1. Click the **Show Equalizer and Settings button**. A graphic equalizer appears onscreen.

From here you can change audio quality settings.

2. Click the **Next Preset button**. The equalizer settings change.

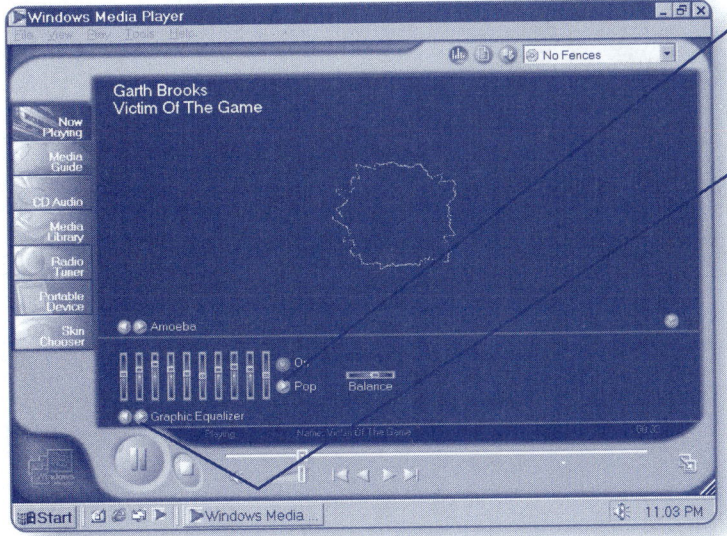

In this figure, the equalizer settings (and sound) change to Pop music settings.

3. Click the **Next Setting button**. A video settings graphic appears.

190 CHAPTER 14: DISCOVERING MULTIMEDIA

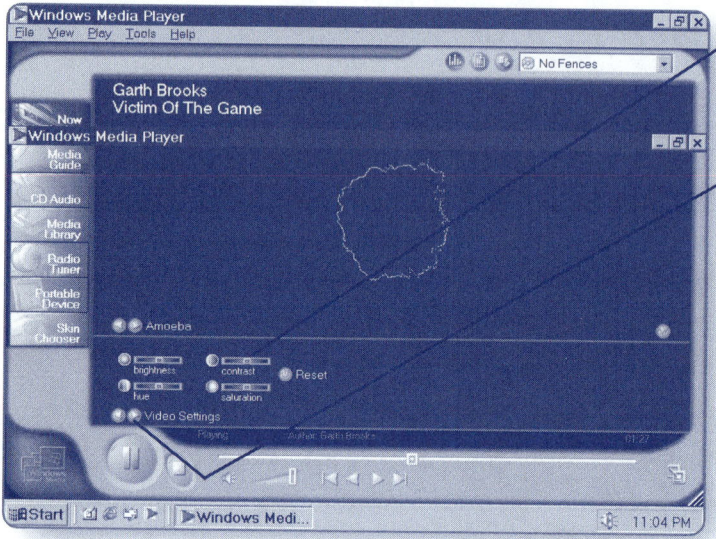

From here, if you are viewing video, you can change video color and other settings.

4. Click the **Next Setting button**. The Media Information graphic appears.

If you're connected to the Internet, you'll see information on the CD currently playing.

USING THE WINDOWS MEDIA PLAYER   191

5. Make a **selection** from the information list to view additional information on the current CD including biography of the artist, reviews, and other album information.

6. Click the **Next Setting button**. The Captions graphic appears.

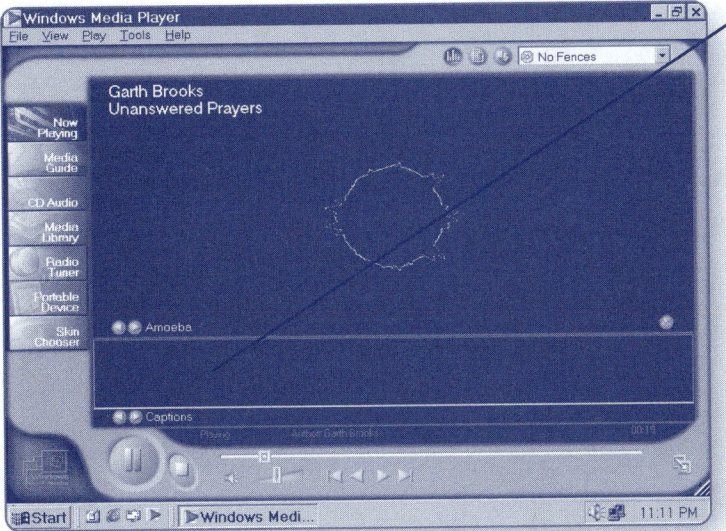

Captions appear when you use Windows Media Player to create video shows.

TIP

Click the Show Equalizer and Settings button again to close the equalizer.

Listening to Web Radio

With Internet access and the Windows Media Player, you can listen to music, news, or sports from more than 1,500 live Internet radio stations from around the world.

1. **Click** on **Radio Tuner**. A list of preset radio stations appears.

2. **Double-click** a **radio station** from either the presets window pane or the station locator pane. Internet Explorer opens and connects to the Web page associated with the radio station. In a few seconds, the radio broadcast begins.

The current station indicator.

Click on the Internet Explorer icon to view the Web page associated with the radio station.

USING THE WINDOWS MEDIA PLAYER 193

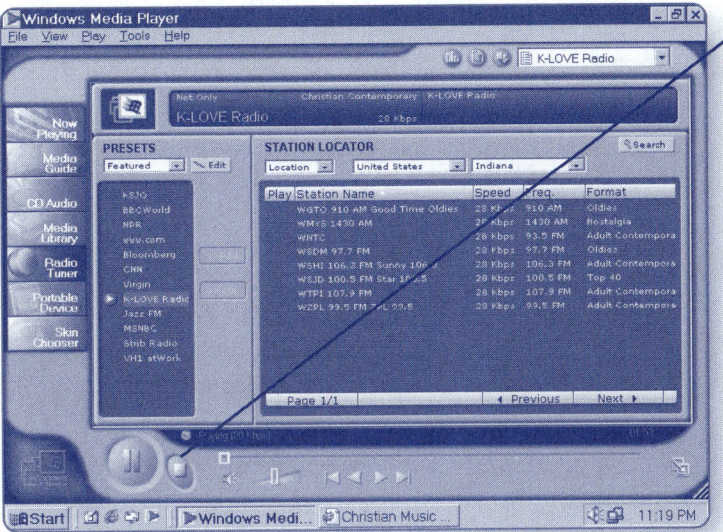

3. Click on **Stop**. The radio broadcast stops.

> **NOTE**
> Although you can customize Windows Media Player to recognize radio stations that match your personal preferences, setting those preferences are beyond the scope of this book.

Using the Media Guide

Use Media Guide to find, download, and play movies, music, and video on the Internet. Media Guide is a live Web page with links to movies, music, and video. Although you can play everything listed in Media Guide using Windows Media Player, you must connect to the Internet to use Media Guide.

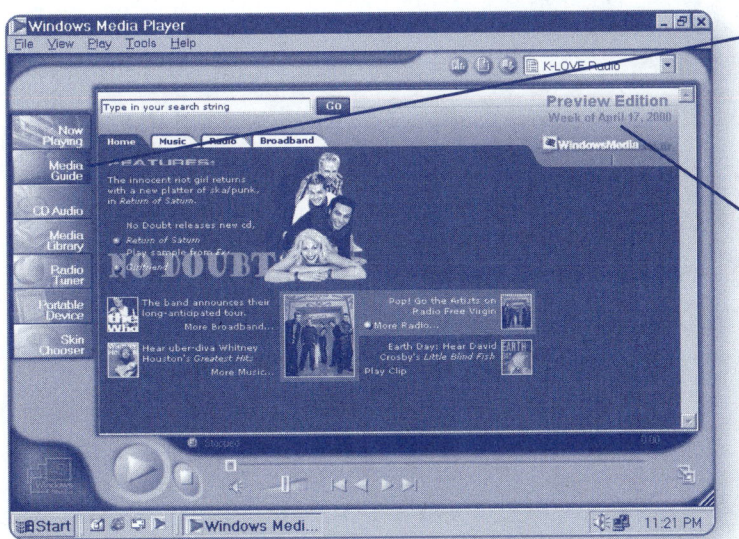

1. Click on **Media Guide**. If you're not already connected to the Internet, a connection establishes.

The Media Guide window changes frequently.

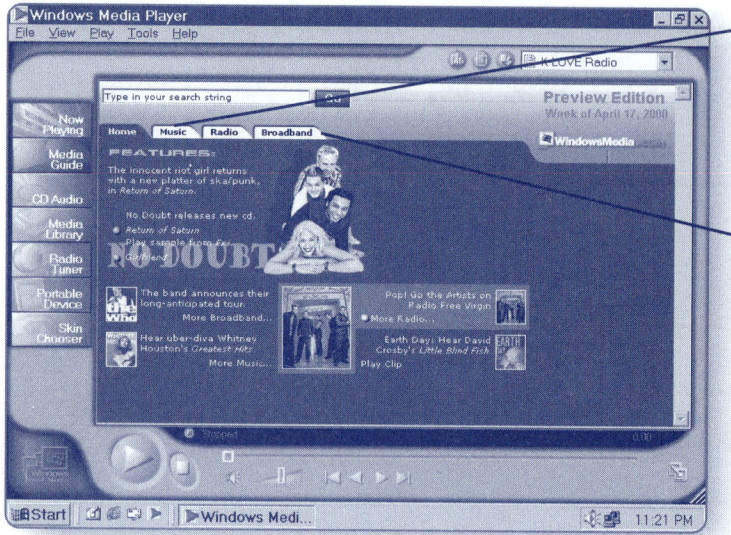

2. Click the **type of media** you want to preview. A selection of choices appears.

TIP

Without a cable modem, ADSL line, T1 connection, or other broadband connection type, you may find the Broadband selections extremely slow.

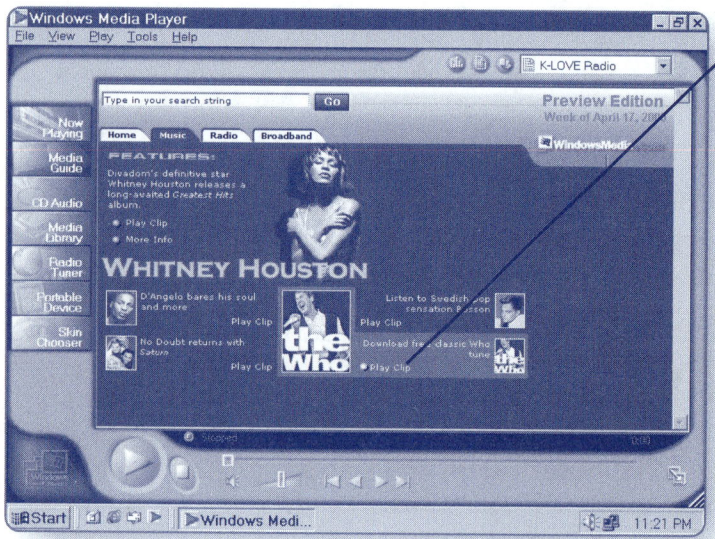

3. Click on **Play Clip** next to the song or video you want to preview. Enjoy!

Cataloging Media

Let the Windows Media Player locate and organize all the different media on your computer so that you won't need to remember the location where you saved these files when you want to play them.

Creating a Media Library

Depending on selected options, the Media Library can check your hard drives or the Internet.

1. Click on **Media Library**. If you're not already connected to the Internet, a connection establishes.

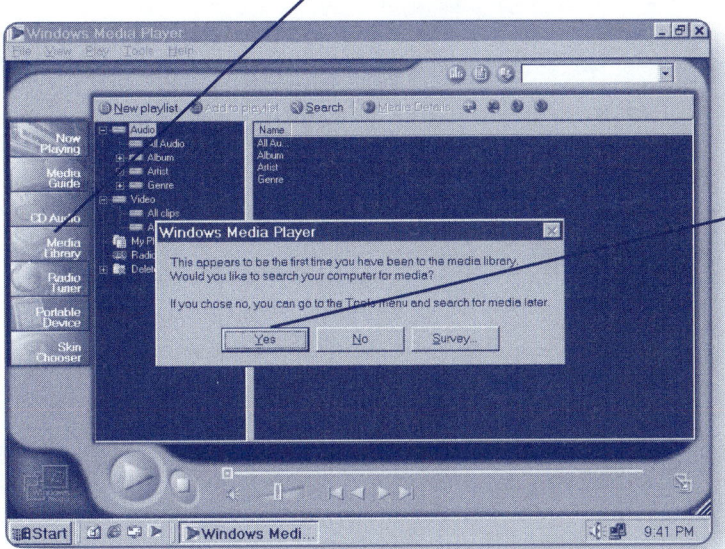

The first time you access the Media Library, Windows Media Player prompts you to search your computer for media.

2. Click on **Yes**. The Search Options dialog box appears.

196 CHAPTER 14: DISCOVERING MULTIMEDIA

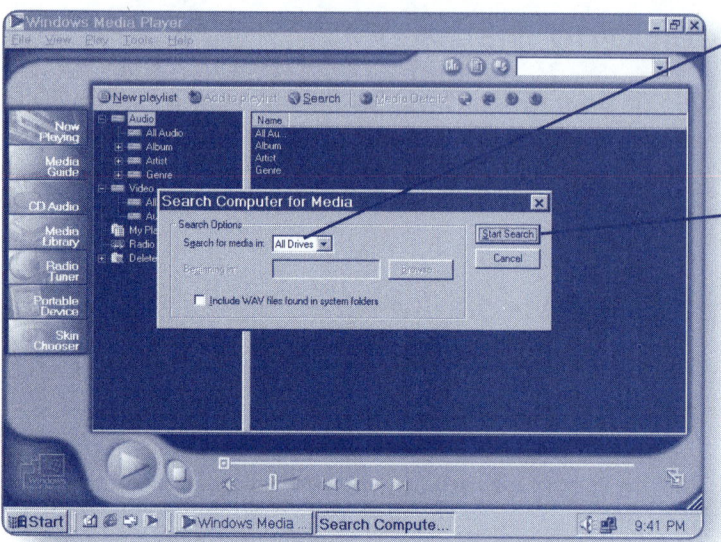

3. Click the **disk drive** you want to search. By default, Media Library searches all available disk drives.

4. Click on **Start Search**. Windows Media Player searches your hard drive for media files.

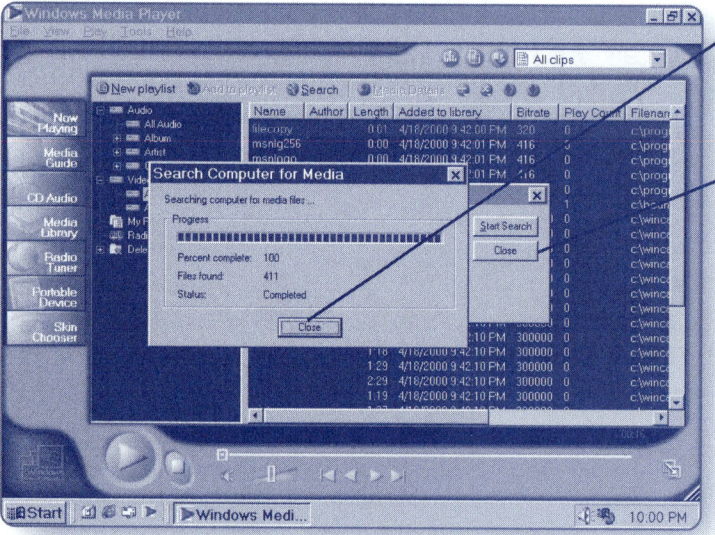

5. Click on **Close**. The Search Computer for Media dialog box closes.

6. Click on **Close**. The bottom Search Computer for Media dialog box closes.

USING THE WINDOWS MEDIA PLAYER   197

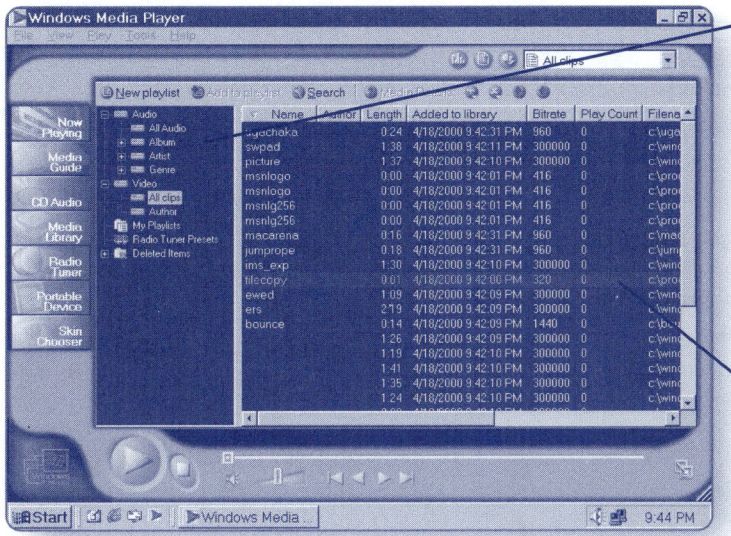

Media Library separates your stored media into audio and video. Within the audio category, Media Library creates subcategories such as Album title, Artist name, and Genre (category). For video, Media Library creates one subcategory—the author.

Double-click on any file to play the media file.

Deleting a Library Media File

If you have a media file you don't want included in the Media Library, you can easily delete it. When you delete the file, you're not deleting the file from your computer; you're only deleting the *link* to it.

1. Click on the **file name** you want to delete. Media Library highlights the file name.

2. Click on the **Delete button**. A menu appears.

3. Click on **Delete from Library**. Media Library removes the file link from the library list.

Viewing Modes and Choosing Skins

Windows Media Player includes two different modes of viewing the player—full mode and compact mode. Up until now, you've been viewing the player in full mode, the non-customizable view that allows access to all Windows Media Player features. The second view, compact mode, uses Windows Media Player skins. Skins are files that customize the look and functionality of the Windows Media Player.

In compact mode, depending on the selected skin, the Windows Media Player may not have access to all features.

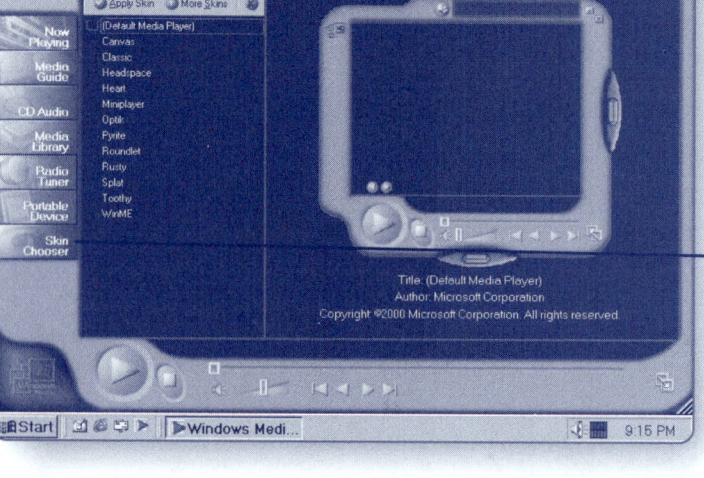

1. Click on **Skin Chooser**. A preview and list of skins appears.

TIP
Depending on the size of your window and the size and resolution of your screen, you may need to scroll down to see the Skin Chooser selection.

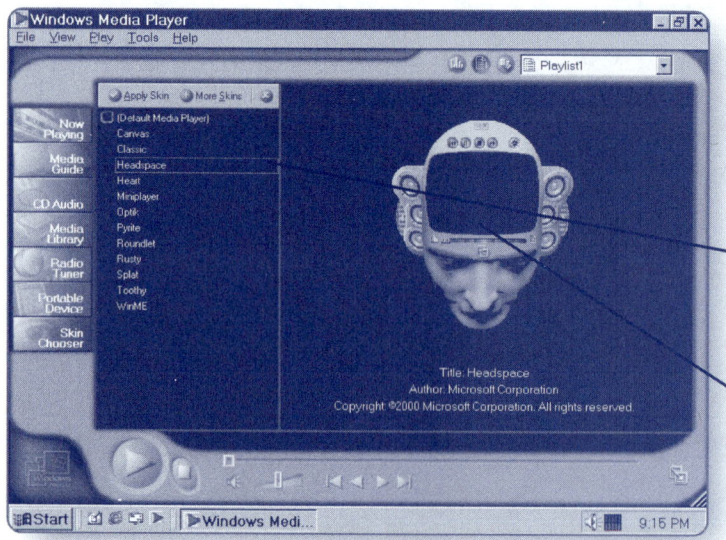

2. Click on a **skin name**. Windows Media Player highlights the skin name.

A preview of the skin appears in the right window pane.

USING THE WINDOWS MEDIA PLAYER   199

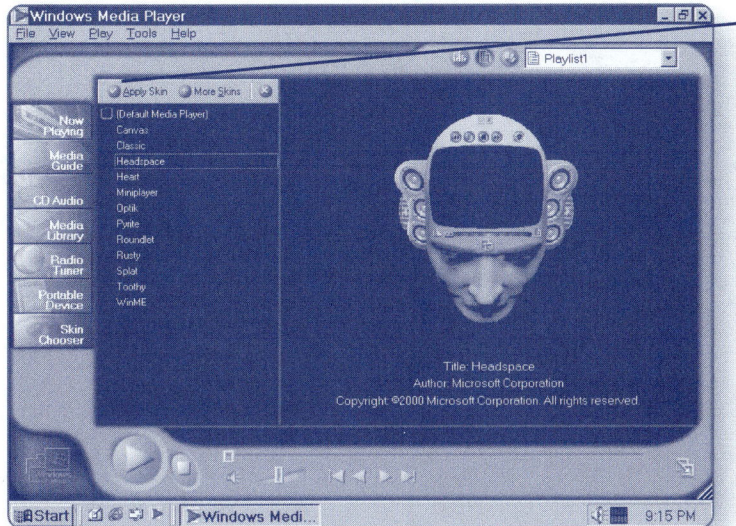

3. Click on **Apply Skin**. The window switches to compact mode with the Windows Media Player skin appearing on your desktop.

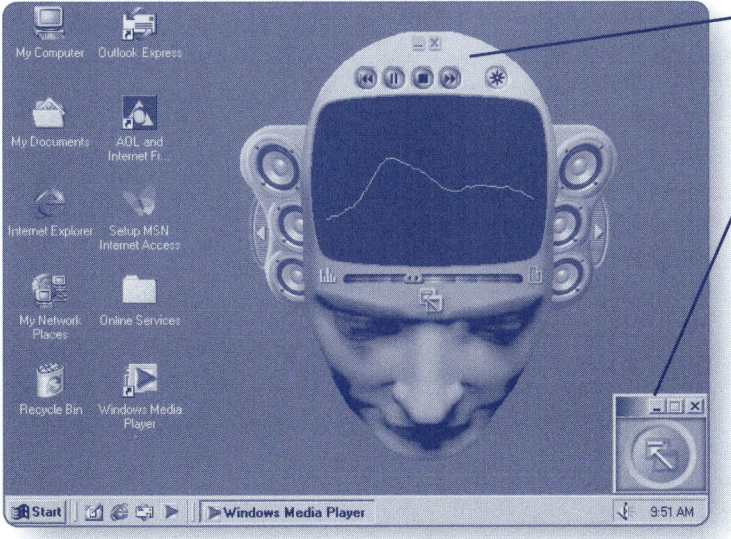

The Windows Media Player in compact mode with the selected skin.

The Control window.

200 CHAPTER 14: DISCOVERING MULTIMEDIA

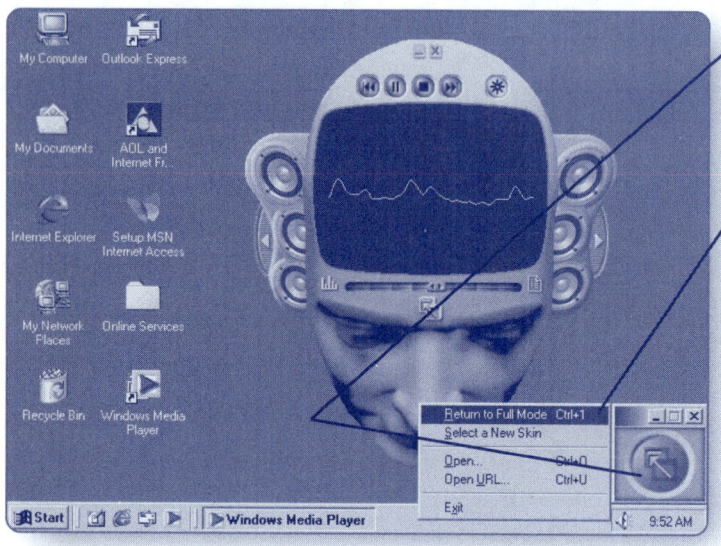

4. Click on the **Control window icon**. A submenu appears.

5. Click on **Return to Full Mode**. The Windows Media Player returns to full mode.

Click here to return to Compact mode.

6. Click the **Close box**. The Windows Media Player window closes.

Using the Windows Volume Control

It's almost like having a remote control right at your fingertips! The volume control allows you to set different settings for the sounds and other audible objects you play on your computer. You'll learn how to assign sounds to your computer functions in Chapter 17, "Having Fun with the Control Panel."

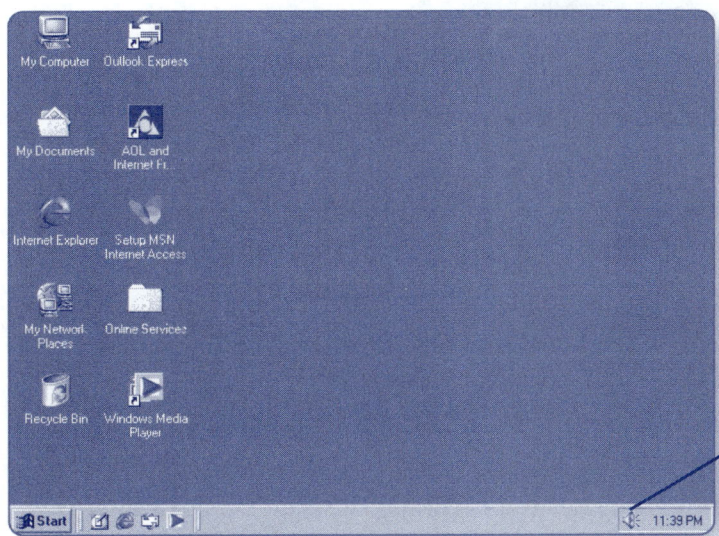

1. Click on the **speaker icon** in the System Tray. The Volume slider appears.

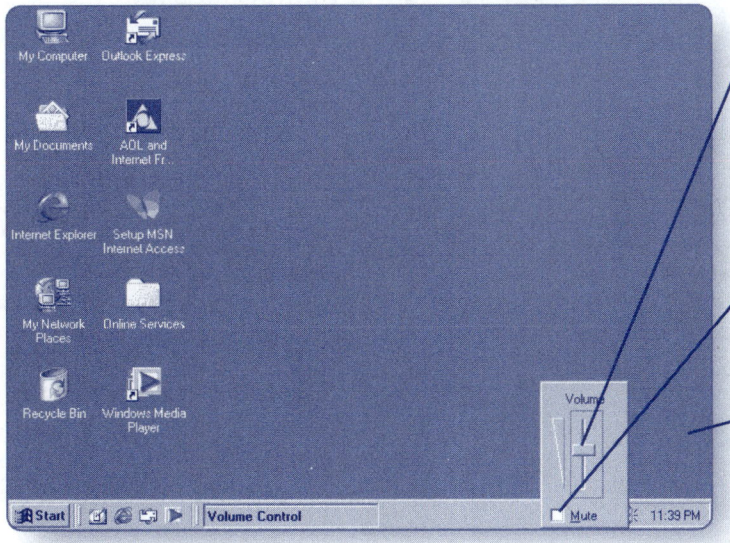

2. Click and **drag** the **volume slider** up or down. The volume level increases or decreases.

> **TIP**
> Click the Mute check box to mute all speaker volume.

3. Click anywhere on the **desktop**. The Volume slider closes.

202 CHAPTER 14: DISCOVERING MULTIMEDIA

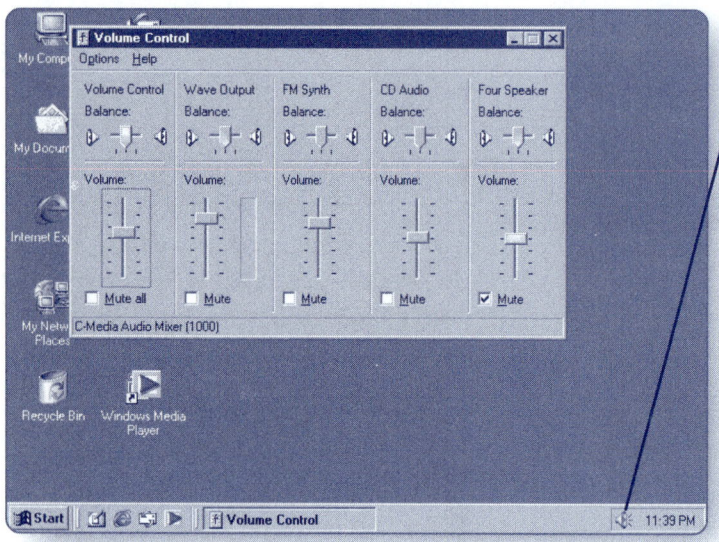

4. Double-click on the **speaker** in the System Tray. The Volume Control window opens.

The Volume Control window allows you to balance and adjust other mixer properties as well as the volume. The options available in the Volume Control window vary with the type of sound card installed in your computer.

5. Adjust any desired **settings**. The slide bars indicate the new settings.

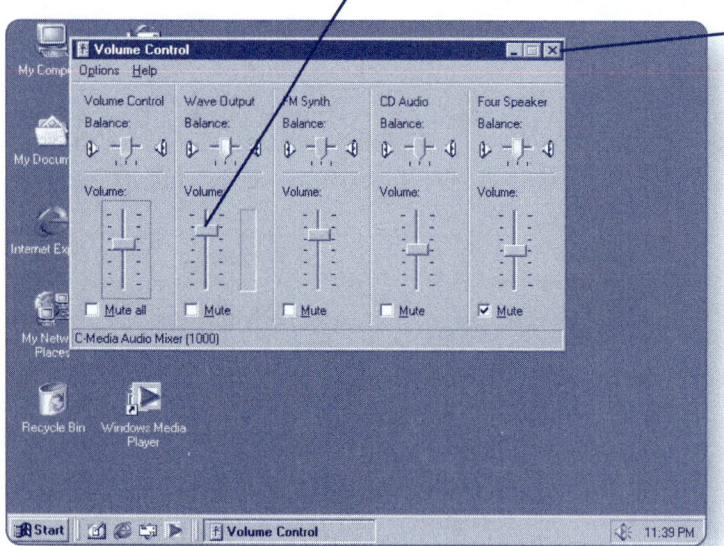

6. Click on the **Close button** (X). The Volume Control window closes.

TIP
You can also open the Volume Control window by clicking on Start, Programs, Accessories, Entertainment, and Volume Control.

Adding a Media Clip to a Document

Today's applications, such as Word, WordPerfect, Excel, Lotus 1-2-3, and many others, have the capability to embed media files within documents. Adding sound or video to a file sent electronically can add more pizzazz. The only limitation is that the person receiving the file must have multimedia capabilities (speakers and a sound card).

1. Locate the **media file** you want to include in your document. Use the Windows Explorer, the Windows Search feature, or if the file is located in My Documents, open the My Documents folder.

2. Right-click on the **media file** you want to place in the document. A shortcut menu appears.

3. Click on **Copy**. Although it looks like nothing happened, Windows copies the media file to the Windows Clipboard.

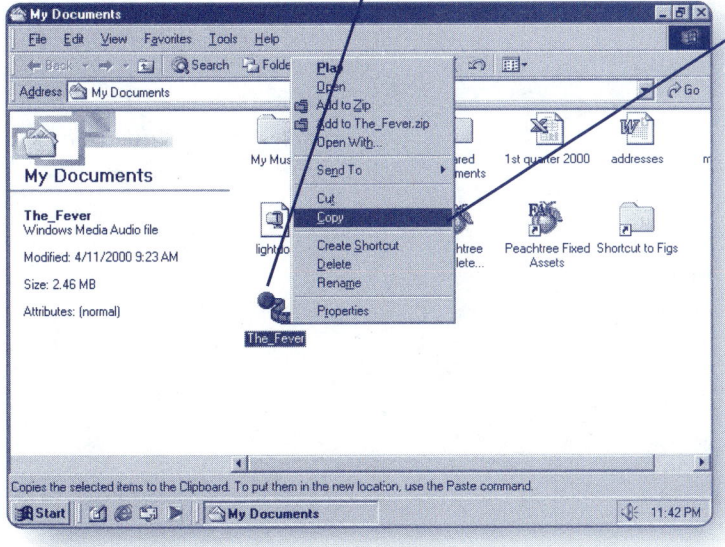

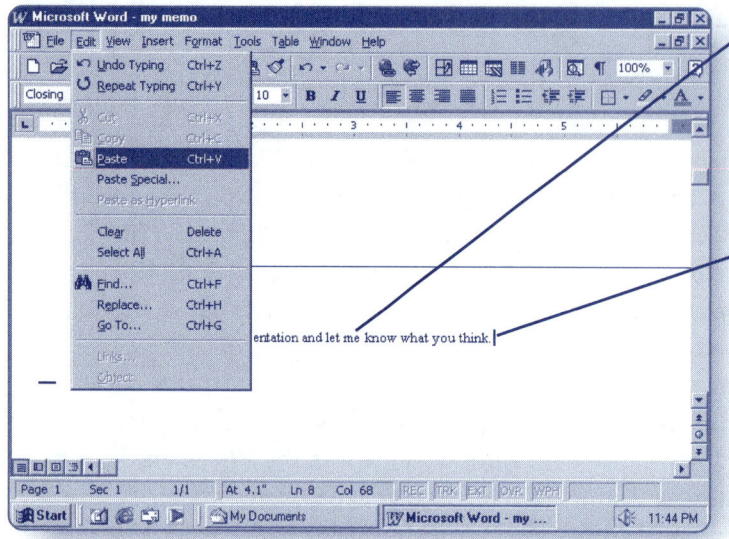

4. Create or open the **document** in which you want to place the media file. In our example, we're opening a Microsoft Word document.

5. Click the **mouse** where you want to place the media file. The insertion point moves to the selected location.

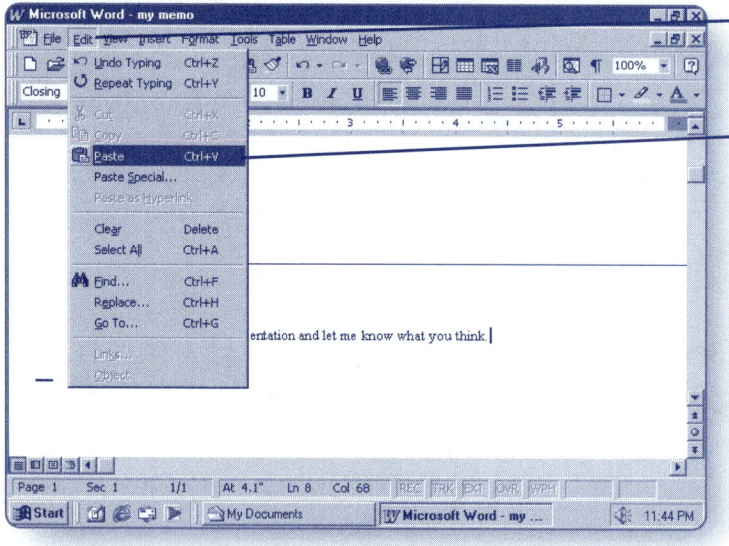

6. Click on **Edit**. The Edit menu appears.

7. Click on **Paste**. An object box appears in the document as Windows adds an icon for the media file.

ADDING A MEDIA CLIP TO A DOCUMENT

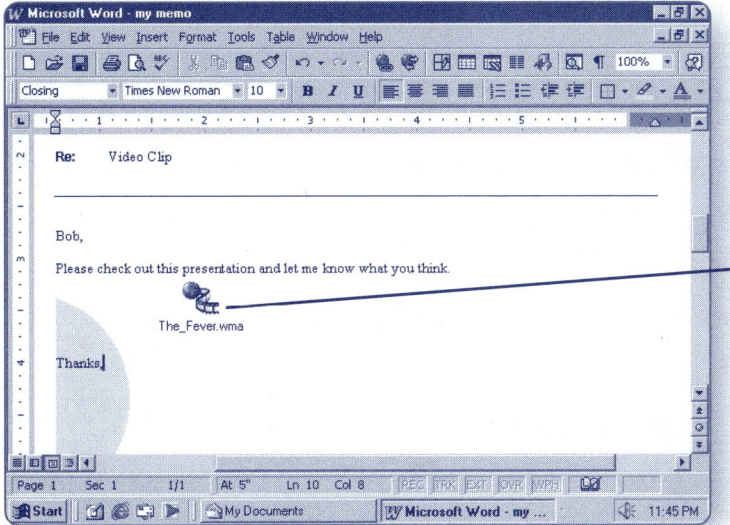

The appearance of the object in the document varies between applications and the type of media file.

TIP

Double-click on a media clip to play it.

Part III Review Questions

1. What Windows feature assists you with issues such as personalizing your computer or connecting to a network? *See "Starting Windows Help" in Chapter 10*

2. Why should you defragment your files? *See "Defragmenting Your Hard Drive" in Chapter 11*

3. What Windows program checks your hard drive for potential errors? *See "Scanning Your Hard Disk for Problems" in Chapter 11*

4. What happens to a file when it is fragmented? *See "Defragmenting Your Hard Drive" in Chapter 11*

5. What does the Maintenance Wizard do? *See "Using the Maintenance Wizard" in Chapter 11*

6. What program is a graphic illustration of the files and folder contents of your computer? *See "Looking in the Explorer Window" in Chapter 12*

7. What type of information is displayed when you show your files in Detail View? *See "Changing the Way Files Are Displayed" in Chapter 12*

8. When a file is deleted, where is it placed? *See "Deleting Files " in Chapter 12*

9. What types of items can you search for using the Find feature? *See "Finding Files, Folders, and People" in Chapter 13*

10. What can you do with the Windows Media Player? *See "Using the Windows Media Player" in Chapter 14*

PART IV

Customizing Windows

Chapter 15
  Customizing the Desktop 209

Chapter 16
  Tinkering with the Control Panel 231

Chapter 17
  Having Fun with the Control Panel 261

Chapter 18
  Working with Printers 279

15
Customizing the Desktop

As you've noticed, there are many different items on the Windows desktop. In Chapter 2, you took a brief look at some of the desktop items, such as My Network Places, My Computer, the Taskbar, and the System Tray. You'll find you will use the right mouse button quite a bit when working on the Windows desktop. In this chapter, you'll learn how to:

- Create new desktop folders
- Move and delete icons
- Create a shortcut
- Rename an icon
- Edit the Start menu
- Customize the Taskbar

Creating a New Folder

Occasionally you might want a folder to organize some of the shortcut icons that appear on the desktop.

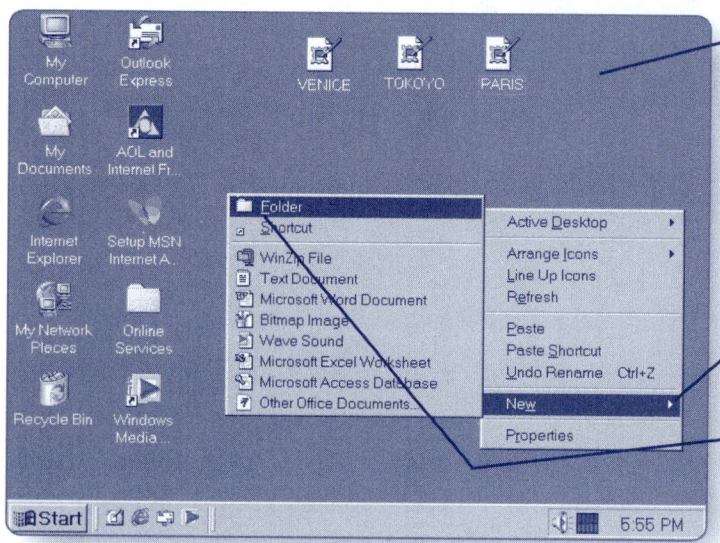

1. Position the **mouse pointer** anywhere over a blank area of the desktop.

2. Click the **right mouse button**. A shortcut menu appears.

3. Click on **New**. The New submenu appears.

4. Click on **Folder**. A new folder appears on the desktop ready to be named.

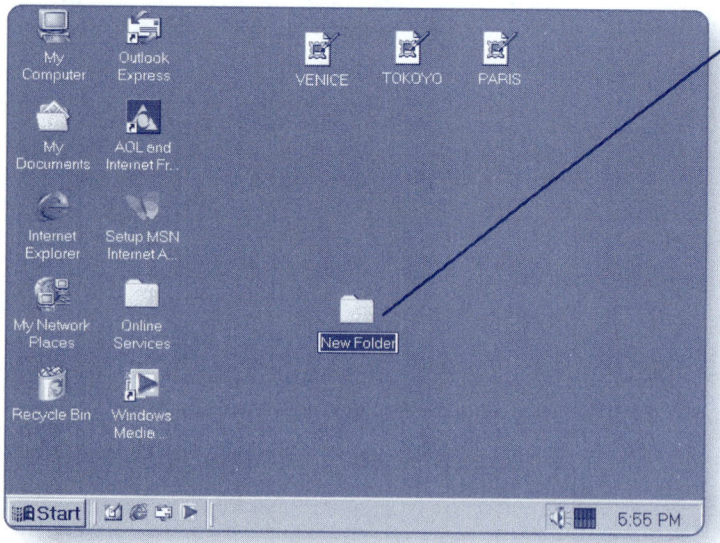

5. Type a **name** for the new folder. The words "New Folder" are replaced with the text you type.

6. Press the **Enter key**. The folder is ready to use.

Moving and Deleting Icons

Icons appear all over the desktop—some you want and some you don't. Icons can be moved or deleted with a click of the mouse.

Moving an Icon

If you want to move an icon to a different location, a feature called *Auto Arrange* must be turned off. If Auto Arrange is activated, you can move an icon, but it will pop right back into its previous location.

1. Position the **mouse pointer** anywhere over a blank area of the desktop.

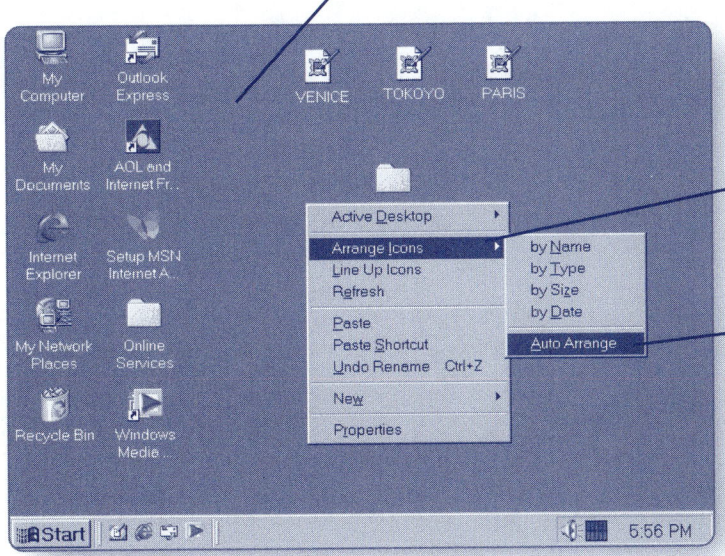

2. Click the **right mouse button**. A shortcut menu appears.

3. Click on **Arrange Icons**. The Arrange Icons submenu appears.

4a. Click on **Auto Arrange** if there is a ✔ already next to it. The feature is deactivated, and the shortcut menu closes.

OR

4b. Click anywhere on the desktop if no ✔ appears next to Auto Arrange. The shortcut menu closes with no changes made.

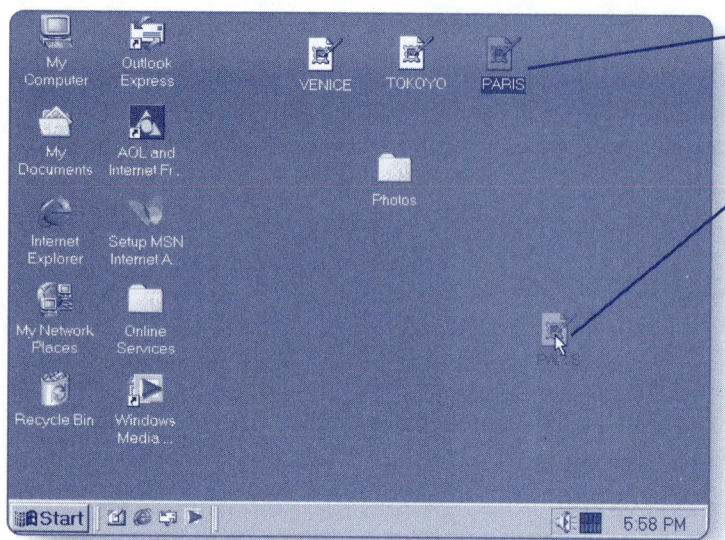

5. Position the **mouse pointer** over the icon to be moved. The icon is selected.

6. Press and **hold** the **mouse button** as you move the mouse. The icon moves with the mouse.

7. Release the **mouse button**. The icon remains in the new location.

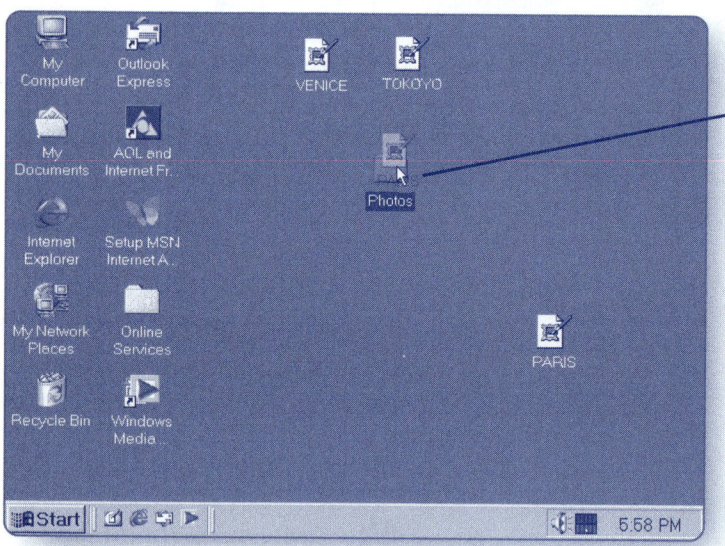

TIP

To move an icon into a folder on the desktop, drop the icon on top of the folder.

MOVING AND DELETING ICONS   213

Deleting an Icon

If the icon you want to delete has a small white arrow in the lower-left corner of it, you will not be deleting the program or document to which the icon refers. You will be deleting only the shortcut to the program or document.

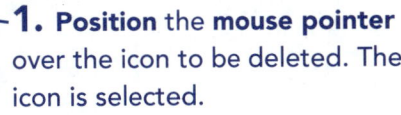

1. Position the **mouse pointer** over the icon to be deleted. The icon is selected.

2. Click the **right mouse button**. A shortcut menu appears.

3. Click on **Delete**. The Confirm File Delete dialog box opens.

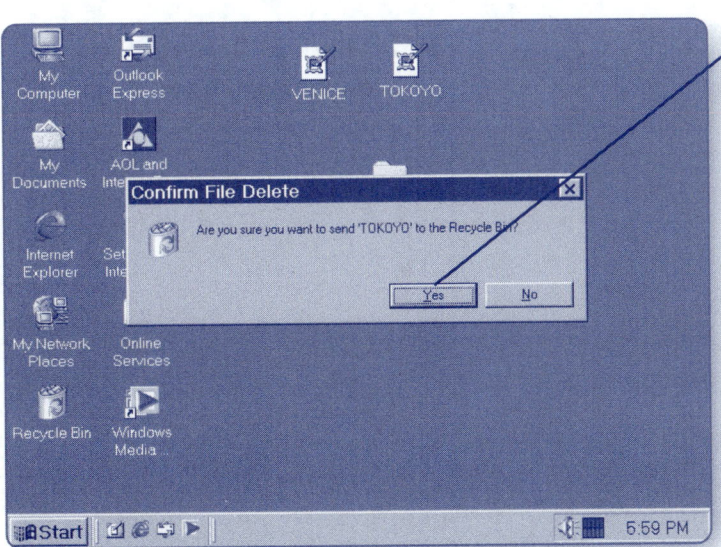

4. Click on **Yes**. The icon is deleted and placed in the Recycle Bin.

TIP

An optional method of deleting icons or files is to drag them directly to the Recycle Bin.

Creating a Shortcut

It can be an annoyance to dig through the profusion of selections on the Start menu just to get to your favorite program. Create a shortcut on your desktop!

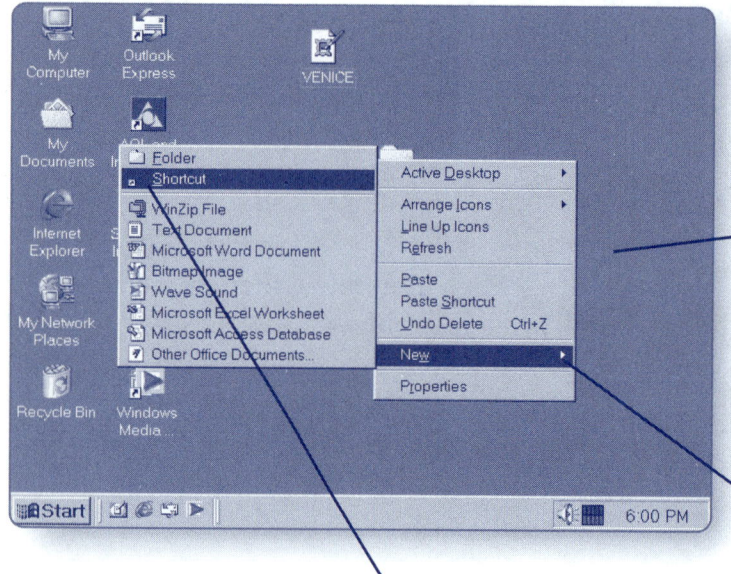

You can even create a shortcut for a document that you use frequently. Windows will open the creating program and that specific file for you.

1. Position the **mouse pointer** over a blank area of the Windows desktop.

2. Click the **right mouse button**. A shortcut menu appears.

3. Click on **New**. The New submenu appears.

4. Click on **Shortcut**. The Create Shortcut dialog box opens.

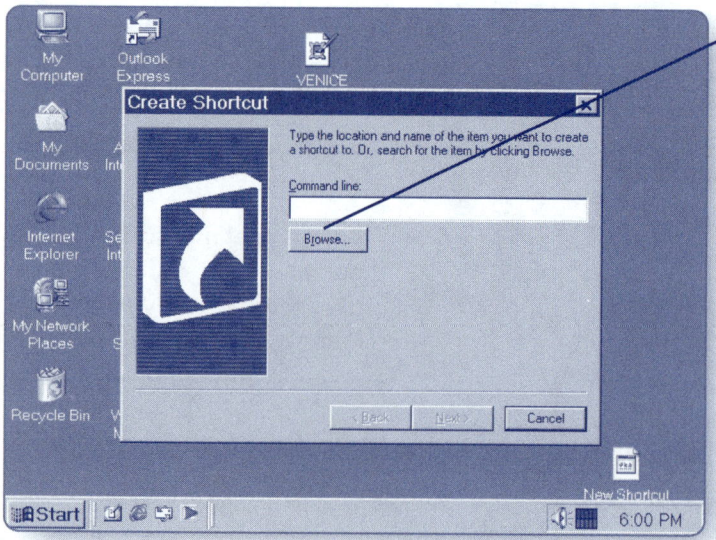

5. Click on **Browse**. The Browse dialog box opens.

CREATING A SHORTCUT

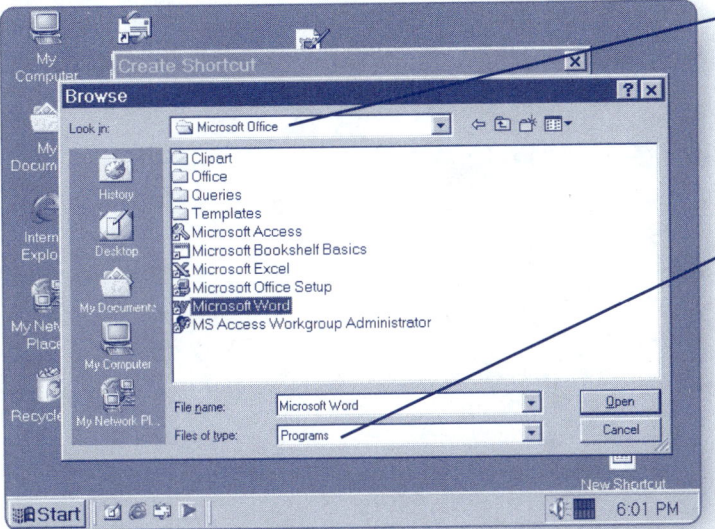

6. **Locate** the **folder** that has the program or document to which you want to create a shortcut. A list of all available programs in that folder appears.

If you are looking for a document and not a program, change the Files of type: list box to All Files instead of Programs. You will then see documents as well as programs.

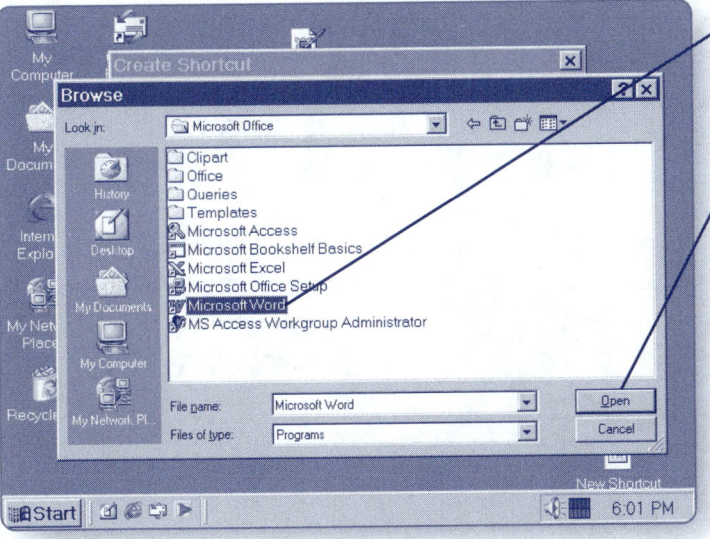

7. **Select** the **desired program** or **document**. The item is highlighted.

8. **Click** on **Open**. The Browse dialog box closes, and the program or document name (including the location) appears in the Create Shortcut dialog box.

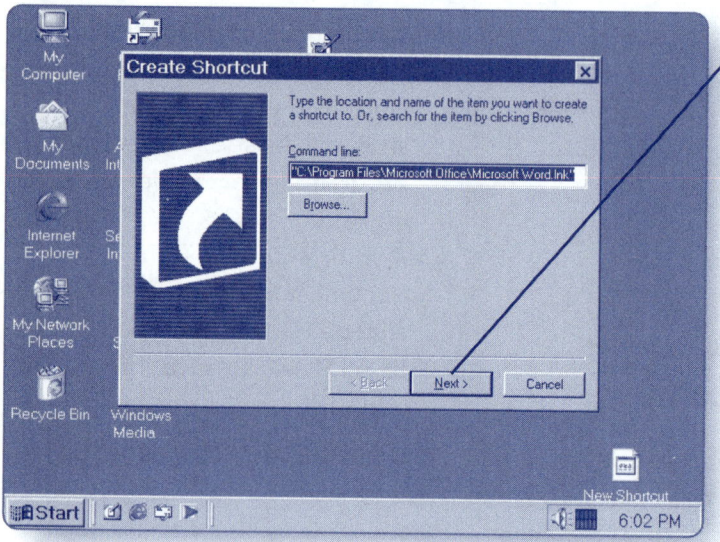

9. Click on **Next**. The Select a Title for the Program dialog box opens.

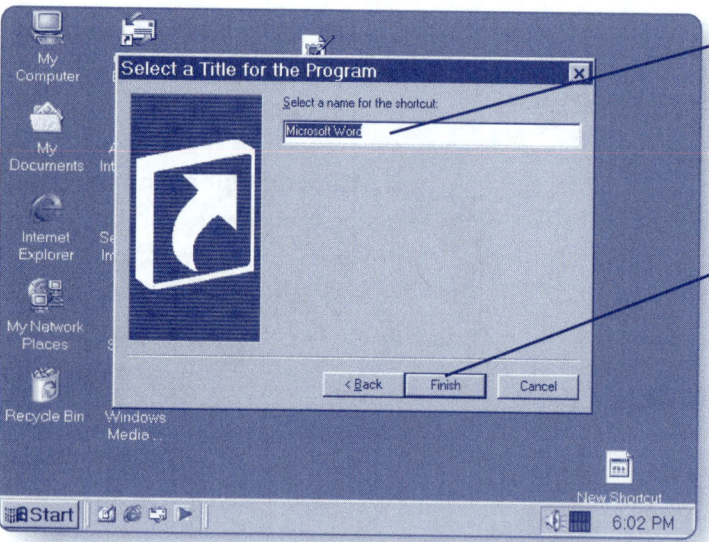

10. Optionally, **type** a **new name** for the icon if desired. This name represents only what you see on the desktop, not the actual file name.

11. Click on **Finish**. The Select a Title for the Program dialog box closes, and the new shortcut appears on your desktop.

CREATING A SHORTCUT   217

Changing an Icon

Shortcuts that you create have an icon associated with them. If you've created a shortcut to a document, the icon used is the one associated with the document's program icon. You can select from other icons.

Shortcuts can be identified by a small arrow in the lower-left corner of the shortcut icon.

> **TIP**
> Click on any shortcut to launch the program and/or document associated with it.

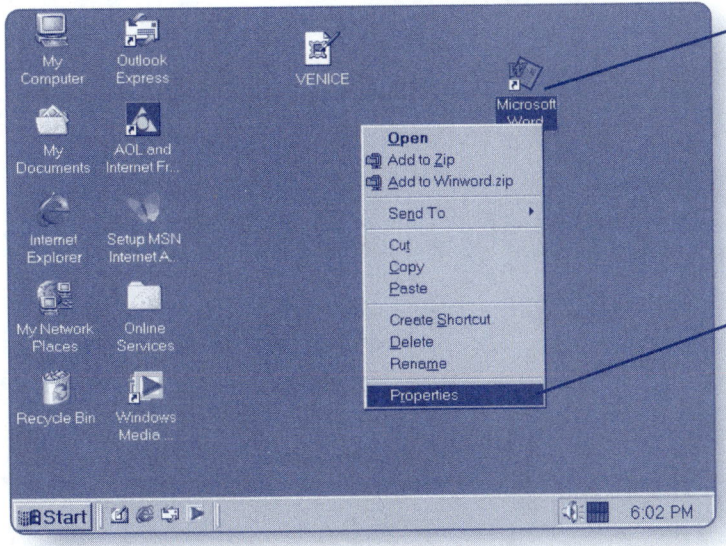

1. Position the **mouse pointer** over the icon you want to change. The icon is selected.

2. Click the **right mouse button**. A shortcut menu appears.

3. Click on **Properties**. The Properties dialog box opens.

CHAPTER 15: CUSTOMIZING THE DESKTOP

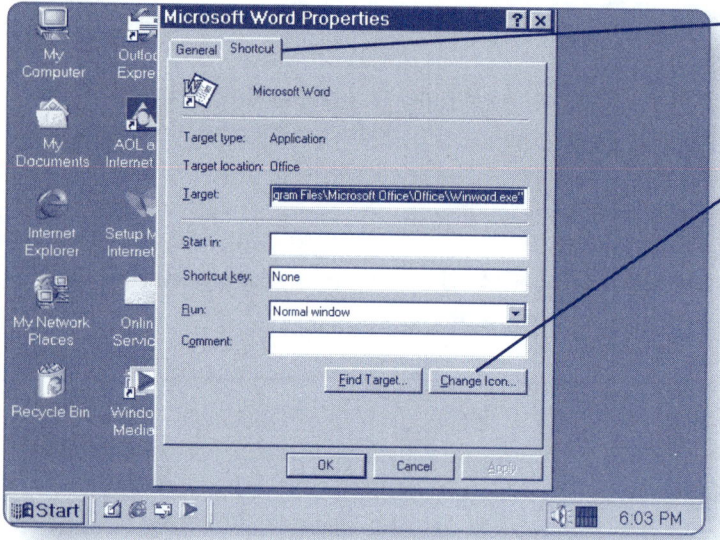

4. Click on the **Shortcut tab** if necessary. The Shortcut tab comes to the front.

5. Click on **Change Icon**. The Change Icon dialog box opens.

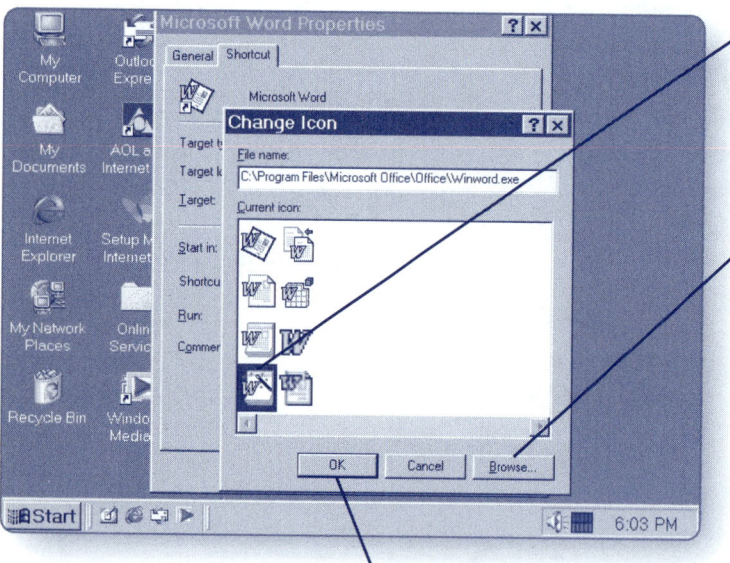

6. Click on the **icon** you want to use. The icon is highlighted.

NOTE

If you have purchased other icon software, click on the Browse button to navigate to the folder that contains the other icons.

7. Click on **OK**. The Properties dialog box returns.

RENAMING AN ICON 219

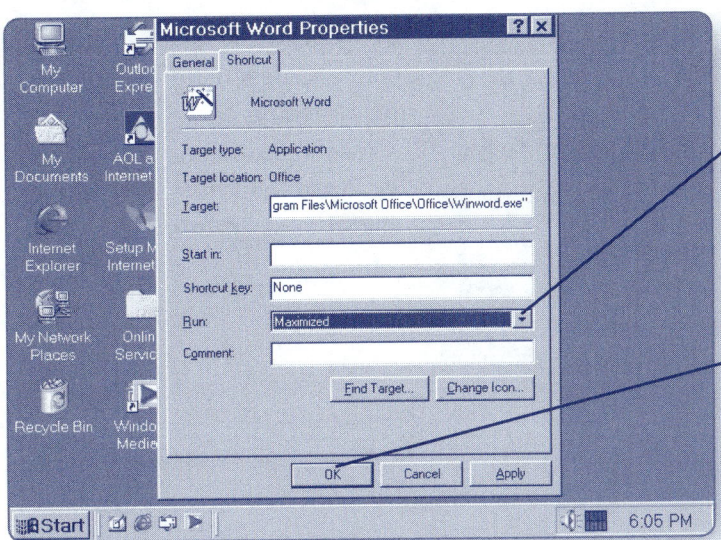

TIP
To always have a full screen when you launch the shortcut, click on the Run: down arrow (▼) and then select Maximized.

8. Click on **OK**. The Properties dialog box closes, and the current icon is replaced with the newly selected one.

Renaming an Icon

You can rename any icon on your desktop except the Recycle Bin and the Set Up The Microsoft Network icons.

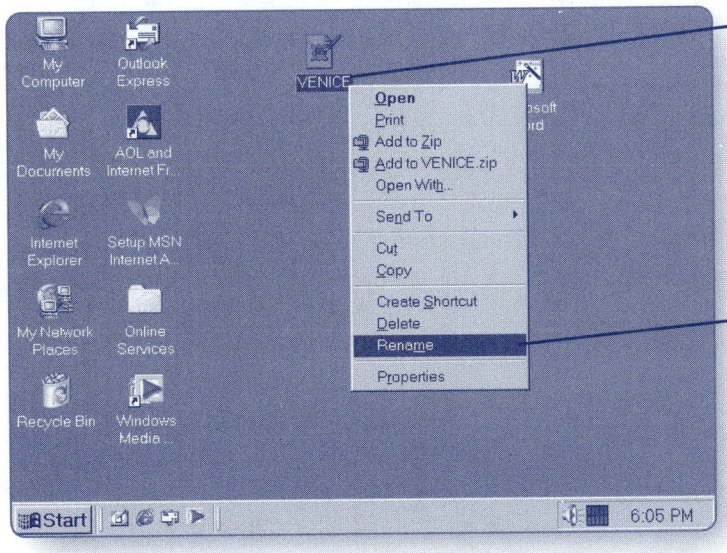

1. Position the **mouse pointer** over the icon you want to rename. The icon is selected.

2. Click the **right mouse button**. A shortcut menu appears.

3. Click on **Rename**. The current icon name appears highlighted.

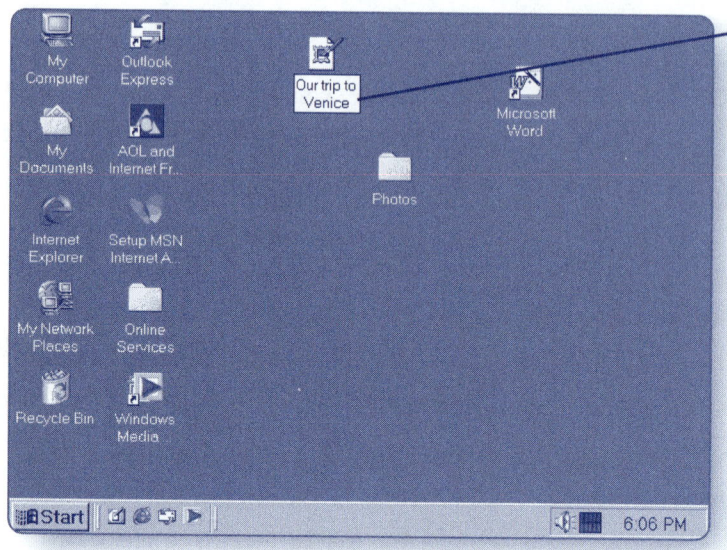

4. Type a **new name** for the icon. The new name replaces the old name.

5. Press the **Enter key**. The change is accepted.

Editing the Start Menu

If you look in Windows Explorer, in the Windows folder you will see another folder called *Start Menu*. The items you see when you click on the Start button are stored in this folder. You can control which items are accessible from the Start menu and in which order they are displayed.

Reorganizing the Start Menu

You have the capability to easily reorganize the Start menu in Windows.

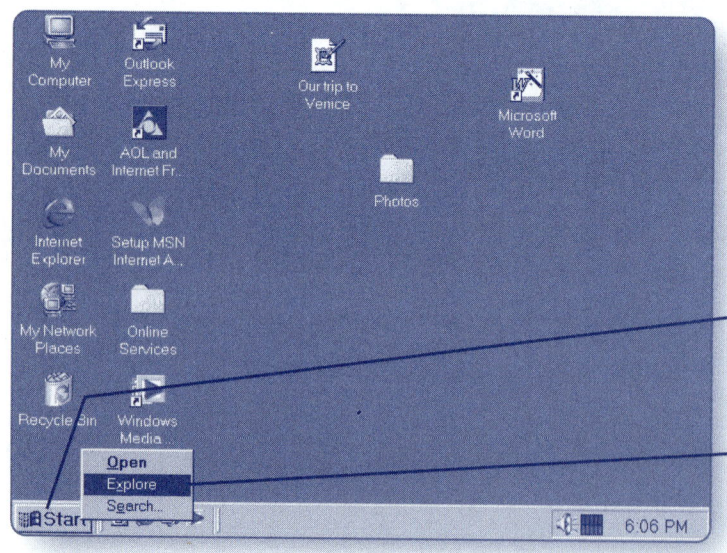

1. Right-click on the **Start button**. A shortcut menu appears.

2. Click on **Explore**. The Explorer window opens at the Start Menu folder.

EDITING THE START MENU 221

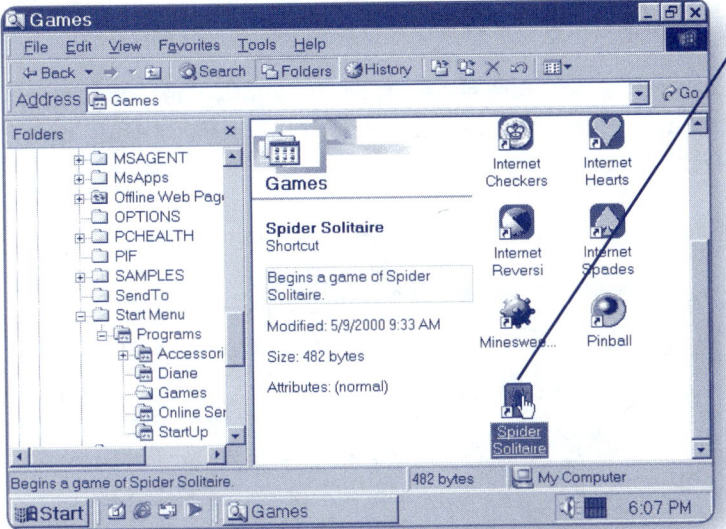

3. Locate, **press**, and **hold** the **mouse button** on the folder or shortcut to be moved. The selected item is highlighted.

TIP

Hold down the Ctrl key to select multiple items to move at the same time or hold down the Shift key to select a consecutive list of items.

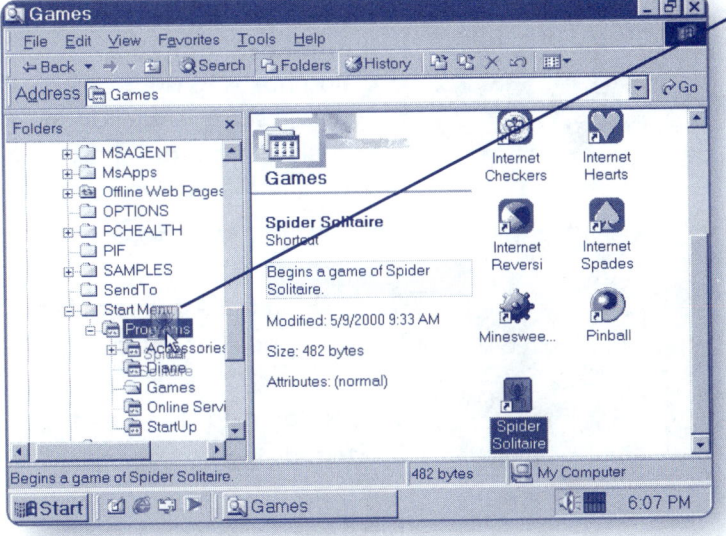

4. Drag the **item** to the new desired folder or location. You'll see an outline of the moved item as you are dragging it.

5. Release the **mouse button**. The selected item(s) drop into the new location.

Adding an Item to the Start Menu

You can add a program shortcut or frequently-used document to the Start menu. You can accomplish this several ways, but here is the easiest method.

1. **Click** on the **Start button**. The Start menu appears.

2. **Click** on **Settings**. The Settings submenu appears.

3. **Click** on **Taskbar and Start Menu**. The Taskbar and Start Menu Properties dialog box opens.

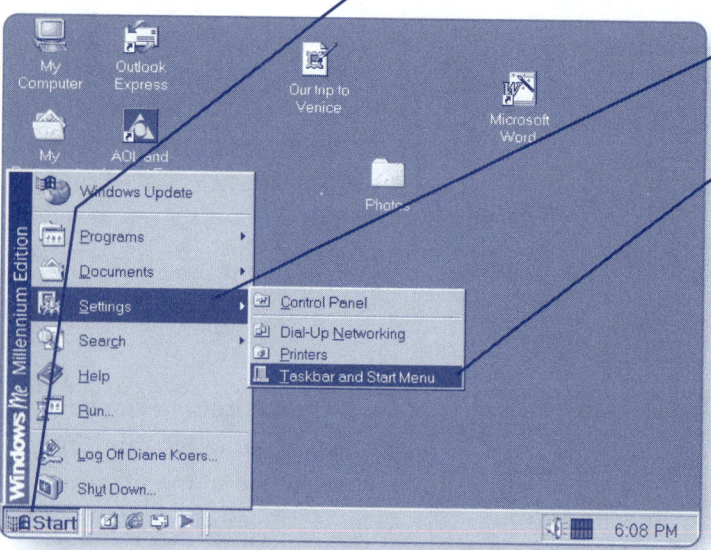

> **TIP**
>
> An alternative way to open the Taskbar Properties dialog box is to right-click on the Taskbar, and click on Properties from the short-cut menu that appears.

4. **Click** on the **Advanced tab**. The tab appears in the front.

5. **Click** on **Add**. The Create Shortcut dialog box opens.

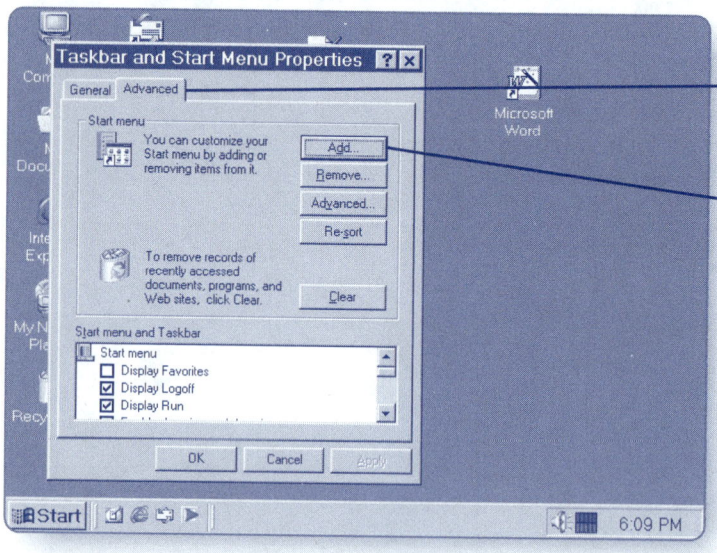

EDITING THE START MENU   223

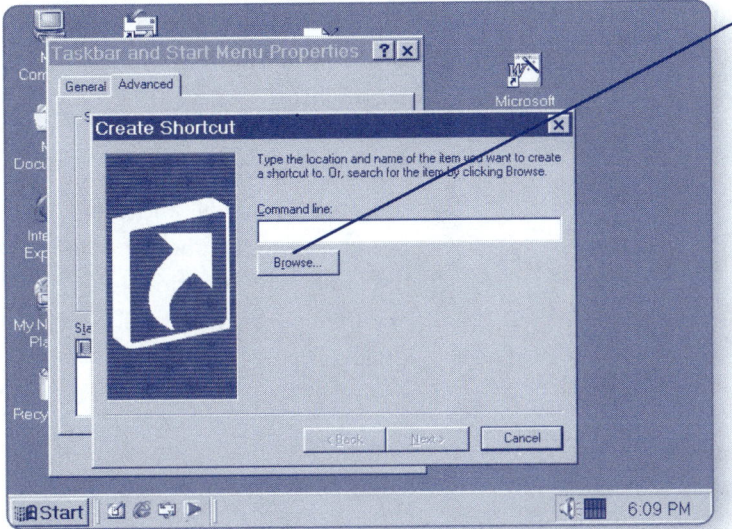

6. Click on **Browse**. The Browse dialog box opens.

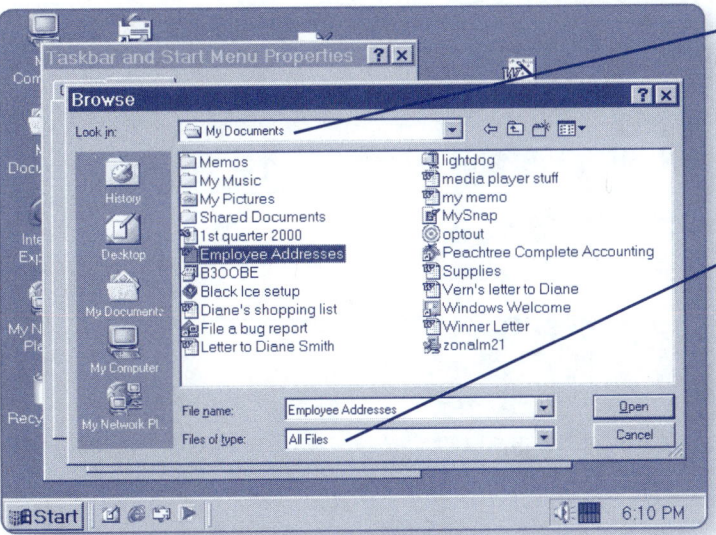

7. Locate the **folder** that has the program or document to which you want to create a shortcut. A list of all available programs in that folder appears.

If you are looking for a document rather than a program, change the Files of type: list box to All Files instead of Programs. You will then see documents as well as programs.

224 CHAPTER 15: CUSTOMIZING THE DESKTOP

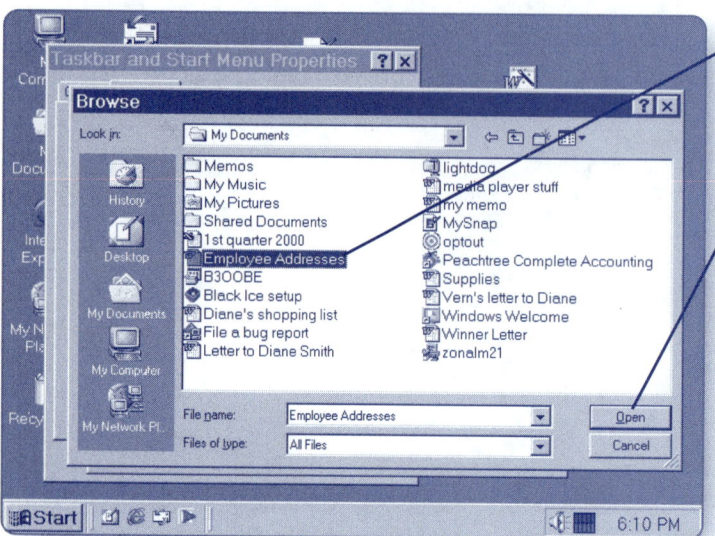

8. Select the **desired program** or **document**. The item is highlighted.

9. Click on **Open**. The Browse dialog box closes, and the program or document name (including the location) appears in the Create Shortcut dialog box.

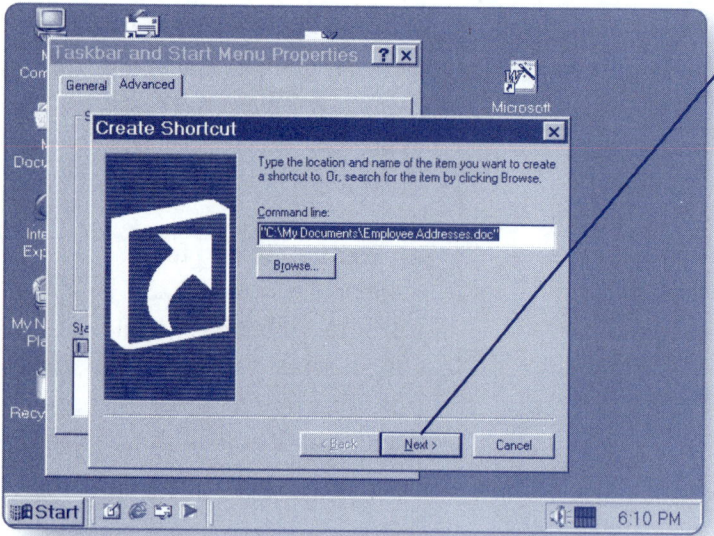

10. Click on **Next**. The Select Program Folder dialog box opens.

EDITING THE START MENU 225

11. **Click** on the **folder** in which you want the shortcut to appear. The folder is selected. If you want the item to be stored on the first level of the Start menu, click on the Start Menu folder.

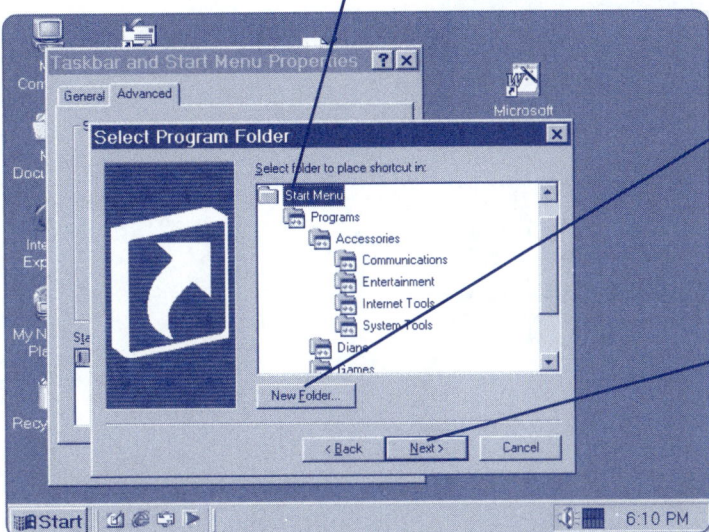

TIP

You can also create a new folder to store the shortcut in by clicking on the New Folder button and typing a name for the new folder.

12. **Click** on **Next**. The Select a Title for the Program dialog box opens.

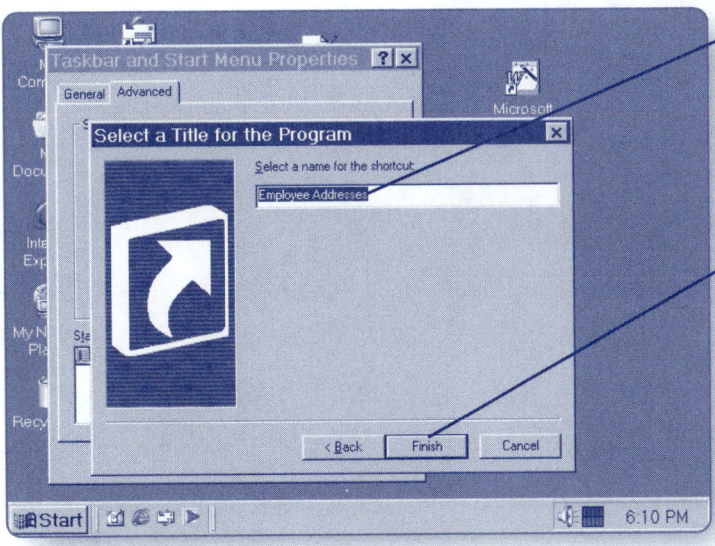

13. **Type** a **new name** for this icon if desired. This name represents what you see on the Start menu, not the actual file name.

14. **Click** on **Finish**. The Select a Title for the Program dialog box closes.

226 CHAPTER 15: CUSTOMIZING THE DESKTOP

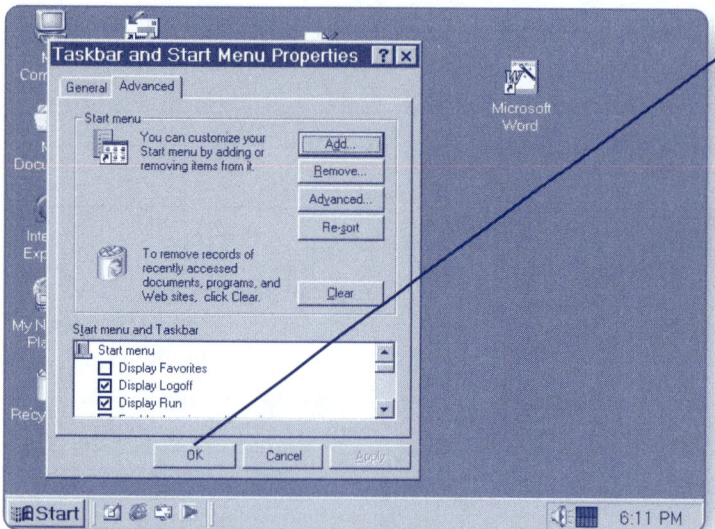

15. **Click** on **OK**. The Taskbar Properties dialog box closes.

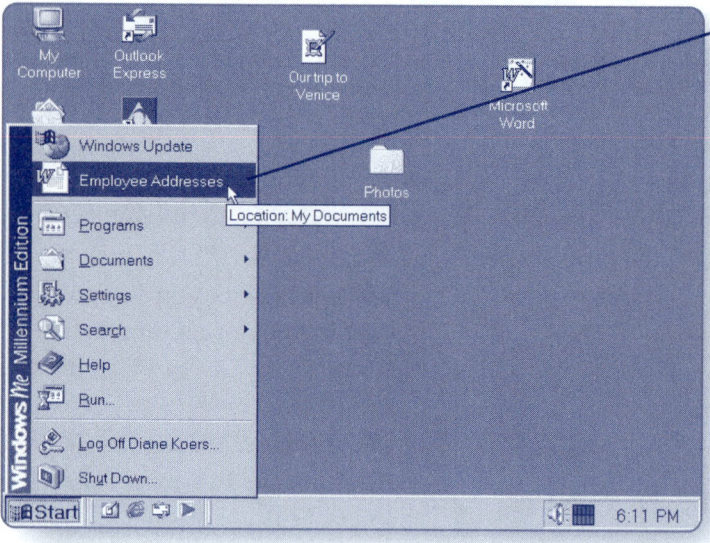

The new item is displayed on the Start menu. Click on the item to launch it.

Removing an Item from the Start Menu

When you delete an item from the Start menu, you are not deleting a program or document itself, only the shortcut that points to that particular program or document. The shortcut is then placed in the Recycle Bin.

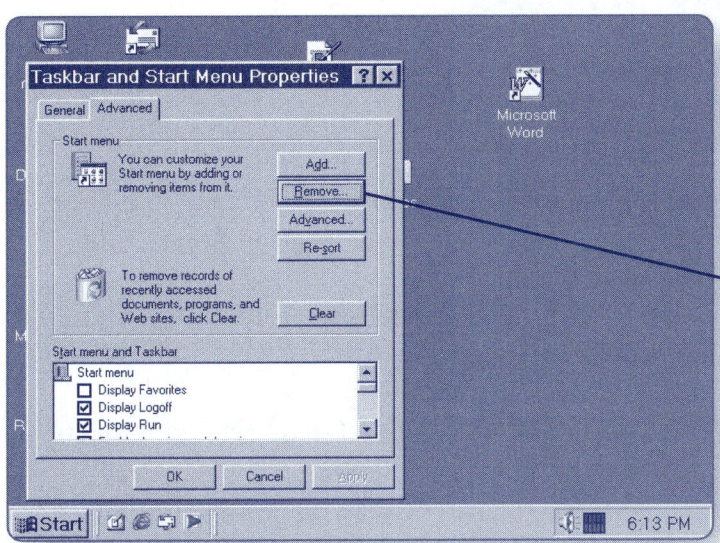

1. **Follow steps 1** through **4** in "Adding an Item to the Start Menu." The Advanced tab moves to the front of the Taskbar and Start Menu Properties dialog box.

2. **Click** on **Remove**. The Remove Shortcuts/Folders dialog box opens with a list of all folders and documents on the Start Menu displayed.

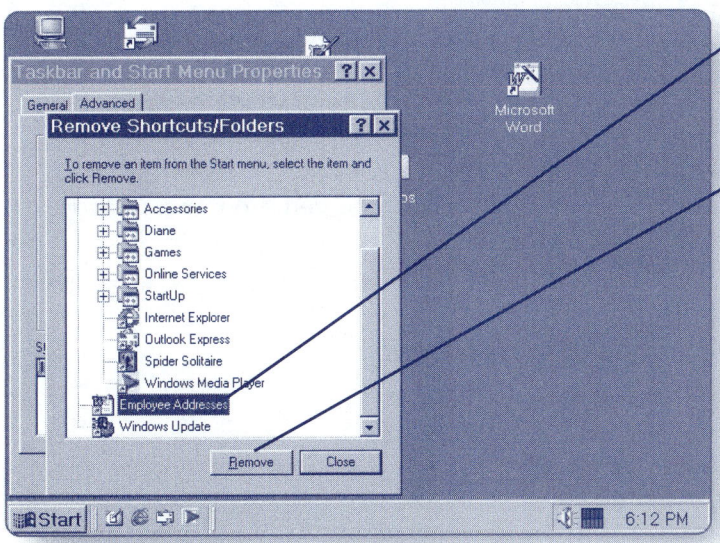

3. **Click** on the **folder** or **shortcut** you want to delete. The item is selected.

4. **Click** on **Remove**. The item is removed from the Start menu.

228 CHAPTER 15: CUSTOMIZING THE DESKTOP

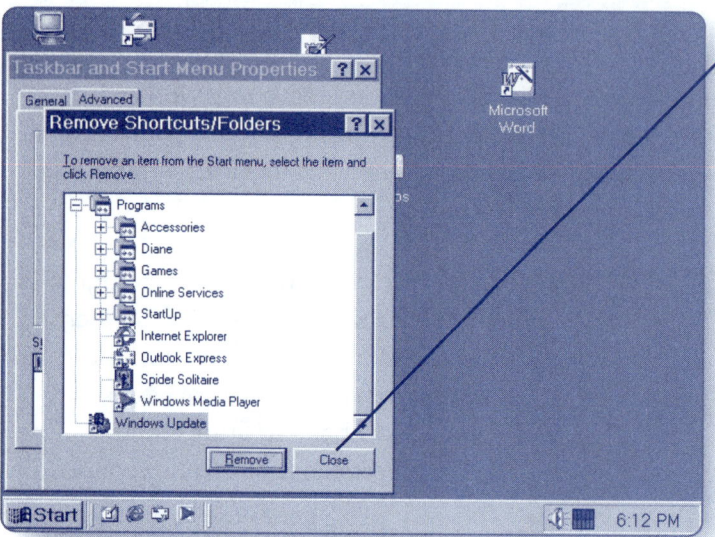

5. Click on **Close**. The Remove Shortcuts/Folders dialog box closes.

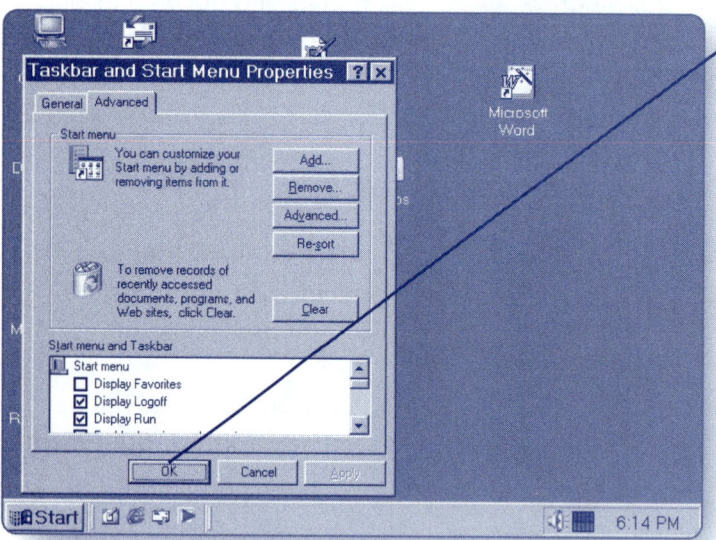

6. Click on **OK**. The Taskbar and Start Menu Properties dialog box closes.

TIP
Another way to remove an item from the Start menu is to drag the undesired item on to the Windows desktop, and then drag the item from the desktop to the Recycle Bin.

Customizing the Taskbar

You can control the actions of the Taskbar. You can decide when and where the Taskbar is displayed or even add more toolbars to the Taskbar.

Moving the Taskbar

By default, the Taskbar is located at the bottom of the screen. However, you can move it to any side of your screen.

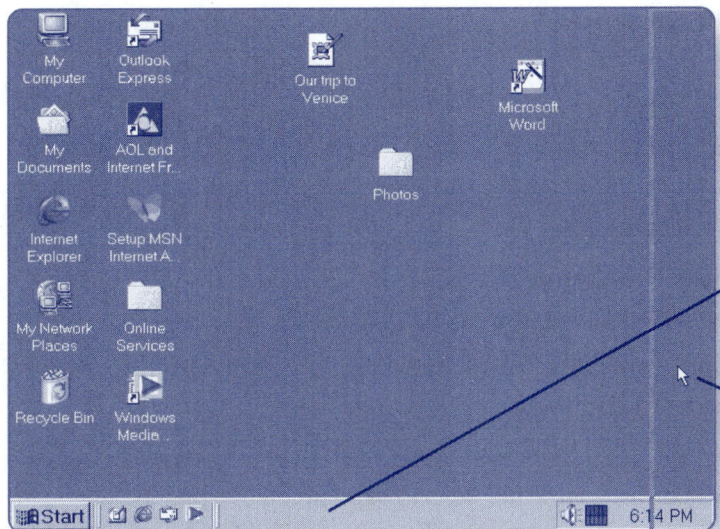

1. **Press** and **hold** the **mouse button** on a blank area of the Taskbar.

2. Drag the **Taskbar** to the desired side of the screen. An outline of the Taskbar appears at the new location.

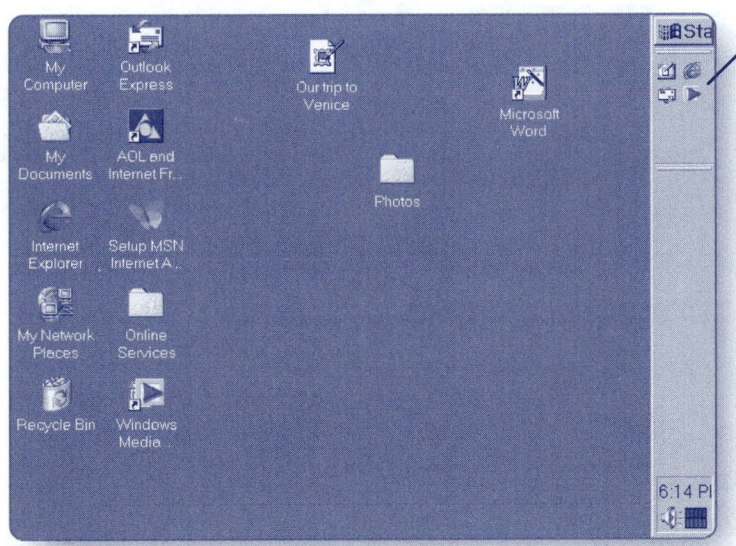

3. Release the **mouse button**.

The Taskbar is displayed at the new location.

Changing Taskbar Options

You can change the display of the Taskbar so that it will remain hidden until you call for it.

The Taskbar display options include the following:

- **Always on top.** Guarantees that the Taskbar is always visible, even when running a program in a maximized window.

- **Auto hide.** Allows the Taskbar to be hidden until you point to the location where the Taskbar usually resides, and then the Taskbar reappears.

- **Show small icons in Start menu.** Reduces the size of the menu items on the Start menu.

- **Show clock.** Controls whether the clock displays in the corner of the Taskbar.

- **Use personalized menus.** Applies to the Programs menu and controls whether Windows keeps track of the programs you use most often and hides the programs you haven't used in a long time.

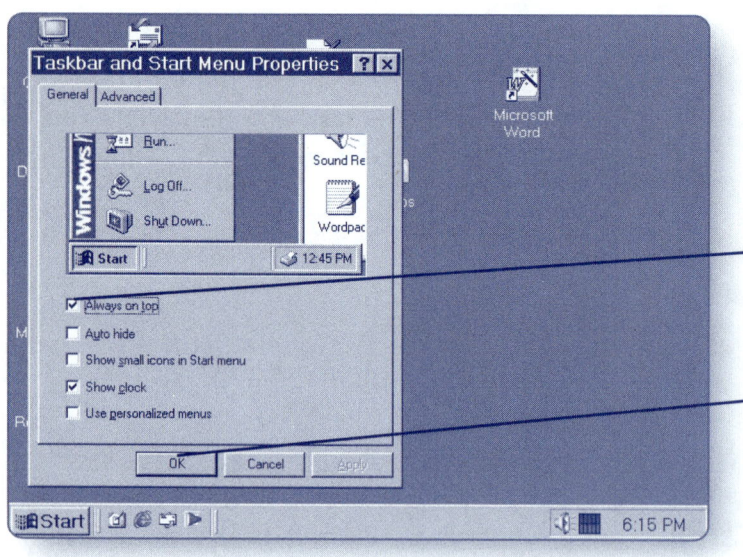

1. Follow steps 1 through **3** in "Adding an Item to the Start Menu." The Taskbar and Start Menu Properties dialog box opens.

2. Click on the desired **options**. A ✔ appears in each selected choice.

3. Click on **OK**. The dialog box closes, and the new options are applied.

16

Tinkering with the Control Panel

How can I make my mouse less sensitive? Where do I set the current date? You'll find the answers to these questions, as well as others related to fine-tuning your computer, in the Control Panel. In this chapter, you'll learn how to:

- Change the current date and time
- Change the way the mouse works
- Add new software and Windows components
- Create a Windows startup disk
- Set up and change passwords
- Set up multiple users
- Change accessibility options

Opening the Control Panel

The Control Panel can be accessed from the Start menu or from the My Computer icon.

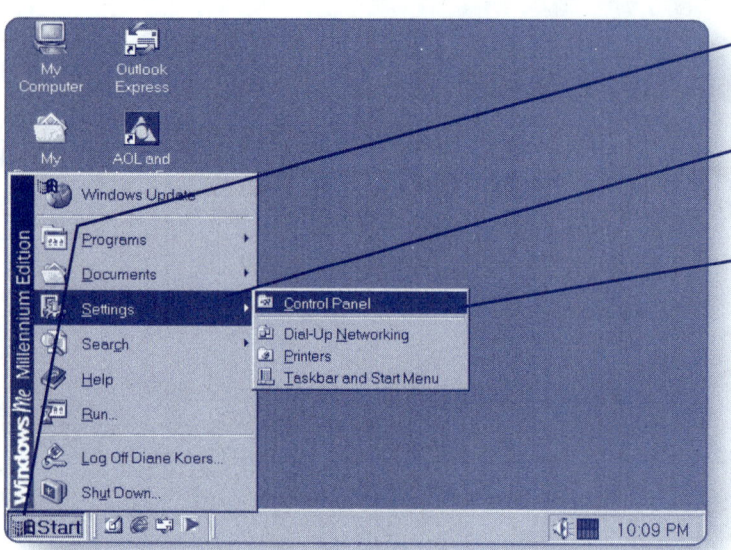

1. **Click** on the **Start button**. The Start menu appears.

2. **Click** on **Settings**. The Settings menu appears.

3. **Click** on **Control Panel**. The Control Panel window opens displaying commonly used Control Panel options.

Changing the Current Date and Time

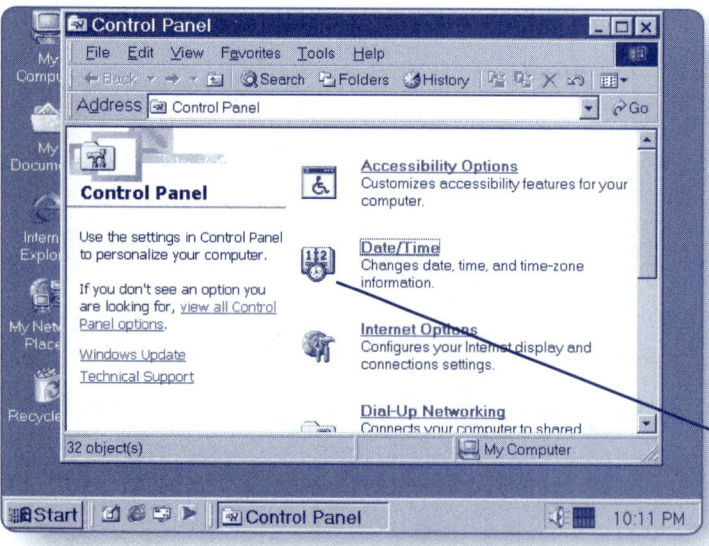

It's important to have the correct date and time, especially when you need to insert the current date into a document on which you are working.

1. **Click** on **Date/Time**. The Date/Time Properties dialog box opens.

CHANGING THE CURRENT DATE AND TIME 233

From here you have four options that you can set:

- **The current month.** Click on the down arrow (▼) to choose the current month.
- **The current year.** Click on the up/down arrows (♦) to select the current year.
- **The current day.** Click on the current day of the month.
- **The current time.** Click on the portion of the time you want to change, and then click on the up/down arrows (♦).

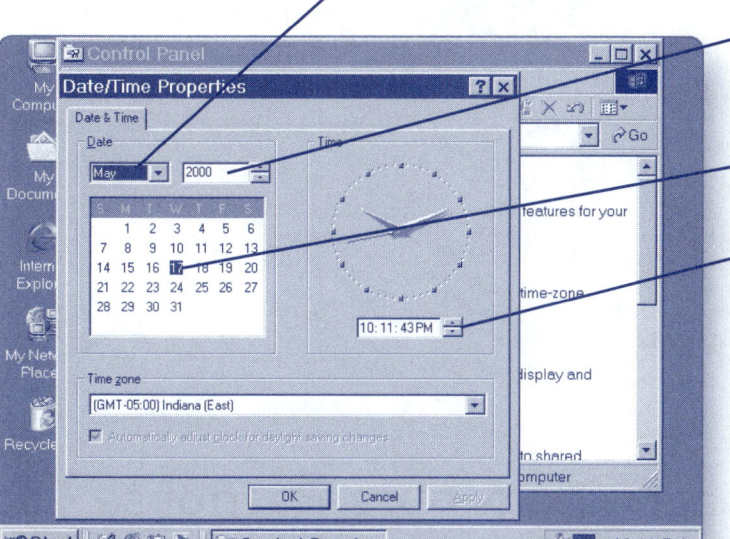

2. Make any desired **changes** to the date or time.

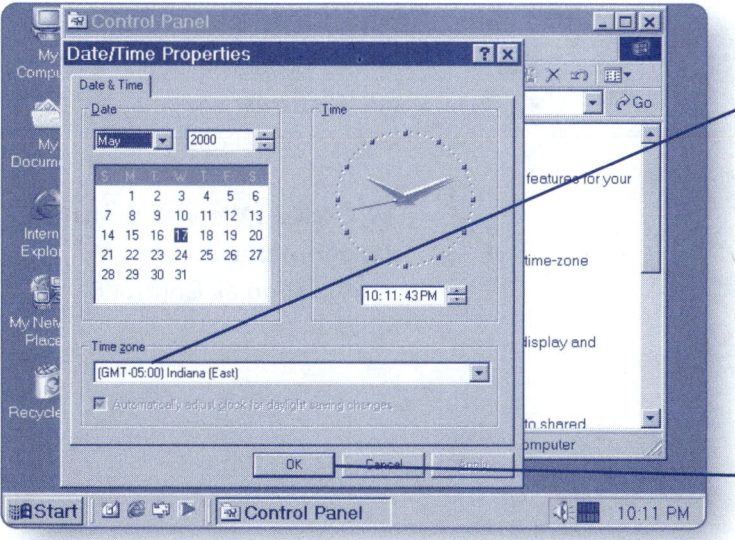

NOTE

Be sure you make adjustments according to your time zone. Windows knows when time changes (such as Daylight Savings Time) occur and will adjust the time accordingly. Click on the Time Zone tab to select your zone.

3. Click on **OK**. The Date/Time Properties dialog box closes.

234 CHAPTER 16: TINKERING WITH THE CONTROL PANEL

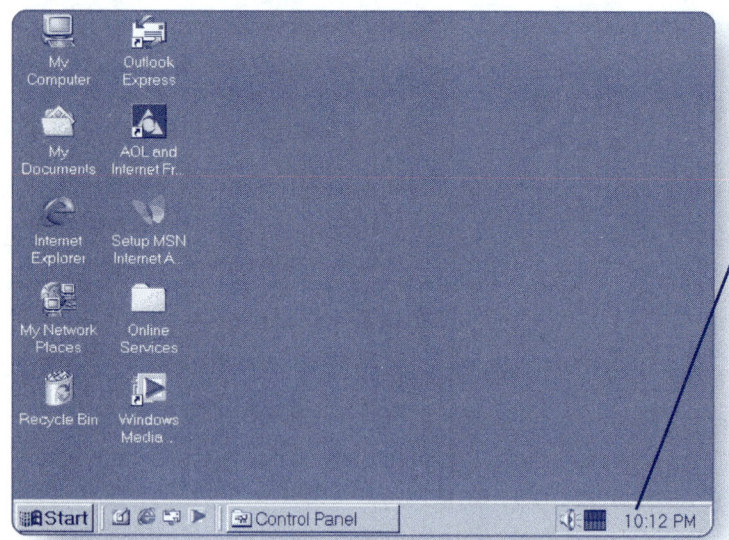

TIP
A quick way to access the Date/Time Properties dialog box is to double-click on the current time in the System Tray.

Changing Mouse Response

You can make the mouse respond according to your preferences. You can temper the motion of the mouse, select different pointers, or even reverse the mouse buttons.

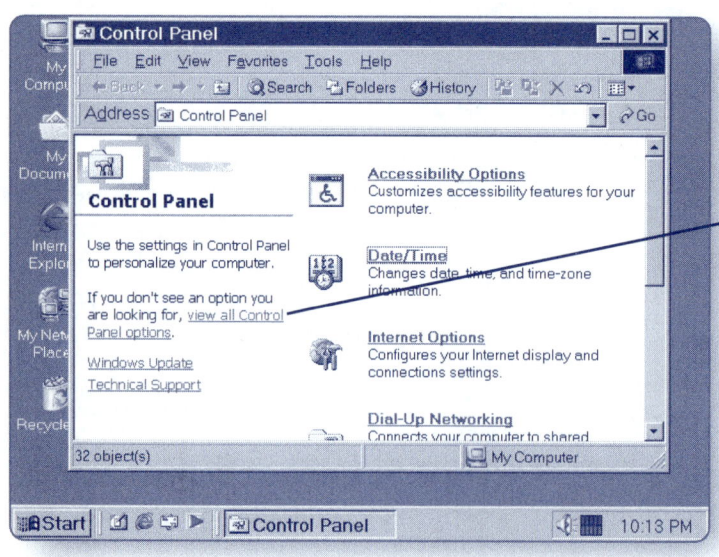

Before you can change the mouse properties, you need to tell Windows to display all Control Panel options.

1. Click on **View all Control Panel options**. Icons representing all Control Panel functions appear.

CHANGING MOUSE RESPONSE   235

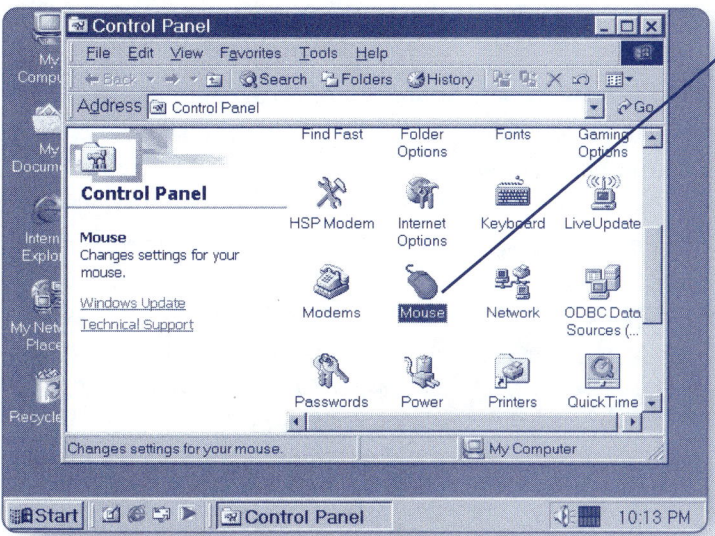

2. From the Control Panel window, **click** on **Mouse**. The Mouse Properties dialog box opens.

The choices displayed in the Mouse Properties dialog box vary depending on the brand of mouse you have installed on your computer. The selections displayed in this section are specific to the Microsoft IntelliPoint mouse.

Changing Basic Mouse Responses

1. If necessary, **click** on the **Buttons tab**. The Buttons tab appears in front. From here you can:

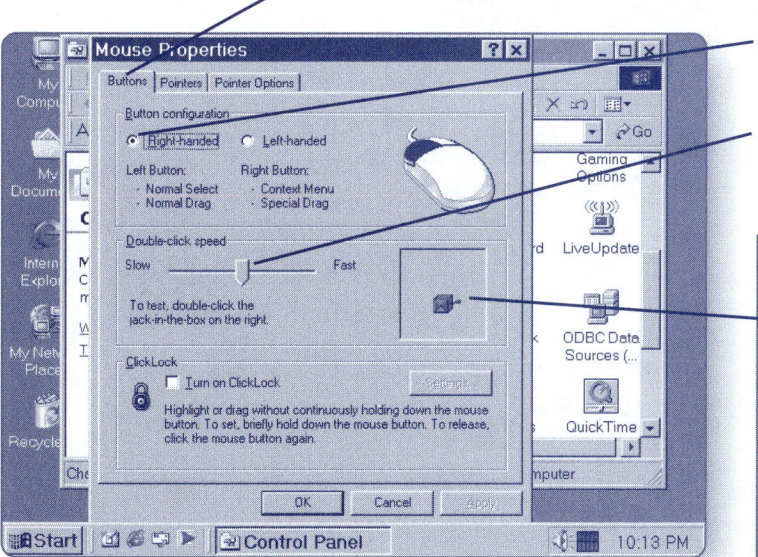

- Choose your main mouse button (right or left).
- Select the speed at which double-clicks initiate action.

TIP

Test the double-click speed by double-clicking in the test area. If you can easily make the jack-in-the-box pop up or down, you have correctly set the double-click speed.

Changing Mouse Pointers

Instead of the traditional hourglass or arrowhead on the mouse pointer, how about an apple or a hand? You can choose from a variety of pointers.

1. Click on the **Pointers tab**. The Pointers tab appears in front.

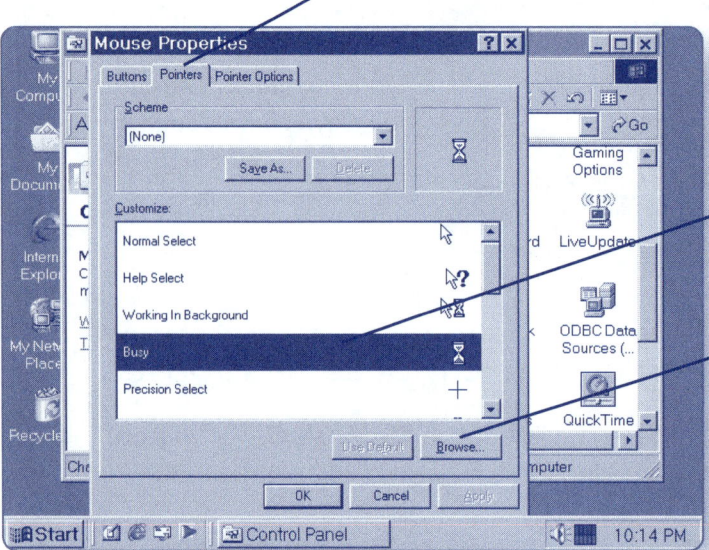

You'll see the current selection of mouse pointers for various tasks. You can choose from many others.

2. Click on the **pointer** you want to change. The pointer is selected.

3. Click on **Browse**. The Browse dialog box opens and displays a selection of mouse pointers.

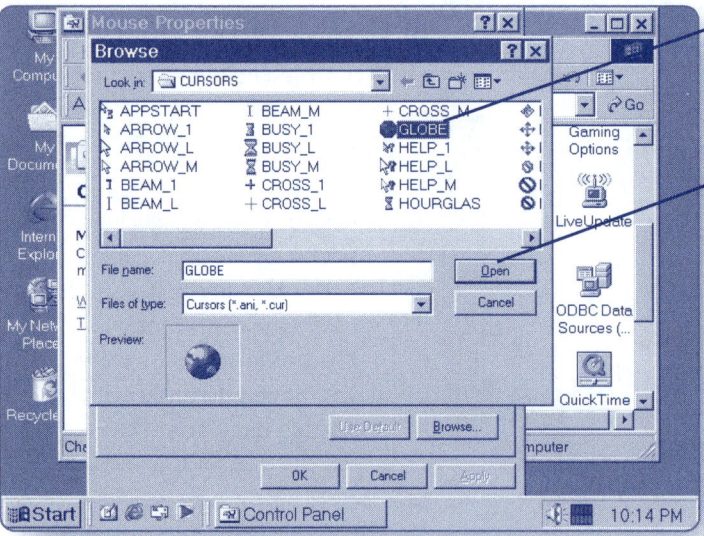

4. Click on the **pointer** you want to use. A sample appears in the Preview: box.

5. Click on **Open** to accept the selection. The Browse dialog box closes.

CHANGING MOUSE RESPONSE 237

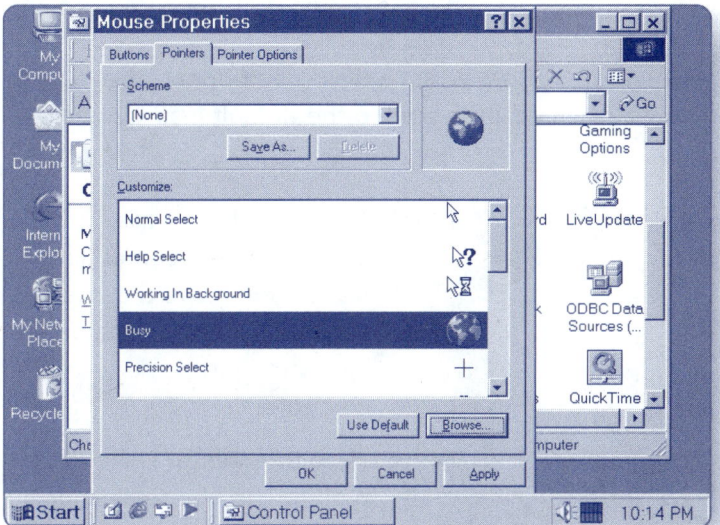

6. Repeat Steps 2 through **5** for each additional mouse pointer you want to change.

Changing Mouse Visibility

Changing the visibility of the mouse arrow can be very helpful, especially when using a laptop computer. Sometimes the mouse appears to get "lost."

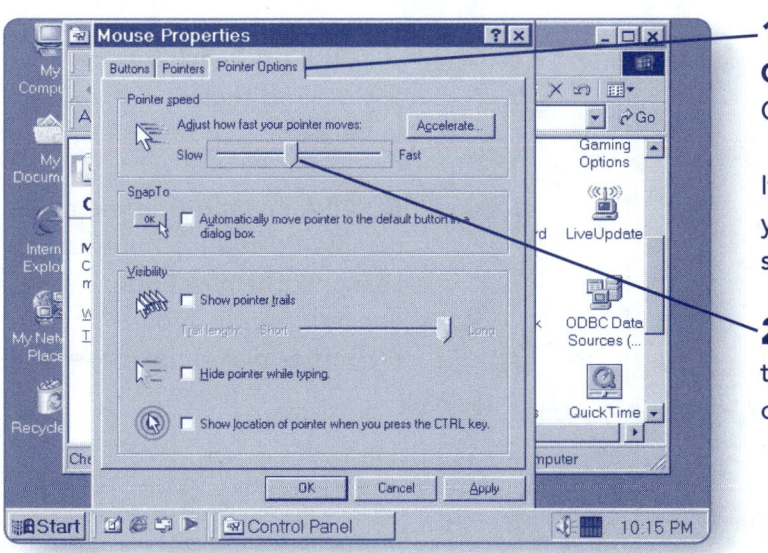

1. Click on the **Pointer Options tab**. The Pointer Options tab appears in front.

If your mouse moves faster than you'd like it to, change the speed.

2. Click and drag the **slide bar** to make the mouse move faster or slower across the screen.

Other options you can change include:

- Use the snap option. When a dialog box opens, the mouse pointer automatically moves to the default (usually the OK) button.

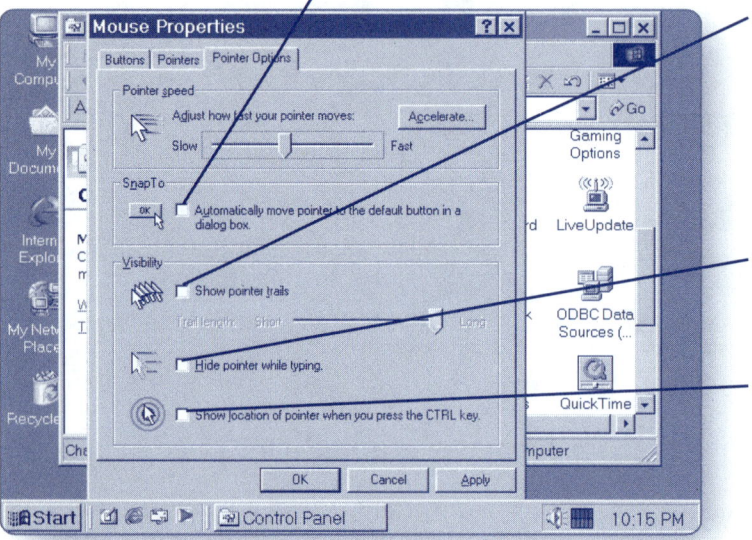

- Display pointer trails. This option shows a comet-like trail as you move the mouse arrow. This one is especially handy on notebook computers.

- Hide the pointer while typing. The pointer reappears when you move the mouse.

- Show the location of the pointer when you press the Ctrl key. A series of gray circles helps you quickly locate the mouse.

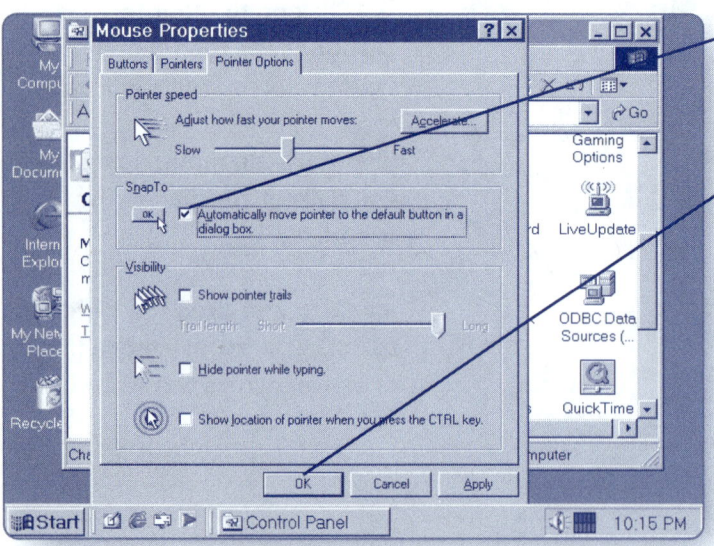

3. Click the **check box** next to any desired choice. A ✔ appears in the box.

4. Click on **OK** when you have completed making mouse-arrow changes. The new options are applied, and the Mouse Properties dialog box closes.

Adding and Removing Programs

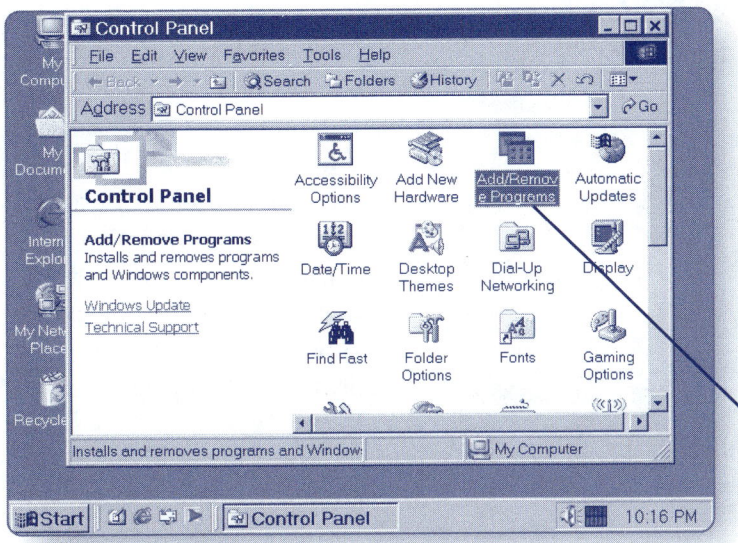

When it comes time to install or uninstall software on your computer, the Add/Remove Programs icon simplifies the process. This is also the place to go when you need to add more Windows components (such as Accessibility Options) or additional Systems tools (such as Microsoft Backup).

1. Click on **Add/Remove Programs**. The Add/Remove Programs Properties dialog box opens.

Installing a New Program

When installing a new software program, follow the manufacturer's instructions or these steps.

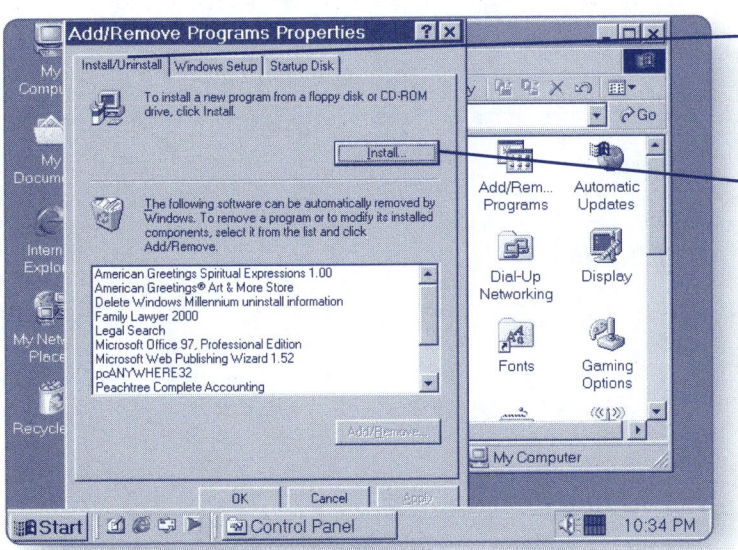

1. Click on the **Install/Uninstall tab**. The Install/Uninstall tab moves to the front.

2. Click on **Install**. The Install Wizard begins.

240 CHAPTER 16: TINKERING WITH THE CONTROL PANEL

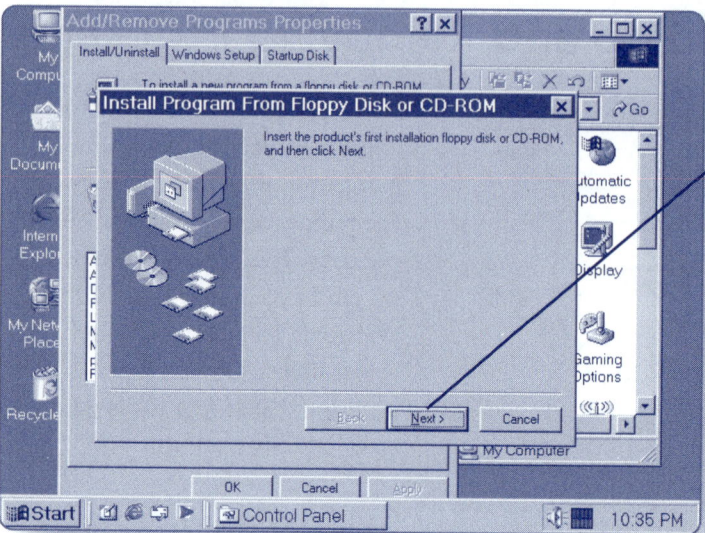

3. Insert the software installation **disk** or **CD**.

4. Click on **Next**. The next screen appears.

Windows searches the floppy disk drive first; then, if it doesn't find any type of installation or setup program, it searches the CD-ROM drive. The suggested setup program that it finds is usually the correct program.

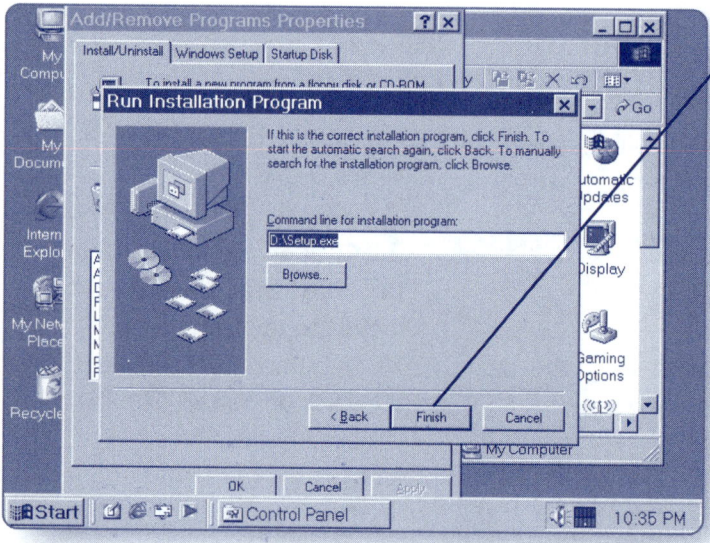

5. Click on **Finish**. The installation begins. You may need to answer individual questions from the software manufacturer. It's probably a good idea to accept the installation selections offered by the manufacturer.

Uninstalling a Program

If you have a program you no longer want on your computer, you usually can use the Windows uninstaller to remove the program. This is usually the cleanest way to remove a program, because Windows not only deletes the program files, but also cleans the Windows registry of any markers related to that program. Also, any extra files frequently stored in the Windows directory, such as .dll or .ini files, will safely be removed. Not all programs are available to uninstall using this method.

> **NOTE**
> The Windows registry is an encoded central database file that Windows uses to store information about the hardware, software, and preferences on your computer.

1. Click on the **Install/Uninstall tab**. The Install/Uninstall tab appears in front. You'll see a list of programs that can be automatically removed by Windows.

2. Click on the **program** you want to uninstall. The selected item is highlighted.

3. Click on **Add/Remove**. The Confirm File Deletion dialog box opens.

Depending upon the application you're removing, you may be prompted to insert the original CD.

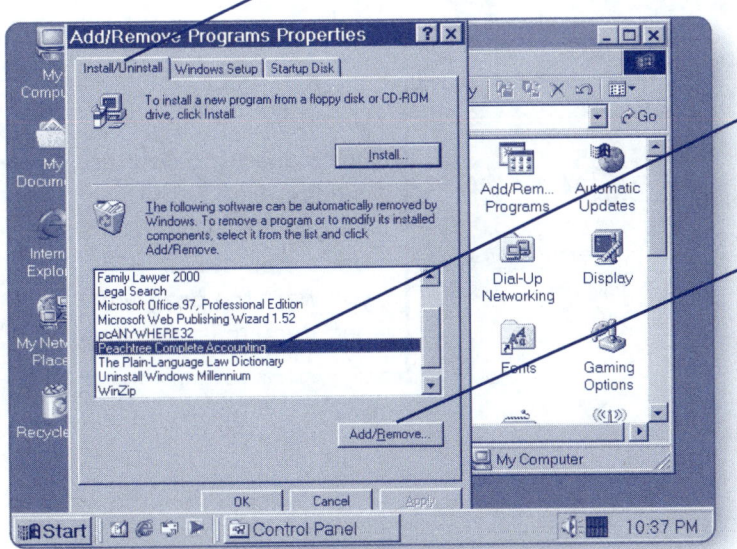

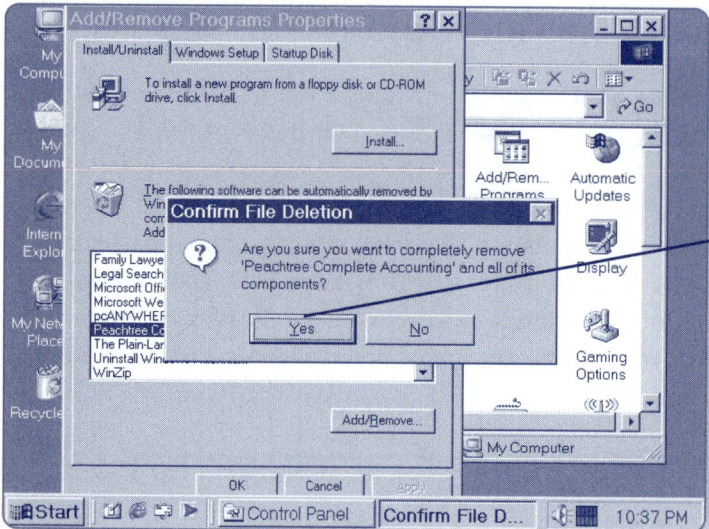

> **NOTE**
> Your screens may vary from the ones shown.

4. Click on **Yes**. The Remove Programs From Your Computer dialog box opens, and Windows begins the removal process.

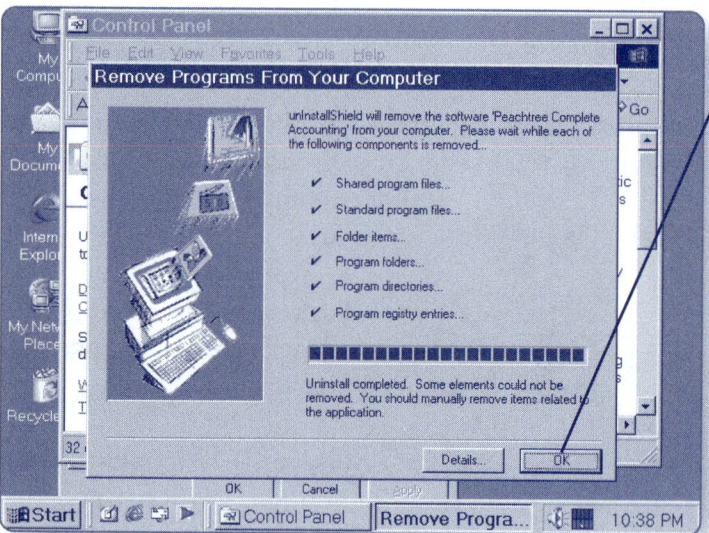

5. Click on **OK** when the uninstall process is completed. The Remove Programs From Your Computer dialog box closes.

> **NOTE**
> When a program is uninstalled and deleted, it is not placed in the Recycle Bin. There is no Undo step available. If you want the program back, you must reinstall it.

Creating a Windows Startup Disk

A Windows Millennium Edition emergency startup disk is an absolute *must have* item. If your system refuses to boot up, this disk stores the most critical files needed to get you back up and running again. When you install Windows Millennium Edition, you are advised to create a startup disk at that time. If you didn't, you should do it now. You will need one disk for this process.

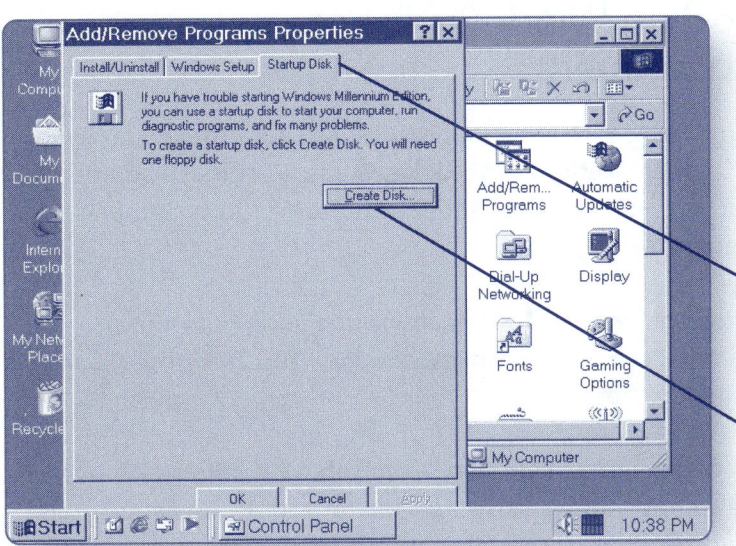

1. **Click** on the **Startup Disk tab**. The Startup Disk tab appears in front.

2. **Click** on **Create Disk**. Windows prepares to copy files.

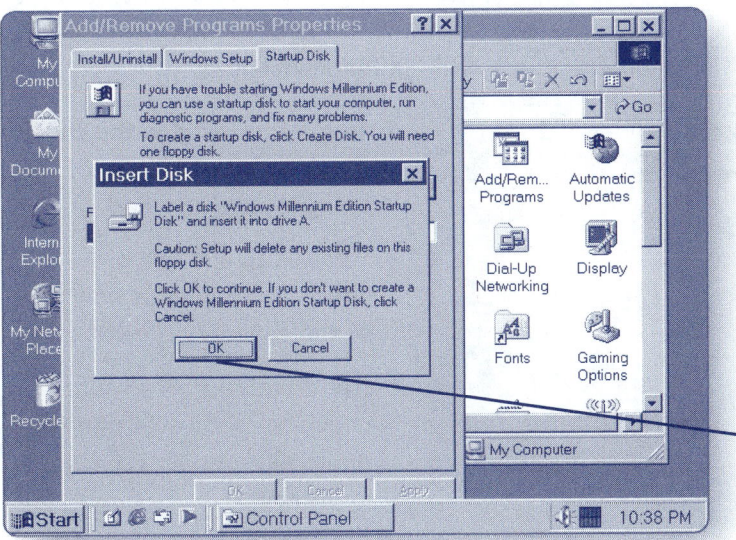

3. **Insert** the **disk** that will hold the startup files. Windows will delete any existing files on this disk.

> **NOTE**
> You may be prompted to insert the Windows Millennium Edition CD-ROM.

4. **Click** on **OK**. Windows begins the process of preparing the startup disk.

If you need to use the emergency startup disk, place the disk in the disk drive before you turn on the power to your computer. Windows will recognize it as a startup disk and will take over from there.

Adding Windows Program Components

Some items discussed in this book are not installed during a default installation of Windows. If you want these additional features, you must add them with the Windows Setup program.

Items not installed by default include additional mouse pointers, some Accessibility options, Web TV options, and some Internet tools.

1. Click on the **Windows Setup tab**. Windows searches for the components already installed on your PC. A list of Windows component categories is displayed.

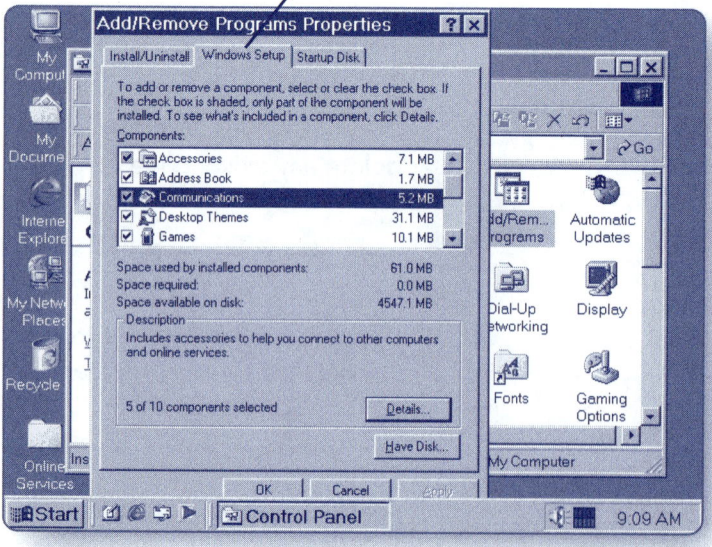

Windows uses the following designations to indicate if any, all, or no parts of a category are already installed:

- Items with no ✔ in the check box indicates no parts of that category are installed.

- Items with a ✔ in a gray check box indicates only part of the category is installed.

- Items with a ✔ in a white check box indicates that the entire category is already installed.

ADDING AND REMOVING PROGRAMS   245

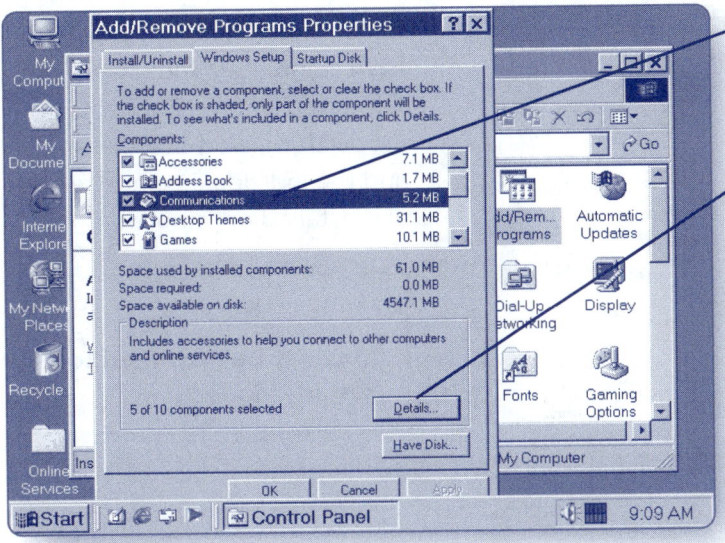

2. Click on the **category** you want to install. The category is selected.

3. Click on **Details**. The dialog box for that category opens.

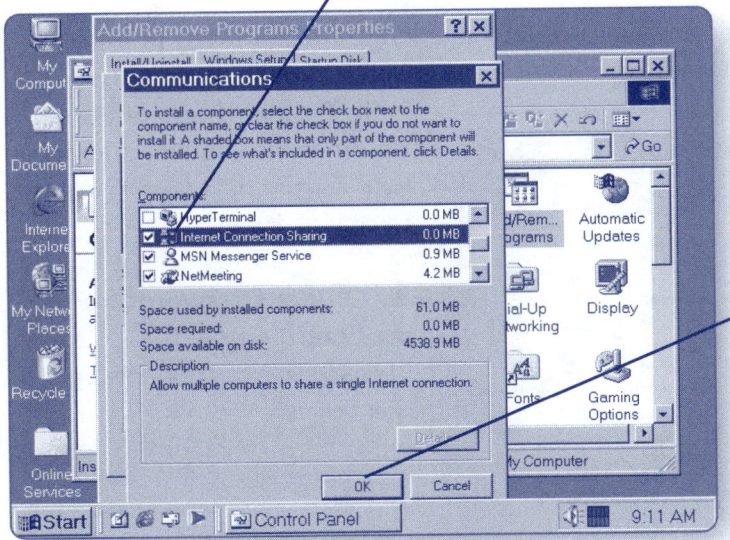

4. Click on as many **components** of that category that you want to install. A ✔ appears in the check box.

NOTE
Some components require additional choices to operate correctly. Windows Setup advises you of this.

5. Click on **OK**. The category dialog box closes.

TIP
To remove a Windows component, remove the ✔ from the items you want to uninstall and continue with Step 6.

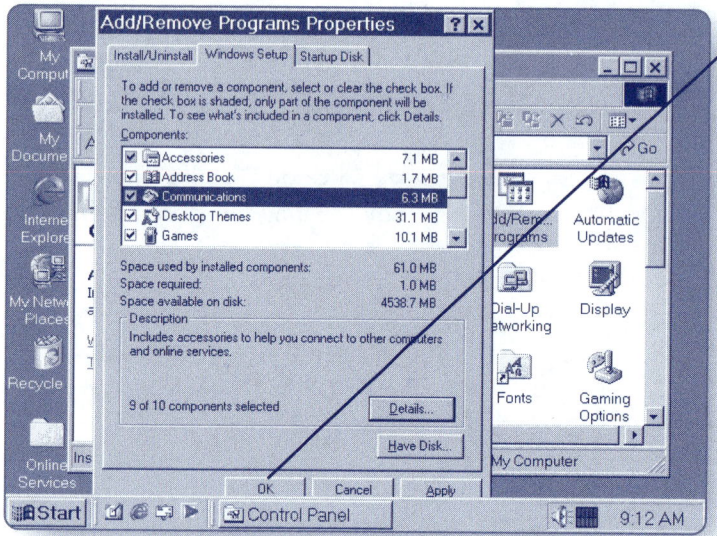

6. Click on **OK** when you have completed your selections. The Add/Remove Programs Properties dialog box closes, and the individual components are installed or removed.

> **NOTE**
> You may be prompted to restart Windows.

Changing Your Windows Password

If you are connected to a network, Windows may prompt you for a password when Windows starts up. This setting is stored in the Password area of the Control Panel. You must know your current password in order to change it.

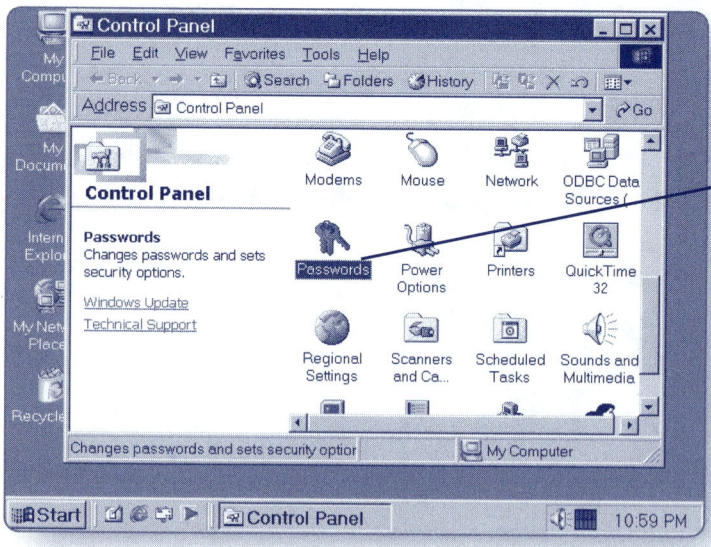

1. Click on **Passwords** from the Control Panel. The Passwords Properties dialog box opens.

CHANGING YOUR WINDOWS PASSWORD   247

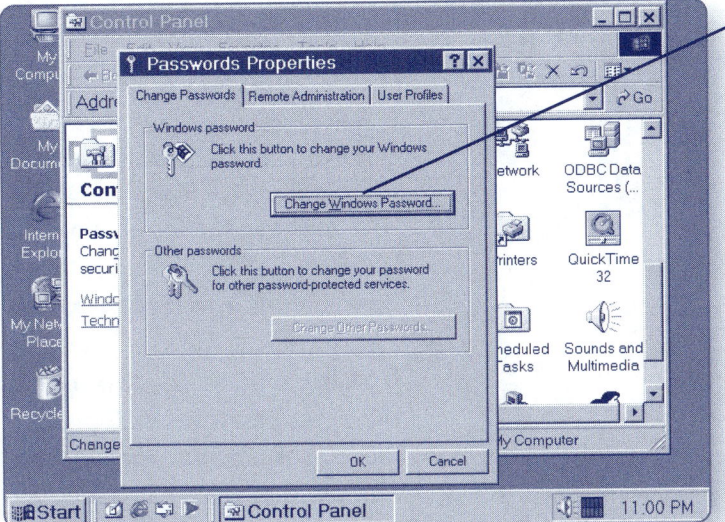

2. Click on **Change Windows Password**. The Change Windows Password dialog box opens.

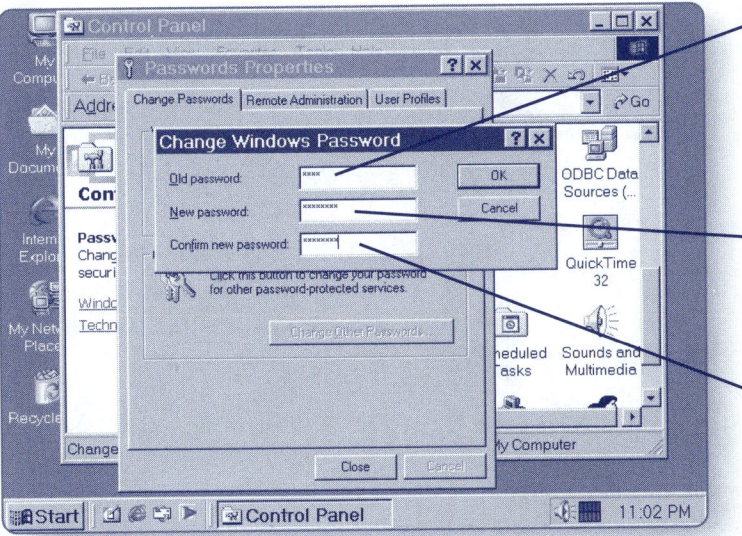

3. Type your **old password** in the Old password: text box. A series of asterisks appears. If you didn't previously have a password, leave this field blank.

4. Type your **new password** in the New password: text box. A series of asterisks appears.

5. Type your **new password** in the Confirm new Password: text box. A series of asterisks appears.

TIP

To remove your password completely, enter the existing password in the Old password: text box and leave both of the new password text boxes blank.

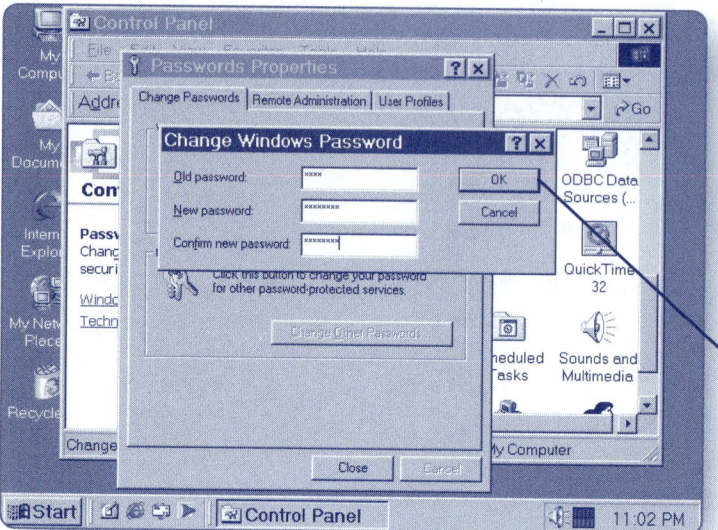

NOTE
You are asked to type your new password twice to make sure you didn't make a typing error (because you cannot see the letters you are typing).

6. Click on **OK**. The Change Windows Password dialog box closes, and you are advised that the password has been changed.

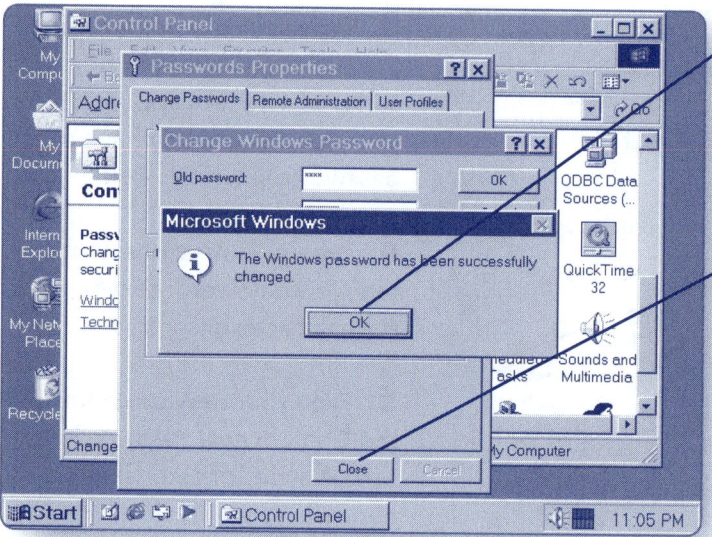

7. Click on **OK**. The acknowledgment message closes, and your new password takes effect the next time you start Windows.

8. Click on **Close**. The Passwords Properties dialog box closes.

Setting Up Multiple Users

Windows enables you to set up your computer to be used by more than one person. Each user can have his or her own set of preferences, such as wallpaper, backgrounds, screen savers, and icons. The settings used by Windows are determined by which user is logged on.

1. Click on **Users**. The Enable Multi-User Settings dialog box opens.

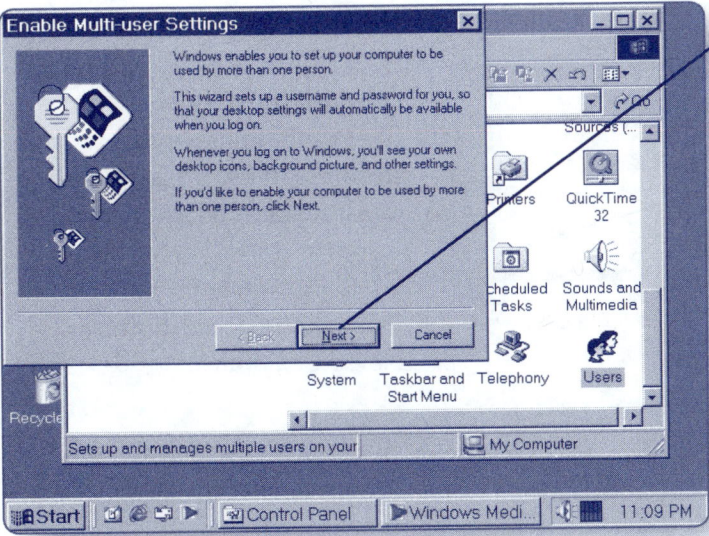

2. Click on **Next**. The next screen appears.

250 CHAPTER 16: TINKERING WITH THE CONTROL PANEL

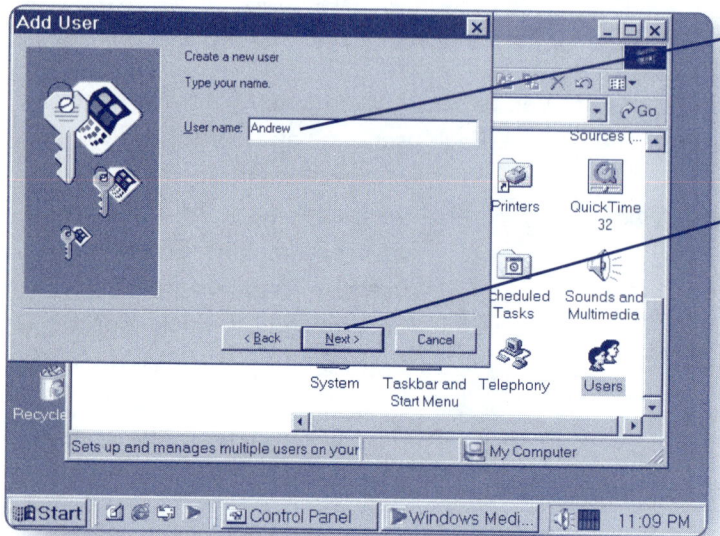

3. **Enter** a **name** for the new user in the User name: text box. The name you type is used to identify the user.

4. **Click** on **Next**. The Enter New Password dialog box opens.

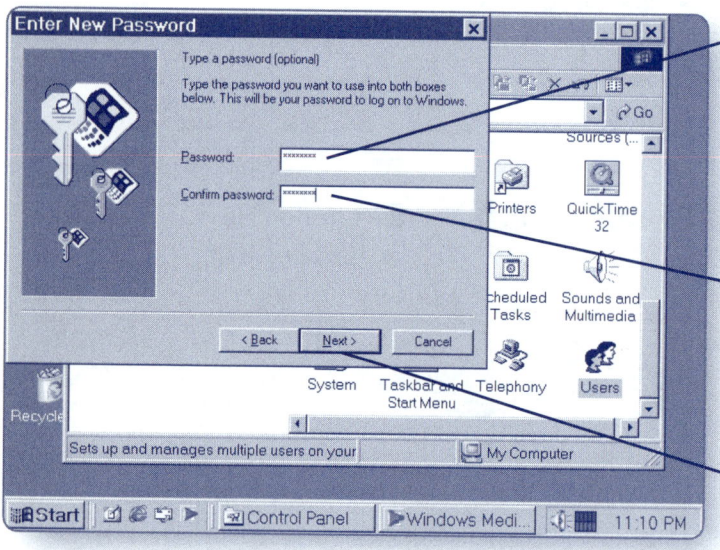

5. **Type** a **password** to use when logging on to Windows. A series of asterisks appears. You can leave this text box blank if the new user doesn't want to use a password.

6. **Type** the **new password** in the Confirm password: text box to confirm your typing. A series of asterisks appears.

7. **Click** on **Next**. The Personalized Items Settings dialog box opens.

SETTING UP MULTIPLE USERS 251

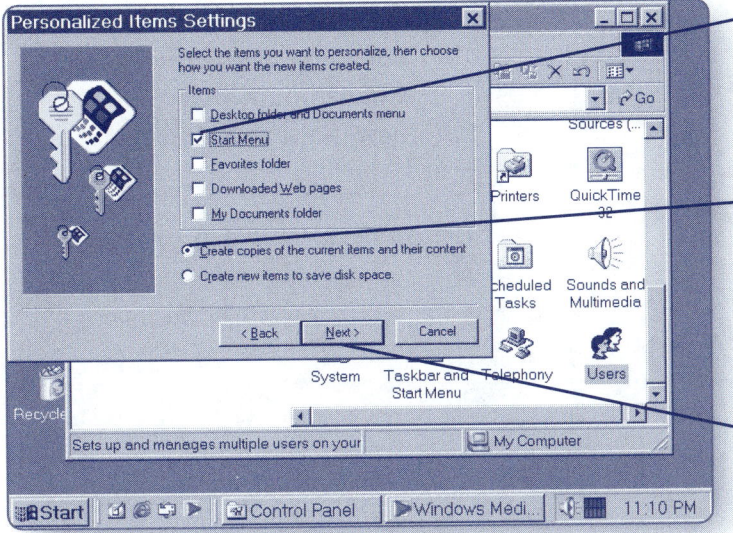

8. Click on each **item** you want to personalize. A ✔ appears in the check box for each selected item.

9. Click on **Create copies of the current items and their content**. The current user's settings are duplicated for the new user.

10. Click on **Next**. The Enable Multi-User Settings dialog box opens.

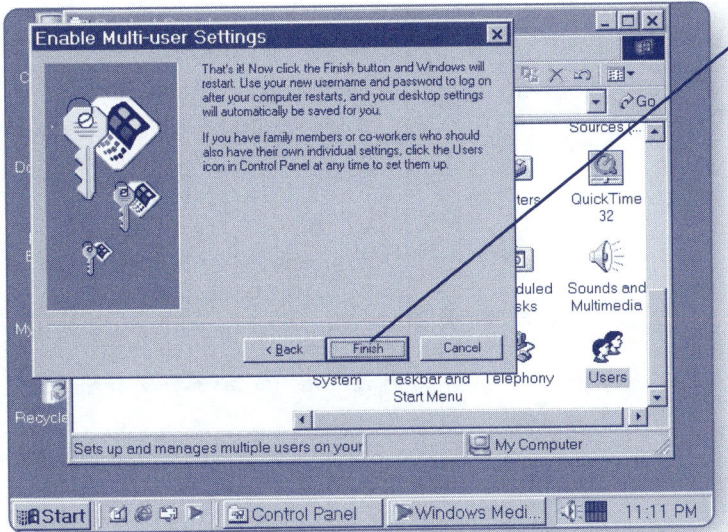

11. Click on **Finish**. Windows creates personalized settings folders for the new user, and you are prompted to restart your computer.

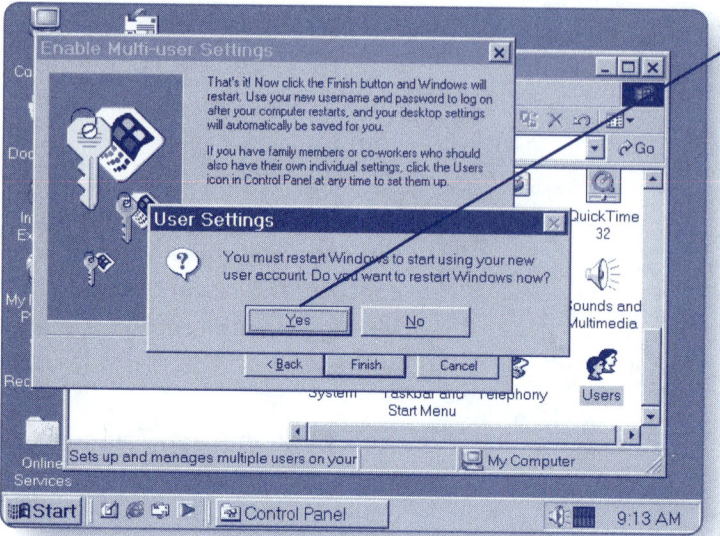

12. Click on **Yes**. Your computer will be restarted; when Windows starts up, the new user name displays.

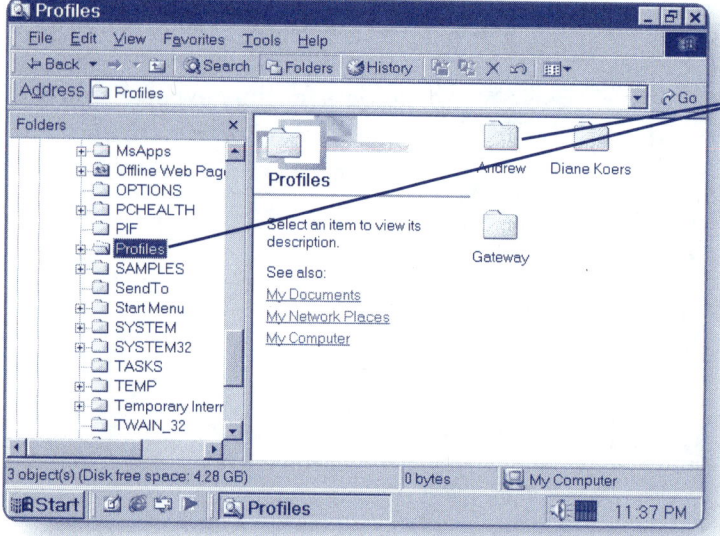

NOTE

Windows creates a new folder called Profiles when there are multiple users. It is located in the Windows folder. Each user has his or her own folder in the Profiles folder.

Changing Accessibility Options

Windows offers many enhancements designed to make using a PC easier for people with certain physical limitations. The accessibility options are not installed by default. You need to add them through the Add/Remove Programs feature.

Accessibility features include enhancements for easier keyboard and mouse input for those users who have mobility impairments as well as features for users who are visually or hearing impaired.

1. Click on **Accessibility Options**. The Accessibility Properties dialog box opens.

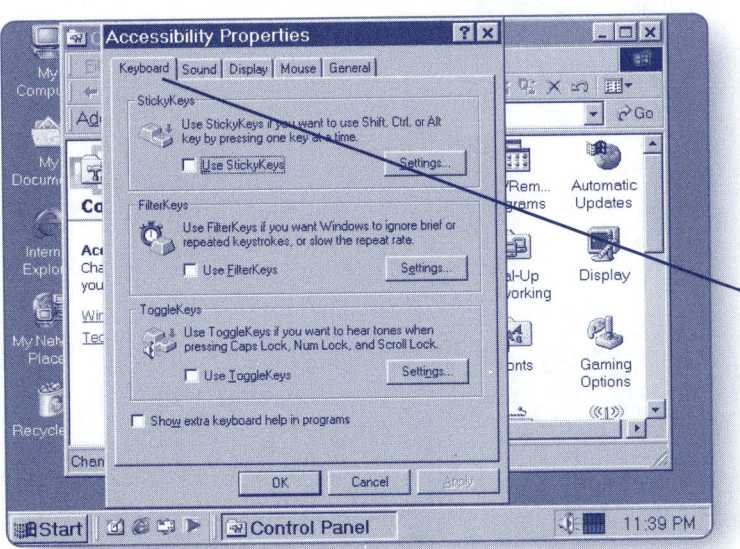

Changing Keyboard Options

Keyboard options include enhancements for easier keyboard use.

1. Click on the **Keyboard tab** if necessary. The Keyboard tab appears in front.

Three main options are available on the Keyboard tab:

- **StickyKeys.** Turn this feature on if you want to be able to press the Ctrl, Alt, or Shift key and have it remain operative until another key is pressed. This feature is very useful for someone who has difficulty pressing two keys at the same time.

- **FilterKeys.** Turn this feature on if you have a tendency to hold a key down too long and it repeats itself. When this feature is activated, Windows ignores brief or repeated keystrokes.

- **ToggleKeys.** Turn this feature on to hear a light tone when you press the Caps Lock, Num Lock, or Scroll Lock keys. When you press one of these keys, you hear a low, soft click.

2. Click on the **features** you want to use. A ✔ appears next to the activated features.

3. Click on **Settings** for each feature you activate if desired. The Settings dialog box opens.

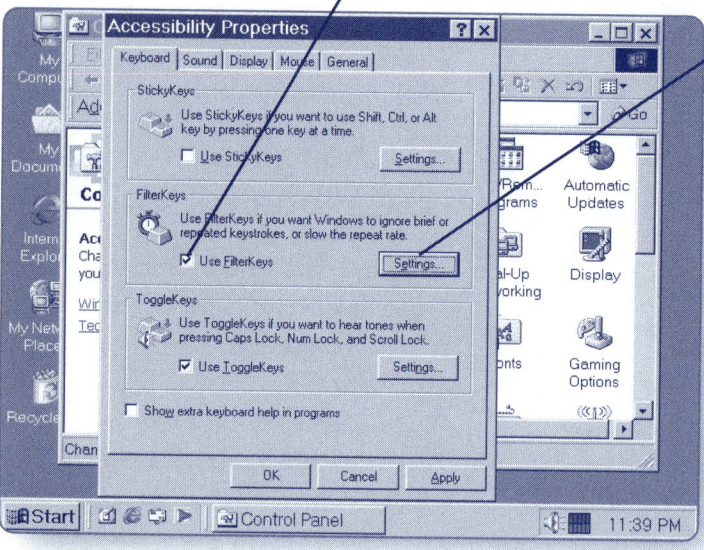

CHANGING ACCESSIBILITY OPTIONS   255

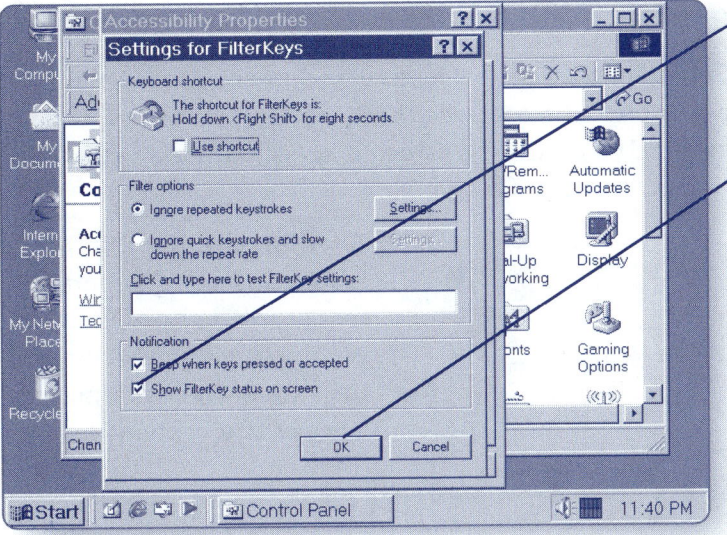

4. Click on any additional **options** you want for the selected keyboard option.

5. Click on **OK**. The Settings dialog box closes.

TIP

See the section "Using MouseKeys" later in this chapter for information on an additional feature to aid those with hand impairments.

Setting Options for the Hearing Impaired

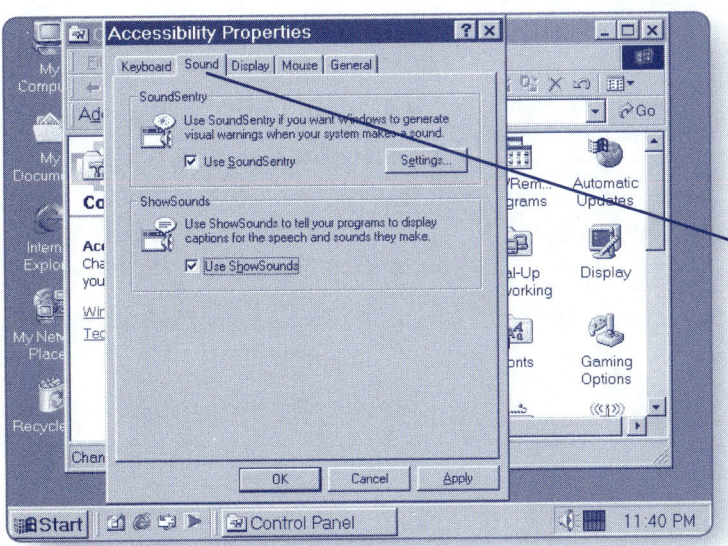

These options can assist the hearing impaired by turning normal computer sounds from the computer into visible reminders.

1. Click on the **Sound tab**. The Sound tab appears in front.

Two options appear here:

- **SoundSentry.** Use this feature if you want Windows to flash a part of your screen each time the computer plays a sound. The part of the screen is specified in the Settings for SoundSentry dialog box.

- **ShowSounds.** Use this feature to instruct programs that usually relay information only by sound to also provide the information by displaying icons or text captions.

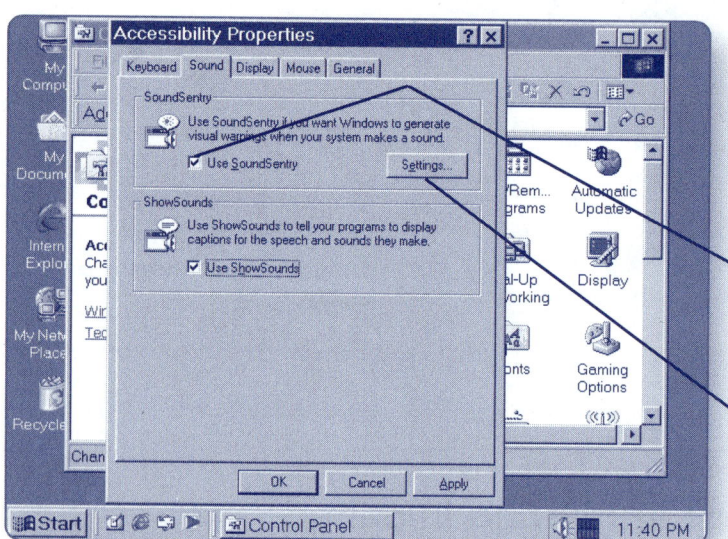

2. **Click** on the **features** you want to use. A ✔ appears next to activated features.

3. If you've elected to use SoundSentry, **click** on **Settings.** The Settings dialog box for the selected feature opens.

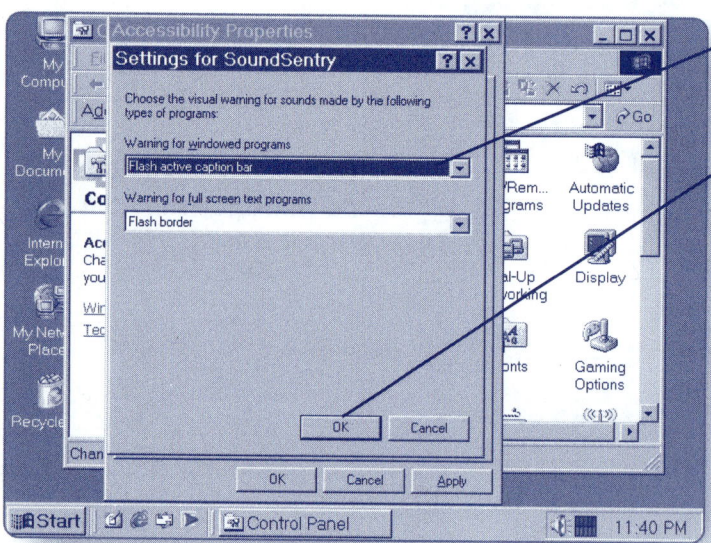

4. **Click** on any desired **setting changes**. The options appear.

5. **Click** on **OK**. The Settings option box closes.

CHANGING ACCESSIBILITY OPTIONS 257

Setting Options for the Visually Impaired

The Display option has a feature for those with limited vision. For better visibility, it can instruct a program to use a specified color scheme instead of the one indicated by a specific program.

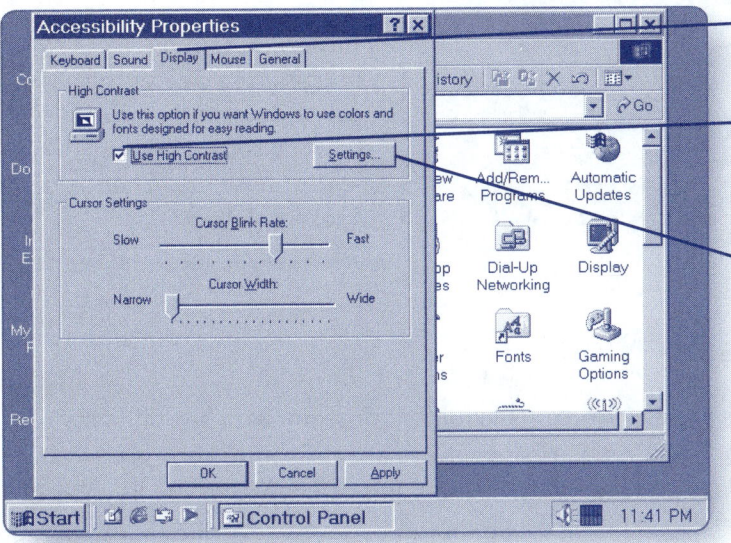

1. Click on the **Display tab**. The Display tab appears in front.

2. Click on the **Use High Contrast check box**. A ✔ appears in the check box.

3. Click on **Settings**. The Settings for High Contrast dialog box opens.

Several high-contrast color schemes are available. Options include displaying white on black, black on white, or one of several high-contrast options.

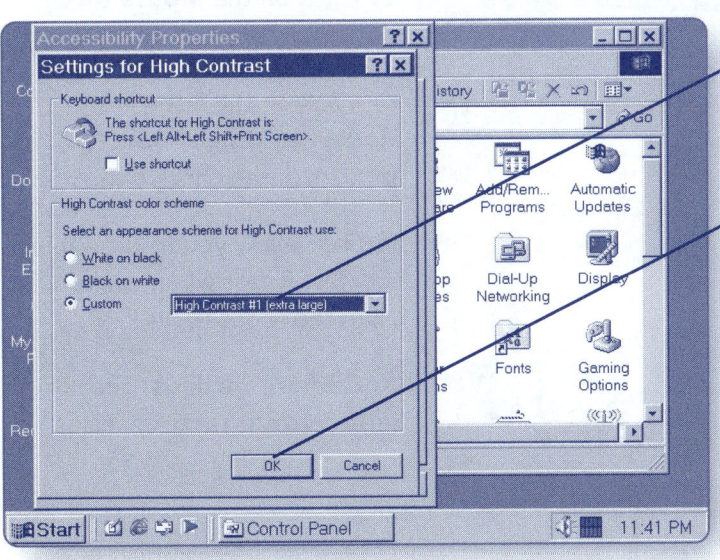

4. Click on the **color scheme** you want to use. The option is selected.

5. Click on **OK**. The Settings for High Contrast dialog box closes.

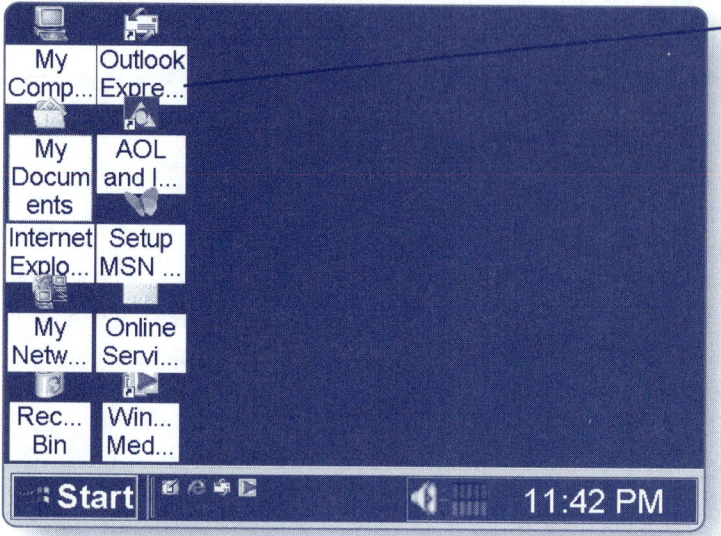

This figure indicates a screen with High Contrast #1, extra-large fonts selected.

TIP

An additional aid for the visually impaired is to make the mouse pointer larger. For information on changing the size of the mouse pointer, see the previous section in this chapter entitled "Changing Mouse Pointers."

Using MouseKeys

MouseKeys are very useful for someone who has difficulty handling a mouse. MouseKeys enable you to control the mouse pointer by using the numeric keypad of the keyboard.

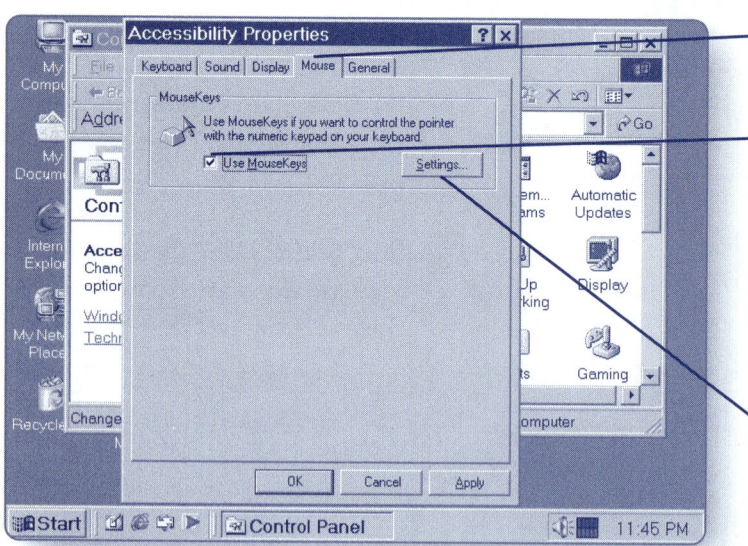

1. Click on the **Mouse tab**. The Mouse tab appears in front.

2. Click on the **Use MouseKeys check box**. A ✔ appears in the check box.

Settings allow you to determine how fast is fast when you are using the MouseKeys.

3. Click on **Settings**. The Settings dialog box opens.

CHANGING ACCESSIBILITY OPTIONS 259

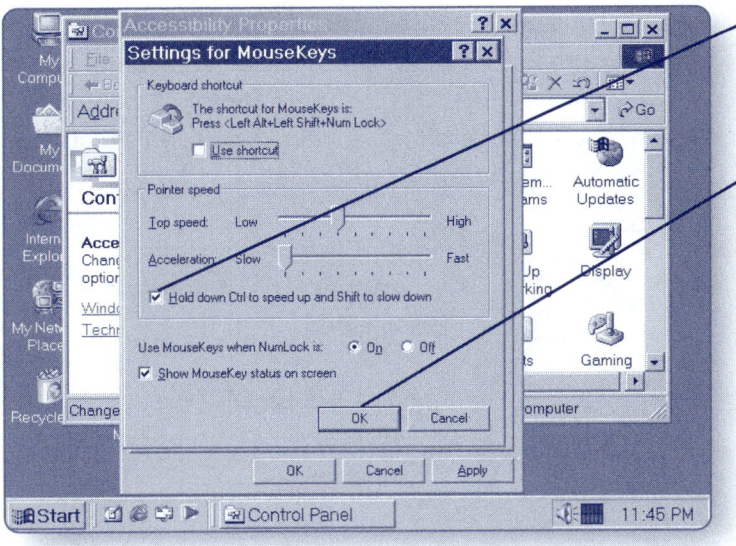

4. Change any desired **settings**. The options are selected.

5. Click on **OK**. The MouseKeys options are applied immediately.

Setting General Accessibility Options

The General options are for the overall properties and actions of accessibility features.

1. Click on the **General tab**. The General tab appears in front.

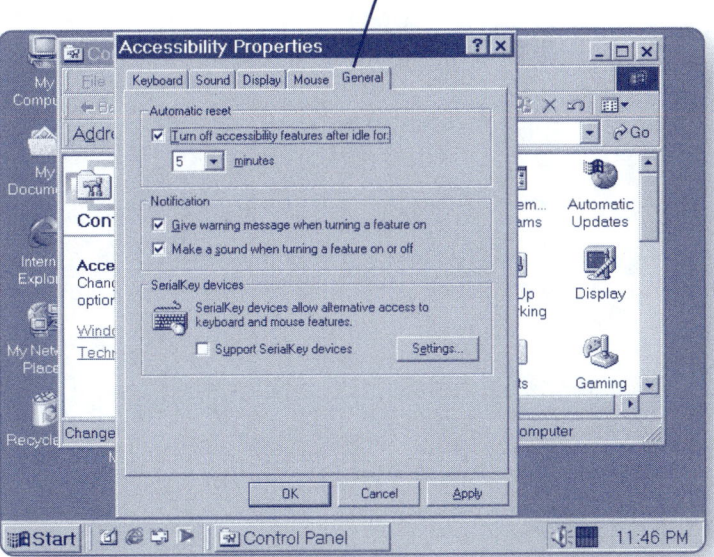

Windows offers several general options that can affect the operations of the Accessibility features:

- **Automatic Reset.** Turns off the accessibility features if your computer has been idle for a specified period of time.

- **Notification.** Notifies you when you have activated accessibility features via shortcut keys.

- **SerialKey Devices.** Indicates whether Windows is to support an alternative input device (called an *augmentative communication device*). This feature is for those who are unable to use a standard mouse or keyboard. This feature is not affected by the Automatic Reset.

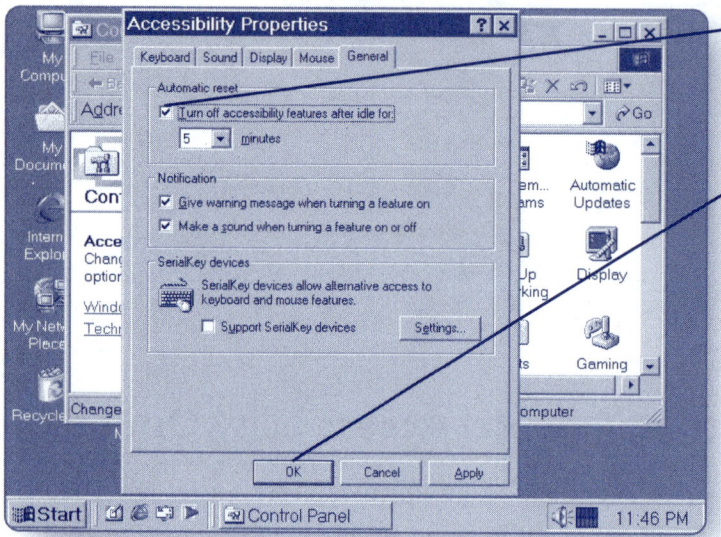

2. **Click** on any desired **options**. The options are selected.

3. Click on **OK**. The Accessibility Properties dialog box closes.

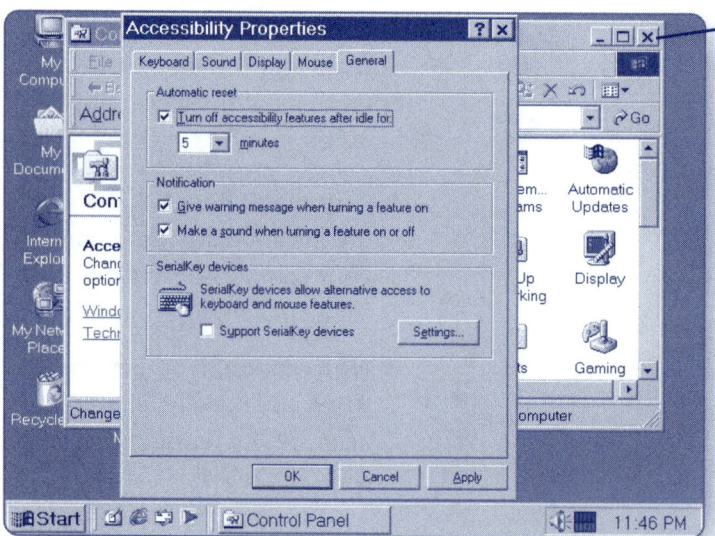

4. Click on the **Close box** ([X]). The Control Panel window closes.

17

Having Fun with the Control Panel

In the preceding chapter, you learned how to use some of the system support items that the Control Panel offers. Now you'll learn how to use the Control Panel to maximize the fun you can have with your computer. Do you want something prettier than the standard Windows desktop? How about changing the sound you hear every time a message appears? In this chapter, you'll learn how to:

- Change sounds
- Choose a wallpaper
- Change desktop colors
- Subscribe to channels
- Use the Desktop Themes

Changing Sounds

You might hear a sound when you attempt to complete a particular task in Windows. It could sound like a ding or a chord, even a drum roll or an owl. These sounds are established through the Windows Control Panel.

> **TIP**
> To open the Control Panel, click on Start, Settings, and choose Control Panel.

1. Open the **Control Panel**. The Control Panel window opens.

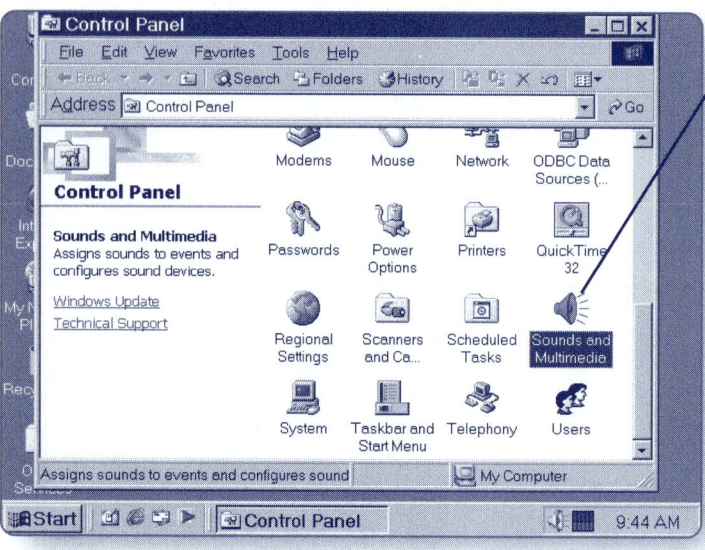

2. Click on **Sounds and Multimedia**. The Sounds and Multimedia Properties dialog box opens. The dialog box lists various Windows events, such as closing a program or the appearance of a warning message. A speaker icon indicates those events that already have a sound assigned to them.

> **TIP**
> If you don't see a Sounds and Multimedia icon, click on View All Control Panel options.

CHANGING SOUNDS   263

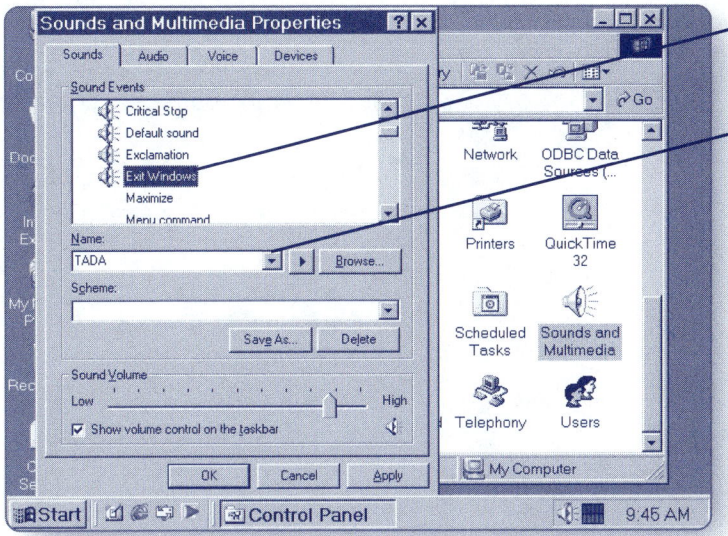

3. Click on a **Sound Event**. The event is selected.

4. Click on the **down arrow** (▼) by the Name: list box. A list of available sounds appears.

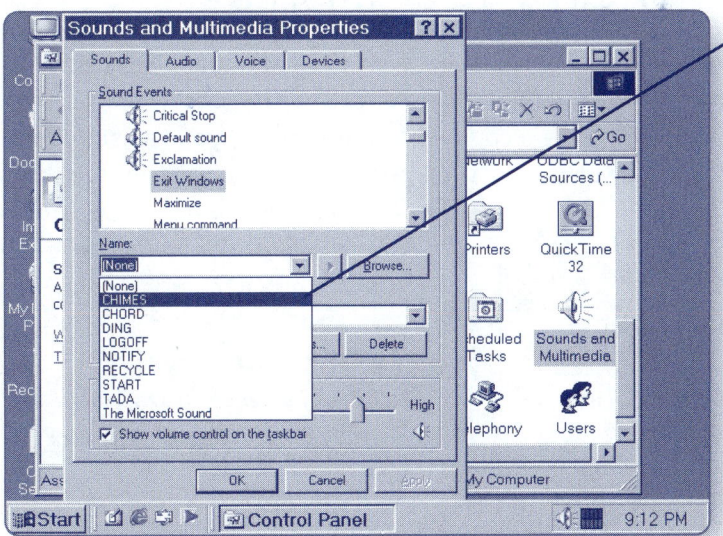

5. Click on the **sound name** you want to associate with the event. The sound name appears in the Name: list box.

TIP

If you do not want a sound associated with an event, click on [None] from the Name: list box.

264 CHAPTER 17: HAVING FUN WITH THE CONTROL PANEL

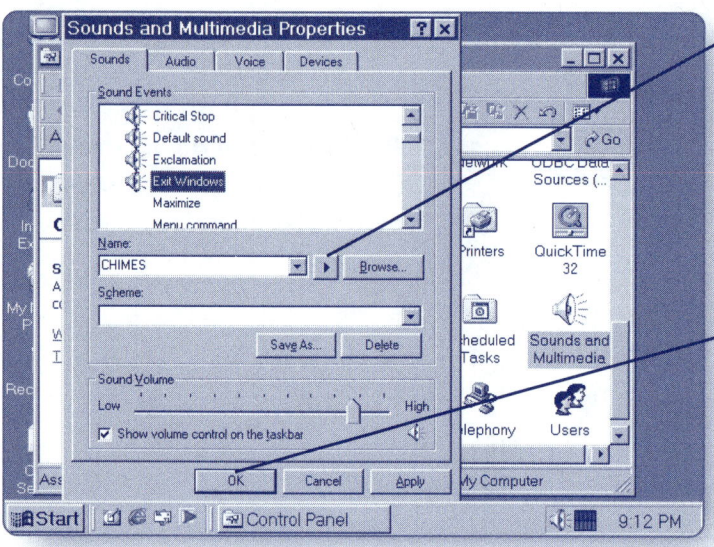

6. **Click** on the **Play button** to preview the sound. The sound plays through your speakers.

7. Repeat Steps 3 through **5** for each event you want to change.

8. Click on **OK**. The Sounds and Multimedia Properties dialog box closes.

Enhancing Your Display

Windows Millennium Edition adds several major changes to your desktop. You might not notice the changes at first; however, with only a couple of mouse clicks, you can set your eyes on the world—via the Internet. This feature is called the *Active Desktop*. Active Desktop is only one of the many changes you can make to your display.

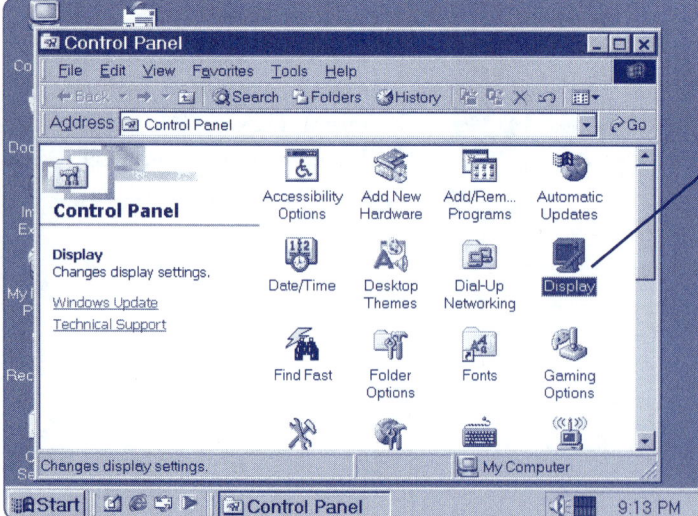

1. Click on **Display** in the Control Panel window. The Display Properties dialog box opens.

Changing Backgrounds

Many different graphic types and .html files can be displayed as wallpaper for your Windows desktop! Windows Millennium Edition also includes many new choices from which you can select.

1. Click on the **Background tab** (if necessary). The Background tab appears in front.

2. Click on a **wallpaper** from the selections provided. A sample of the wallpaper appears in the Preview box.

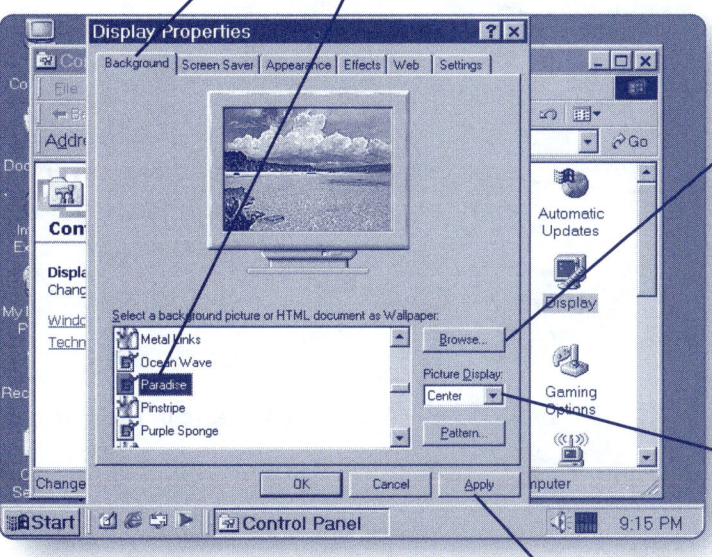

TIP
If you don't find wallpaper that you like, click the Browse button and navigate to the folder that contains the image you want to display. Double-click on the image you want to use.

3. Click on the **down arrow** (▼) next to the Picture Display: list box. A list of choices appears.

4. Click an **option**. This affects the way the wallpaper displays on your screen.

5. Click on **Apply**. Your new background selection is applied.

Selecting a Screen Saver

Screen savers display moving images that appear on your screen when the computer is idle for a specified amount of time. You can choose from the abundance of screen savers included with Windows, or you can purchase many different themes from third-party software manufacturers.

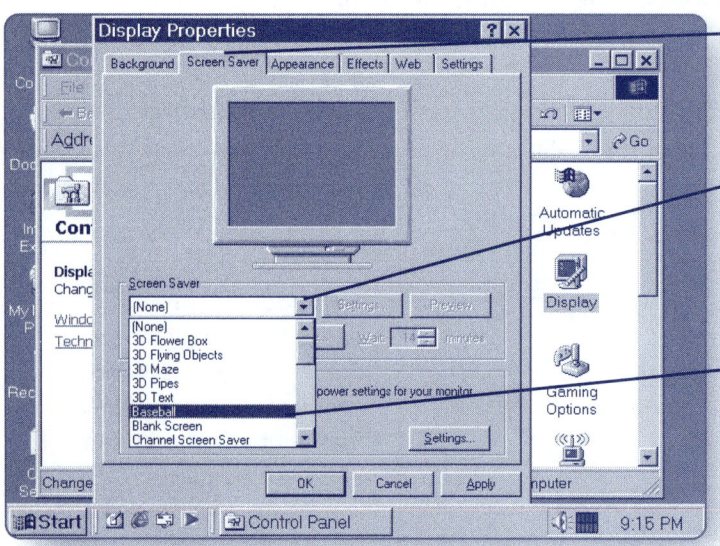

1. Click on the **Screen Saver tab**. The Screen Saver tab appears in front.

2. Click on the **down arrow** (▼) of the Screen Saver list box. A list of available choices appears.

3. Click on the **screen saver** you want to use. Your selection appears in the Screen Saver list box.

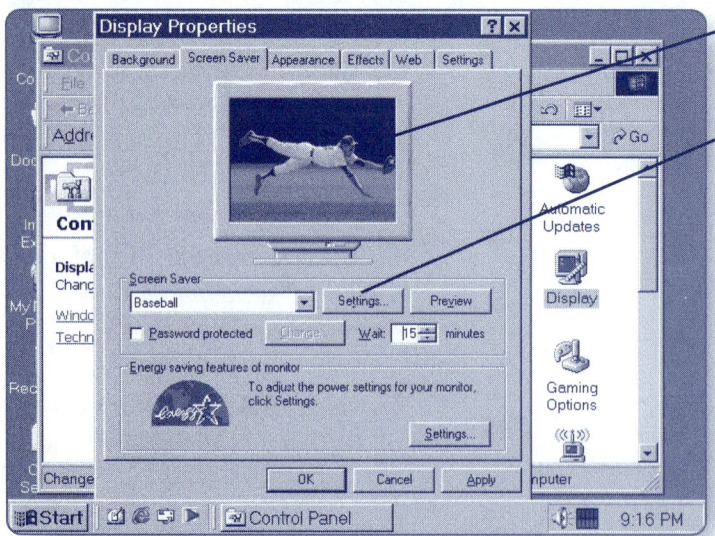

A sample appears in the Preview box.

4. Click on **Settings**. A Screen Saver Properties dialog box specific to the screen saver you have selected opens.

From here, you can set various options, such as speed, sound, and sometimes color or size. The options will vary with each screen saver.

ENHANCING YOUR DISPLAY   267

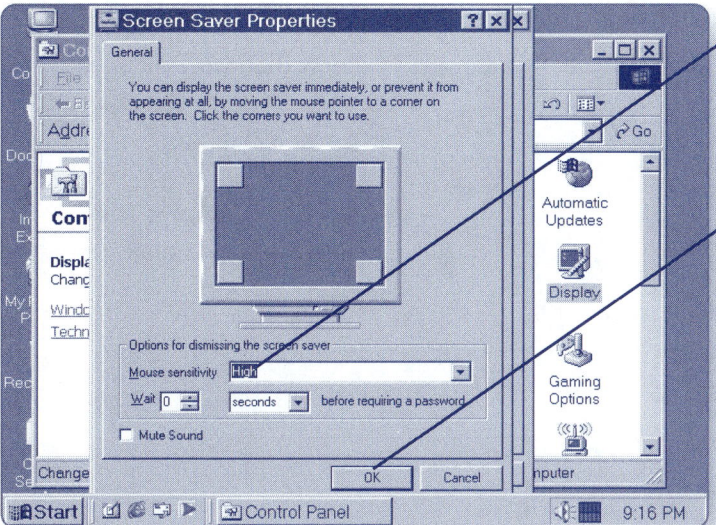

5. Change any desired **options** in the Screen Saver Properties dialog box. The options are selected.

6. Click on **OK**. The Screen Saver Properties dialog box closes.

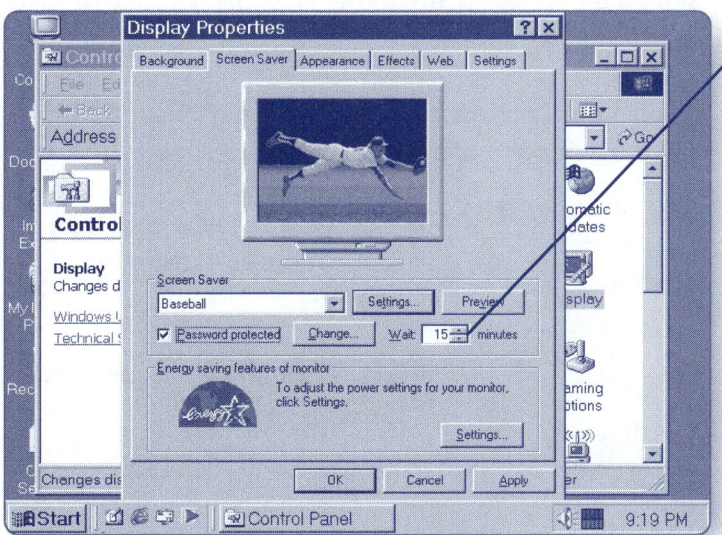

7. Click on the **up** or **down arrow** (✦) next to the Wait spin box to set the number of minutes that elapse before the screen saver starts. An average time is 10 to 15 minutes.

Optionally, you can set a password to lock your screen when the screen saver is activated. This feature prevents curious eyes from exploring your computer while you are otherwise occupied.

268 CHAPTER 17: HAVING FUN WITH THE CONTROL PANEL

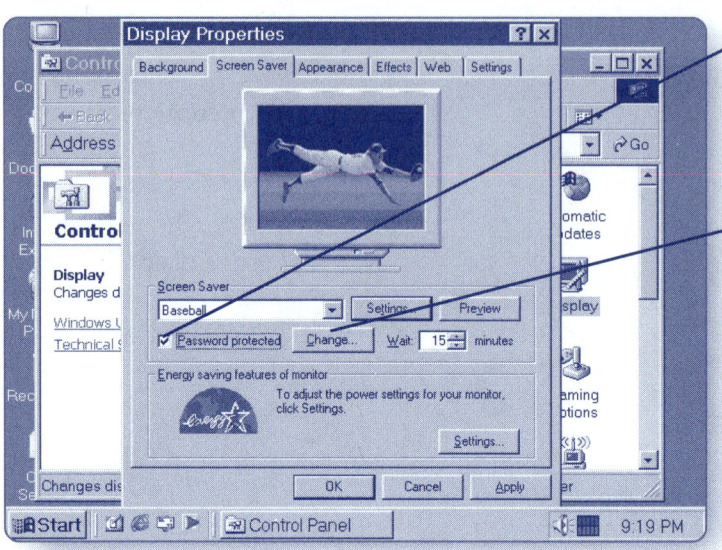

8. **Click** on the **Password Protected check box**. A ✔ appears, and the Change button becomes available.

9. **Click** on **Change**. The Change Password dialog box opens.

10. **Type** the **new password** in the New password: text box. A series of asterisks appears.

11. **Click** in the **Confirm new password: text box**. A blinking insertion point appears.

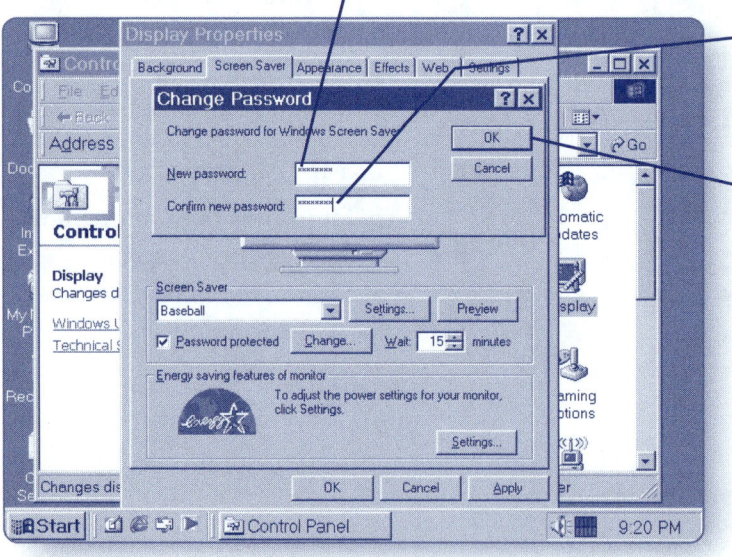

12. **Type** the **new password** again. A series of asterisks appears.

13. **Click** on **OK**. A confirmation box opens.

ENHANCING YOUR DISPLAY

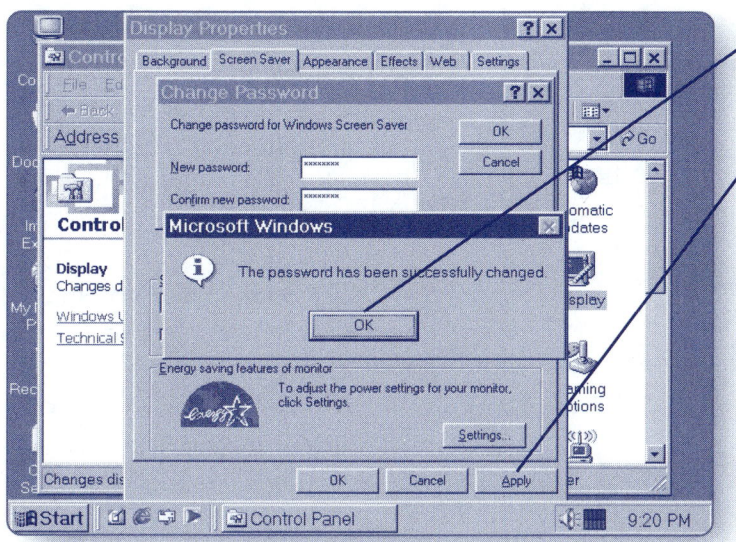

14. Click on **OK**. The Change Password dialog box closes.

15. Click on **Apply**. Your new screen saver selection is applied.

Changing the Colors of Your Windows

You can adjust the appearance of your screen by changing the colors that are displayed in any Windows program. Windows includes some pretty (and some not so pretty) color combinations from which you can choose. Color schemes affect everything from the color of a window title bar to the text displayed in a menu.

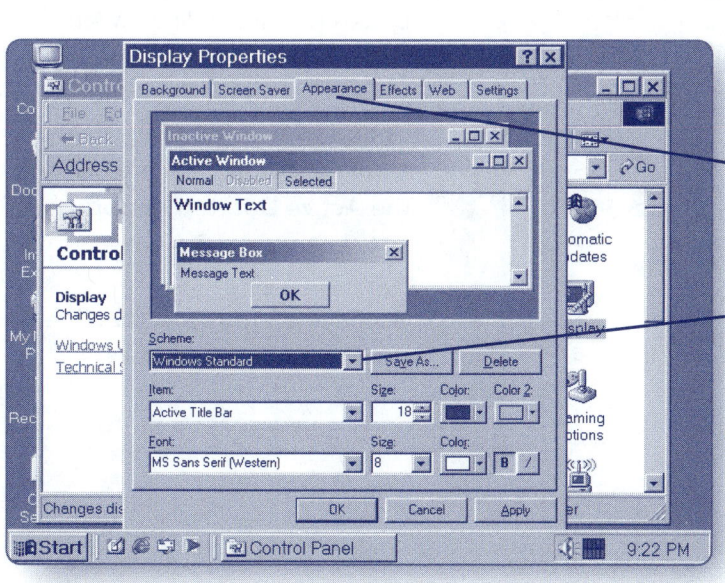

1. Click on the **Appearance tab**. The Appearance tab appears in front.

2. Click on the **down arrow (▼) next to** the Scheme: list box. A selection of color schemes appears.

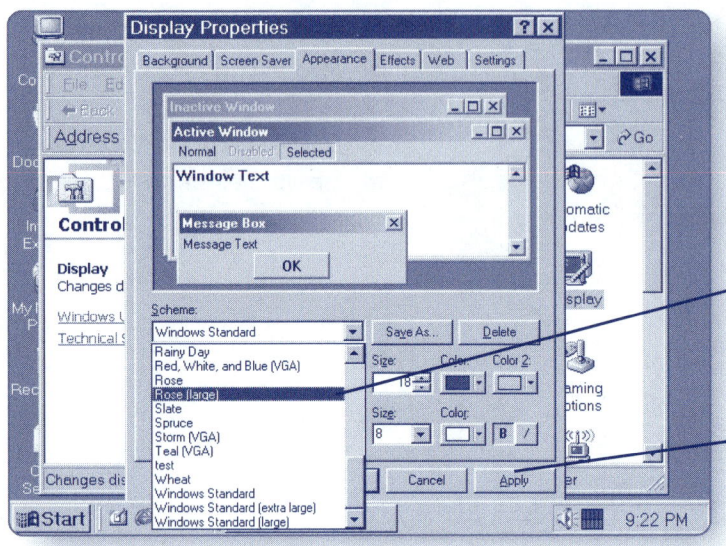

3. Press the **up** or **down arrow keys** on your keyboard or **use** the **scroll bar** to preview the different color schemes. Each choice appears in the Preview box.

4. Click on the **color scheme** you want to use. It appears in the Scheme: list box.

5. Click on **Apply**. The new color settings are applied.

Integrating Your Desktop with the Web

You can activate one of the newer features to Windows—the Active Desktop. Active Desktop makes your desktop come alive with content, such as continuous stock information, sports scores, or weather updates. Icons on an Active Desktop function like a Web page in that they require only a single click to be activated. This book was written on the assumption that you are using the Active Desktop as opposed to the Standard Desktop.

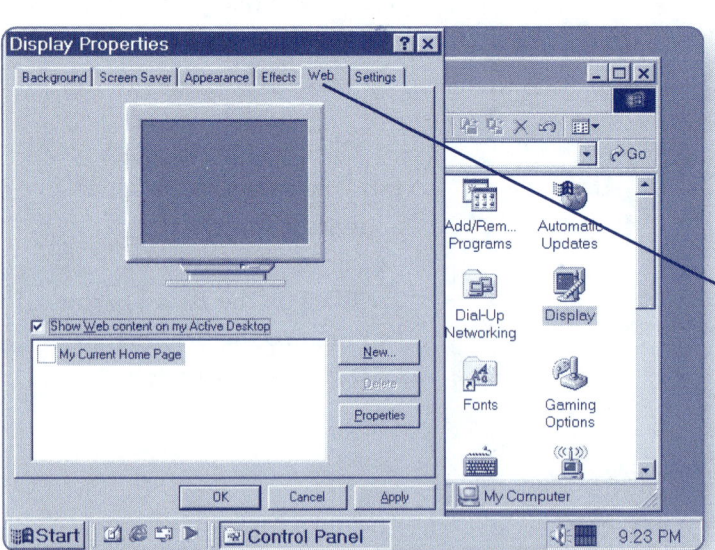

1. Click on the **Web tab**. The Web tab appears in front.

ENHANCING YOUR DISPLAY 271

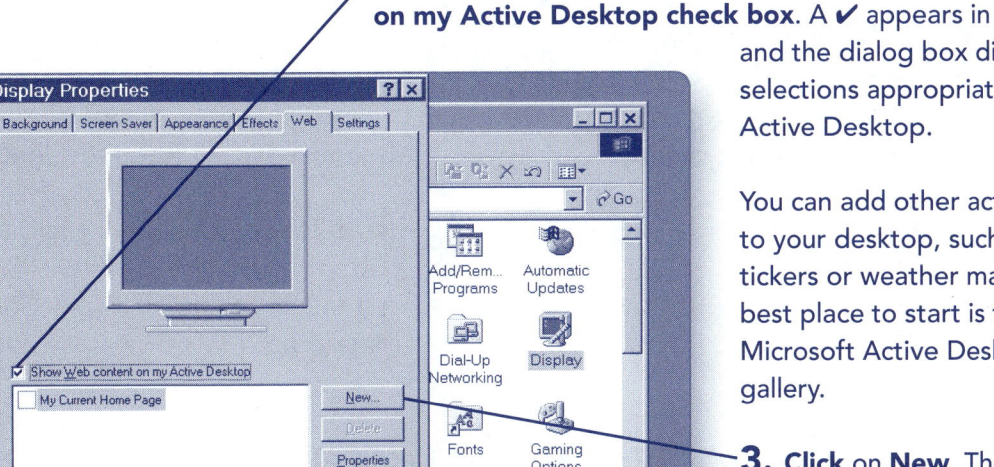

2. If not already checked, **click** on the **Show Web content on my Active Desktop check box**. A ✔ appears in the box, and the dialog box displays selections appropriate to the Active Desktop.

You can add other active items to your desktop, such as stock tickers or weather maps. The best place to start is the Microsoft Active Desktop gallery.

3. Click on **New**. The New Active Desktop Item dialog box opens.

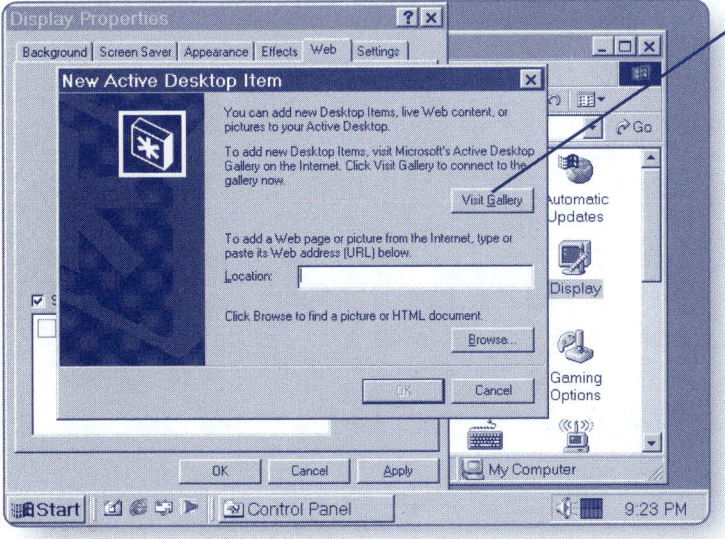

4. Click on **Visit Gallery**. Your Web browser launches and connects to your Internet service provider.

Your Web browser automatically displays the Microsoft Active Desktop Gallery page.

272 CHAPTER 17: HAVING FUN WITH THE CONTROL PANEL

NOTE
Your screen may look a little different. This Web page changes frequently.

5. Click on the **category** to which you want to subscribe. A list of items under that category appears.

6. Click on the **item** you want to add to your desktop. The Web page for that gallery item appears.

ENHANCING YOUR DISPLAY 273

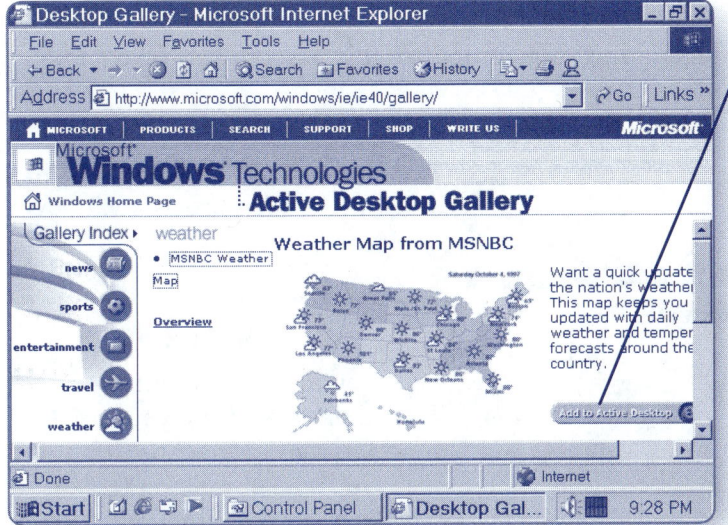

7. **Click** on **Add to Active Desktop**. A Security Alert message box appears.

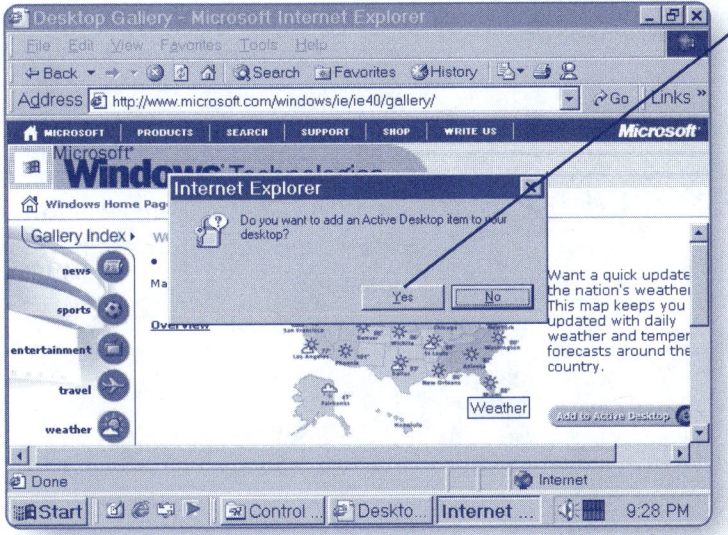

8. **Click** on **Yes**. A message appears asking you to confirm your subscription.

NOTE
A channel subscription is a free automatic update to a specific Web site.

274 CHAPTER 17: HAVING FUN WITH THE CONTROL PANEL

9. **Click** on **OK**. The Active Desktop Gallery item is downloaded to your computer. This process may take a few minutes.

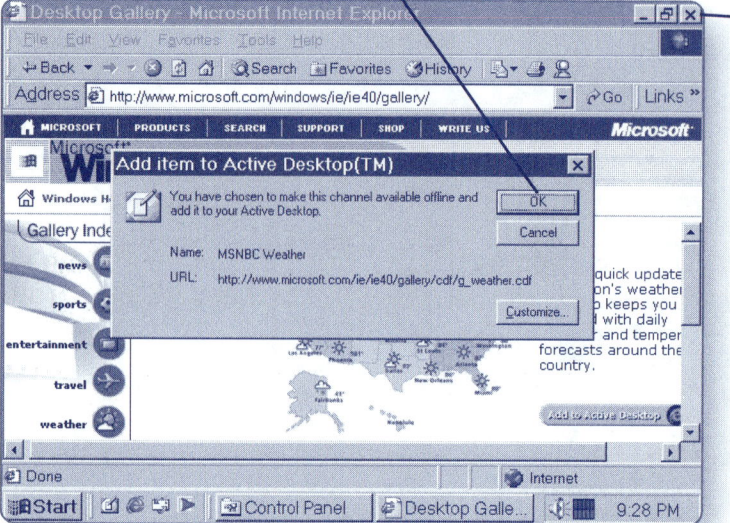

10. **Click** on the **Close button** (X). The Web browser window closes.

NOTE

You may be prompted to disconnect from your Internet connection. If you are subscribing to a channel with frequent updates, such as stock market items, you may want to keep your Internet connection open.

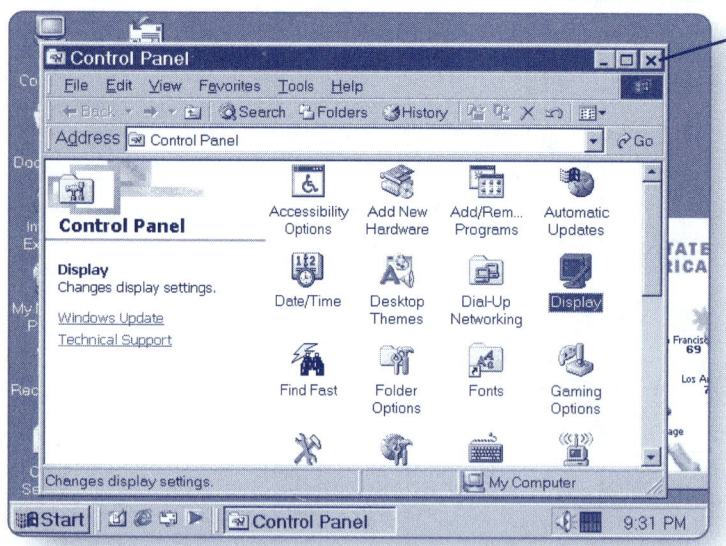

11. **Click** on the **Close button** (X). The Control Panel window closes, and you return to the desktop.

ENHANCING YOUR DISPLAY 275

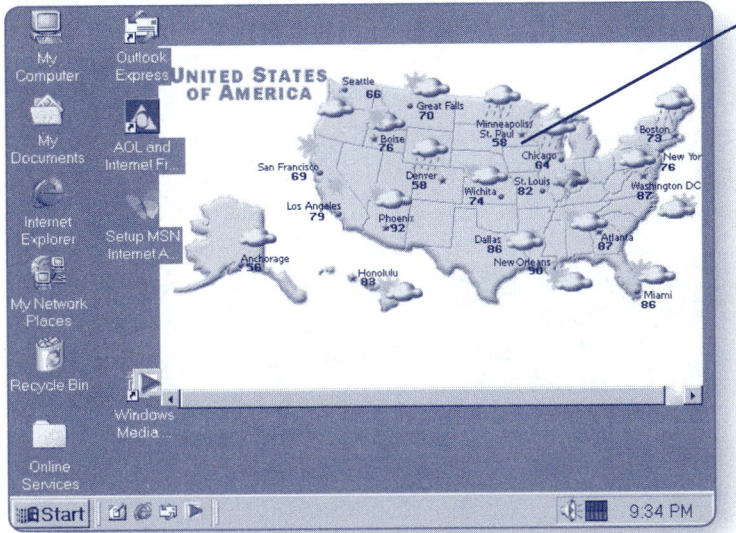

In this example, the MSNBC Weather Map has been added to the Active Desktop.

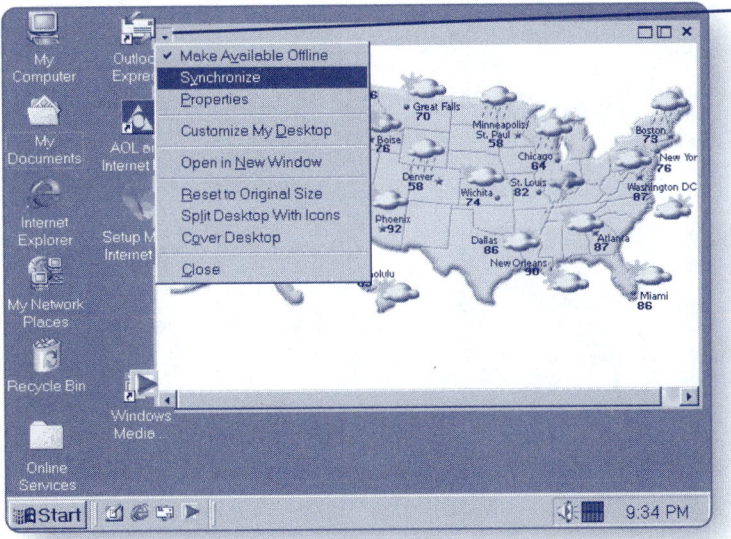

As you position your mouse pointer on top of an Active Desktop item, a small gray bar appears. From the bar you can edit the properties of the Active Desktop item or close it. You'll want to choose Synchronize to update the channel.

Using Desktop Themes

Instead of going to the trouble of picking out wallpaper, screen savers, colors, and other choices for your desktop, try one of the Desktop Themes. Microsoft Windows Millennium Edition supplies some really cool themes (such as Jungle, Tropical Fish, Leonardo da Vinci, Science, Travel, Sports, or The 60s—just to name a few). These themes include background wallpapers, sounds, screen savers, icons, and other Windows items all coordinated together.

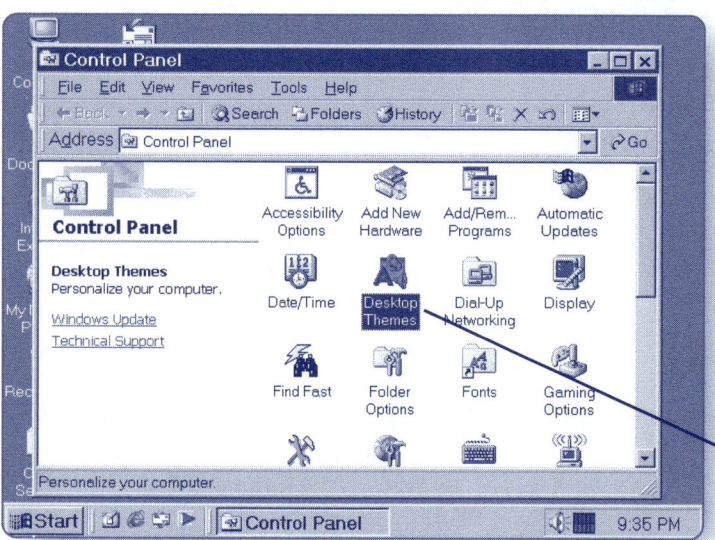

1. **Open** the **Control Panel**. The Control Panel window appears.

2. **Click** on **Desktop Themes**. The Desktop Themes window opens.

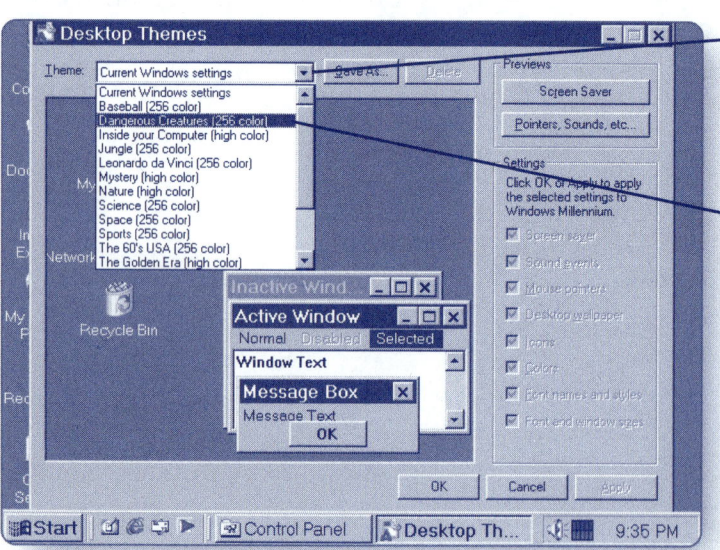

3. **Click** on the **down arrow** (▼) next to the Theme: list box. A list of available themes appears.

4. **Click** on your favorite **theme**. The theme appears in the Theme: list box, and you will see it in the Preview box.

USING DESKTOP THEMES 277

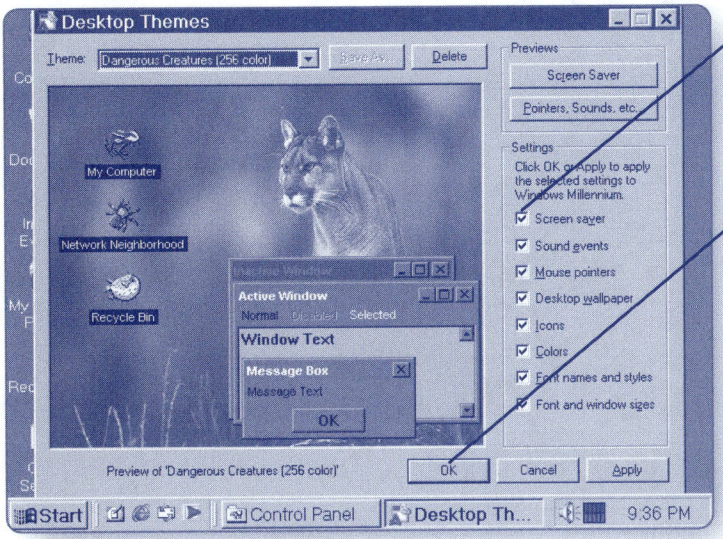

5. **Click** on the **check boxes** you want in the Settings area. You can include or exclude any combinations you want.

6. **Click** on **OK**. The Desktop Themes window closes.

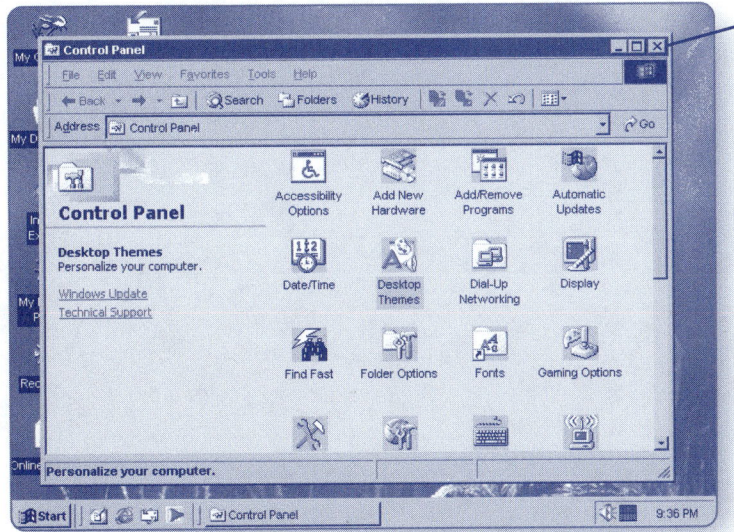

7. **Click** on the **Close box** (X). The Control Panel window closes.

278 CHAPTER 17: HAVING FUN WITH THE CONTROL PANEL

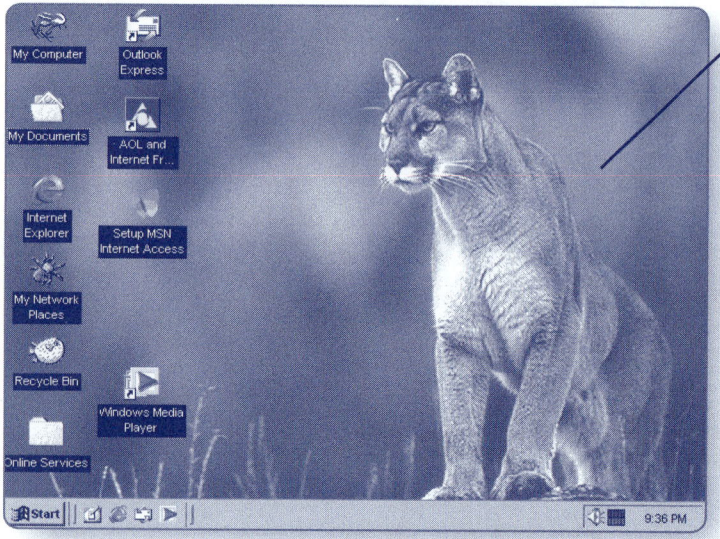

This example shows the Dangerous Creature Theme. The wallpaper, icons, display fonts, colors, mouse pointers, and sounds were changed to follow the theme. To revert to the standard Windows Millennium Edition theme, choose Windows Default from the Theme: list box.

18

Working with Printers

Printing is still the most common way to distribute information to others. When you work with a Windows-based program, all the printing is controlled by Windows—not by the individual software program. This has the advantage of consistency and the ability to resolve all printing issues in one central area. In this chapter, you'll learn how to:

- Install a new printer
- Share a printer
- Connect to a network printer
- Make a printer the default printer
- Control printing jobs

Installing a New Printer

Most of the time, when you hook up a printer to your computer, Windows' Plug & Play feature will detect the new printer and automatically install the necessary printer settings. Occasionally, however, you must manually tell the computer what type of printer you're using. Windows includes the Add Printer Wizard to assist you in installing a new printer.

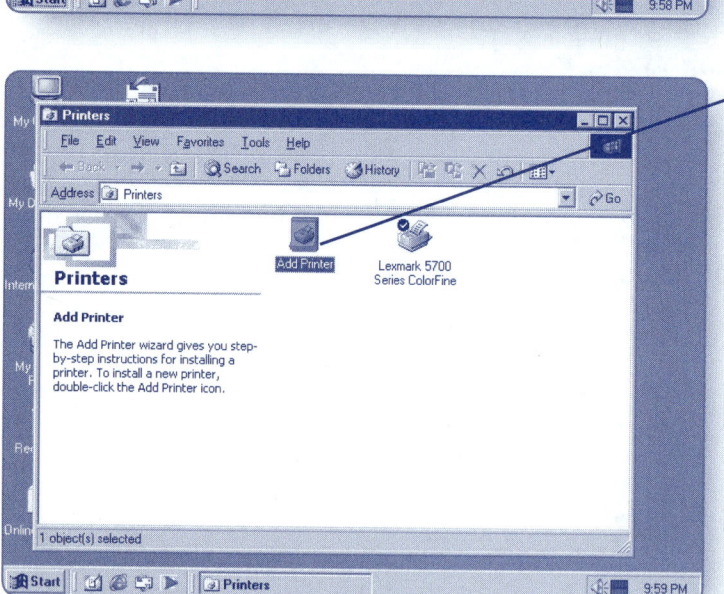

1. **Click** on the **Start button**. The Start menu appears.

2. **Click** on **Settings**. The Settings submenu appears.

3. **Click** on **Printers**. The Printers window opens.

4. **Click** on **Add Printer**. The Add Printer Wizard opens.

INSTALLING A NEW PRINTER   281

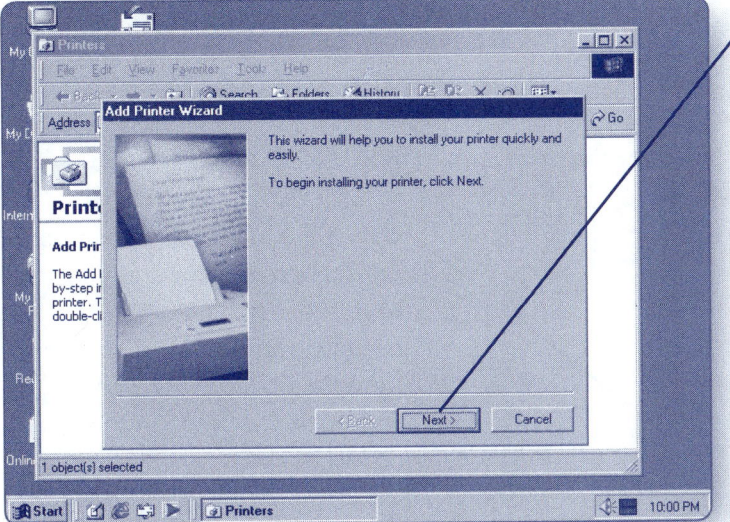

5. Click on **Next**. The next screen appears.

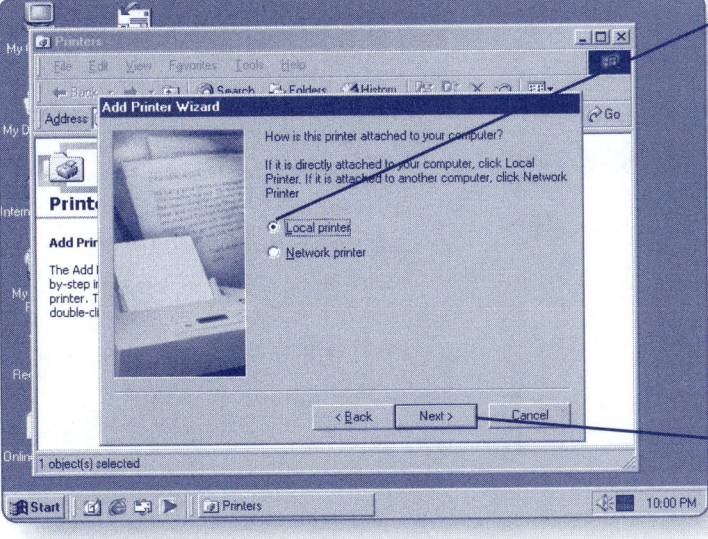

6. Click on **Local printer**. The option is selected.

NOTE
Hooking up to a network printer is discussed in the section "Connecting to a Network Printer" later in this chapter.

7. Click on **Next**. The next screen appears.

8a. Click on the **Manufacturer** and, in the **Printers** window, choose the model of your printer. The manufacturer and model names are selected.

OR

8b. Click on **Have Disk** if your printer is not listed and you have the installation disk that came with the printer. The Install from Disk dialog box opens. Follow the prompts in this dialog box.

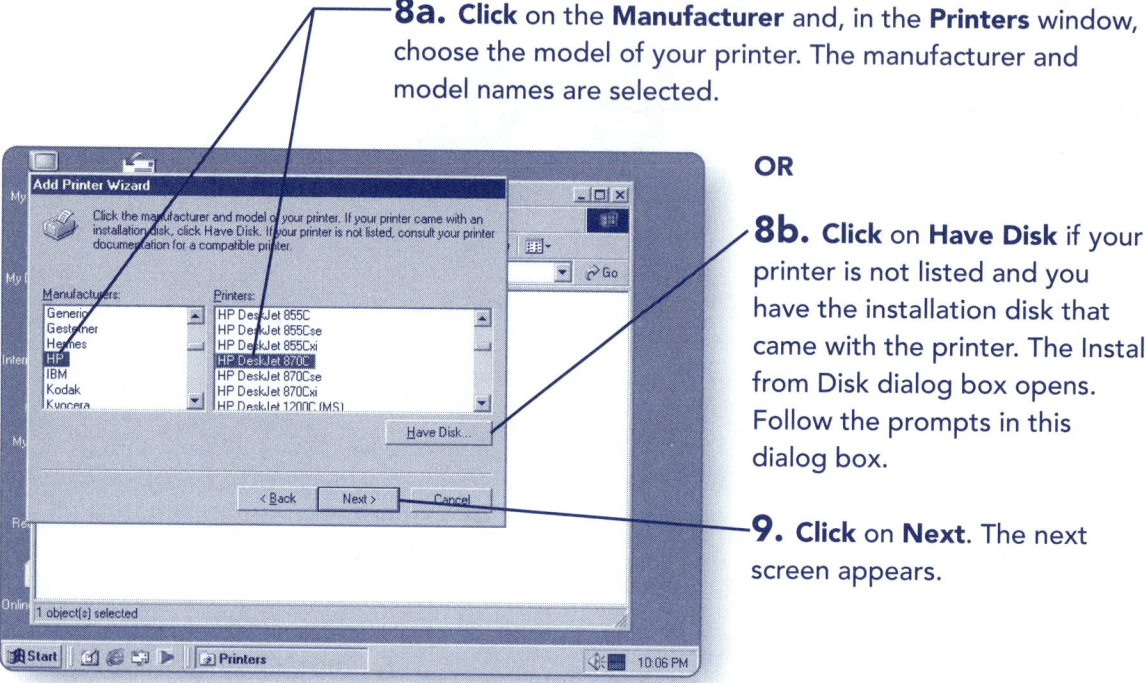

9. Click on **Next**. The next screen appears.

10. Click on **LPT1** or whatever printer port to which you attached the printer cable. The printer port name is selected.

11. Click on **Next**. The next screen appears.

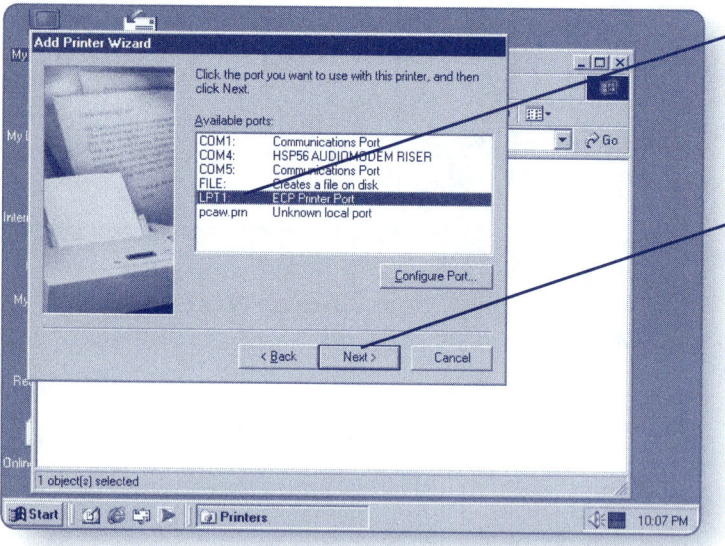

INSTALLING A NEW PRINTER 283

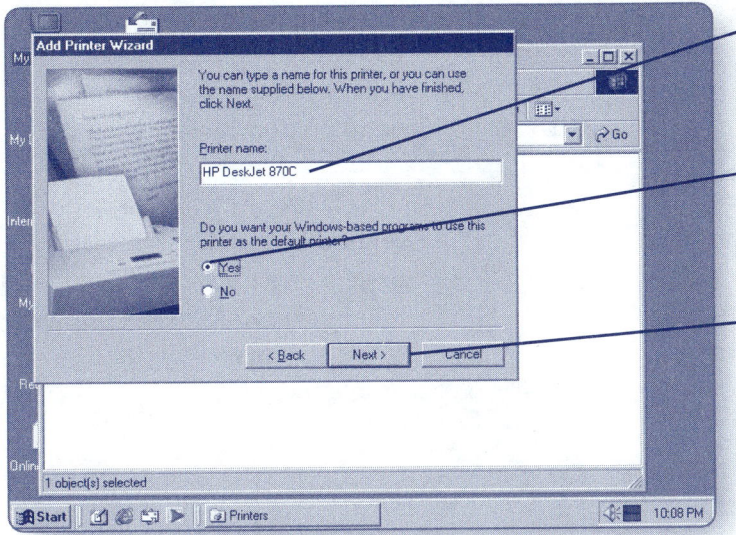

12. **Type** a descriptive **name** for the printer, if desired, in the Printer name: text box.

13. **Click** on **Yes** if this printer is your main printer. The option is selected.

14. **Click** on **Next**. The next screen appears.

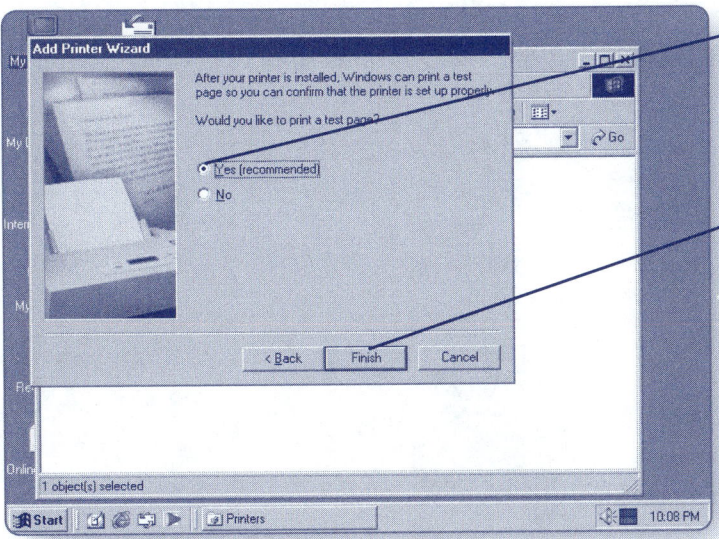

15. **Click** on **Yes** if you want to print a test page to check the connections to your printer. The option is selected.

16. **Click** on **Finish**. The Add Printer Wizard closes. The necessary files are copied to your computer and you might be prompted to insert the Windows CD-ROM or another specified disk.

284 CHAPTER 18: WORKING WITH PRINTERS

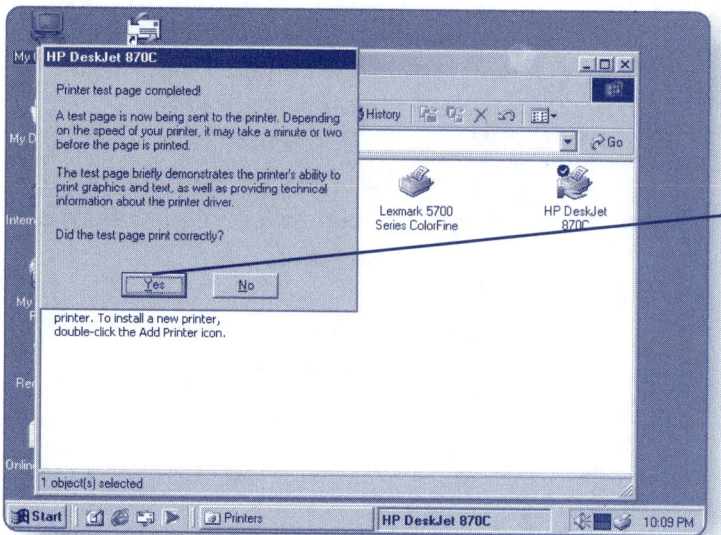

If you elected to print a test page, a dialog box opens, asking you whether the test page printed correctly.

17. Click on **Yes** if the page printed correctly. If the test page didn't print correctly, the Printing Troubleshooter appears to assist in resolving the problem.

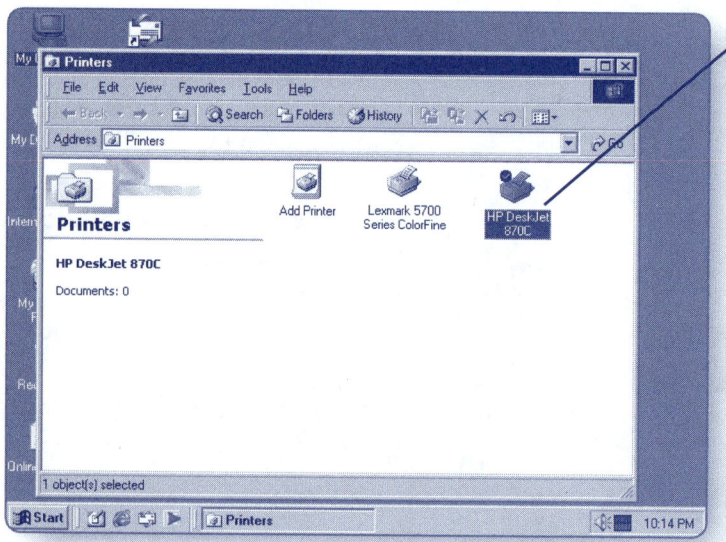

An icon representing the new printer appears in your printer folder.

Discovering Printer Properties

Printers have options that determine the default settings for a specific printer. These options are called *properties*.

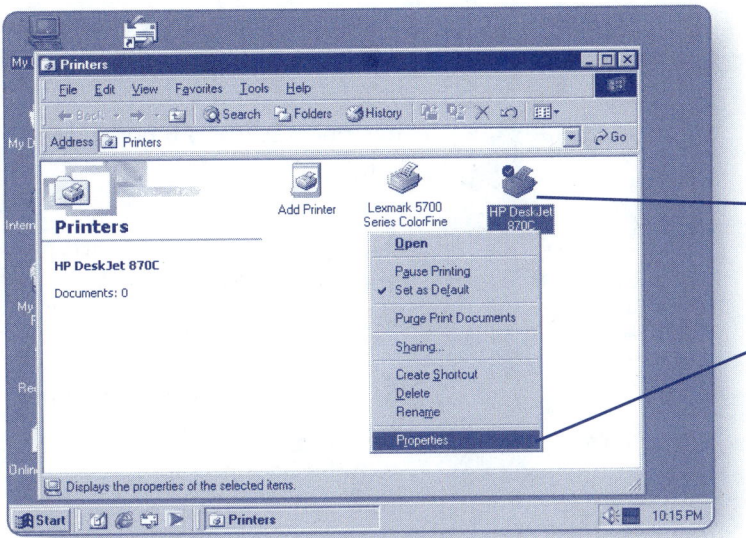

1. Right-click on the **printer** you want to modify. A shortcut menu appears.

2. Click on **Properties**. A Properties dialog box specific to your printer opens.

The Properties dialog box varies depending on the type of printer you have selected. Some printers have more choices available than others.

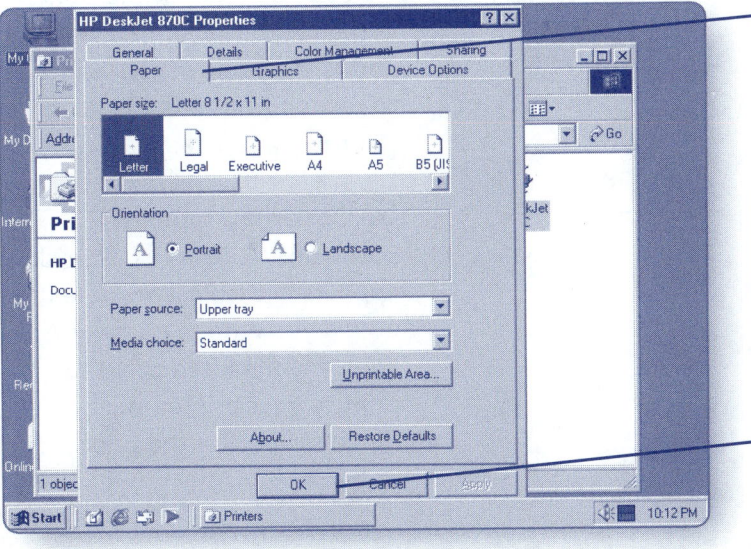

3. Click on the **Paper tab**. From here you can change the standard paper size, source, or orientation.

NOTE
Other tabs allow you to set timeout settings and various other options.

4. Click on **OK** when you have finished making any property changes. The Properties dialog box closes.

Sharing a Printer

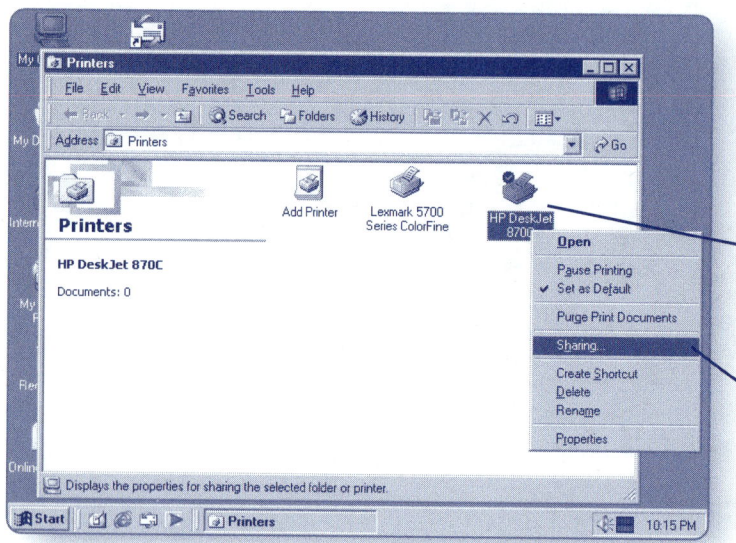

If you want to share your printer with others on your network, you must first tell the printer it has permission to be used by others.

1. Right-click on the **printer** that you want to share. A shortcut menu appears.

2. Click on **Sharing**. The Printer Properties dialog box opens with the Sharing tab at the front.

3. Click on **Shared As**. The option is selected, and the Shared As choices become available.

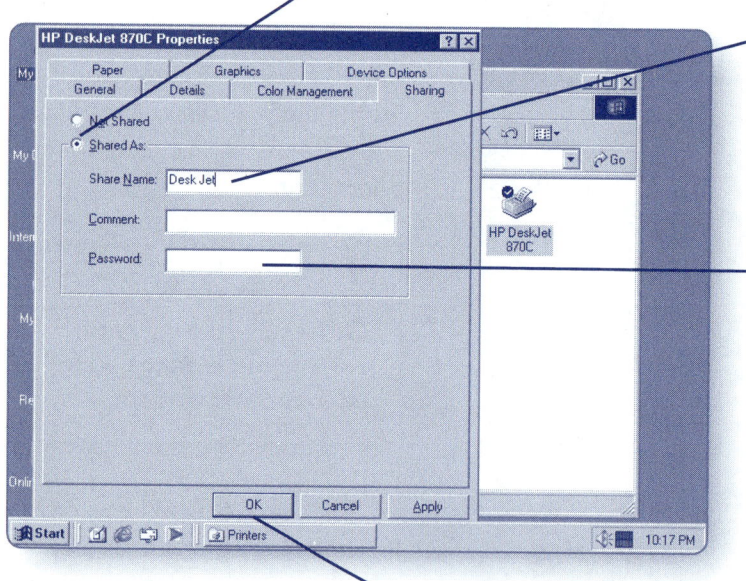

4. Type a **name** for the printer in the Share Name: text box. This is the name others will use to recognize that this is your printer.

5. Optionally, **type** a **password**. A series of asterisks appears in the Password: text box. If you enter a password here, anyone attempting to print to your printer must enter the password for the print job to begin.

6. Click on **OK**. The Printer Properties dialog box closes.

CONNECTING TO A NETWORK PRINTER   287

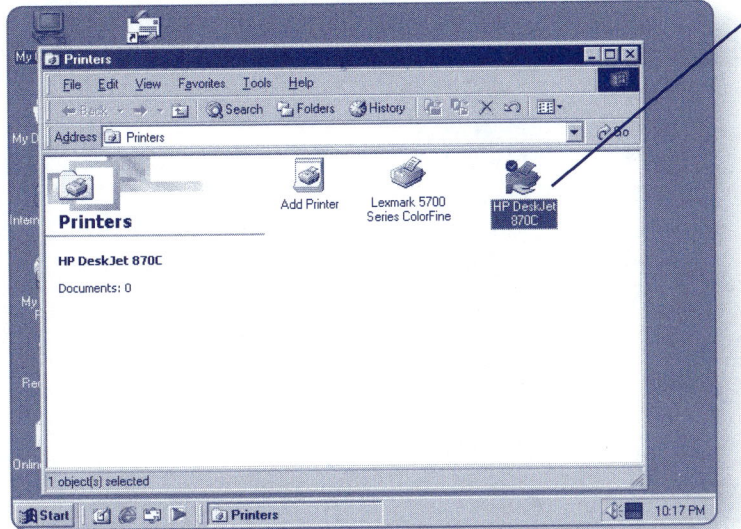

A shared printer is represented with a small hand under it.

Connecting to a Network Printer

If you want to print to a printer across a network, the printer must be a shared printer.

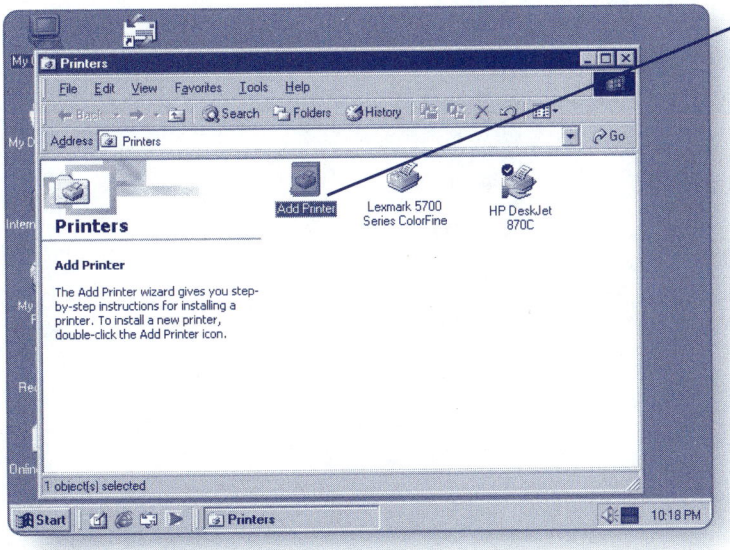

1. Click on **Add Printer**. The Add Printer Wizard opens.

288 CHAPTER 18: WORKING WITH PRINTERS

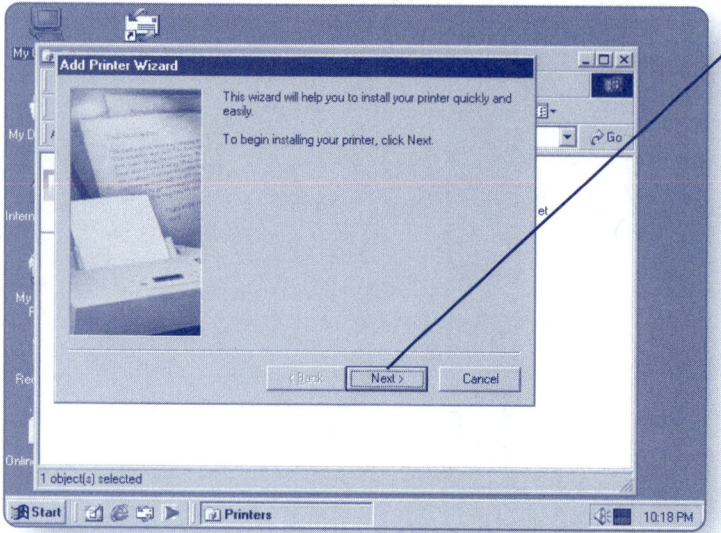

2. **Click** on **Next**. The next screen appears.

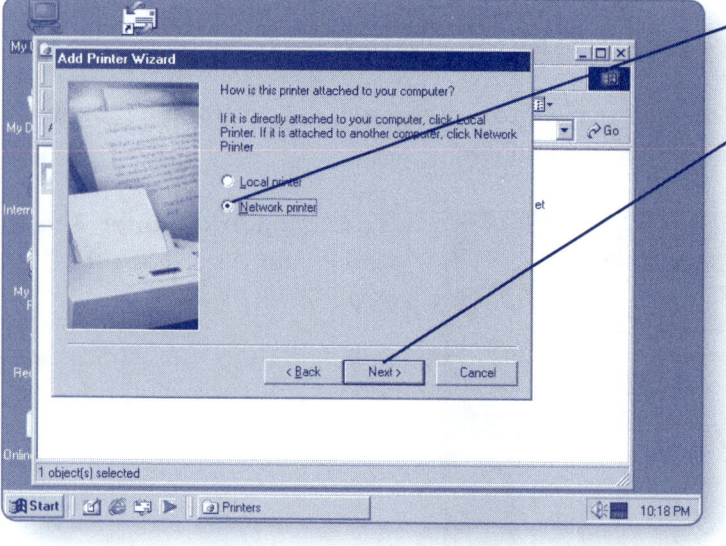

3. **Click** on **Network printer**. The option is selected.

4. **Click** on **Next**. The next screen appears.

CONNECTING TO A NETWORK PRINTER 289

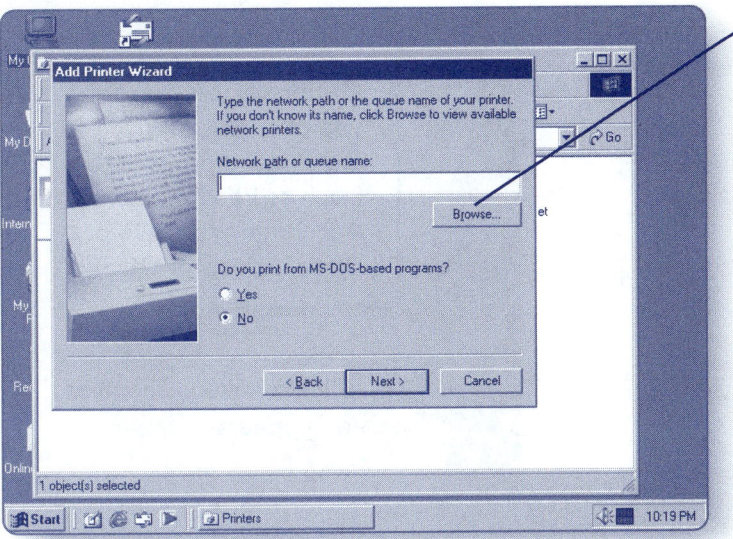

5. **Click** on **Browse**. The Browse for Printer dialog box opens.

6. **Click** on the **+ (plus sign)** next to the computer that has the printer to which you want to connect. The plus sign turns into a **− (minus sign)**, and a list of available printers appears.

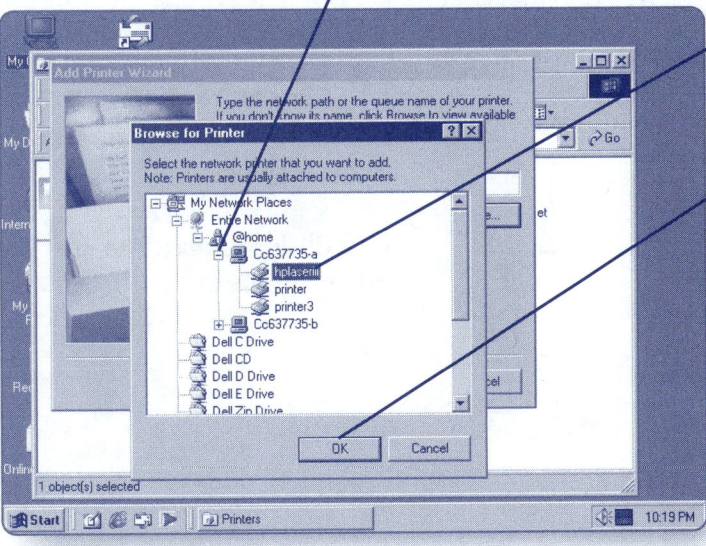

7. **Click** on the **printer** you want to use. The printer is highlighted.

8. **Click** on **OK**. The Browse for Printer dialog box closes, and the network path appears in the Add Printer Wizard dialog box.

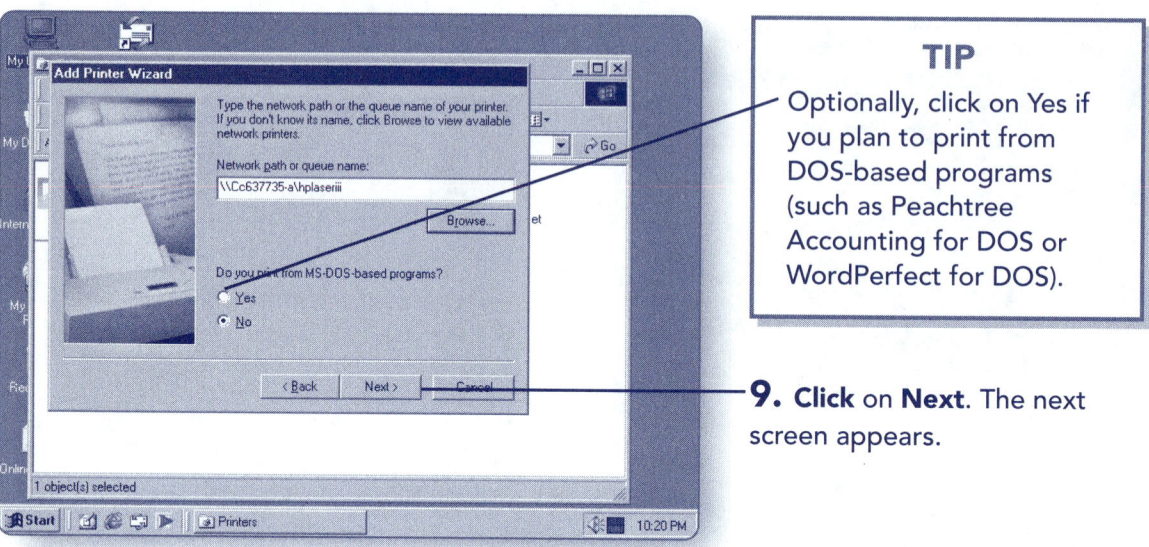

TIP

Optionally, click on Yes if you plan to print from DOS-based programs (such as Peachtree Accounting for DOS or WordPerfect for DOS).

9. Click on **Next**. The next screen appears.

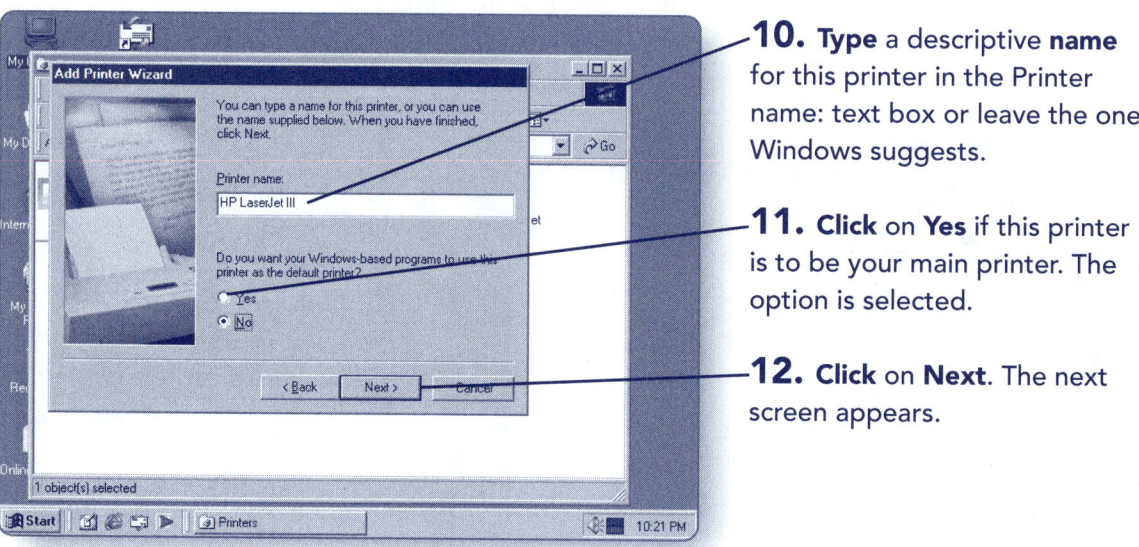

10. Type a descriptive **name** for this printer in the Printer name: text box or leave the one Windows suggests.

11. Click on **Yes** if this printer is to be your main printer. The option is selected.

12. Click on **Next**. The next screen appears.

CONNECTING TO A NETWORK PRINTER   291

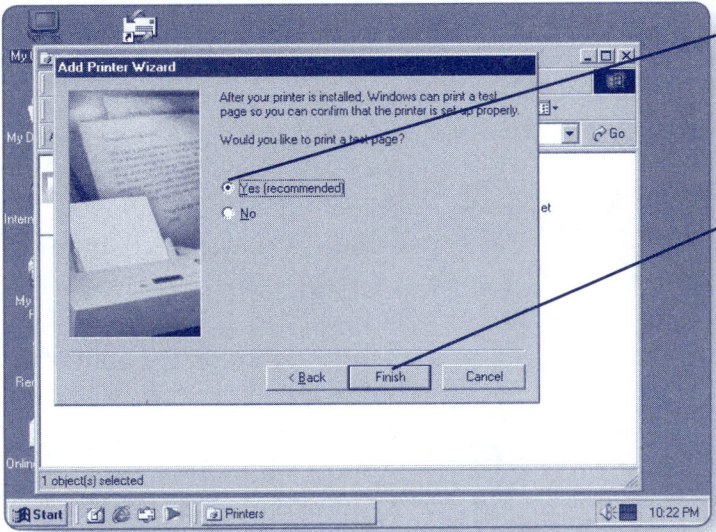

13. **Click** on **Yes** if you want Windows to print a test page to check the connections to your printer.

14. **Click** on **Finish**. The Add Printer Wizard closes, and the necessary files are copied to your computer. You may be prompted to insert the Windows CD-ROM or other specified disks.

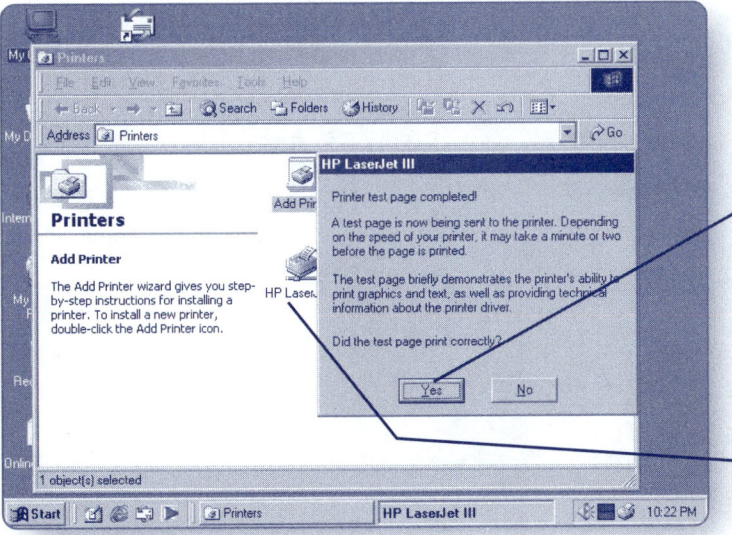

If you elected to print a test page, a dialog box opens, asking you whether the test page printed correctly.

15. **Click** on **Yes** if the page printed correctly. If the test page didn't print correctly, the Printing Troubleshooter appears to assist in resolving the problem.

A printer icon is displayed in the Printers window. A network printer is designated by what looks like a cable running underneath it.

Making a Printer the Default

You might have several printers to which you can print, including a fax or other device. One of these must be set as a default printer. The default printer is the one Windows assumes you want to print to unless you tell it otherwise.

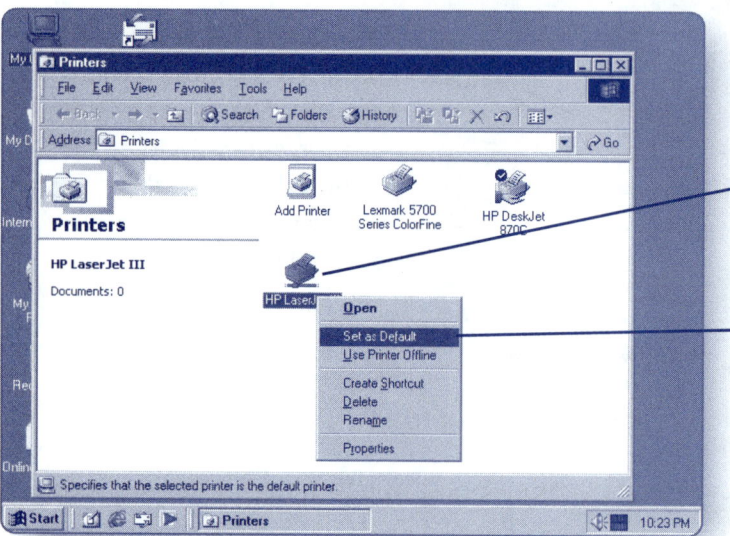

1. Right-click on the **printer** to be the default printer. A shortcut menu appears.

2. Click on **Set as Default**. The shortcut menu closes.

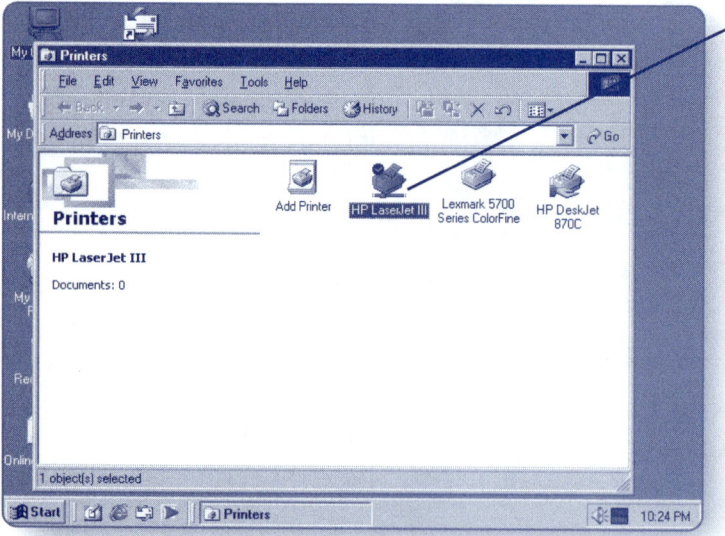

A ✔ appears on the printer icon to indicate it is the default printer.

Creating a Desktop Shortcut to the Printer

Having a printer icon on the desktop allows for "drag-and-drop" printing.

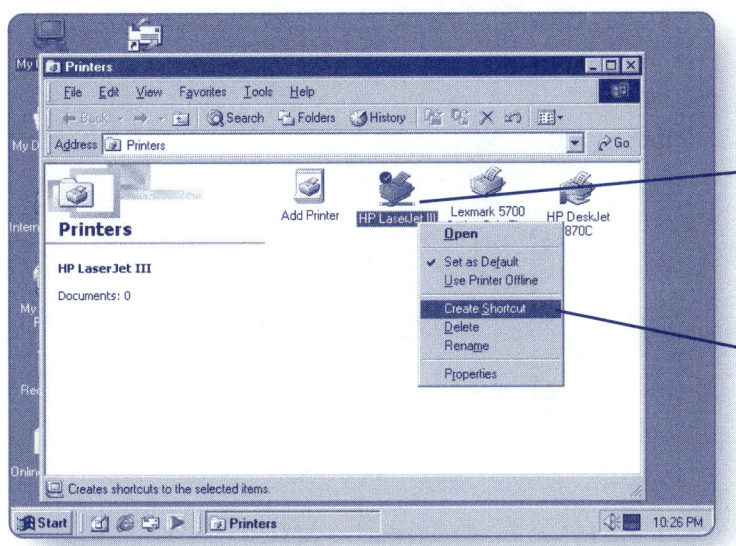

1. Right-click on the **printer** to which you want to create a shortcut. A shortcut menu appears.

2. Click on **Create Shortcut**. The Shortcut dialog box opens.

3. Click on **Yes**. The Shortcut dialog box closes.

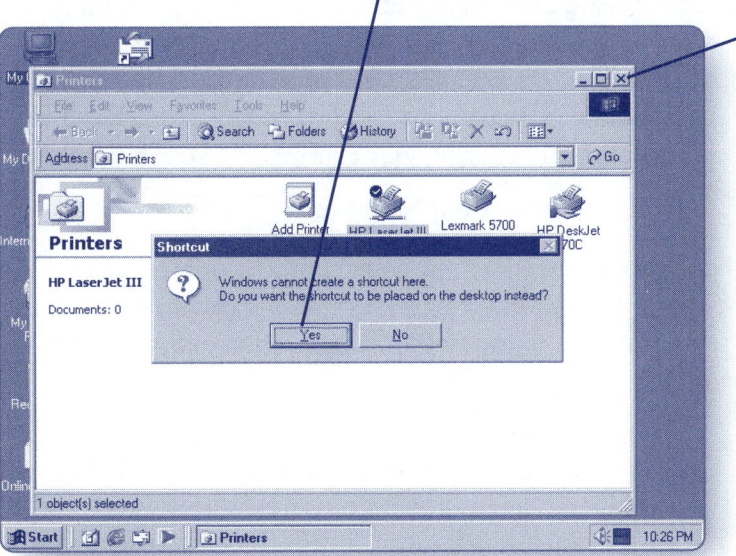

4. Click on the **Close button** ([X]). The Printers window closes, and a printer shortcut appears on your desktop.

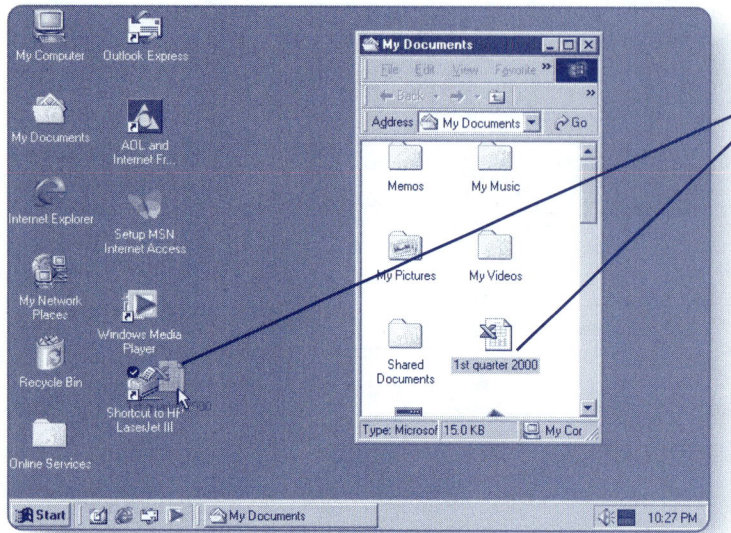

NOTE

To take advantage of drag-and-drop printing from the Windows desktop, Windows Explorer, or any Windows Open or Save File dialog box, click on the document you want to print and drag it to the printer shortcut icon. The document prints with any default settings installed for that printer.

Controlling Print Jobs

In previous chapters you learned how to print by pressing Ctrl+P, by clicking on the File menu and choosing Print, or even by clicking on a Printer button on a program toolbar. Sometimes, however, printing problems occur. Occasionally, you might need to stop a job from printing either temporarily or permanently, or you might need to "rush" a job ahead of others waiting in line. Printing is controlled through the print *queue*.

When you choose to print a document, the printer icon appears in the System Tray. If no printer is displayed in the System Tray, you're too late—the job has already gone to the printer.

CONTROLLING PRINT JOBS 295

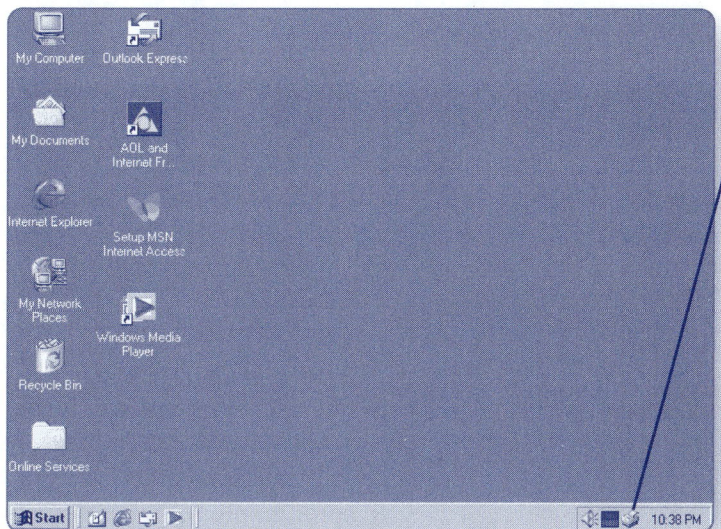

1. Double-click on the **printer icon** in the System Tray. The Printer window opens, displaying all jobs in the print queue.

TIP
Optionally, you can open the Printer window by clicking on Start, Settings, and then Printers.

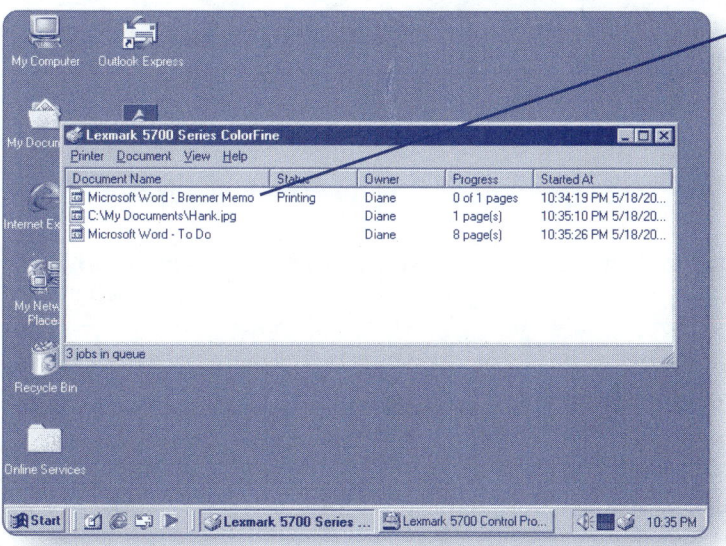

The job currently being printed is at the top of the list.

Pausing a Print Job

In many cases, you can use the Printer window to temporarily stop, or pause, a print job.

1. Click on the **print job** you want to pause. The job is selected.

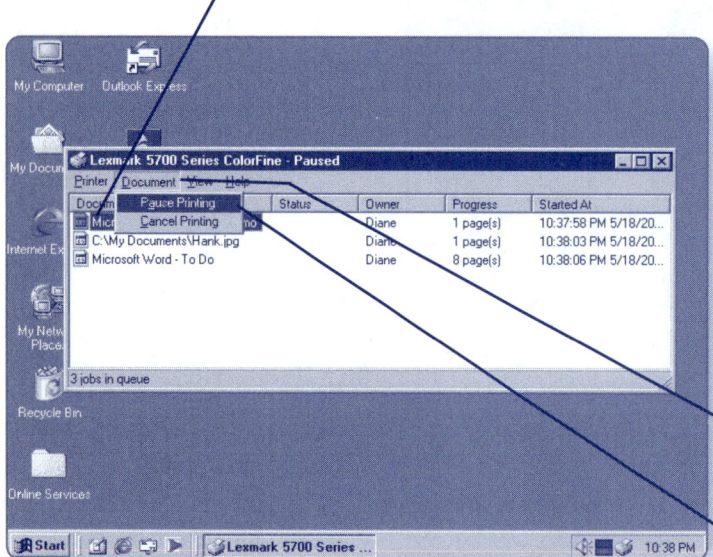

NOTE

If a print job isn't listed, it's because the job has already left the print queue and is in the printer memory. Turning off the printer is the only way to cancel the job.

2. Click on **Document**. The Document menu appears.

3. Click on **Pause Printing**. The print job temporarily stops.

4. Repeat these **steps** to resume printing. The print job resumes.

Deleting a Print Job

If you want to completely stop the printing of a particular print job, you can delete the print job from the Printer window.

CONTROLLING PRINT JOBS 297

1. Click on the **print job** you want to stop. The job is selected.

2. Click on **Document**. The Document menu appears.

3. Click on **Cancel Printing**. The print job is deleted from the print queue.

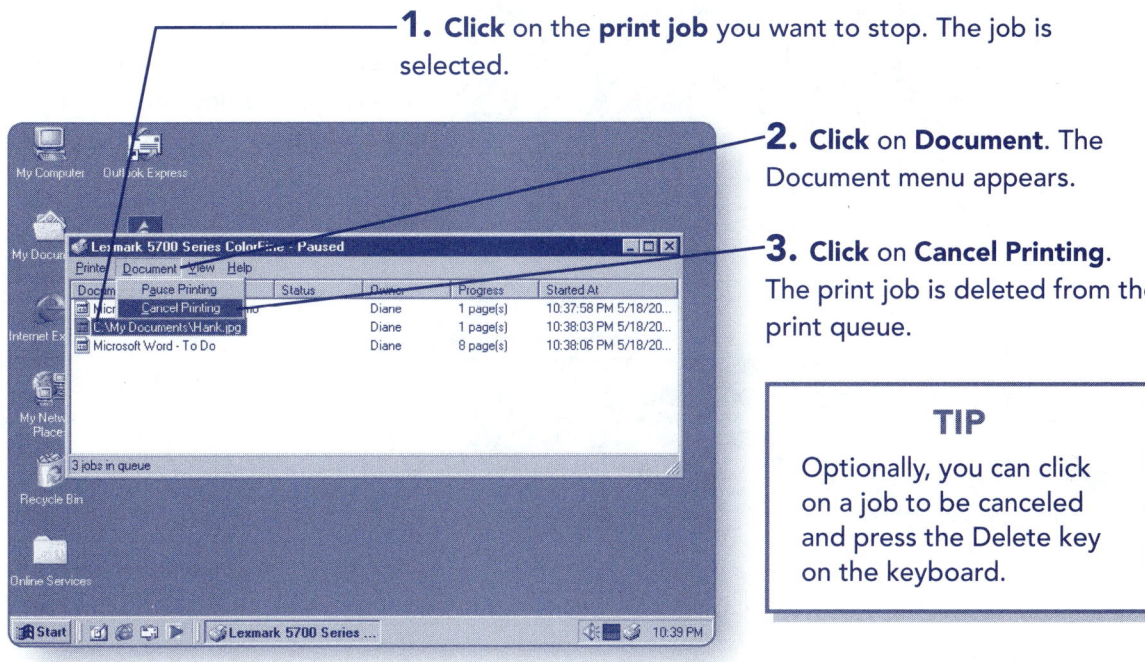

TIP
Optionally, you can click on a job to be canceled and press the Delete key on the keyboard.

Rushing a Print Job

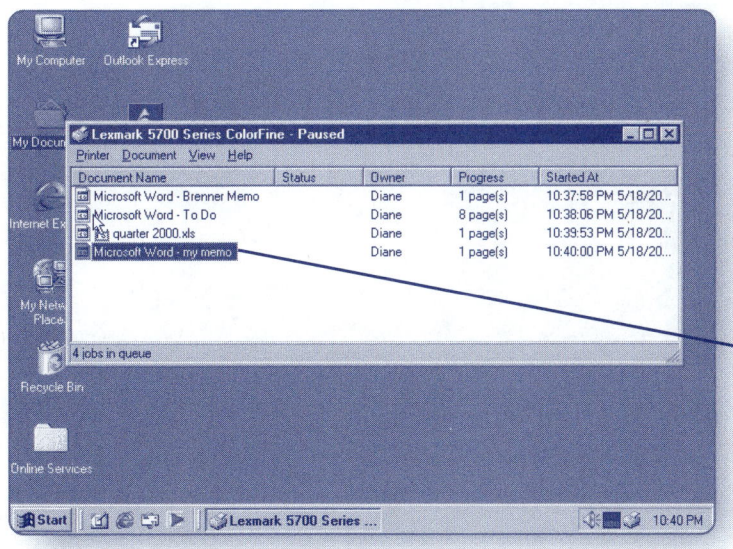

If there are several print jobs waiting in line to be printed, you can change the order of the jobs to be printed. You cannot send a print job ahead of a job currently in the process of printing, but you can place it next in line.

1. Click on the **print job** you want to move. The job is selected.

298 CHAPTER 18: WORKING WITH PRINTERS

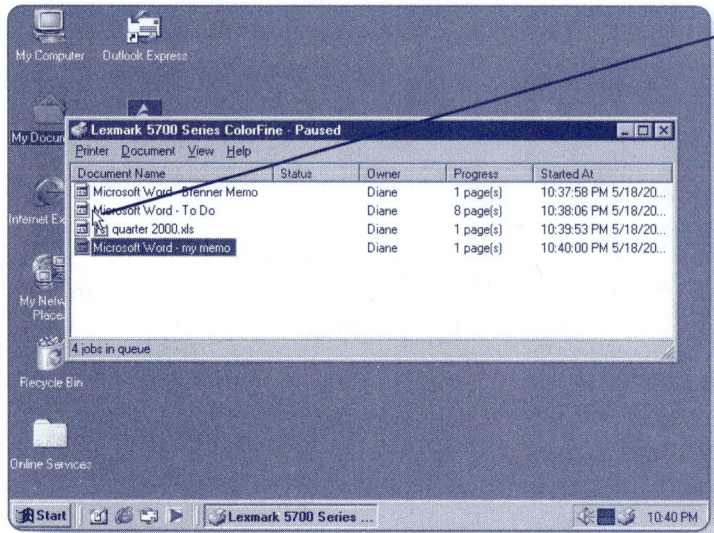

2. Drag the **print job** to the desired position in the list. The mouse pointer indicates the new position.

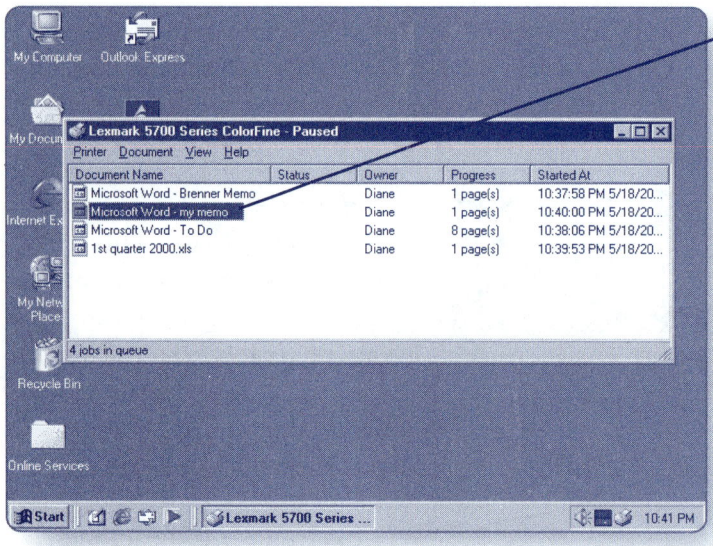

3. Release the mouse **button**. The job is moved to the new location and priority.

Part IV Review Questions

1. How can you turn off the Auto Arrange feature? *See "Moving and Deleting Icons" in Chapter 15*

2. What two icons located on your desktop cannot be renamed? *See "Renaming an Icon" in Chapter 15*

3. What does Auto Hide do to the Windows taskbar? *See "Changing Taskbar Options" in Chapter 15*

4. When are mouse trails handy to use? *See "Changing Mouse Visibility" in Chapter 16*

5. Why should you have a Windows Millennium Edition startup disk? *See "Creating a Windows Startup Disk" in Chapter 16*

6. What do MouseKeys do? *See "Using MouseKeys" in Chapter 16*

7. What do screen savers do? *See "Selecting a Screen Saver" in Chapter 17*

8. What can activating the Active Desktop do? *See "Integrating Your Desktop with the Web" in Chapter 17*

9. What is the name of the tool furnished with Windows Millennium Edition to assist you with installing a new printer? *See "Installing a New Printer" in Chapter 18*

10. How can you tell whether your printer is shared? *See "Sharing a Printer" in Chapter 18*

PART V

Using the Internet

Chapter 19
　　Connecting to the Internet **303**

Chapter 20
　　Surfing with Internet Explorer **323**

Chapter 21
　　E-Mailing with Outlook Express **339**

Chapter 22
　　Using the Windows Address Book **365**

19

Connecting to the Internet

Whether you plan on surfing the Internet or just need to send an e-mail message to a friend, you need to get connected. Windows provides several tools to assist you with your connectivity needs. In this chapter, you'll learn how to:

- Subscribe to an online service
- Create an Internet connection
- Start your Web browser

Subscribing to an Online Service

When you install Windows Millennium, Windows places the Online Services folder on your desktop. This folder contains setup icons that connect to several online services or Internet service providers (ISPs). By selecting an online service or ISP, you establish an account with that company directly.

Internet service providers in the Online Services folder include:

- America Online
- Prodigy Internet
- AT&T WorldNet
- Earthlink Internet

Online service providers charge a fee for these services. The fee varies with the plan you subscribe to, but you can expect to pay $10–$50 per month. You make payment arrangements directly with the online service or ISP. Many services also offer a predetermined number of free trial hours.

> **NOTE**
> To set up an online service, you'll need a credit card to bill for the services. The service won't bill you during the free trial hours, but you can't even get connected without a credit card number. If you decide to cancel an online service, you'll need to notify the service provider.

Signing Up for MSN Internet Access

You'll find the setup process for each service similar, but each varies slightly from the others. In this chapter, we'll subscribe to The Microsoft Network (MSN).

SUBSCRIBING TO AN ONLINE SERVICE   305

1a. Click on **Setup MSN Internet Access**. The MSN Setup screen appears.

OR

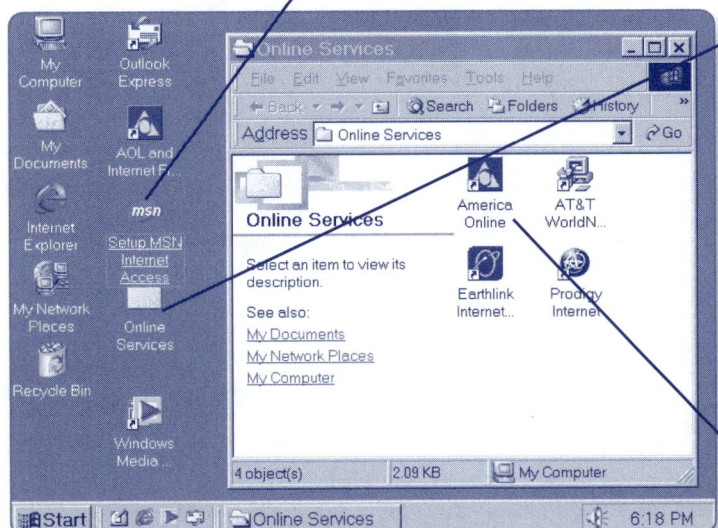

1b. Click on the **Online Services folder**. The Online Services window opens.

NOTE

Before you can connect to any of these services, you must have a modem in your computer that connects to a telephone line.

2. Click on the **service** you want to set up. The online service's setup screen appears.

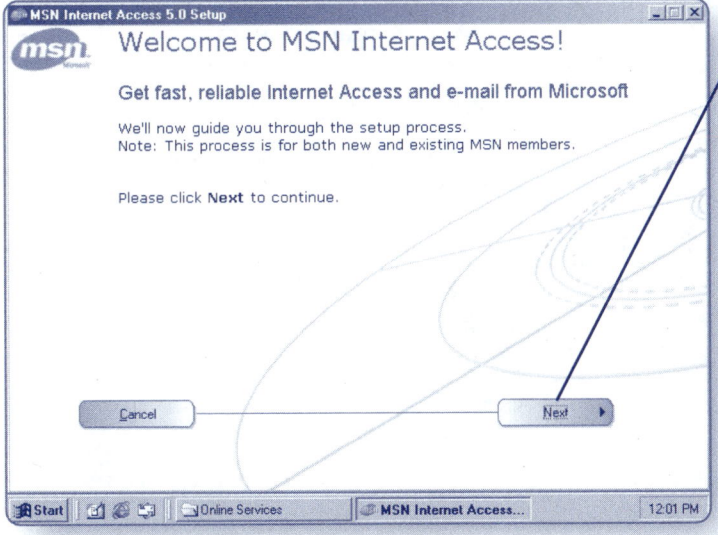

3. Click on **Next**. The Using Your Modem to Connect screen appears.

306 CHAPTER 19: CONNECTING TO THE INTERNET

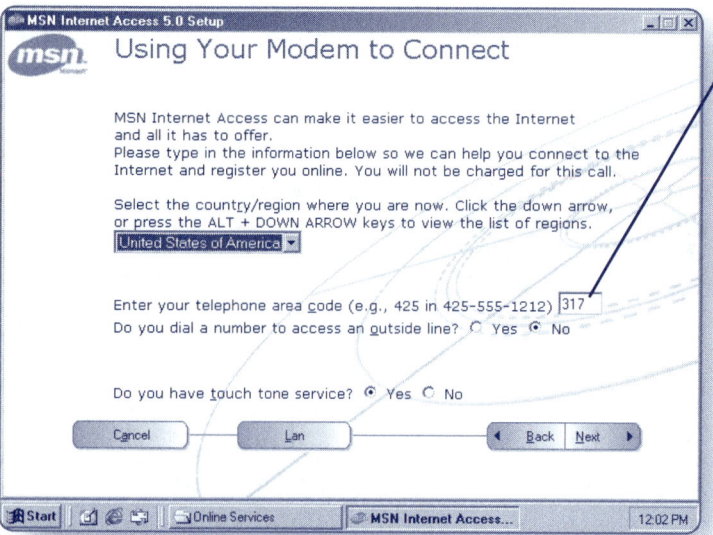

4. **Enter** your **area code**. The area code you enter appears in the area code box.

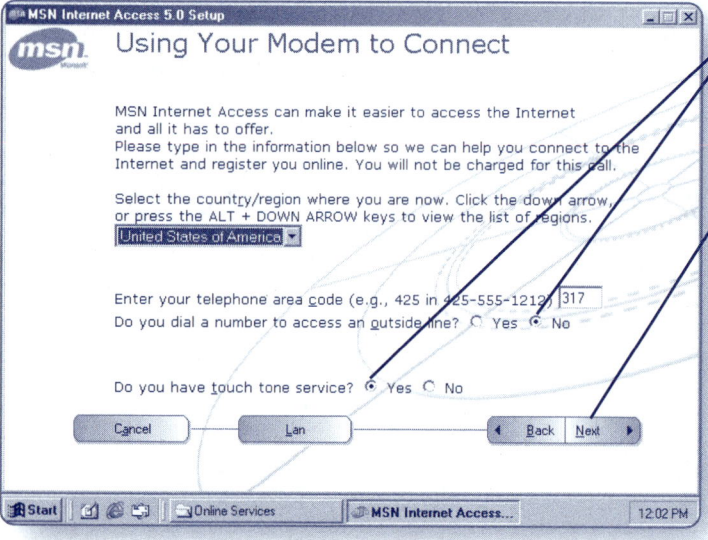

5. **Make choices** from the other screen selections. The options are selected.

6. **Click** on **Next**. The Welcome screen appears.

SUBSCRIBING TO AN ONLINE SERVICE 307

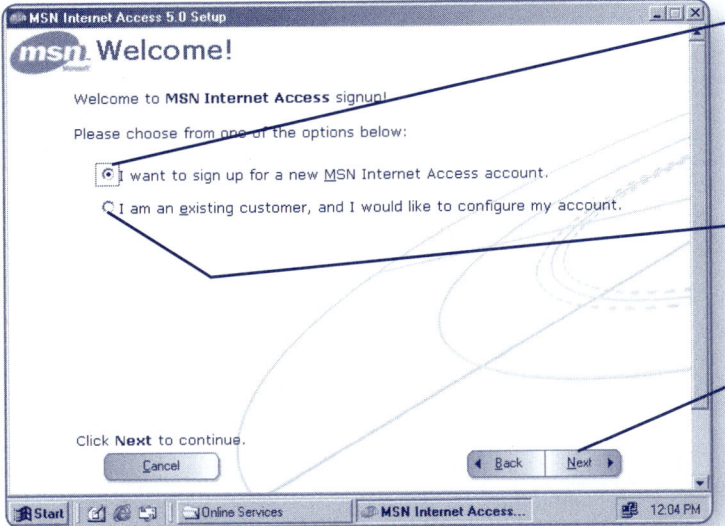

7a. **Click** on **I want to sign up for a new MSN Internet Access account**. The option is selected.

OR

7b. **Click** on **I am an existing customer, and I would like to configure my account**.

8. Click on **Next**. The Billing Plan screen appears.

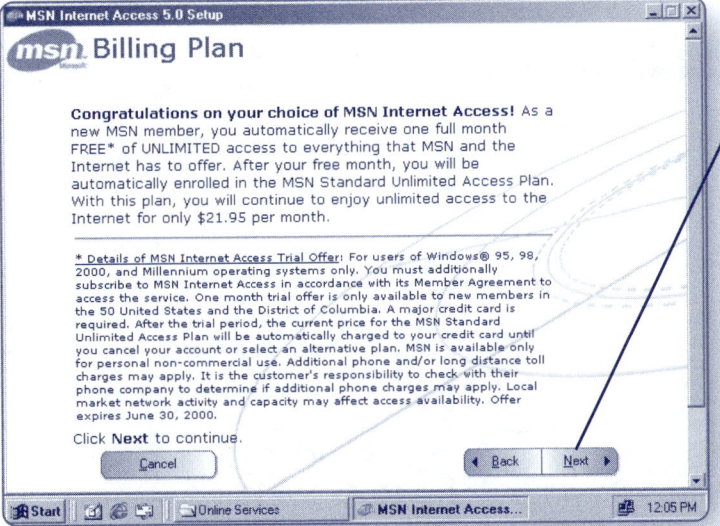

Read the billing plan carefully.

9. Click on **Next**. The User Information screen appears.

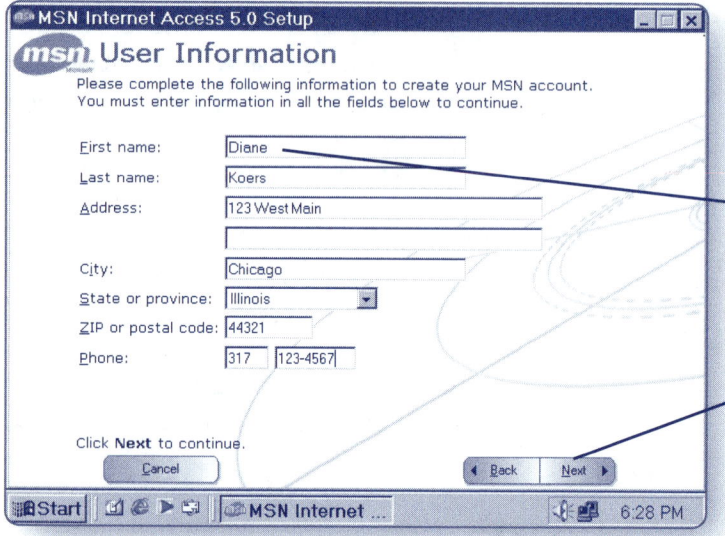

MSN Setup prompts you for personal information, such as name, address, and phone number.

10. Enter the requested **information**. Each piece of information appears in the appropriate text box.

11. Click on **Next**. The Member ID & Password screen appears.

12. Choose a **Member ID**. The option is selected.

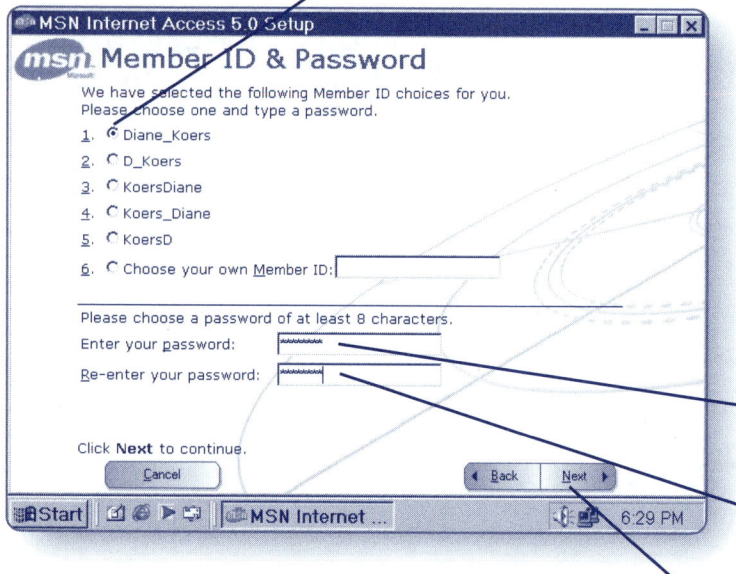

NOTE

If you create your own member ID, you can use any combination of letters, numbers, hyphens, or the underscore characters, but don't use spaces or other special characters.

13. Enter a **password**. A series of asterisks appears.

14. Re-enter the same **password**. A series of asterisks appears.

15. Click on **Next**. The MSN License Agreement appears.

SUBSCRIBING TO AN ONLINE SERVICE 309

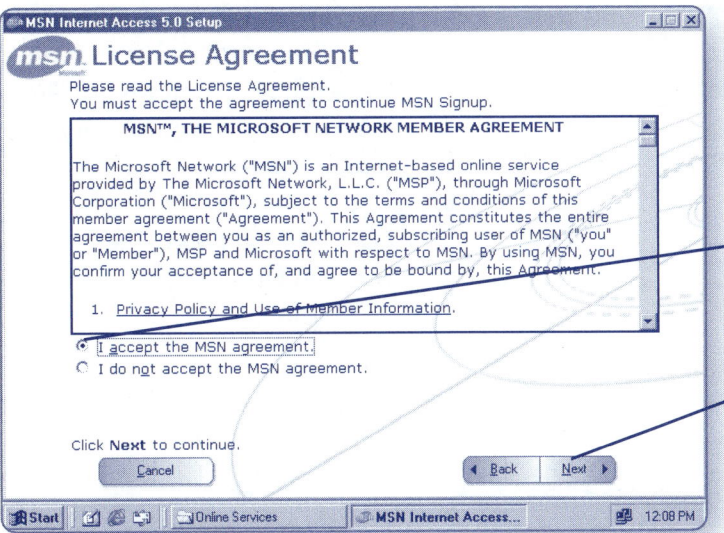

TIP
Read the agreement carefully.

16. **Click** on **I accept the MSN agreement**. The option is selected.

17. **Click** on **Next**. The Payment Method screen appears.

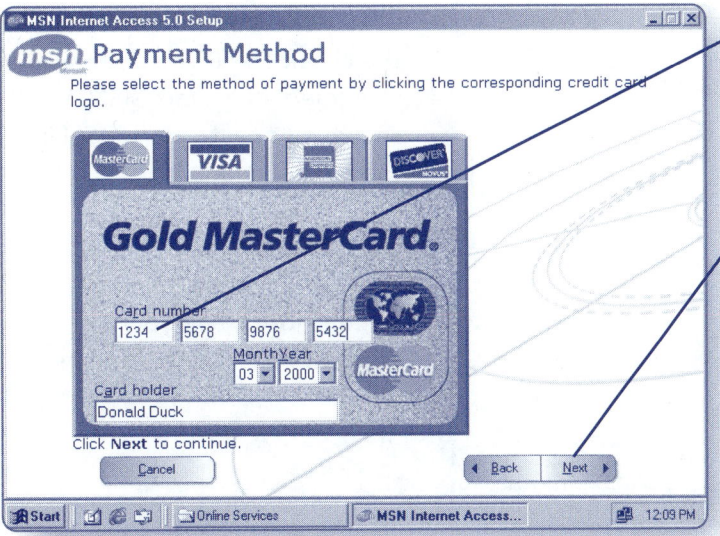

18. **Enter** your **credit card information**. Don't put any dashes or spaces in the credit card number.

19. **Click** on **Next**. The Settings screen appears.

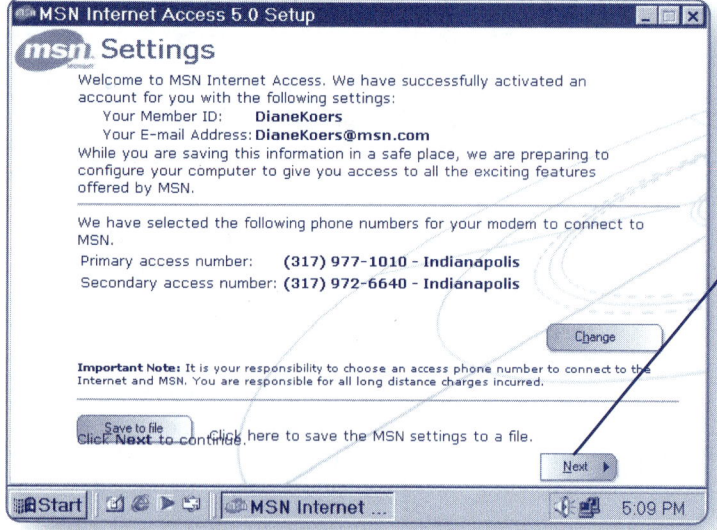

The Settings screen confirms your member ID, e-mail address (write it down somewhere), and your primary and secondary access phone numbers.

20. **Click** on **Next**. The Congratulations screen appears.

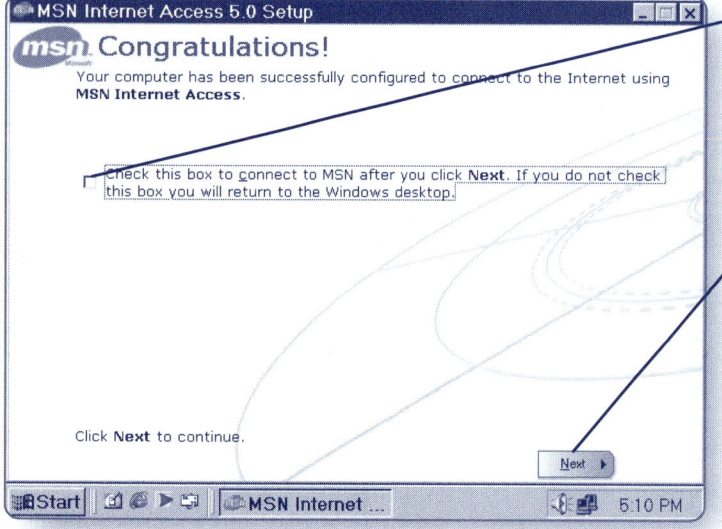

21. **Remove** the **check** from the check box if you don't want to immediately start MSN. We'll show you how to start MSN in the next section.

22. **Click** on **Next**. The MSN Internet Access 5.0 Setup screen closes, and your Windows desktop reappears.

SUBSCRIBING TO AN ONLINE SERVICE 311

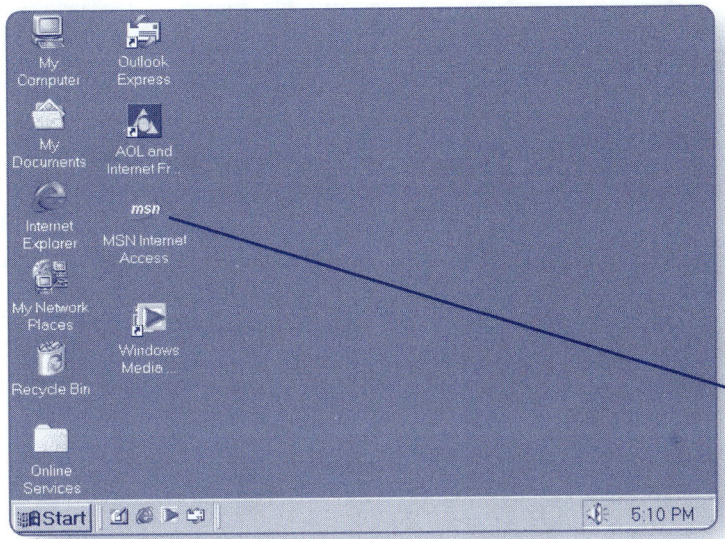

Starting MSN Internet Access

Did you notice the MSN icon changed? Before you signed up, it read "Setup MSN Internet Access." Now it reads "MSN Internet Access." The appearance of the icon changed also.

1. Click on the **MSN Internet Access icon**. The MSN Sign-In window appears.

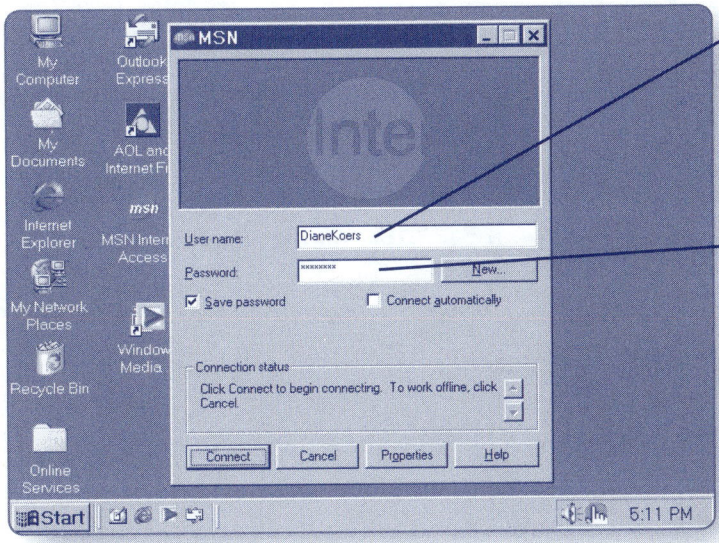

2. If not already displayed, **type** your **user name** in the User name: text box. Your user name is the same as your Member ID.

3. Type your **password** in the Password: text box. A series of asterisks appears.

312 CHAPTER 19: CONNECTING TO THE INTERNET

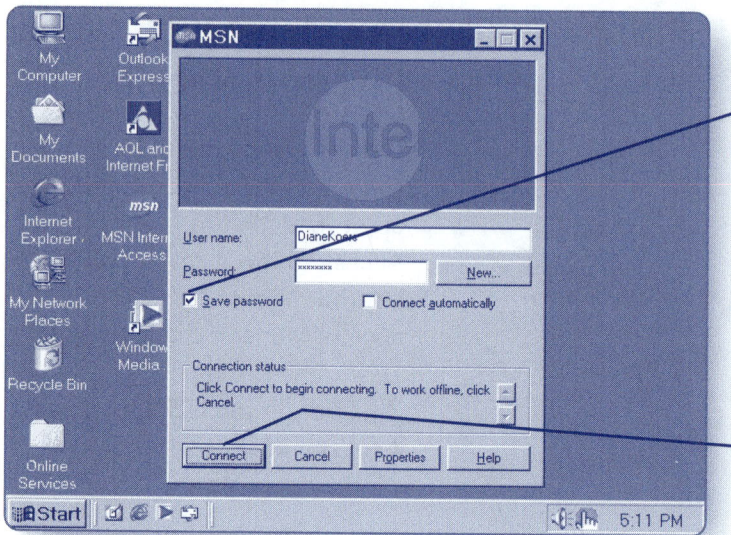

TIP
Click on the Save password check box, and you won't have to type your password each time; however, this also gives anyone who uses your computer free access to your Internet account.

4. Click on **Connect**. The modem dials The Microsoft Network.

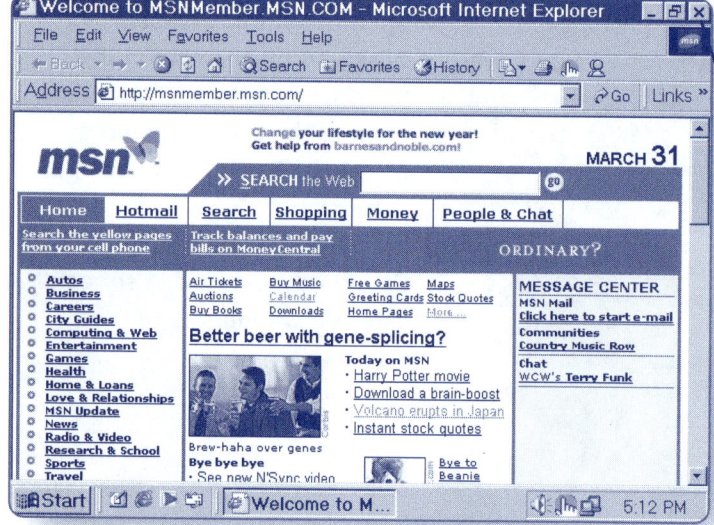

Congratulations! When you're connected, the Microsoft Internet Explorer launches to the MSN member home page.

5. Click the **Close button**. The Internet Explorer window closes.

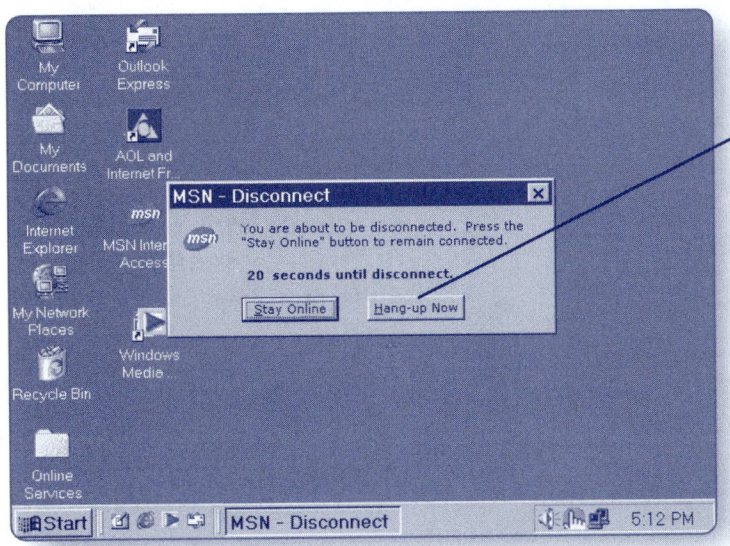

You'll probably want to close your Internet connection.

6. Click on **Hang-Up Now**. MSN disconnects.

Creating a Dial-Up Connection

If you already have a direct Internet access provider, you'll need to tell Windows how to connect to your ISP. Windows stores information about your connections in the Dial-Up Networking folder. Some people refer to Dial-Up Networking as *DUN* or *DUNS*.

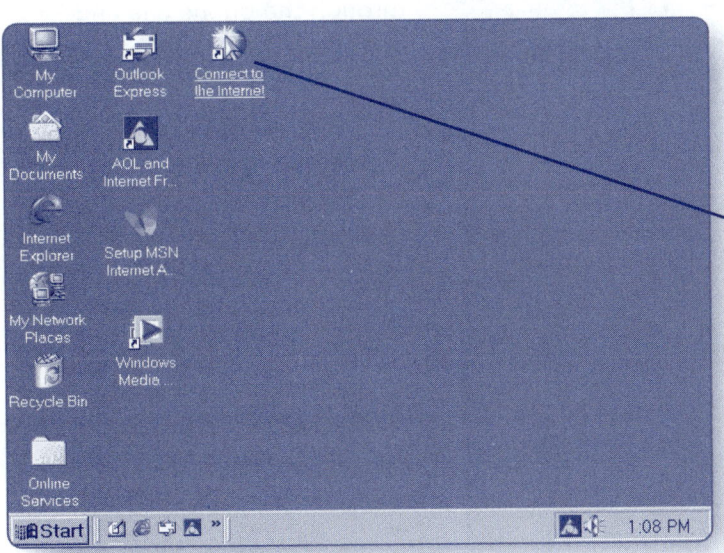

1. Click on **Connect to the Internet**. The Internet Connection Wizard begins.

314 CHAPTER 19: CONNECTING TO THE INTERNET

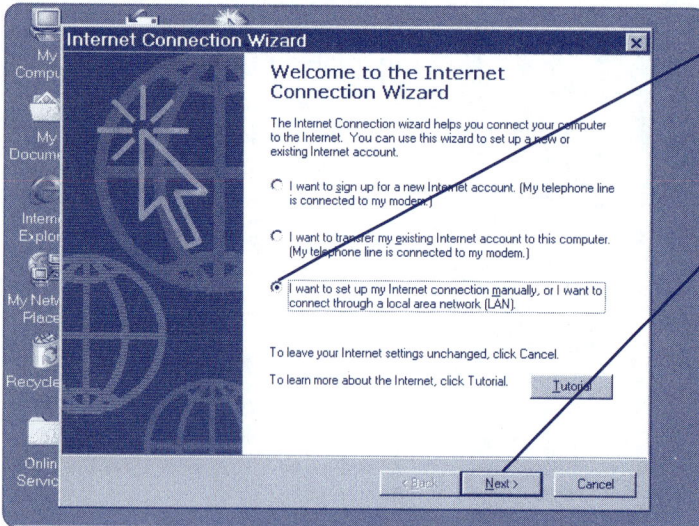

2. Click on **I want to set up my Internet connection manually**. The option is selected.

3. Click on **Next**. The Setting Up Your Internet Connection screen appears.

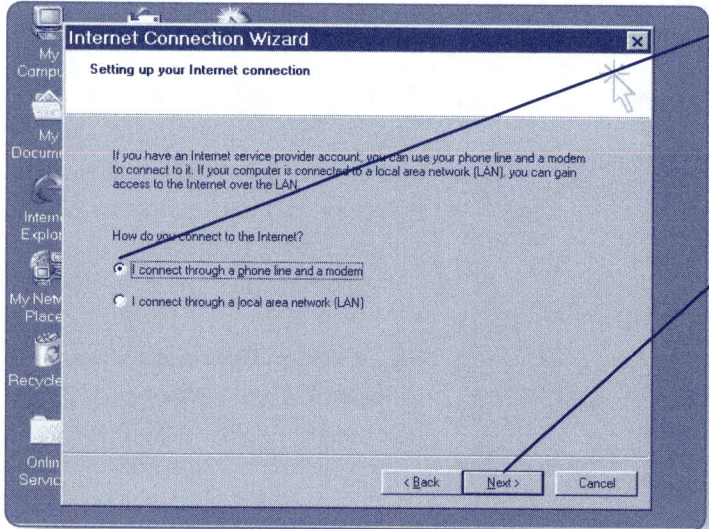

4. Choose the **connection type**. The option is selected. In our example, we're connecting through the phone line and modem.

5. Click on **Next**. The Step 1 of 3 screen appears.

CREATING A DIAL-UP CONNECTION   315

6. Enter the **area code, telephone number**, and **country** you'll call. Your Internet service provider provides this information.

7. If you don't need to dial an area code to reach your ISP, **remove** the **check** from Dial using the area code and country code.

8. Click on **Next**. The Step 2 of 3 screen appears.

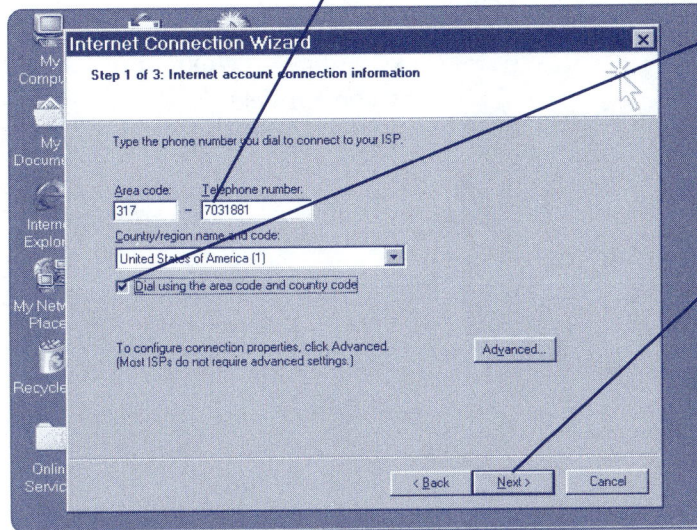

9. Enter your **user name**. This is also provided by your ISP. The user name appears in the User name: text box.

10. Enter your **password**. The password appears as a series of asterisks.

11. Click on **Next**. The Step 3 of 3 screen appears.

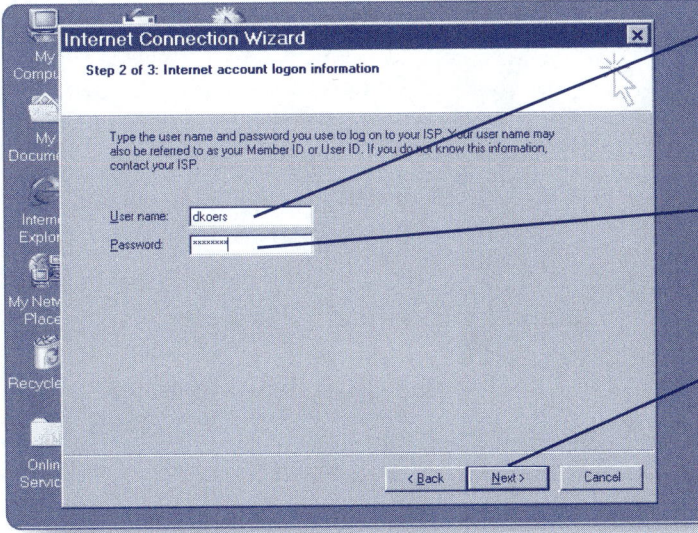

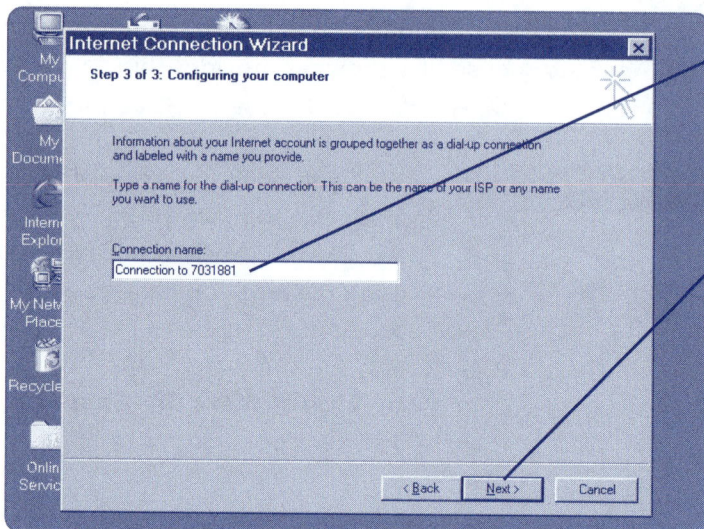

12. **Type** a **name** for the connection (one that you'll recognize as a connection to your ISP).

13. **Click** on **Next**. The next screen appears.

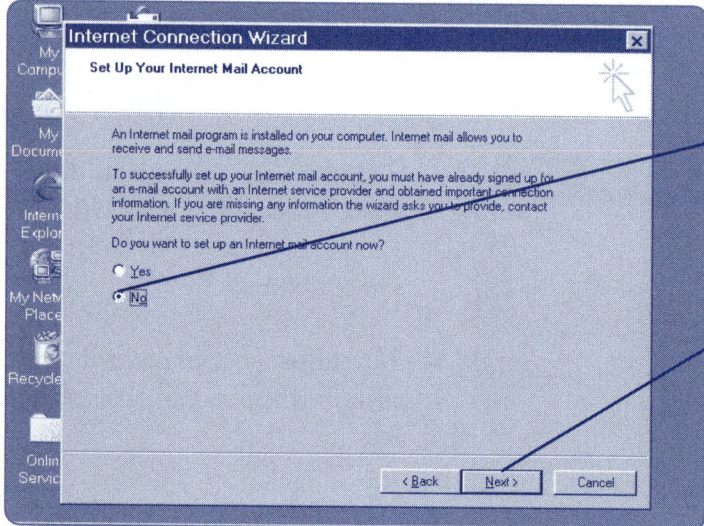

Next you're prompted to set up your mail accounts.

14. For now, **click** on **No**. We'll set up the mail account in Chapter 21, "E-mailing with Outlook Express."

15. **Click** on **Next**. The Internet Connection Wizard final screen appears.

CREATING A DIAL-UP CONNECTION   317

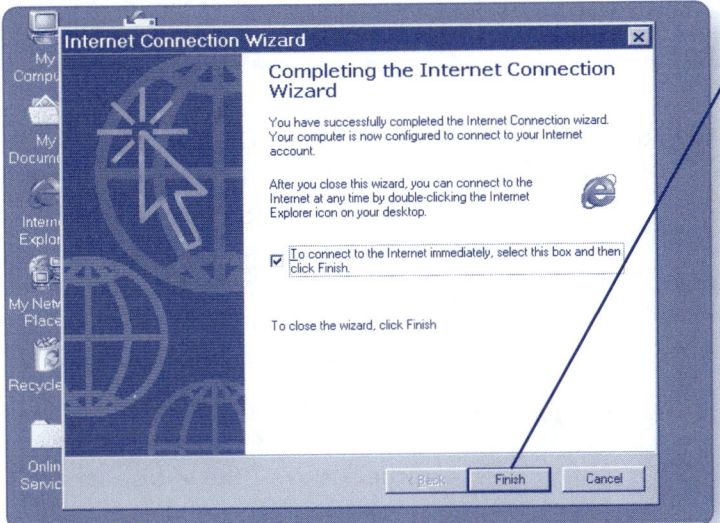

16. Click on **Finish**. The Connect To dialog box appears.

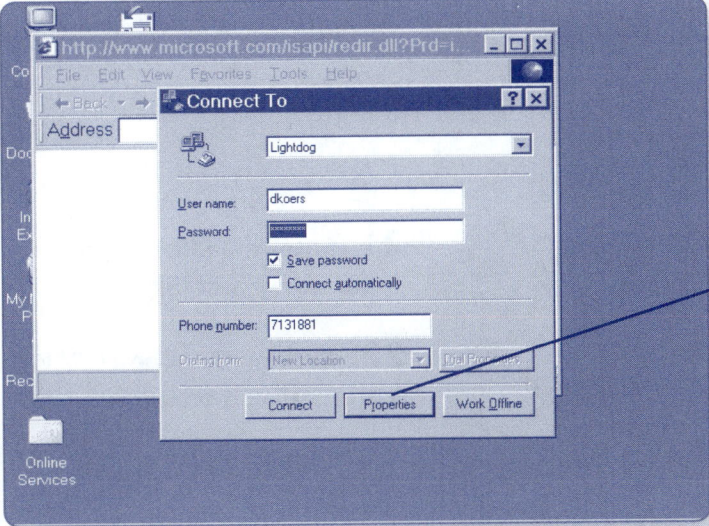

Although it appears you're ready to connect to your ISP, you might not be quite finished yet. Most ISPs have other information you'll need to enter that applies to their operation.

17. Click on **Properties**. The properties dialog box for your connection opens.

18. Click on the **Networking tab**. The Networking tab appears in front.

The type of information you enter here varies between the different ISPs. If you don't have written instructions for these steps from your ISP, call them and ask them to talk you through the choices you'll need to make for their connection.

19. Click on any necessary **choices**. A ✔ appears in the check boxes (the ✔ disappears from check boxes already selected).

20. If instructed by your ISP, **click** on **TCP/IP Settings**. The TCP/IP Settings dialog box opens.

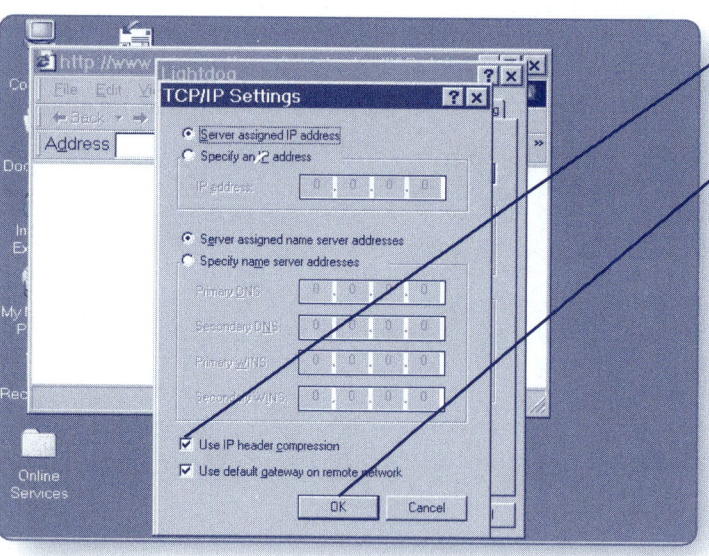

21. Enter the **information** as specified by your ISP.

22. Click on **OK**. The TCP/IP Settings dialog box closes.

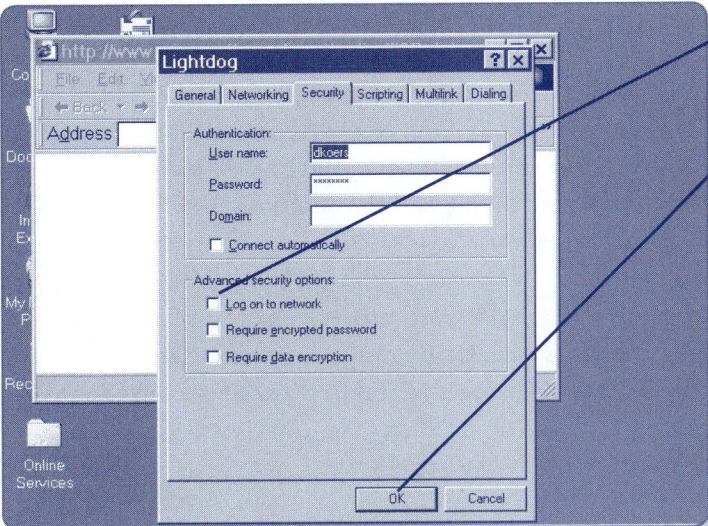

23. **Change** any other **settings** as specified by your ISP.

24. **Click** on **OK** when you have completed making any changes to your connection. The properties dialog box closes.

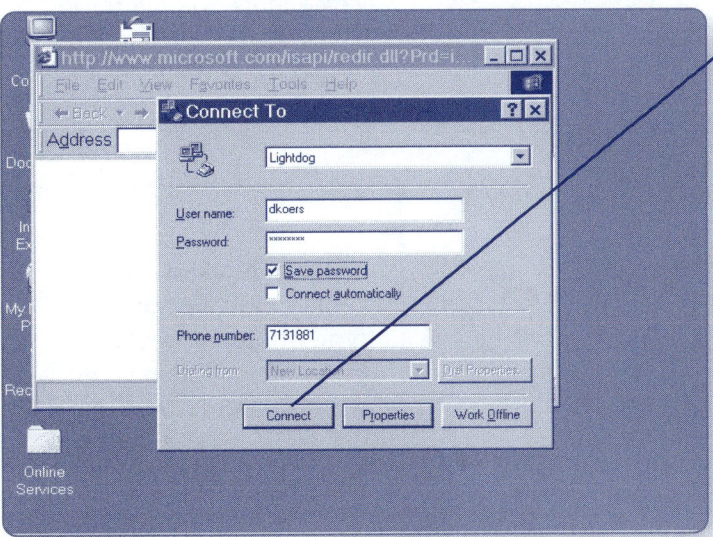

25. **Click** on **Connect**. A connection to your ISP is established, and your Web browser opens.

Starting Your Web Browser

With an Internet connection, you'll use a type of application to view the HTML documents created for the World Wide Web, called a *Web browser*. Several types of Web browsers exist on the market today, and the features that each offers are updated frequently.

Two of the most popular Web browsers are Microsoft Internet Explorer and Netscape Navigator. Windows includes Internet Explorer 5.5 with Windows Millennium Edition. Netscape Navigator also is a free product. You can download Netscape Navigator from http://www.netscape.com.

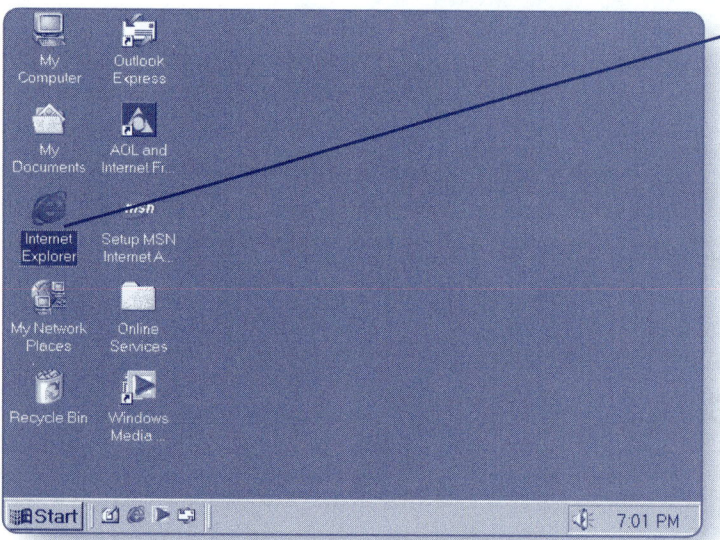

1. Click on the **icon** representing the browser you want to use. In our example, we're connecting on Internet Explorer. If you're using a dial-up connection, the Connect To dialog box appears.

> **NOTE**
>
> If you're hooked up to a cable modem or other type of permanent Internet connection, you won't see the Connect To dialog box. The browser starts and displays a starting page.

STARTING YOUR WEB BROWSER 321

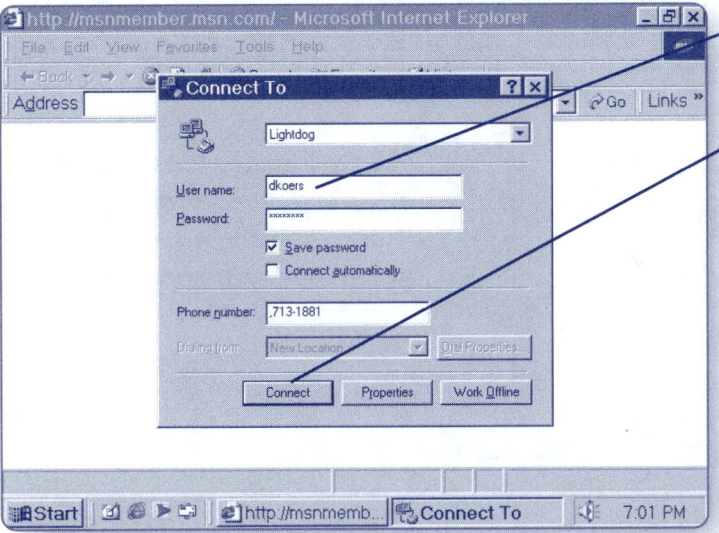

2. **Type** your **user name** and **password** if prompted to do so.

3. **Click** on **Connect**. Your modem dials in to your ISP. As it establishes a connection, you might hear some screeching and strange noises from your computer. That's okay—it's one computer saying "hello" to the other.

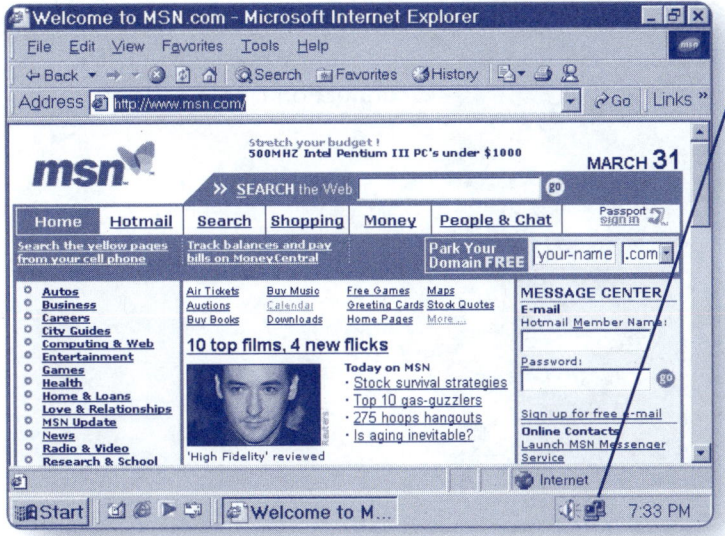

When connected, an icon representing two small computers appears on the Windows System Tray.

TIP

To disconnect from your ISP, double-click on the connection icon in the System Tray and click on Disconnect.

The Web browser launches and displays a starting page.

From here you can "surf the Net." When you finish with the Web browser, close it.

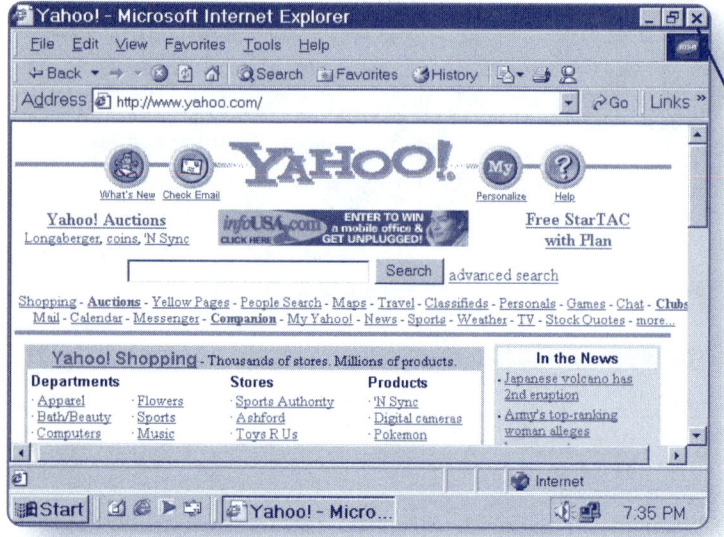

You'll learn more about Internet Explorer in Chapter 20, "Surfing with Internet Explorer."

4. **Click** on the **Close button** (X). The browser window closes. You might see a prompt to disconnect from your ISP.

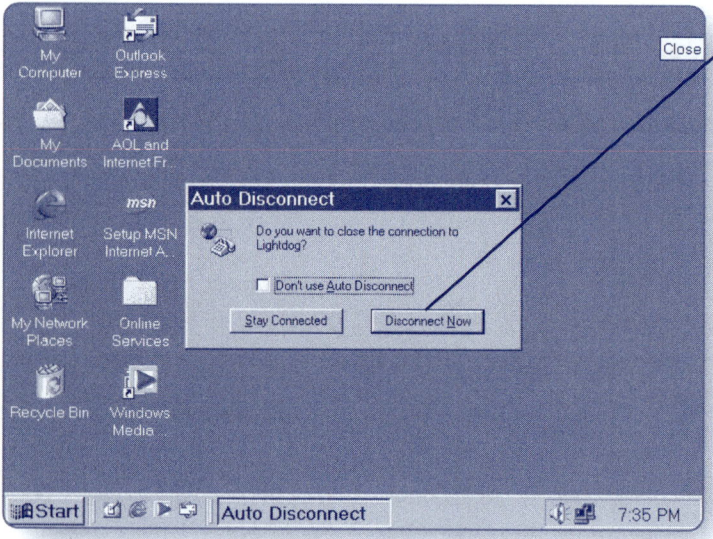

5. **Click** on **Disconnect Now** if you want to disconnect. The connection closes.

20

Surfing with Internet Explorer

The Internet is a collection of millions of computers around the world. Learning opportunities and hours of fun are at your fingertips. But how do you get to these computers? Internet Explorer version 5.5 enables you to gain access to the vast stores of information on these computers. How can you protect children from undesirable material? In this chapter, you'll learn how to:

- Browse the Web with Internet Explorer
- Set and use Favorites
- Set parental controls

Browsing the Web with Internet Explorer

Screens that you access on the Internet are called *Web pages* or *home pages*. You call the starting point of a series of connected Web pages a *home page*. Web pages have *addresses*. A typical Web address usually starts with http://www. Then you need to specify an exact address such as microsoft.com or whitehouse.gov. Therefore, a completed Web address might look something like http://www.microsoft.com or http://www.whitehouse.gov.

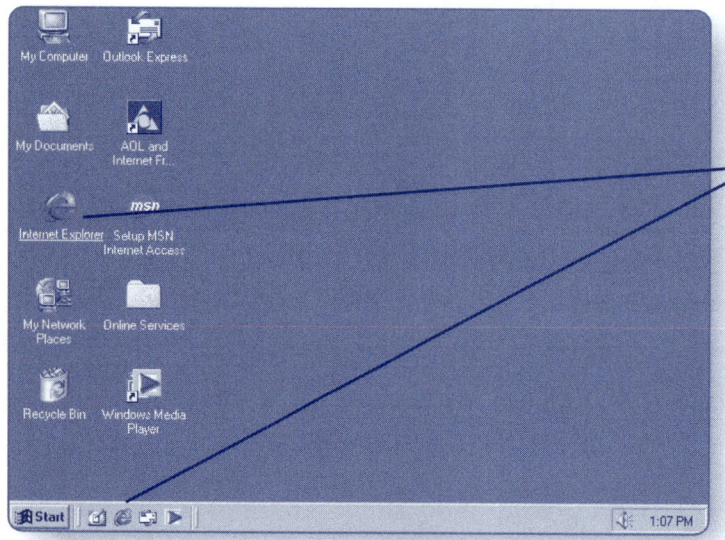

Access Internet Explorer from the desktop or from the Quick Launch bar.

1. Click on **Internet Explorer**. The Connect To dialog box opens.

> **NOTE**
> If you have a permanent connection such as cable modem, DSL, or T1, you won't see the Connect To box.

2. Type your **password**, if not already entered in the Password: text box. A series of asterisks appears.

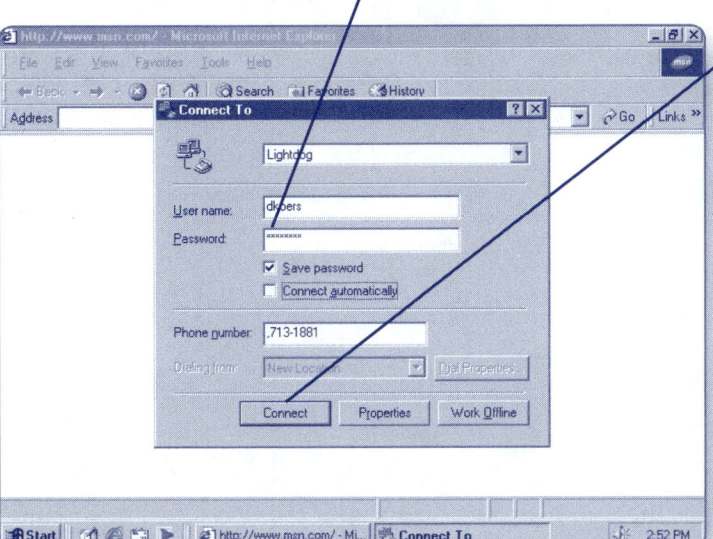

3. Click on **Connect**. Your ISP establishes a connection, and the Internet Explorer start page displays. A *start page* is the first page a browser looks at when you launch your Web browser.

> **NOTE**
>
> The terms *start page* and *home page* are sometimes interchangeable.

You can type a specific address to go to, or you can search the Internet for specific information.

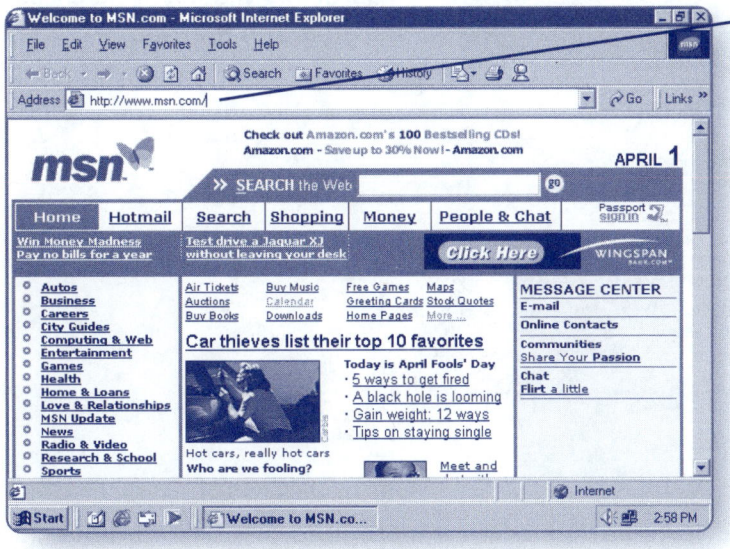

4. Type the specific Web **address.** The address appears in the Address list box.

5. Press the **Enter key**. Internet Explorer displays the home page for the address you specified.

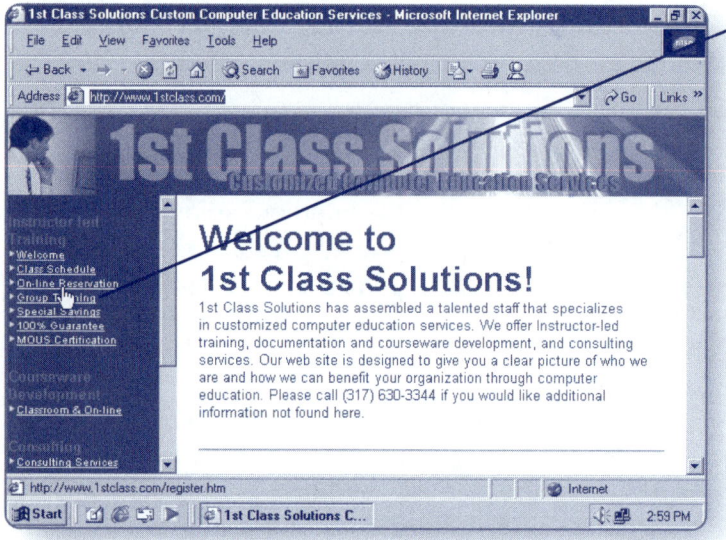

When you position your mouse on underlined text or pictures and the mouse turns into a hand, you are pointing to a hyperlink. You click a *hyperlink* to go to a Web page referenced by the hyperlink.

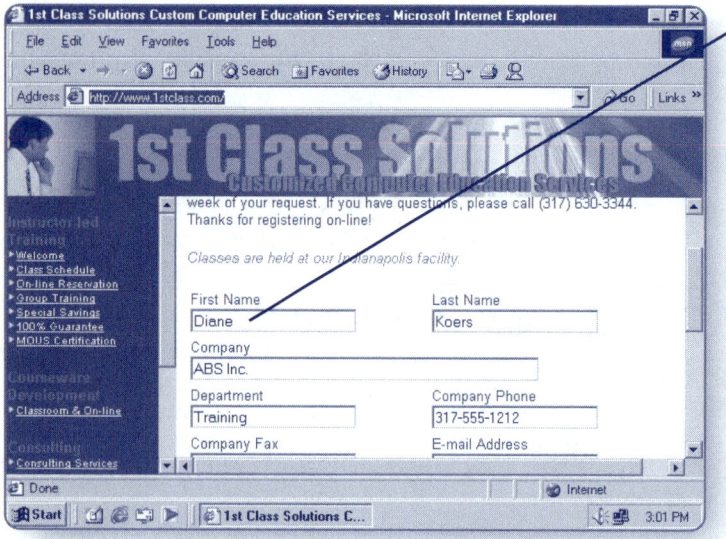

Many Web pages have forms that you can fill out and submit. You usually see forms if you request information or purchase something on the Web.

EXPLORING THE INTERNET EXPLORER WINDOW 327

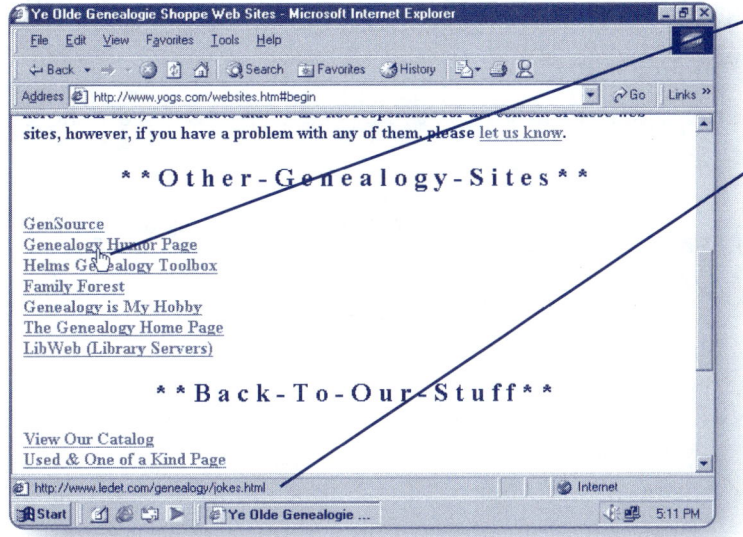

Many Web pages have hyperlinks to other Web pages that might interest you.

When you point to a hyperlink, its Web address appears at the bottom of the Internet Explorer window.

Exploring the Internet Explorer Window

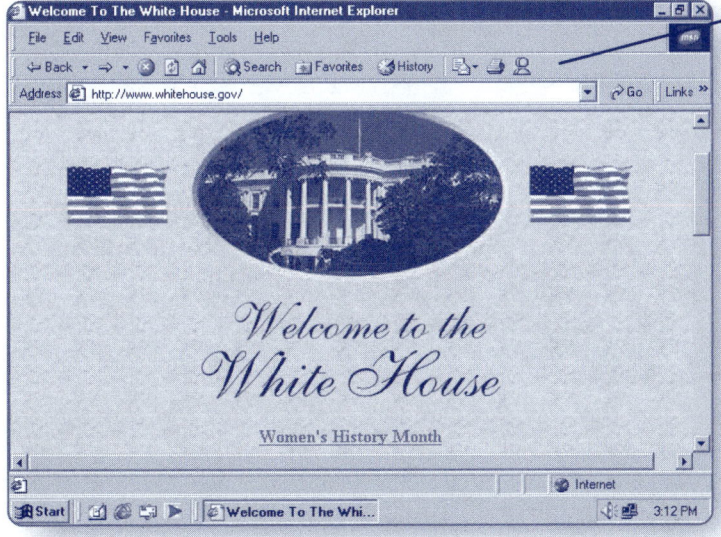

The Internet Explorer window has a toolbar with buttons to help you navigate the Web.

TIP
If you don't have a toolbar showing, click on View, Toolbars, and then Standard Buttons.

328 CHAPTER 20: SURFING WITH INTERNET EXPLORER

- **Back.** Sends Internet Explorer to the previously viewed Web page.
- **Forward.** Returns Internet Explorer to the next Web page.
- **Stop.** Stops the loading of the current Web page.
- **Refresh.** Reloads the current Web page.
- **Home.** Returns you to your start page.

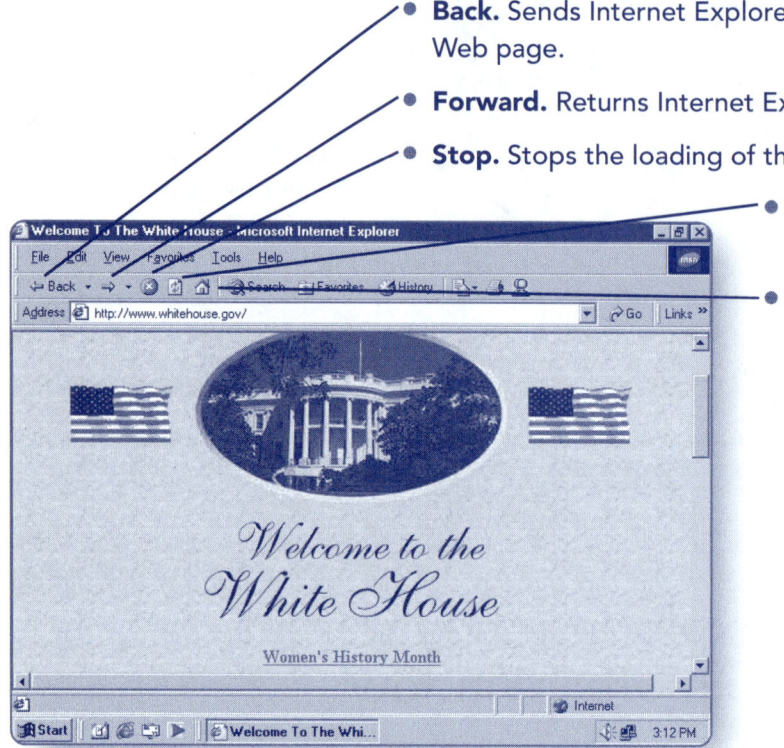

- **Search.** Displays a list of search engines to help you find a topic. (Click the Search button again to close the Search window.)

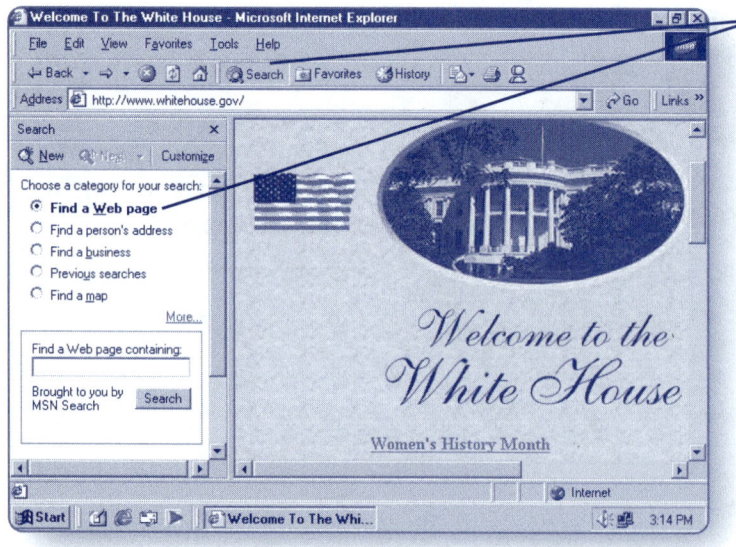

EXPLORING THE INTERNET EXPLORER WINDOW

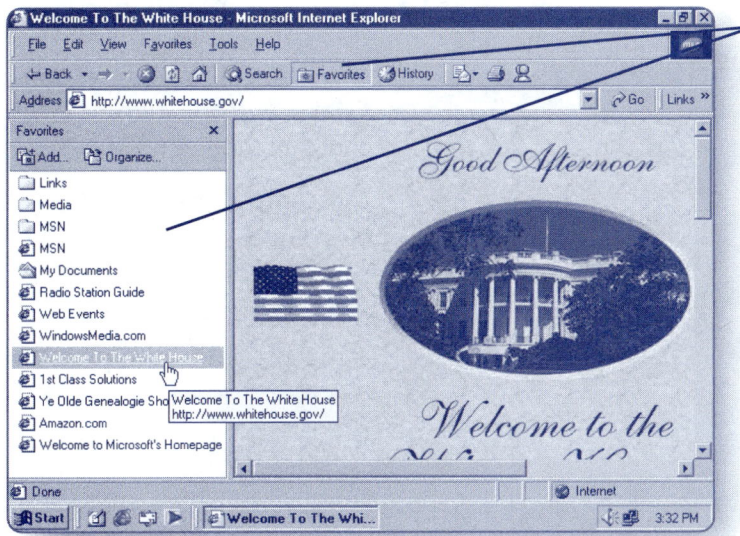

- **Favorites.** Displays a collection of Web sites you frequently access. (Click the Favorites button again to close the Favorites window.)

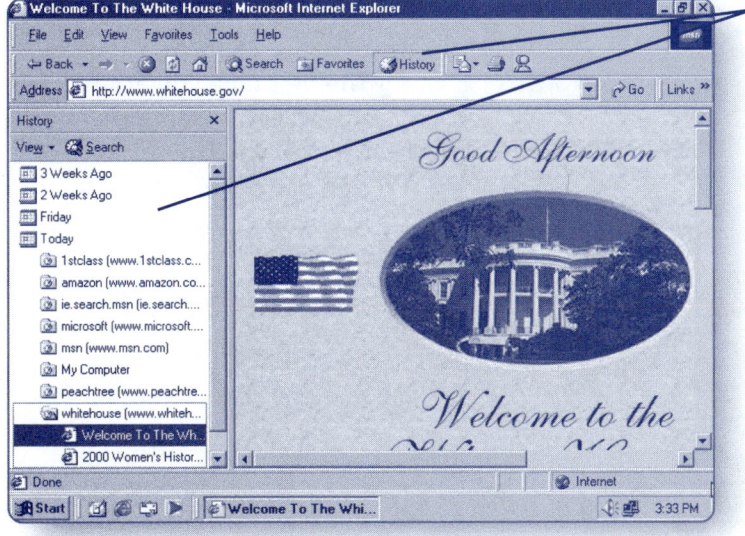

- **History.** Displays a list of Web sites you have previously viewed. (Click the History button again to close the History window.)

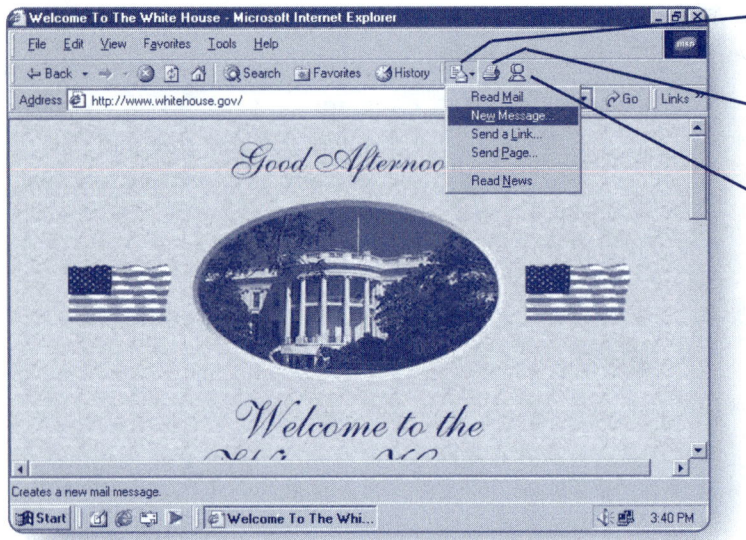

- **Mail.** Displays Internet mail options.
- **Print.** Prints the current page.
- **Messenger.** Loads MSN Messenger—A program to help you stay in touch online with friends and family.

> **NOTE**
> The first time you access the MSN Messenger Service, you'll need to sign up for MSN Hot Mail, Microsoft's free e-mail service.

Playing Favorites

If you have a special poem that you like to read often, you might place a bookmark at the location of that poem. You'll find Internet Explorer Favorites similar to bookmarks to your favorite Web sites. Favorites are a convenient way to organize and link to Web sites you visit frequently.

Adding Favorites

Keep track of Web sites you like by adding them to your Favorites list.

1. Display the **Web page** you want to add to your collection of favorite pages. The page appears in the Internet Explorer window.

> **NOTE**
> Favorites aren't limited to Web pages. You can make any document or folder on your computer a Favorite.

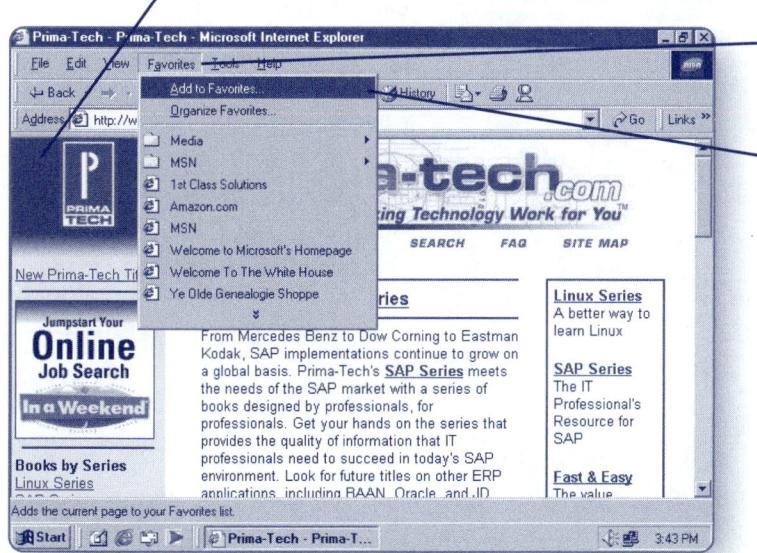

2. Click on **Favorites**. The Favorites menu appears.

3. Click on **Add to Favorites**. The Add Favorite dialog box opens.

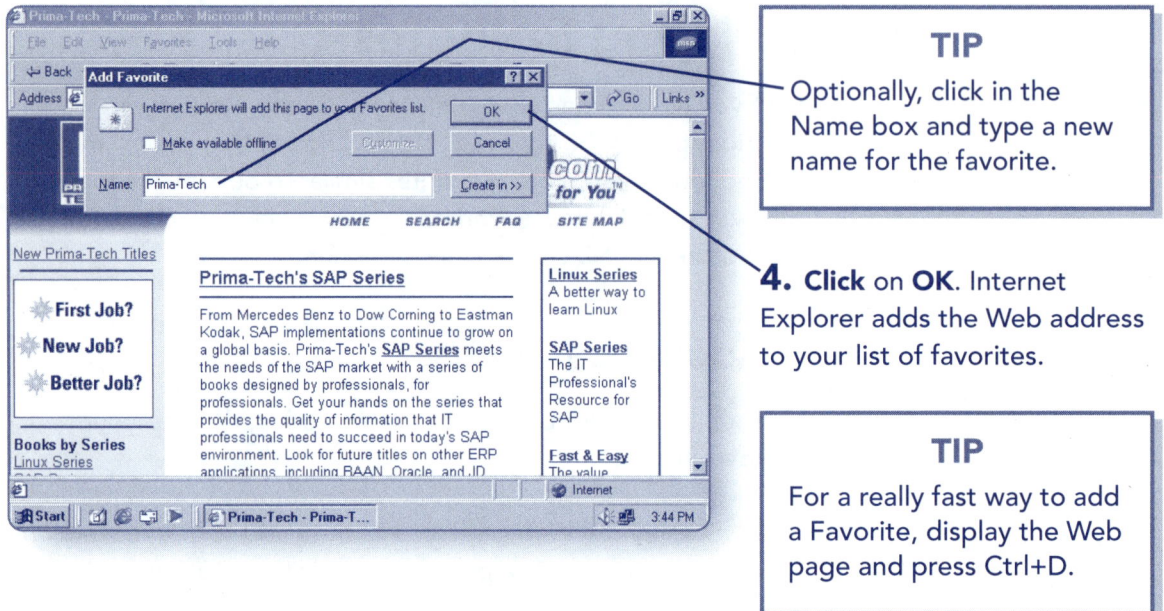

TIP

Optionally, click in the Name box and type a new name for the favorite.

4. Click on **OK**. Internet Explorer adds the Web address to your list of favorites.

TIP

For a really fast way to add a Favorite, display the Web page and press Ctrl+D.

Accessing Your Favorite Sites

Now to get to one of your favorite sites, you don't have to remember the Web address or even type it. You can access your favorite site with a simple click of the mouse.

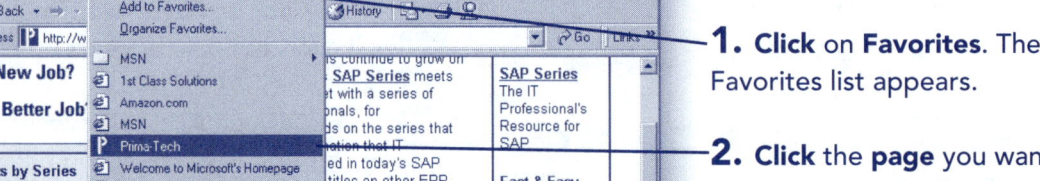

1. Click on **Favorites**. The Favorites list appears.

2. Click the **page** you want to open. Internet Explorer opens the specified Web page.

SETTING PARENTAL CONTROLS 333

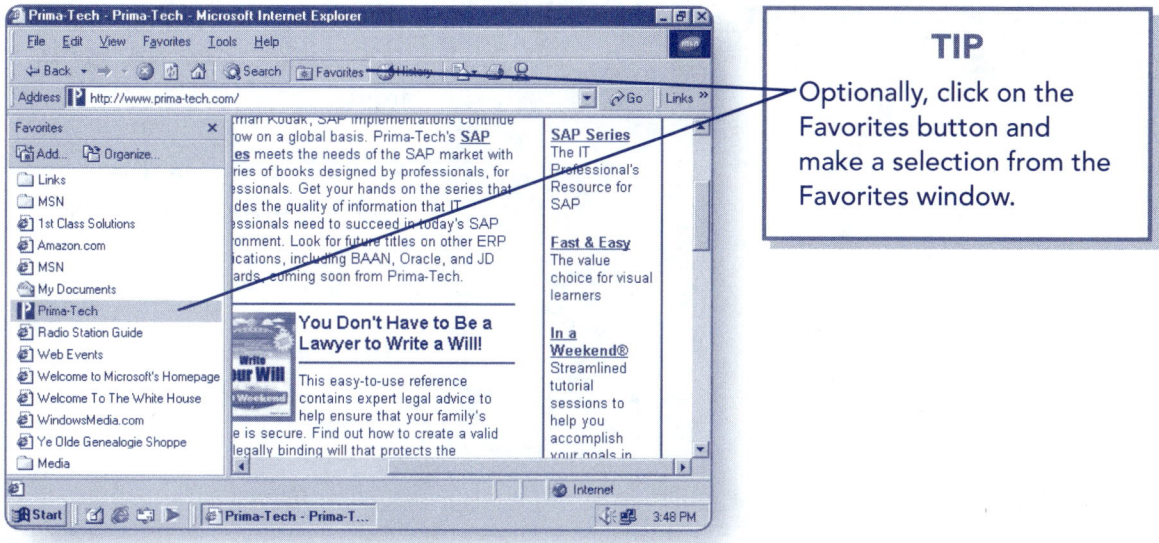

TIP
Optionally, click on the Favorites button and make a selection from the Favorites window.

Setting Parental Controls

NOTE
Many Web pages are not rated.

You'll find the Web filled with information. Any topic you want to research, you'll find on the Web. However, you might want to monitor the information you or your children can access. With the Content Advisor, you can screen out objectionable or offensive content by using voluntary industry-standard ratings defined independently by the Platform for Internet Content Selection (PICS) committee.

1. Right-click on the **Internet Explorer icon**. A shortcut menu appears.

2. Click on **Properties**. The Internet Properties dialog box appears.

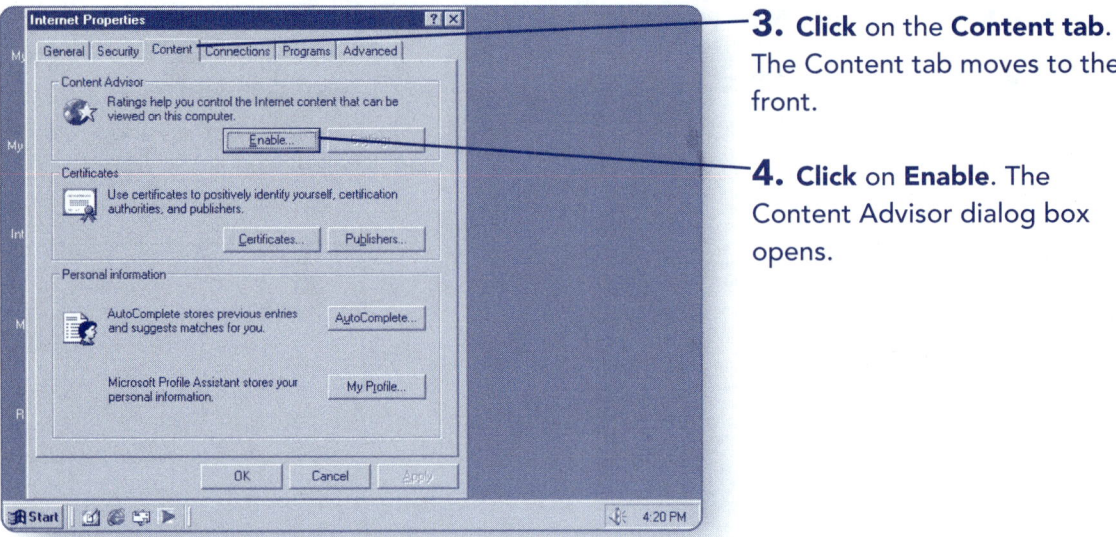

3. Click on the **Content tab**. The Content tab moves to the front.

4. Click on **Enable**. The Content Advisor dialog box opens.

Here you can control the level of language, nudity, sex, and violence of the Web pages displayed.

Each category has a five-level rating beginning with zero (the strictest rating) and extending to four (the most lenient rating).

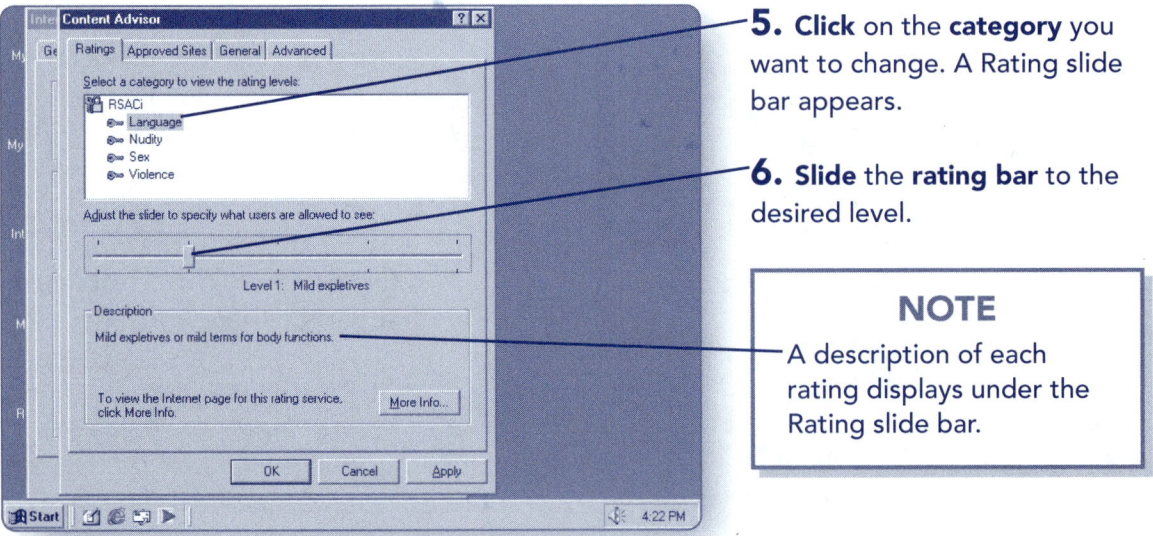

5. Click on the **category** you want to change. A Rating slide bar appears.

6. Slide the **rating bar** to the desired level.

> **NOTE**
> A description of each rating displays under the Rating slide bar.

SETTING PARENTAL CONTROLS   335

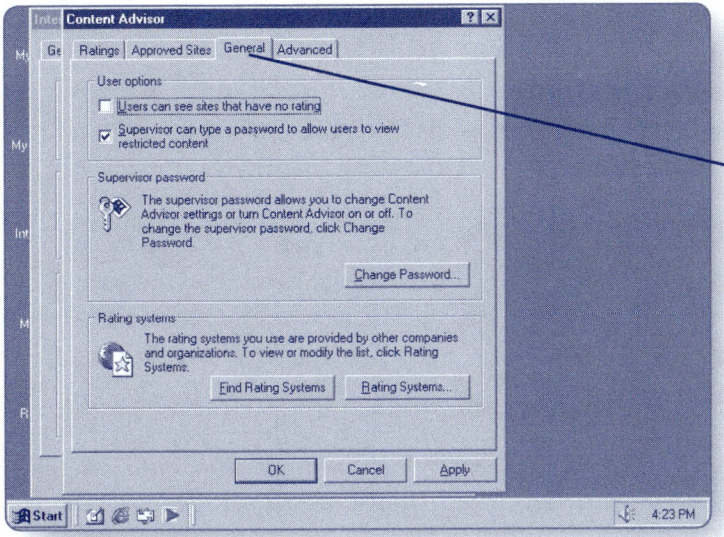

7. Repeat steps 8 and **9** for each category you want to restrict.

8. Click on the **General tab**. The General tab moves to the front.

The General tab has additional options from which you can select.

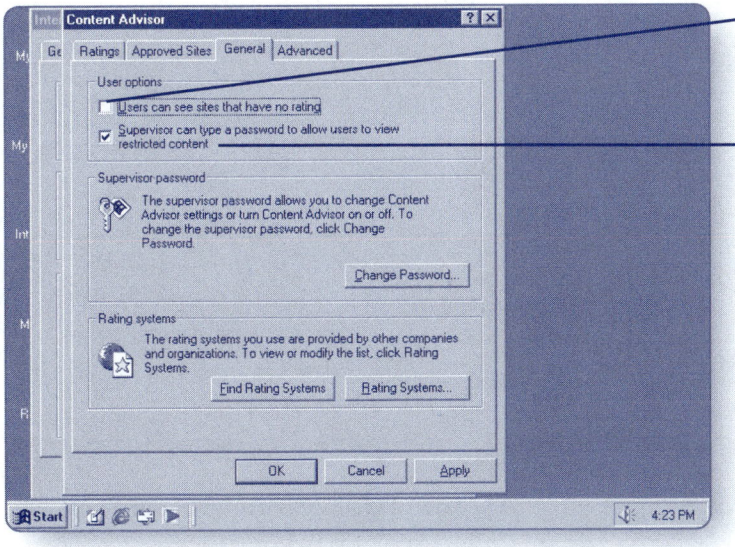

- Users can see sites that have no rating. Enables access to an unrated site.

- Supervisor can type a password to allow users to view restricted content. Enables access to a restricted Web site for anyone who has access to the supervisor password.

9. Click any desired User options **check boxes**. A ✔ appears in the box next to a selected item.

Tell the Content Advisor if you have specific Web sites you want to allow or disallow.

10. **Click** on the **Approved Sites tab**. The Approved Sites tab appears in front.

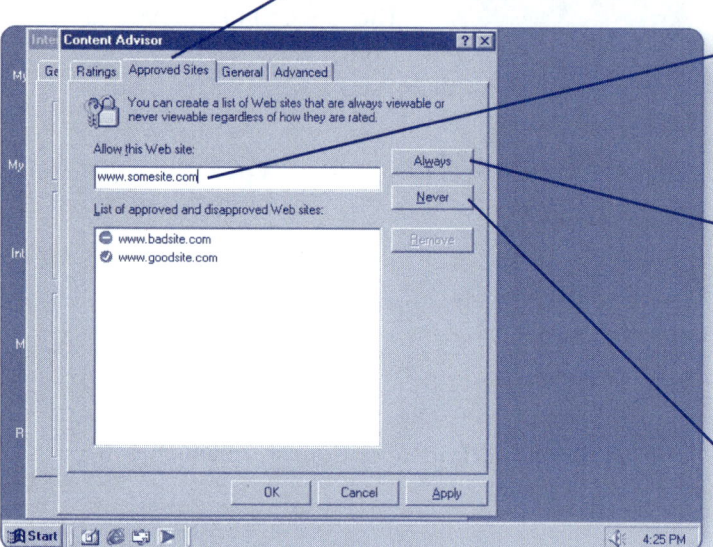

11. **Type** the **Web address** you want to allow or disallow. The address appears in the Allow this Web site: text box.

12a. **Click** on **Always**. Internet Explorer adds the Web site to the List of approved and disapproved Web sites.

OR

12b. **Click** on **Never**. Internet Explorer adds the Web site to the List of approved and disapproved Web sites.

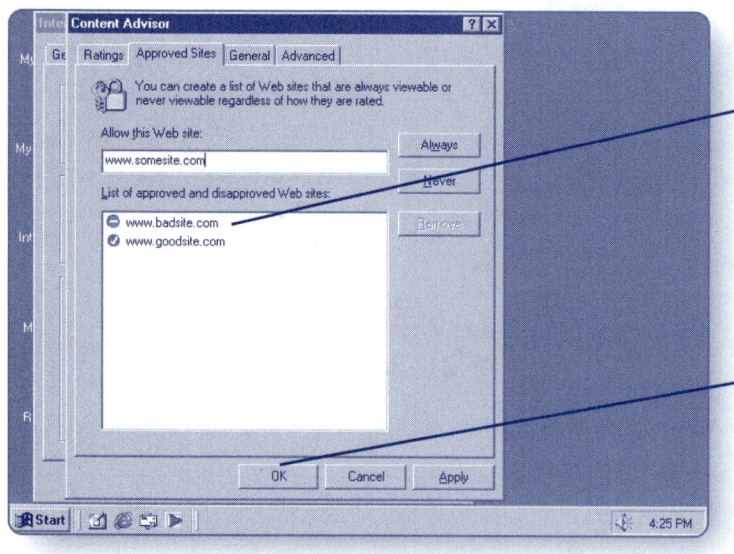

TIP

Internet Explorer indicates allowed Web sites with a green check mark, whereas disallowed Web sites are indicated with a red minus sign.

13. **Click** on **OK**. The Create Supervisor Password box appears.

SETTING PARENTAL CONTROLS 337

When you enable the Content Advisor, you must assign a supervisor password to prevent others from changing the settings. Only someone who knows the password can modify the settings.

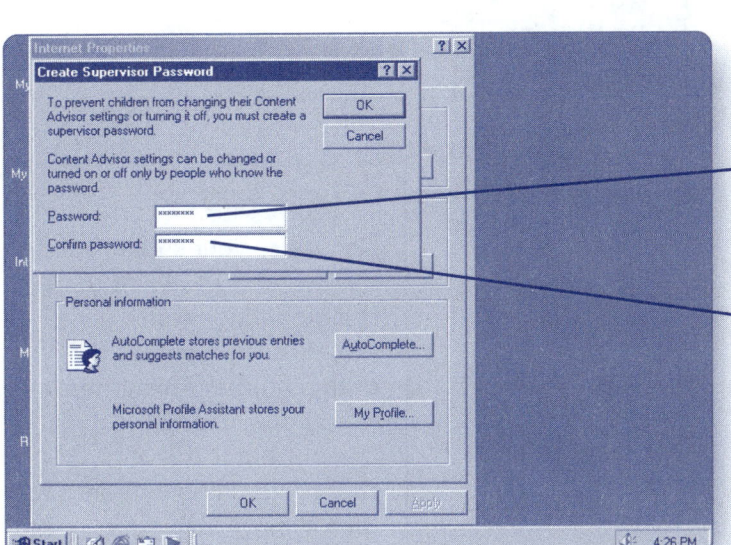

14. **Type** a **password** in the Password: text box. Asterisks appear in the text box.

15. **Type** the same **password** in the Confirm password: text box. Asterisks appear in the text box.

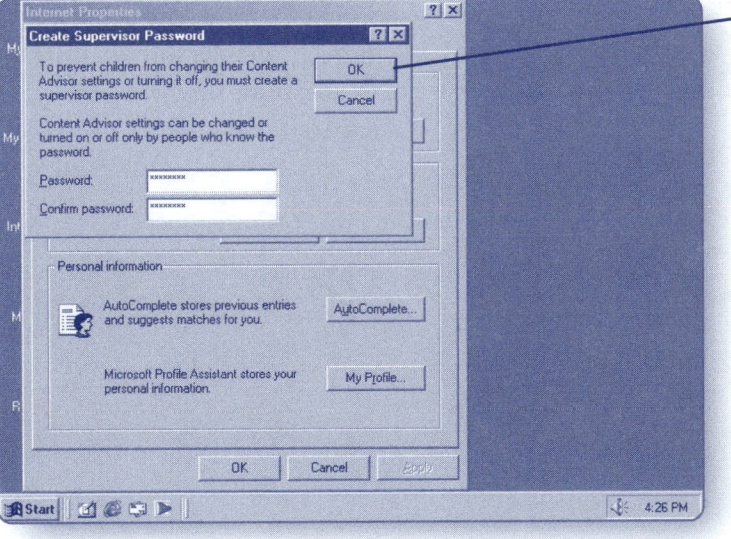

16. **Click** on **OK**. A Content Advisor confirmation box appears.

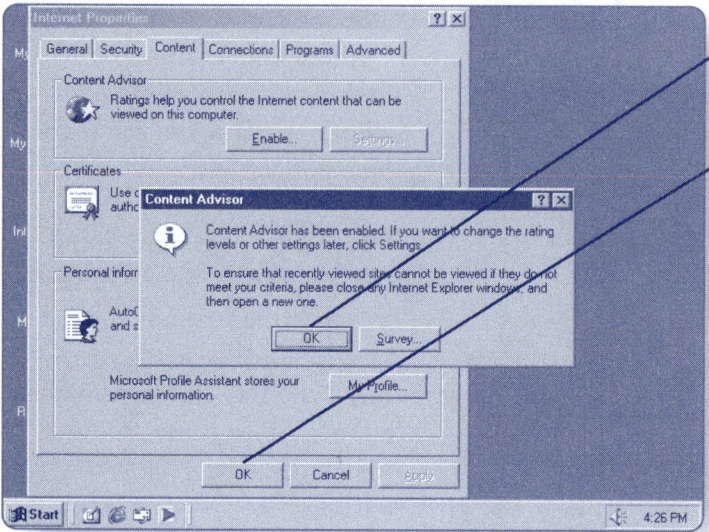

17. **Click** on **OK**. The Content Advisor confirmation box closes.

18. **Click** on **OK**. The Internet Properties dialog box closes.

> **NOTE**
> Don't lose your supervisor password! If you want to disable ratings restrictions, return to the Content tab of the Internet Properties dialog box, click on Disable, enter the supervisor password, and then click on OK.

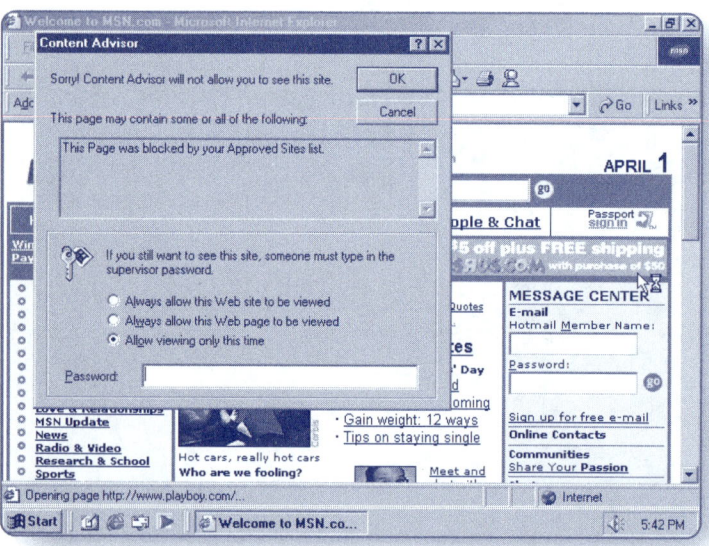

If you try to access a blocked site, the Content Advisor appears advising the site is blocked. You see the requested site only after providing the supervisor password.

21

E-mailing with Outlook Express

The capability to send and receive e-mail is one of the most important functions of a computer. What is e-mail? Well, e-mail is defined as the exchange of text messages and computer files over a communications network, such as the Internet or an intracompany network. You'll find Outlook Express a full-featured e-mail and news-reading client that comes with Windows Millennium Edition. In this chapter, you'll learn how to:

- Create e-mail accounts
- Create and send e-mail
- Attach a file to an e-mail
- Receive and manage e-mail

Starting Outlook Express

To send or receive e-mail or to access newsgroups, your computer must have a modem that is connected to a telephone line, and you must have access to some type of online service.

Windows Millennium Edition provides three ways you can start the Outlook Express program:

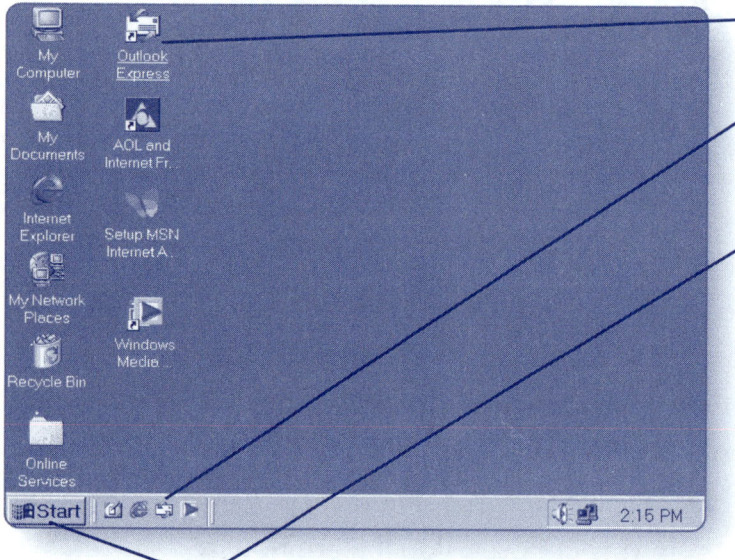

- Click on the Outlook Express icon on the desktop.

- Click on the Outlook Express icon on the Quick Launch toolbar.

- Click on the Start button, and then Programs, and choose Outlook Express.

1. Click on **either** of the **Outlook Express icons**. The Outlook Express program starts.

Working with E-mail

Before you can use Outlook Express to create and send e-mail, you need to set up an e-mail mail account.

Creating an E-mail Account

Before you can send or receive e-mail, you must first set up a mail account. Outlook Express uses the Internet Connection Wizard to quickly lead you through the process of setting up a new or additional e-mail account.

WORKING WITH E-MAIL   341

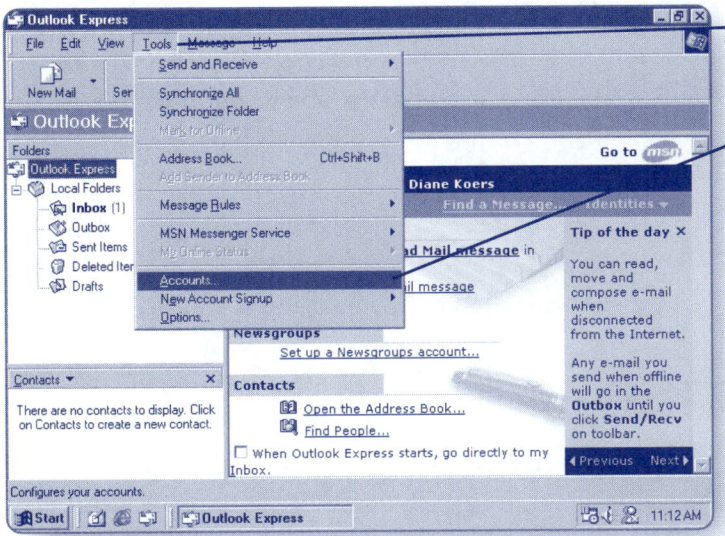

1. Click on **Tools**. The Tools menu appears.

2. Click on **Accounts**. The Internet Accounts dialog box opens.

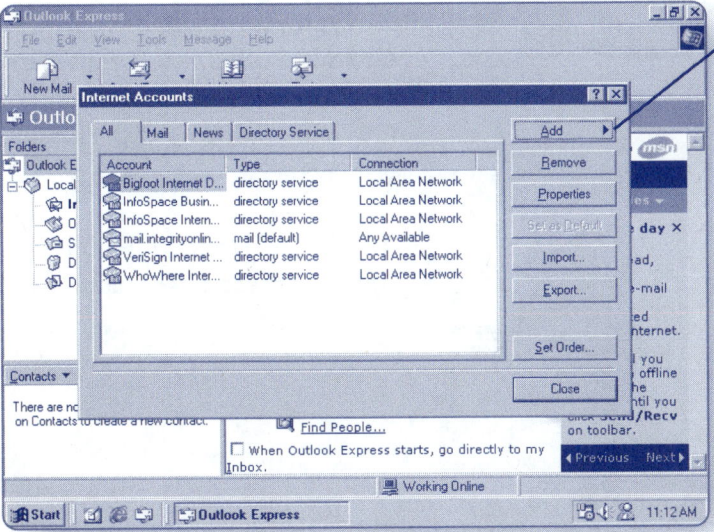

3. Click on **Add**. The Add menu appears.

342 CHAPTER 21: E-MAILING WITH OUTLOOK EXPRESS

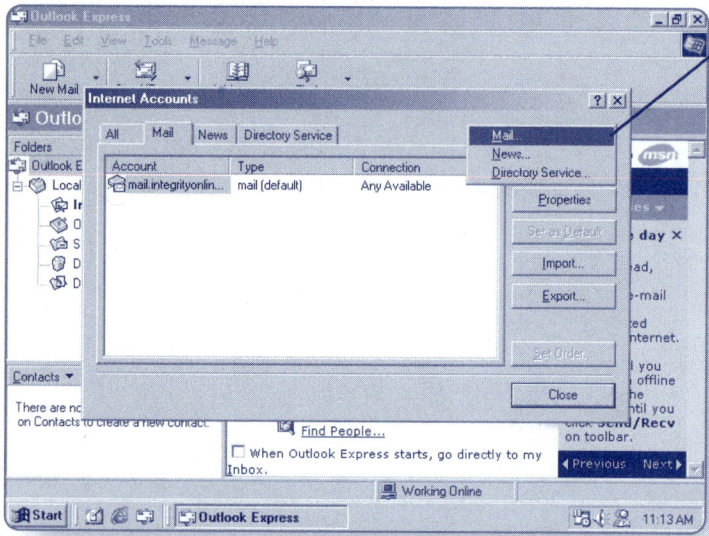

4. Click on **Mail**. The Internet Connection Wizard opens to assist you through the e-mail account setup process.

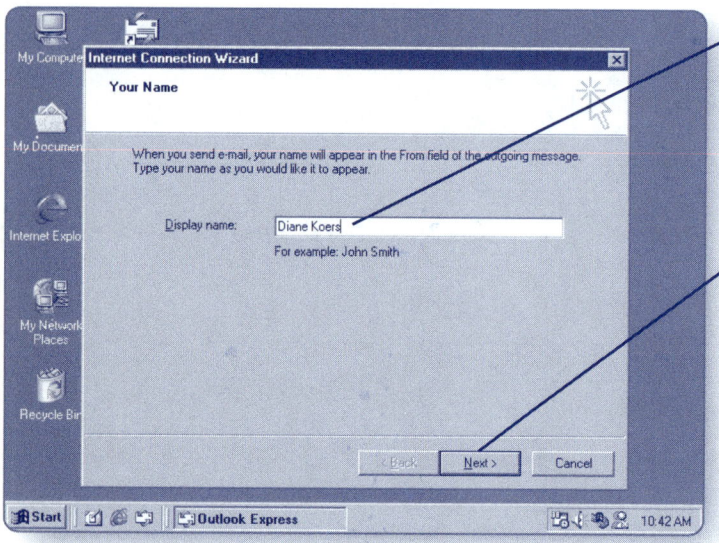

5. Type your **name** as you would like others to see it when they receive e-mail from you. Your name appears in the Display name: text box.

6. Click on **Next**. The Internet E-mail Address screen appears.

WORKING WITH E-MAIL 343

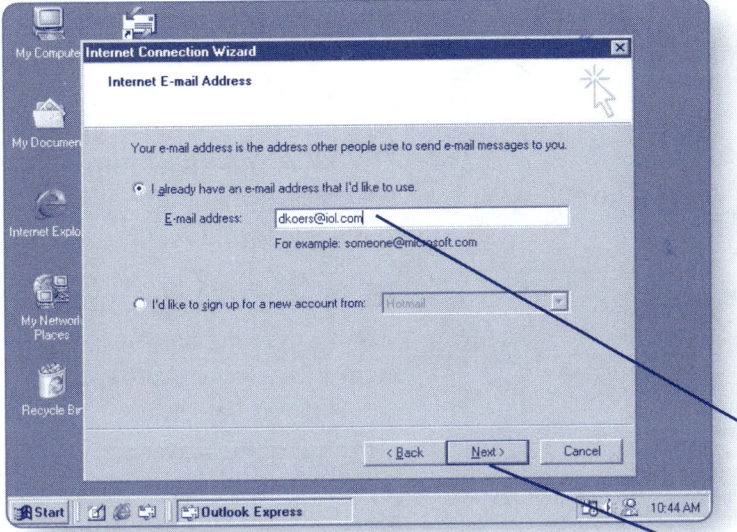

In this chapter, we're assuming you have already established an Internet connection.

NOTE
See Chapter 19, "Connecting to the Internet," to create an Internet connection.

7. Type your **e-mail address**. The address appears in the E-mail address: text box.

8. Click on **Next**. The E-mail Server Names screen appears.

It gets a little trickier here. When you get to this screen, contact your ISP and ask for the information. They'll be happy to provide it to you.

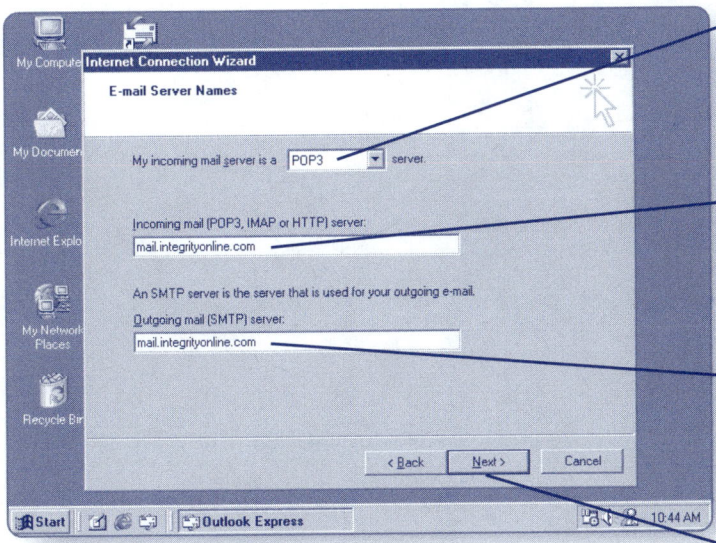

9. Click on the correct type of **mail server** (POP3 or IMAP). Your selection appears in the list box.

10. Type the **incoming mail server name**. The text you type appears in the Incoming mail server: text box.

11. Type the **outgoing mail server name**. The text you type appears in the Outgoing mail server: text box.

12. Click on **Next**. The Internet Mail Logon screen appears.

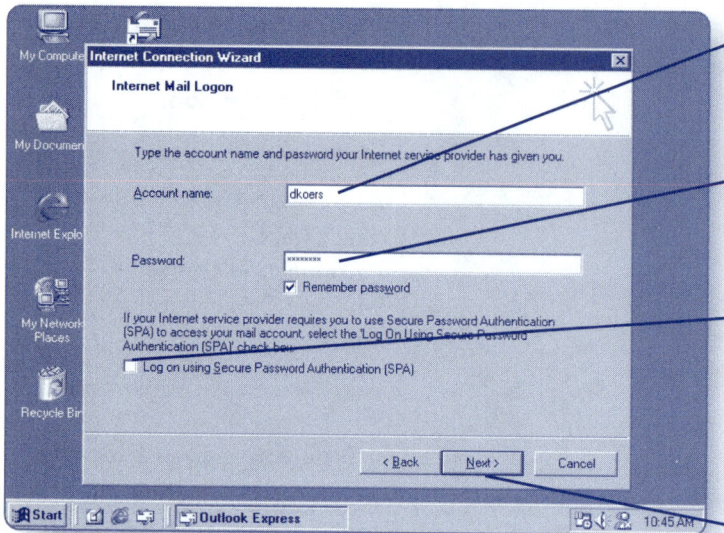

13. **Type** your **account name**. Again, your ISP provides this information.

14. **Enter** your **password**. Asterisks appear in the Password: text box.

15. If required by your ISP, **click** on the **Log on using Secure Password Authentication (SPA)** box. (Most ISPs do *not* require this feature.)

16. **Click** on **Next**. The Congratulations screen appears.

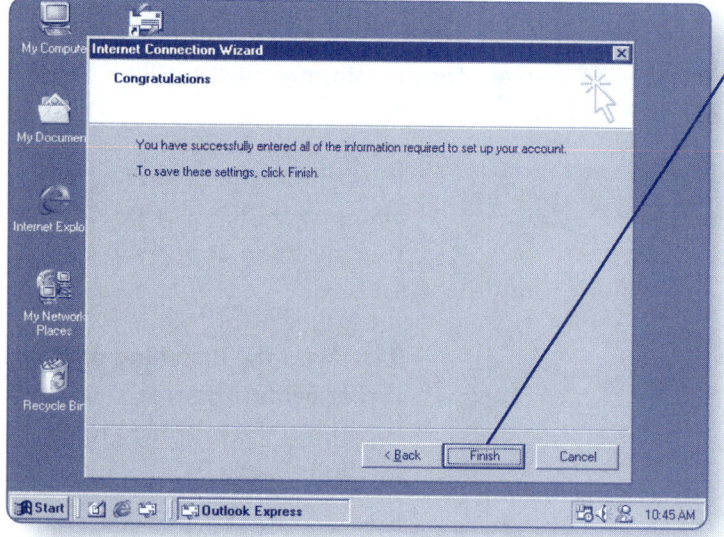

17. **Click** on **Finish**. The Outlook Express opening screen appears.

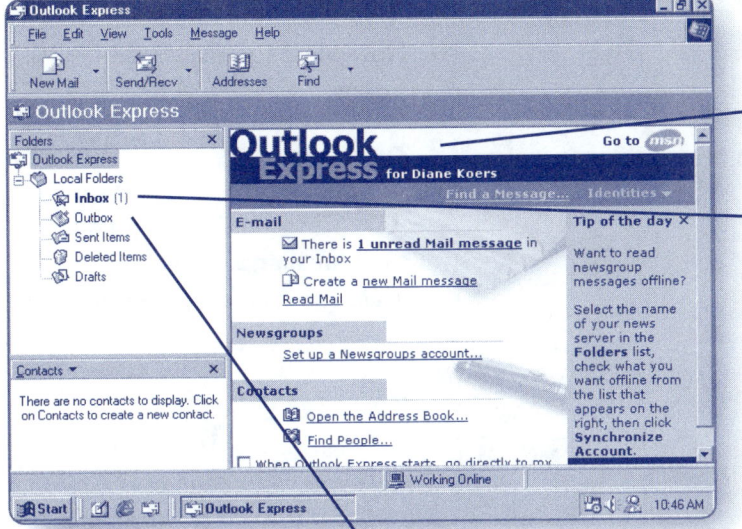

Outlook Express lists several folders in the folder list.

The Outlook Express Start page appears on the right side.

The Inbox folder is the next folder under the Outlook Express folder. When you are connected to your ISP, Outlook Express places any incoming mail in the Inbox folder. A number (in parentheses) on the right side of the Inbox folder indicates new messages.

When you create e-mail messages, you have the option to send them immediately or send them at a later time. The Outbox folder indicates any messages waiting to be sent.

Other folders created with Outlook Express include a Sent Items folder to keep copies of any e-mail you send, a Deleted Items folder to throw away e-mail, and a Drafts folder in which to keep unfinished messages.

Creating an E-mail Message

If you want to communicate with someone quickly, send him or her an e-mail message. In Outlook Express, you can read, create, and send your e-mail messages.

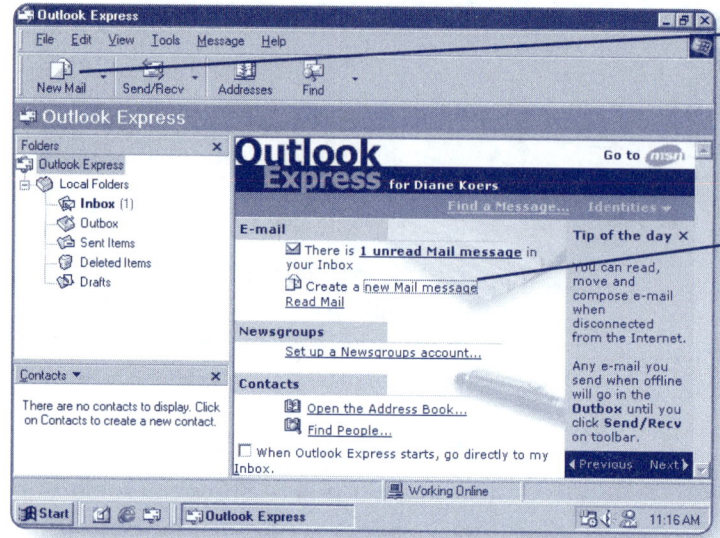

1a. Click on **New Mail**. The New Message dialog box opens.

OR

1b. Click on **Create a new Mail message**. The New Message dialog box opens.

TIP

If you can't see your toolbar, click on View and choose Toolbar.

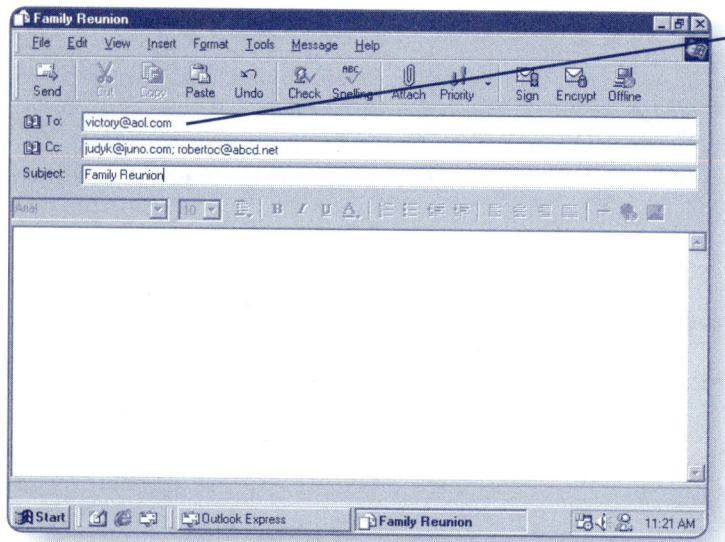

2. Type the **e-mail address** of the person to which you want to send the message. The name appears in the To: line.

NOTE

In Chapter 22, "Using the Windows Address Book," you'll learn how to save and use names and e-mail addresses in the Windows Millennium Edition Address Book.

3. Press the **Tab key**. The insertion point moves to the Cc: line.

WORKING WITH E-MAIL   347

4. Type an **e-mail address** of anyone to whom you want to send a carbon copy (CC) of the message. The e-mail address appears in the Cc: box.

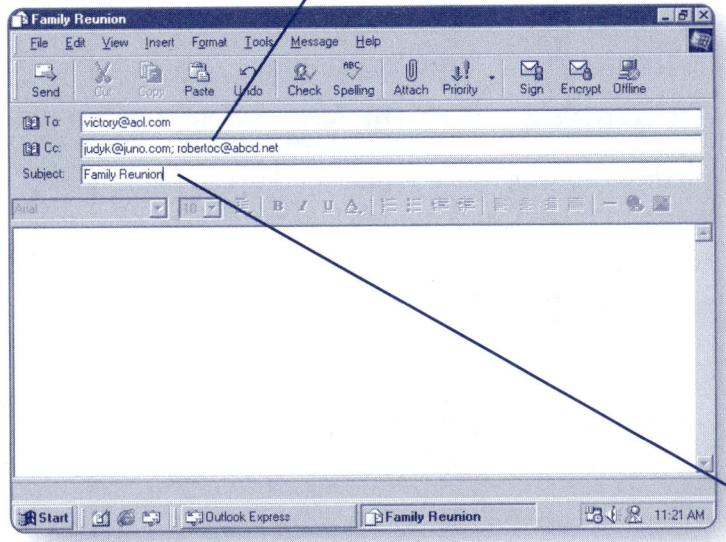

NOTE

If you have more than one person to list on any of the address lines, separate the e-mail name of each recipient by a comma or a semicolon.

5. Press the **Tab key**. The insertion point moves to the Subject: line.

6. Type a **subject** for the message. The text appears in the Subject: line.

An e-mail message doesn't require a Subject: line, but I recommend you enter one. If you try to send a message without a subject, Outlook Express asks if you're sure you want to send it without a subject.

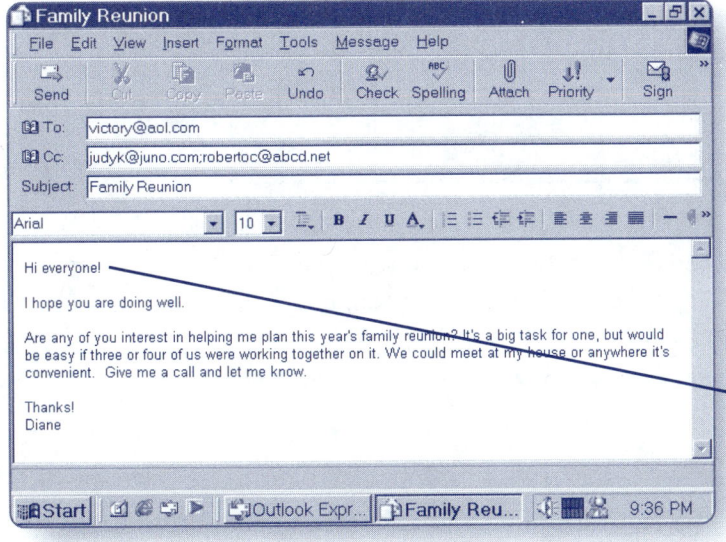

7. Press the **Tab key**. The insertion point moves to the body of the message.

8. Type your **message** in the body of the message box. The typed text appears in the lower half of the window.

> **TIP**
> Don't type in ALL CAPS.
> That's considered SHOUTING!

Formatting an E-mail Message

You can dress up your e-mail messages. Instead of plain text, you can insert bullets, images, and horizontal lines. Add color and style with different fonts and sizes or add a graphic background. You'll format text in Outlook Express almost identical to formatting text in WordPad or other word-processing programs.

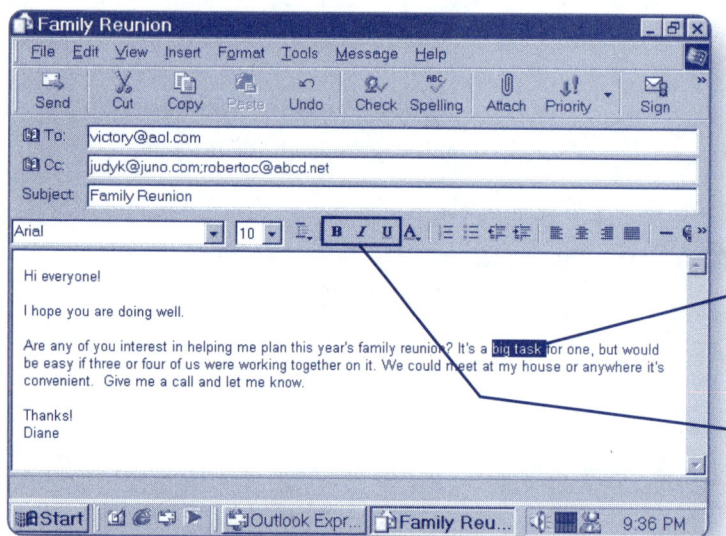

1. Click and **drag** across the **text** you want to modify. The text is highlighted.

2. Click on the **Bold, Italic,** or **Underline buttons**. The text is bolded, italicized, and/or underlined.

> **TIP**
> If you don't see the toolbar with the Bold, Italic, or Underline button, click on Format and choose Rich Text.

WORKING WITH E-MAIL 349

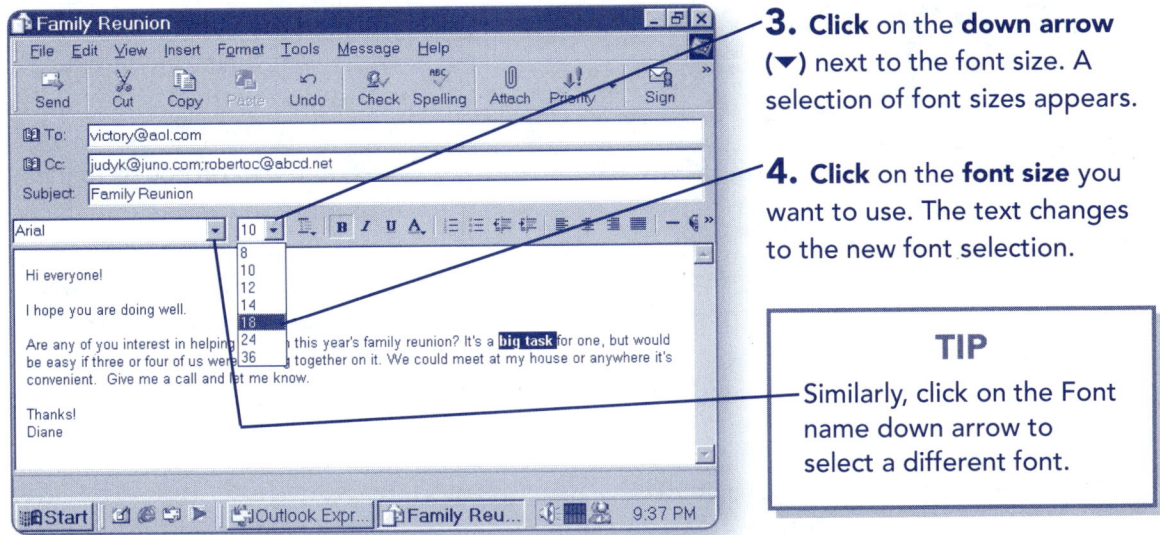

3. Click on the **down arrow** (▼) next to the font size. A selection of font sizes appears.

4. Click on the **font size** you want to use. The text changes to the new font selection.

TIP
Similarly, click on the Font name down arrow to select a different font.

You can add bullet points or numbering to lists in your e-mail messages.

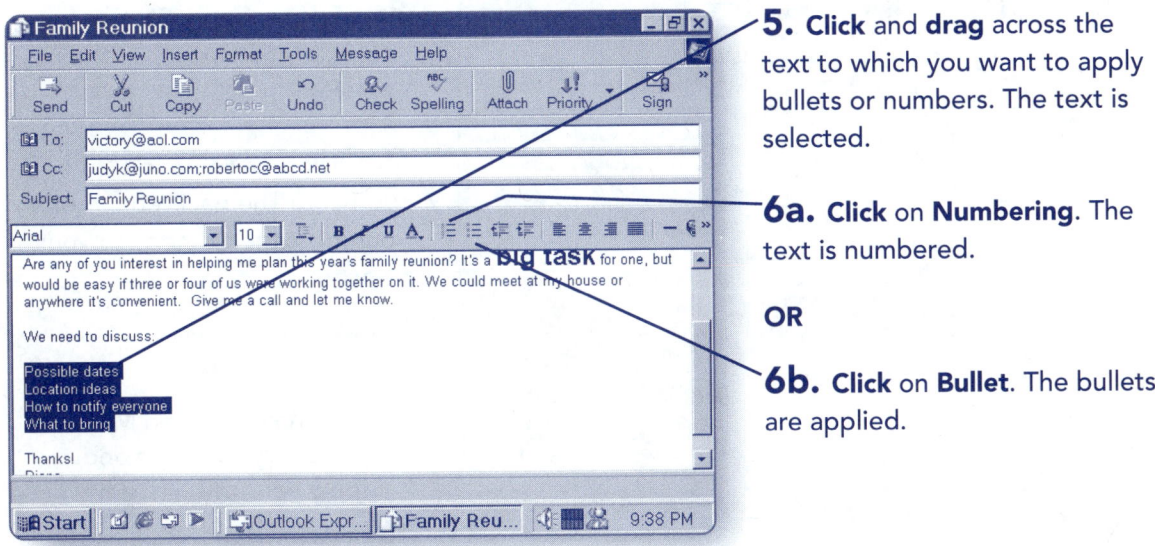

5. Click and **drag** across the text to which you want to apply bullets or numbers. The text is selected.

6a. Click on **Numbering**. The text is numbered.

OR

6b. Click on **Bullet**. The bullets are applied.

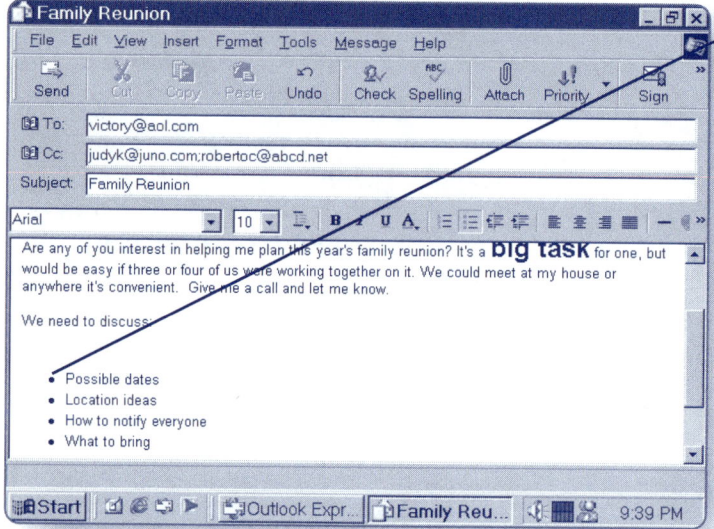

Each line of the selected text has a bullet point or number applied to the front of it.

Next, add a background to your message. You can use one that comes supplied with Outlook Express, or you can apply your own .jpeg or .gif image.

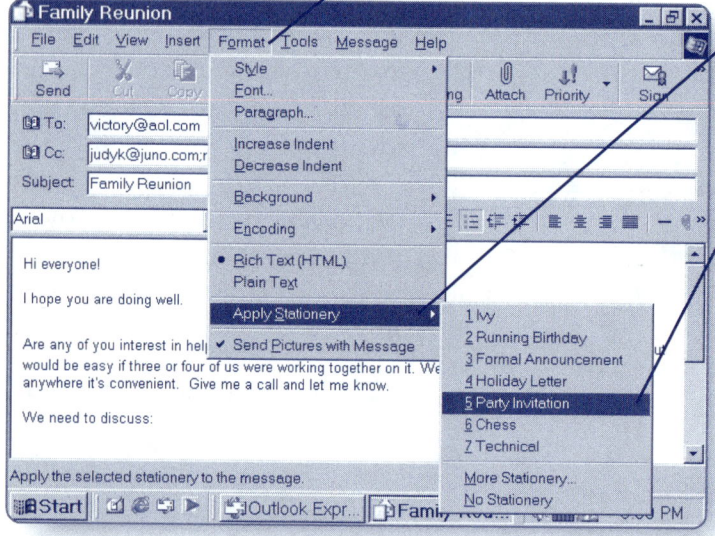

7. Click on **Format**. The Format menu appears.

8. Click on **Apply Stationery**. The Apply Stationery submenu appears.

9. Click on a **selection** from the submenu. The background of your message changes to your selection.

TIP

Optionally, click on More Stationery to locate and apply your own image.

WORKING WITH E-MAIL   351

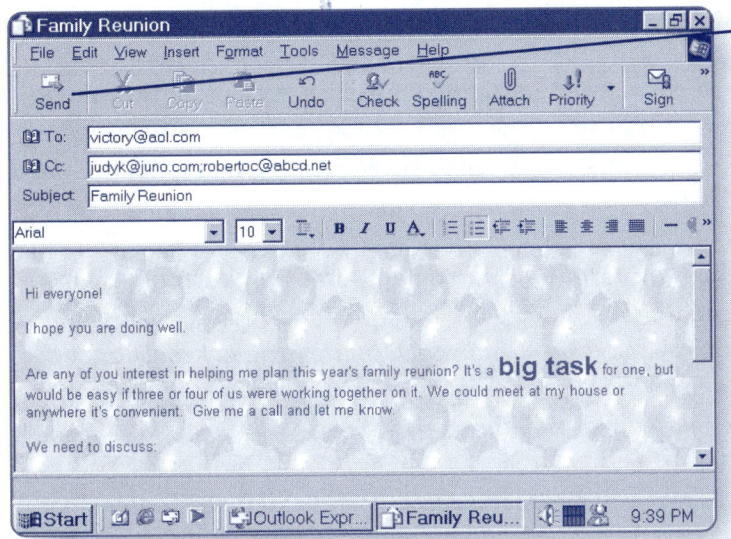

10. Click on the **Send button**. Outlook immediately sends the message to the recipients.

TIP
If you don't want to send the message immediately, click on File and then choose Send Later.

Windows also places a copy of the message in the Sent Items folder.

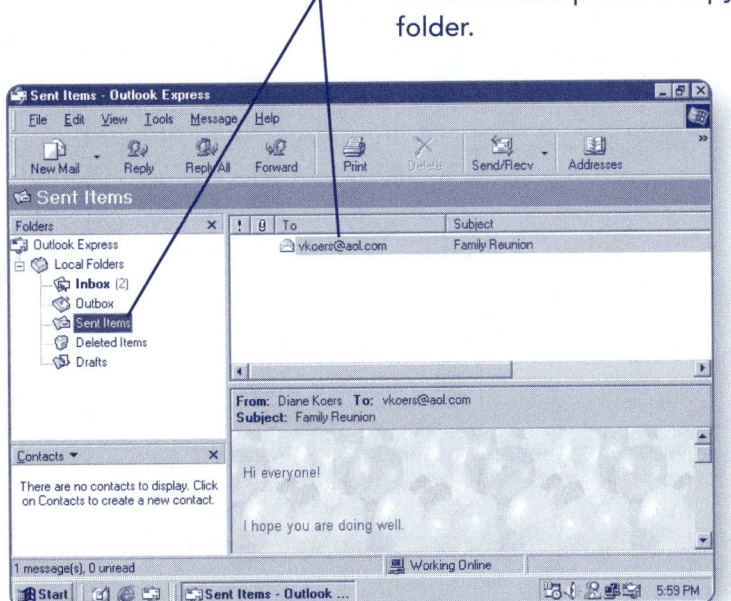

NOTE
Formatting an e-mail message applies special formatting called HTML codes to the message. If you send an e-mail to someone whose e-mail program doesn't support HTML, the recipient might see additional HTML coding in the message. The recipient can simply ignore any HTML codes.

Attaching Files to E-mail

You might want to include a spreadsheet or other document with an e-mail message. Outlook Express can send files of any type—pictures, documents, spreadsheets, or any text or binary files.

To open the additional document, the recipient must have a program that supports the file format you are sending. For example, if you send an Excel file, the recipient must either have Excel on his or her system, or a spreadsheet application that can read Excel files.

1. Create the e-mail **message**. The message appears on your screen.

2. Click the **Attach button**. The Insert Attachment dialog box opens.

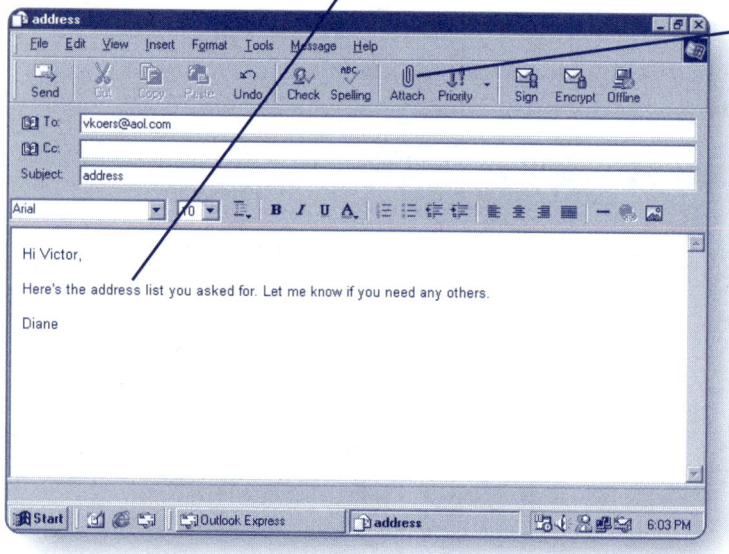

WORKING WITH E-MAIL   353

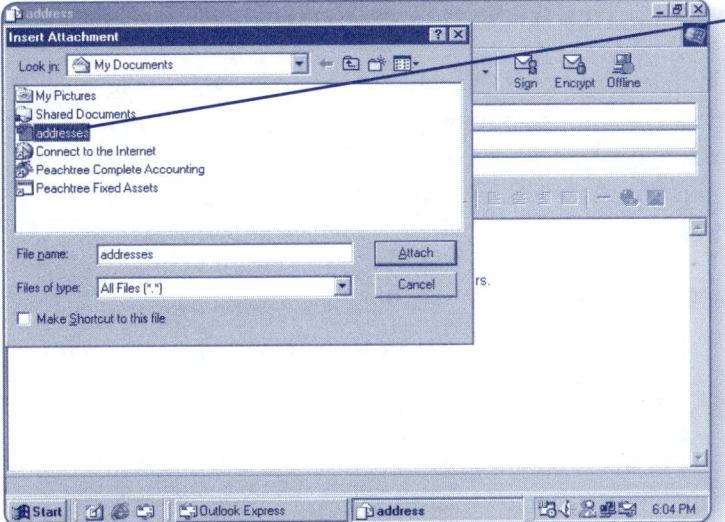

3. Locate and **click** the **file** you want to attach to the message. The Insert Attachment dialog box closes.

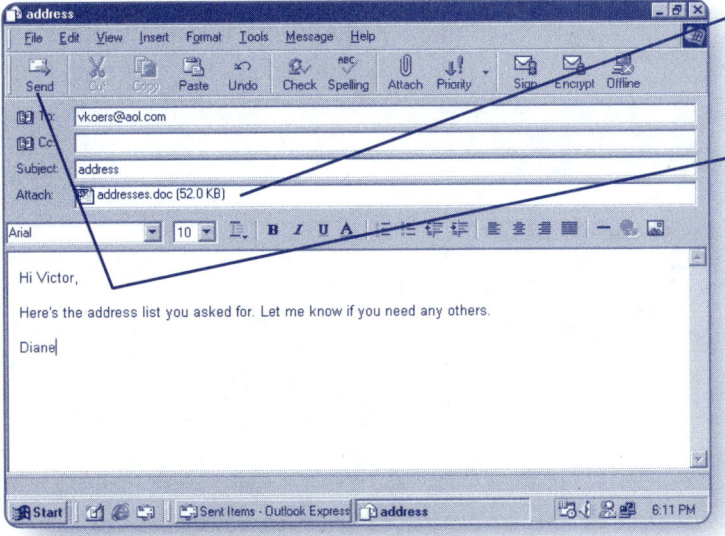

Outlook Express displays an icon representing the attached file.

4. Click on **Send**. Outlook Express sends the file along with the message.

CHAPTER 21: E-MAILING WITH OUTLOOK EXPRESS

Retrieving Incoming E-mail

Outlook Express tells you when you have new messages by putting the number of new messages in parentheses (and in boldface) next to the Inbox. If you are online, Outlook Express checks for new messages at specified intervals. A light tone notifies you when you receive a new message.

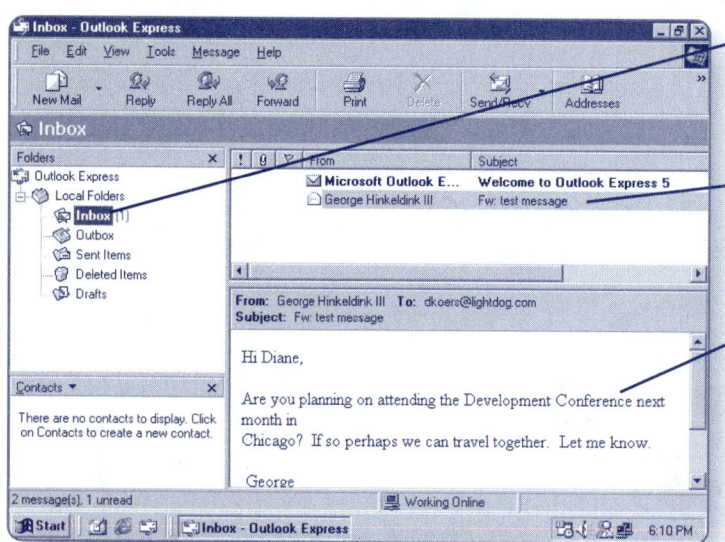

1. Click on the **Inbox**. A list of new messages appears on the right side of the screen.

2. Click on a **message** to read. The message appears in the Preview pane.

3. Read the **message** in the Preview pane. Use the scroll bar to see more of the message.

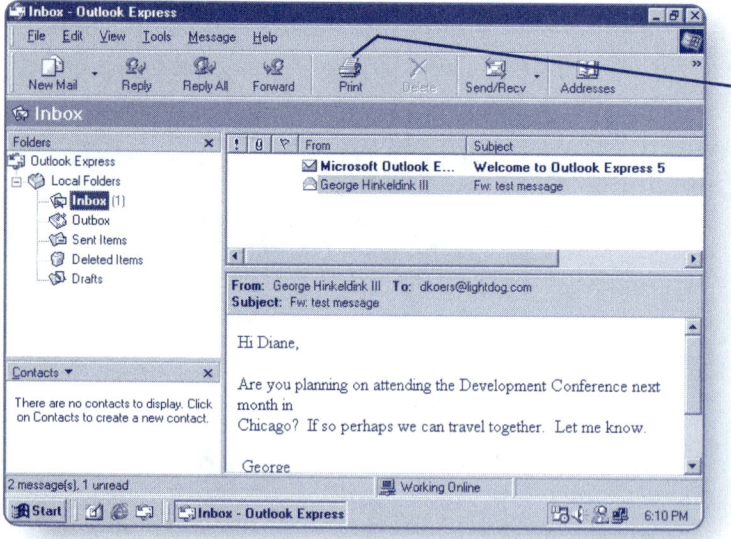

> **TIP**
> You can print any message by clicking the Print button.

4. Click on the **next message** you want to read. The next message appears in the Preview pane.

WORKING WITH E-MAIL   355

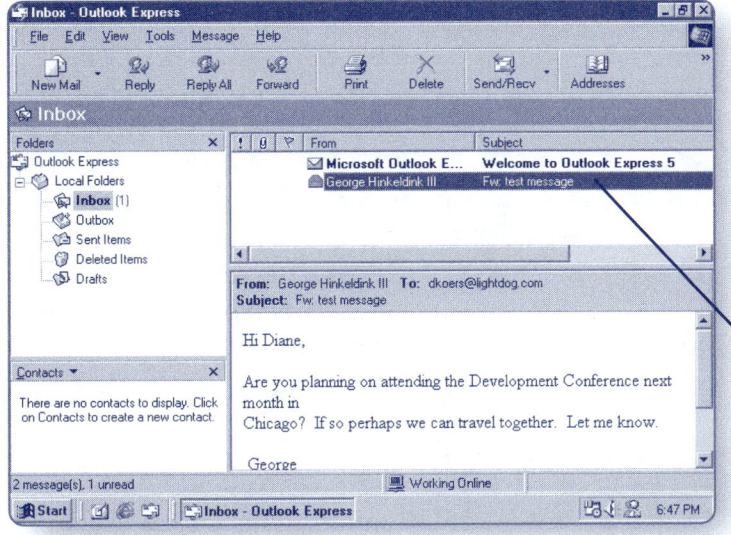

Replying to a Message

Now that you've read the message, you might want to reply to the sender. Outlook Express enables you to answer a message.

1. Click on the **message** to which you want to reply. The message is selected.

2. Click the **Reply button**. A mail message window appears with the sender's e-mail address and subject already entered.

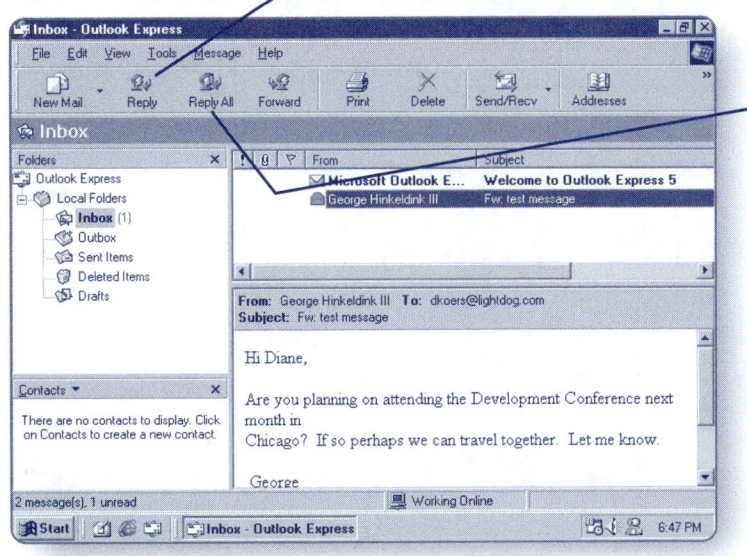

TIP
If the original message was sent to more than one person, you can click on Reply All instead of Reply. Outlook Express sends your reply to each person who received the original message.

356 CHAPTER 21: E-MAILING WITH OUTLOOK EXPRESS

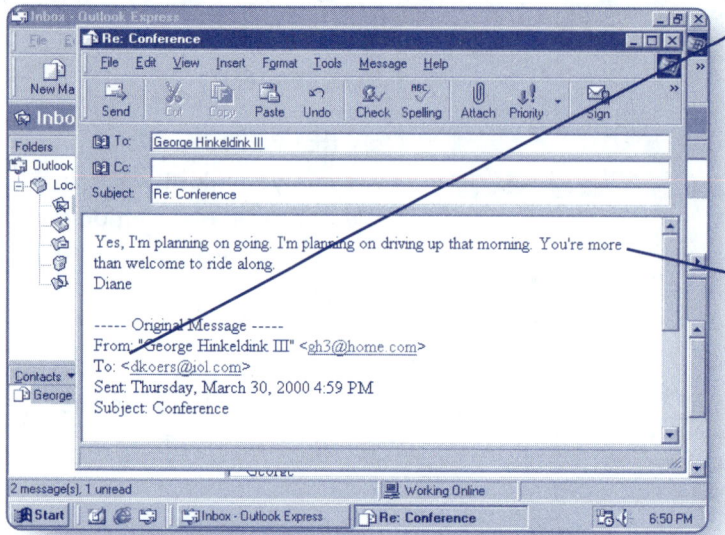

In the body of the new e-mail message, the original message is displayed. Some of the message might have a carat sign (<) in front of it, denoting it is part of the original message.

3. Type the **reply** in the message body. The text appears in the bottom half of the window.

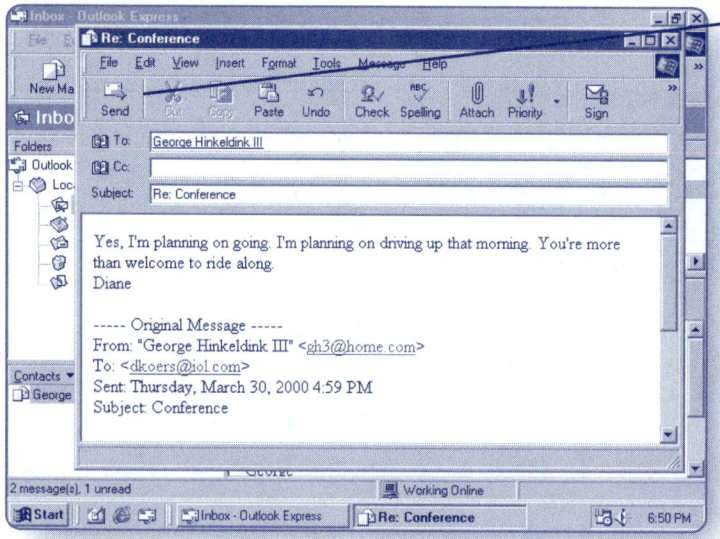

4. Click on the **Send button**. Outlook Express sends the reply immediately and places a copy of the reply in the Sent Items folder.

Forwarding a Message

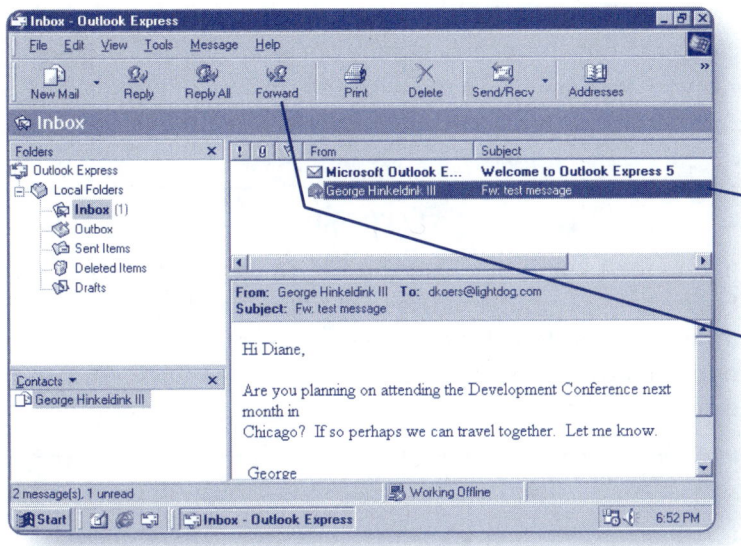

You can send a received message on to another person by forwarding it. You can even add your own message along with it.

1. Click on the **message** you want to forward. The message is highlighted.

2. Click on the **Forward button**. A new mail message window opens and the e-mail address appears blank in the To: line. The Subject: line contains the same subject as the mail you received and places the original message in the body of the new e-mail message.

3. Type the recipient's **e-mail address**. The address appears in the To: line.

4. Click in the **body** of the e-mail message. The insertion point flashes in the bottom half of the window.

5. Type the **message** you want to send in addition to the original message if desired. The text appears in addition to the original message.

6. Click on the **Send button**. The message is sent to the new recipient immediately, and a copy is placed in the Sent Items folder.

Receiving E-mail with Attachments

You've seen how to attach a file to a message you send, and you've seen how to receive e-mail, but what about if someone sends you an e-mail message with an attachment? What should you do with the file you receive?

> **CAUTION**
> If you don't know who sent the file, DON'T OPEN IT! Frequently, computer viruses are transmitted through attached files. This doesn't mean you should never open an attached file; just be sure you know where it came from. Keep your anti-virus software up-to-date.

A paper clip indicates the e-mail has an attachment.

1. Double-click on the e-mail **message**. A window displaying the message opens.

WORKING WITH E-MAIL 359

You can open, print, or save the file.

2. Right-click the e-mail **attachment**. A shortcut menu appears.

3. Click on **Save As**. The Save As dialog box opens.

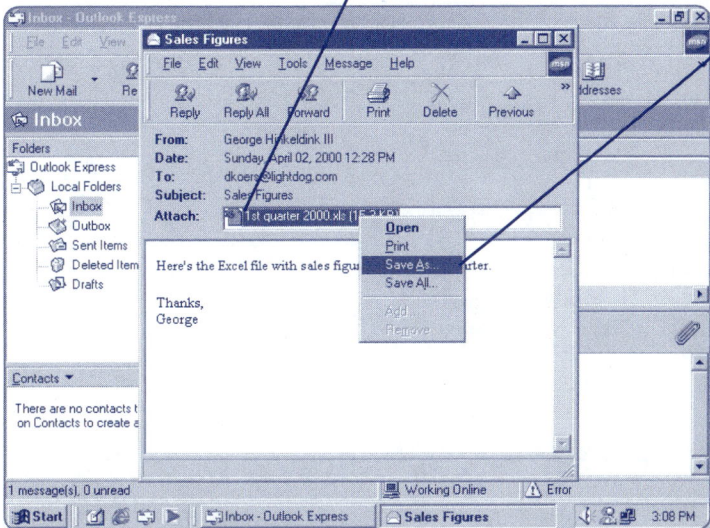

NOTE
To open the received document, you must have a program that supports the file format you are receiving. For example, if you receive an Excel file, you must either have Excel on your system, or a spreadsheet application that can read Excel files.

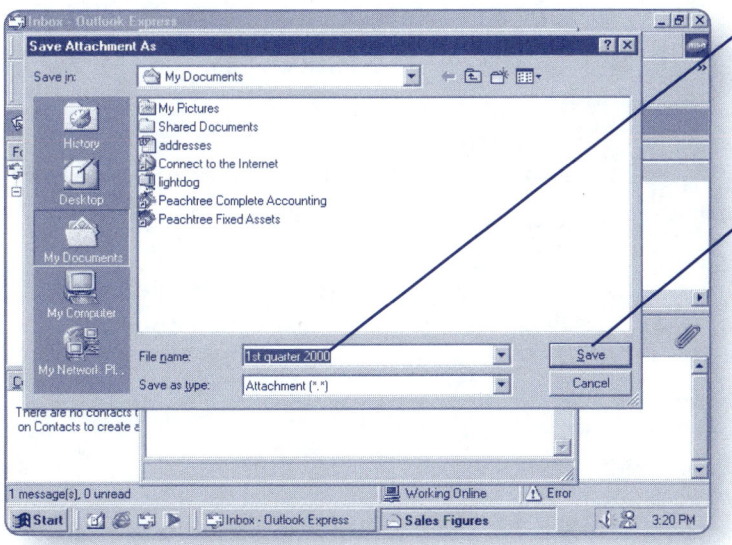

4. Enter a **name** for the file and choose a location. The information appears in the Save As dialog box.

5. Click on **Save**. Windows saves the file in the location you specified.

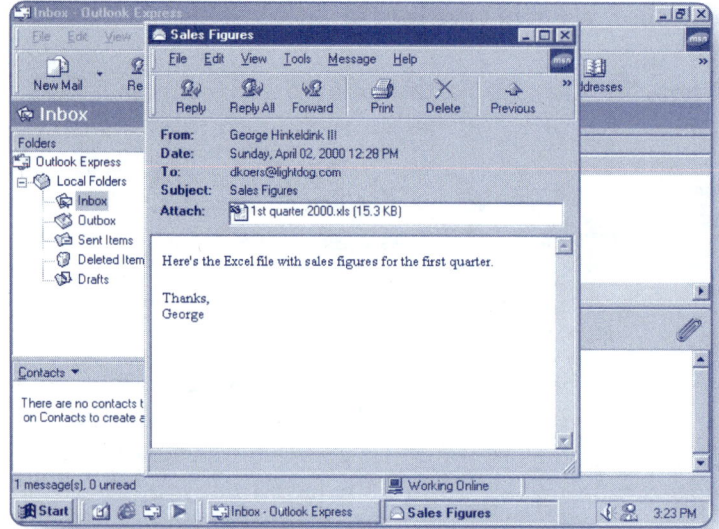

You can now close, reply, delete, forward, or file the e-mail as usual. If you reply to the message, the attachment is not included in the reply. If you forward the message, the attachment *is* included.

Creating an E-mail Folder

Outlook Express stores incoming messages in the Inbox until you do something with them. As more and more e-mail arrives, the Inbox can get very full. Create new folders to organize your mail.

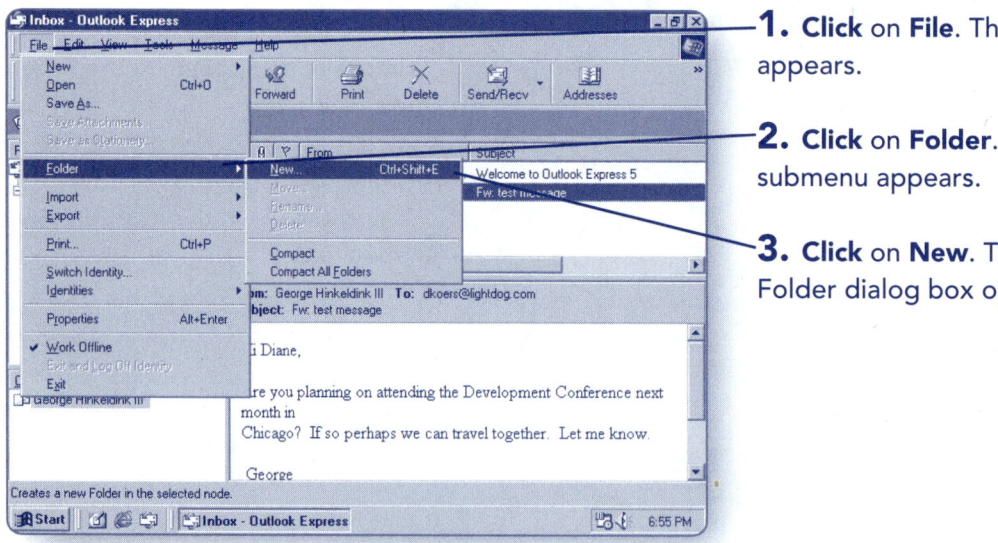

1. Click on **File**. The File menu appears.

2. Click on **Folder**. The Folder submenu appears.

3. Click on **New**. The Create Folder dialog box opens.

WORKING WITH E-MAIL   361

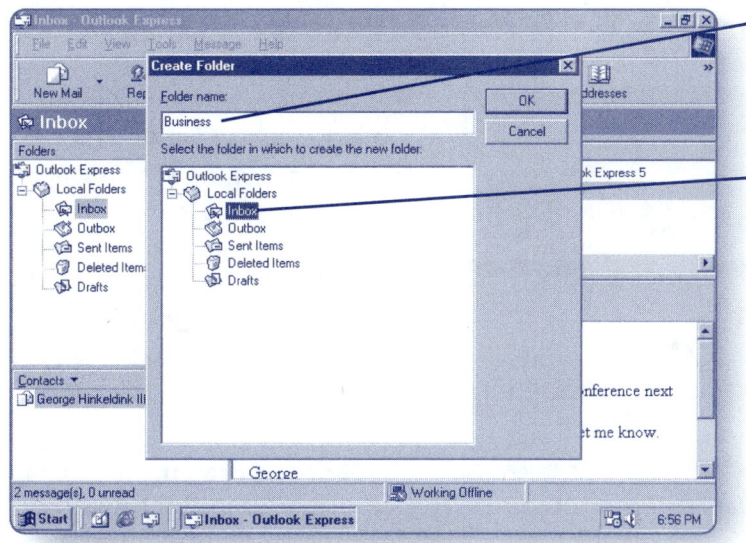

4. Type a **name** for the new folder. The name appears in the Folder name: text box.

5. Click on the **folder** in which you want to place the new folder. The selected folder is highlighted.

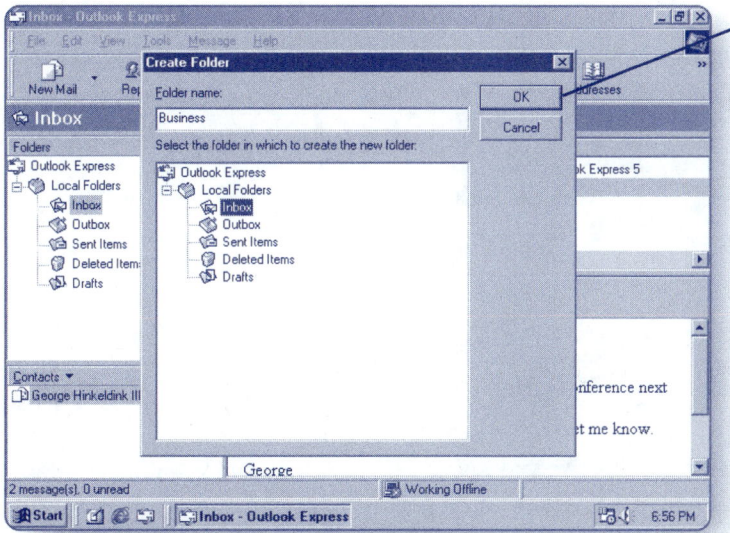

6. Click on **OK**. Outlook Express creates a new folder.

Moving an E-mail Message

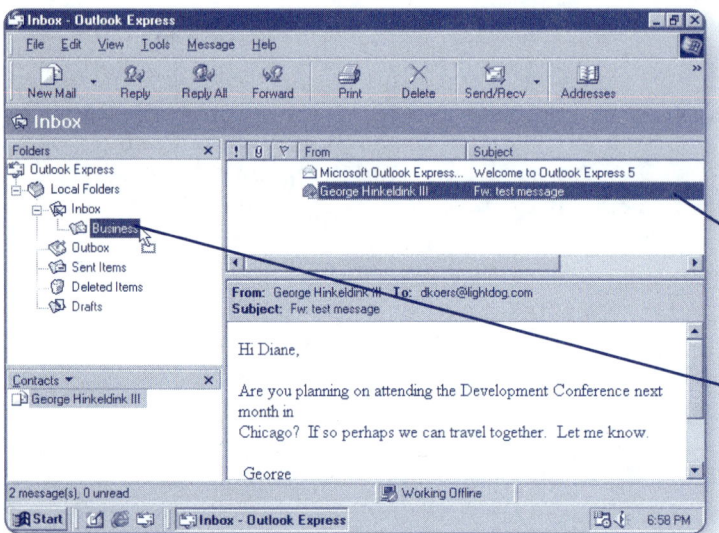

You can move any e-mail from the Inbox to any existing folder. Move e-mail in the same manner as you move files in the Windows Explorer.

1. Click on the **message** you want to move. The message is selected.

2. Click and **drag** the message to the new folder. The message disappears from the current folder.

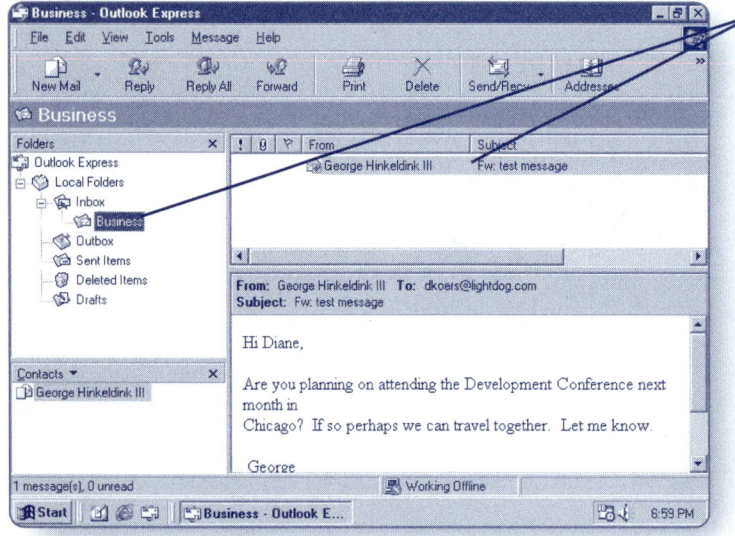

The message appears in the new folder.

Deleting an E-mail Message

Similar to the Windows Recycle Bin, Outlook Express stores deleted messages in a Deleted Items folder.

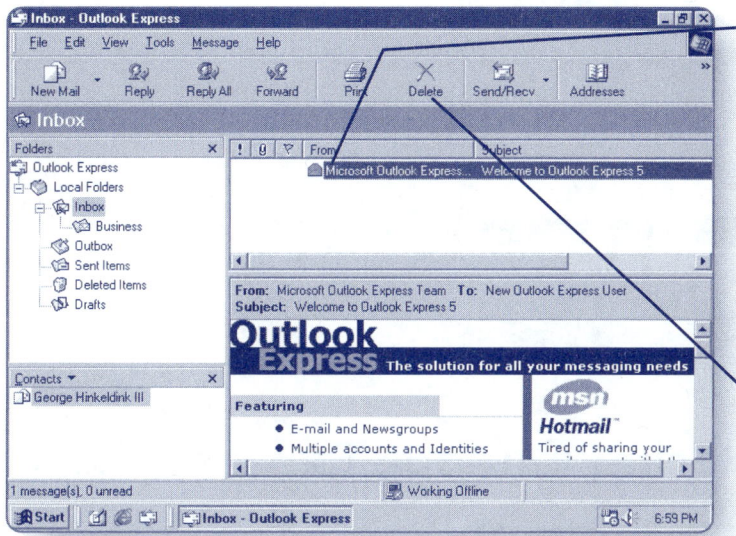

1. Click on the **message** you want to delete. The message is highlighted.

TIP
You should periodically delete old messages from the Sent Items folder.

2. Click the **Delete button**. Outlook Express moves the message to the Deleted Items folder.

TIP
If you want to "undelete" a mail message, click on the Deleted Items folder and drag the message to a different folder.

Like the Windows Recycle Bin, periodically, you'll want to empty the Deleted Items folder.

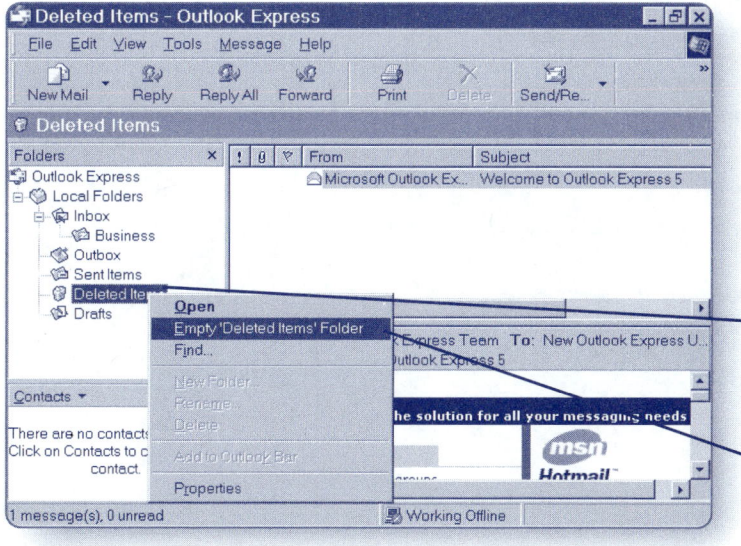

3. Right-click on the **Deleted Items folder**. A shortcut menu appears.

4. Click on **Empty Deleted Items Folder**. A confirmation message appears.

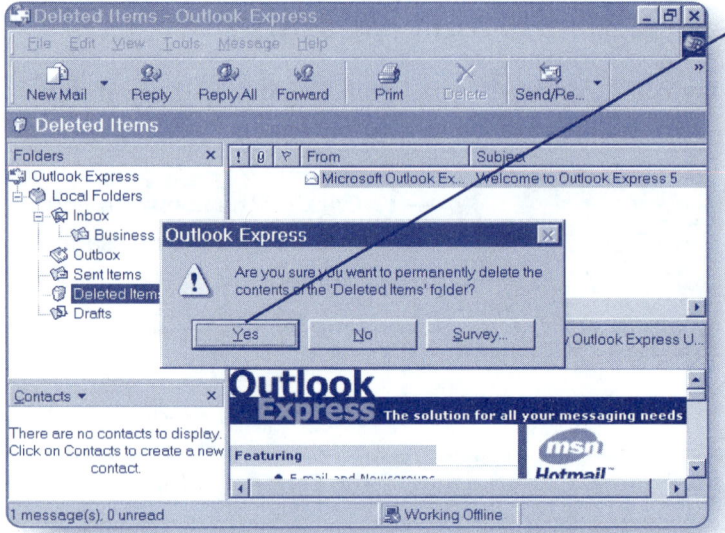

5. **Click** on **Yes**. Outlook Express empties the folder.

Closing Outlook Express

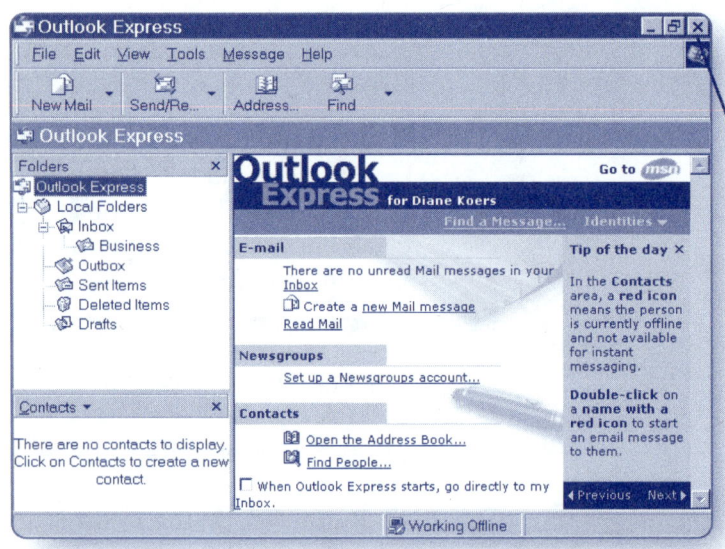

Close the Outlook Express program in the same manner as other Windows Millennium Edition programs.

1. **Click** the **Close button**. The program closes.

22

Using the Windows Address Book

Windows Millennium Edition and Outlook Express join forces to provide an address book that you can use to maintain a variety of information about business and personal contacts. You can use the Address Book to send e-mail to a contact or print a phone list. In this chapter, you'll learn how to:

- Add, edit, or delete an Address Book entry
- Send e-mail from the Address Book
- Sort Address Book entries
- Print a phone list

Managing Address Book Contacts

You can access the Address Book through Outlook Express or through the Windows Start menu.

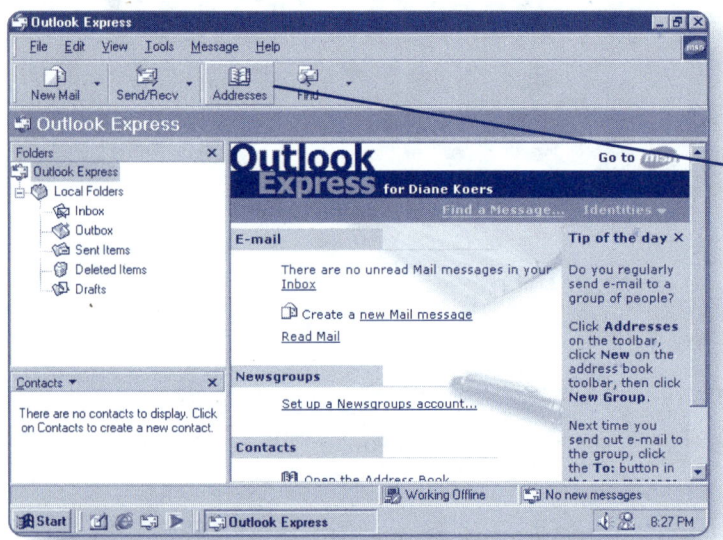

1. Open Outlook Express. The Outlook Express window appears.

2. Click on **Addresses**. The Address Book window appears.

> **TIP**
> Optionally, click on Start, Programs, Accessories, and choose Address Book.

Adding Contacts

It is easy to add entries to the Address Book. As you add contacts, the Address Book lists them in alphabetical order by first name. You'll discover later in this chapter how to sort the entries in a different order.

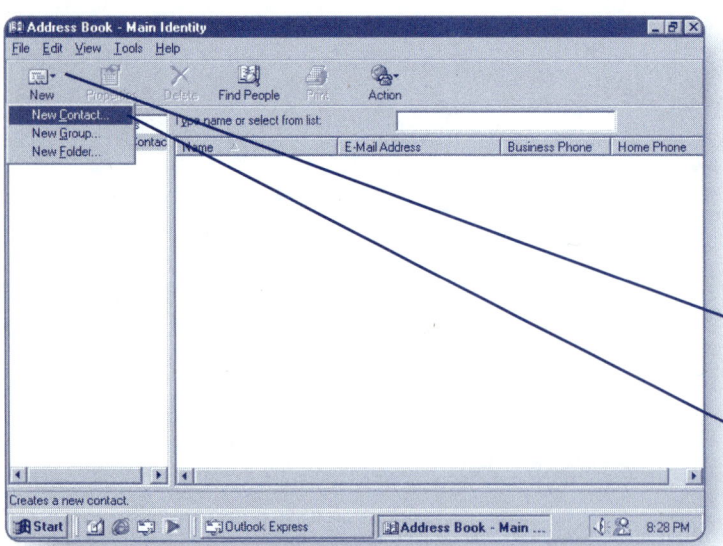

1. Click on the **New button**. A drop-down list appears.

2. Click on **New Contact**. The Properties dialog box opens.

MANAGING ADDRESS BOOK CONTACTS 367

The Name tab appears first. This is where the Address Book stores the contact name and e-mail addresses. All information is optional.

3. Type the contact's **first name**. The name appears in the First: text box.

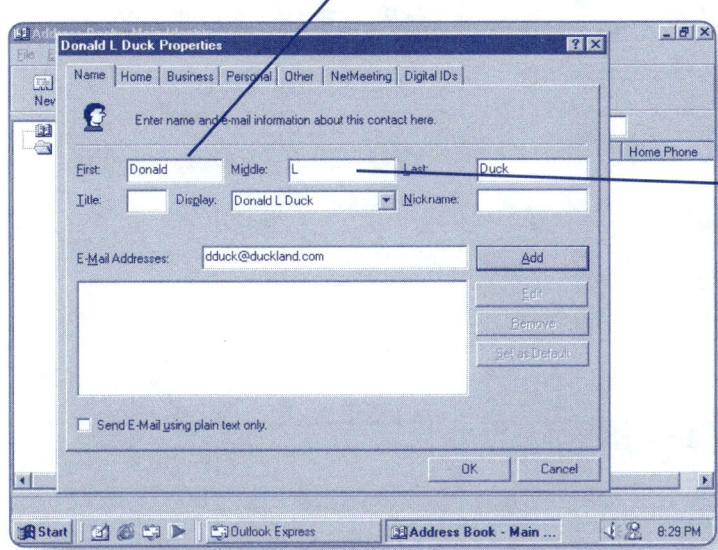

4. Press the **Tab key**. The insertion point moves to the Middle: text box.

5. Enter a **middle name or initial**. The name appears in the Middle: text box.

6. Press the **Tab key**. The insertion point moves to the Last: text box.

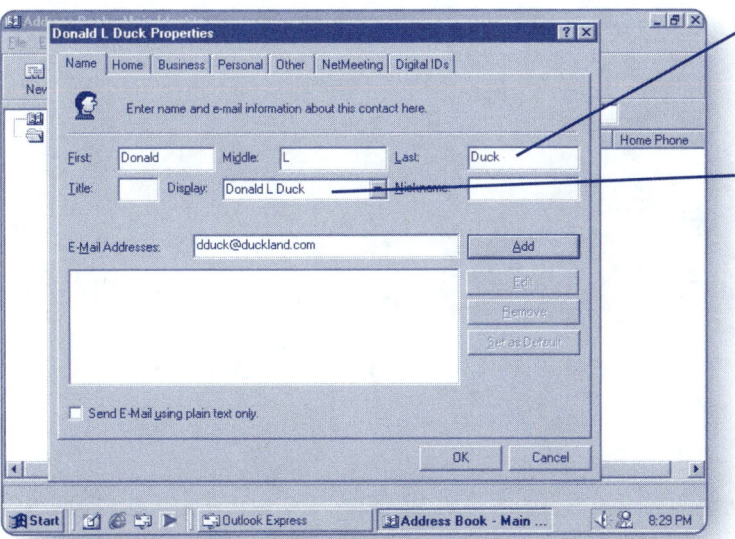

7. Type the contact's **last name**. The name appears in the Last: box.

As you enter the name, Address Book automatically fills in the Display: box. The display name appears in the title bar. If desired, you can change the display name.

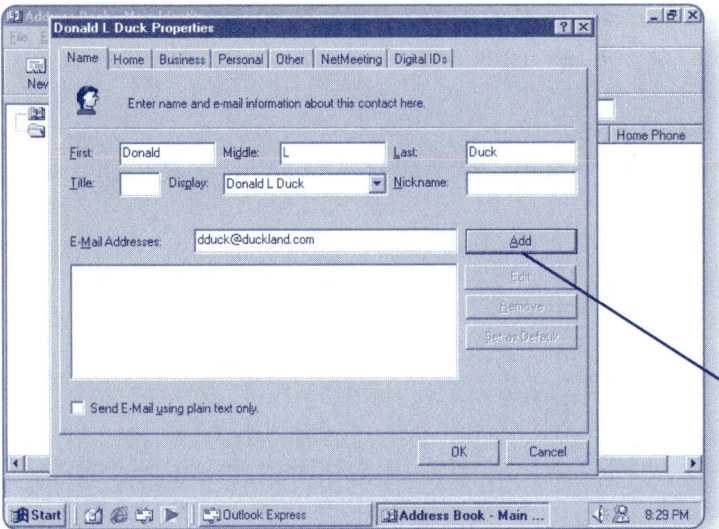

8. Click in the **E-Mail Addresses: text box**. The blinking insertion point is in the E-Mail Addresses: text box.

9. Type the contact's **e-mail address**. The e-mail address appears in the E-Mail Addresses: text box.

10. Click on **Add**. The e-mail address is added.

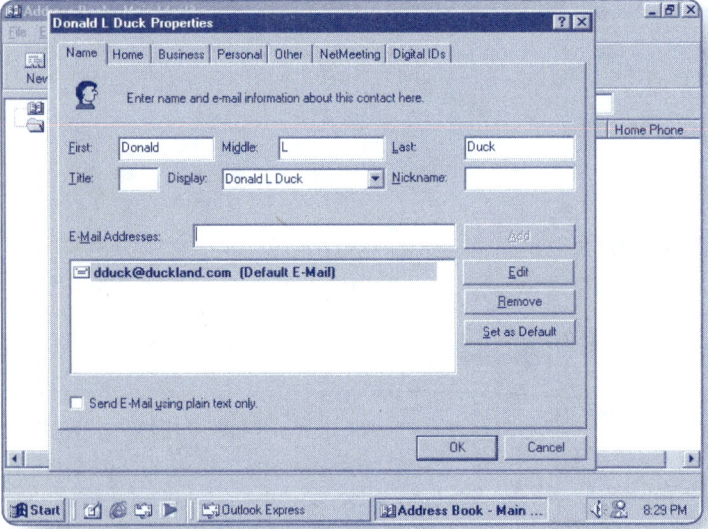

> **TIP**
>
> Repeat Steps 9 and 10 to add as many e-mail addresses as you want for this contact.

MANAGING ADDRESS BOOK CONTACTS 369

11. Click on the **Home tab**. The tab comes to the front.

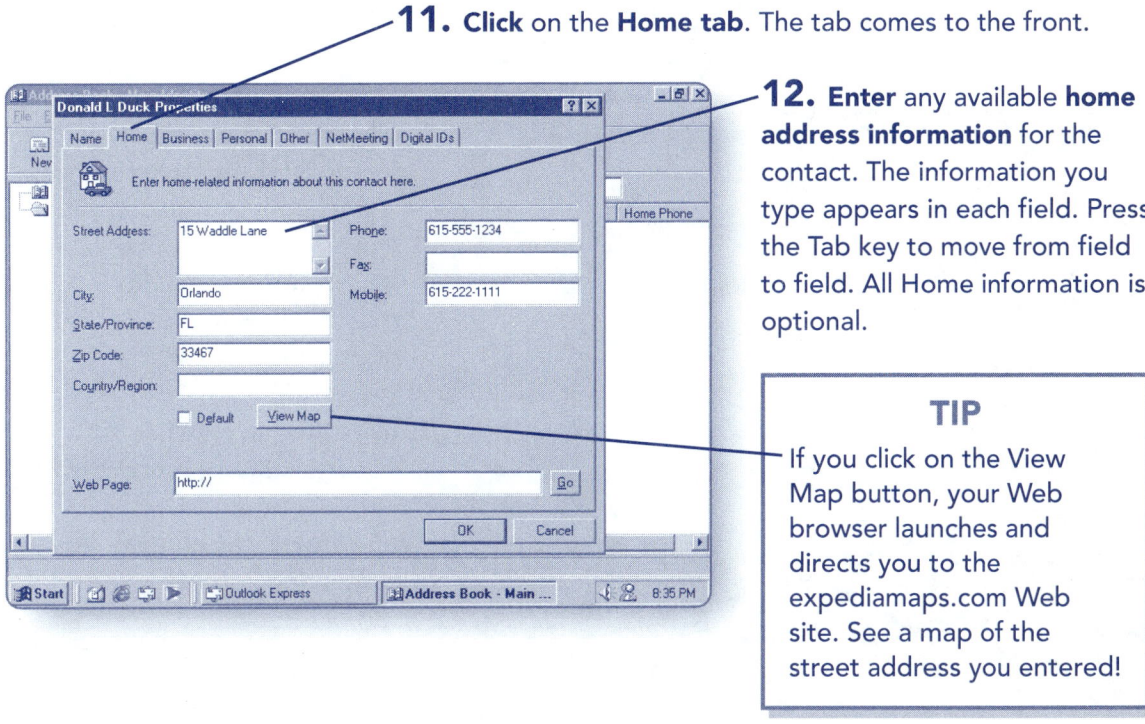

12. Enter any available **home address information** for the contact. The information you type appears in each field. Press the Tab key to move from field to field. All Home information is optional.

TIP

If you click on the View Map button, your Web browser launches and directs you to the expediamaps.com Web site. See a map of the street address you entered!

13. Click on the **Business tab**. The Business tab comes to the front.

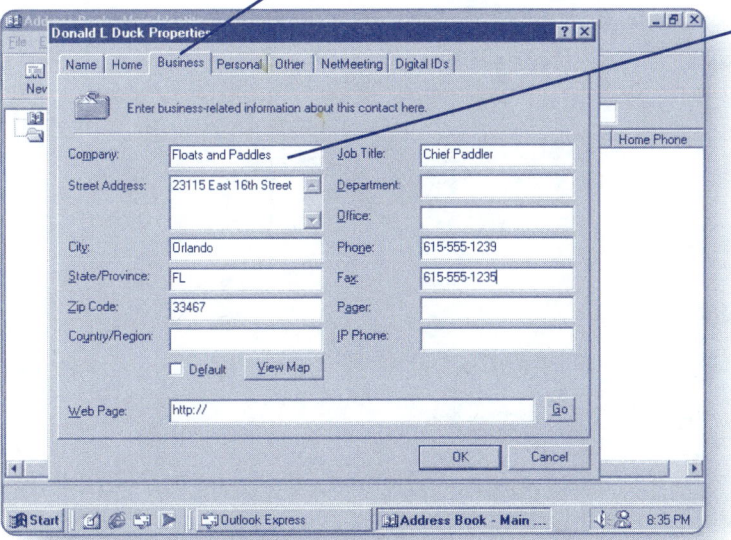

14. Enter any available **business information** for the contact. The information you type appears in each field. Press the Tab key to move from field to field. All business information is optional.

TIP

Click the View Map button to see a map of the street address entered on this screen.

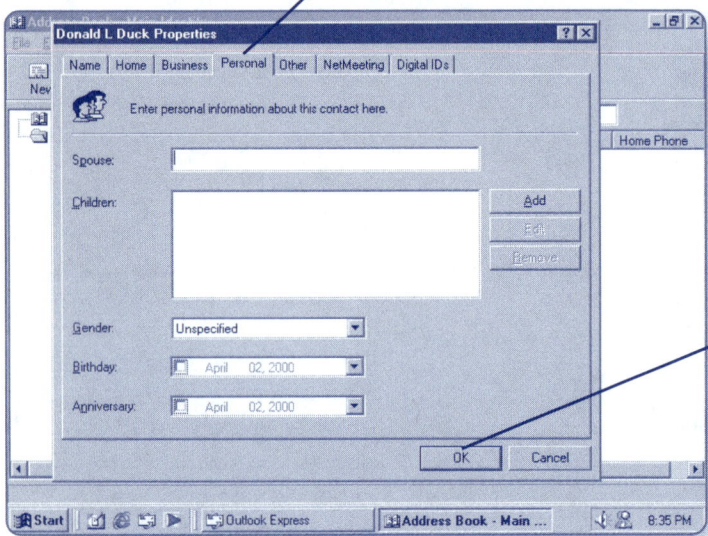

15. Click on the **Personal tab**. The Personal tab comes to the front.

16. Enter any available **personal information** for the contact. The information you type appears in each field. Press the Tab key to move from field to field. All personal information is optional.

17. Click on **OK**. The Properties dialog box closes.

A portion of the contact information appears in the Address Book.

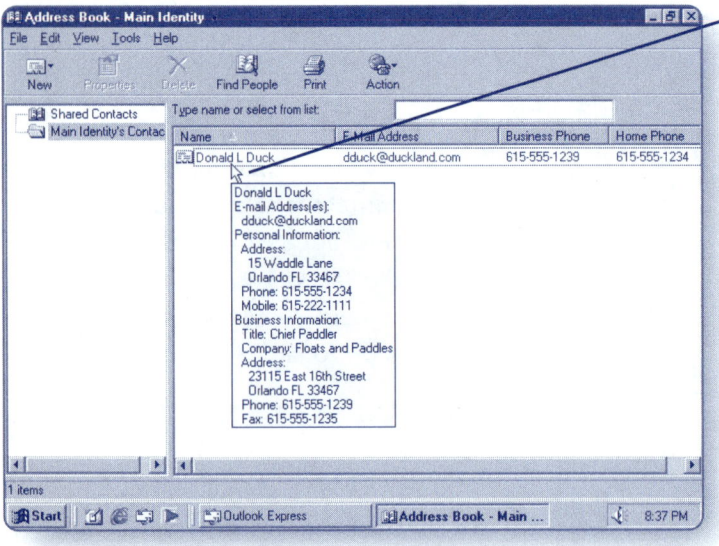

Position the mouse over a contact to see the entire contact information.

MANAGING ADDRESS BOOK CONTACTS 371

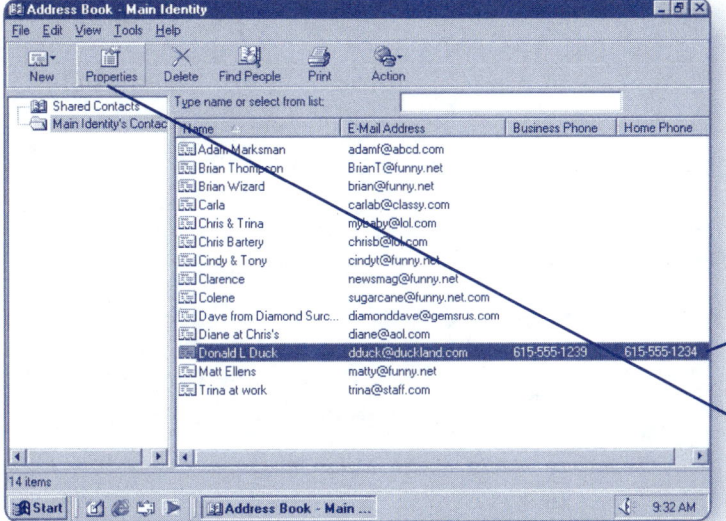

Editing Contacts

Only the display name, e-mail address, and two phone numbers appear in the Address Book. You'll need to open the record to edit or view the entire contact information.

1. Click on the **entry** you want to edit. The entry is highlighted.

2. Click on the **Properties button**. The Properties dialog box opens.

TIP

Optionally, double-click an entry to open the Properties dialog box.

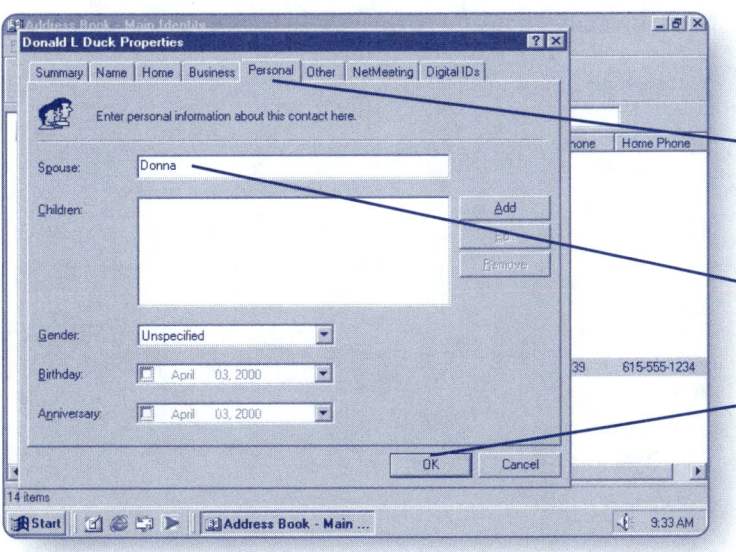

3. Click on the **information tab** you want to edit. The selected contact information appears.

4. Change or add any desired **information**.

5. Click on **OK**. The Properties dialog box closes.

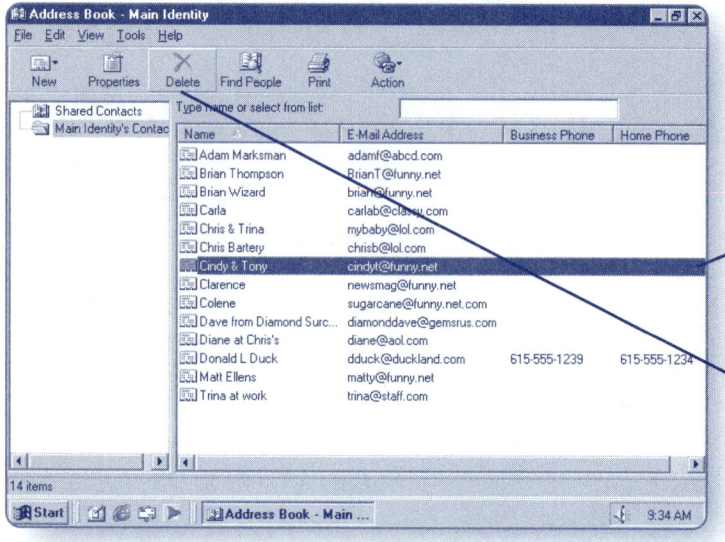

Deleting Contacts

If you no longer want a contact listed in your Address Book, you can easily delete it.

1. **Click** on the **contact name** you want to delete. The name is highlighted.

2. **Click** on the **Delete button**. A confirmation box appears.

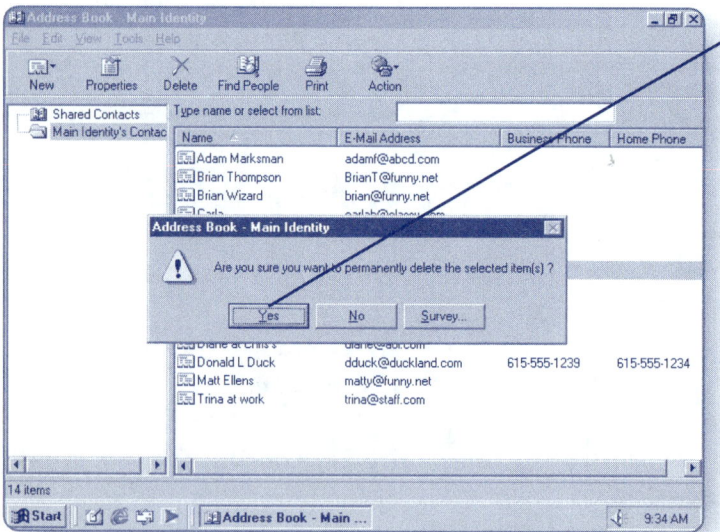

3. **Click** on **Yes**. The contact and all its information is deleted.

> **NOTE**
> You cannot undo the delete action.

Sorting Address Book Contacts

By default, the Address Book lists your contacts by first name. However, you can sort them by last name, e-mail address, business phone number, or home phone number.

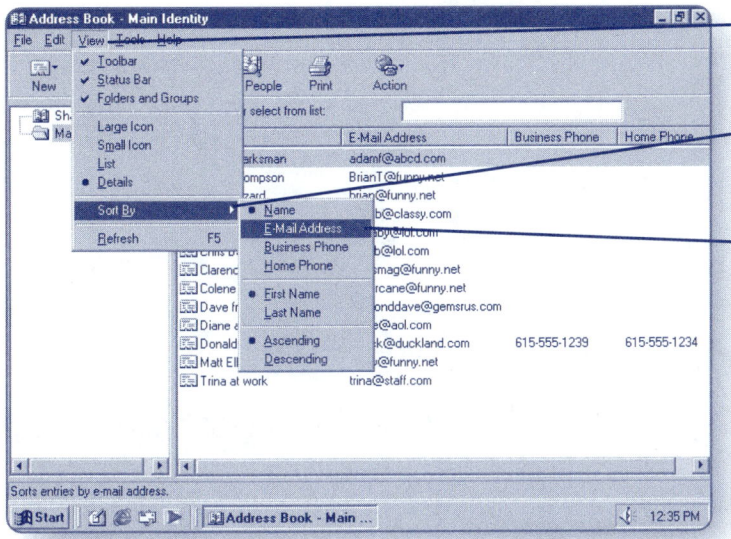

1. Click on **View**. The View menu appears.

2. Click on **Sort By**. The Sort By submenu appears.

3. Click the **method** by which you want to sort. Depending on your selection, you may have additional choices.

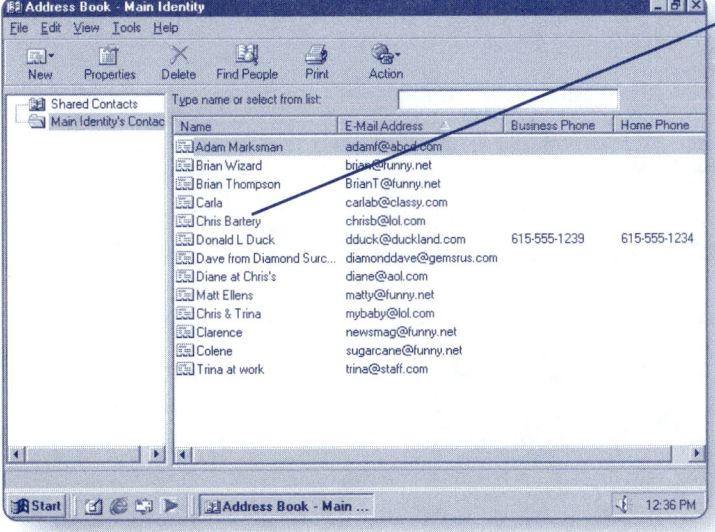

If you select by name, you can choose first name or last name.

You can sort in ascending or descending order.

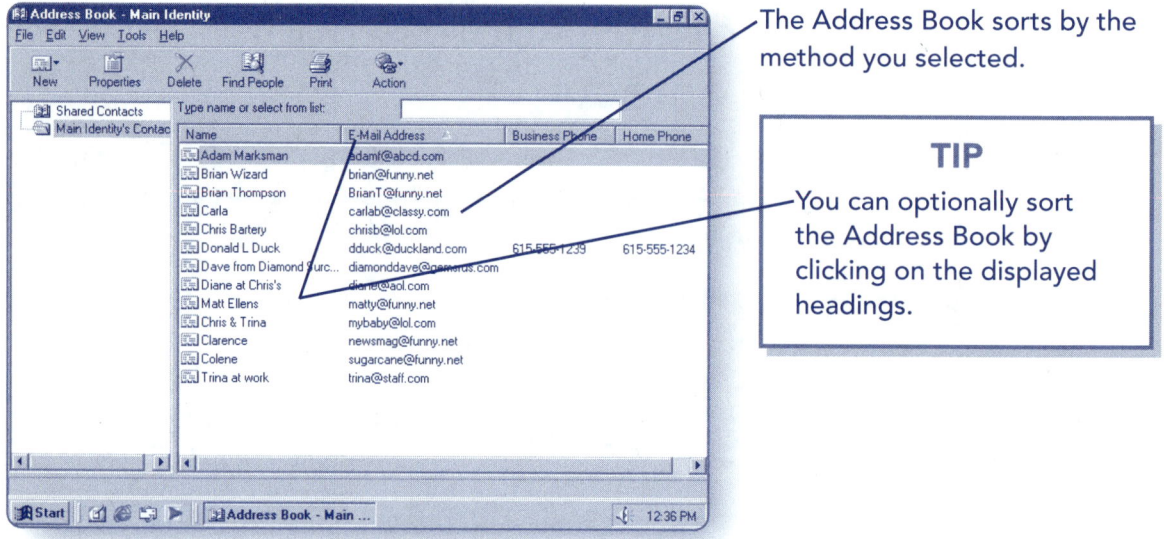

The Address Book sorts by the method you selected.

TIP
You can optionally sort the Address Book by clicking on the displayed headings.

Printing a Phone List

You can print the contact information in any of three formats: Memo Style, Business Card Style, and Phone List Style.

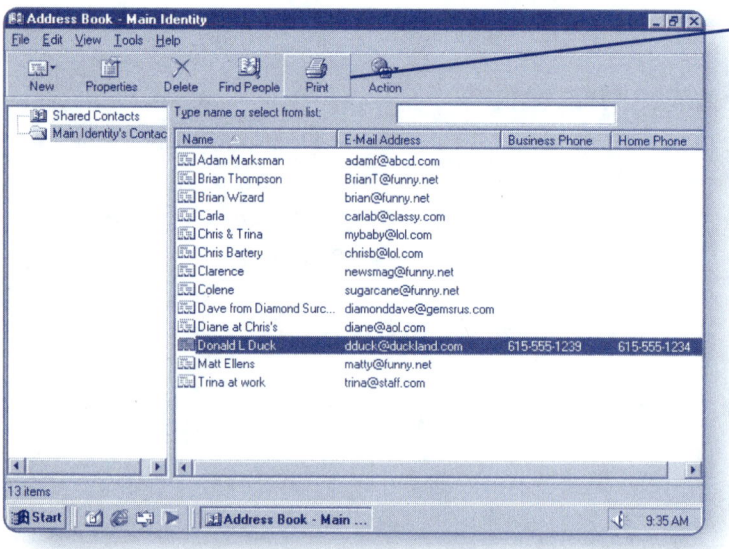

1. Click on the **Print button**. The Print dialog box opens.

PRINTING A PHONE LIST 375

You can print your entire contact list, or only the currently selected record—the one highlighted before you clicked on the Print button.

2. Click on a **print range**. The option is selected.

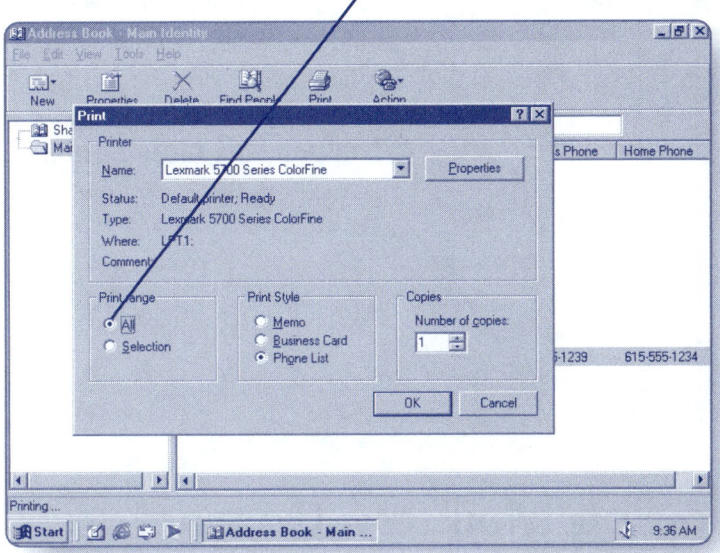

You can print the Address Book in any of three different print styles:

- **Memo**: Prints all available information from the Name, Home, and Business tabs.

- **Business Card**: Prints names, address, phone numbers, and e-mails in a format similar to a traditional business card.

- **Phone List**: Prints an alphabetical list of names and phone numbers. Names are grouped together by alpha letter. For example, all the "A"s print, then all the "B"s, and so forth.

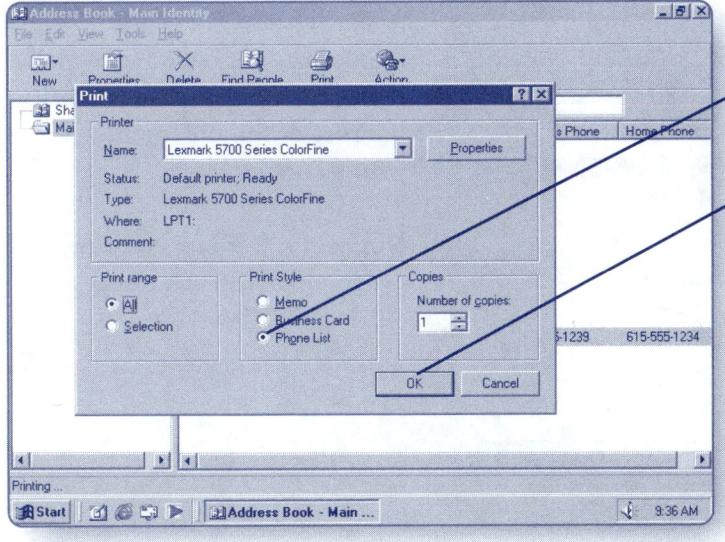

3. Click on a **print style**. The style is highlighted.

4. Click on **OK**. The Address Book contacts print.

Closing the Address Book

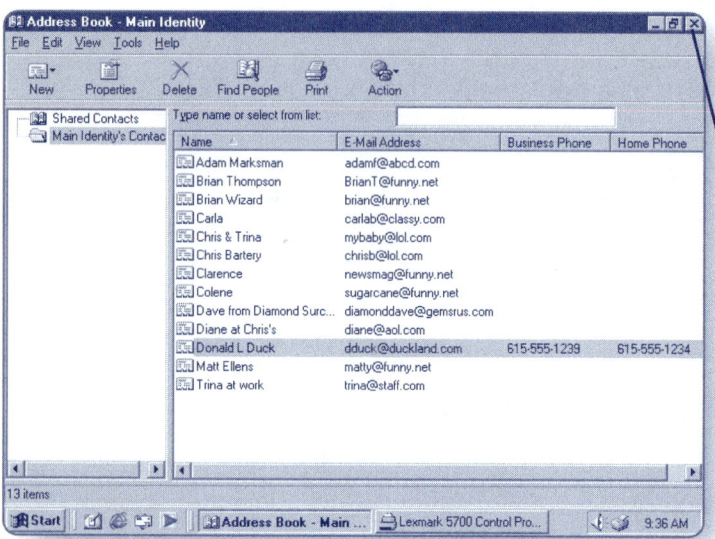

Address Book automatically saves information as you enter it. When you're finished with the Address Book, close it like you would any other Windows application.

1. Click on the **Close button**. The Address Book window closes.

Sending Mail to a Contact

In Chapter 21, "E-mailing with Outlook Express," you learned how to send e-mail with Outlook Express. The Address Book makes sending e-mail even easier. You don't have to memorize—or even type—the sometimes-complicated e-mail address of the person to whom you're sending mail.

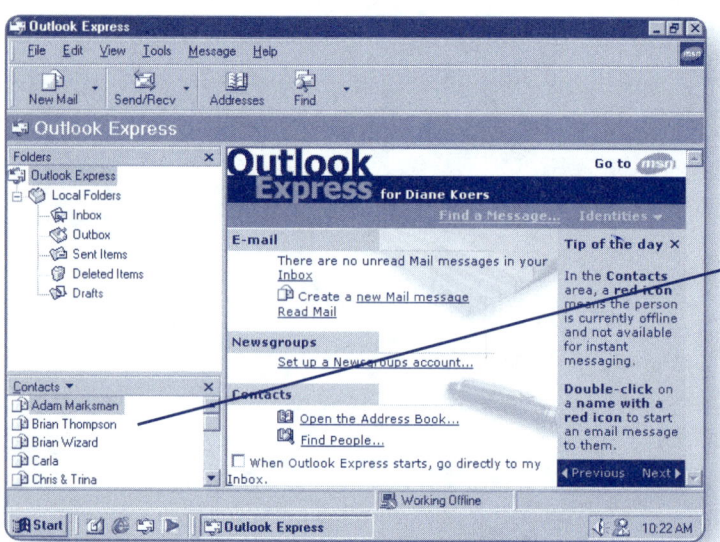

Notice the Contacts window listing your Address Book entries.

SENDING MAIL TO A CONTACT 377

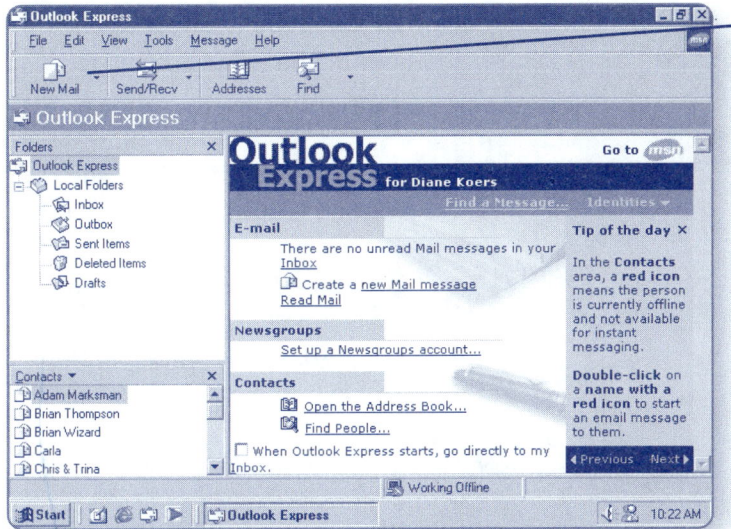

1. From the Outlook Express window, **click** the **New Mail button**. The New Message window appears.

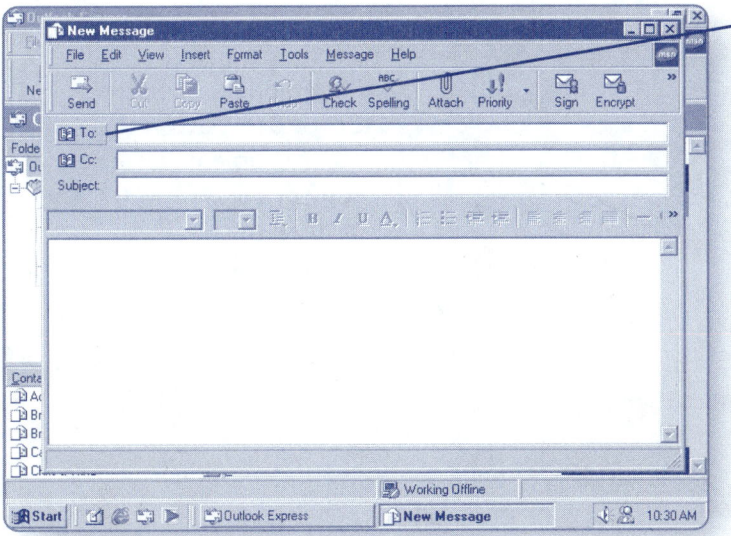

2. Click the **To: button**. The Select Recipients window appears.

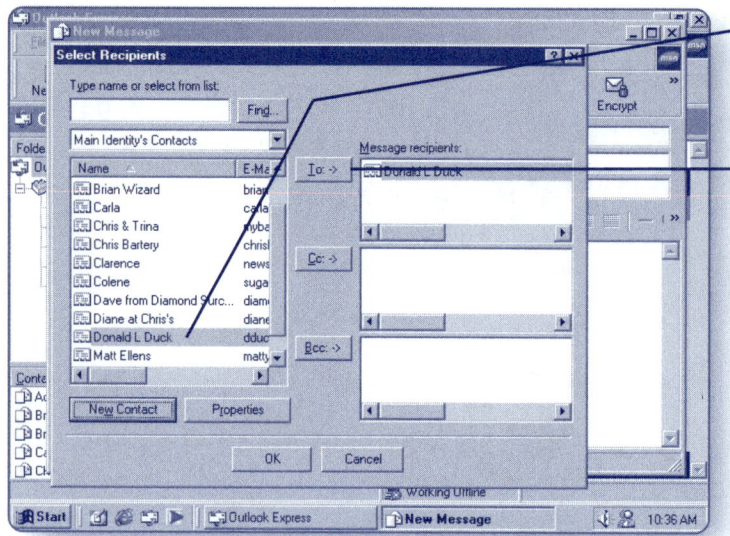

3. Click the e-mail **recipient name**. The contact name is highlighted.

4. Click the **To: arrow**. The contact is added to the To: list.

5. Repeat Steps 3 and 4 for each e-mail recipient. The selected names appear in the To: list.

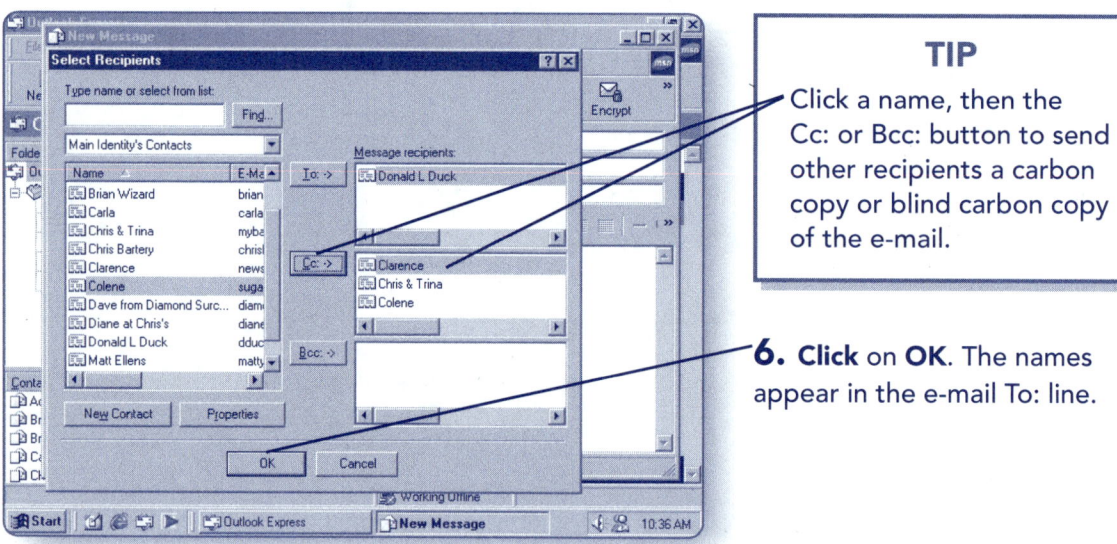

TIP

Click a name, then the Cc: or Bcc: button to send other recipients a carbon copy or blind carbon copy of the e-mail.

6. Click on **OK**. The names appear in the e-mail To: line.

SENDING MAIL TO A CONTACT 379

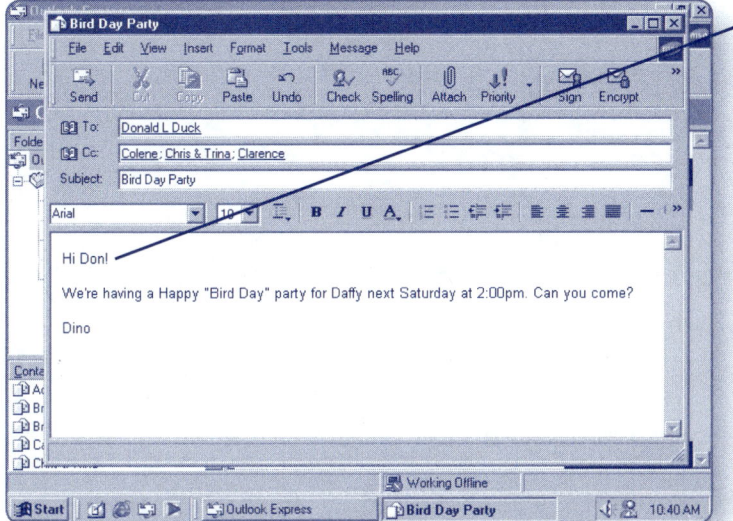

7. Enter the **subject and body** of the e-mail as you learned in Chapter 21. The e-mail is ready to send.

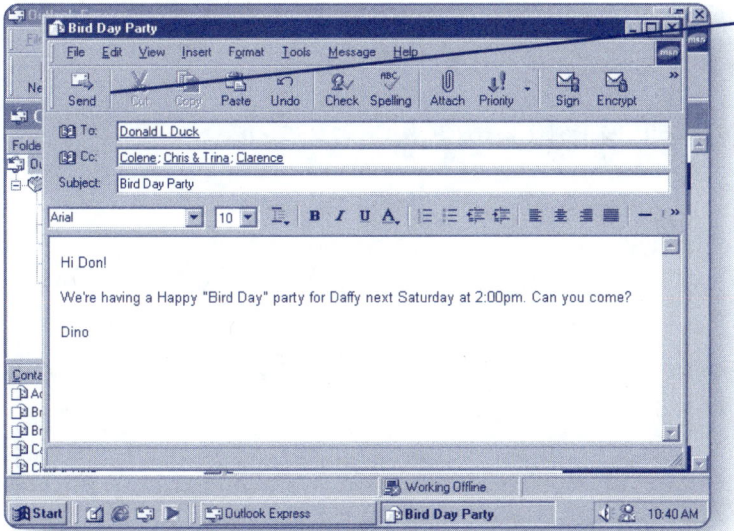

8. Click on **Send**. The e-mail message is sent.

Part V Review Questions

1. What do you need in order to sign up with an online service? *See "Subscribing to an Online Service" in Chapter 19*

2. What are two of the most frequently used Web browsers on the market today? *See "Starting Your Web Browser" in Chapter 19*

3. What does a typical Web address begin with? *See "Browsing the Web with Internet Explorer" in Chapter 20*

4. What does it mean when you point your mouse to underlined text and the mouse pointer turns into a hand? *See "Browsing the Web with Internet Explorer" in Chapter 20*

5. What types of content can you control with Parental Control? *See "Setting Parental Controls" in Chapter 20*

6. What is e-mail? *See "E-mailing with Outlook Express" in Chapter 21*

7. What do you use to separate multiple names on an e-mail message? *See "Creating an E-mail Message" in Chapter 21*

8. How can you add a background to an e-mail message? *See "Formatting an E-mail Message" in Chapter 21*

9. How do you print an e-mail? *See "Retrieving Incoming E-mail" in Chapter 21*

10. What type of information can be stored in the Address Book? *See "Adding Contacts" in Chapter 22*

A

Upgrading to Windows Millennium

If you go out today and buy a new computer, most likely it will have Windows Millennium pre-installed on it. But if you're upgrading from an earlier version of Microsoft Windows, you'll be pleasantly surprised with the ease of installing Windows Millennium. In this appendix you'll learn how to:

- Install Windows Millennium
- Uninstall Windows Millennium
- Register your software online

Understanding the Upgrade Process

Setup is a simple process with Windows Millennium and requires very little interaction between you and the computer. During the Setup process, Windows Millennium recognizes your current configuration on the PC and retains those settings.

Windows Millennium easily detects your hardware and existing software, and it has a built-in setup recovery system. If the setup process should fail in the middle, the process remembers where it left off and begins at that step. This feature saves time because you won't have to redo the successful installation steps.

System Requirements

To install Windows Millennium, your PC must meet the following requirements:

- A Pentium or equivalent machine with a minimum speed of 150 MHz (megahertz).
- 32MB of RAM.
- Disk space requirements vary with the options you install, but you can expect to use anywhere from 320MB to 430MB for a typical installation, but can range between 200MB and 550MB, depending on your system configuration and the options you choose to install.

If you have only the minimum requirements, expect Windows Millennium to run very slowly. If you can add memory to your "minimum" PC, you'll see a marked improvement in performance.

Installing the Windows Millennium Edition Upgrade

Installation of the Windows Millennium upgrade requires five basic parts, all of which are run almost automatically by the Setup program.

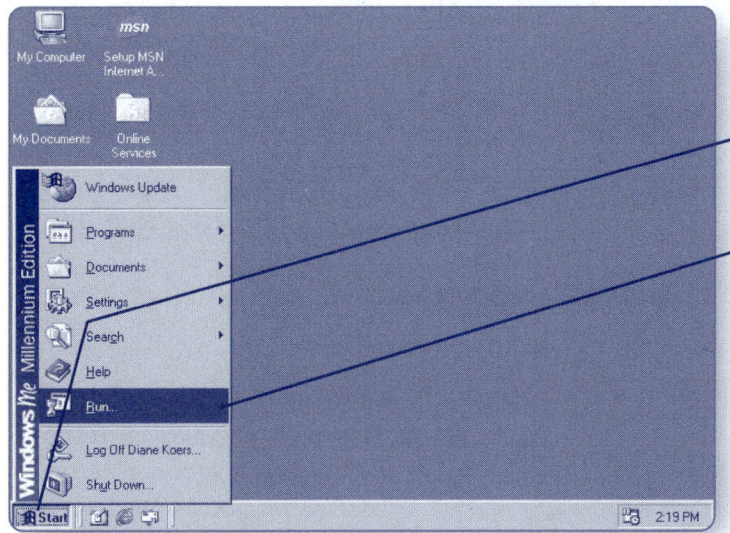

1. **Insert** the **Windows Millennium CD-ROM**.

2. **Click** on **Start**. The Start menu appears.

3. **Click** on **Run**. The Run dialog box opens.

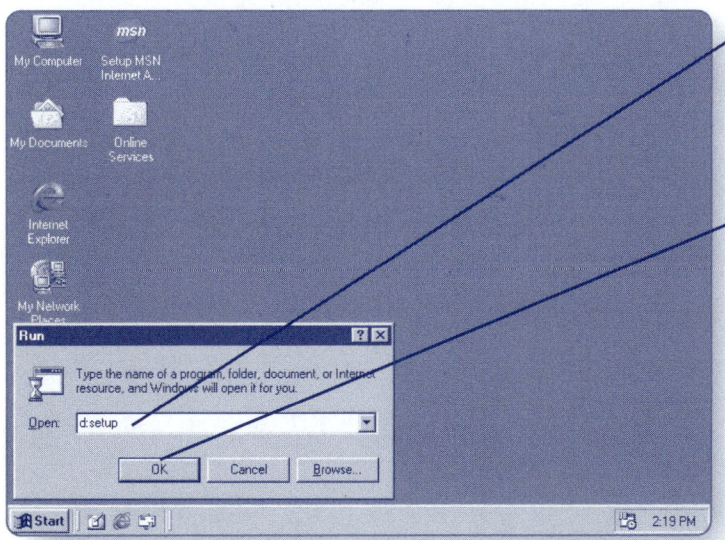

4. Type **D:SETUP** in the Open: text box. If D is not the drive letter for your CD-ROM drive, use the appropriate letter.

5. **Click** on **OK**. The Windows Millennium Edition Setup Wizard launches.

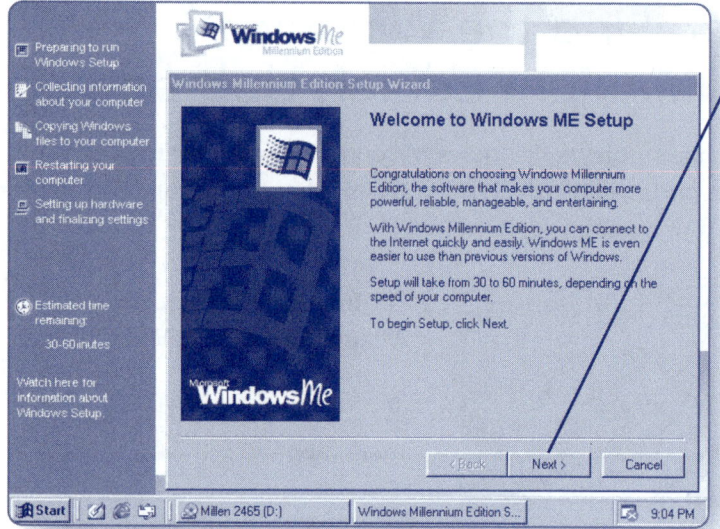

6. Click on **Next**. The setup process begins.

Windows first checks out your existing system; you can track the process with the progress bar. On the left side of your screen, a display lists the steps to be done during the upgrade and the estimated time remaining to accomplish it. The current step is displayed in yellow. The exact time depends on the speed and configuration of your machine.

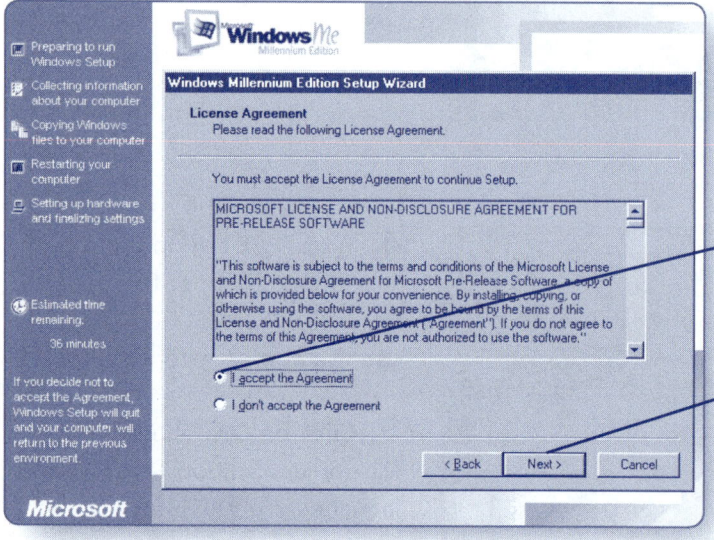

The Microsoft licensing agreement is displayed. You can read through the agreement. Press the Page Down key to see more of it.

7. Click "**I accept the Agreement**". The option will be highlighted.

8. Click on **Next**. The Windows Product Key screen appears.

INSTALLING THE WINDOWS MILLENNIUM EDITION UPGRADE 385

The CD key code that Setup asks for pertains to your license to use Windows Millennium. This code could be located in one of two places. First, look on the CD-ROM case. Second, look on the certificate of authenticity included with the paperwork that came with your Windows Millennium upgrade.

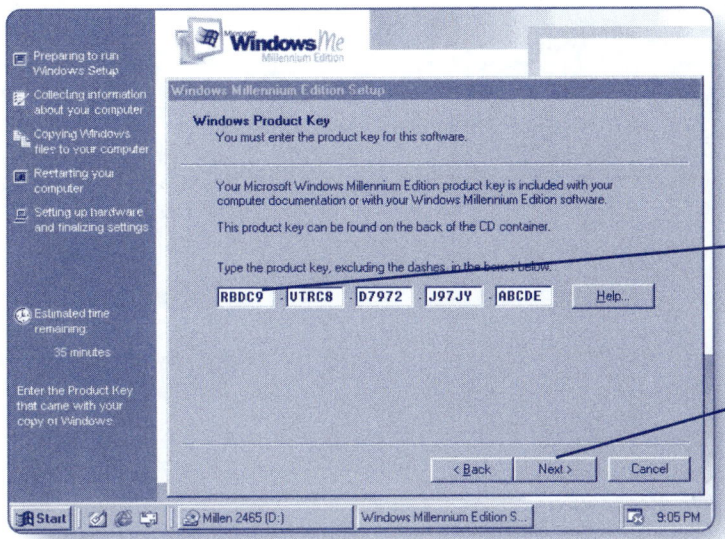

9. Enter the **CD code**. The letters and numbers you type appear in the text box.

10. Click on **Next**. The Save System Files screen appears.

The Setup Wizard next asks about saving the existing system files, so you can uninstall Windows Millennium if necessary. This step requires an additional 110MB of disk space. I recommend you save the system files if at all possible. You can delete them at a later date.

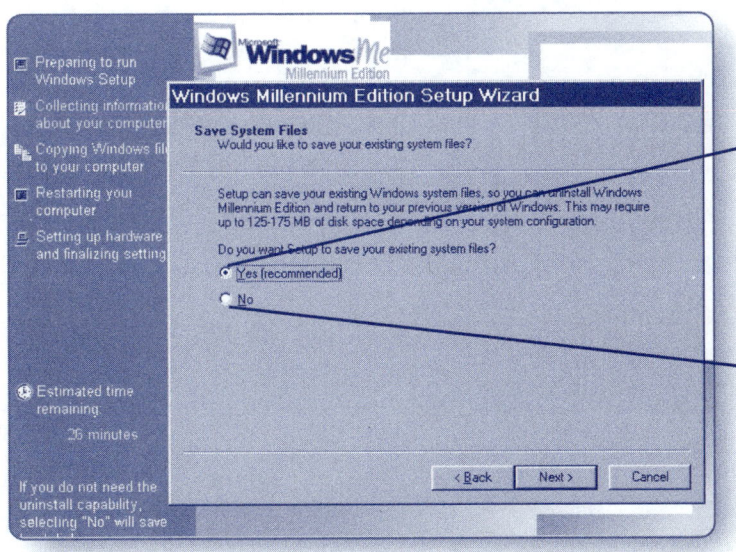

11a. Click on **Yes** if you want to save the existing files. The option will be selected.

OR

11b. Click on **No** if you don't want those files saved. You will not be able to uninstall Windows Millennium if you choose No.

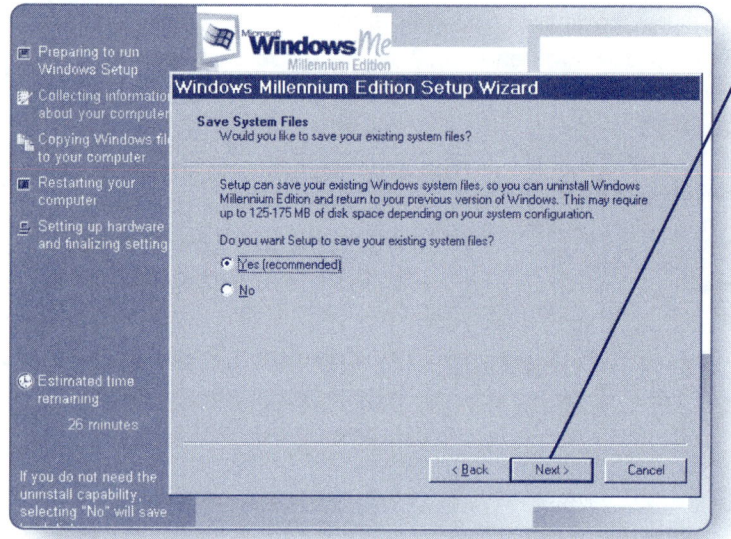

12. Click on **Next**. The Save System Files are created.

Next you are prompted to create a Startup disk to use if you later have trouble starting Windows Millennium. Creating a Startup disk isn't mandatory, but I highly recommend it.

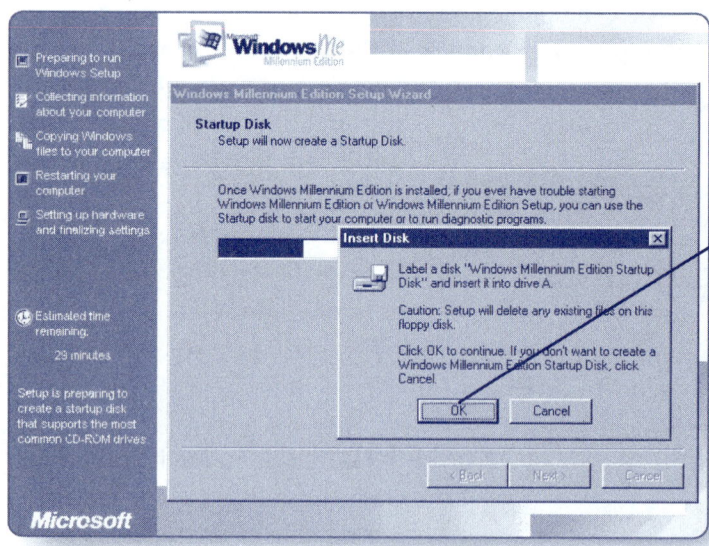

13. Insert a floppy **disk** into the floppy disk drive. If the floppy disk has existing files on it, those files will be erased.

14. Click on **OK**. Setup transfers the necessary startup files to a floppy disk.

INSTALLING THE WINDOWS MILLENNIUM EDITION UPGRADE   387

> **TIP**
> If you do not want to create a Startup disk, click on Cancel. To create a startup disk at a later time, see "Creating a Windows Startup Disk" in Chapter 16, "Tinkering with the Control Panel."

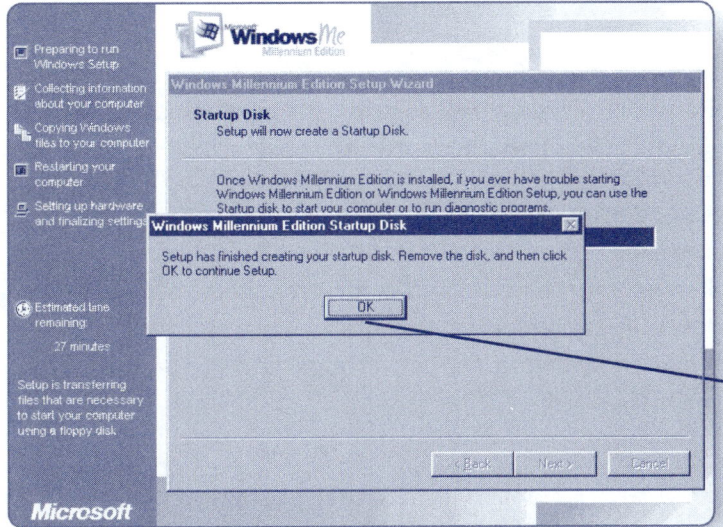

A message box appears when the startup disk is complete.

15. **Remove** the **disk** from the disk drive and label the disk "Emergency Windows Millennium Startup Disk." Store this disk in a safe, convenient place.

16. **Click** on **OK**. The Ready to Begin Copying Files screen appears.

The Setup Wizard has enough information about your systems and is ready to start copying Windows Millennium files to your hard drive.

17. **Click** on **Finish**. The Welcome to Windows Millennium screen appears.

Be patient; this part might take a little while. Read the screens for information about Windows Millennium Edition's new features and enhancements. On the left side of the screen, a progress indicator keeps you up-to-date on the status of the upgrade.

At several different points, the Setup Wizard will restart your machine. It does so automatically, so you don't need to do anything.

Setup detects the hardware on your machine and your current configuration and matches it with Windows Millennium. Setup now configures Control Panel, Start menu items, Help, DOS programs settings, system configuration, and other settings. It is also looking for the various software programs you have installed on your machine and configures them to work with Windows Millennium. A small box announces that Windows Millennium is updating system settings, and Windows restarts one more time!

> **NOTE**
> If the computer stops responding for a long time, turn it off and then back on.

When Windows restarts this time, it finishes building a driver database and sets up personalized settings for other Windows components, such as Internet Explorer, Multimedia, and Accessories. A Setup dialog box appears several times as Windows sets up each component.

Windows Millennium is now installed, and you're ready to use it.

Uninstalling Windows Millennium Edition

Microsoft hopes you'll like Windows Millennium Edition so much you won't want to remove it, but you can if you want to, provided that you allowed Windows to back up your system files on the hard disk when you were installing Windows Millennium Edition.

UNINSTALLING WINDOWS MILLENNIUM EDITION 389

Use the Add/Remove Programs feature you learned about in Chapter 16.

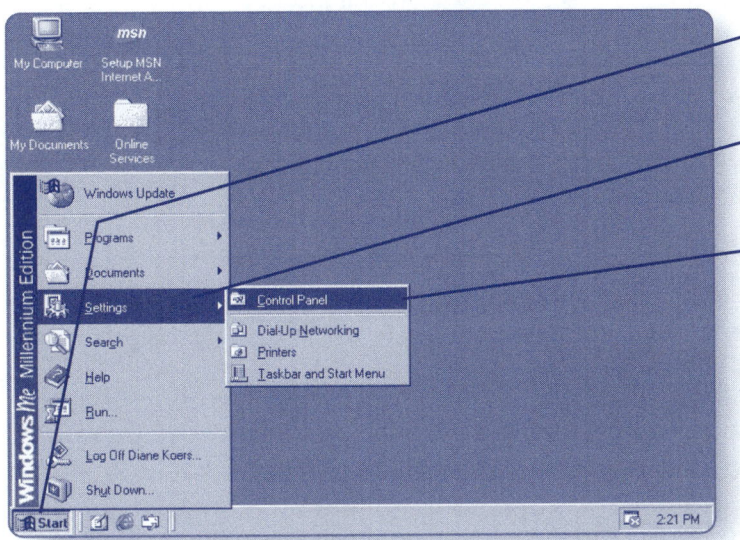

1. Click on **Start**. The Start menu appears.

2. Click on **Settings**. The Settings submenu appears.

3. Click on **Control Panel**. The Control Panel window opens.

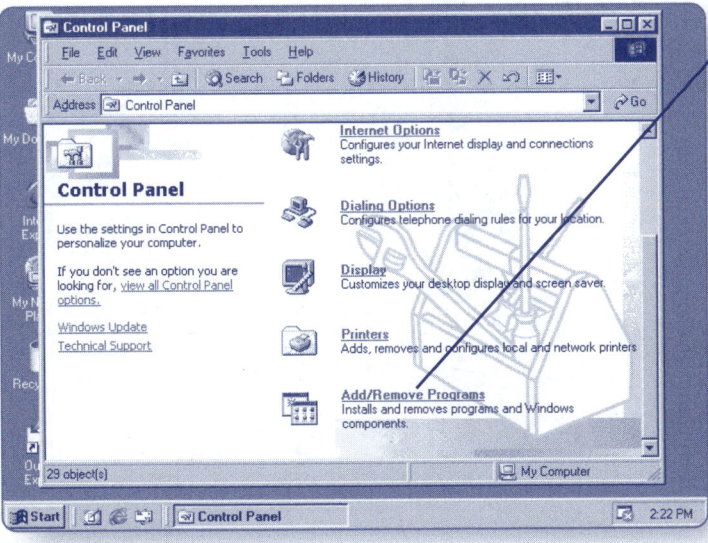

4. Click on **Add/Remove Programs**. The Add/Remove Programs Properties dialog box opens.

390 APPENDIX A: UPGRADING TO WINDOWS MILLENNIUM

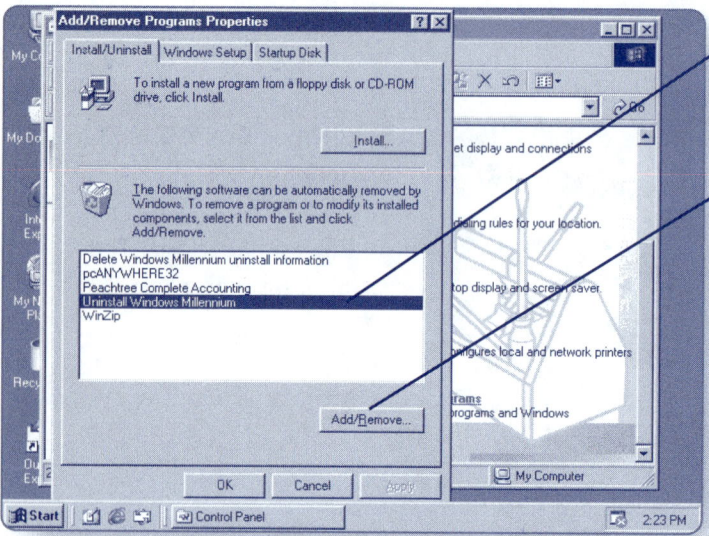

5. **Click** on **Uninstall Windows Millennium**. The option is highlighted.

6. **Click** on **Add/Remove**. A confirmation box opens.

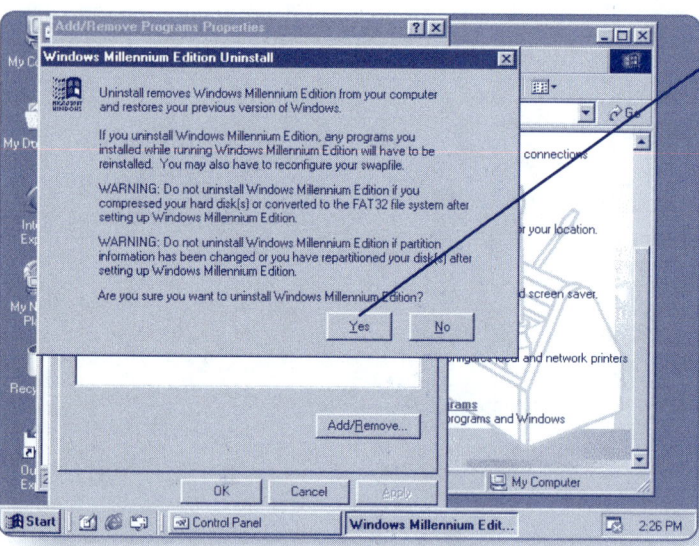

7. **Click** on **Yes**. An uninstall dialog box opens.

UNINSTALLING WINDOWS MILLENNIUM EDITION 391

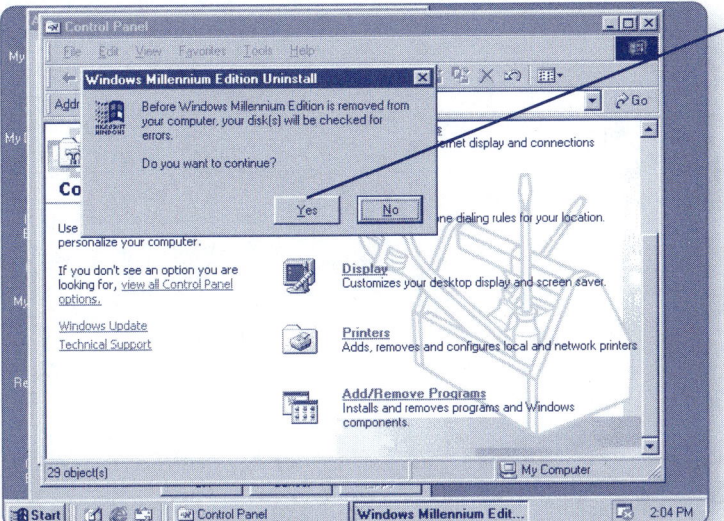

8. Click on **Yes**. Your hard drives are scanned for errors.

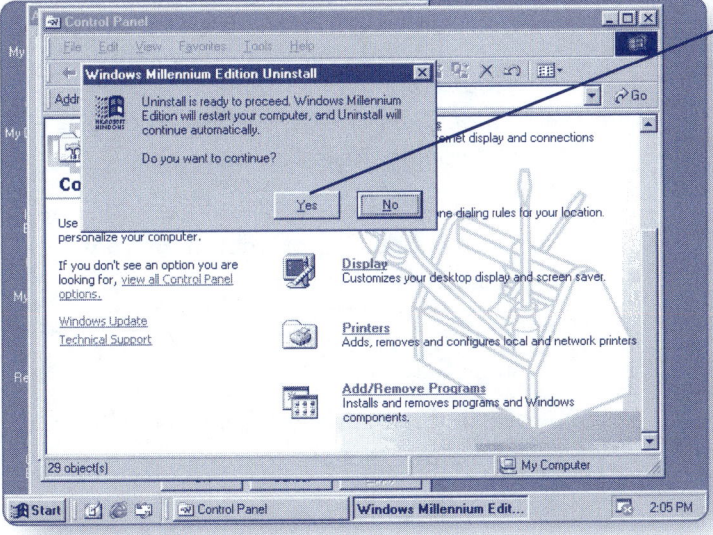

9. Click on **Yes**. Your computer restarts, the uninstallation process begins, and your computer reverts to the previous version of Windows.

If you installed any programs while using Windows Millennium, you'll need to reinstall those applications.

Glossary

Access Number. The telephone number used to dial in to an online service, such as The Microsoft Network, America Online, or CompuServe, or an Internet service provider such as AT&T.

Active Desktop. A feature to customize your desktop to display information, including information you can update from the Internet. A term that is synonymous with viewing your desktop as a Web page.

Active Window. The window that is currently open for use. The active window is designated by a different color toolbar than other open windows.

Alignment. The arrangement of text to the margins of a document or the edges of a table cell. Also called *justification*.

AOL (America Online). A widely used online service offering access service to the Internet as well as proprietary information created by AOL. This proprietary information includes news, financial planning, homework help for students, chat lines, and much more.

Application. Computer program designed to enable users to perform specific job functions. Word-processing, accounting, and engineering programs are examples of applications.

AT&T WorldNet. A widely used online service.

Attributes. Items that determine the appearance of text, such as bolding, underlining, italics, or point size.

Back Up. The process of making additional copies of data to protect them from unexpected disaster.

Bitmap. A graphics file format made up of small dots.

Block. To highlight text that will be affected by the next action.

Bold. A font attribute that makes text thicker and more prominent.

Border. A line or graphic surrounding paragraphs, pages, or objects.

Briefcase. A special folder on the Windows desktop used to keep documents up-to-date when shared between computers.

GLOSSARY

Browser. A software program specifically designed for viewing Web pages on the Internet.

Bullet. A symbol, such as a filled circle, that precedes items in a list.

Button. A graphical representation of an option or a command that activates the option.

Byte. The amount of space needed to store a single character, such as a number or a letter. 1,024 bytes equals one kilobyte (1KB).

Card. A removable circuit board that is plugged into an expansion slot inside the computer (such as a graphics card, sound card, or fax card).

Cascading Menu. An additional list of menu items opening from a single menu item. Sometimes called a *Submenu*.

CD-ROM. Compact Disc–Read–Only Memory. Means of data storage using optical storage technology. A single CD-ROM can hold more than 650MB of information, or one-half billion characters of text.

Channels. A link to Web sites used to collect information from the Internet to your computer.

Check Box. A small box next to an option in a dialog box. Clicking an empty check box selects the option; clicking a marked check box deselects the option.

Choose. To use the mouse or the keyboard to pick a menu item or dialog box option that initiates an immediate action.

Click. To push and release the mouse button.

Clip Art. A piece of artwork that can be inserted into a document.

Clipboard. An area of computer memory where text or graphics can be temporarily stored. It is a holding place for items that have been cut or copied. The item remains on the Clipboard until you cut or copy an additional item or until you turn off the computer.

Close. To shut down or exit a dialog box, a window, or an application.

Command. An instruction given to a computer to carry out a particular action.

Command Button. A button in a dialog box (such as Open, Close, Exit, OK, or Cancel) that carries out a command. The selected command button is indicated by a different appearance, such as a dotted rectangle or another color.

CompuServe. A widely used online service that offers access to the Internet and proprietary content and information.

Connect Charge. The fee a user must pay for the privilege of having access to an online service or Internet access. Generally, a connect charge is based on a monthly rate.

Conversion. A process by which files created in one application are changed to a format that can be used in another application.

Copy. To take a selection from the document and duplicate it on the Clipboard.

Cursor. A symbol (usually a blinking horizontal or vertical bar) that designates the position on the screen where text or codes will be inserted or deleted.

Cut. To take a selection from the document and move it to the Clipboard.

Data. An item of information.

Default. A setting or action predetermined by the program unless changed by the user.

Deselect. To remove the ✔ from a check box, or menu item or to remove highlighting from selected text in a document.

Desktop. The screen background and main area of Windows where you can open and manage files and programs.

Destination Disk. A disk to which data is written. Traditionally used when making a copy of a disk.

Dialog Box. A box that opens and lets you select options, or displays warnings and messages.

Dimmed. Describes the appearance of an icon, a command, or a button that cannot be chosen or selected.

Document. A letter, memo, proposal, or other file that is created in a software application.

Double-Click. Pushing and releasing the left mouse button twice in rapid succession.

Drag and Drop. To move text or an object by positioning the mouse pointer on the item you want to move, pressing and holding the mouse button, moving the mouse, and then releasing the mouse button to drop it into its new location.

Driver. A computer software program that runs a certain device. For example, a printer needs a driver to communicate with the computer.

Ellipsis. A punctuation mark consisting of three successive periods (. . .). Choosing a menu item or command button with an ellipsis opens a dialog box.

E-mail. The exchange of text messages or computer files over a local area network or the Internet.

Endnote. Reference information that prints at the end of a document.

Exit. To leave a program.

FAT. File Allocation Table. A table, or list, within the operating system that keeps track of a user's files and their locations. The system uses this table as users create and modify files.

Fax Modem. An internal or external modem that enables documents to be sent directly from the computer to another fax modem or to a standard facsimile machine.

File. Information stored on a disk under a single name.

File Format. The arrangement and organization of information in a file. File format is determined by the application that created the file.

File Name. The name given to a file that a user uses to identify the contents of that file, or that a program uses to open or save a file.

Fill. The background color or pattern of an object, such as a cell of a table or a paragraph.

Folder. An organizational tool used to store files.

Font. A group of letters, numbers, and symbols with a common typeface.

Format. The arrangement of data. For example, word processing programs offer commands for modifying the appearance of text with fonts, alignment, page numbers, and so on. An alternate use of format relates to the preparation of a disk with sectors so that it can be used for storing data.

Function Keys. A set of keys, usually labeled Fl, F2, F3, and so on, used by themselves or with the Shift, Ctrl, or Alt keys to provide quick access to certain features in an application.

Gigabyte. Approximately one billion bytes. Abbreviated as *GB*.

Group. A set of related options in a dialog box, often with its own subtitle.

Handle. Small black squares that appear when you select an object; the squares enable you to resize the object.

Header. Text entered in an area of the document that will be displayed at the top of each page of the document.

Help. A feature that gives you instructions and additional information on using a program.

Help Topic. An explanation of a specific feature, dialog box, or task. Help topics usually contain instructions on how to use a feature, pop-up terms with glossary definitions, and related topics. You can access Help topics by choosing any command from the Help menu.

Highlight. To change to a reverse-video appearance when a menu item is selected or an area of text is blocked or highlighted.

Hypertext Link. Used to provide a connection from the current document to another document or to a document on the World Wide Web.

Icon. A small graphic image that represents an application, a command, or a tool. An action is performed when an icon is clicked or double-clicked.

Inactive Window. A window that is not currently being used. Its title bar changes appearance, and keystrokes and mouse actions do not affect its contents. An inactive window can be activated by clicking on it.

Indent. To move a complete paragraph one tab stop to the right.

Input. The process of entering data into a computer from a keyboard or other device.

Internet. An international computer network connecting businesses, government agencies, universities, and other organizations for the purposes of sharing information.

GLOSSARY

Internet Explorer. A browser made by Microsoft used to view documents on the World Wide Web.

Intranet. A network designed for information processing within a company or organization. An intranet can distribute information, documents, files, and databases. Similar to the Internet except that it is contained within an organization.

Kilobyte (KB). 1,024 bytes of information or storage space.

Link. A connection between two objects that enables data to be passed between them.

List Box. A box that displays a list of choices. When a list is too long to display all choices, it will have a scroll bar so that you can view additional items.

Log In or Log On. The process a user goes through to begin using a computer system. Usually involves entering some type of identification, followed by a password.

Log Out or Log Off. The process a user goes through to end a session on the computer.

Mailbox. An area of memory or disk that is assigned to store any e-mail messages sent by other users.

Margin. The width of blank space from the edge of the page to the edge of the text. All four sides of a document have a margin.

Maximize. The step of enlarging a window so that it fills all the space available within a larger window or the screen.

Megabyte. Approximately one million bytes (MB) 1,024 kilobytes (1,048,576 bytes) of information or storage space.

Memory. A generic term for storage areas in the computer. The area in a computer where information is stored while being worked on. Information is only temporarily stored in memory.

Menu. A list of options displayed onscreen from which you can select a particular function or command.

Menu Bar. The area at the top of a window containing headings for pull-down menu items.

Message Box. A type of dialog box that appears with information, a warning, an error message, or a request for confirmation to carry out a command.

Microsoft Network. A widely used online service offering access to the Internet and proprietary content and information.

MIDI. Musical Instrument Digital Interface. A format that allows communication of musical data between devices, such as computers and synthesizers.

Mnemonics. Underlined, bolded, or colored letters on menu commands or dialog box options indicating keystroke access for that item or option.

Modem. A device used to connect a personal computer with a telephone line so that the computer can be used for accessing online information or communicating with other computers.

Mouse Pointer. A symbol that indicates a position onscreen as you move the mouse around on your desk.

Movement Keys. Keys that control cursor movement within a document, including the arrow keys, Page Up, Page Down, Home, and End.

Multimedia. A generic term for computer applications and files that combine standard computer capabilities with other media, such as video and sound.

Multitasking. The capability of a computer to perform multiple operations at the same time.

Netiquette. Short for *network etiquette*. Rules of courtesy for sending e-mail and participating in newsgroups whether through the Internet or through a company network.

Netscape Navigator. A popular browser made by Netscape to view documents on the World Wide Web.

Network. An information system based on two or more computers connected through hardware and software for the purpose of sharing files and resources.

Newsgroups. An Internet forum of discussions on a range of topics. They consist of articles and follow-up messages related to specific subjects.

Object. A picture, map, or other graphic element that you can place in a document.

Open. To start an application, to insert a document into a new document window, or to access a dialog box.

Operating System. Software that controls how a computer does basic operations and interfaces between the hardware and software.

Option. A choice inside a dialog box.

Option Button. One of a set of buttons found before options in a dialog box. Only one option button in a set can be selected at a time. Sometimes called *radio buttons*.

Orientation. A setting that designates whether a document will print with text running along the long or short side of a piece of paper.

Page Break. A command that tells an application to begin a new page.

Password. A secret code word that restricts access to a file. Without the password, the file cannot be opened.

Paste. The process of retrieving information stored on the Clipboard and inserting a copy of it into a document.

Path. A pattern of folders used to designate the location of a file.

Pixel. Short for "picture element." A pixel is the smallest dot that can be represented on a screen or within a paint (bitmap) graphic.

Plug & Play. A set of hardware standards followed by computer manufacturers to allow for better compatibility between computers and software. Also known as *PnP*.

Pop-Up List. A list of options that appears when a pop-up button is selected. Most pop-up buttons are marked by double arrows or triangles and display mutually exclusive options. The button itself shows the selected option. Other pop-up lists—marked by single arrows or triangles—show the feature name rather than the selected option.

Pop-Up Term. A box that appears when you click on an underlined word in a Help topic. Pop-ups contain additional information or glossary definitions.

Port. A connection device between a computer and another component, such as a printer or modem. For example, a printer cable is plugged into the printer port on the computer so that information can be sent to the computer.

Print Preview. Enables you to see a preview onscreen of how your printed document will look before you print it.

Print Queue. The list of print jobs waiting to be sent to a particular printer.

Print Spooling. The process of sending documents to a storage area on a disk, called a buffer, where they remain until the printer is ready for each one in turn.

Printer Driver. The software that enables a program to communicate with the printer so that the program's information can be printed.

Prodigy. A widely used online service offering access service to the Internet and proprietary content and information.

Program. A set of instructions for a computer to execute. Software designed for a certain use, such as word processing, e-mail, or spreadsheet entries. Sometimes called an *application*.

Queue. A waiting or holding location, usually for printing or e-mail messages.

Quick Launch Bar. A toolbar on the Taskbar that provides shortcuts to frequently-used features, such as the desktop, the Web browser, Outlook Express, and channels.

Radio Button. *See* Option Button.

RAM. Random Access Memory. The main memory that holds programs and data that are currently being used.

Recycle Bin. An icon on the desktop that represents a temporary holding place for files that are deleted.

Redo. Reverses the last Undo action.

Registry. A central file that Windows Millennium Edition uses to store information about the hardware, software, and preferences on a specific computer.

Restore. Copies files from a backup storage device to their normal location or changes the size of a window.

ROM. Read-Only Memory. The part of a computer's main memory that contains the basic programs that run the computer when it is turned on. ROM cannot be erased.

Ruler. Used to change page format elements, such as tabs and margins.

Save. The process of taking a document residing in the memory of the computer and creating a file to be stored on a disk.

Save As. Saves a previously saved worksheet with a new name or properties.

Scroll Bar. The bars on the right side and bottom of a window that let you move vertically and horizontally through a document.

Select. To identify a command or option (from menus or dialog boxes) to be applied to an object or block of text.

Selection Cursor. The highlighted text, dotted rectangle, or cursor that shows you where the next keystroke or mouse action will apply in a dialog box or window.

Serial Port. A port on a computer through which data is sent and received one bit at a time.

Shortcut. An icon that represents a quick way to start a program or open a file or folder.

Shortcut Key. A keystroke or keystroke combination that gives you quick access to a feature.

Shut Down. The process of saving all settings before a computer is physically turned off. Accessed from the Start menu.

Sizing Handle. The small solid squares that appear on the borders of a graphics box or a graphics line that has been selected. You can drag these handles to size the box and its contents.

Software. The instructions created from computer programs that direct the computer in performing various operations. Software can also include data.

Sort. To arrange data in a specified order. For example, data can be sorted in ascending or descending alphabetical order.

Source Disk. A disk from which data is read. Traditionally used when making a copy of a disk.

Spin Box. A button in a dialog box that lets you specify program-selected amounts by clicking the mouse instead of typing numbers.

Start Button. The button in the lower-left corner of the Taskbar that is used to access programs.

Status Bar. The line at the bottom of a window that shows such information as the path, page information, or location of the insertion point.

Submenu. An additional list of menu items opening from a single menu item. Also called a *cascading menu*.

Subscribe. The capability to receive updated information from a channel on a regular basis.

System Tray. The icons displayed in the lower-right corner that represent programs running in the background.

Taskbar. The bar (usually at the bottom of the screen) that lists all open folders and active programs.

Telephony. A general term for the technology of the telephone, including the conversion of sound into signals that are transmitted to other locations and then converted back into sound. A modem uses telephony.

Template. A document file with customized format, content, and features. Frequently used to create faxes, memos, and proposals.

Temporary File. A file that a program creates when it is running. Temporary files are deleted when the program is exited properly.

Text File. A file saved in ASCII file format. It contains text, spaces, and returns, but no formatting codes.

Tile. A display format for open windows. Tiled windows are displayed side by side, with no window overlapping any other window.

Toggle. A term used to refer to something (such as a feature) that turns on and off with the same switch (such as a keystroke).

Toolbar. Appears at the top of the application window and is used to access the features available in an application.

Trackball. A pointing device consisting of a small platform with a ball resting on it, similar in size to a mouse. The platform remains stationary, while the user manipulates the ball with his or her hand, and thus moves the cursor or arrow on the screen.

Undo. Reverses the last editing action.

Upgrade. To install a new or enhanced version of a product—whether software or hardware—so that the latest features are available for use.

Views. Ways of displaying documents to see different perspectives of the information in that document.

Virus. A computer program that infects computer files by inserting into those files copies of itself. Although not all virus programs are damaging, some can be very destructive, such as destroying a computer hard disk.

Wallpaper. A photograph, drawing, or pattern displayed on the background of the Windows Millennium Edition desktop.

Wildcard. The character used to replace one character (?) or any number of characters (*) in a search string. These two characters are conventions in most applications.

Window. A method of displaying a document so that many of its elements appear graphically and many features are immediately available as onscreen choices. The place where you type your documents is called a document window.

Wizards. The interactive programs supplied with Windows Millennium Edition to assist users through a project or problem by asking a series of questions.

World Wide Web. A series of specially designed documents, all linked together, residing on server computers all over the world to be viewed on the Internet.

WYSIWYG.w What You See Is What You Get. Refers to a computer screen display that approximates the printed page, showing fonts and graphics in correct proportions.

Zoom. Used to enlarge or reduce the way text is displayed onscreen. It does not affect how the document will print.

Index

A

accessibility options, 253–260
- augmentative communication device, 260
- Automatic Reset for, 259
- general options, setting, 259–260
- for hearing impaired persons, 255–256
- MouseKeys, 258–259
- Notification feature, 259
- SerialKey Devices, 260
- for visually impaired persons, 257–258

Accessories menu. *See also* Calculator
- in Paint program, 35, 94
- ScanDisk, opening, 132–133
- for Windows Explorer, 150–151
- WordPad, starting, 72

Active Desktop, 270–275
- adding new items to, 271–273
- backgrounds, changing, 265
- channel subscriptions, 273
- MSNBC Weather Map on, 275
- Security Alert message, 273

Addition key, Calculator, 65

Add Printer Wizard, 280–284

Add/Remove Programs
- accessibility options, installing, 253
- programs, uninstalling, 241–242
- Windows Millennium Edition, uninstalling, 389–391

Address bar, Windows Explorer, 152, 156

Address Book
- adding contacts to, 366–370
- blind carbon copies, sending, 378
- business card style, printing in, 374–375
- business information, entering, 369
- carbon copies, sending, 378
- closing, 376
- deleting contacts, 372
- editing contact information, 371
- home address information, entering, 369
- managing contacts in, 366–372
- map of street address, viewing, 369
- memo style, printing in, 374–375
- name of contact, entering, 367
- personal information on contact, entering, 370
- phone list style, printing in, 374–375
- printing phone list, 374–375
- Properties dialog box, 371–372
- searching for people in, 181–182
- sending e-mail to contacts with, 376–379
- sorting by contacts, 373–374
- View Map button, 369

A drive, 11

ADSL lines, 194

Album title, Media Library subcategory, 197

alignment in WordPad, 85–86

Alt key
- menu choices with, 39–41
- shortcut keys with, 47
- StickyKeys feature, 254

Always on top option, Taskbar, 230

America Online
- Online Services folder including, 304
- searching for people on, 181–182

Artist name, Media Library subcategory, 197

Assisted Support button, 127–130
- in Help and Support system, 121

attachments to e-mail. See Outlook Express
AT&T WorldNet, Online Services folder including, 304
augmentative communication device, 260
Auto Arrange, turning off, 211
Auto hide option, Taskbar, 230
Automatic Reset for accessibility features, 259

B

Back button
    in Help and Support system, 121
    in Internet Explorer, 328
    in My Computer, 14
Backgammon, 107
backgrounds. See wallpaper
Backspace key, 76
    in Calculator, 65
.bmp files for Paint program drawings, 104
boldfacing in e-mail, 348
Broadband selections, 194
Browse button, 218
Browse for Folder dialog box, 165
Browse for Printer dialog box, 289
browsers. See Web browsers
bullets
    in e-mail messages, 348–350
    in WordPad document, 86–87
buttons, displaying features of, 20

C

Calculator
    clearing totals on, 67
    closing, 70
    copying values from, 67–69
    identifying buttons on, 65
    operators for, 66
    scientific calculator, viewing, 69–70
    standard calculator, restoring, 70
    starting, 64
    style, changing, 69–70
    using, 66–67
calendar for System Restore, 147–148
Cancel button, 43
    in dialog boxes, 45
Caps Lock key ToggleKeys option, 254
carbon copies of e-mail, 347, 378
cascading menus, 18, 34
CD key code, 385
C drive, 11
CD-ROM. See also Media Player
    from My Computer, 11
    new programs, adding, 240
centered text in WordPad, 85
Change Windows Password dialog box, 247–248
channel subscriptions, 273
check boxes, 42
circles, drawing, 100
Classic style desktop, 10
Clear All, Calculator, 65
Clear Entry key, Calculator, 65
Clipboard
    Calculator values, copying, 67–69
    media clips to documents, copying, 203–205
clock, Taskbar showing, 230
Close button, 25
Close command, 46
closing
    Calculator, 70
    Paint program, 106
    shortcut menus, 38
    Windows programs, 53–54
    WordPad, 92
Color box, Paint program, 96
colors. See also Paint program
    desktop themes and, 276–278
    to e-mail messages, 348
    screen display, changing colors of, 269–270
    for visually impaired persons, 257–258
commands, list of, 46–47
components of Windows programs, adding, 244–246
Computing Central Forums, assisted help on, 127–129
Confirm File Delete dialog box, 168–169
Content Advisor for parental controls. See Internet Explorer
Control Panel
    accessibility options, 253–260
    components of Windows programs, adding, 244–246
    dates and times, changing, 232–234
    mouse response, changing, 234–238
    multiple users, setting for, 249–252
    My Computer displaying, 12
    opening, 232, 262
    passwords, changing, 246–248
    programs, adding and removing, 239–246
    sounds, changing, 262–264
    startup disk, creating, 243–244
Copy command, 46
copying
    Calculator, values from, 67–69
    Calculator values, 68
    folders, 164–166
    media clips to documents, 203–205
Create Shortcut dialog box, 214–216
    Start menu, adding item to, 224
credit cards for online services, 304

INDEX

Ctrl+Alt+Delete keys, shutting down with, 55
Ctrl key
  shortcut keys with, 47
  StickyKeys feature, 254
Cut command, 46
  in WordPad, 81–82

D

Dangerous Creature desktop theme, 278
Date and Time dialog box, WordPad, 77–78
dates and times
  Control Panel, changing dates and times with, 232–234
  finding files by date, 178–180
  sorting files by date, 159–160
  WordPad, inserting dates and times in, 77–78
Date/Time Properties dialog box, 232–234
Daylight Savings Time, setting, 233
D drive (CD-ROM drive), 11
Decimal key, Calculator, 65
Defragmenting dialog box, 135–136
Defragmenting hard drive. See Disk Defragmenter
Delete key, 76
deleting
  Address Book contacts, 372
  bullets from WordPad document, 87
  components of Windows programs, 245
  defragmenting after, 135
  e-mail messages, 363–364
  files, 172
  icons from desktop, 213
  Media Library file, 197
  passwords, 247

print job, 296–297
programs, uninstalling, 241–242
Start menu, items from, 227–228
WordPad text, 76
desktop, 4. *See also* Active Desktop; screen savers; wallpaper
  Classic style desktop, 10
  colors, changing, 269–270
  deleting icons from, 213
  drag-and-drop printing, 293–294
  Internet Explorer, accessing, 324
  moving icons on, 211–212
  new folders, creating, 210
  opening programs from, 51–52
  renaming icons on, 219–220
  screen savers, 266–269
  shortcuts, creating, 214–216
  themes, using, 276–278
  Web style desktop, 10
Desktop Themes, using, 276–278
diagnostics, 4
dialog boxes, 18
  keyboard, selecting with, 45
  working in, 42–45
dial-up connections
  creating, 313–319
  name for connection, 316
  networking information, 318
  passwords for, 315
  TCP/IP settings for, 318
Disk Defragmenter, 134–136
  Maintenance Wizard for, 137–138
disk drives
  from My Computer, 11
  network, sharing on, 12
  viewing contents of, 13
display. *See* desktop
Display option for visually impaired persons, 257–258
Division key, Calculator, 65

document area, WordPad, 73
documents. *See also* WordPad
  e-mail, attaching files to, 352–353
  as Favorites, 331
  media clips, adding, 203–205
  searching in body of, 176
  Start menu, adding item to, 222–226
Documents menu, 18
double-clicking, 6
  testing speed for, 235
downloading
  Netscape Navigator, 320
  Windows updates, 140–143
drag-and-drop printing, 293–294
Drives and Folders section. See Windows Explorer
drop-down list boxes, 43
DSL connections, 324

E

Earthlink Internet, Online Services folder including, 304
editing
  Address Book contact information, 371
  Start menu, 220–228
  WordPad text, 75–76
Edit menu, 34
  Calculator values, copying, 68
E drive (removable zip disk drive), 11
Ellipse tool, Paint program, 98
ellipsis, 18
  with dialog boxes, 42–45
  menu items with, 37
e-mail. *See also* Outlook Express
  Address Book, sending from, 376–379
  searching for addresses, 181–182

INDEX

emergency startup disk, creating, 243–244, 386–387
emptying Recycle Bin, 172
Enable Multi-User Settings dialog box, 251
End Task button, 55
equalizer, Media Player, 189–191
Erase/Color Eraser tool, Paint program, 95
error messages
　illegal or fatal message, 54
　network error messages, 16
Excel
　e-mail attachments requiring, 359
　media clips, adding, 203–205
Exit command, 46
Explorer. *See* Internet Explorer; Windows Explorer

F

Fatal Exception message, 54
Favorites. *See* Internet Explorer
Favorites menu, 18
fees for online services, 304
File menu, 34
　closing programs from, 53–54
file names
　for Paint program drawings, 104
　renaming files, 166–167
　for WordPad documents, 88
files. *See also* Windows Explorer
　attaching files to e-mail, 352–353
　copying files, 164–166
　date, finding files by, 178–180
　deleting files, 168–172
　moving files, 164–166
　recovering file from Recycle Bin, 170–171
　Recycle Bin, sending files to, 168–172
　renaming files, 166–167
Fill with Color tool, Paint program, 96

FilterKeys option, 254
finding. *See* searching
Find menu, 18
Find People dialog box, 181–182
floppy disk drive
　from My Computer, 11
　new programs, adding, 240
Folder Options dialog box, Windows Explorer, 160–161
folders. *See also* Outlook Express; Windows Explorer
　Browse for Folder dialog box, 165
　copying folders, 164–166
　as Favorites, 331
　finding folders, 174–180
　moving folders, 164–166
　new folders, creating, 162–163, 210
　Profiles folder for multiple users, 252
　renaming folders, 166–167
　shortcuts, creating, 215
　Start menu, adding item to, 222–226
　for WordPad files, 88
Font dialog box, WordPad, 83–84
fonts
　desktop themes and, 276–278
　for e-mail messages, 348–349
　in WordPad, 83–84
formatting
　e-mail messages, 348–351
　in WordPad, 83–84
Forward button
　in Help and Support system, 121
　Internet Explorer, 328
forwarding e-mail messages, 357
FreeCell, 107
Free-Form Select tool, Paint program, 95, 102
frozen applications. *See* locked-up computers

G

games, 107. *See also* Internet Hearts; Spider Solitaire
Genre, Media Library subcategory, 197
Get Assistance window, 127
gif images in e-mail, 350
graphics. *See* Paint program

H

hard disk
　defragmenting, 134–136
　ScanDisk, using, 132–134
hearing impaired persons, options for, 255–256
Hearts, 107. *See also* Internet Hearts
Help and Support system, 19
　Assisted Support, 127–130
　Help Index, using, 124–125
　Index, using, 124–125
　Look for Help window, 122–123
　printing Help topics, 123
　searching for help, 125–127
　starting, 120
　topics, using, 122–123
　window, exploring, 120–127
Help command, 46
Help menu, 34
hibernation feature, 57
high contrast option for visually impaired, 257–258
History button, Internet Explorer, 329
Home button
　in Help and Support system, 121
　in Internet Explorer, 328
Home Networking Wizard, 15
home page, 324–325
horizontal scroll bar, 26
Hot Mail, MSN, 330

INDEX

HTML codes in e-mail, 351
hyperlinks, 326–327

I

icons
  changing icons, 217–219
  deleting, 213
  moving desktop icons, 211–212
  for multiple users, 249
  Outlook Express icon, 21
  Properties dialog box for, 217–218
  renaming icons, 219–220
  System Tray icons, 20
Illegal Operation message, 54
IMAP servers, 343
Index, Help and Support system, 121, 124–125
insertion point, WordPad, 73
insert mode, WordPad, 75
installing. *See also* uninstalling
  accessibility options, 253
  CD key code, 385
  printers, 280–284
  programs, 239–240
  Windows Millennium, 383–388
Install Wizard, 239–240
Internet. *See also* Active Desktop; Internet Explorer; Microsoft Network (MSN); Web browsers; Web pages
  Assisted Support on, 127–130
  dial-up connections, creating, 313–319
  help on, 127–130
  Media Player with, 185
  online service, subscribing to, 304–313
  Windows Update Wizard with, 139–143
Internet Accounts dialog box, 341–342

Internet Connection Wizard. *See also* Outlook Express
  dial-up connections, creating, 313–319
Internet E-mail Address screen, 342–343
Internet Explorer, 22, 320
  accessing, 324
  Back button, 328
  Content Advisor, 333–338
    allowed sites, 336
    General tab options, 335–338
    passwords, 336–338
    supervisor password, 336–338
  Favorites
    accessing favorite sites, 332–333
    adding Favorites, 331–332
  Favorites button, 329
  Forward button, 328
  History button, 329
  Mail button, 330
  Messenger button, 330
  parental controls, setting, 333–338
  passwords, 325, 336–338
  Print button, 330
  on Quick Launch toolbar, 19
  Search button, 328
  Stop button, 328
  toolbar, 327–328
  using, 324–327
  window, exploring, 327–330
Internet Hearts
  connecting to, 111–115
  messages, sending, 114
Internet service providers (ISPs). *See also* dial-up connections; Microsoft Network (MSN); Outlook Express
  disconnecting from, 321

italicizing in e-mail, 348

J

jpeg images in e-mail, 350
Jungle desktop theme, 276

K

keyboard
  accessibility options for, 253–255
  augmentative communication device, 260
  dialog boxes, selecting in, 45
  FilterKeys option, 254
  menu choices with, 39–41
  SerialKey Devices, 260
  StickyKeys feature, 254
  ToggleKeys option, 254

L

language for Internet Hearts, 12
laptop computers
  mouse visibility in, 237–238
  System Tray power options, 20
left-aligned text, WordPad, 85
left mouse button, 6–7
Leonardo da Vinci desktop theme, 276
licensing agreements
  Microsoft licensing agreement, 384
  Microsoft Network (MSN) licensing agreement, 308–309
list boxes, 42
  drop-down list boxes, 43
locked-up computers, 54–55
  shutting down, 58
Log Off, 18
Lotus 1-2-3, media clips in, 203–205

M

Magnifier tool, Paint program, 96
Mail button, Internet Explorer, 330
mail servers, 343
Maintenance Wizard, 137–138
maps
    Address Book street address, viewing map of, 369
    Weather Map on Active Desktop, 275
Maximize button, 25, 30
Media Guide, using, 193–194
Media Library
    creating, 195–196
    deleting file from, 197
    subcategories in, 197
Media Player, 22
    Broadband selections, 194
    Captions graphic, 191
    cataloging media, 195–198
    closing equalizer, 191
    compact mode, 198–200
    documents, adding media clip to, 203–205
    equalizing settings with, 189–191
    fast forward button, 188
    full mode, 198–200
    with Internet Connection, 185
    Media Guide, using, 193–194
    Media Information graphic, 190–191
    modes for viewing in, 198–200
    muting speakers, 188, 201
    next track button, 188
    pause/(Play) button, 188
    playing music CDs, 184–187
    playlist, choosing from, 187
    previous track button, 188
    on Quick Launch toolbar, 19
    radio stations, listening to, 192–193
    rewind button, 188
    skins, 198–200
    starting music CD, 184–185
    stop button, 188
    video settings graphic, 189–190
    visualizations, choosing, 186
    volume controls, 188, 201–202
    Volume Control window, 202
    Web Radio, 192–193
    window, exploring, 187–188
menu bar
    in Windows Explorer, 151–152
    in WordPad, 73
menus. *See also* shortcut menus
    cascading menus, 18, 34
    closing, 36
    keyboard shortcuts on, 47
    mouse, selecting with, 34–37
    three-dimensional menus, 35
Messenger button, Internet Explorer, 330
Microsoft Active Desktop gallery, 271–275
Microsoft licensing agreement, 384
Microsoft Network (MSN), 22
    billing plan, 307
    Computing Central Forums, assisted help on, 127–129
    Hot Mail, 330
    license agreement, 308–309
    member ID, choosing, 308
    Messenger Service, 330
    passwords
        saving passwords, 312
        selecting password, 308
    payment method, selecting, 309
    personal information, entering, 308
    Settings screen, 309–310
    signing up for, 304–310
    starting Internet access with, 311–313
    Welcome screen, 306–307
Microsoft Word
    media clips, adding, 203–205
    shortcut menus in, 37
Minesweeper, 107
Minimize button, 25, 31, 38
modems
    cable modems, 324
    for e-mail, 340
    for Web browsers, 320
month, setting, 233
mouse
    augmentative communication device, 260
    basic responses, changing, 235
    Calculator with, 66
    Control Panel, changing mouse in, 234–238
    desktop themes and, 276–278
    double-clicking speed, testing, 235
    hiding mouse pointer, 238
    left mouse button, 6–7
    location of pointer, showing, 238
    menu choices with, 34–37
    pointers, changing, 236–237
    pointer trails, displaying, 238
    right mouse button, 7
    selecting with, 5–7
    SerialKey Devices, 260
    snap option for, 238
    visibility of arrow, changing, 237–238
    visually impaired persons, mouse point for, 258
    WordPad, selecting in, 79–80
MouseKeys, 255, 258–259
Mouse Properties dialog box, 235–238
moving
    desktop icons, 211–212
    e-mail messages, 362
    folders, 164–166
    Paint program, objects in, 102–103

INDEX

Spider Solitaire cards, 109–110
Taskbar, 229
windows, 32
MSNBC Weather Map, 275
MSN Gaming Zone, 107
Internet Hearts, connecting to, 112–115
MSN Setup screen, 305
multiple programs, switching between, 52–53
multiple users
passwords for, 250
personalized item settings for, 250–251
Profiles folder for, 252
setting up for, 249–252
Multiplication key, Calculator, 65
muting speakers, Media Player, 188, 201
My Computer, 10–14
Back button in, 14
Control Panel, opening, 232
finding, 10
searching all drives with, 176
viewing drive contents with, 13
My Digital Camera, 12
My Documents, 21
Browse for Folder dialog box, 165
copying folders in, 164–166
Files and Documents section, 162–163
moving folders in, 164–166
new folders, creating, 162–163
My Network Places, 15–16
Windows Explorer Drives and Folders section and, 154

N

names. *See also* file names
for dial-up connections, 316
for new folders, 163
for printers, 283

for shared printers, 290
skin name, Media Player, 198–199
Netscape Navigator, 320
networks. *See also* My Network Places; shared printers
connecting to shared printers, 287–291
dial-up connections, networking information for, 318
disk drives shared on, 12
Hearts game, connecting to, 111–115
Windows Millennium Edition on, 5
New Active Desktop Item dialog box, 271
new folders, creating, 162–163, 210
New Password dialog box, 250–251
Notification for accessibility features, 259
numeric keypad, MouseKeys with, 258
Num Lock key, ToggleKeys option, 254

O

OK button, 43
in dialog boxes, 45
online service, subscribing to, 304–313
Online Services folder, 22
Open command, 46
Open dialog box
deleting files from, 169
renaming files in, 167
for WordPad, 91
opening
Control Panel, 232
Windows Explorer, 151
Windows program, 50–52
Option buttons, 44

Outlook Express. *See also* Address Book
account for e-mail, creating, 340–345
addressing e-mail, 346–347
ALL CAPS messages, 348
attachments, 352–353
receiving e-mail with, 358–360
backgrounds for messages, 350
boldfacing in message, 348
bullets in e-mail messages, 348–350
carbon copies (CC), sending, 347
closing, 364
colors in messages, 348
colors to e-mail, adding, 348
Deleted Items folder, 345, 363–364
deleting messages, 363–364
Drafts folder, 345
fonts for messages, 348
formatting messages, 348–351
forwarding messages, 357
HTML codes in message, 351
icon, 21
Inbox folder, 345
incoming mail server name, entering, 343
italicizing in message, 348
messages, creating, 345–348
moving e-mail messages, 362
multiple persons, replying to, 355
New Message dialog box, 346
numbering in message, 349
organizing mail, folders for, 360–361
Outbox folder, 345
outgoing mail server name, entering, 343
password feature, 344
printing messages, 354
on Quick Launch toolbar, 19

Outlook Express (continued)

replying to messages, 355–356
retrieving incoming e-mail, 354
Save As dialog box for attachments, 359
sending messages, 351
Sent Items folder, 345
servers for e-mail, 343
starting, 340
Start page, 345
stationery for e-mail messages, 350
subject, messages including, 347
undeleting e-mail messages, 363
underlining in message, 348

P

Page Setup dialog box, WordPad, 44–45
Paintbrush tool, Paint program, 96–98
Paint menu, 35
Paint program, 34–37
   background colors, filling in, 101
   circles, drawing, 100
   Color box, 96
   deselecting objects in, 103
   Erase/Color Eraser tool, 95
   exiting, 106
   fill colors, 99
   Fill with Color tool, 96
   Free-Form Select tool, 95, 102
   Magnifier tool, 96
   moving objects in, 102–103
   Paintbrush tool, 96–98
   Pencil tool, 95
   Pick Color tool, 95
   printing drawings, 106
   rectangles, drawing, 98–100
   resizing objects in, 103
   saving
      drawings, 104
      wallpaper, saving drawing as, 105
   selecting objects in, 102–103
   Select tool, 96, 102
   squares, drawing, 100
   starting, 94
   Tool box, 95–96
   undoing mistakes, 98
   wallpaper, saving drawing as, 105
paper size for printers, 285
parental controls on Web, setting, 333–338
Part I review questions, 59
Part II review questions, 116
Part III review questions, 206
Part IV review questions, 299
Part V review questions, 380
passwords. *See also* Microsoft Network (MSN)
   changing Windows password, 246–248
   deleting, 247
   for dial-up connections, 315
   for e-mail, 344
   for Internet Explorer, 325, 336–338
   for multiple users, 250
   for network use, 5
   screen savers and, 267–268
   for shared printers, 286
   for Web browsers, 321
Passwords Properties dialog box, 246–248
Paste command, 46
   Calculator values, copying, 68
   media clips into documents, 204–205
   in WordPad, 81–82
Peachtree Accounting for DOS, 290

Pencil tool, Paint program, 95
Percentage key, Calculator, 65
Personalized Items Settings dialog box, 250–251
Pick Color tool, Paint program, 95
Pinball, 107
Plug & Play feature, 280
POP3 servers, 343
power, shutting off, 55
power options, System Tray managing, 20
Print button, Internet Explorer, 330
Print command, 46
Print dialog box, WordPad, 90
printers
   default printer, setting, 191
   default settings for, 285
   installing new printers, 280–284
   naming printer, 283
   paper size, selecting, 285
   printer port, choosing, 282
   Printing Troubleshooter, 284
   properties of, 285
   sharing printers, 286–291
   shortcuts to, 293–294
   test page, printing, 283–284
   timeout settings for, 285
printer window
   deleting print job from, 296–297
   opening, 295
printing
   Address Book phone list, 374–375
   canceling print job, 296
   deleting print job, 296–297
   drag-and-drop printing, 293–294
   e-mail messages, 354
   Help topics, 123
   Paint program drawings, 106
   pausing print job, 296

INDEX

print jobs, controlling, 294–298
queue, controlling, 294–298
rushing print job, 297–298
Print Preview, WordPad, 89
Prodigy Internet, Online Services folder including, 304
Profiles folder, 252
programs
closing, 53–54
components of Windows programs, adding, 244–246
Control Panel, adding and removing programs in, 239–246
installing new programs, 239–240
opening Windows programs, 50–52
switching between, 52–53
uninstalling programs, 241–242
Programs menu, 18
in Windows Paint program, 35

Q

queue for print, controlling, 294–298
Quick Launch toolbar, 19–20
Internet Explorer, accessing, 324
Outlook Express, starting, 340
Show Desktop button, 51

R

radio, listening to, 192–193
rectangles, drawing, 98–100
Rectangle tool, Paint program, 98
Recycle Bin, 21
emptying, 172
icons, deleting, 213
programs, uninstalling, 242
recovering file from, 170–171
sending files to, 168–172

Start menu, removing items from, 228
Refresh button, Internet Explorer, 328
Remove Programs From Your Computer dialog box, 242
Remove Shortcuts/Folders dialog box, 227–228
renaming
files and folders, 166–167
icons, 219–220
resizing
Paint program objects, 103
windows, 28–29
restarting computer, 55, 58
after hibernation, 57
restoring system. *See* System Restore
Reversi, 107
review questions
Part I review questions, 59
Part II review questions, 116
Part III review questions, 206
Part IV review questions, 299
Part V review questions, 380
right-aligned text, WordPad, 85
right mouse button, 7
Rounded Corner Rectangle tool, Paint program, 98
Ruler, WordPad, 73
Run, 18

S

Save As dialog box
deleting files from, 169
for e-mail attachments, 359
in Paint program, 104
renaming files in, 167
in WordPad, 87–88
Save command, 46
Save in: list box, WordPad, 88
Save System files, creating, 386

saving. *See also* Paint program; WordPad
Spider Solitaire game, 110
ScanDisk
locked-up computers, powering off, 58
Maintenance Wizard for, 137–138
multiple disks, scanning, 133
running, 4
using, 132–134
Science desktop theme, 276
scientific calculator, viewing, 69–70
Screen Saver Properties dialog box, 266–267
screen savers
desktop themes and, 276–278
elapsed time for starting, 267
for multiple users, 249
passwords and, 267–268
selecting, 266–269
scroll bars, 25–26
dragging, 28
pages, moving through, 27
using, 26–28
scroll box, 26
Scroll Lock key, ToggleKeys option, 254
Search button, Internet Explorer, 328
Search Help and Support text box, 125–126
searching
in Address Book, 181–182
date, finding files by, 178–180
for files, 174–180
in Help and Support system, 125–127
for media, 195–196
Select All command, 46
Select All option, WordPad, 79
Select a Title for the Program dialog box, 225

INDEX

selecting
 Paint program, objects in, 102–103
 in WordPad, 78–80
Select Program Folder dialog box, 224–225
Select tool, Paint program, 96, 102
SerialKey Devices, 260
Settings dialog box, 255
Settings menu, 18
shared printers, 286–291
 connecting to, 287–291
 default printer, setting, 191
 installing network printers, 281
 names for, 290
 passwords for, 286
 Printing Troubleshooter for, 291
Shift key, StickyKeys feature, 254
shortcut keys, 39–41
 accessibility options Notification feature, 259
 for commands, 46
 switching between programs, 53
shortcut menus
 right mouse button opening, 7
 underlined letters, selecting with, 41
 using, 37–38
shortcuts. See also shortcut keys; shortcut menus; Start menu
 desktop shortcuts, creating, 214–216
 icons, changing, 217–219
 to printers, 293–294
 storing shortcuts in folders, 225
Show clock option, Taskbar, 230
Show Desktop button, 51
Show small icons in Start menu option, Taskbar, 230
Show Web Content on My Active Desktop check box, 271
Shut Down Windows dialog box, 56

shutting down, 18
 correct method for, 55–57
 for locked-up computer, 58
skins, Media Player, 198–200
snap option for mouse, 238
software. See programs
Solitaire, 107. See also Spider Solitaire
sorting
 Address Book contacts, 373–374
 Windows Explorer files, 159–160
sounds. See also Media Player
 changing sounds, 262–264
 desktop themes and, 276–278
 for hearing impaired persons, 255–256
Sounds and Multimedia Properties dialog box, 262–264
SoundSentry option, 256
SoundShows option, 256
Spades, 107
Spider Solitaire, 107–111
 moving cards, 109–110
 saving game, 110
Sports desktop theme, 276
squares, drawing, 100
Standard toolbar, Windows Explorer, 156
Start button, 17–19
 opening programs from, 50–51
starting
 Calculator, 64
 Outlook Express, 340
 Paint program, 94
 Spider Solitaire, 108
 Windows Millennium Edition, 4
 WordPad, 72–73
Start menu
 adding items to, 222–226
 Address Book accessing, 366
 Control Panel, opening, 232
 deleting items from, 227–228

 editing, 220–228
 opening programs from, 50–51
 Paint program, 94
 reorganizing, 220–221
 Taskbar displaying, 17
start page, 324–325
startup disk, creating, 243–244, 386–387
stationery for e-mail, 350–351
statistical functions with Calculator, 69
status bar, Windows Explorer, 152
StickyKeys feature, 254
Stop button, Internet Explorer, 328
subfolders, Windows Explorer, 153
subscriptions
 channel subscriptions, 273
 to Microsoft Network (MSN), 304–310
 to online services, 304–313
Subtraction key, Calculator, 65
switching between programs, 52–53
System Checkpoints, 147
system requirements, 382
System Restore, 144–148
 calendar for, 147–148
 restore point, creating, 144–146
 restoring system, 146–148
 System Checkpoints, 147
System Tray, 20–21
 Date/Time Properties dialog box, accessing, 234
 ISPs, disconnecting from, 321
 print queue and, 294

T

Taskbar, 11
 changing options, 230
 moving, 229
 multiple programs, switching between, 52–53

INDEX

working with, 17
Taskbar Properties dialog box, 222–226
TCP/IP settings for ISP, 318
telephone numbers. *See also* Address Book
    for dial-up connections, 315
    for Microsoft Network (MSN), 308
three-dimensional menus, 35
thumbnails view, Windows Explorer, 158
times. *See* dates and times
Times New Roman, WordPad, 83
time zone, adjusting to, 233
tips
    Address Book
        carbon copies, sending, 378
        entire entry, viewing, 182
        map of street address, viewing, 369
        Properties dialog box, opening, 371
        several addresses for contact, creating, 368
        sorting contacts in, 374
        starting, 366
        View Map button, 369
    Backspace key, 76
    buttons, displaying features of, 20
    Calculator
        clearing totals on, 67
        closing, 70
    check boxes, selecting in, 42
    components, removing, 245
    Control Panel, opening, 262
    copying multiple items, 164
    dates, finding files by, 179
    Date/Time Properties dialog box, accessing, 234
    defragmenting hard drive, 135
        visual representation of, 136
    Delete key, 76

deleting
    files, 169
    icons, 213
Favorites, adding, 332–333
Find feature, opening files from, 177
folders, creating, 162–163
Help and Support system
    accessing, 120
    printing Help topics, 123
icons
    deleting, 213
    moving, 212
Internet Explorer
    Content Advisor allowed sites, 336
    Favorites, adding, 332
    toolbar, 327–328
Internet service provider (ISP), disconnecting from, 321
maximizing windows, 30
Media Player
    documents, playing media clip in, 205
    equalizer, closing, 191
    manually starting, 184
    muting speakers, 201
    playlist, closing, 187
    Skin Chooser selection, viewing, 198
    Volume Control window, opening, 202
menus, closing, 36
Microsoft Network (MSN) passwords, saving, 312
mouse
    double-clicking speed, testing, 235
    left mouse button, 7
MouseKeys, 255
moving
    icons, 212
    multiple items, 164
    new folder, file to, 166

My Computer
    Back button in, 14
    finding, 10
    searching all drives with, 176
My Network Places, Windows Explorer Drives and Folders section and, 154
option buttons, choosing, 44
Outlook Express
    ALL CAPS messages, 348
    fonts in messages, 349
    formatting e-mail, 348
    formatting toolbar, 348
    printing messages, 354
    replying to multiple persons, 355
    sending messages, 351
    stationery for e-mail messages, 350
    toolbar, locating, 346
    undeleting e-mail messages, 363
Paint program
    background area, filling in, 101
    circles, drawing, 100
    deselecting objects in, 103
    exiting, 106
    resizing objects in, 103
    squares, drawing, 100
    Tool box, viewing, 95
    tools, description of, 96
    undoing mistakes, 98
    wallpaper, viewing, 105
passwords, deleting, 247
powering off, 57
Printer window, opening, 295
print job, canceling, 297
renaming files, 167
restarting computer, 55
ScanDisk for multiple disks, 133
scroll bars, dragging, 28
selecting multiple items, 221

tips *(continued)*
    shared printers for DOS-based programs, 290
    shortcut keys with Ctrl or Alt, 47
    shortcut menus, closing, 38
    shortcuts
        folders for storing, 225
        launching programs with, 217
        maximizing screen for launching, 219
    sounds
        events, associating sounds with, 263
        Sounds and Multimedia Properties icon, locating, 262
    Sounds and Multimedia Properties icon, locating, 262
    Spider Solitaire
        moving cards, 109–110
        returning to saved game, 111
        starting, 108
    Start menu, deleting items from, 228
    startup disk, creating, 387
    switching between programs, 53
    Taskbar Properties dialog box, opening, 222
    visually impaired persons, mouse point for, 258
    wallpaper
        changing, 265
        viewing, 105
    Windows Explorer
        active choices, indication of, 155
        columns, changing width of, 158
        Details view, 160
        Drives and Folders section, 152
        opening, 151
        Views button, 159
    Windows Update Wizard, 139–143

WordPad
    Backspace and Delete keys in, 76
    cutting text in, 81
    deselecting text, 78
    multiple paragraphs, modifying, 85
    pasting text in, 82
    Print Preview, 89
    print setting, changing, 90
    removing bullets, 87
title bar, 25
    maximizing windows from, 30
Title for the Program dialog box, 216
ToggleKeys option, 254
toggle switches, 36
T1 connections, 324
toolbars, 25. *See also* Windows Explorer
    Internet Explorer toolbar, 327–328
    Quick Launch toolbar, 19–20
    in WordPad, 73
ToolTips, 17, 24
Total key, Calculator, 65
touchpads, 5
Tours & Tutorials button, Help and Support system, 121
trackballs, 5
Travel desktop theme, 276
trigonometric functions with Calculator, 69
Tropical Fish desktop theme, 276
troubleshooting printer installation, 284, 291

U

underlining in e-mail, 348
Undo feature, 46
    Address Book contacts, 372
    in Paint program, 98
    programs, uninstalling, 242

unfreezing applications. *See* locked-up computers
uninstalling
    programs, 241–242
    Windows Millennium Edition, 388–391
Update Wizard, 139–143
updating system, 139–143
upgrading to Windows Millennium, 382–388
Use personalized menus option, Taskbar, 230
User Name text box, 5
Using Your Modem to Connect screen, 305–306

V

vertical scroll bar, 25–26
View menu, 34
    scientific calculator, viewing, 69–70
Views button, Windows Explorer, 159
View the Entire Contents of This Drive, 13
visualizations with Media Player, 186
visually impaired persons, options for, 257–258
volume controls, Media Player, 201–202
Volume Control window, Media Player, 202

W

wallpaper
    changing, 265
    for desktop, 265
    desktop themes and, 276–278
    for e-mail messages, 350
    for multiple users, 249
    Paint program drawing as, 105
Weather Map on Active Desktop, 275

INDEX

Web browsers. *See also* Internet Explorer
  disconnecting from, 322
  Netscape Navigator, 320
  starting, 320–322
Web pages
  address for, 324
  forms on, 326
  home page, 324
  hyperlinks, 326–327
  ratings for, 333–335
Web radio, 192–193
Web style desktop, 10
windows
  manually resizing windows, 28–29
  maximizing windows, 30
  minimizing windows, 31
  moving, 32
  resizing windows, 28–29
  restoring size of, 31
  WordPad window, 24
Windows Explorer
  active choices, indication of, 155
  Address bar, 156
  address bar, 152
  columns, changing width of, 158
  components of, 151–152
  date, sorting files by, 159–160
  deleting files with, 168–172
  Details view, 158, 160
  display options, changing, 154–155
  drag-and-drop printing, 293–294
  Drives and Folders section, 152
    hiding, 154–155
      My Network Places, viewing, 154
  expanding folders in, 153–154
  file display, changing, 156–159
  Find feature, using, 174–180

  Folder Options dialog box, 160–161
  large icons view in, 156
  list view, 157
  menu bar, 151
  modifying folder options, 160–161
  name, sorting files by, 159–160
  new folder, creating, 162–163
  renaming files and folders, 166–167
  size, sorting files by, 159–160
  small icons view in, 157
  sorting files in, 159–160
  Standard toolbar, 156
  status bar, 152
  subfolders in, 153
  thumbnails view in, 158
  toolbars, 152
    displaying, 155–156
  type, sorting files by, 159–160
  using, 150–151
  Views button, 159
Windows Help. *See* Help and Support system
Windows key, 19
Windows Millennium Edition
  installing, 383–388
  on networks, 5
  starting, 4
  uninstalling, 388–391
Windows Millennium Edition Setup Wizard, 383–388
Windows Paint program. *See* Paint program
Windows Product Key screen, 384–385
Windows registry, 241
Windows Setup program, 244–246
Windows Update Wizard, 139–143
WordPad
  adding text in, 75

  alignment, modifying, 85–86
  bullets, adding, 86–87
  closing program, 92
  cutting text in, 81–82
  date, inserting, 77–78
  deleting text in, 76
  deselecting text, 78
  editing text, 75–76
  entering text, 73–74
  folders for files in, 88
  fonts, changing, 83
  formatting text in, 83–84
  insert mode, 75
  justifying text in, 85
  opening
    documents, 91
    screen, 73
  Page Setup dialog box, 44–45
  paragraph, selecting, 79
  pasting text in, 81–82
  Print dialog box in, 90
  printing documents, 89–90
  Print Preview in, 89
  Save As dialog box in, 87–88
  saving
    on closing, 92
    documents, 87–89
  Select All option, 79
  selecting text in, 78–80
  starting, 72–73
  time, inserting, 77–78
  window, 24–26
WordPerfect
  for DOS, 290
  media clips in, 203–205
word wrap, WordPad, 73

Y

year, setting, 233

Learning Microsoft® Office 2000 is a breeze with PRIMA TECH's bestselling *fast & easy*™ guides

Offering extraordinary value at a bargain price, the *fast & easy* series is dedicated to one idea: To help readers accomplish tasks as quickly and easily as possible. There's no need to wade through endless pages of boring text. The unique and carefully developed visual teaching method combines concise tutorials and hundreds of WYSIWYG (what-you-see-is-what-you-get) screen shots to dramatically increase learning speed and retention of the material. With PRIMA TECH's *fast & easy* series, you simply look and learn.

A Division of Prima Publishing
www.prima-tech.com

Call now to order
(800)632-8676
ext. 4444

Prima Publishing and Fast & Easy are trademarks of Prima Communications, Inc. All other product and company names are trademarks of their respective companies.

Microsoft® Office 2000
0-7615-1762-6
$16.99

Microsoft® Word 2000
0-7615-1402-3
$16.99

Microsoft® Excel 2000
0-7615-1761-8
$16.99

Microsoft® Outlook™ 2000
0-7615-1927-0
$16.99

Microsoft® PowerPoint® 2000
0-7615-1763-4
$16.99

Microsoft® Publisher 2000
0-7615-2033-3
$16.99

Microsoft® FrontPage® 2000
0-7615-1931-9
$16.99

Microsoft® Access 2000
0-7615-1404-X
$16.99

Microsoft® PhotoDraw 2000
0-7615-2034-1
$16.99

Microsoft® Internet Explorer 5
0-7615-1742-1
$16.99

Microsoft® Office 2000 Professional "Six-Pack" Edition
0-7615-2032-5
$29.99

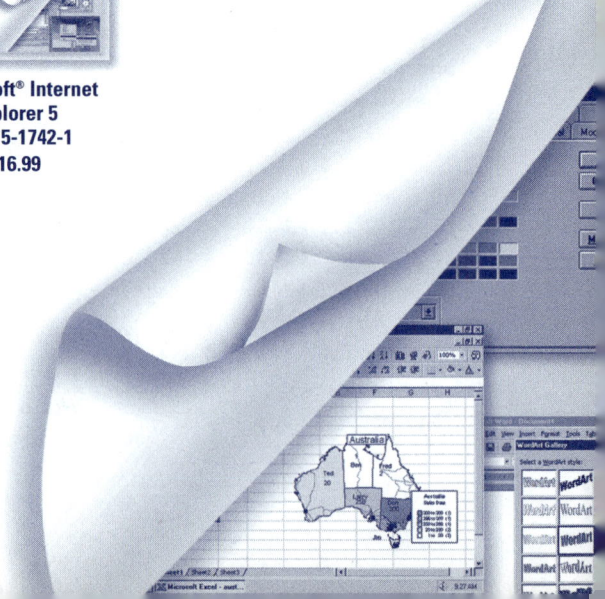